Gregory of Nyssa: Contra Eunomium II

Supplements
to
Vigiliae Christianae

Formerly Philosophia Patrum

Texts and Studies of Early
Christian Life and Language

VOLUME 82

Andreas Spira in memoriam

Gregory of Nyssa: Contra Eunomium II

An English Version with Supporting Studies

Proceedings of the 10th International Colloquium on Gregory of Nyssa (Olomouc, September 15–18, 2004)

Edited by

Lenka Karfíková, Scot Douglass and Johannes Zachhuber

With the assistance of

Vít Hušek and Ladislav Chvátal

BRILL

LEIDEN • BOSTON
2007

This book is printed on acid-free paper.

Library of Congress Cataloging-in-Publication Data

International Colloquium on Gregory of Nyssa (10th : 2004 : Olomouc, Czech Republic)
Gregory of Nyssa : Contra Eunomium II : an English version with supporting studies : proceedings of the 10th International Colloquium on Gregory of Nyssa (Olomouc, September 15–18, 2004) / edited by Lenka Karfíková . . . [et al.] with the assistance of Vít Hušek and Ladislav Chvátal.
p. cm. — (Supplements to Vigiliae Christianae, ISSN 0920-623X ; v. 82)
English, French, and German.
Contra Eunomium II translated from the Greek by Stuart George Hall.
Includes bibliographical references and indexes.
ISBN-13: 978-90-04-15518-3
ISBN-10: 90-04-15518-X (hardback : alk. paper) 1. Gregory, of Nyssa, Saint, ca. 335-ca. 394—Congresses. 2. Eunomius, Bp. of Cyzicus, ca. 335-ca. 394—Congresses. 3. Eunomianism—Congresses. 4. Church history—Primitive and early church, ca. 30-600—Congresses. I. Karfíková, Lenka. II. Hall, Stuart George. III. Gregory, of Nyssa, Saint, ca. 335-ca. 394. Contra Eunomium. Book II. English. IV. Title. V. Title: Contra Eunomium II. VI. Series.

BR65.G75C666 2004
273'.4—dc22

ISSN 0920-623x
ISBN-13 978 90 04 15518 3
ISBN-10 90 04 15518 X

PRINTED IN THE NETHERLANDS

CONTENTS

PART III

COMMENTARY

PART IV

SUPPORTING STUDIES

IV.1. Philosophical questions

IV.2. Theological motives

PREFACE

This volume contains the contributions presented during the 10th International Colloquium on Gregory of Nyssa, *Contra Eunomium II*, held in Olomouc, the Czech Republic, on September 15–18, 2004. It is organized into four major sections. The first offers two papers (Th. Kobusch, B. Studer) that contextualize the main problematic of the *Second Book Against Eunomius* – the theory of language and the problem of naming God – from a broader philosophical and theological perspective. The next three sections follow what has become the customary pattern for the proceedings of the recent Gregory of Nyssa Colloquiums: a new English translation of the text (S. G. Hall), a series of main papers providing commentary on its passages and numerous short essays discussing related issues. The *CE* II has a complex and layered structure. It is a polemic against Eunomius' polemic that followed Basil's polemic against Eunomius (see the structure of *CE* II given by S. G. Hall in the introduction to his translation). As a result, the commentaries (Th. Böhm, M. Ludlow, Ch. Apostolopoulos, A. Meredith, J. Zachhuber, L. Karfíková, J. S. O'Leary, V. H. Drecoll) focus not only on specific passages but also on the main topics found throughout the text and the larger debate regarding language between Gregory, his brother Basil and their Neo-Arian opponent. The short essays develop a range of related themes: various philosophical questions raised by the text (E. Moutsopoulos, G. Arabatzis, J. Demetracopoulos, L. Chvátal, Th. Alexopoulos, G. Lekkas, T. Tollefsen), as well as theological motives connected with the *CE* II (T. Dolidze, S. Douglass, A. Ojell, A.-G. Keidel, T. Aptsiauri, J. Rexer).

This gathering was the tenth in a series of international colloquia on Gregory of Nyssa dating back to 1969 in Chevetogne (M. Harl, ed., *Écriture et culture philosophique dans la pensée de Grégoire de Nysse*, Leiden 1971). This initial effort began a long and rich tradition of scholarly interaction and production: the 2nd, Freckenhorst bei Münster 1972 (H. Dörrie – M. Altenburger – U. Schramm, eds., *Gregor von Nyssa und die Philosophie*, Leiden 1976); the 3rd, Leiden 1974 (J. C. M. van Winden – A. van Heck, eds., *De infantibus praemature abreptis. Colloquii Gregoriani III Leidensis 18/23–IX–1974 Acta*, Leiden 1976, *pro manuscripto*), the 4th, Cambridge, England 1978 (A. Spira – Ch. Klock, eds., *The Easter Sermons of Gregory of Nyssa*, introduction by G. Ch. Stead, Cambridge, Mass., 1981), the 5th, Mainz 1982 (A. Spira – Ch. Klock, eds., *The Biographical Works of Gregory of Nyssa*, Cambridge, Mass., 1984), the 6th, Pamplona 1986 (L. F. Mateo-Seco – J. L. Bastero, eds., *El "Contra Eunomium I" en la produccion literaria de Gregorio de Nisa*, Pamplona 1988), the 7th, St. Andrews 1990 (S. G. Hall, ed., *Gregory of Nyssa, Homilies on Ecclesiastes*, Berlin – New York 1993), the 8th, Paderborn 1998 (H. R. Drobner – A. Viciano, eds., *Gregory of Nyssa, Homilies on the Beatitudes*, Leiden – Boston – Köln 2000), the 9th, Athens 2000 (*Jesus Christ in the Theology of St. Gregory of Nyssa*, yet unpublished).

The Olomouc Colloquium was organized by the *Centre for Patristic, Medieval and Renaissance Texts* at the Palacký University Olomouc, a project sponsored by the Ministry of Education of the Czech Republic from 2000 to 2004. We are particularly grateful for the kind and generous support of the Olomouc Region, the City of Olomouc, the St. Cyril and Methodius Faculty of Theology (Palacký University Olomouc) and the OK Design Ltd. (Olomouc). The Colloquium was convened under the auspices of His Magnificence the Rector of the Palacký University Olomouc, Jana Mačáková; His Excellency the Archbishop of Olomouc, Mons. Jan Graubner; His Excellency the Ambassador of Greece in the Czech Republic, Vassilios Eikosipentarchos; and the Mayor of Olomouc, Martin Tesařík.

The editors would like to express their warmest thanks to Vít Hušek and Ladislav Chvátal from the *Centre for Patristic, Medieval and Renaissance Texts* in Olomouc who graciously took on the responsibility for the technical preparation of the proceedings. Without their help, this publication would have never been completed. We are also very grateful to Johan Leemans from Leuven for looking at the French papers included in the volume.

At this time I would like to remember the initiative of Andreas Spira and Friedhelm Mann who, during the Gregory of Nyssa Congress in Athens 2000, encouraged me to organize the next Colloquium in the Czech Republic and who, together with my friends and co-editors Thomas Böhm, Scot Douglass and Johannes Zachhuber, were actively involved in its preparation.

The death of Andreas Spira on May 18th, 2004, only a few months before the Olomouc Colloquium, was and continues to be a source of deep grief for all the participants in our Colloquium and the wider world of Gregory of Nyssa scholarship. This volume is dedicated to his memory.

Lenka Karfíková

LIST OF PARTICIPANTS

Theodoros ALEXOPOULOS, Heidelberg, Germany
Charalambos APOSTOLOPOULOS, Ioannina, Greece
Tamara APTSIAURI, Tbilisi, Georgia
Georges ARABATZIS, Athenes, Greece
David BARTOŇ, Praha, Czech Republic
Thomas BÖHM, Freiburg i.B., Germany
Konstantinos BOZINIS, Athens, Greece
Sibbele DE BOER, Castricum, The Netherlands
Ladislav CHVÁTAL, Olomouc, Czech Republic
Tina DOLIDZE, Tbilisi, Georgia
Scot DOUGLASS, Boulder, Colorado, USA
Volker Henning DRECOLL, Tübingen, Germany
Pavel DUDZIK, Brno, Czech Republic
Christopher GRAHAM, Dallas, Texas, USA
Stuart G. HALL, Elie, Leven (Fife), Scotland
Filip KARFÍK, Praha, Czech Republic
Lenka KARFÍKOVÁ, Praha – Olomouc, Czech Republic
Anne-Gordon KEIDEL, West Newton, Massachusetts, USA
Theo KOBUSCH, Bonn, Germany
Morwenna LUDLOW, Oxford, England
Giulio MASPERO, Roma, Italy
Lucas Francisco MATEO-SECO, Pamplona, Spain
Anthony MEREDITH, London, England
Edgars NARKEVICS, Riga, Latvija
Joseph S. O'LEARY, Tokyo, Japan
Ari OJELL, Mäntsälä, Finland
Jana PLÁTOVÁ, Olomouc, Czech Republic
Jochen REXER, Tübingen, Germany
Adolf Martin RITTER, Heidelberg, Germany
Ekaterina SCODRA, Kalamata, Greece
Louise SCHOUTEN, Leiden, The Netherlands
Heleni SKOUMPOU, Byronas, Greece
Basil STUDER, Engelberg, Switzerland
Abraham THOMAS, London, England

Torstein Tollefsen, Oslo, Norway
Judit Toth, Debrecen, Hungary
Antonia Varkintzoglou, Athens, Greece
Sandra Wenger, Zürich, Switzerland
Johannes Zachhuber, Oxford, England
Nektarios Zarras, Athens, Greece

Written contributions by:
John Demetracopoulos, Patras, Greece
Georgios Lekkas, Athenes, Greece
Evanghélos Moutsopoulos, Athens, Greece

ANDREAS SPIRA (29.12.1929–18.5.2004) ZUM GEDENKEN[1]

Adolf Martin Ritter

Am 18. Mai dieses Jahres ist, für die meisten, die ihn kannten, völlig überraschend, unser Kollege Prof. Dr. Andreas Spira in Mainz verstorben. Da er sich noch im unmittelbaren Vorfeld dieses Symposiums, bis in die letzten Wochen seines Lebens hinein, als Ratgeber große Verdienste erworben hat, ist es nur billig, ehe wir mit unserer Arbeit beginnen, seiner zu gedenken.

Ich bin verschiedentlich gefragt worden: *Woran* ist er gestorben? Ich weiß es nicht genau. Nur dass es eine schwere Erkrankung war, die rasch fortschritt und ihm keine Chance zum Überleben ließ. Umso sicherer weiß ich, *wie* er gestorben ist: In großer Tapferkeit. Er hat auch nahe Freunde nichts von seiner schweren Erkrankung wissen und spüren lassen und stattdessen, in aller Stille, "das Haus bestellt". Es hat ihn auch in dieser schweren Zeit sein wohlbekannter Humor nicht verlassen. In Gedanken entwarf und versandte er, wie er einem nahen Freund wenige Tage vor seinem Ableben gestand, selbst die Todesanzeigen, einige von ihnen mit persönlichen Notizen versehend. So war einem Mathematikerfreund die Bemerkung zugedacht: "Einer von uns musste ohnehin als Erster gehen." Vor allem aber ist zu sagen: Andreas Spira ist die letzte Strecke seines Erdenweges als gläubiger katholischer Christ gegangen. Er hat alles gerichtet und bis ins einzelne geplant: wo das Requiem stattfinden (in St. Stephan, Mainz-Gonsenheim) und wer es leiten solle (die Freunde Hubertus Drobner und Christoph Klock), wer die Orgel spielen (Christoph Riedweg) und was er musizieren solle. Auf dem Waldfriedhof in Mainz-Gonsenheim ist er zur letzten Ruhe bestattet worden.

Wer war Andreas Spira? In Ostpreußen geboren und nach der Flucht im Raum Frankfurt-Wiesbaden aufgewachsen, hat er u.a. in Freiburg, Münster und Frankfurt a.M. studiert; bei Harald Patzer

---

[1] Gedenkwort, gesprochen am 16. September 2004, zu Beginn des 1. Arbeitstages des Olomoucer Kolloquiums. Ich verdanke wesentliche Informationen über Andreas Spira, seine Tätigkeit in Mainz und seine letzten Lebenstage meinem und seinem Freund Christoph Riedweg sowie seinem Schüler und Christoph Riedwegs Doktoranden Wolfram Brinker.

verfasste er eine Dissertation über Sophokles und Euripides,[2] aufgrund deren er 1957 in Frankfurt a.M. zum Dr. phil. promoviert wurde. Anschließend an einen Oxford-Aufenthalt übernahm er eine Assistentur in Mainz bei Andreas Thierfelder und Walter Marg und wurde ebendort 1967 mit einer Arbeit über "Die Grabrede Gregors von Nyssa auf Meletios von Antiochien"[3] habilitiert. Ab 1972 war er dann bis zum Eintritt in den Ruhestand (1995) in Mainz als Professor für Klassische Philologie tätig und hat in dieser Zeit zahlreiche Staatsexamens- und Magisterarbeiten sowie mehrere Doktorarbeiten (u.a. von Henriette Meissner, Jürgen-André Röder, Kristijan Domiter und Christoph Klock) betreut.

In der Traueranzeige der Familie (Allgemeine Zeitung Mainz, 22.5.2004) heißt es: "Sein Leben war geprägt von großer Fürsorge für seine Familie"; aber nicht nur für sie. Sondern: "Allen Menschen, die sich in ihren Anliegen an ihn wandten, begegnete er mit freundlicher Zuwendung und Hilfsbereitschaft." Das haben, wie ich weiß, auch manche unter uns dankbar erfahren. Selbst ihm bis dahin nahezu Unbekannten hat er in seinem Haus Gastfreundschaft gewähren können, aus dem einzigen Grund, dass sie dessen bedürftig waren.

In der Anzeige der Mainzer Universität (vier Tage später in derselben Zeitung) werden als "Schwerpunkte seiner Forschung" "die griechische Tragödie und die griechische Patristik" hervorgehoben und heißt es zur Kennzeichnung des Lehrers Andreas Spira: "Er war ein akademischer Lehrer aus Leidenschaft, insbesondere seine Rhetorikvorlesungen wurden weit über die Fachgrenzen hinaus gerühmt." Die Anzeige des Mainzer Seminars (ebenda) berücksichtigt im Hinblick auf den Lehrer noch mehr das Persönliche und Atmosphärische und sagt: "Als akademischer Lehrer hat er am Seminar persönliche Tutorien nach englischem Vorbild eingeführt, seine Studenten unermüdlich und in vielfältigster Weise gefördert . . . Andreas Spira war gleichsam der verbindende Mittelpunkt des Seminars, sein soziales Gewissen und sein *arbiter dignitatis et elegantiae.*

---

[2] *Untersuchungen zum Deus ex machina bei Sophokles und Euripides*, Kallmünz 1960 (= Diss. Frankfurt 1957).

[3] Vgl. Nachrichten des *Gnomon* 40 (1968) 112; die Habilitationsschrift liegt auch der Edition der Leichenrede auf Meletius in der Jaegerschen Ausgabe der *Gregorius Nyssenus. Opera* (GNO IX/1, Leiden 1967) zugrunde, in der A. Spira auch für die kritische Ausgabe der Trauerrede auf Kaiserin Flacilla und die Trostrede für Pulcheria verantwortlich zeichnete (Praefationes, 345ff; Text, 441ff).

Wo es die Interessen der Wissenschaft und der Lehre zu verteidigen galt, scheute er auch nicht vor dem Konflikt mit übergeordneten Instanzen zurück . . ."

Viele unter uns, meine Damen und Herren, die Andreas Spira als Teilnehmer an den Gregor von Nyssa-Kolloquien (seit Cambridge [11.–15.9.1978]) erlebt haben, können das unmittelbar nachvollziehen. Genau so haben sie ihn erlebt: als *arbiter dignitatis et elegantiae*, auch wenn er sie – gelegentlich nicht ohne Schärfe – kritisieren zu müssen meinte.

Was bedeutet der in den zitierten Anzeigen genannte 2. Schwerpunkt in der Forschung Andreas Spiras ("griechische Patristik") konkret? Er bedeutet, wenn man sich die Themen seiner Veröffentlichungen vergegenwärtigt, zuerst und zuletzt – und auch dazwischen immer wieder –: *Gregor von Nyssa*; dessen Grabreden war der (auf einem paper vor der Oxforder internationalen Patristikerkonferenz basierende) erste patristische Aufsatz[4] und dessen beiden Reden über die Liebe zu den Armen war die erste (ebenso kritische wie sachkundige) Rezension[5] gewidmet, die im Druck erschienen. Es folgten u.a. die Herausgabe der Akten des 4. internationalen Gregor von Nyssa-Kolloquiums in Cambridge (11.–15. Sept. 1978) über die Osterpredigten des Nysseners (Mitherausgeber: Chr. Klock),[6] mit einem eigenen Beitrag über den "Descensus ad Inferos in der Osterpredigt Gregors von Nyssa *De tridui spatio*",[7] und die Herausgabe der Akten des nächsten, 5., von ihm in Mainz organisierten Kolloquiums über die biographischen Werke Gregors von Nyssa,[8] mit einer eigenen, langen Einleitung zum Thema.

Schaut man sich jedoch zumal die letzte Veröffentlichung, den im Jahre 2000 erschienenen überarbeiteten und mit umfangreichen Anmerkungen und einer langen Bibliographie versehenen Text seines Vortrages bei dem 8. Colloquium Gregorianum in Paderborn (14.–18. Sept. 1998) über Gregors Reden über die Seligpreisungen

[4] "Rhetorik und Theologie in den Grabreden Gregors von Nyssa", *StPatr* 9 (= TU 94, Berlin) (1966) 106–114.

[5] "A. v. Heck (ed.), Gregorii Nysseni *De pauperibus amandis* orationes duo (1964)", *Gnomon* 38 (1966) 666–671.

[6] Cambridge 1981 (Patristic Monographs Ser. IX).

[7] Samt einem textkritischen Anhang, in dem er sich recht kritisch mit der Ausgabe dieser Predigt in den GNO IX (s.o., Anm. 3) auseinandersetzt, bezeichnend für die Skrupulosität, mit der er zu Werke zu gehen pflegte.

[8] A. Spira (Hrsg.), *The Biographical Works of Gregory of Nyssa. Proceedings of the Fifth International Colloquium on Gregory of Nyssa (Mainz, 6–10 September 1982)*, Cambridge 1984.

der Bergpredigt,[9] der der Interpretation und Kommentierung der 2. Seligpreisung ("Selig sind die Sanftmütigen; denn sie werden das Erdreich besitzen") gewidmet ist, näher an, so zeigt sich, welches Maß an Vertrautheit der Verstorbene sich nicht nur mit klassisch-antiker Rhetorik und Philosophie und dem Werk Gregors, sondern auch mit der griechischen (Clemens Alexandrinus und Origenes vor allem) und lateinischen Patristik (Augustin) überhaupt erworben hat. Es ist so eine nahezu vollkommene Kommentierung gelungen, die dem auszulegenden Text nach Form und Inhalt wie seiner geistes- und theologiegeschichtlichen Einordnung gleichermaßen gerecht wird; und das war es offenbar, worum es ihm stets zu tun war.

Man kann sagen: Andreas Spira ist in den letzten anderthalb bis zwei Jahrzehnten immer mehr zum philologischen Gewissen im Kreis der Gregorianer geworden und hat die Lücke schließen helfen, die zuletzt der Tod H. Dörries gerissen hatte. Es bedarf ernster Anstrengung, dass dieser Platz nicht allzu lange leer bleibt, sondern sich Kolleginnen und Kollegen vergleichbarer Kompetenz und Sensibilität finden und als Gesprächspartner den Gregorianern aller Schattierungen, nicht zuletzt den Theologen unter ihnen, zur Verfügung stellen; sie haben es bitter nötig. Ich werde allerdings von Olomouc scheiden können in dem Gefühl, dass man sich in dieser Hinsicht über die Zukunft der *Studia Gregoriana* nicht zu viel Sorgen machen muss!

Andreas Spira war, wie wir hörten, bereits in seiner ersten patristischen Veröffentlichung – für ihn bezeichnenderweise – "Rhetorik *und* Theologie" bei seinem geliebten Gregor auf der Spur, hat sich also von Anfang an auch für dessen Theologie interessiert und auf diesem Feld immer sicherer zu bewegen verstanden. Er hat deshalb auch, mehr als H. Dörrie, zu versöhnen gesucht – und vermocht, was sonst in der Gregorforschung seit langem eher auseinanderstrebt und in Konkurrenz zueinander tritt: eine eher 'philosophische' und eine eher 'mystische' Gregordeutung, repräsentiert zum einen durch die Schule W. Jaegers, zum andern durch Hans Urs von Balthasar, Jean Daniélou und Henri de Lubac samt deren zahlreicher Schülerschaft. Dieser auf Versöhnung statt auf Polarisierung bedachte Ansatz kommt in der veröffentlichten Fassung seiner Paderborner Interpretation

[9] H. R. Drobner – A. Viciano (Hrsg.), *Gregory of Nyssa: Homilies on the Beatitudes. An English Version with Commentary and Supporting Studies. Proceedings of the Eighth International Colloquium on Gregory of Nyssa (Paderborn, 14–18 September 1998)*, Leiden 2000, 111–138.

der zweiten Seligpreisung Jesu (*Mt* 5,4) in der homiletischen Auslegung durch Gregor eindrucksvoll zum Ausdruck. So kann diese Interpretation nun nachträglich gleichsam als Vermächtnis unseres verstorbenen Kollegen gelten.

Man hätte es sich, nicht zuletzt um seinetwillen, sehr gewünscht, dieses Vermächtnis hätte die von vielen sehnlich erwartete Edition von Gregors *De anima et resurrectione* sein können, an der er so lange gearbeitet hatte und deren Abschluss er schon vor mindestens zwei Jahren als unmittelbar bevorstehend anzukündigen sich getraute. Sie zu vollenden aber ist ihm nicht mehr vergönnt gewesen. Wer ihn in den vergangenen Jahren nach dem Stand dieses Projektes fragte, der konnte ihn, vor allem wenn sich auch nur ein Anflug von Spott in die Frage mischte, außer sich geraten sehen. D.h. man hatte – unbeabsichtigt – eine Wunde getroffen; Andreas Spira wusste um seine Grenzen und litt darunter. Seine meisterhafte Interpretation von Gregors *De beatitudinibus*, hom. 2, mit der stupenden Quellenkenntnis, die sich darin niedergeschlagen hat, auch ihren zahlreichen Ergänzungsvorschlägen für den Testimonienapparat der Textausgabe in den GNO, aber auch ältere Rezensionen verraten etwas von dem enorm hohen Anspruch, den Andreas Spira an andere und, mehr noch, an sich selbst stellte. Das ist schwerlich der einzige, aller Wahrscheinlichkeit nach aber ein wichtiger Grund, weshalb wir so lange auf die genannte Edition haben warten müssen, am Ende vergeblich. Denn diese ungewöhnliche Skrupulosität wirkte sich ersichtlich auch hemmend auf seine eigene Arbeit aus.

Vor ein paar Tagen habe ich an der Beisetzung eines aus Siebenbürgen stammenden 'sächsischen' Pfarrers teilgenommen und etwas erlebt, das mich dermaßen beeindruckte, dass ich es Ihnen gern weitererzählen möchte. Zum Abschluss der Beerdigung, am noch offenen Grab, trat ein Freund des Verstorbenen auf, wie es unter den Lutherischen Siebenbürgens der Brauch war, und bat im Namen des Verstorbenen alle Anwesenden von Herzen um Verzeihung, wo sie sich von diesem ungerecht behandelt oder gar verletzt fühlten, so wie dieser allen seinen 'Schuldigern' von Herzen vergeben habe. – Das geht, finde ich, noch einen wesentlichen Schritt weiter als das gewiss ehrenwerte Prinzip: *De mortuis nil nisi bene*, zumal, wenn ein süffisanter Unterton kaum zu überhören ist, mit dem man sich darauf beruft.

REQUIEM AETERNAM DONA, DOMINE,
ET LUX AETERNA LUCEAT EI ET LUCEAT NOBIS.

PART I

INTRODUCTION

DIE EPINOIA – DAS MENSCHLICHE BEWUSSTSEIN IN DER ANTIKEN PHILOSOPHIE

Theo Kobusch

Die Griechen hatten lange Zeit kein Bewusstsein von dem, was wir heute – dabei der Terminologie des Deutschen Idealismus folgend – das endliche Bewusstsein als den Inbegriff aller intellektiven Tätigkeiten nennen, die als das Subjektive einer objektiven Wirklichkeit gegenüberstehen. Dafür gibt es einen sicheren Hinweis: Lange Zeit gibt es im Griechischen keinen terminologisch gebrauchten Begriff für das spezifisch menschliche, d.h. endliche Bewusstsein. Der Begriff der Seele kann dafür nicht in Anspruch genommen werden, denn in seiner Bedeutung als Lebensprinzip kann er alles Lebendige, von der Pflanze bis zur Weltseele, bezeichnen. Auch der 'Geist' (νοῦς) entspricht nicht dem, was wir das menschliche Bewusstsein nennen, ja sogar er gerade nicht, denn er bezeichnet das göttliche Prinzip, sei es im Menschen, sei es als separate Wesenheit. Am nächsten scheint dem noch der Begriff der Dianoia zu stehen, denn er drückt in der Tat *per se* etwas dem endlichen Bewusstsein Eigentümliches aus, nämlich die Diskursivität des Denkens. Allerdings kommt gerade auch in der späteren neuplatonischen Diskussion, in der die Dianoia neben dem Nus und der Phantasie u.a. genannt wird, deutlich zum Ausdruck, als was sie im Griechentum schon immer angesehen wurde: nämlich als ein Vermögen der Seele neben anderen. Hier aber soll die Rede sein von dem der Wirklichkeit gegenüberstehenden, spezifisch menschlichen Bewusstsein. Die Stoiker haben dafür den Terminus 'Epinoia' geprägt.[1] Zwar scheint auf den ersten Blick schon Antisthenes in seiner berühmten Kritik an der platonischen Ideenlehre – "ein Pferd sehe ich zwar, aber eine Pferdheit sehe ich nicht" – das Allgemeine als das charakterisiert zu haben, was 'bloß im Denken' (ἐν ψιλαῖς ἐπινοίαις) ist, aber offenkundig ist es Ammonius selbst, der die Deutung des Antisthenischen Fragmentes in stoischen Termini

[1] Zur Geschichte des Begriffs vgl. T. Kobusch, *Sein und Sprache. Historische Grundlegung einer Ontologie der Sprache*, Leiden 1987, 23ff, 33ff.

und besonders mit dem erst spät belegbaren Ausdruck des 'bloßen Denkens' vorgenommen hat.[2] Die Stoiker waren es und nicht Aristoteles, die das menschliche Denken mitsamt seinem Inhalt unter dem Titel der Epinoia philosophisch offenbar ausführlich diskutierten, wie aus den wenigen Fragmenten über dieses Thema geschlossen werden kann. Danach müssen verschiedene Bewusstseinsweisen, Modi des Denkens (τρόποι νοήσεως), auseinandergehalten werden. Alles Gedachte kommt nämlich zustande entweder durch eine Annäherung an das sinnlich Evidente oder durch eine Entfernung von ihm, die sich in Form einer Metabasis vollzieht. Der unmittelbaren Berührung mit dem sinnlich Manifesten verdanken sich solche Begriffe wie das Weiße und Schwarze, das Süße und Bittere. Denn "dieses wird, auch wenn es sinnlich wahrnehmbar ist, trotzdem gedacht". Dieser Übergang von einem zum anderen kann wiederum verschiedene Formen annehmen, z.B. die Form der Ähnlichkeit, wenn der abwesende Sokrates aufgrund eines Bildes von ihm erkannt wird, oder die Form der Zusammensetzung, indem der Begriff des 'Bockhirsches' aus dem Menschen und dem Pferd zusammengesetzt wird. Schließlich stellt auch die Analogie einen Modus des Übergangs von einem zum anderen dar, und das in zweifacher Form: Das menschliche Bewusstsein kann vergrößern und verkleinern, es kann, wenn es einen mittelmäßig großen Menschen wahrgenommen hat, sich einen Riesen vom Schlage des Zyklopen vorstellen, aber auch einen Pygmäen, die als solche beide nicht sinnfällig sind.[3] Der Skeptiker Sextus Empiricus, der uns diese Lehre überliefert, sagt uns auch, gegen wen das gesagt ist. Platon und Demokrit waren es nämlich, die die sinnlichen Wahrnehmungen praktisch ausgeklammert haben und "nur dem Intelligiblen gefolgt sind". Dadurch haben sie aber nicht nur die Wahrheit der Dinge auf den Kopf gestellt, sondern auch das Bewusstsein von ihnen, ihre Epinoia. Denn jedes Denken beruht auf sinnlicher Erfahrung oder ist doch nicht ohne sie möglich, und alle Modi des Bewusstseins bis hin zu den falschesten Einbildungen der Phantasie, ob sie gleich Traumgebilde oder

---

[2] Ammonius, *In Porphyrii Isagogen* (CAG IV/3 40,6–8): ὁ τοίνυν Ἀντισθένης ἔλεγε τὰ γένη καὶ τὰ εἴδη ἐν ψιλαῖς ἐπινοίαις εἶναι λέγων ὅτι « ἵππον μὲν ὁρῶ, ἱππότητα δὲ οὐχ ὁρῶ » καὶ πάλιν « ἄνθρωπον μὲν ὁρῶ, ἀνθρωπότητα δὲ οὐχ ὁρῶ ». Vgl. Antisthenes, *Fr.* 50C (Caizzi 42).

[3] Vgl. Sextus Empiricus, *Adversus Mathematicos* IX 393–402 (Mutschmann II 293–294). Ähnlich auch *Adversus Mathematicos* III 40–49 (Mau III 115–117).

Wahnvorstellungen sind, hängen von den sinnlichen Erfahrungen ab. Daher gilt ganz allgemein, dass "nichts im Bewusstsein zu finden ist, was einer nicht als von ihm durch sinnliche Erfahrung Erkanntes hätte". Und ein weiteres Mal zählt Sextus an dieser Stelle die schon erläuterten Modi des Bewusstseins auf,[4] denen Diogenes Laertius noch weitere hinzufügt, nämlich die Metapher, wenn wir von den Augen der Brust sprechen, und die konträre Entgegensetzung, aufgrund derer wir z.B. den Tod denken können, bevor wir ihn erfahren. Zuletzt ist das menschliche Bewusstsein in der Lage, etwas auf 'natürliche Weise' zu denken, wie z.B. das Gute und das Gerechte, oder auch Fehlendes zu bemerken, also etwas wie das, dem eine Hand fehlt, im Sinne einer Privation zu erkennen.[5] Die stoische Position scheint in dieser Frage der Bewusstseinsweisen nicht einheitlich gewesen zu sein, denn in dem zitierten Fragment bei Diogenes Laertius wird das κατὰ μετάβασιν Erkannte nicht im Sinne eines schlichten Übergangs von einem zum anderen verstanden, sondern als das, was die Stoiker das 'Unkörperliche' nennen, wie z.B. die Lekta, d.h. die gedachten Sachverhalte als solche, oder der Raum, die neben der Zeit und dem Leeren die Arten der Gedankendinge darstellen, denen eine nur gedankliche Existenz (ὑφιστάναι) zukommt.[6] Wir haben es hier also mit Begriffen zu tun, die als 'transzendente' bezeichnet werden könnten, weil sie gewonnen werden, indem die Welt der empirischen Erfahrung im Ganzen überschritten wird. Auf diese Weise entwickelte sich zuerst in der Stoa ein Bewusstsein von den verschiedenen Modi des menschlichen Denkens und seiner Begriffe. Die epikureische Philosophie scheint davon nicht sehr weit entfernt gewesen zu sein.[7] Was als bedeutsames Resultat dieser innergriechischen Entwicklung festgehalten werden muss, ist die Etablierung eines Begriffs des menschlichen Bewusstseins als einer festen Größe, als eines eigenen Bereichs gegenüber einer objektiven (sinnlichen oder intelligiblen) Wirklichkeit. Etwas ist entweder nur bewusstseinsmäßig (ἐν ἐπινοίαις) oder außerhalb des Bewußtseins, entweder nur ein Begriff oder etwas Wirkliches. Das hat sich auch terminologisch in dem Gegensatz von 'Epinoia' und 'Hypostasis' niedergeschlagen, die

[4] Sextus Empiricus, *Adversus Mathematicos* VIII 56–60 (SVF II 88).
[5] Vgl. Diogenes Laertius VII 52 (SVF II 87).
[6] Vgl. dazu T. Kobusch, *Sein und Sprache*, 30ff und 362ff.
[7] Vgl. *Vita Epicuri* (= Diogenes Laertius X 32) (Laks 30,2ff) und Epicurus, *Epistula ad Herodotum* I 40 (Arrighetti 39).

der im mittelalterlichen Denken gängigen Unterscheidung zwischen *ens rationis* und *ens naturae* oder *ens reale* entspricht. In diesem Sinne hat offenbar Poseidonios als erster, aber beileibe nicht als letzter – wenn wir an Avicennas und R. Bacons Regenbogentheorie, an Teile der mittelalterlichen Farbenlehre bis hin zur Goetheschen Denken – im Bereich des Sinnlichen eine rein phänomenale Existenz (κατ' ἔμφασιν) der metarsischen Erscheinungen wie z.B. des Regenbogens von dem wirklichen Vorhandensein eines Dinges (καθ' ὑπόστασιν) unterschieden.[8] Es scheint auch Poseidonios oder doch jedenfalls die stoische Philosophie gewesen zu sein, die den Gegensatz zwischen objektiver Realität und menschlichem Bewusstsein terminologisch als 'Hypostasis' und 'Epinoia' zuerst festgelegt hat.[9] Doch wirkt sich dieser Gegensatz zwischen bewusstseinsabhängiger und bewusstseinsunabhängiger Existenz nicht nur in besonderen Fragen der Meteorologie aus. Vielmehr wird er im weiteren Verlaufe der paganen spätantiken Philosophie zu einem tragenden Element. Plotins Zahlenschrift (*Enn.* VI 6 [34]), die gerade auch diese Terminologie aufgenommen hat und den Begriff der Epinoia terminologisch für das endliche, menschliche Bewusstsein im Unterschied zum Nus gebraucht, lebt in ihrer Kritik an der stoischen Vorstellung doch von diesem Gegensatz zwischen ἐπίνοια und οὐσία. Auch wenn wir allgemein von der Hypostasenlehre des Plotin sprechen, muss dieser begriffliche Gegensatz zur Epinoia beachtet werden. Es ist ein weitverbreitetes Vorurteil in der Forschung, das möglicherweise durch eine einflussreiche Abhandlung von H. Dörrie festgeschrieben und unterstützt wurde,[10] dass die Rede von den drei Hypostasen des Einen, des Nus und der Seele – die nicht dem Sprachgebrauch Plotins selbst entspricht – die Vorstellung von einer Stufung notwendig impliziere. H. G. Thümmel hat mit Recht diese Verknüpfung kritisiert und darauf hingewiesen, dass im Hintergrund des neuplatonischen Hypostasis-Begriffs Origenes stehe.[11] Ob es wirklich Origenes ist – wer weiß das schon? Aber

---

[8] Vgl. T. Kobusch, *Sein und Sprache*, 304–327.

[9] Vgl. R. E. Witt, "ΥΠΟΣΤΑΣΙΣ", in: H. G. Wood (Hrsg.), *Amicitiae Corolla*, London 1933, 319–343, hier 325: "The contrast between objective actuality and purely mind-dependent existence very often appears in the verbal form καθ' ὑπόστασιν, κατ' ἐπίνοιαν, an antithesis first formulated, it seems, by Posidonius."

[10] H. Dörrie, "Hypostasis. Wort- und Bedeutungsgeschichte", *Nachrichten der Akademie der Wissenschaften zu Göttingen, Philologisch-historische Klasse* 3 (1955) 35–92.

[11] H. G. Thümmel, "Logos und Hypostasis", in: D. Wyrwa (Hrsg.), *Weltlichkeit des Glaubens in der Alten Kirche. FS für U. Wickert zum 70. Geb.*, Berlin – New York 1997, 347–398, hier 383–394.

eines scheint ganz sicher zu sein: Immer, wenn in dieser Zeit der Begriff der Hypostasis gebraucht wird, ist auch der Gegenbegriff der Epinoia, und damit das stoische Begriffspaar präsent. Hypostasis bezeichnet daher in der Tat, wie H. G. Thümmel, wenngleich ohne den Gegenbegriff der Epinoia zu nennen, das dargelegt hat, das 'selbständige Sein' oder das, was später die 'Subsistenz' genannt wird im Unterschied zum vom menschlichen Bewusstsein abhängigen Sein.[12] Von Alexander von Aphrodisias an, bei Porphyrios und den späteren Aristoteleskommentatoren, hat diese Disjunktion zudem bei den Erörterungen über den ontologischen Charakter des Allgemeinen den Charakter einer Bifurkation, an der sich die Geister scheiden.[13] Die mathematische Existenz kann, wie ein Blick auf Alexander von Aphrodisias, Proklos und andere spätantike Autoren zeigt, ohne diese Unterscheidung gar nicht verständlich gemacht werden.[14] Kurzum: Die Unterscheidung von Bewusstsein und Realität, von Gedachtsein und Wirklichsein, von Begriff und Sache ist von universaler philosophischer Bedeutung, denn sie wird bei der Gelegenheit verschiedener Probleme zur Geltung gebracht.[15] Ganz am Ende der Antike bringt sie zudem eine Problematik in den Blick, die so noch nicht vorher gedacht worden war und geradezu schon hinüberweist in eine scholastische Dimension: Bei David, der zur Enkelgeneration der Ammoniusschule gehört, wird die in dieser Schule übliche Unterscheidung zwischen der Epinoia und der bloßen Epinoia noch einmal thematisch behandelt. Was ist jenes, was ist dieses? David sagt, was in der Natur zusammenhängend ist, aber durch unser Denken getrennt wird, wie z.B. die Farbe eines Körpers, das ist unsere Epinoia. Wir könnten also sagen, was durch eine Form der Abstraktion

---

[12] Sehr gut erkannt hat den stoischen Gegensatz als Grundlage des plotinischen Hypostasenverständnisses C. Rutten, "ΥΠΑΡΞΙΣ et ΥΠΟΣΤΑΣΙΣ chez Plotin", in: F. Romano – D. P. Taormina (Hrsg.), *HYPARXIS e HYPOSTASIS nel Neoplatonismo (Atti del I Colloquio Internazionale del Centro di Ricerca sul Neoplatonismo)*, Firenze 1994, 25–32.

[13] Vgl. z.B. Alexander von Aphrodisias, *In Aristotelis Metaphysica Commentarius* (CAG I 483,23–28): ἔλεγον γὰρ ὅτι ὁ μὲν καθόλου ἄνθρωπος, ὃν ὁ νοῦς ὁ ἡμέτερος ἀπὸ τῶν καθ᾽ ἕκαστα ἀπεσύλησε καὶ τὸ εἶναι αὐτῷ ἀπεχαρίσατο, ὁμοίωμα τῶν κατὰ μέρος ἀνθρώπων ἐστὶ καὶ ὁ αὐτός ἐστι τοῖς καθ᾽ ἕκαστα καὶ ἐν ἐπινοίᾳ μόνῃ τὸ εἶναι ἔχει, ὁ δὲ αὐτοάνθρωπος ἡ ἰδέα, ἥτις καθ᾽ αὑτήν ἐστι καὶ ἐν ὑπάρξει, οὐκ ἔστιν ὁ αὐτὸς τοῖς καθ᾽ ἕκαστα ἀνθρώποις.

[14] Alexander von Aphrodisias, *In Aristotelis Metaphysica Commentarius* (CAG I 52,13–16): τὰ δὲ μαθηματικὰ τὴν ἐν τοῖς πολλοῖς, τουτέστι τοῖς αἰσθητοῖς καὶ τοῖς καθ᾽ ἕκαστα, δηλοῦν ὁμοιότητα, ἐνυπάρχοντα τούτοις. οὐ γάρ ἐστιν αὐτὰ καθ᾽ αὑτὰ ὑφεστῶτα, ἀλλ᾽ ἐπινοίᾳ.

[15] Vgl. T. Kobusch, *Sein und Sprache*, s.v. "Gedachtes".

hervorgebracht wird, das ist in der 'Epinoia'. Was dagegen überhaupt nicht ist, wie z.B. der Bockhirsch, dessen Teile in der Natur zwar gegeben sind, aber doch willkürlich von unserer Phantasie zusammengesetzt werden, das ist in der 'bloßen Epinoia'.[16] Doch damit nicht genug. David berichtet davon, dass diese Ansicht der aristotelischen entspreche. Danach ist also das ganz und gar Nichtseiende dasjenige, was keine aktuelle Existenz haben kann, aber – wie der Bockhirsch – als Begriff im Bewusstsein sein kann. Nach der platonischen Ansicht dagegen ist das eigentlich Nichtseiende dasjenige, was weder eine gedankliche noch eine aktuelle Existenz haben kann.[17] Wie man leicht sehen kann, führen so schon die antiken Erörterungen über das menschliche Bewusstsein hin zu jenen Fragen, die die Grenzen der Möglichkeit desselben und damit das Denkmögliche und das Realmögliche und schließlich die Negation dieser Möglichkeit betreffen. Es sind die modalontologischen Probleme, die dann im Mittelalter, bei Abaelard und besonders im Scotismus, bei Suarez und in der Jesuitentradition auf je eigene Weise einer Lösung zugeführt werden.

Die christliche Philosophie hat sich in die Diskussionen um die Epinoia, ihren ontologischen Status, ihre Rolle bei der Bewältigung der äußeren Realität (von der Namengebung bis zur Technik) und ihre Möglichkeiten der Erkenntnis eingemischt und sich die (auch terminologische) Entdeckung der Stoiker auf breiter Front zu eigen gemacht. Das kommt zunächst am deutlichsten im Zusammenhang theologischer Probleme im engeren Sinne zum Ausdruck. So haben Origenes und die Origenesschule (Didymus der Blinde), Athanasius und die Kappadozier, also vor allem auch das 4. Jahrhundert, die

---

[16] David, *In Porphyrii Isagogen Commentarius* (CAG XVIII 2, 119,17–24): Ἄξιόν ἐστι ζητῆσαι τί διαφέρει ἐπίνοια τῆς ψιλῆς ἐπινοίας. ἐπίνοια μέν ἐστιν, ὅταν διαχωρίζειν τῷ λόγῳ τολμῶμεν τὸ συνημμένον ἐκ τῆς φύσεως δημιούργημα· οἷον ἡ φύσις ὁμοῦ τὸ σῶμα καὶ τὸ χρῶμα δημιουργεῖ, καὶ οὐκ ἔστι σῶμα μὴ ἔχον χρῶμα. τοῦτο οὖν τὸ ὁμοῦ συνημμένον, φημὶ δὲ τὸ λευκὸν καὶ τὸ σῶμα, διαχωρίζομεν λέγοντες τὸ μὲν λευκὸν χρῶμα διακριτικὸν ὄψεως, τὸ δὲ σῶμα τριχῇ διαστατόν. αὕτη οὖν ἐστιν ἡ ἐπίνοια. ψιλὴν δὲ ἐπίνοιάν φαμεν, ὅταν τὰ μηδαμῇ μηδαμῶς ἐν τῇ ἡμετέρᾳ διανοίᾳ οἰκοδομῶμεν, τὸν τραγέλαφον καὶ τὰ ὅμοια.

[17] David, *In Porphyrii Isagogen Commentarius* (CAG XVIII 2, 189,6–11): ἰστέον δὲ ὡς ἄλλο μέν φησιν ὁ Πλάτων τὸ μηδαμῇ μηδαμῶς, ἄλλο δὲ ὁ Ἀριστοτέλης· ὁ μὲν γὰρ Πλάτων ἔλεγε τὸ μηδαμῇ τὸ μηδαμῶς μήτε ἐπινοίᾳ μήτε ἐνεργείᾳ ὑπάρχον (ἀμέλει τὸν τραγέλαφον οὔ φησι μηδαμῇ μηδαμῶς, ἐπειδὴ ἔχει τὸ εἶναι ἐν ἐπινοίᾳ), Ἀριστοτέλης δέ μηδαμῇ μηδαμῶς ἔλεγε τὸ τῇ μὲν ἐπινοίᾳ ὑφιστάμενον, ἐνεργείᾳ δὲ οὐκέτι, οἷον τὸν τραγέλαφον καὶ τὰ τοιαῦτα.

Lehre der Sabellianer und Monarchianer kritisiert, nach der zwischen den göttlichen Personen ein nur begrifflicher Unterschied (ἐπίνοια) anzunehmen sei. Vielmehr entsprechen den Differenzierungen unseres Bewusstseins auch bestimmte Formen der Wirklichkeit (ὑπόστασις). So kommt der ursprünglich stoische Gegensatz von ἐπίνοια und ὑπόστασις in der christlichen Trinitätslehre zur Geltung. Man kann deswegen davon ausgehen, dass die Formulierung von den τρεῖς ὑποστάσεις, die schon bei Origenes belegbar ist, ein Resultat der Auseinandersetzungen um den ontologischen Status der drei göttlichen Personen sind.[18] Ähnlich wichtig ist der Begriff der Epinoia auch in der Lehre von den göttlichen Attributen bzw. in der Christologie, in der es ebenfalls Origenes war, der die entscheidenden Anstöße gab. Mit Hilfe der stoischen Unterscheidung von ἐπίνοια und ὑπόστασις kann erklärt werden, wie Jesus, diese eine, reale historische Person, durch viele Namen wie z.B. 'Licht der Welt', 'Wahrheit' oder 'Tür' bezeichnet werden kann. Ähnliches gilt auch für die dritte göttliche Person oder für das eine, göttliche Wesen selbst.[19] Den

[18] Origenes, *Johanneskommentar* II 75 (GCS 10, 65,16). Dazu R. E. Witt, "ΥΠΟΣΤΑΣΙΣ", 335. Vgl. auch Pseudo-Athanasius, *De sancta Trinitate dialogus* 1 (PG 28, 1144d–1145a): Ἀλλὰ αὐτὴ ἡ ὑπόστασις καὶ ἀθανασία ἐστί· καὶ οὐ μόνον ἀθανασία, ἀλλὰ καὶ ἀφθαρσία, καὶ δικαιοσύνη, καὶ ἁγιασμὸς, καὶ ἀπολύτρωσις, καὶ κυριότης, καὶ δύναμις. Καὶ οὐκ ἔστι κατὰ σύνθεσιν ταῦτα ὁ Θεός, ἀλλὰ κατὰ διαφόρους ἐπινοίας λεγόμενος· . . . καὶ διὰ τοῦτο δύο μὲν ὑποστάσεις λέγομεν Πατρὸς καὶ Υἱοῦ, μίαν δὲ θεότητα, δύναμιν, κυριότητα, καὶ ἀθανασίαν, καὶ ἀφθαρσίαν, καὶ ὅσα . . .

Athanasius, *Oratio quarta contra Arianos* (Stegmann 2,24–29): ἃ λέγεται, κατ' ἐπίνοιαν καὶ ἁπλῶς λεγόμενα. Εἰ δὲ φευκτέον τὸ ἐκ τῆς ἐπινοίας ἄτοπον, ἄρα ἀληθὴς λόγος οὐσιώδης ἐστίν. Ὥσπερ γὰρ ἀληθῶς πατήρ, οὕτως ἀληθῶς σοφία. Κατὰ τοῦτο οὖν δύο μέν, ὅτι μὴ κατὰ Σαβέλλιον ὁ αὐτὸς πατὴρ καὶ υἱός, ἀλλ' ὁ πατὴρ πατήρ, καὶ ὁ υἱὸς υἱός, ἓν δέ, ὅτι υἱὸς τῆς οὐσίας τοῦ πατρός ἐστι φύσει, ἴδιος ὑπάρχων λόγος αὐτοῦ.

Basilius muss quasi entschuldigend darauf hinweisen (*Ep.* 210,5,9–11, Courtonne II 195), dass Gregor Thaumaturgos im Disput mit einem Gegner die sabellianische Formel verwendet habe: ὡς ἄρα Γρηγορίου εἰπόντος ἐν ἐκθέσει πίστεως Πατέρα καὶ Υἱὸν ἐπινοίᾳ μὲν εἶναι δύο, ὑποστάσει δὲ ἕν, um im Sinne der christlich richtigen Lehre hinzuzufügen: ἀλλὰ χρὴ ἕκαστον πρόσωπον ἐν ὑποστάσει ἀληθινῇ ὑπάρχον ὁμολογεῖν.

Cyrill, *Thesaurus de sancta consubstantiali Trinitate* (PG 75, 141c): Οὐκοῦν ἁπλῆ τις οὖσα καὶ ἀσύνθετος ἡ τῆς θεότητος φύσις, οὐκ ἂν ἐτμήθη ποτὲ ταῖς ἐπινοίαις εἰς δυάδα Πατρὸς καὶ Υἱοῦ, εἰ μή τις εὐδόκει προκεῖσθαι διαφορά, οὐ κατὰ τὴν οὐσίαν φημί, ἀλλ' ἔξωθεν ἐπινοουμένη, δι' ἧς τὸ ἑκατέρου πρόσωπον εἰσφέρεται ἐν ἰδιαζούσῃ μὲν ὑποστάσει κείμενον, εἰς ἑνότητα δὲ θεότητος διὰ ταυτότητος φυσικῆς σφιγγόμενον, ἵνα μή τις ἀνάχυσις καὶ οἱονεὶ φυρμὸς γένηται Πατρὸς καὶ Υἱοῦ, εἰς μόνην ἑνάδα τρεχούσης τῆς ὑποστάσεως, τῆς πολλῆς λίαν ὁμοιότητος οὐκ ἐώσης φαίνεσθαι δυάδα.

[19] Vgl. z.B. Didymus, *Commentarius in Psalmos* 109,16–20 (Gronewald II 230–232):

vielen Namen entspricht jeweils etwas in der bezeichneten, realen Person. Sie sind die vielen, durch die Begrenztheit des menschlichen Bewusstseins bedingten Aspekte des einen realen Wesens. Origenes hat so in der Lehre von den Christusprädikaten die stoische Unterscheidung zwischen den Seinsbereichen des wesenhaften, hypostatischen Seins einerseits und des menschlichen Bewusstseins bzw. des gedachten Seins (*cum et sine fundamento in re*) in die christliche Philosophie als Fundamentalunterscheidung eingeführt.[20]

Die Kappadozier, allen voran Basilius und sein Bruder Gregor von Nyssa, haben vollendet, was Origenes durch die Rezeption der stoischen Lehre von der Epinoia innerhalb der christlichen Philosophie begonnen hatte, indem sie in der Auseinandersetzung mit Eunomius, dem philosophisch gebildeten Vertreter der Jungarianer, diese Lehre zu einer Sprachphilosophie ausbauten und damit gewissermaßen auch die Ansätze der antiken Theorie vom menschlichen Bewusstsein vollendeten. Genauer gesagt haben sie den Begriff der Epinoia innerhalb der christlichen Philosophie rehabilitiert, indem sie das kulturstiftende, erfinderische, methodisch vorgehende Element der endlichen Vernunft und damit ihre Kompetenz für den Bereich der endlichen Dinge unterstrichen. Sie haben damit epochal bedeutungsvoll der Diskreditierung des menschlichen Bewusstseins entgegengewirkt, die nicht nur im Arianismus, sondern durchaus auch bei Athanasius zu spüren ist. Der dogmatische Streit mit den Neuarianern ist in einer literarischen Kontroverse dokumentiert, die weder nur einen provinziellen Charakter hatte noch bloß eine Wiederauflage des alten arianischen Streits darstellt. Vielmehr sind die bedeutendsten Autoren des 4. Jh. in diesen Streit involviert, der obendrein auch philosophisch neue bedeutsame philosophische Entwürfe, wie z.B. die Sprachphilosophie, zutage gefördert hat.[21] Neben dem 359 entstandenen *Syntagmation* des Aetios sind es besonders die Schriften seines Schülers Eunomius gewesen, die die Antwort der Großen, des

τὸ πνεῦμα δὲ ἓν ὂν κατὰ τὰ διάφορα αὐτοῦ χαρίσματα πλῆθος ἀγαθῶν ἐστιν· ὁ γὰρ τὸ ἅγιον πνεῦμα ἔχων ἔχει τὰ χαρίσματα τοῦ πνεύματος ἀγαθὰ ὄντα πλείονα. καὶ τῇ μὲν οὐσίᾳ ἕν ἐστιν, ταῖς δὲ ἐπινοίαις πολλὰ ἀγαθά. ὡς καὶ ὁ θεὸς εἷς ἐστιν κατ᾽ οὐσίαν. λέγεται δέ καὶ κατὰ διαφόρους ἐπινοίας πολλά· ἀγαθός, ἄτρεπτος, ἀναλλοίωτος, πηγή, φῶς· καὶ πάλιν ὁ σωτὴρ ὡσαύτως εἷς ὢν κατ᾽ ὑποκείμενον λέγεται ζωή, ἀλήθεια.

[20] Zur genaueren Bedeutung der Epinoia bei Origenes vgl. meinen Aufsatz "Die philosophische Bedeutung des Kirchenvaters Origenes", *ThQ* 165 (1985) 94–105, hier 95–97.

[21] Vgl. A. M. Ritter, "Arianismus", *TRE* III, 1978, 692–719.

Basilius, des Gregor von Nyssa, Theodors von Mopsuestia, Johannes Chrysostomus u.a. herausforderten. Der Auftakt dieser Auseinandersetzung war die wohl um das Jahr 360 zu datierende *Apologie* des Eunomius, auf die Basilius mit seinem *Anatreptikos* oder *Adversus Eunomium* kritisch antwortete. Eunomius ließ darauf hin seine *Apologia apologiae* zunächst in drei Büchern von 377 bis 381 peu à peu erscheinen, auf die Gregor von Nyssa mit seinem monumentalen Werk *Contra Eunomium* (381–383) reagierte. Schließlich legte Eunomius im Jahre 383 sein *Glaubensbekenntnis* (ἔκθεσις πίστεως) vor, das wiederum Gregor im selben Jahr einer eingehenden Kritik unterzog in der Schrift *Refutatio confessionis Eunomii*.[22] In der Auseinandersetzung zwischen Eunomius einerseits und Basilius und Gregor andererseits geht es eigentlich und zuletzt und vor allem um das Problem der Epinoia. Basilius stellt die entscheidende Frage, "was denn eigentlich die Epinoia sei". Wie man es mit der menschlichen Vernunft, d.h. mit dem endlichen Bewusstsein und seinen inneren Resultaten, den Begriffen halte, das war die sprachphilosophische Gretchenfrage, die das vierte Jahrhundert in Atem hält. Eunomius' Antwort lässt an Klarheit nichts zu wünschen übrig: "Das, was durch das menschliche Denken ausgesagt wird, hat sein Sein nur in den Namen und in der Äußerung und verschwindet naturgemäß zusammen mit den Lauten der Stimme."[23] Hier ist deutlich erkennbar, als was die Epinoia von Eunomius angesehen wird: Sie ist in ihrer Äußerung nichts weiter als ein *flatus vocis*, die flüchtige Gestalt einer äußeren Bezeichnung. Sie ist nicht konstitutiv für den Wesensbegriff einer Sache. Was sie hervorbringt, hat keine Bedeutung (im Wortsinne), ist Falsches, Trügerisches, Fiktionales und hat mit der wahren Erkenntnis der Dinge nichts zu tun. Die Produkte des menschlichen Bewusstseins sind nach dieser Ansicht *per se* Verkehrungen der Wahrheit. In diesem Sinne sind alle Äußerungen der endlichen Vernunft entweder nur bedeutungslose Ausdrücke, bei denen man sich nichts denken kann, wie z.B. 'Skindapsos' oder 'Blityri', jene aus der Stoa stammenden Standardbeispiele für die sog. *voces non significativae*, oder sie beruhen, wie im Falle des Kolossalen, auf einer künstlichen Vergrößerung oder auch einer Verkleinerung, wie beim Begriff des

[22] Zu diesen Angaben und mehr Details vgl. die zuverlässige Studie von J.-A. Röder, *Gregor von Nyssa, Contra Eunomium I 1–146*, eingel., übers. und kommentiert, Frankfurt a.M. u.a. 1993, Einleitung 40–72.

[23] Eunomius, *Apologia* 8,4 (SC 305, 248). Vgl. auch *CE* II 44 (GNO I 238,26ff).

Pygmäen, oder sie gehen auf eine Art der Hinzufügung zurück, z.B. wenn wir die Polykephalen denken, oder auf eine Zusammensetzung wie bei den Mischtieren.[24] Die Ähnlichkeit dieses Beispielkatalogs mit stoischen oder epikureischen Texten darf nicht darüber hinwegtäuschen, dass die Funktion der Epinoia hier bei Eunomius von anderer Art ist als in den Philosophenschulen. Wollten die Stoiker die Epinoia als schöpferische Potenz, als das bei jedem Erkenntnisakt konstitutiv beteiligte endliche Bewusstsein charakterisieren, so wird sie bei Eunomius zum Urheber des Nichtigen, Phantastischen und Fiktiven, d.h. des bloß zufällig Gedachten. Auch nach Gregor verbindet Eunomius die Epinoia immer nur mit der leeren Phantasie.[25] Der philosophiegeschichtliche Hintergrund dieser Depotenzierung der menschlichen Vernunft ist schwer auszumachen. Man hat auf Zusammenhänge mit dem Neuplatonismus hingewiesen. In der Tat hat Plotin die stoische Epinoia ähnlich scharf kritisiert. Aber Terminologie und Gedanken haben sonst nicht viel mit dem Neuplatonismus zu tun.[26] Ob nicht doch Epikureisches im Hintergrund steht? Die Tatsache, dass die stoische Lehre von den σημαινόμενα, die ja für Basilius und Gregor sehr wichtig ist, von Eunomius implizit abgelehnt wird, indem der Name das individuelle wirkliche Wesen der Sache unmittelbar bezeichne,[27] könnte ein Hinweis sein. Zudem verdächtigt auch Gregor die eunomianische Lehre von der Epinoia des Epikureismus.[28]

---

[24] Vgl. Eunomius bei Gregor von Nyssa, *CE* II 179 (GNO I 276,22ff). Zu dem Beispielkatalog vgl. bes. Sextus Empiricus, *Adversus Mathematicos* IX 393–394 (Mutschmann II 293) und VIII 58ff (Mutschmann II 115ff), ferner SVF II 87.88 und Epicurus, *Fr.* 36 (Usener 105–106). Als Beispiele der bei Eunomius genannten *voces non significativae* nennt Gregor von Nyssa, *CE* III/V 44 (GNO II 176,6f) selbst die stoischen Ausdrücke 'Skindapsos' und das bis Leibniz gebräuchliche 'Blityri'. Vgl. SVF II 149; III 20. Gregor hat solche sinnlosen Ausdrücke in *In Ecclesiasten* 1 (GNO V 281,4ff) beschrieben als das "Nichtexistierende, das allein im Hervorbringen des Wortes sein Sein hat", also genau so wie Eunomius.

[25] Vgl. *CE* II 11 (GNO I, 229,29ff).

[26] Kritisch zur Neuplatonismusthese J. M. Rist, "Basil's 'Neoplatonism'. Its Background and Nature", in: P. J. Fedwick (Hrsg.), *Basil of Caesarea. Christian, Humanist, Ascetic. A Sixteen-hundredth Anniversary Symposium*, Toronto 1981, 137–220. Vgl. auch die Erörterungen bei L. Abramowski, "Eunomius", *RAC* VI, 943f und A. M. Ritter, "Eunomius", *TRE* X, 1982, 527.

[27] Eunomius, *Apologia* 12,9 (SC 305, 258).

[28] Vgl. *CE* II 410 (GNO I 345,25ff). Zum epikureischen (und arianischen) Hintergrund der Lehre von der Epinoia des Eunomius vgl. auch Th. Kobusch, "Name und Sein. Zu den sprachphilosophischen Grundlagen in der Schrift 'Contra Eunomium'

Basilius und Gregor versuchen die durch diesen arianischen Generalangriff beschädigte Würde des menschlichen Bewusstseins wiederherzustellen, indem sie es als eine schöpferische, sprachbegabte, bedeutungskonstitutive und methodisch disziplinierte Vernunft darstellen. Basilius macht in seiner gegen Eunomius gerichteten Schrift, sobald die Rede auf die Epinoia kommt, auf die tiefe Kluft, die sie trennt, aufmerksam.[29] Wäre die Epinoia – wie Eunomius behauptet – nur ein Schall, nur ein *flatus vocis*, dann müsste man sie viel eher 'Unsinn' (παράνοια) nennen und könnte sie nicht als eine Form der Sinnfindung begreifen. Gibt man aber zu, dass die Epinoia eine semantische Funktion hat, dass sie also etwas bezeichnet, dann muß, so schließt der in der stoischen Philosophie wohlbewanderte Kirchenvater, zwischen dem Bezeichnenden und dem Bezeichneten unterschieden werden, und das Bezeichnete ist nicht identisch mit dem bezeichneten zufälligen Gegenstand, sondern stellt eine eigene Ebene dar. Wie aber soll dann gedacht werden können, was Eunomius auch gesagt hatte, nämlich dass das durch die Epinoia bezeichnete Falsche und Nichtige mit dem Schall des Wortes verschwinde? Selbst wenn es wirklich immer falsch wäre, so bliebe doch dieses Falsche auch nach dem Verklingen des lautlichen Wortes als ein Gedachtes (νόημα) im Bewusstsein. Die Epinoia kann nämlich sowohl den Akt des Bewusstseins wie auch sein inneres Resultat, eben das Noema bezeichnen.[30] Mit anderen Worten: Wenn die Epinoia eine bezeichnende Funktion hat, muss immer die Ebene des lautlichen Sprechens von der Ebene der Bedeutung, die etwas Gedachtes in der Seele darstellt, unterschieden werden. Ein Hauptanliegen sowohl des Basilius wie Gregors liegt darin, die Ebene der Bedeutung eines Wortes zur Geltung zu bringen. Die Bedeutung, die bei beiden Autoren mit den stoischen Ausdrücken des σημαινόμενον oder auch der ἔμφασις bezeichnet wird, ist das durch die Epinoia Konstituierte, das niemals mit einem anderen austauschbar ist und so einem Erkannten erst eigentlich Bestimmtheit verleiht.[31] Im Reich der Bedeutung allein gibt es

---

des Gregor von Nyssa", in: L. F. Mateo-Seco – J. L. Bastero (Hrsg.), *El „Contra Eunomium I" en la Produccion Literaria De Gregorio De Nisa. VI. Coloquio Internacional sobre Gregorio de Nisa*, Pamplona 1988, 247–268, hier 252–254.

[29] Basilius, *Adversus Eunomium* I 6–7 (SC 299, 182–192).

[30] Vgl. Th. Dams (zitiert in SC 299, 182): "Le mot ἐπίνοια peut signifier l'acte mental et le resultat de cet acte, le νόημα en nous."

[31] Vgl. z.B. *CE* II 24 (GNO I 233,17–22): πρὸς οὓς τοῦτό φαμεν, ὅτι ἕτερον τοῦ

Eindeutigkeit. Wäre eine Konfusion unter den Bedeutungen möglich, dann verlöre die Bezeichnung der Dinge, besonders die vielheitliche Benennung desselben Dinges ihr Recht.[32] Würde man die Epinoia aber, wie Eunomius das ja in Wirklichkeit auch tut, als eine bedeutungslose Bezeichnung (ἄσημον ὄνομα) verstehen, die ausschließlich in der Pronunciation ihr Sein hätte, dann wären die Begriffe nicht mehr von den sinnlosen Ausdrücken unterscheidbar. Die eunomianische Beschreibung der Epinoia greift nach Basilius zu kurz. Sie begreift sie ausschließlich als die Urheberin des bloß Fiktiven, Nichtigen und Phantasierten. Eine solche Auffassung wird der wahren Rolle des menschlichen Bewusstseins nicht gerecht. Sie verkennt auch völlig die positiv-konstitutive Funktion der menschlichen Vernunft bei jeder Art von Erkenntnis. Deswegen sind die Begriffe des endlichen Bewusstseins nach Basilius eher als die subtileren und präzisierenden Bestätigungen (ἐπενθυμήσεις) des sinnlichkeitsbedingt gebildeten allgemeinen Begriffs anzusehen. So kann z.B. der Weizen je nach seinen verschiedenen Eigentümlichkeiten mal als 'Same', mal als 'Frucht' oder auch als 'Nahrung' verstanden werden. Was Basilius wie auch sein Bruder durch dieses Beispiel verdeutlichen wollen, ist die Aspektgebundenheit und insofern die Begrenztheit des menschlichen Denkens. Was immer vom Menschen gedacht wird, es ist aus einer bestimmten Sicht, d.h. im Hinblick auf ein bestimmtes Bezeichnetes oder in einer bestimmten Bedeutung erfasst.[33] In diesem Sinne offenbaren auch die vielen Epinoiai Christi (wie z.B. Wahrheit, Tür, Weinstock usw.), die schon Origenes so nachhaltig beschäftigt hatten, je verschiedene Aspekte oder Bedeutungen der einen Realität.[34]

ἀσυνθέτου καὶ ἕτερον τοῦ ἀγεννήτου τὸ σημαινόμενον. τὸ μὲν γὰρ τὴν ἁπλότητα τοῦ ὑποκειμένου, τὸ δὲ τὸ μὴ ἐξ αἰτίας εἶναι παρίστησι, καὶ οὐκ ἐπαλλάσσονται πρὸς ἀλλήλας αἱ τῶν ὀνομάτων ἐμφάσεις, κἂν περὶ τὸ ἓν ἀμφότερα λέγηται. Vgl. *CE* I 560 (GNO I 188,15): οὗτος τὴν παντελῆ τοῦ σημαινομένου μετάληψιν ἀπὸ τῆς συνήθους τῶν ὀνομάτων ἐμφάσεως ποιησάμενος εἰς ἄτοπον δῆθεν ἐκβάλλει τὸν λόγον. Zur "gewöhnlichen Bedeutung" s. auch *CE* I 643 (GNO I 211,16).

[32] *CE* II 474 (GNO I 364,26ff).

[33] Vgl. Basilius, *Adversus Eunomium* I 6,51–54 (SC 299, 186): Τούτων δὲ ἕκαστον τῶν λεγομένων καὶ κατ' ἐπίνοιαν θεωρεῖται, καὶ τῷ ψόφῳ τῆς γλώσσης οὐ συναπέρχεται· ἀλλὰ τῇ ψυχῇ τοῦ νενοηκότος ἐνίδρυται τὰ νοήματα. Vgl. auch *CE* I 560 (GNO I 188,13: κατά τι σημαινόμενον) und *CE* I 599 (GNO I 199,1).

[34] Basilius, *Adversus Eunomium* I 7,10ff (SC 299, 188): Ἄλλο γὰρ τὸ σημαινόμενον φωτὸς, καὶ ἄλλο ἀμπέλου, καὶ ἄλλο ὁδοῦ, καὶ ἄλλο ποιμένος. Vgl. auch Basilius, *Ep.* 8,8,6 (Courtonne I 32).

Gregors gegen Eunomius gerichtete Schrift ist ein einziger Protest gegen die Verunglimpfung der menschlichen Vernunft. Eine solche Geringschätzung der Epinoia nimmt uns alle Möglichkeit, so wendet Gregor ein, das Menschliche des menschlichen Lebens zu begreifen. Woher haben wir denn, so fragt Gregor in seinem hohen Lied auf die endliche Vernunft, die Errungenschaften der Geometrie, der Arithmetik, der Logik und der Physik, woher die Erfindungen der Maschinen, woher kommt so etwas wie die Metaphysik in beiderlei Gestalt, als Ontologie und als philosophische Theologie? Was ist zudem mit den später sog. knechtischen Künsten, was ist mit Ackerbau und Schifffahrt? Wie konnte das Meer dem Menschen zugänglich werden, wie die wildesten Tiere gezähmt? Wurde das nicht alles durch die Epinoia im Dienste des menschlichen Lebens erfunden? Indem Gregor auf diese Weise die menschliche Vernunft als die Stifterin der Kultur überhaupt präsentiert, setzt er einerseits die hellenistische Tradition der Kulturentstehungslehren fort, andererseits avanciert er dadurch zum vielgelesenen Vorbild in der Aufklärungszeit, ja sogar zum Aufklärer der Spätantike. Denn das II. Buch von *Contra Eunomium* (zitiert als Buch XII), in dem dieses Loblied steht, war es ausschließlich, was in der Renaissance und in der Aufklärungszeit von dieser Schrift bekannt war und rezipiert wurde.[35] Im Sinne der kulturstiftenden Funktion definiert Gregor die Epinoia durchaus nicht ohne bestimmte Anklänge an Aristoteles als die inventive Annäherung an das Unbekannte, die von intuitiv erfassten ersten Gedanken ausgeht und das daraus Folgende mit dem Ersten zusammenfügt.[36] Der in diesem Zusammenhang verwendete Ausdruck der ἔφοδος εὑρετική verweist auf die aristotelische Methode der *via inventionis* in der *Topik* oder, wie aus einer späteren Stelle deutlich wird,[37] allgemein auf die syllogistische Methode des Aristoteles. Wie immer es damit im Detail stehen mag, fest steht doch dies, dass das hohe Lied Gregors auf die Epinoia die Glorifizierung der aristotelisch verstandenen menschlichen Vernunft darstellt. Das ist umso bemerkenswerter, als Gregor im Zusammenhang mit dem Problem der Gotteserkenntnis eben diesen Vernunftbegriff einer unbarmherzigen Kritik unterzieht. Weswegen Gregor die Epinoia gleichwohl zu den höchsten Gütern zählt, liegt

[35] Vgl. dazu T. Kobusch, "Name und Sein", 248ff und Anm. 42.
[36] *CE* II 182 (GNO I 277,21).
[37] *CE* III/V 5 (GNO II 162,10).

in einem Element begründet, das in der patristischen Zeit allgemein ein hohes Bewertungskriterium darstellte. Die Epinoia ist nämlich auch die lebensdienliche Vernunft. "Alles, was die Zeit an Lebensnützlichem und -dienlichem . . . erfand, ist nur durch die Epinoia erfunden worden."[38] Die Künste und technischen Disziplinen helfen in diesem Sinne, leichter zu leben. So erfand sich das Leben auch die Medizin, die gleichwohl ein Geschenk Gottes genannt werden kann, denn "der Geist ist ein Werk Gottes". Wenn eben dieser selbe Geist in menschlicher Gestalt, eben die Epinoia, auch Trügerisches und Falsches hervorbringt – wie ja Eunomius hervorzuheben nicht müde wird –, dann ist dieser Hinweis nach Gregor durchaus ein Beitrag auch im Hinblick "auf unser Ziel". Denn "auch wir behaupten", dass die Epinoia wie auch die anderen Wissenschaften sowohl zum Dienst an der Wahrheit gebraucht wie auch in den Dienst der Lüge und der Falschheit gestellt werden können. Doch ist die Epinoia eigentlich zu einem guten Zweck von Gott der menschlichen Natur verliehen worden. Es steht mit ihr so ähnlich wie mit der Freiheit selbst: Zu einem guten Zweck gegeben kann sie doch jederzeit missbraucht werden.[39] Hier ist zugleich jene markante Stelle des Gedankengangs, wo sich die Wege des Eunomius und Gregors am deutlichsten trennen. Denn Gregor nimmt ausdrücklich den Grundgedanken des Eunomius auf, um ihn zu zerstören. Der Grundgedanke des Eunomius ist aber, dass Gott der Urheber der Sprache ist, indem er, bevor der Mensch existierte, den Dingen die Namen gab. Das ist Grund genug für Gregor, auf die absurden Implikationen einer solchen Annahme hinzuweisen. Offenbar hat Gott dieser Annahme gemäß ganz anthropomorph gedacht eine diskursive Begrifflichkeit benutzt und mit Stimme und Laut die einzelnen Begriffe geprägt. Wenn das aber richtig ist, dann muss sein Logos, wie der menschliche auch, bestimmte sinnliche Teile zur Äußerung benutzt haben, wie z.B. die Luftröhren, die Zunge, die Zähne, den Mund. Ja, sogar die Wangen sind nach Gregors höhnischer Gedankenführung, bei der er die stoische Lehre von den Stimmwerkzeugen heranzieht, Mitarbeiter am Werk des Logos.[40] Was Gregor somit Eunomius'

[38] *CE* II 183 (GNO I 277,30).
[39] *CE* II 185–192 (GNO I 278–280).
[40] *CE* II 198–203 (GNO I 282–284). Vgl. *De hominis opificio* IX (PG 44, 149b ff). Zur stoischen Lehre vgl. SVF II 836.

These von der göttlichen Setzung der Sprache entgegenhält, sind die notwendigen Implikationen körperlicher Vorstellungen, die die Grundvoraussetzung der Geistigkeit des göttlichen Wesens desavouieren. Deswegen kann es nach Gregor darüber keinen Zweifel geben, dass die lautliche Sprache eine Eigentümlichkeit einer inkarnierten Natur ist, die in artikulierten Worten die Gedanken des Herzens äußert.[41]

Ähnliches gilt für die physischen Verhältnisse des Redens und Zuhörens, über die Gregor feine phänomenologische Beobachtungen macht. Für die nicht allzu weit Entfernten benutzen wir die Stimme, um uns Gehör zu verschaffen. Sind die Adressaten weit entfernt, dann äußern wir unsere Meinung in der Schrift. Gegenüber den Anwesenden erheben wir entweder die Stimmlage oder, je nach der Distanz, senken sie. Bisweilen bedeuten wir den in der Nähe Stehenden nur durch einen Wink – im Mittelalter nach einigen Theorien die wortlose Sprache der Engel –, was zu tun ist, wir äußern ohne Worte einen Willensentschluss, wir geben durch eine Augenbewegung oder Handbewegung unser Ge- oder Missfallen kund. Kurzum, wenn schon die inkarnierte menschliche Existenz den Nächststehenden die geheimen Bewegungen des Herzens ohne Stimme, Wort und Schrift kundtun kann, sollte dann jene immaterielle, unberührbare oberste und erste Wesenheit, von der Eunomius spricht, auf Worte angewiesen sein – von denen Eunomius obendrein sagt, sie vergingen mit der Stimme –, um sich mitzuteilen? Auch wer, wie Eunomius, vom Hören Gottes spricht, setzt unweigerlich sinnliche Verhältnisse voraus, die dem angenommenen Wesen Gottes nicht gerecht werden. Nicht nur, weil eine Stimme immer nur durch ein Vermittelndes, wie z.B. die Luft, zu dem Hörenden gelangt, sondern vor allem, weil die Trennung der fünf Sinne mit ihren jeweiligen eigenen, unvertauschbaren Gegenstandsbereichen ein besonderer Ausdruck der Endlichkeit des menschlichen Bewusstseins ist, während das göttliche als ganzes Sehen, als ganzes Hören, als ganzes Erkennen ist oder mit dem Ausdruck aus der stoischen Mischungslehre: ὅλον δι' ὅλου. Diese intelligible Mischung ist eine zwar in sich unterschiedene, aber distanzlose, ganz und gar miteinander verbundene Einheit, die durch die Identität des Willens garantiert wird.[42]

---

[41] *CE* II 207 (GNO I 285,18f): ἴδιον γὰρ τῆς ἐνσωμάτου φύσεως τὸ διὰ ῥημάτων ἐξαγγέλλειν τὰ τῆς καρδίας νοήματα. Vgl. auch *CE* II 391 (GNO I 340,21ff).

[42] *CE* II 208–214 (GNO I 285–288).

Wenn aus diesen und anderen Gründen die eunomianische Vorstellung aufgegeben werden muss, dass Gott der Ursprung der Sprache sei und als "Pädagoge und Schulmeister" die ersten Menschen unmittelbar gelehrt habe, fragt es sich, wie sonst die Sprache in diese Welt gekommen sein sollte. Um diese Frage beantworten zu können, muss man sich nach Gregor zunächst die Funktion der Sprache klarmachen. Wie die dargelegte Argumentation gezeigt hat, bedarf Gott selbst nicht der Worte und Bezeichnungen, um sich mitteilen zu können. Die Erfindung der einzelnen Worte genügte vielmehr dem menschlichen Bedürfnis nach der Bezeichnung der Dinge. Die Sprache wurde deswegen allein "von uns selbst erdacht" (ἐπενοήθη).[43] Gott ist der Schöpfer der Dinge, nicht der Sprache. Das hat er der menschlichen Vernunft selbst überlassen.[44] Sprache und Vernunft – das ist dasselbe. Die Rede von der Erschaffung des Menschen meint notwendig immer auch die Verleihung dieser sprachbegabten Vernunft. Es ist keine Epoche denkbar, in der es Menschen ohne Sprache, ohne Vernunft, ohne Kultur gegeben hätte. Eunomius hatte dagegen die These vertreten, dass die ersten Menschen "in Unvernunft und Sprachlosigkeit zusammengelebt" hätten, wenn Gott sie nicht die Namen der Dinge gelehrt hätte.[45] Seitdem aber ist es nach Eunomius ein von Gott in die Natur gelegtes Gesetz, dass aus den Dingen selbst die Namen hervorgehen. Namen und Begriffe sind in diesem Sinne für Eunomius "natürlich".[46] Das ist für Gregor die eigentliche Crux des Gedankengangs. Wenn Eunomius recht hätte, müssten doch alle Menschen dieselbe Sprache sprechen. Die Sprache kann daher nicht die Sache der Natur sein. Vielmehr ist sie nach Gregor Ausdruck der Freiheit.[47] Gott hat ja auch nicht 'von oben' die Lebewesen mit bestimmten Bezeichnungen belegt, sondern Adam die Freiheit der Namensgebung gegeben. Diese Freiheit, das Erkannte

[43] *CE* II 237 (GNO I 295,27).

[44] *CE* II 246 (GNO I 298,10ff). Vgl. auch *CE* II 281 (GNO I 309,13ff): ὅτι θεὸς πραγμάτων ἐστὶ δημιουργός, οὐ ῥημάτων ψιλῶν. οὐδὲ γὰρ ἐκείνου χάριν, ἀλλ' ἡμῶν ἕνεκεν ἐπίκειται τοῖς πράγμασι τὰ ὀνόματα.

[45] *CE* II 398 (GNO I 342,22ff). Vgl. auch *CE* II 549 (GNO I 386,30ff).

[46] Zu Eunomius' Lehre von der ἔννοια φυσική vgl. bes. L. Abramowski, "Eunomius", *RAC* VI, 943; 946.

[47] *CE* II 546 (GNO I 385,28–386,2): εἰ οὖν ὁ νόμος τῆς φύσεως ἐκ τῶν πραγμάτων ἡμῖν ἀναφύεσθαι τὰς προσηγορίας ἐποίει ὥσπερ ἐκ τῶν σπερμάτων ἢ τῶν ῥιζῶν τὰ βλαστήματα, καὶ μὴ τῇ προαιρέσει τῶν δηλούντων τὰ πράγματα τὰς σημαντικὰς τῶν ὑποκειμένων ἐπωνυμίας ἐπέτρεπε, πάντες ἂν ἦμεν οἱ ἄνθρωποι πρὸς ἀλλήλους ὁμόγλωσσοι.

so oder anders zu nennen, liegt in der Natur. Wenn man das 'Bewusstsein' (ἐπίνοια) nennen will – Gregor kümmert sich nicht um austauschbare Namen.[48] Wenn es aber bei Gregor – mit den schönen Worten Wilhelm von Humboldts, aber durchaus im Sinne Gregors – die "Untrennbarkeit des menschlichen Bewusstseins und der menschlichen Sprache" gibt, dann gilt auch für die Epinoia, dass sie auf Freiheit beruht, oder mit den eigenen Worten Gregors: "Die Epinoia ist eine Tätigkeit unserer diskursiven Vernunft und hängt von dem Entschluß (προαίρεσις) der Sprechenden ab, nicht in sich subsistierend, sondern aufgrund des Antriebs der Mitunterredner seiend."[49] Man muss sich vergegenwärtigen, was hier, in den wunderbaren Texten eines großen Geistes des 4. Jh. geschieht. Da wird zum ersten Mal *expressis verbis* das menschliche Sprechen und Denken, Bewusstsein überhaupt, wenn man so sagen kann, als die Sache der Freiheit bezeichnet. Vernunft aber ist in allen Menschen. Gregor sagt es ausdrücklich: Da das Vernünftige in allen Menschen ist, müssen je nach den Unterschieden der Völker auch die Verschiedenheiten der Namen, d.h. der Sprachen betrachtet werden.[50] Die Vielheit der Sprachen und die durch das menschliche Bewusstsein konstituierten verschiedenen Bedeutungen der Wörter sind nicht mehr als Abfall von einer Ursprache zu verstehen, sondern als Ausdruck der von Gott geschenkten Freiheit. A. Borst hat in seiner bewundernswerten Arbeit dieses Verständnis von Sprache und Bewusstsein des Menschen mit Recht 'revolutionär' genannt. Wird es jemanden noch wundern, dass gerade das II. Buch von *Contra Eunomium* eine entscheidende Auseinandersetzung der neuzeitlichen Sprachphilosophie, in die berühmte Autoren wie Maupertuis, Süßmilch, Herder, Humboldt u.a. involviert waren, mitbestimmt hat?[51] Die Aufklärung hat ihn als Bundesgenossen im Kampf gegen falsche Vorurteile betrachtet. Sie hat ihn sogar in den Rang des ersten christlichen Aufklärers erhoben, der auf dem Gebiet der Sprachphilosophie die Sache der autonomen Vernunft vertreten hat. Aber Aufklärer haben es schwer, zumal dann, wenn sie so differenziert argumentieren wie Gregor von Nyssa, dessen hohes Lied

---

[48] *CE* II 396 (GNO I 342,10ff): ἡ δὲ ἐξουσία τοῦ τὰ νοηθέντα πάντα τοιῶσδε ἢ ὡς ἑτέρως κατονομάζειν ἐν τῇ φύσει κεῖται· ἣν εἴτε τις ἐπίνοιαν εἴτε ἄλλο τι βούλοιτο λέγειν, οὐ διοισόμεθα. Vgl. auch *CE* II 304–305 (GNO I 315,27ff).

[49] *CE* II 334 (GNO I 323,29).

[50] *CE* II 246 (GNO I 298,17).

[51] Vgl. T. Kobusch, "Name und Sein", 247–268.

auf die Epinoia nur die eine Seite der Medaille ist. Die andere besteht in einer unverwechselbaren Kritik an jener Theorie, nach der diese Epinoia, d.h. die endliche, nach einer bestimmten Methode erforschende, neugierige, menschliche Vernunft auch die göttliche Wesenheit wie ein Ding unter anderen ergründen könne.[52] Doch das ist ein weites Feld.

[52] Vgl. dazu T. Kobusch, "Zeit und Grenze. Zur Kritik des Gregor von Nyssa an der Einseitigkeit der Naturphilosophie", in: S. G. Hall (Hrsg.), *Gregory of Nyssa, Homelies on Ecclesiastes. An English Version with Supporting Studies. Proceedings of the Seventh International Colloquium on Gregory of Nyssa*, Berlin – New York 1993, 299–317; ferner "Metaphysik als Lebensform bei Gregor von Nyssa", in: H. R. Drobner – A. Viciano (Hrsg.), *Gregory of Nyssa: Homilies on the Beatitudes. An English Version with Commentary and Supporting Studies, Proceedings of the Eighth International Colloquium on Gregory of Nyssa*, Leiden – Boston – Köln 2000, 467–485, hier 467–471.

DER THEOLOGIEGESCHICHTLICHE HINTERGRUND DER EPINOIAI-LEHRE GREGORS VON NYSSA

Basil Studer

Einleitung

In einem bemerkenswerten Aufsatz geht H. J. Sieben der Frage nach, in welchem Sinn Gregor von Nyssa in seiner Schrift *De perfectione* die Epinoiai-Lehre des Origenes übernommen hat.[1] Er zeigt dabei auf, dass bei ihm die Namen Jesu zu Vorbildern des christlichen Lebens geworden sind. Wer bedenkt, welchen Wert die ἐπίνοιαι des Origenes in der Frömmigkeit Gregors bekommen haben, wird nicht überrascht sein, dass die Erwägungen über sie auch in seiner Polemik gegen Eunomius weiten Raum einnehmen.[2]

Gewiss steht im zweiten Buch *Contra Eunomium*, das uns hier beschäftigt, die Inkarnation nicht im Vordergrund.[3] Im Anschluss an die Kontroverse zwischen seinem Bruder Basilius und dem Bischof von Cyzicus diskutiert Gregor darin vielmehr die Fragen der damaligen Trinitätstheologie und im Zusammenhang damit im besonderen jene der Gotteserkenntnis. Weil dabei jedoch der Gebrauch der Gottesnamen mit dem der Christusnamen verglichen wird, kommt die Epinoiai-Lehre des Origenes dennoch voll zur Geltung.[4] Sieben selbst weist denn auch im Abschnitt "Beiläufiges Vorkommen der Epinoiai-Lehre bei den Kappadoziern" auf Stellen im ersten Buch *Adversus Eunomium* des Basilius und auf Stellen im zweiten und dritten Buch *Contra Eunomium* Gregors hin.[5] Dabei ist er von seiner Fragestellung

---

[1] H. J. Sieben, "Vom Heil in den vielen 'Namen Christi' zur 'Nachahmung' derselben. Zur Rezeption der Epinoiai-Lehre des Origenes durch die kappadokischen Väter", *ThPh* 73 (1998) 1–28.

[2] Vgl. H. J. Sieben, "Zur Rezeption der Epinoiai-Lehre", 18–21.

[3] Vgl. R. P. C. Hanson, *The Search for the Christian Doctrine of God: The Arian Controversy 318–381*, Edinburgh 1988, 627.

[4] Origenes übernimmt, wie sich zeigen wird, von der Überlieferung die Lehre von den vielen Namen Gottes. Aber er entfaltet vor allem die Auffassungen von den vielen Bezeichnungen und Titeln Christi.

[5] Vgl. H. J. Sieben, "Zur Rezeption der Epinoiai-Lehre", 12f, mit Basilius, *Adversus*

her nicht genötigt, genauer auf die theologische Problematik des Origenes und des Nysseners einzugehen.

Tatsächlich erscheint in der Entfaltung der origenischen Epinoiai-Lehre, wie sie in der eunomianischen Kontroverse geschehen ist, viel stärker als zuvor eine doppelte Spannung. Einerseits ist die Aufmerksamkeit darin sehr stark auf die Gottesaussagen gerichtet, welche mit der Kosmologie zusammenhängen und darum einen philosophischen Charakter besitzen. Die biblischen Ansatzpunkte treten demgemäß, besonders im Vergleich zum *Johanneskommentar* des Origenes, zurück. Auf der anderen Seite führt die Diskussion über die Erkenntnis der göttlichen Natur zu einer Betonung des göttlichen Wirkens in der Geschichte und damit, wenn vielleicht auch nicht sehr ausdrücklich, zu einer größeren Beachtung des Verhältnisses der θεολογία zur οἰκονομία.[6] Wer auf diese zweifache Spannung zwischen den mehr kosmologischen und den mehr soteriologischen Aussagen sowie zwischen dem ewigen Sein Gottes und dessen Wirken in der Zeit achtet, muss sich zudem fragen, welche Bedeutung Gregor dem Glauben und der Geschichte zumisst. Offensichtlich hilft eine solche Betrachtungsweise die theologische Eigenart des zweiten Buches *Contra Eunomium* Gregors klarer zu begreifen.

Um den Fragestand noch etwas besser zu erklären, sei mir erlaubt, an den Vortrag zu erinnern, den ich am Gregor-Symposion in Pamplona gehalten habe.[7] Unter dem Titel "Der geschichtliche Hintergrund des ersten Buches *Contra Eunomium* Gregors von Nyssa" behandelte ich im ersten Abschnitt die kirchengeschichtliche Lage um 380. Im zweiten Abschnitt hingegen ging ich auf die damalige Rezeption des nizänischen Glaubens sowie auf die dabei verwendete theologische Methode ein. In den folgenden Ausführungen werde ich nicht mehr so weit ausholen. Ich möchte mich vielmehr allein mit der Frage befassen, in welcher Weise Gregor sich in seinem zweiten Buch *Contra Eunomium* an die Kontroverse zwischen Eunomius und Basilius angeschlossen und dabei die aus einer breiten Tradition herausgewach-

---

Eunomium I 5–7 (SC 299, 180–188), sowie 18ff; *CE* II 179; 182 (GNO I 276; 277); *CE* II 344; 347; 350 (GNO I 326; 327; 328).

[6] Vgl. G. Maspero, *Theologia, Oikonomia e Historia: La teologia della storia di Gregorio di Nissa*, Diss. Pamplona 2003.

[7] B. Studer, "Der geschichtliche Hintergrund des ersten Buches Contra Eunomium Gregors von Nyssa", in: L. F. Mateo-Seco – J. Bastero (Hrsg.), *El „Contra Eunomium I" en la Produccion Literaria De Gregorio De Nisa. VI Coloquio Internacional sobre Gregorio de Nisa*, Pamplona 1988, 139–171.

sene Epinoiai-Lehre des Origenes übernommen hat. Aus diesem Fragestand ergibt sich die Einteilung meiner Darlegungen. In diesen geht es zuerst um die Epinoiai-Lehre Gregors selbst, weiter um ihr Verhältnis zu den Auffassungen des Basilius, ferner um ihre origenische Herkunft und schließlich um ihre Verwurzelung in der biblischen und kirchlichen Überlieferung.

I. *Die Epinoiai-Lehre im zweiten Buch* Contra Eunomium *Gregors*

Im zweiten Buch *Contra Eunomium*, in dem Gregor sich im Anschluss an die vorausgehende Kontroverse zwischen Basilius und Eunomius mit diesem auseinandersetzt, stehen zwei Thesen im Vordergrund. Nach der ersten identifiziert Eunomius das Wesen Gottes mit der göttlichen ἀγεννησία.[8] Laut der zweiten These hingegen entsprechen die Namen sosehr dem Wesen einer Sache, dass verschiedene Namen auf verschiedene Wesen verweisen.[9] In den Augen seiner kappadozischen Gegner vertritt Eunomius diese beiden Thesen, um damit die nizänische Lehre von der Gleichheit von Vater und Sohn abzulehnen.[10] Weil nämlich der Sohn nicht ἀγέννητος ist wie der Vater, ist er dem Wesen nach von ihm verschieden.[11] Er steht zwar über allen Geschöpfen, ist aber dennoch geworden und damit mit dem Vater nicht vergleichbar.[12]

---

[8] Vgl. besonders *CE* II 12–23 (GNO I 230–233, mit einem Zitat aus Eunomius); *CE* II 141 (GNO I 266); *CE* II 158 (GNO I 271); *CE* II 177 (GNO I 276); *CE* II 377B-386 (GNO I 336–339); *CE* II 504–523A (GNO I 373–379, mit Zitaten des Eunomius); *CE* II 623f (GNO I 408). Vgl. ausserdem Eunomius, *Apologia* 7–11 (SC 305, 244–256), zit. bei Basilius, *Adversus Eunomium* I 5 (SC 299, 176); Basilius, *Adversus Eunomium* I 4 (SC 299, 164, mit der Formel, welche nach B. Sesboüé die Hauptthese des Aëtius zusammenfasst). Dazu R. P. C. Hanson, *The Search*, 619–622.

[9] Vgl. *CE* II 177 (GNO I 276); *CE* II 481 (GNO I 366); *CE* II 487 (GNO I 368). Vgl. ferner Basilius, *Adversus Eunomium* II 3–4 (SC 305, 18); II 9 (SC 305, 36). Dazu R. P. C. Hanson, *The Search*, 630.

[10] Vgl. *CE* II 50–60 (GNO I 240–243), bes. *CE* II 54 (GNO I 241); *CE* II 125 (GNO I 262, mit einem Hinweis auf Basilius).

[11] Vgl. *CE* II 21 (GNO I 232).

[12] Vgl. Basilius, *Adversus Eunomium* I 22 (SC 299, 250ff), mit den Hinweisen auf Eunomius, *Apologia* 11,1–13 und 17–19 (SC 305, 254–256). Hinsichtlich dieses Textes stellt sich die Frage, ob Eunomius wie Aëtius als Anhomäer zu betrachten ist. R. P. C. Hanson, *The Search*, 613 und 627 verneint diese Frage und betrachtet Eunomius, gestützt auf Philostorgius, als Homöer. B. Sesboüé, in SC 299, 19, bejaht die Frage, betont aber in SC 299, 27, mit E. Cavalcanti, Eunomius hätte es vermieden, von der Unähnlichkeit des Sohnes zu sprechen.

Basilius hatte die beiden Thesen und ihre negativen Konsequenzen in der Widerlegung der ersten Apologie vor allem mit der Lehre von den ἐπίνοιαι zurückzuweisen versucht.[13] Eunomius hatte in seiner Replik speziell diese Auffassung bekämpft.[14] Darum legt Gregor bei der Verteidigung seines Bruders großes Gewicht auf die genaue Umschreibung des Begriffes ἐπίνοια und weist damit seinerseits die beiden Hauptthesen des Eunomius zurück.[15]

Es ist nicht leicht den Gedankengängen Gregors zu folgen. Sie sind allzu sehr von der recht subtilen Beweisführung des Gegners bestimmt und deswegen selbst gewunden und schwer nachzuvollziehen. Allein schon der Umstand, dass Gregor sich oft auf Basilius stützt, wie ihn Eunomius verstanden hatte, erschwert das Verständnis ungemein. Es sei dennoch versucht, seine Meinung von den ἐπίνοιαι Gottes kurz zu umreißen.

Wie sonst in den Diskussionen um den nizänischen Glauben geht es auch in *CE* II vorrangig um die Weise, im Anschluss an die Bibel und die kirchliche Lehre von Vater und Sohn sowie auch vom Heiligen Geist zu sprechen. Im Vordergrund stehen darum die Namen (ὀνόματα) und Benennungen (προσηγορίαι). Diese charakterisierenden Aussagen beruhen auf einer tieferen Überlegung, auf der ἐπίνοια im aktiven Sinn.[16] Wer nämlich eine Sache vordergründig erfasst hat, müht sich, ihre verschiedenen Aspekte, die ἐπίνοιαι in der passiven Bedeutung, herauszubringen.[17] Im Falle Gottes gründet diese vertiefte Erkenntnis auf der Offenbarung seiner Werke.[18] Die Namen und die von ihnen ausgedrückten Begriffe bestimmen jedoch nicht die Natur einer Sache.[19]

---

[13] Vgl. *CE* II 42–50 (GNO I 238ff).

[14] Vgl. *CE* II 42–50 (GNO I 238ff); *CE* II 66 (GNO I 245); *CE* II 125 (GNO I 262).

[15] Vgl. die Texte in *Lexicon Gregorianum* III 791–793: ἐπινοέω; III 793–799: ἐπίνοια. Dazu E. Mühlenberg, *Die Unendlichkeit Gottes bei Gregor von Nyssa*, Göttingen 1966, 183–196, bes. 192ff, mit *CE* II 94–105; 119–124 (GNO I 254–257; 260–262).

[16] Vgl. *CE* II 192 (GNO I 280); *CE* II 194 (GNO I 281). Dazu *Lexikon Gregorianum* III 795f, II.C: ἐπίνοιαι als Aspekte differenzierendes Denken.

[17] *CE* II 182 (GNO I 277).

[18] *CE* II 13 (GNO I 230): analoge Erkenntnis aus der Schönheit der Schöpfung; *CE* II 298f (GNO I 314), mit einer Definition von ἐπίνοια; *CE* II 304 (GNO I 315); *CE* II 353 (GNO I 329); *CE* II 148–158 (GNO I 268–271); *CE* II 581–587 (GNO I 395–397), besonders 583–584 (GNO I 396–397).

[19] Vgl. *CE* II 386 (GNO I 338f): nicht die οὐσία, sondern τὸ πῶς oder τὸ ποιόν werden erkannt. Dazu Basilius, *Adversus Eunomium* II 9 (SC 305, 38); II 28 (SC 305, 120).

Gregor kommt immer wieder auf diese These zurück. Um sie zu erhärten, entfaltet er seine Auffassung von dem alle Erkenntnis übersteigenden Gott.[20] Ergänzend dazu spricht er vom Glauben Abrahams,[21] äußert seine Bedenken gegenüber der Neugierde[22] und betont die Unmöglichkeit, die eigene Seele zu erkennen.[23] Ohne eine eigene Existenz zu besitzen,[24] verweisen die Namen und Begriffe auf ihr Subjekt, auf die οὐσία sofern sie ὑποκείμενον ist. Dabei sind es gewöhnlich ihrer viele.[25] Aber sie sind nicht zerstreut, sondern kommen einem einzigen ὑποκείμενον zu.[26]

Gregor wendet nun den so verstandenen Begriff der ἐπίνοια auf das Verhältnis Gottes zu seinem Sohn an. Die ἀγεννησία ist nicht mit dem Wesen Gottes gleichzusetzen.[27] Sie ist nur eine ἐπίνοια Gottes und nicht einmal die einzige.[28] Wie die anderen göttlichen Attribute lässt sie nicht das Wesen Gottes als solches verstehen, selbst wenn sie auf das eine ὑποκείμενον verweist. Um sich dazu weiter abzusichern,[29] unterscheidet Gregor fortwährend zwischen den ἐπίνοιαι oder νοήματα und den ὀνόματα, welche sich auf die πράγματα und besonders auf die ἐνέργειαι beziehen.[30] Dazu verteidigt er die Berechtigung über eine Sache weiter nachzudenken und so ihre verschiedenen Aspekte herauszuschälen.[31] Vor allem findet er eine Bestätigung

---

[20] *CE* II 63–83 (GNO I 244–251), besonders *CE* II 71 (GNO I 248f).

[21] *CE* II 84–96 (GNO I 251–254), besonders *CE* II 93 (GNO I 254), mit einer Definition des Glaubens.

[22] *CE* II 97–105 (GNO I 255–257).

[23] *CE* II 106–120 (GNO I 257–261).

[24] Vgl. *CE* II 589 (GNO I 398).

[25] Vgl. *CE* II 133 (GNO I 264).

[26] Vgl. *CE* II 353–356 (GNO I 329f); *CE* II 469–479 (GNO I 363–366), besonders 473 und 475. Dazu *CE* III/V 56 (GNO II 180).

[27] Vgl. *CE* II 270 (GNO I 305); *CE* II 612 (GNO I 404f), mit einem Basiliuszitat.

[28] *CE* II 137–141 (GNO I 265f); *CE* II 271 (GNO I 305f); *CE* II 473 (GNO I 364) (Ablehnung der Auffassung des Eunomius).

[29] Zu beachten ist, dass Gregor die διάνοια, die begriffliche Deutung der von den biblischen Namen bezeichneten Wirklichkeiten als Aufgabe der Theologie betrachtet. Vgl. *CE* II 136 (GNO I 265).

[30] Die Dreiheit von Name oder Bezeichnung – von eingehender Überlegung oder Hinsicht – von Sache oder Kräfte findet sich in zahlreichen Texten. Vgl. *CE* II 12 (GNO I 230); *CE* II 125–195 (GNO I 262–281); über das Benennen und Erdenken Gottes, besonders *CE* II 160 (GNO I 271) und *CE* II 174 (GNO I 275); *CE* II 513 (GNO I 376); *CE* II 515 (GNO I 377); *CE* II 589 (GNO I 398).

[31] Vgl. die in Anm. 18 zitierten Texte über die Offenbarung Gottes aus den Werken. Dazu *CE* II 391f (GNO I 340), wo es heisst, dass der Mensch seine Gedanken wegen seiner körperlichen Verfassung den anderen nicht ohne Worte vermitteln kann.

seines theologischen Vorgehens in der Christologie, in der Christus verschiedene Namen zugesprochen werden, seien es Namen, die in den Heiligen Schriften vorkommen,[32] oder seien es Namen, mit denen sich der Herr selbst benannt hat.[33]

Eunomius hingegen stellt sich gegen die Vielfalt der Namen Gottes.[34] Er lehnt es im Besonderen ab, den Begriff ἀγεννησία und den damit oft verbundenen Begriff ἀφθαρσία als ἐπίνοια zu verstehen.[35] Für ihn ist Gott 'wesenhaft' ohne Anfang und ohne Ende.[36] Offenbar fürchtet er, dass bei einer Verwendung von ἐπίνοια die göttliche Wirklichkeit in Frage gestellt wird. Vielleicht im Hinblick auf die Antithese κατ' ἐπίνοιαν – καθ' ὑπόστασιν betrachtet er die ἐπίνοια als reines Gedankending.[37] Jedenfalls weist er das Beispiel des Weizenkornes ab, in dem verschiedene Aspekte unterschieden werden können.[38] Er zeigt sich selbst sehr skeptisch gegenüber der Meinung von den verschiedenen ἐπίνοιαι Christi.[39] Er lässt sich also in seinen Auffassungen über die ἀγεννησία Gottes nicht erschüttern. Nach seiner Meinung teilt Basilius mit seinen ἐπίνοιαι das Wesen Gottes auf.[40] Während er die Wirklichkeit der ἐπίνοια ablehnt, hält er am Realismus der Namen im allgemeinen und der Aussagen über Gott im besonderen fest.[41] Laut seinem Sprachverständnis stammen diese Namen wie alle Namen von Gott und nicht von den Menschen.[42] Im übrigen geht es Eunomius letztlich nicht einfach um die Ablehnung der Epinoiai-

---

[32] *CE* II 343–358 (GNO I 326–331).

[33] *CE* II 294–332 (GNO I 313–323); Ausgangspunkt der Diskussion: Basilius, *Adversus Eunomium* I 12 (SC 299, 212ff); *CE* II 350–358 (GNO I 328–331).

[34] *CE* II 359–365 (GNO I 331ff); *CE* II 469–479 (GNO I 363–366), besonders *CE* II 475 (GNO I 364f).

[35] Vgl. besonders *CE* II 42–50 (GNO I 238–240). Dazu Eunomius, *Apologia* 6–8 (SC 305, 242–250). Weiter, *CE* II 66 (GNO I 245); *CE* II 350–370 (GNO I 331–334).

[36] Vgl. *CE* II 125 (GNO I 262); *CE* II 336–339 (GNO I 324f); *CE* II 377–386 (GNO I 336–339).

[37] *CE* II 45–49 (GNO I 239f); *CE* II 180 (GNO I 276f); *CE* II 387 (GNO I 339); *CE* II 492–503 (GNO I 370–373). Dazu Eunomius, *Apologia* 8,1–6 (SC 305, 246–248), zitiert von Basilius, *Adversus Eunomium* I 5 (SC 299, 180).

[38] *CE* II 195 (GNO I 282); *CE* II 364f (GNO I 332f); *CE* II 387f (GNO I 339).

[39] *CE* II 310ff (GNO I 317); *CE* II 347–350 (GNO I 327f).

[40] *CE* II 462–468 (GNO I 361ff).

[41] *CE* II 42–50 (GNO I 238ff); *CE* II 334 (GNO I 323f); *CE* II 589 (GNO I 389). Dazu Eunomius, *Apologia* 18 (SC 305, 268–270).

[42] *CE* II 195–204 (GNO I 281–284); *CE* II 246–293 (GNO I 298–313, über den Ursprung der menschlichen Sprache); *CE* II 281–288 (GNO I 309ff, Gegenargument: die menschliche Sprache ist nicht gegen die Vorsehung); *CE* II 389–394 (GNO I 339ff); *CE* II 413–422 (GNO I 346–350).

Lehre. Entscheidend ist für ihn, selbst wenn er dies vielleicht ungenügend zum Ausdruck bringt, die Ordnung (τάξις) zu wahren, in welcher die real verschiedenen Personen der Dreifaltigkeit aufeinander bezogen sind.[43]

Um die Stellung Gregors noch besser zu verstehen, mag es nützlich sein, näher auf seinen methodologischen Ansatz zu achten. Er hält sich einerseits an die Bibel und die kirchliche Tradition und gebraucht andererseits die Dialektik seiner Zeit. Dieses zweifache Vorgehen ist im Grunde genommen von dem des Eunomius nicht verschieden.[44] Auf jeden Fall ist die doppelte Orientierung der theologischen Methode Gregors offensichtlich.[45] Auf der einen Seite stützt er sich auf die Heilige Schrift und auf die kirchliche Tradition. Die biblische Autorität erscheint vor allem in der Verwendung der Christusnamen, die größtenteils auf die Heiligen Schriften zurückgehen.[46] Auf Grund seiner Einstellung zur Bibel lehnt er den Verweis des Eunomius auf die 'Heiligen', d.h. auf die Propheten und die Apostel, nicht ab.[47] Er kritisiert nur die Art und Weise seines Gegners, sich auf die 'Heiligen' zu berufen. Dasselbe gilt auch für die Art des Eunomius, sich auf das Glaubensbekenntnis zu stützen.[48] Gregor selbst stellt dem Symbol des Eunomius nicht das der Väter von Nizäa entgegen. Auf der anderen Seite ist die theologische Methode des Gregor von der Dialektik seiner Zeit geprägt. Darin unterscheidet er sich jedoch kaum von Eunomius, selbst wenn er diesen als

---

[43] Vgl. die Darstellung der trinitarischen Aussagen bei Eunomius, *Apologia* 27 (SC 305,290–294). Dazu Basilius, *Adversus Eunomium* I 20 (SC 299, 244–246).

[44] Vgl. *CE* II 11 (GNO I 229f): Basilius, der Vorkämpfer der Wahrheit, führt den Kampf gegen Eunomius mit Hilfe der ἔννοιαι κοιναί und der Zeugnisse der Schrift; *CE* II 49 (GNO I 240). Dazu B. Sesboüé, in SC 305, 179ff, mit Eunomius, *Apologia* 1–6 (SC 305, 234–244), sowie die Polemik dagegen in Basilius, *Adversus Eunomium* I 4 (SC 299, 166 gegen das Glaubensbekenntnis des Eunomius) und *Adversus Eunomium* I 5 (SC 299, 170) gegen *Apologia* 7 (SC 305, 244).

[45] Vgl. *CE* II 98 (GNO I 255); *CE* II 319 (GNO I 319). Dazu die verschiedenen Studien in M. Harl (Hrsg.), *Écriture et culture philosophique dans la pensée de Grégoire de Nysse. Actes de Chevetogne, 1969*, Leiden 1971; B. Studer, *Schola Christiana. Die Theologie zwischen Nizäa und Chalzedon*, Paderborn 1998, 158f; 180–186.

[46] Vgl. *CE* II 293–358 (GNO I 312–331).

[47] Vgl. *CE* II 310 (GNO I 317), sowie Basilius, *Adversus Eunomium* II 18 (SC 305, 70ff). Dazu R. P. C. Hanson, *The Search*, 624f, wo es heisst, dass Eunomius viele Schrifttexte anführte.

[48] Vgl. *CE* II 11ff (GNO I 229ff). Dazu Basilius, *Adversus Eunomium* II 4–5 (SC 299, 162–170), der den Hinweis des Eunomius auf das alte Glaubensbekenntnis stark kritisiert.

'Technologen' abzufertigen sucht.[49] Inhaltlich gesehen, hält sich Gregor an die stoische Kategorienlehre.[50] Danach existieren die ἐπίνοιαι wie die ὀνόματα nicht für sich selbst. Zusammen mit den Namen verweisen sie aber auf etwas, was in den Dingen wirklich existiert.[51] Sie kommen einem ὑποκείμενον zu, wie Gregor öfter betont.[52] Sie bringen damit zum Ausdruck, auf welche Weise die fragliche οὐσία sich verwirklicht. Gregor unterscheidet also mit der stoischen Dialektik 'das, was ist' (τί ἐστιν) und 'wie es ist' (ὅπως ἐστίν). B. Sesboüé deckt in seiner Einleitung zum *Adversus Eunomium* des Basilius diesen Zusammenhang klar auf.[53] Es kann jedoch nicht übersehen werden, dass die Kappadozier die gemeinsamen und individuellen ποιότητες nicht klar unterscheiden. Sie haben vielmehr die Tendenz, die gemeinsamen Eigentümlichkeiten, die κοινά oder das κοινόν, von den ἰδιώματα zu unterscheiden und auf die οὐσία zu reduzieren.[54]

Wer dieses doppelte Vorgehen beurteilen will, muss sicher zugeben, dass der dialektischen Bestimmung der Begriffe ein sehr wichtiger Platz zukommt. Die Widerlegung des Eunomius spielt sich vor allem auf der Ebene der philosophischen Analyse ab. In dieser Einschätzung ist der Rückgriff auf die göttlichen Attribute, die sich aus der Kosmologie ergeben, mit eingeschlossen. Immer und immer wieder ist vom Schöpfer die Rede. Die ἀγεννησία bezieht sich nach Eunomius und demgemäß weitgehend auch nach seinen Gegnern weniger auf die Herkunft des Sohnes als auf den Ursprung der Welt. Ἀγεννησία bedeutet vor allem, dass Gott keinen Anfang hat.[55] Doch der erste Eindruck darf nicht täuschen. Die Geschichte in der Bedeutung von Erzählung des Handelns Gottes ist in keiner Weise

[49] Vgl. *CE* I 282 (GNO I 109); *CE* II 65 (GNO I 244); *CE* III/I 63 (GNO II 26,7–11). Dazu Basilius, *Adversus Eunomium* I 9 (SC 299, 200ff), mit der Erklärung von B. Sesboüé in SC 299, 35–38, mit der früheren Literatur und den Texten.

[50] Vgl. R. M. Hübner, "Gregor von Nyssa als Verfasser der sog. ep. 38 des Basilius", in: J. Fontaine – C. Kannengiesser (Hrsg.), *Epektasis*, Paris 1972, 463–490, besonders 476–482. Ausserdem B. Sesboüé in SC 299, 78–82, zur stoischen Kategorienlehre bei Basilius, sowie L. I. Scipioni, *Ricerche sulla cristologia del „Libro di Eraclide" di Nestorio*, Friburgo 1956, 98–106.

[51] Vgl. *CE* II 334 (GNO I 232f); *CE* II 589 (GNO I 398).

[52] Vgl. *CE* II 334 (GNO I 323f); *CE* II 354 (GNO I 329); *CE* II 356 (GNO I 330); *CE* II 448 (GNO I 357).

[53] Vgl. B. Sesboüé in SC 299, 78–82.

[54] Vgl. Basilius, *Adversus Eunomium* II 28 (SC 305, 118); Basilius, *Ep.* 38,4–5 (Courtonne I 84–89).

[55] Vgl. Basilius, *Adversus Eunomium* I 5 (SC 299, 174); *CE* II 174–177 (GNO I 275f), und öfters.

zu unterschätzen. Aus der biblischen Geschichte kennt der Theologe die Taten, die Krafterweise Gottes (ἐνέργειαι), aus denen er dessen ἐπίνοιαι ableitet.[56] Die οἰκονομία, von der in der Geschichte oder in den Geschichten die Rede ist, bleibt für Gregor die Grundlage der Erkenntnis der Trinität.[57] Wie sehr dies zutrifft, wird durch die häufigen Hinweise auf die ἱστορία, auf die ἱστορίαι oder auf die ἱστορία εὐαγγελική bestätigt.[58] Obwohl Gregor die Offenbarung Gottes in der Schöpfung von der in der Heiligen Schrift erzählten geschichtlichen Offenbarung Gottes nicht streng unterscheidet,[59] besteht also kein Zweifel darüber, dass nach seiner Auffassung die ἐπίνοιαι, welche das Verhältnis des Vaters zum Sohn zum Ausdruck bringen, letztlich auf dem Glauben an das menschgewordene Wort Gottes beruhen.

II. *Die Epinoiai-Lehre des Meisters*

Wie bereits betont, schließt sich Gregor an die Kontroverse zwischen seinem Bruder Basilius und Eunomius an. Er bekämpft in *CE* II die ersten zwei Bücher der *Apologia Apologiae* des Eunomius. Darin setzt sich dieser mit dem ersten Buch von *Adversus Eunomium* des Basilius auseinander, in dem dieser seine erste Apologie diskutiert.[60]

---

[56] Vgl. *CE* II 581–587 (GNO I 359ff).

[57] Vgl. zum Thema der οἰκονομία als Offenbarung der θεολογία J. Rexer, *Die Festtheologie Gregors von Nyssa*, Frankfurt 2002, 262–272 (Lit.); G. Maspero, *Theologia*, 97–300; V. Corbellini, *La dottrina dell'incarnazione del Verbo nell'Adversus Eunomium di Gregorio di Nissa*, Diss. Augustinianum, Roma, 2003.

[58] Vgl. u.a. *CE* II 84–96 (GNO I 251–254, Geschichte Abrahams mit Hinweisen auf Glaube und Hoffung); *CE* II 119 (GNO I 260f: εὐαγγελικὴ ἱστορία, mit dem Hinweis auf *Joh* 21,25); *CE* II 226 (GNO I 291); *CE* II 255 (GNO I 300); *CE* II 269–281 (GNO I 305–309, Diskussion des Schöpfungsberichtes); *CE* II 426 (GNO I 351); *CE* II 434 (GNO I 353, Hinweis auf die Mythen). Weiter Texte in *Lexikon Gregorianum* III 487–491. Dazu G. Maspero, *Theologia*, 301–447: *Historia*.

[59] Wie wichtig für Gregor die οἰκονομία der Schöpfung ist, zeigt sich auch in der *Oratio catechetica magna*, in der dieser Begriff vor allem mit der Schöpfung verbunden wird. Vgl. Gregor von Nyssa, *Oratio catechetica magna* (GNO III/4 6,14–14,13).

[60] Zum Zusammenhang der Schriften der drei Autoren vgl. E. Cavalcanti, *Studi Eunomiani*, Roma 1976, besonders 67–105, sowie die Angaben über die Schriften des Eunomius in CPG II 3455–3460. Zur Bedeutung der Polemik des Basilius vgl. B. Sesboüé, in SC 299, 15–49, und A. Smets und M. Van Esbroeck in SC 160, 99–115, sowie vor allem M. V. Anastos, "Basil's *Kata Eunomiou*. A Critical Analysis", in: P. J. Fedwick (Hrsg.), *Basil of Caesarea, Christian, Humanist, Ascetic*, Toronto 1981, 67–136; G. L. Kustas, "Saint Basil and the Rhetorical Tradition", in: P. J. Fedwick

Wie weit Gregor in *CE* II die Auseinandersetzung zwischen Basilius und Eunomius weiterführt, erscheint allein schon darin, dass er sich fortwährend auf seinen Lehrer und Meister bezieht.[61] Basilius ist für ihn der Vorkämpfer (πρόμαχος) im Streit für den rechten Glauben.[62] Er ist der Lehrer der Orthodoxie (εὐσέβεια).[63] Folglich unterlässt es Gregor nicht, die Stellungnahme seines Bruders gegenüber seinem Gegner zu umschreiben.[64] Bemerkenswert sind außerdem die Zitate, in denen Gregor Basilius zu Wort kommen lässt.[65] Soweit man aus der kritischen Ausgabe von Jaeger schließen kann, sind es nicht sehr viele. Sie sind auch nicht immer ganz wörtlich angeführt. Dazu stammen sie zum Teil aus der *Apologia Apologiae* des Eunomius, sind also bereits interpretiert und gewertet.[66] Auffallenderweise beziehen sich diese Verweise auf Basilius zu einem großen Teil auf dessen Epinoiai-Lehre.[67] Darin kommt sicher klar zum Ausdruck, dass sich in der ganzen Diskussion der Streit vorwiegend um die ἐπίνοιαι dreht. Um diese Auseinandersetzung zu verstehen, muss man sich ohne Zweifel vor Augen halten, dass die Ausdrucksweise des Basilius von der stoischen Tradition abhängt. Wie B. Sesboüé aufzeigt, sind dabei drei Punkte zu beachten.[68] Basilius setzt an der stoischen Erkenntnislehre an. Dazu nimmt auch er an, dass die Namen von den Menschen erfunden sind. Schließlich rezipiert er die stoische Kategorienlehre, welche zwischen dem Wesen (οὐσία) und den Qualitäten (ποιότητες) unterscheidet.

Bei der Weiterführung der Diskussion um die Berechtigung des Begriffes ἐπίνοια ist grundlegend, dass Gregor von Basilius dessen

(Hrsg.), *Basil of Caesarea*, 221–279. Die Untersuchung von J. M. Rist im gleichen Band beschränkt sich auf das Verhältnis des Basilius zu Plotin.

[61] Vgl. z.B. *CE* II 66 (GNO I 245); *CE* II 130 (GNO I 263); *CE* II 141 (GNO I 266); *CE* II 195 (GNO I 281).

[62] *CE* II 10f (GNO I 229f).

[63] *CE* II 197 (GNO I 282).

[64] Vgl. *CE* II 125 (GNO I 262).

[65] Vgl. *CE* II 65–66 (GNO I 244–245); Eunomius, *Apologia* 8 (SC 305, 250; zit. auch von Basilius, *Adversus Eunomium* I 11, SC 299, 208); *CE* II 446 (GNO I 356f; Basilius, *Adversus Eunomium* I 7, SC 299, 192); *CE* II 506 (GNO I 374; Basilius, *Adversus Eunomium* I 7, SC 299, 192).

[66] Vgl. *CE* II 294 (GNO I 313), mit der Anmerkung von Jaeger: Basilius, *Adversus Eunomium* I 7 (SC 299, 188), aus Eunomius; *CE* II 344 (GNO I 326: ungenaue Zitation aus Basilius, *Adversus Eunomium* I 6, SC 299, 186); *CE* II 351ff (GNO I 328f; Basilius, *Adversus Eunomium* I 6, SC 299, 186f).

[67] Vgl. *CE* II 65f (GNO I 244f).

[68] B. Sesboüé, in SC 299, 76–83.

Definition gegenüber Eunomius präzisiert.[69] Ebenso macht er sich die Beweisführung für die Geltung dieses Begriffes zu eigen. Er deutet darauf hin, dass Basilius dazu ein Beispiel aus der körperlichen Welt heranzieht.[70] Er erklärt, wie man in einer vertieften Reflexion dazu kommt, die verschiedenen Aspekte eines Weizenkornes zu unterscheiden. Den Hauptbeweis liefert ihm die Art, wie Basilius aus der Verwendung der vielen Namen des einen Christus, die in der Bibel[71] und im besonderen in den Worten des Herrn selbst vorkommen.[72] Aus diesen Überlegungen schließt Gregor zusammen mit Basilius, dass die ἀγεννησία weder als einziges Attribut Gottes betrachtet noch mit dem Wesen Gottes identifiziert werden darf.[73]

Es stellt sich indes die Frage, wie weit sich Gregor an die Auffassungen des Basilius über den Begriff ἐπίνοια und seine Anwendung auf die Diskussion der ἀγεννησία Gottes und der Bedeutung der Gottesnamen hält und wie weit er über ihn hinausgeht. Für die Beantwortung dieser entscheidenden Frage sind die Überlegungen hilfreich, die M. V. Anastos in seiner Darstellung von Basilius' *Contra Eunomium* vorlegt.[74] Sie sind sicher nicht endgültig. Ihr Autor betont selbst, wie schwierig ein Vergleich zwischen Basilius und Gregor ist. Aber er möchte sich dennoch wenigstens einige knappe Bemerkungen erlauben. Danach schließt sich Gregor ziemlich eng an die Widerlegung seines Bruders an.[75] Dabei ist er jedoch ausführlicher als dieser und erweitert dessen Argumente und Beispiele. Im Grossen und Ganzen ist seine Dialektik schärfer. In Bezug auf die Einzelheiten hebt Anastos

---

69 *CE* II 345 (GNO I 326). Vgl. Basilius, *Adversus Eunomium* I 6 (SC 299, 186).

70 *CE* II 352 (GNO I 328f).

71 *CE* II 343–349 (GNO I 326ff).

72 *CE* II 350–358 (GNO I 328–331), besonders 353 (GNO I 329), sowie *CE* II 356 (GNO I 330): der Herr ist eins κατὰ τὸ ὑποκείμενον, hat aber verschiedene Namen entsprechend seinen ἐνέργειαι.

73 Vgl. vor allem *CE* II 475ff (GNO I 364f). Dazu Basilius, *Adversus Eunomium* II 4 (SC 305, 18–23): Unterscheidung von οὐσία und ἰδιώματα.

74 M. V. Anastos, "Basil's *Kata Eunomiou*", 121f. Vgl. auch M. Van Esbroeck, in SC 160, 109–114.

75 Im besonderen ist zu beachten, dass Gregor wie Basilius sich auf die kirchliche Tradition und auf die Philosophie seiner Zeit, speziell auf die stoische Kategorienlehre stützt und wie dieser die Epinoiai-Lehre im Anschluss an die antimonarchianische Überlieferung theologisch auswertet. Ferner ist zu bedenken, dass Basilius in *Ep.* 210,3–4 (Courtonne II 191–194), ausdrücklich nicht nur gegen die Anhomöer, sondern auch gegen die Sabellianer Stellung nimmt. Dabei diskutiert er die Meinung, nach welcher der Vater und der Sohn ἐπινοίᾳ zwei, hingegen ὑποστάσει eins seien, und stellt ihr seine Auffassung von τὸ κοινὸν τῆς οὐσίας und τὸ ἰδιάζον τῶν ὑποστάσεων entgegen.

im besonderen hervor, dass Gregor die Kritik des Eunomius an der Auffassung des Basilius von der οὐσία ernst nimmt. Es ist nicht richtig, die Gleichwesentlichkeit von Vater und Sohn mit der gemeinsamen οὐσία zu vergleichen, die alle Menschen als ὑλικὸν ὑποκείμενον vereint.[76] Die Einheit des Wesens, das die Einheit der Menschheit begründet, darf nicht als materielles Substrat verstanden werden.

In diesem Zusammenhang mag es am Platz sein, darauf hinzuweisen, dass Anastos in seiner Gegenüberstellung von Basilius und Gregor von einer unhaltbaren Voraussetzung ausgeht.[77] Nach seiner Meinung macht Basilius keinen Gebrauch des Glaubens von Nizäa um seine Stellungnahme zu festigen. Das sei umso bemerkenswerter, als das Bekenntnis des Eunomius, dem Basilius skeptisch gegenüberstehe, dem nizänischen *Credo* und seinem eigenen Taufbekenntnis ähnlich sei. Diese Zurückhaltung gegenüber dem nizänischen Glauben erklärt Anastos vor allem im Anschluss an die Äußerungen des Gregor von Nazianz als Rücksichtnahme auf die damaligen kirchenpolitischen Verhältnisse. Aber er setzt dabei voraus, dass das ὁμοούσιος die Hauptaussage des *Credo* von 325 bildet. Diese Voraussetzung muss jedoch als übertrieben betrachtet werden. Ὁμοούσιος ist nämlich nur eine Präzisierung von γεννηθέντα οὐ ποιηθέντα. Wenn Basilius in seiner Auseinandersetzung mit Eunomius so wenig Gewicht auf die Autorität des ὁμοούσιος legt, das von Athanasius und anderen als Schlüsselwort angesehen wird, dann tut er dies offenbar aus der Überzeugung heraus, dass es in erster Linie auf den richtigen Begriff der Sohnschaft Christi ankommt. Die Aussage "Licht vom Licht, gezeugt, nicht geschaffen" ist ihm wichtiger als das ὁμοούσιος. Wie die westlichen Theologen, Ambrosius und Augustinus miteingeschlossen, vertritt er den nizänischen Glauben, ohne deswegen dem ὁμοούσιος einen großen Wert beizumessen.[78] Im übrigen stehen hier die Unterschiede in der Pneumatologie nicht in Frage. Gregor diskutiert in *CE* II nur die Kritik, die Eunomius im Hinblick auf *Adv. Eun.* I und nicht jene von *Adv. Eun.* III des Basilius angestellt hat.

---

[76] Vgl. Basilius, *Adversus Eunomium* I 15 (SC 299, 226); II 4 (SC 305, 20). Die gegenteiligen Texte Gregors, die Anastos in der Anmerkung 185, S. 121 nach D. Balas zitiert, sind allerdings dem dritten Buch *CE* entnommen, das hier direkt nicht zur Diskussion steht.

[77] M. V. Anastos, "Basil's *Kata Eunomiou*", 128f.

[78] Vgl. dazu meine Kritik der Theorie des Neunizänismus in „Una valutazione critica del neonicenismo", in: *Mysterium Caritatis*, Roma 1999, 425–444, sowie in *Adamantius* 8 (2002), 152–159.

Immerhin muss bei der Beurteilung des Umstandes, dass Basilius das Wort θεός nicht auf den Heiligen Geist anwenden will, auch bedacht werden, wie sehr der neutestamentliche Sprachgebrauch, nach welchem θεός ein Eigenname des Vaters ist, nachwirkt und in Konkurrenz mit θεός als der gemeinsamen Bezeichnung der drei Personen und der ganzen Trinität steht.

In einem Vergleich der Epinoiai-Lehre des Basilius mit derjenigen Gregors darf die Feststellung nicht fehlen, dass beide in einer Überlieferung stehen, welche auf Origenes zurückgeht. Natürlich folgt Gregor dem Meister von Alexandrien nicht allein in dem Maße, wie es Basilius zuvor getan hat. Er kannte Origenes nicht weniger gut als sein Bruder. Er konnte sich dessen origenischen Ansichten gerade deswegen zu eigen machen, weil er Origenes selber kannte. Ebenso ist zu beachten, dass sowohl Basilius als auch Gregor nicht einfach auf die Schriften des Origenes zurückgehen. Sie schließen sich vielmehr weitgehend an eine Tradition an, die sich im Anschluss an den *Johanneskommentar* und an *De principiis* gebildet hat. Vor allem ist die Vermittlung des Eusebius von Cäsarea nicht zu übersehen, der schon vor den Kappadoziern im Blick auf die origenische Epinoiai-Lehre theologisch argumentiert hat. Doch das alles ist noch genauer aufzuzeigen.

III. *Die origenische Herkunft der Epinoiai-Lehre*

Wie schon in früheren Studien betont worden ist, verweist auch die neueste Forschung darauf hin, dass Basilius und damit auch Gregor in ihrer Epinoiai-Lehre von Origenes abhängen.[79] Wenn es angeht, weiterhin in Basilius den Mitverfasser der *Philokalie* anzusehen,[80] dann drängt sich dieser Zusammenhang geradezu auf. Allerdings ist nicht

[79] Vgl. H. J. Sieben, "Zur Rezeption der Epinoiai-Lehre", 1f, mit den bibliographischen Angaben. Dazu im besonderen, B. Sesboüé, in SC 299, 65–74; J. Wolinski, "Le recours aux ἐπίνοιαι du Christ dans le Commentaire de Jean d'Origène", in: G. Dorival – A. Le Boulluec (Hrsg.), *Origeniana Sexta*, Leuven 1995, 465–492.

[80] Während M. Harl, in SC 302, 24. 37–41, in Bezug auf die kappadozische Verfasserschaft der *Philokalie* eher skeptisch bleibt, verteidigt sie E. Prinzivalli, in: A. Monaci Castagno (Hrsg.), *Origene. Dizionario, La cultura, il pensiero, le opere*, Roma 2000, 326. Vgl. B. Sesboüé, in SC 299, 39, der die vielfach angenommene Abfassungszeit von 358 vertritt.

zu übersehen, dass die Philokalisten die trinitarischen und christologischen Darlegungen in *De principiis* nicht berücksichtigt[81] und auch die ersten Bücher des *Johanneskommentars* übergangen haben.[82] Jedenfalls ist es besser, nicht einfach von einer Abhängigkeit der Kappadozier seitens des Origenes als vielmehr von der Rezeption der origenischen Überlieferung zu sprechen.[83] Vor allem darf die Rolle des Eusebius von Cäsarea, den man als Tor zur Theologie des vierten Jahrhunderts ansehen kann, nicht Außeracht gelassen werden.[84]

Origenes selbst entfaltet seine Epinoiai-Lehre im ersten Buch seines *Johanneskommentars*, das er vor 226 noch in Alexandrien abgefasst hat.[85] Er kommt nur wenig später in *De principiis* im nur lateinisch überlieferten Kapitel über den Sohn auf seine Auffassung von den ἐπίνοιαι Christi zurück.[86] Mehr nebenbei berührt er diese Frage an zahlreichen Stellen seiner Schriften. Er tut dies in bemerkenswerter Weise in den anderen Büchern seiner *Erklärungen des Johannesevangeliums*,[87] in der um 234/5 verfassten Schrift über das Gebet,[88] in den spät verfassten *Homilien zum Propheten Jeremias*,[89] im *Kommentar zu Matthäus*[90] und in der Apologie *Contra Celsum*.[91] Diese zum Teil nur flüchtigen Hinweise erlauben es vielfach, die Hauptzeugnisse besser zu verstehen.[92]

---

[81] Vgl. M. Harl, in SC 302, 35ff.

[82] Vgl. die Bemerkungen von M. Harl, in SC 303, 263 u. 283.

[83] Vgl. E. Prinzivalli, "Origenismo (in Oriente, secc. III–IV)", in: A. Monaci Castagno (Hrsg.), *Origene. Dizionario*, 322–329.

[84] Vgl. B. Studer, "Die historische Theologie des Eusebius von Cäsarea", *Adamantius* 10 (2004) 138–166. Dazu auch die zahlreichen Verweise auf Origenes in H. Strutwolf, *Die Trinitätslehre und Christologie des Euseb von Caesarea*, Göttingen 1999. Welche Rolle Eusebius in der Vermittlung origenischen Gedankengutes spielte, müsste jedoch systematisch untersucht werden. Es gibt diesbezüglich nur sporadische Hinweise. B. Sesboüé, in SC 299, 73, hält etwa fest, dass Basilius durch die Vermittlung des Eusebius die Hexapla des Origenes kannte. Sicher ist zudem, wie gezeigt werden soll, dass Eusebius in der kontroverstheologischen Verwendung der Epinoiai-Lehre des Origenes den Kappadoziern vorangegangen ist.

[85] Origenes, *Comm. in Io.* I 21,125–39,292 (SC 120, 126–206).

[86] Origenes, *De principiis* I 2 (SC 252, 110–142).

[87] Vgl. besonders Origenes, *Comm. in Io.* XIX 5,26–28 (SC 290, 60–64).

[88] Vgl. Origenes, *Or.* 24 (PG 11, 492a–496b): Erklärung der Bitte: "Geheiligt werde dein Name."

[89] Vgl. Origenes, *Hom. in Ier.* VIII 2 (SC 232, 356–362).

[90] Vgl. Origenes, *Comm. in Mt.* XIV 7 (PG 13, 1197cd).

[91] Vgl. Origenes, *Contra Celsum* II 64 (SC 132, 434ff): Über die vielen ἐπίνοιαι Jesu.

[92] Vgl. H. J. Sieben, "Zur Rezeption der Epinoiai-Lehre", 2–8: Zusammenstellung und Beurteilung der wichtigsten Texte.

Im ersten Buch von *Johanneskommentar* macht sich Origenes zur Aufgabe, die ersten Worte des vierten Evangeliums zu erklären.[93] Im ersten Teil befasst er sich mit den Worten "Im Anfang war das Wort" (*Joh* 1,1).[94] Er gebraucht dabei den Paralleltext im Buch der Sprüche (8,22): "Der Herr hat mich gebildet als Anfang seiner Wege im Hinblick auf seine Werke."[95] Der Vergleich von *Joh* 1,1 mit dieser Stelle führt ihn dazu, in der Weisheit, die Gott am Anfang gebildet hat, den Anfang zu sehen, in dem der Logos immer war. Die Weisheit ist danach vor dem Logos. Der Sohn Gottes ist nicht als Logos Anfang der Dinge, sondern als Weisheit. Als Weisheit enthält er alle ἐπίνοιαι, welche in seinen Namen offenbart werden. In der vielfältigen Weisheit sind die unzähligen Titel des Sohnes verwurzelt, welche durch den Logos den geistigen Wesen mitgeteilt werden.[96] Die Weisheit und der Logos selbst sind verschiedene Aspekte des einen Sohnes. Wie sehr sie eins sind, kommt allerdings erst am Ende des ersten Buches zur Sprache, wo es heißt: "Christus ist ein Logos, der im Anfang, in der Weisheit eine eigene Existenz (ὑπόστασις) besitzt."[97] Damit unterscheidet Origenes den ganz einfachen Gott und den vielfältigen Erlöser: den Gott, der ist, und den Erlöser, der wird.[98] Im Hinblick auf diese grundsätzliche Feststellung sammelt Origenes eine ganze Reihe von Aussagen, welche an jene von Weisheit und Wort anschließen: Licht, Erstgeborener von den Toten, Hirt und andere Titel. Dabei unterscheidet er die Namen, die auch außerhalb der Erlösungsordnung anzunehmen sind: Weisheit, Wort, Leben und Wahrheit, von jenen, welche von der Rückkehr zur ursprünglichen Seligkeit erfordert sind.[99] Außerdem unterscheidet er die Titel Christi hinsichtlich der Gottheit und der Menschheit.[100] Dabei gibt er klar zu verstehen, dass die Mittel, welche mit der Menschwerdung

---

[93] Die folgenden Ausführungen stützen sich weitgehend auf J. Wolinski, "Le Recours", 465–492. Vgl. auch D. Pazzini, "Il prologo di Giovanni in Origene e in Gregorio di Nissa", in: W. A. Bienert – L. Perrone e. a. (Hrsg.), *Origeniana Septima*, Leuven 1999, 497–504.

[94] Origenes, *Comm. in Io.* I 16,90–20,124 (SC 120, 106–124).

[95] Origenes, *Comm. in Io.* I 17,101 (SC 120, 112).

[96] Vgl. Origenes, *Comm. in Io.* I 19,109–20,14 (SC 120, 118–124).

[97] Vgl. Origenes, *Comm. in Io.* I 39,291f (SC 120, 206).

[98] Vgl. J. Wolinski, "Le Recours", 471f, mit Origenes, *Comm. in Io.* I 20,119 (SC 120, 122).

[99] Origenes, *Comm. in Io.* I 20,123f (SC 120, 124).

[100] Vgl. Origenes, *Comm. in Io.* I 18,107 (SC 120, 116).

des Wortes verbunden sind, beim Aufstieg zu Gott den Anfang bilden müssen. Durch sie gelangt der Christ zu den höheren Titeln: zur Weisheit, zum Logos, zum Leben, zur Wahrheit und zur Gerechtigkeit.[101]

Im zweiten Teil des ersten Buches stellt Origenes die ἐπίνοια 'Logos' den anderen ἐπίνοιαι gegenüber.[102] Er wendet sich dabei gegen Leute, welche nur den Titel Logos annehmen und außerdem vielleicht die anderen Aussagen im übertragenen Sinn verstehen.[103] In dieser Polemik handelt es sich offenbar um eine Auseinandersetzung mit den Monarchianern, welche die Einheit von Vater und Sohn überbetonen und mit denen Origenes auch in seinem *Dialog mit Heraklides* zu tun hat.[104] Origenes legt ihnen gegenüber eine Liste von vierzig anderen Titeln vor.[105] Im Anschluss daran sucht er zu erklären, in welchem Sinn der Sohn 'Logos' genannt werden kann. Paulus, der von der 'Macht und der Weisheit' spricht und zudem hervorhebt, was Christus für uns geworden ist, veranlasst ihn, zwischen 'für uns' und 'für sich' (ἁπλῶς) zu unterscheiden.[106] So stellt er wiederum zwei Reihen von Aussagen auf, solche, welche im Hinblick auf uns gemacht werden und demgemäß die Menschwerdung betreffen, und solche, die einfach vom Logos gemacht werden, aber auch für uns Bedeutung haben. Dabei schließt er nicht aus, dass der Sohn den Vater erkennt und dass auch der Mensch an der Gottheit des Vaters teilhaben kann.[107] Es geht ihm vielmehr darum, die Eigenständigkeit jeder der beiden Personen zu wahren. Im übrigen bringt er die Überlegungen über die ἐπίνοιαι auch mit der Auslegung der Bibel in Verbindung. Was den Logos im besonderen angeht, sucht Origenes, seine Eigenart im Zusammenhang mit seiner Kosmologie näher zu bestimmen. Er stellt dabei fest, dass der Logos fest umschrieben ist (περιγραφή) und eine eigene Wirklichkeit (ὑπόστασις) besitzt.[108] Außerdem betont er, dass der Sohn als Logos aus den geistigen Geschöpfen 'logische' Wesen macht, indem er ihnen die Fähigkeit schenkt, ihre

[101] Vgl. Origenes, *Comm. in Io.* I 20,124 (SC 120, 124).
[102] Origenes, *Comm. in Io.* I 21,125–39,292 (SC 120, 126–206).
[103] Origenes, *Comm. in Io.* I 21,125 (SC 120, 126).
[104] Vgl. Origenes, *Dial.* 4,6–10 (SC 67, 60–76).
[105] Origenes, *Comm. in Io.* I 21,126–23,150 (SC 120,126–136).
[106] Vgl. J. Wolinski, "Le Recours", 476, mit Origenes, *Comm. in Io.* I 34,251 (SC 120, 184).
[107] Vgl.. Origenes, *Comm. in Io.* II 2,16f (SC 120, 216ff).
[108] Origenes, *Comm. in Io.* I 39,291 (SC 120, 206).

Verantwortung wahrzunehmen und sich voll zu entfalten.[109] Diese Möglichkeiten verwirklichen sich auf Grund der Menschwerdung des Wortes.[110]

Um voll zu begreifen, wie wichtig es für Origenes ist, das Verhältnis des Logos zur Weisheit und zu den anderen ἐπίνοιαι zu klären, ist es hilfreich, die Einleitung zum erstem Buch des *Johanneskommentars* genauer ins Auge zu fassen.[111] Origenes behandelt darin weit ausholend die Bedeutung von 'Evangelium'.[112] Dabei bezieht er sich auf eine Stelle im Buch Jesaja, an der steht: "Wie schön sind die Füße derer, welche die guten Dinge verkünden" (*Jes* 52,7).[113] Er setzt diese guten Dinge (ἀγαθά) mit Jesus gleich und schließt darin die Wirklichkeiten (πράγματα) ein, welche in den ihm gegebenen Namen zu erkennen sind.[114] Als ἐπίνοιαι zählt er ausdrücklich auf: das Leben – das Licht – die Wahrheit, welche sich κατ' ἐπίνοιαν vom Leben und vom Licht unterscheidet – der Weg – die Auferstehung – die Türe – die Weisheit – die Kraft Gottes – das Wort.[115] Er unterlässt es jedoch nicht hinzuzufügen, dass all diese Güter nur denen zugänglich sind, welche Jesus als den Gekreuzigten annehmen. Allein sie begreifen, dass Jesus für uns Gerechtigkeit, Heiligkeit und Erlösung geworden ist.[116] Auf Grund zahlreicher einschlägiger Schriftstellen also ist es möglich aufzuzeigen, was Jesus alles ist, und den Reichtum zu erahnen, den kein Buch zum Ausdruck bringen kann.[117] In diesen einleitenden Gedanken gibt Origenes nicht nur zu verstehen, was er mit ἐπίνοιαι meint. Es sind Aspekte einer Sache, welche man mit Hilfe einer Überlegung aus den vorgegebenen Namen ableitet.[118] Darin ist vor allem ausgesprochen, dass sie die 'guten Dinge' sind, die uns für den Weg zu Gott gegeben sind.[119]

Im ersten Buch von *De principiis* entwickelt Origenes im Kapitel über den Sohn seine Gedanken über die ἐπίνοιαι Christi in kürzerer

---

[109] Origenes, *Comm. in Io.* I 37,273 (SC 120, 196).
[110] Origenes, *Comm. in Io.* I 37,276 (SC 120, 198).
[111] Origenes, *Comm. in Io.* I 1,1–15,89 (SC 120, 56–104).
[112] Origenes, *Comm. in Io.* I 5,27–15,89 (SC 120, 74–104).
[113] Origenes, *Comm. in Io.* I 8,51 (SC 120, 86).
[114] Origenes, *Comm. in Io.* I 9,52 (SC 120, 88).
[115] Origenes, *Comm. in Io.* I 9,53–57 (SC 120, 88ff).
[116] Origenes, *Comm. in Io.* I 9,58f (SC 120,90), mit *1 Kor* 1,22, u. 1,30 sowie *Röm* 6,10.
[117] Origenes, *Comm. in Io.* I 9,60f (SC 120, 90).
[118] Origenes, *Comm. in Io.* I 9,52 (SC 120, 88).
[119] Vgl. Origenes, *Comm. in Io.* I 8,51 (SC 120, 86).

Form.[120] Er geht dabei von der Unterscheidung zwischen der Gottheit und der menschlichen Natur aus. Dazu, so meint er, ist zu untersuchen, "was der eingeborene Sohn Gottes ist, der ja mit vielen verschiedenen Namen benannt wird, die entweder in der Sache oder in den Ansichten derer begründet sind, die sie gebrauchen" (n. 1). Unter Hinweis auf die entsprechenden Schrifttexte befasst er sich zuerst eingehend mit dem Namen 'Gottes Weisheit'. Dabei betont er vor allem, dass die Weisheit eine eigene Wirklichkeit ist (*sapientia, substantialiter subsistens*) und seit Ewigkeit alle Kräfte und Gestalten für die Schöpfung in sich enthält (n. 2). Diese ewige Weisheit heißt auch Wort Gottes, weil sie das Verständnis für die Geheimnisse eröffnet, die in ihr enthalten sind (n. 3). Origenes erklärt weiter, in welchem Sinn der Sohn auch Wahrheit und Leben sowie Weg ist. Dabei unterstreicht er, dass diese Benennungen von den Wirkungen und Kräften des Sohnes genommen sind (n. 4). Er vertieft seine Darlegungen mit einer Erklärung der Zeugung des Sohnes, indem er die Bibeltexte heranzieht, in denen der Sohn als Bild Gottes und als Abglanz der göttlichen Herrlichkeit bezeichnet wird (nn. 4–13, vor allem mit *Kol* 1,15; *Hebr* 1,3; *Weish* 7,25f). Dabei stellt er heraus, dass es keine Zeit gibt, zu der die Weisheit nicht war (n. 9). Von Interesse ist in diesen Ausführungen über die Ewigkeit der göttlichen Zeugung und der eigenen Wirklichkeit der Weisheit besonders die Art und Weise, wie Origenes die fünf in *Weish* 7,25f enthaltenen Gottesbezeichnungen: Macht, Herrlichkeit, Licht, Tätigkeit und Güte auf die Weisheit Gottes überträgt.[121] Er geht selbst soweit, dass man von einem Austausch der Namen sprechen kann. Origenes deutet nämlich einen solchen an, wenn er sagt: "Wie niemand daran Anstoß nehmen darf, dass, nachdem der Vater Gott ist, auch der Erlöser Gott ist, so darf auch, sofern der Vater allmächtig heißt, niemand daran Anstoß nehmen, dass der Gottes Sohn allmächtig genannt wird."[122] Abschließend stellt Origenes fest, dass es zu weit führen würde, alle Benennungen des Sohnes Gottes zu sammeln und dabei darzulegen, aus welchen Gründen, Kräften und Eigenheiten ein jeder dieser Ausdrücke gebraucht wird:

[120] Origenes, *De principiis* I 2 (SC 252, 110–142 = Görgemanns-Karpp 122–156 für die deutsche Übersetzung der Zitate).

[121] Origenes, *De principiis* I 2,9 (SC 252, 128).

[122] Origenes, *De principiis* I 2,10 (SC 252, 134).

> *Multum autem est et alterius vel operis vel temporis, congregare omnes filii dei appellationes, verbi causa, quomodo vel lumen verum est vel ostium vel iustitia vel sanctificatio vel redemptio et alia innumera, et quibus ex causis vel virtutibus vel affectibus unumquodque horum nominetur, exponere.*[123]

Ohne jeden Zweifel steht im Hintergrund dieser Darlegungen über die ἐπίνοιαι des Sohnes im *Johanneskommentar* und in *De principiis* die antike Problematik des Einen und des Vielen.[124] Origenes selbst stellt die Einfachheit Gottes der Vielfalt des Sohnes gegenüber. Er macht zudem deutlich, dass der Sohn als Weisheit, in der alle Gedanken Gottes enthalten sind, und als dem offenbarenden Wort zwischen dem transzendenten, ungewordenen Gott und der vielfältigen, gewordenen Schöpfung vermittelt.[125] In diesem Zusammenhang nimmt er offensichtlich gegen die Äonenlehre der Valentinianer Stellung.[126] Dabei stellt er gewiss Gedanken über die Erkenntnis der vielen Aussagen über Gott und den Logos an.[127] Doch will er offensichtlich mit seinen Überlegungen über die Namen Christi, des eingeborenen Sohnes Gottes, nicht so sehr eine philosophische Frage beantworten, als vor allem ein pastorales Ziel verfolgen. Es geht ihm nicht sosehr um die Frage des Einen und des Vielen als vielmehr um die Anpassung Gottes an seine Geschöpfe sowie um den fortschreitenden Aufstieg des Menschen zur Fülle der Gottheit.[128] Die ἐπίνοιαι Christi sind, wie es in den späteren Büchern des *Johanneskommentars* heißt, die Tugenden, welche stufenweise zu Gott zurückführen.[129] Die pastorale Ausrichtung der Epinoiai-Lehre kennzeichnet sicher in erster Linie

---

[123] Origenes, *De principiis* I 2,13 (SC 252, 142).

[124] Vgl. M. Harl, *Origène et la fonction révélatrice du Verbe incarné*, Paris 1958, 334ff. Dazu Origenes, *Hom. in Ier.* VIII 2 (SC 232, 358).

[125] Vgl. B. Studer, *Gott und unsere Erlösung im Glauben der Alten Kirche*, Düsseldorf 1985, 105f.

[126] Vgl. J. Wolinski, "Le Recours", 266f; H. J. Sieben, "Zur Rezeption der Epinoiai-Lehre", 3–5.

[127] Vgl. dazu besonders *Or.* 24 (PG 11, 492b–493b), wo Origenes die Namen als umfassende Aussage über die Eigenart des Benannten definiert und betont, dass in Bezug auf Gott der Hinweis auf seine Eigenart nur zutrifft, wenn die betreffende aus der Bibel übernommene ἔννοια ihm in richtiger Weise zugesprochen wird. Zu den an dieser Stelle vorgetragenen Gedanken über den Ursprung der Sprache und die Magie, vgl. unten.

[128] Vgl. M. Harl, *Origène et la fonction révélatrice*, 234–243; J. Wolinski, "Le Recours", 468.

[129] Vgl. Origenes, *Comm. in Io.* XIX 6,33–39 (SC 290, 66–70), sowie auch *Comm. in Mt.* 14,7 (PG 13,1197c). Dazu M. Harl, *Origène et la fonction révélatrice*, 290ff; D. Pazzini, "Virtù", in: A. Monaci Castagno (Hrsg.), *Origene. Dizionario*, 468f.

die Erklärungen des vierten Evangeliums. Sie liegt aber ebenso *De principiis* zugrunde, in welchem es darum geht aufzuzeigen, wie jene, welche an die Christus-Wahrheit glauben, diesen Glauben mit Hilfe der 'Worte Christi' vertiefen und in ihr Leben umsetzen können.[130]

Vielleicht weniger wichtig, aber kaum weniger entscheidend ist die eigentlich theologische Ausrichtung der Epinoiai-Lehre des Origenes. Sowohl in *De principiis*, seinem theologischsten Werk, als auch im *Johanneskommentar* nimmt er gegenüber der Tendenz Stellung, den Sohn mit dem Vater zu identifizieren, den Logos Gottes nur als ein Attribut oder eine Tätigkeit des Vaters zu betrachten. Die Polemik gegen die so genannten Monarchianer, welche zur Zeit des Origenes auch bei anderen Autoren, dem Verfasser des *Contra Noetum*, bei Tertullian und Hippolyt anzutreffen ist,[131] beherrscht offensichtlich das erste Buch von *De principiis*. Auch wenn die lateinische Übersetzung diese Stoßrichtung etwas verstärken mag, scheint sie in allen Texten auf, in denen von der *substantia* oder der *subsistentia* des Sohnes oder der Weisheit oder des Wortes die Rede ist.[132] Die Betonung der eigenen Wirklichkeit des Wortes macht sich jedoch auch im ersten Buch des *Johanneskommentars* geltend. Sie zeigt sich speziell an seinem Ende, wo von der Umgrenzung (περιγραφή) und von der Eigenständigkeit (ὑπόστασις) des Logos die Rede ist. Wie sehr Origenes daran interessiert ist, bestätigt sich in anderen Texten des Kommentars. So spricht er an einer Stelle, in der es um die durch den Sohn vermittelte Herkunft des Heiligen Geistes geht, von den drei Hypostasen.[133] Ebenso kritisiert er anderswo Leute, welche die Eigenheit des Sohnes nicht von derjenigen des Vaters unterscheiden und dem Sohn die Eigenheit (ἰδιότης) und die individuelle Wesenheit (οὐσία κατὰ περιγραφήν) absprechen.[134] Noch entschiedener bezeugt Origenes im *Dialog mit Heraklides* seine Ablehnung der Monarchianer. In Aussagen

---

[130] Origenes, *De principiis* I prol. 1 (SC 252, 76): "*Omnes qui credunt et certi sunt quod gratia et veritas per Iesum Christum facta sit, et Christum esse veritatem norunt, secundum quod ipse dixit: Ego sum veritas, scientiam quae provocat homines ad bene beateque vivendum non aliunde quam ab ipsis Christi verbis doctrinaque suscipiunt.*"

[131] Vgl. B. Studer, *Gott und unsere Erlösung*, 99ff.

[132] Vgl. D. Pazzini, "Cristo Logos e Cristo Dynamis nel I Libro del Commentario a Giovanni di Origene", in: R. J. Daly (Hrsg.), *Origeniana Quinta*, Leuven 1992, 424–429, besonders 427, mit *Comm. in Io.* I 24,151ff (SC 120, 136ff).

[133] Origenes, *Comm. in Io.* II 10,75 (SC 120, 234).

[134] Origenes, *Comm. in Io.* II 2,16 (SC 120, 216). Dazu *Comm. in Io.* X 37,246 (SC 157, 528ff), mit der Anmerkung von E. Corsini in der italienischen Übersetzung: 436, Anm. 51.

(φωναί) wie *Jes* 43,10 und *Joh* 10,30 darf man die Einheit Gottes nicht ohne Christus auf den Gott des Alls anwenden.[135]

Wie nicht eigens betont werden muss, ist in unserem Zusammenhang die theologische Orientierung der origenischen Auffassung von den ἐπίνοιαι Christi von besonderer Wichtigkeit. In seiner Auseinandersetzung mit den monarchianischen Tendenzen seiner Zeit hat Origenes der Methode vorgearbeitet, die Basilius und Gregor gegen Eunomius anwenden werden. Die Kappadozier sind allerdings – und das ist ebenso bemerkenswert – nicht die ersten gewesen, welche das Vorgehen des Origenes rezipiert haben. Vor ihnen hatte schon Eusebius in ähnlicher Weise wie dieser gegenüber Marcellus die eigene Wirklichkeit des Logos verteidigt.[136] Wenn man die vor 360 verfassten Schriften durchgehen würde, könnte man vielleicht noch andere Beispiele ausfindig machen.

Um den Einfluss der Epinoiai-Lehre des Origenes auf Basilius und Gregor noch genauer abzuschätzen, mag es hilfreich sein, nochmals an ihre Hauptelemente zu erinnern. Es ist gewiss zuzugeben, dass Origenes weder über die Berechtigung der ἐπίνοιαι noch über ihr Verhältnis zu den Namen und zu den Trägern der Namen weiter nachdenkt. Doch erscheinen bei ihm dennoch Ansätze zu einer solchen Reflexion.[137] So betont er ausdrücklich die Unterschiede der ἐπίνοιαι. Der Logos muss von der Weisheit unterschieden werden. Brot und Weinstock sind nicht dasselbe.[138] Ebenso hebt Origenes die Unterschiede hervor, welche sich aus den verschiedenen Namen ergeben.[139] Die Unterscheidungen selbst beruhen nach seiner Meinung auf Überlegungen.[140] Solche Reflexionen beziehen sich vor allem auf

---

[135] Origenes, *Dialogus cum Heraclide* 4 (SC 67, 62). Vgl. *Comm. in Mt.* XVII 14 (PG 13, 1517b–1520b).

[136] Eusebius, *De ecclesiastica theologia* I 8 (PG 24, 837a–d), I 19–20 (PG 24, 864c–896c): mit dreissig Titeln Christi wird bewiesen, dass dieser eine eigene Existenz hat. Vgl. bes. PG 24, 864c u. 893, wo die Abhängigkeit von Origenes offensichtlich ist.

[137] Vgl. C. Blanc in SC 120, 841, die für den *Comm. in Io.*, unter Angabe von Texten, eine zweifache Bedeutung von ἐπίνοια unterscheidet: "aspect, attribut de l'objet pensé" und "notion, point de vue du sujet pensant".

[138] Origenes, *Comm. in Io.* I 30,207 (SC 120, 162).

[139] Vgl. M. Harl, in SC 302, 275–279: zur Unterscheidung der φωναί, σημαινόμενα (ἐπίνοιαι), πράγματα.

[140] Vgl. den Ausdruck in Origenes, *Comm. in Io.* I 9,53 (SC 120, 88). Vgl. Origenes, *De principiis* IV 4,1 (SC 268, 402). Die Idee der Überlegung kommt auch mit den Worten νοητόν und κατανοεῖν zum Ausdruck. Vgl. Origenes, *Comm. in Io.* I 9,55 (SC 120, 88).

die Wirkungen, welche das benannte Subjekt hervorbringt.[141] Vor allem sollten nach seiner fortwährend wiederholten Überzeugung die verschiedenen Aspekte, welche in den verschiedenen Namen zum Ausdruck kommen, nicht dazuführen, die Einheit des Substrates (ὑποκείμενον) in Frage zu stellen.[142] Sehr klar drückt er dies im *Johanneskommentar* aus, wenn er meint: "Niemand soll sich daran stoßen, dass wir die dem Erlöser zugeschriebenen ἐπίνοιαι unterscheiden, in der Meinung wir würden dasselbe für seine οὐσία tun."[143] Noch ausdrücklicher äußert er sich in einer *Jeremiahomilie*, in welcher er nach der Aufzählung einer Reihe von Attributen Christi erklärt: "Das Substrat ist eines; die vielen Namen jedoch beziehen sich aufgrund der ἐπίνοιαι auf verschiedenes. Du verstehst in Bezug auf Christus nicht dasselbe, wenn du ihn als Weisheit oder wenn du ihn als Gerechtigkeit denkst."[144] Es ist nicht zu übersehen, dass in solchen Erklärungen das eine Subjekt als ὑποκείμενον, als οὐσία oder auch als ὑπόστασις bezeichnet wird. Schließlich bringt Origenes seine Auffassungen von den ἐπίνοιαι nicht nur in der Erklärung der biblischen Titel Christi zur Anwendung. Er tut es auch, obgleich weniger oft und mehr nebenbei, wenn Gott oder die Erkenntnis Gottes in Frage stehen.[145] Aus diesen Hinweisen sollte es klar geworden sein, dass Origenes und seine Schüler – sicher Eusebius – die theologische Diskussion über die ἐπίνοιαι, die Basilius und Gregor mit Eunomius führten, vorbereitet hatten. Doch muss diese Rezeption der origenischen Epinoiai-Lehre sicher in einem weiteren geistesgeschichtlichen Zusammenhang gesehen werden. Wie sehr dies zutrifft, soll im Folgenden näher erklärt werden.

---

[141] Vgl. Origenes, *Comm. in Io.* I 37,267 (SC 120, 192).

[142] Vgl. die Texthinweise in M. Harl, *Origène et la fonction révélatrice*, 236, Anm. 63.

[143] Origenes, *Comm. in Io.* I 28,200 (SC 136, 158).

[144] Origenes, *Hom. in Ier.* VIII 2 (SC 232, 358). Dazu *Contra Celsum* III 41 (SC 136, 96), mit der Anmerkung, in welcher M. Borret die Ausdrücke: αὐτολόγος, αὐτοσοφία und αὐταλήθεια erklärt.

[145] Vgl. Origenes, *Comm. in Io.* XIX 5,26f (SC 290, 60ff), mit dem Hinweis auf die verschiedenen ἐπίνοιαι von 'Gott' und 'Vater'. Ausserdem ist zu beachten, dass die Vielfalt der Namen, wie sie schon in der hellenistischen Kultur vertreten wurde, gerade auch vom Vater gilt. Vgl. Origenes, *Contra Celsum* I 24 (SC 132, 134–140), mit den Anmerkungen von M. Borret. Weiteres dazu unten.

IV. *Die Wurzeln der origenischen Überlieferung*

In seiner bemerkenswerten Studie über die ἐπίνοιαι Christi im *Johanneskommentar* des Origenes, schickt J. Wolinski einen Abschnitt über die Vorgeschichte voraus.[146] Nach einer vorläufigen Erklärung des Begriffs ἐπίνοια spricht er von seinen ersten christlichen Verwendungen, vom 'Namen' in der Bibel, von Justin und Irenäus. Die Tatsache, dass das Wort ἐπίνοια im einzigen Text des Neuen Testamentes im Zusammenhang mit Simon Magus vorkommt, führt ihn dazu von seinem Gebrauch bei den Gnostikern und bei Plotin zu sprechen. Damit berührt er, wie zu erwarten, die Problematik des Einen und des Vielen. Bei Plotin kommen die ἐπίνοιαι bei der Unterscheidung zwischen der 'Erkenntnis in der Ruhe' und der 'Erkenntnis in der Bewegung' zur Sprache.[147] Die Valentinianer wiederum stellen eine Hierarchie der Äonen auf, welche eine gewisse Ähnlichkeit mit den Klassifizierungen der ἐπίνοιαι bei Origenes besitzen.[148] Ohne jeden Zweifel wird dieser selbst weitgehend von der fundamentalen Fragestellung des Einen und Vielen der antiken Philosophie bestimmt. Manche seiner Formulierungen und vor allem die Unterscheidung der zum Vater hingewendeten Weisheit und des die Gedanken des Vaters offenbarenden Logos hängen damit zusammen. Doch dieser mehr philosophische Hintergrund war für Origenes bei weitem nicht allein entscheidend.

Wichtig war ebenso, wenn nicht wichtiger, die Auffassung des 'Namens' in der Bibel.[149] In den Schriften des Alten Testamentes sind die Offenbarung und die Heiligung des Namens Gottes grundlegend. In den apostolischen Schriften ist fortwährend die Rede vom Namen Jesu. Dabei wird vorausgesetzt, wie immer wieder betont wird, dass der Name mit dem Wesen einer Sache zu tun hat, für die Person steht, die benannt wird, die Aufgabe betrifft, zu der Gott einen Menschen erwählt. Origenes selbst übernimmt die biblische Theologie des Namens in besonders eindrücklicher Weise in seiner Erklärung der Vaterunser-Bitte "Geheiligt werde dein Name".[150] Die

---

[146] J. Wolinski, "Le Recours", 466–471.
[147] Plotin, *Enn.* II 9 [33] 1,40–44.
[148] Vgl. Ireneus, *Adversus haereses* II 13,9 (SC 294, 126).
[149] Vgl. J. Wolinski, "Le Recours", 467f, sowie R. Gögler, *Zur Theologie des biblischen Wortes bei Origenes*, Düsseldorf 1963, 211–217.
[150] Origenes, *Or.* 24 (PG 11, 492a–496b).

biblische Auffassung von der Wirksamkeit der Namen spielt bei ihm eine wichtige Rolle. In der Auseinandersetzung mit der heidnischen Umwelt passt er sich selbst weitgehend deren Überzeugung an, man könne mit der Anrufung eines geheimnisvollen, von oben stammenden Namens eine besondere Gunst der höheren Mächte erreichen. Er vertritt diese Meinung vor allem in seiner Apologie *Contra Celsum*[151] sowie in einer zum Teil griechisch erhaltenen *Homilie zum Buch Josua.*[152] Interessanterweise zieht er bei der Umschreibung des Wertes von Namensanrufungen und Beschwörungen auch die antiken Diskussionen über die menschliche Sprache heran.[153] Weil ihm das dient, hält er sich dabei an die stoische Überlieferung, nach welcher die Namen nicht aus der menschlichen Konvention, sondern aus der Natur stammen.[154] Bei der Anrufung von mysteriösen Namen handelt es sich allerdings um ein spezielles, wenn auch häufiges Phänomen. Wenn Origenes dazu in einer Art Stellung bezieht, die uns heute befremdet, will er damit nicht die allgemeine Frage nach dem Ursprung der menschlichen Sprache beantworten.[155] Jedenfalls betont er immer wieder den menschlichen Charakter der biblischen Redeweise.[156] Darum steht er den Kappadoziern, die gegenüber Eunomius den menschlichen Ursprung der Namen Gottes und der Namen Christi verteidigen, viel näher als es auf den ersten Blick erscheint. Wie sehr dies zutrifft, wird durch die Art und Weise bestätigt, wie Origenes die Vielfältigkeit der göttlichen Namen begründet, welche mit der christlichen wie mit der heidnischen Anrufung Gottes eng verbunden ist. Er betont indes, dass die Namen der Wahrheit entsprechen müssen und von den gläubigen Christen auf die Bibel zurückgeführt werden.[157] Nach seiner Auffassung beruht die Anerkennung der vielen Namen letztlich auf zwei Gründen. Auf der einen Seite kann der Mensch als vielfältiges Geschöpf den ganz einfachen Gott nur mit vielen Namen bekennen. Auf der anderen Seite hat Gott sich

---

[151] Origenes, *Contra Celsum* I 24 (SC 132, 134–140).

[152] Origenes, *Hom. in Iesu N.*, fragm. (SC 302, 388–392), mit der Analyse von M. Harl, in SC 302, 394–397.

[153] Vgl. R. Gögler, *Zur Theologie*, 218–229: "Wort und Wirklichkeit"; W. Gessel, *Die Theologie des Gebetes*, Paderborn 1975, 233, Anm. 96.

[154] Vgl. R. Gögler, *Zur Theologie*, 275–281: "Das Urwort und die Worte".

[155] Vgl. M. Harl, in SC 302, 131f.

[156] Vgl. R. Gögler, *Zur Theologie*, 307–319.

[157] Vgl. R. Gögler, *Zur Theologie*, 216f; W. Gessel, *Die Theologie*, 233–236, der den Zusammenhang des Gebetes mit der liturgischen Verlesung der *historia Iesu* hervorhebt.

den Menschen angepasst, in dem er sich durch die vielen Namen Christi offenbart.[158] Damit wird von neuem bestätigt, wie grundlegend die Bibel für die Theorie von den ἐπίνοιαι gewesen ist.

Es ist sicher hilfreich, in der Vorgeschichte der origenischen Epinoiai-Lehre auf Justinus und Irenäus zu verweisen. Der erste fügt in den *Dialog mit Tryphon* ganze Reihen von Christus-Titeln ein.[159] Er legt besonderen Wert auf den Logos-Titel, mit dem er die Präexistenz Christi zu beweisen sucht. Außerdem geht es nach seiner Überzeugung nicht an, dem Vater des Alls, der ungezeugt ist, einen Namen zulegen zu wollen. "Vater, Gott, Schöpfer, Herr, Meister" seien keine Namen, sondern Aussagen, welche ihren Grund in den Wohltaten und Werken Gottes haben.[160] Schließlich ist bemerkenswert, dass Justinus sich sowohl mit den Namen Gottes wie mit jenen des Sohnes befasst. Der Namen 'Christus' hat einen verborgenen Sinn, so gut wie die Aussage 'Gott' eigentlich kein Name ist, sondern eine dem Menschen angepasste Weise, eine unsagbare Wirklichkeit zu umschreiben.[161] Was Irenäus betrifft, sind zwei Gedanken festzuhalten.[162] Gott kann nicht in seiner Größe, sondern nur in seiner Liebe, mit der er sich mitteilen will, erfasst werden. Seine Natur bleibt verborgen, in seinen Werken hingegen macht er sich sichtbar.[163] Andererseits nimmt Irenäus einen Fortschritt in der Gotteserkenntnis an,[164] welcher der Fähigkeit des einzelnen Menschen entspricht,[165] und bereitet damit die Auffassung des Origenes von der Herablassung Gottes vor.[166]

J. Wolinski berücksichtigt leider in seiner Vorgeschichte zwei einflussreiche Autoren nicht: Philo und Klemens von Alexandrien. Die Schriften des ersten bestätigen den Zusammenhang der origenischen Epinoiai-Lehre mit der Interpretation der Bibel. Die beiden Vorläufer des Origenes geben zudem klar zu verstehen, dass dessen Lehre, wie schon oben betont wurde, einen stoischen Hintergrund besitzt. Wie M. Harl mit Recht bemerkt hat, sind die fragmentarischen Hinweise,

---

158 Vgl. M. Harl, *Origène et la fonction révélatrice*, 234–238.

159 Vgl. J. Wolinski, "Le Recours", 468ff.

160 Iustinus Martyr, *Apologia secunda* 6,1–2 (Wartelle 204).

161 Iustinus Martyr, *Apologia secunda* 6,3–4 (Wartelle 204). Vgl. *Apologia secunda* 6,6 (Wartelle 204), wo von der 'Beschwörung' im Namen des Gekreuzigten die Rede ist.

162 Vgl. J. Wolinski, "Le Recours", 470f.

163 Ireneus, *Adversus haereses* IV 20,4 (SC 100, 634).

164 Ireneus, *Adversus haereses* IV 20,7 (SC 100, 646ff).

165 Ireneus, *Adversus haereses* IV 38,2 (SC 100,948ff).

166 Vgl. Origenes, *Comm. in Io.* XIII 34,203–225 (SC 222,145–153), mit dem Thema von Milch und fester Speise.

die gewöhnlich in Bezug auf den stoischen Hintergrund zitiert werden, zu einem großen Teil Schriften des Philo und des Klemens entnommen.[167] Zu beachten ist im besonderen Philos Traktat *Quis rerum divinarum heres*, der offensichtlich auf die wichtige, oben zitierte Stelle in Origenes' *Homilien über Jeremias* eingewirkt hat.[168]

In der Darstellung, in der J. Wolinski die früheren Ansätze zur Lehre von den ἐπίνοιαι des Origenes kurz zusammenfasst, fehlt weiter ein ganz wichtiger Gesichtspunkt. Wer berücksichtigt, wie sehr diese Lehre mit der Exegese zusammenhängt, wird sich sogleich daran erinnern, dass in der antiken Hermeneutik die Deutung der Wörter grundlegend gewesen ist. Die eigentliche Texterklärung – die *enarratio*, wie es in der lateinischen Tradition heißt – umfasste bekanntlich die *cognitio verborum* und die *cognitio rerum*.[169] Die Worterklärung bestand in einer Art Etymologie und vor allem in der Beachtung der verschiedenen Bedeutungen der Wörter. Das trifft auch für Origenes zu, wie aus den Studien von M. Harl und B. Neuschäfer entnommen werden kann.[170] Bemerkenswert ist besonders ein Abschnitt der *Philokalie*, in dem Origenes betont, dass es bei der Behandlung sowohl ethischer als auch physischer und theologischer Fragen darauf ankommt, die Begriffe (σημαινόμενα) genau zu bestimmen. Ohne die Kenntnis der Sprache würde man die Schwierigkeiten nicht lösen können, welche die Homonymie, die Mehrdeutigkeit, der übertragene und der eigentliche Sinn der Wörter mit sich bringen.[171] Ebenso ist beachtlich, wie Origenes bei der Erklärung der biblischen Texte, besonders der Gleichnisse, Wort für Wort genauer zu verstehen sucht.[172] Offensichtlich verdankt er dieses philologische Vorgehen der Schule seiner Zeit.[173] Wie bedeutend dieser exegetische Rahmen anzusehen ist, illustriert allein schon die Erklärung des Wortes ἀρχή, die im Hinblick auf *Gen* 1,1 und *Joh* 1,1 immer wieder vorgelegt wird.[174]

---

[167] M. Harl, in SC 302, 276. Vgl. P. Nautin, in SC 232, 358f, Anm. 3 zu Origenes, *Hom. in Ier.* VIII 2.

[168] Vgl. Philo, *Quis rerum* 22–23 (Wendland III 6–7), und Origenes, *Hom. in Ier.* VIII 2 (SC 232, 356ff).

[169] Vgl. B. Studer, *Schola Christiana*, 131.

[170] Vgl. M. Harl, in SC 302, 414–426, und B. Neuschäfer, *Origenes als Philologe*, Basel 1987, 140–202.

[171] *Philocalia* 14,2 (SC 302, 408ff).

[172] Vgl. M. Harl, in SC 302, 135–140.

[173] Vgl. besonders B. Neuschäfer, *Origenes als Philologe*, wo auch die Frage der Verwendung von etymologischen und semantischen Lexika besprochen wird (vgl. besonders 154f).

[174] Vgl. Origenes, *Comm. in Io.* I 16,90–18,108 (SC 120, 106–118).

Zweifelsohne ist die Epinoiai-Lehre des Origenes unter dem Einfluss mannigfaltiger geschichtlicher Faktoren entstanden. Wer sie begreifen will, muss sich darum über ihre Vorgeschichte Rechenschaft geben. Die verschiedenen Einflüsse bestimmten nicht allein das Denken des Origenes und dann die Rezeption seiner Schriften durch seine Freunde und Feinde. Sofern sie auch später aktuell blieben, wirkten sie vielmehr oft unmittelbar auf diese selbst ein.[175] Es seien dazu drei Beispiele angeführt. Die Schrifterklärung im allgemeinen, die auch die eunomianische Kontroverse bestimmt, wurde nicht allein von den exegetischen Schriften des Origenes und der darin befolgten Auslegungsmethode beeinflusst. Die Überlieferungen der antiken Schule, welche hinter der Bibelarbeit des Origenes stehen, wurden auch nach ihm von den Grammatikern und Rhetoren vertreten.[176] Zudem dreht sich die Diskussion zwischen Eunomius und Basilius offensichtlich weitgehend um die Interpretation der ersten Kapitel der Genesis.[177] Diese exegetische Auseinandersetzung ist natürlich nicht allein von Origenes her zu verstehen. Es sind auch andere Autoren, vor allem Philo zu berücksichtigen. Ferner sind die Fragen über den Ursprung der menschlichen Sprache und über die verschiedenen Formen der Aussagen in einen breiten Rahmen hineinzustellen.[178] Gewiss übte, wie vor allem die *Philokalie* nahe legt, Origenes selbst in dieser Hinsicht einen direkten Einfluss auf die Kappadozier aus. Aber auch in diesem Bereich blieben die selbst im vierten Jahrhundert nachhaltig wirkenden Schultraditionen der Antike eine nichtversiegende Quelle. Im übrigen sind, wie zu erwarten, in der Rezeption des Origenes, sofern sie von neuen Fragestellungen bestimmt wurde, manche Gegebenheiten neu überdacht worden.[179]

Rückblick und Ausblick

Im zweiten Buch *Contra Eunomium* befasst sich Gregor von Nyssa, wie aus vielen Stellen hervorgeht, in besonderer Weise mit den Ansichten,

---

[175] Vgl. B. Sesboüé, in SC 299, 75–95: Philosophische Einflüsse. Dazu J. M. Rist, "Basil's 'Neoplatonism'. Its Background and Nature", in: P. J. Fedwick (Hrsg.), *Basil of Caesarea*, 137–220.

[176] Vgl. B. Studer, *Schola Christiana*, 198–229.

[177] Vgl. M. Van Esbroeck, in SC 160, 99–115, mit *CE* I 151f (GNO I 71ff); *CE* II 198–205 (GNO I 282–285); *CE* II 226 (GNO I 291f).

[178] *CE* II 246–293 (GNO I 298–313); *CE* II 403–445 (GNO I 344–356).

[179] Vgl. B. Sesboüé, in SC 299, 65–95.

welche sein Gegner in Bezug auf die Ungezeugtheit Gottes und den Zusammenhang der Namen und der von ihnen bezeichneten Wesen vertritt. Um diese Auffassungen und damit die (an)homöische Stellungnahme des Bischofs von Cyzicus zu erschüttern, greift er auf die Lehre von den ἐπίνοιαι zurück. Dabei lässt er sich offensichtlich von den Überlegungen leiten, die schon sein Bruder Basilius gegenüber Eunomius vertreten hatte. Er geht indes in zweifacher Hinsicht darüber hinaus. Er benutzt eine noch subtilere Dialektik an. Zudem gibt er sich eingehender über die Berechtigung der Reflexion Rechenschaft, welche der Unterscheidung der ἐπίνοιαι zugrunde liegt. Basilius selbst schließt sich eindeutig der origenischen Tradition an. Origenes selbst hatte keine eigentliche Theorie über die Frage vorgelegt. Aber in seinen Schriften finden sich wichtige Ansätze zur Epinoiai-Lehre, mit der Basilius und nach ihm Gregor Eunomius bekämpfen. Zu beachten sind vor allem das dreifache Schema: Laute – Begriffe – Sachen sowie die Betonung der Einheit des Subjektes, dem verschiedene Aspekte zugeschrieben werden. Außerdem hat Origenes die Epinoiai-Lehre nicht allein in einer eher spirituellen Weise, sondern auch eigentlich theologisch verwendet. In seiner Polemik gegenüber den Monarchianern hat er den Weg gezeigt, wie die ἐπίνοιαι in der trinitarischen Kontroverse gebraucht werden können. Vor den Kappadoziern hatte schon Eusebius diese Anregung verstanden. Die Art und Weise wie Origenes von den ἐπίνοιαι sowohl Christi als auch Gottes spricht, muss indes in einen größeren geistesgeschichtlichen Zusammenhang gestellt werden. Dabei sind vor allem drei Dinge gut zu beachten: die Namenstheologie der Bibel, die alexandrinische Erklärung der Wörter sowie die stoische Dialektik, wie sie schon Philo und Klemens von Alexandrien übernommen hatten. Methodologisch gesehen verdient festgehalten zu werden, dass die Kappadozier wie schon Origenes exegetisch und dialektisch vorgehen.[180] Dabei wurden sie von der Stoßrichtung der Polemik dazu gebracht, weniger historisch vorzugehen, als dieser und Eusebius es getan hatten. Aber sie geben dennoch zu verstehen, dass der Taufglaube letztlich in der οἰκονομία verwurzelt ist und darum über die κοιναὶ ἔννοιαι hinausgeht.

Um die Auseinandersetzung zwischen Eunomius und den beiden Kappadoziern voll zu verstehen, mag es hilfreich sein, sie auch einer

[180] Vgl. Origenes, *Contra Celsum* IV 9 (SC 136, 206).

kritischen Überlegung zu unterziehen. In der Diskussion über die Art und Weise, von der Eigenheit des Vaters zu sprechen, halten Basilius und Gregor auseinander, was dem Vater und dem Sohn gemeinsam und was ihnen eigentlich zukommt.[181] In Bezug auf die Aussagen, die sowohl den Vater als auch den Sohn bezeichnen, machen sie mit den stoischen Denkformen: 'was etwas' und 'wie etwas ist' zu wenig ernst. Sie beschränken das Gemeinsame auf die οὐσία, das Eigene beziehen sie auf die Hypostasen.[182] In der stoischen Dialektik findet sich aber auch die Unterscheidung zwischen den gemeinsamen und eigenen ποιότητες. Augustinus wird sich in dieser Hinsicht klarer ausdrücken. Er unterscheidet über das gemeinsame Substrat hinaus zwischen gemeinsamen und individuellen Zuweisungen. Darum schreibt er die Weisheit, die Liebe, die Geistigkeit sowohl *communiter* allen drei Personen zusammen als auch *proprie* den einzelnen Personen zu.[183] Wenn die Kappadozier nicht so weit gelangt sind, scheint mir der Hauptgrund darin zu liegen, dass Eunomius sie dazu gedrängt hat, in Gott vor allem den Schöpfer und Herrn des Alls zu sehen. Die Anfanglosigkeit und Endlosigkeit, auf die sie immer wieder zurückkommen, trifft auch für den Sohn zu. Die Kappadozier übersehen zwar nicht, dass diese zwei Attribute dem Vater und Sohn auf eine andere Weise zugesprochen werden, aber sie bringen das nicht eindeutig zum Ausdruck. Nach meiner Meinung ist es jedenfalls nicht unwichtig mit Augustinus herauszustellen, dass der Vater *principium sine principio*, der Sohn hingegen *principium de principio* ist. Damit wird die einseitig kosmologische Sicht überwunden, welche die Diskussion mit Eunomius kennzeichnet. Die heilsgeschichtliche Orientierung, ohne welche ein Taufglauben undenkbar ist, kommt damit zum Tragen.

---

[181] Vgl. Basilius, *Adversus Eunomium* I 19 (SC 299, 242); *Ep.* 210,5 (Courtonne II 195f); *Ep.* 38,5 (Courtonne I 84–87).

[182] Vgl. Basilius, *Adversus Eunomium* II 28 (SC 305, 118–122).

[183] Augustinus, *De Trinitate* VII 1,1–3,6 (CCL 50, 244–254). Vgl. B. Studer, *Gratia Christi – Gratia Dei bei Augustinus von Hippo*, Roma 1993, 194.

PART II

TRANSLATION

THE SECOND BOOK AGAINST EUNOMIUS. AN INTRODUCTION TO THE TRANSLATION

Stuart George Hall

Translating Gregory is never easy. I must acknowledge with thanks my debt to members of the Gregory of Nyssa Colloquium, and especially Lenka Karfíková, Joseph S. O'Leary and Johannes Zachhuber, all of whom corrected errors and made useful suggestions.

The text presented by Jaeger in GNO has been followed with rare exceptions, all of which are indicated in the footnotes. Most of them are matters of punctuation, such as the exact location of a question mark, or a difference of opinion as to whether Gregory is quoting from Eunomius or representing his opponent's views in his own words.

Technical terms are sometimes difficult to translate consistently. I have generally followed the practice adopted in translating *Contra Eunomium* I.[1] The principles are usually discussed in the footnotes when a word first occurs, e.g. 'being' for οὐσία and 'concept' for ἐπίνοια. Eunomius' key term, ἀγεννησία and its cognates are not so discussed, but I have as before used 'unbegotten' and 'unbegottenness', which are in English so ugly and unusual that they correspond well to the Eunomian use which Gregory criticizes.

The general aim has been to present all the thoughts of Gregory as he might have written them, had he been using modern, philosophically informed, English. Nothing can make him easy to read, but we have done our best.

An important problem is the structure of the work. Older editions and translations are unhelpful. Jaeger introduced numbered sections, which are here treated as basic, and larger paragraphs which are generally, but not always, followed. Since some scholars habitually refer to lines and pages, the page-turns in GNO I are indicated by numbers in square brackets.

[1] L. F. Mateo-Seco – J. L. Bastero (eds.), *El "Contra Eunomium I" en la producción literaria de Gregorio de Nisa. VI Coloquio Internacional sobre Gregorio de Nisa*, Pamplona 1988, esp. 31–33.

I have also added fifteen main headings and numerous subheadings to Gregory's text in order to help in understanding. The reader must not suppose that this is part of what Gregory himself wrote. The headings are an hermeneutic tool. Arriving at them is not easy, and colleagues in the Colloquium had different opinions of the structure of the work. What we offer is my own analysis, altered in the light of Lenka Karfíková's independent proposals, Joseph S. O'Leary's penetrating criticisms, and the published scheme of Bernard Pottier.[2] The result cannot be regarded as infallible, but is offered to help the reader understand what Gregory is trying to say.

[2] B. Pottier, *Dieu et le Christ selon Grégoire de Nysse*, Namur 1996, 425–430.

I. Introduction (1–11)
- 1.–9. Eunomius, the headless Goliath
- 10.–11. Basil, our champion

II. Unbegottenness (12–66)
- 12.–22a. Orthodox faith and Eunomius' attack on it
- 22b.–43. Unbegottenness, simplicity and being
- 44.–50a. Eunomius on 'unbegotten' not being a concept
- 50b.–66. Eunomius' true aim: degrading Christ

III. Limitations of human knowledge (67–124)
- 67.–83. The impossibility of knowing divine things
- 84.–96. The example of Abraham's faith
- 97.–105. Curiosity beyond what scripture says leads to error
- 106.–124. We lack essential knowledge of soul, body and universe

IV. Naming and conceiving God (125–195a)
- 125.–147. Positive and negative words for God
- 148.–158. God is named for his actions, not for his being
- 159.–176. God's being is prior to human conceptions of him
- 177.–195a. The power and limits of conceptual thought.

V. Words spoken by God (195b–236)
- 195b.–204. Eunomius makes God speak physically
- 205.–218. To whom does Eunomius think God speaks?
- 219.–236. Speech without sound in a Psalm

VI. Human language (237–293a)
- 237.–246a. God gives man the power to create words
- 246b.–261. The varieties of human language
- 262.–268. Eunomius falsely claims Moses in his support
- 269.–281a. Evidence from the creation narrative in Genesis
- 281b.–288. Words are invented for man's benefit, not God's
- 289.–293a. Human invention of words does not impugn divine providence

VII. Conceptual thought and Christological titles (293b–366a)
- 293b.–332. Basil and Eunomius on names given to Christ
- 333.–342. Contradictions and evasions in Eunomius
- 343.–350a. Words applied to the Lord by the scriptures
- 350b.–358. Words applied to the Lord by himself
- 359.–366a. Eunomius alleges that applying concepts to God is blasphemous

VIII. Divine indestructibility (366b–386)

366b.–377a. Eunomius makes 'indestructible' part of God's Being, 'Father' a mere activity

377b.–386. Eunomius identifies God's indestructibility and unbegottenness with his being

IX. Divine attributes and human concepts (387–402)

387.–394. The naming of God is a function of human corporeality

395.–402. The power to name by conceptual thought is God's gift to Man

X. Further arguments on the alleged divine origin of words (403–444)

403.–422. Philosophical and literary aspects of the arguments about the origin of speech

423.–442. A Psalm-verse about counting and naming

443.–444. Eunomius misuses Paul's interpretation of Adam

XI. Eunomius' charges against Basil (445–468)

445.–454a. The charge that Basil denies God is by nature indestructible

454b.–461. The charge that Basil denies that God is by nature unbegotten

462.–468. The charge that Basil divides the being of God

XII. Eunomius reduces all divine attributes to one (469–542)

469.–479. God is one, but has various attributes

480.–485. The claim that different attributes divide God's being

486.–491. Eunomius' arguments apply equally to the Son

492.–503. The absurdity of making divine attributes all identical

504.–523a. The syllogism: indestructibility and unbegottenness are incompatible unless identical

523b.–536. Logical games with the endless and the unbegun

537.–542. Eunomius nonsensically identifies 'unbegotten' with 'endless'

XIII. Eunomius' claim that words for God originate in God (543–560)

543.–553. The claim that words for God are prior to man's concepts

554.–560. A dilemma for Eunomius, who identifies God's attributes with his being

GREGORY, BISHOP OF NYSSA
THE SECOND BOOK AGAINST EUNOMIUS

Translated by Stuart George Hall

I. *Introduction (1–11)*

1.–9. *Eunomius, the headless Goliath*

1. Our first disputes with Eunomius were with God's help adequately dealt with in our previous efforts, as those who wish may discover from our works: in our previous book the fraud is forcefully exposed, and in the topics then considered the lie has no more power against the truth, save for those who are fanatically shameless in opposing the truth. **2**. Since, however, a second work has been assembled by him against true religion, like a bandit's ambush, once again with God's aid Truth is being armed by us to resist the array of her foes, marching ahead of our words like a commanding officer, and directing them as she sees fit against the enemy. Following her steps we shall boldly commit ourselves to the second contest, quite undeterred by the onslaught of falsehood, displayed though it is in a host of words; **3**. for faithful is he who promised that thousands would be put to flight by one, and tens of thousands dislodged by two,[3] because true religion, not numerical superiority, prevails in war.

4. In the case of the huge figure of Goliath, brandishing that massive spear of his at the Israelites, he struck no fear in a shepherd, a man with no training in [227] military arts, but when he tangled with him he came out of the battle headless, contrary to his expectation.[4] In the same way our Goliath, the imparter of Philistine knowledge, brandishing his blasphemy at his opponents unsheathed and bare like a sword, and glittering also with newly whetted tricks,

---

[3] *Deut* 32,30.
[4] *1 Sam* 17,23–51.

did not seem frightening or formidable to us simpletons so as to leave him able to boast a field clear of resistance; rather he found that we, the impromptu warriors of the Lord's flock, who were never trained to fight with words and do not reckon that want of training a disadvantage, have shot at him the Word of Truth, simple and rustic. **5**. Furthermore, that shepherd we mentioned, when he had knocked down the Philistine with his sling, and when the stone had pierced the helmet and by the force of the shot penetrated inside, did not limit his valour merely to seeing his adversary dead, but ran up and beheaded the foeman, and then went back to his own people parading that loud-mouthed head in the camp of his compatriots. We too therefore have a duty, following his example, not to quail at the prospect of a second task, but so far as possible to imitate the heroic act of David, and like him follow up the first blow with an attack on the fallen, so that the enemy of the truth may be shown to be totally headless. **6**. One who is cut off from faith is more decapitated than the Philistine was; for since "the head of every man is Christ", as the Apostle says,[5] and the believer is presumably what is meant by 'man' (for Christ would not also be the head of unbelievers), then surely [228] the one cut off from saving faith would be as headless as Goliath: by his own sword, which he whetted against the truth, he is parted from his true Head; it is not our task to cut it off from him, but to demonstrate that it is cut off already.

7. Let none suppose that it is out of a sort of ambition and desire for human glory that I set out readily on this "war without truce or parley",[6] and engage the enemy. If it were possible in leisurely silence to spend our life in peace, it would be out of character deliberately to disturb that silence, of our own accord stirring up war against ourselves by a challenge. **8**. But when siege is laid to the Church, the City of God, and the great wall of Faith shudders, pounded all round by the siege-engines of heresy, and there is no small danger that the Word of the Lord might be seized by the onslaught of the demons and be taken away captive, I reckoned it a dreadful thing not to engage in the Christian struggle, and did

[5] *1 Cor* 11,3.
[6] A rhetorical cliché at least as old as Demosthenes XVIII 262 (Dindorf I 324).

not retreat into silence. I reckoned the sweat of labour much to be preferred to the ease which silence brings, knowing very well that, just as every one will get his reward, in the Apostle's words, in accordance with his own work,[7] so he will certainly also get his punishment for neglecting labours he is capable of. **9**. That was also the reason why I readily undertook the first verbal battle, using missiles from the shepherd's wallet, that is those uncut and natural words from the Church's formularies, for the defeat of blasphemy, and [229] in need of no outsider's verbal weapons for the fray. Now also I do not draw back from the second battle, but set my hope as great David did on one "who trains hands for battle and fingers for war",[8] hoping we may be vouchsafed by the divine Power a writing hand directed to the destruction of heretical teachings, and fingers serviceable to overthrow the army of evil, skilful and masterful in deploying argument against the foe.

10.–11. *Basil, our champion*

10. In wars among men there are those superior to the rest in courage and strength, who are protected by armour and have acquired skill in warfare by practice in dealing with its dangers; these stand at the head of the formation, exposed to danger ahead of those drawn up deeper, while the rest of the troops try to give the appearance of large numbers and thus to make some contribution to the common effort. Such in our battles is Christ's noble soldier and frequent protagonist against the Philistines, that great spiritual man-at-arms Basil, wearing the full apostolic armour, protected by the shield of faith, and ever wielding his fighting weapon – the sword, I mean, of the Spirit.[9] He leads the Lord's army in battle, living and fighting and performing valiantly against the enemy in the work he painfully wrote, while we, the multitude, sheltering behind the shield of our champion's faith, inasmuch as our commander has advanced against the foe, shall not flinch from such combat as we can sustain. **11**. In refuting, therefore, the erroneous and insubstantial illusion of heresy, [230] he asserts that the title 'unbegotten' is applied to God only

[7] *1 Cor* 3,8.
[8] *Ps* 143/144,1.
[9] *Eph* 6,16–17.

conceptually,[10] and he puts forward arguments based on general principles and on scriptural proofs. Eunomius, however, the inventor of error, neither concurs with his arguments, nor is able to refute them. Pressed towards the truth, the clearer the light of orthodox doctrine shines, the more, being dazzled by the light in the manner of nocturnal animals, and unable even to find his usual sophistic bolt-holes, he wanders aimlessly, gets into the impenetrable tangle of falsehood, and is trapped in a circle of repetition: nearly all his second work is devoted to this nonsense. Consequently it is right that we too should do battle with our opponents on this ground, where our champion himself led the way in his own book.

II. *Unbegottenness (12–66)*

12.–22a. *Orthodox faith and Eunomius' attack on it*

12. I suggest that we ought first of all to summarize briefly our whole understanding of dogmatic principles and the disagreement of our opponents with us, so that our treatment of the subject may be methodical. The chief point, then, of the Christian religion is the belief that the Only-begotten God, who is Truth, and true Light, and Power of God, and Life, truly is all that he is said to be; and especially and supremely this, that he is God and Truth, which means God in truth, being always what the thought and word imply, never not being, and never ceasing to be, one whose Being,[11] what he essentially is, eludes all attempt at comprehension and investigation. **13**. For us, as the word of Wisdom somewhere says, from the greatness and beauty of created things, by some analogy based on what we do know, he comes to be known as existing,[12] by means of his activities bestowing only faith, not the knowledge of what he

---

[10] The central term ἐπίνοια is rendered by variations on 'concept', 'conception', 'conceptual', or 'conceptual thought'. It can be used both of the mental activity which conceives, and the thought or attribute which is conceived. Similarly the verb ἐπινοεῖν is rendered 'conceive', with or without an adverb such as 'mentally'.

[11] Parts of the verb εἶναι, 'to be', and the cognate noun οὐσία, 'being', are here regularly rendered with parts of 'be' and 'being' in English. Other terms, such as 'substance' and 'exist', are generally reserved for other Greek words.

[12] *Wis* 13,5.

is. **14**. Whereas this view has come [231] to prevail generally among Christians, at least among those who really deserve the name, those (I mean) who have learnt from the Law[13] not to worship any thing that is not True God, confessing by their very worship that the Only-begotten God is in truth and not falsely called God, there has come the corrosion of church-rust, which corrupts the devout seeds of faith; it advocates Judaistic fraud and has something also of Greek god-lessness. **15**. By fashioning a created God it becomes an advocate of Greek fraud, and by not accepting the Son it establishes the error of the Jews. This heresy therefore, which abolishes the true godhead of the Lord, and makes out a case that he ought to be understood as a created thing, and not that which in essence and power and rank the Father is; – since, with truth shining all about, these opaque notions have no substance, and they have despised all the titles for a proper expression of divine praise found in the scriptures, which are applied alike to Father and Son, they have arrived at the term 'unbegottenness', itself manufactured by these very people in order to deny the majesty of the Only-begotten God.

16. Whereas the orthodox confession stipulates faith in the Only-begotten God, "so that all may honour the Son as they honour the Father",[14] these people reject the orthodox words, in which the majesty of the Son is declared to be as honourable as the rank of the Father, and then conceive for themselves the principles and propositions of godless doctrinal criminality. **17**. Whereas, as the Gospel language teaches, the Only-begotten God came forth out of the Father and is from him,[15] they replace this idea with other terminology, and use it [232] to tear up the true faith. **18**. Whereas truth teaches that the Father is not from some superior cause, these have named that thought 'unbegottenness', and the constitution (ὑπόστασις) of the Only-begotten from the Father they call 'begetting'; then they put together the two words, 'unbegottenness' and 'begetting', as directly contradicting each other, and proceed to lead their silly followers astray.

---

[13] That is, Scripture.
[14] *Jn* 5,23.
[15] *Jn* 8,42 etc.

To make the matter clear with an example, 'was begotten' and 'was not begotten' are just like 'is seated' and 'is not seated' and any other expression of the same kind. **19**. These people however, separating these expressions from the natural meaning of the terms, strive to attach to them another sense in order to get rid of orthodoxy. The terms 'is seated' and 'is not seated' have indeed, as already stated, not the same force, for the meaning of the one is negated by the other. They therefore argue that this contrast in the mode of origin denotes a difference of being: they define the being of one as 'begotten' and that of the other as 'not begotten'. **20**. One may not reckon, however, that the being of a man is that he is seated or not seated, for one would not give the same definition of a man's sitting posture as of the man himself; in the same way, the being which has not been begotten, on the analogy of the example we have used, is surely something different in its proper definition from what is meant by not having been begotten.

21. Yet our opponents, eyes fixed on their wicked aim of securing as far as possible the denial of the godhead of the Only-begotten, do not say that the being of the Father is in fact unbegotten, but by a perversion of language define 'unbegottenness' as 'being', in order to use the contrast with 'begotten' [233] to demonstrate a difference of nature from the contradiction in the words. **22**. For seeing wickedness they have ten thousand eyes, but for the uselessness of this effort they are blind; the eyes of their mind are shut. Who is there, unless his mind's senses are totally blunted, that does not perceive that the foundation of their doctrine is weak and flimsy, and that their argument is based on nothing, when it makes 'unbegottenness' into 'being'? – for that is how their lie is concocted.

22b.–43. *Unbegottenness, simplicity and being*

I shall, however, state my opponents' argument for them in my own words as strongly as I can. **23**. They assert: "God is called Unbegotten; but the Divinity is by nature simple; and what is simple admits of no composition. If therefore God is by nature uncompounded, and the name 'Unbegotten' applies to him, then 'Unbegotten' is the name of his very nature, and his nature is nothing else than unbegottenness." **24**. In response to this we assert that 'uncompounded' means one thing and 'unbegotten' another: one expresses the simplicity of the subject, the other the fact that it derives from no cause; the connotations of the terms do not overlap, even though both are used of the one subject. Rather, we learn from the adjective 'unbegotten' that what is so described has no causal origin, from 'simple' that it is free from composition; neither term is used as substitute for the other. **25**. So it does not necessarily follow that, because the Divinity is by nature simple, his nature is defined as 'unbegottenness'; rather, inasmuch as he is without parts and uncompounded, he is said to be simple, and inasmuch as he has not been begotten, unbegotten.

If the word 'unbegotten' did not mean that he is 'without a cause', but 'simplicity' were to intrude into the connotation of such a word, and if he were for that reason (following the heretical argument) called 'unbegotten', merely because [234] he is simple and uncompounded, and if the connotation of 'simple' and 'unbegotten' is one and the same, then surely the simplicity of the Son must also be called 'unbegottenness'. **26**. They will not deny that the Only-begotten God is also simple by nature, unless indeed they would also deny that he is God. Simplicity therefore will have no shared meaning with 'unbegotten', such that the nature, because it is uncompounded, must be 'unbegottenness'. Otherwise, they bring on themselves one of two absurdities: either they deny the godhead of the Only-begotten or they attribute unbegottenness to him too. **27**. For, since the Divinity is by nature simple, and 'unbegotten' is in their view a word for simplicity, they are either arguing that the Son is compounded, by which it is at the same time implied that he is not God either, or else, if they confess his godhead, and the Divinity is (as has been said) simple, they will surely be arguing that the same person is also unbegotten because of his simplicity, if indeed simplicity is deemed to be the same as unbegottenness.

To make what we are saying clearer, I will repeat the argument. **28**. What we assert is this: each of the words has its own connotation, and 'indivisible' is not implied by 'unbegotten', nor 'unbegotten' by 'simple'. Rather, by 'simple' we understand 'uncompounded', and by 'unbegotten' we learn that something has no originating cause. **29**. We think that we should believe that the Son, being God from God, is himself also simple, because the Divine is free from any composition; and similarly in his case, too, that we neither signify simplicity of being by the title 'Son', nor conversely do we express the meaning of 'Son' by 'simplicity'; but that by the one word his existence deriving from the Father is expressed, and by 'simplicity' just what that word connotes. Since then the phrase [235] "simplicity of being" is exactly the same, whether it is applied to Father or Son, differing neither by subtraction nor by addition, while 'begotten' is very different from 'unbegotten', because in each word there is a meaning which is absent in the other, we therefore claim that there is no necessity, the Father being unbegotten, just because his Being is simple, for his Being to be called 'unbegottenness'. **30**. In the Son's case too we do not, because his being is simple, and the same person is also believed to be begotten, call his being 'simplicity'. Rather, just as the <Father's>[16] being is simple and not 'simplicity', so too the being is unbegotten and not 'unbegottenness'. In the same way, if the Son is also begotten, it is quite unnecessary to conclude that, because his being is simple, his being is defined as 'begottenness'. Rather, in this case too each word has its own meaning: the term 'begotten' points you to a source, and 'simple' to absence of composition.

31. This however does not satisfy our opponents. They insist that, because the Father's being is simple, it must be reckoned nothing else but unbegottenness, since it is also said to be unbegotten. To them we may also reply that, because the Father is also called Creator and Designer,[17] and the one so called is also simple in being, it is time these clever people announced that the Being of the Father is 'creation' and 'design', since no doubt the argument from simplicity attaches to his being the meaning of every word which applies to him. **32**. So they should either separate unbegottenness from their definition of the divine being, letting it retain its own proper meaning, or, if, because of the simplicity of the Subject, they do define the being by unbegottenness, [236] they should on the same grounds envisage both creation and design in the Father's being, not as though the potency in the being were what creates and designs, but as though that potency itself were seen as creation and design. **33**. If

[16] This word is not in the Greek, but is added to make the meaning clear.

[17] Δημιουργός is commonly used in Greek philosophy and patristic theology for the one who skilfully or intelligently creates the world. It may be rendered by various words such as 'craftsman', 'artificer', 'artisan', or transliterated as 'Demiurge'. We have opted for 'Designer', a word with a notable history in English natural theology, which is inexact because design is not quite the same as product: but it comes close enough.

however they reject this as wicked and wrong, let them be persuaded by the logic to reject that other argument with it: as the being of the Designer is not design, so the being of the Unbegotten is not unbegottenness. To be concise and clear I will again repeat the same argument: If it is not as a function of being begotten, but because the Father is a simple and uncompounded being, that he is described as 'unbegotten', for the same reason the Son too will be called 'unbegotten'; for he too is a being uniform and uncompounded. **34**. If however, because the Son has been begotten, we are obliged to confess him as 'begotten', then plainly, because the Father has not been begotten, we shall also address him as 'unbegotten'. If truth and the logic of the case require this conclusion, then 'unbegotten' is not a word for being, but points to a difference of idea, which distinguishes what has been begotten from what has not.

35. There is another point we should add to what has been said. If they allege that the word 'unbegotten' signifies the Being, and not existence without prior cause, what word will they use to denote the fact that the Father has no prior cause, since they have given 'unbegottenness' the function of indicating his being? **36**. If we do not learn from the word 'unbegotten' the difference which distinguishes the Individuals (ὑποστάσεις),[18] but are to understand that this word indicates the Nature itself, as though it emerged immediately from the subject-matter and [237] revealed what we want to know by the enunciation of the syllables, then it must follow that God is either not unbegotten, or is not so described, there being no word specifically to provide such a connotation. **37**. Since, by their account, 'unbegottenness' does not connote the absence of originating cause, but indicates the nature itself, the logical trick will surely backfire against them, and 'unbegotten' as a word for God will end up escaping from their doctrine. In the absence of any other word or expression to indicate that the Father has not been begotten, and with 'unbegotten' by their ingenuity made to mean something else, and not that he was not begotten, their argument fails, slides into Sabellianism[19]

[18] 'Individual' is the term used in modern Anglophone philosophy for what the Greeks meant by a personal ὑπόστασις.

[19] Sabellius, who wrote in the late second or early third century, so stated his understanding of God that he is widely viewed as teaching that there is only one person in God, who manifests himself in different ways, especially as Father and

and collapses. **38**. By this logic it must follow that the Father is deemed the same as the Son, once their doctrine is robbed of the distinction of 'begotten' and 'unbegotten'. So it is one or the other: either they must withdraw their opinion about this word, because it connotes a difference in the character of each and not the nature, or else they must abide by their judgments about the word and agree with Sabellius; for there is no way that the difference between the Individuals can avoid confusion without the distinction of 'begotten' from 'unbegotten'. **39**. If therefore the word indicates a difference, then the being is not what that term will indicate: there is one word for the difference, another for the being; but if they force the meaning of the term to apply to the nature, they will as a consequence be dragged into the error of the so-called 'Sonfatherists', the distinction between Individuals having been removed from the account. **40**. If however they are saying that there is nothing to prevent both the contrast with 'begotten' being expressed by 'unbegottenness', and the same term denoting the being, they must distinguish for us the additional connotations of the word, so that we can effectively connect with each other [238] the distinct senses of 'unbegotten'. **41**. The clear indication of difference given by this term is beyond doubt, as is confirmed by the verbal contrast: we ourselves agree that instead of, "The Son was begotten", and, "The Father was not begotten", the one is by a verbal equivalence called 'unbegotten' and the other 'begotten'; but to tell us on what interpretation the being is denoted by this use of the word is apparently beyond them.

42. This is something our New Theologian says nothing about, but as his writing advances he takes us deceitfully through fresh nonsense. "Because God, being simple," he says, "is unbegotten, therefore God is unbegottenness." What has the thought of simplicity to do with the idea of 'unbegotten'? The Only-begotten, after all, is undoubtedly both begotten and simple. "But also without parts," he says, "and uncompounded." What has that got to do with the question? The Son is not pluriform and composite either, but that does not make him unbegotten. **43**. "But he is utterly without quantity," he says, "and magnitude." That too may be granted: and the Son

Son. What he actually taught was probably more subtle. The term 'Son-father' (υἱοπάτωρ), which Gregory refers to in 39, was attributed to him.

too is unrestricted by size and without quantity, and still Son. But that also is not the question. The object is to show which meaning of 'unbegotten' describes being. Just as the idea of difference of characteristics is understood in this word, so they claim the connotation 'being' is unambiguously present as one of the meanings of exactly the same expression.

44.–50a. *Eunomius on 'unbegotten' not being a concept*

44. He says nothing about that, but tells us that we "should not apply 'unbegotten' to God conceptually. For what is so spoken," he says, "is as fleeting as the words themselves." But what [239] word is not fleeting as soon as it is spoken? We are not like potters or brick-makers; when the words have once been formed in our mouth, we do not keep intact what is expressed in speech, but as soon as the word is uttered, what is said is no more. **45**. When the breath of speech is uttered and returns to the air no trace of the words is left imprinted on the place where the sound was uttered. If therefore what makes him characterize the word as a concept is that it does not remain a word but vanishes together with the sound of the voice, he cannot avoid calling every word a concept, since no substance remains to any word once it is uttered. **46**. He will not be able to prove that even 'unbegottenness', which he exempts from the status of concept, is indissoluble and solid once it is uttered, since the word uttered from the mouth in the sound does not remain intact. The insubstantiality of spoken words may also be observed by this: if we write down in silence the thoughts of the mind, it is not the case that the substantial thoughts will be those denoted by the written letters, while the insubstantial will fail to share that written denotation. **47**. It is possible, whatever the thought may be that comes into the mind, whether it is understood as substantial or has some other status, to record it in writing at will, and for exhibiting meaning the voice is the same as the written record, for we express our thought equally by either. **48**. What his case is therefore for making the concept "dissolve along with the mere utterance",[20] I fail to understand. When any word is orally expressed, the breath that

[20] Cf. below, 159.

conveys the sound is assimilated to its kind, yet the sense of what is said is impressed through the hearing on that part of the hearer's mind which remembers, whether [240] it be true or illusory. **49**. It is therefore a feeble interpretation of this 'concept' which our wordsmith produces, when he characterizes and defines it in terms of dissolving sound. Hence that "shrewd listener" (in Isaiah's phrase)[21] rejects this unintelligible account of the nature of a concept, demonstrating it to be, on Eunomius' argument, incoherent and insubstantial; and he discusses scientifically the connotation contained in the term, using familiar examples to apply the argument to doctrinal ideas. **50**. In opposition to him Eunomius, elevating himself with this noble work of literature, tries in this way to undo what has been so clearly articulated on the subject of 'concept'.

50b.–66. *Eunomius' true aim: degrading Christ*

It would perhaps be best, however, before refuting what has been written, to consider the object of the exercise, why he is anxious to prevent 'unbegotten' being applied to God as a concept. The doctrine prevails among all those who have received the Word of true religion that we should set all our hope of salvation on Christ, because there is no other possibility of enjoying good things unless faith in Christ provides what we desire. **51**. Whereas this thought is firmly fixed in the minds of believers, and all honour, worship and glory offered up by all to the Only-begotten God as the Prince of Life who does all his Father's works, as the Lord himself in the Gospel says,[22] who falls short of no excellence in things that can be thought of as good, these people, provoked by malice and jealousy of the Lord's honour, reckoning the [241] worship offered by believers to the Only-begotten God an injury to themselves, they rise against his divine honours and try to persuade us that none of the things said about them is said in truth. **52**. Though he be named God by scripture, he is not true God, nor when called Son does he have the nature which truly corresponds to the title, nor is there any sharing of rank or nature between him and his Father; for, they say, it is

[21] *Is* 3,3; the reference is to Basil: cf. Basilius, *Adversus Eunomium* I 5 (PG 29, 520c ff).

[22] *Jn* 10,37–38.

impossible for the one begotten to be of like honour with his Maker "in rank or power or nature", since the one has infinite life and existence from eternity, while the Son's life is somehow restricted, because the beginning at which he was made marks off his emergence at the start of his life, and precludes an extension equal to the Father's eternity. **53**. Thus even the life of the latter is to be deemed defective, and he is not always the Father, as he actually is and is called, but when he was formerly something else he afterwards decided to become Father, – or rather, not to become, but to be called, Father, since he is not even named in truth the Father of the Son, but 'Creature' has been substituted for the title 'Son'. **54**. "And surely," says he, "the one begotten Junior by the Senior, the Finite by the Eternal, the Intended by his Maker, is necessarily inferior to the Maker himself in power, rank and nature, in temporal precedence and all honours. **55**. When someone is far from perfection in divine attributes, how can any one properly venerate him with the honours due to the true God?" On this basis it is argued by them that the one imperfect in power, deficient in life, subject to his Sovereign, doing nothing of himself but only what is laid down by his Governor's command, that he [242] must be held to be devoid of divine honour and recognition, entitled God, but flaunting the title devoid of all majestic meaning.

56. Put like that, not dressed up in syllogisms, these things rouse the hearer to anger and make him shudder at their outlandishness. How can any one accept, naked and unadorned, evil advice which directs to the abolition of the majesty of Christ? For this reason they have hidden this pernicious logical trap in plausible twists and deceits, and use alien concepts to pervert unsophisticated hearers. Having presented the rest of the case by which it might be possible to set the mind of hearers moving by itself in this direction, they leave it to the listener to draw the final conclusion. **57**. Having said that the Only-begotten God is not the same in being as the true Father, and having reached that conclusion through the cunning contrast of 'unbegotten' and 'begotten', they are silent as they work out the consequence: impiety wins by a spontaneous logic. It is like the druggist who makes the poison acceptable by sweetening the fatal dose for the victim with honey; he only has to administer it, and the mixture gets into the organs and without further intervention by the druggists works destruction. These people do something similar:

58. first they honey-flavour their poisonous dogma with clever tricks, then when they pour into the mind of the hearer their lie that the Only-begotten is not true God, they achieve everything else at the same time without another word. From the conviction that he is not truly God it follows that none of the other words implying his divinity are truly [243] spoken of him; for if he is in truth neither Son nor God, and each of those names is inexact, then surely all the other titles accorded to him by divine scripture are far from true. **59**. It is not a matter of one being truly spoken of him and another being void of truth; rather, surely, all belong together, so that if he is truly God, then 'Judge' and 'King' and his other titles mean what they say, whereas if the godhead is a lie, nothing else is true about him. Thus when those deceived have been convinced that the title of godhead is falsely applied to the Only-begotten, the case is made at the same time that worship should not be offered, nor veneration, nor anything else at all which we owe to God.

60. To make effective their attack on the Saviour, the method of slander they have adopted is this. They recommend that we should not observe what is common to the other titles by which the equality of rank between the Son and the Father is indicated, but to take account only of the difference of nature implied by the contradictory titles 'unbegotten' and 'begotten', on the ground that the divine nature is what the word 'unbegottenness' connotes. **61**. Then, whereas all men of sense reckon it is impossible for the ineffable nature to be expressed in the meaning of any words, and our knowledge cannot extend so far as to reach things transcending knowledge, and our competence with words has not been endowed with such power as to describe what is being thought of when something utterly sublime and divine comes to mind, then these sophisticates condemn the rest for stupidity and ignorance in the science of logic, and claim that they themselves know these things and are able to [244] impart that knowledge to whomsoever they please. **62**. That is why they say that the divine nature is nothing other than 'unbegottenness' itself, and naming it the 'supreme and highest' title they restrict the majesty of the Godhead to this word. Thus they can argue that, if 'unbegottenness' is supreme in the being, and the remainder of the divine titles, godhead, immortality, power, and the rest, depend upon this one; – so if these and the like are 'unbegottenness', then surely, if something is not called the one, it will not be the others. **63**. In the case of a man, reason, sense of humour, and capacity to learn are all characteristic properties, and if something is not a man, it will certainly not have those properties in its nature; just so, if 'unbegottenness' is indeed true godhead, then one to whom that name does not belong will surely have none of the other characteristics of godhead applied to him. Therefore, if unbegottenness is not attributed to the Son, it is proved that none of the other sublime and divine titles is properly used of him either. **64**. This then is how they define what it is to apprehend the secrets of divinity: it is to set aside the deity of the Son. They come near to shouting aloud to any who will lend an ear, "You can be perfect in knowledge, if you do not believe in the Only-begotten God, that he is truly God; if you do not honour the Son as the Father is honoured; if you reckon that he is not Son, but creature by nature, not Lord, not Sovereign, but slave and subject." That is the direction in which their counsel points, even if their slander is wrapped up in other words.

65. That is why, in his former publication, as he twists about multifariously through the ingenious convolutions of his logic-chopping, and in various ways artfully discusses 'unbegotten', he deceives the mind of those easily led astray [245] by saying, "Therefore, if it is neither conceptual nor privative, nor partial (since he has no parts), nor in him as something alien {(since he is simple and uncompounded), nor something alien outside him}[23] (since he is one and only unbegotten), it must itself be unbegotten being." **66**. Our Instructor[24] is aware of the damage inflicted by this fraud on those perverted by it, because to concede that he is not truly God contravenes the very confession of the Lord, and that is indeed the end to which the logic of these words bends the argument. For this reason, while he does not deny that unbegottenness cannot be applied to God as a part, since he also agrees that the divine is simple and has no quantity, size, or composition, nevertheless, that this designation should not be applied to him as a concept, he does deny, and proves it. Our wordsmith does not leave the matter there, but

[23] The words bracketed {. . . .} are missing in the MSS, restored by Jaeger.
[24] Basil is meant.

once more opposes us with his own subtlety in his second book, and resisting what had been written about conceptual thought.

III. *Limitations of human knowledge (67–124)*

67.–83. *The impossibility of knowing divine things*

67. It is time now to consider the case for this, with just this preliminary argument: human nature has not the potential in it to understand precisely the being of God. It may perhaps not be enough to make that declaration only about human potential, and it might not be wrong to say that even the incorporeal order of creation falls short of taking in and embracing with knowledge the infinite nature. **68**. One might understand this from examples near to hand. There are many and various fleshly creatures in existence, some with wings and some earth-bound, and what [246] rises above the clouds by the power of wings, and what crawls on the belly and burrows, if they were compared with each other, they would appear considerably different, the aerial from the earth-bound; if however the comparison were with the stars and the fixed sphere, the high-flyers with wings would be reckoned just as far from heaven as the animals on the ground. **69**. Similarly, the potential of the angels when compared with ours would seem to be vastly superior, because with no intervening sense-organs it seeks out sublime things by sheer unimpeded power of knowledge; but even their comprehension, if it is looked at alongside the majesty of him who really is, one might dare say that their ability also falls almost as far short of understanding the divine as does ours, and not be far wrong. The barrier which separates uncreated nature from created being is great and impenetrable. **70**. One is finite, the other infinite; the one is confined within its proper measure as the wisdom of its Maker determined, the limit of the other is infinity. The one stretches out in measurable extension, being bounded by time and space, the other transcends any notion of measure, eluding investigation however far one casts the mind. In this life one may perceive both a beginning and an end of what exists, but the Blessedness transcending creation approaches neither beginning nor end, but is by nature beyond the meaning of both, always remaining the same and self-consistent, with no measurable progress from one state of life to another. It does not come to life by partaking of the life of another, which might lead to the thought of the beginning and end of that participation, but what it actually is, is life acting in itself; [247] it becomes neither greater nor less by addition or subtraction. There is no room for increase by growth in the infinite, and what is by nature invulnerable cannot suffer what we conceive as diminution.

71. As we look at the sky, and somehow grasp with our visual senses its exalted beauty, we have no doubt that what we see exists; yet if we are asked what it is, we cannot explain its nature in words. We can only marvel as we see the revolving orb of the universe, the harmonious contrary movement of the planets and what is called a bestiary cycle or zodiac incised on the ecliptic round the pole, by which those skilled in these things observe the annual revolutions, and the different magnitudes and peculiar radiance of heavenly bodies, their appearances and settings, which always occur at the same season without fail in accordance with their annual cycle, the conjunctions of the planets, the inferior courses of those which pass below, the eclipses of those set above, the overshadowing of the earth, the restoration of eclipsed bodies, the pluriform phases of the moon, the middle course of the sun between the poles, and how full he is with his own light, ringed with his radiant corona, and totally enveloped in his luminous power when he is himself eclipsed, the body of the moon, they say, covering him, and how in accordance with the decree of its Disposer it always follows the same path in revolving through its appointed rising and decline, thereby unfolding the four seasons of the year; – seeing all this, we do not doubt the existence of things apparent to our sight, but we are as far from being able to account for the being of each of them as if [248] we had never in the first place known what is apparent to perception. So with the Maker of the world: we know that he Is, but admit we are unable to understand his Being.

72. The people who boast of knowing these things should first tell us about the lower movements – what they think is the material of the sky, and what the mechanism is which revolves continuously, and wherein its movement has its origin. Whatever reasoning the mind may apply, when rational thought approaches the impossible and incomprehensible, it will surely fail. **73**. For if one were to suggest that another body of exactly the same shape, fitted round its exterior, controls its impetus, so that its movement is continually turned back to repeat the same revolution around itself, and is restrained by the strength of its container from flying off at a tangent, how could one explain how these material bodies persist, and are not worn out by their constant friction against each other? **74**. How, furthermore, is the motion stimulated, if two bodies of the same kind fit exactly together, when one remains unmoved? What is inside is gripped tight by the immobility of what holds it in, and will surely not be able to achieve its proper impetus. What, too, is the frame that gives that container its stability, so that it remains solid, and is not shaken up by the movement fitted inside it. **75**. If one were to speculate mentally and suppose that this too has a frame which ensures that it stays firmly in place, then surely the argument must logically go on to postulate a framework for that framework, and for that another, and for the next yet another, so that the enquiry repeats itself and goes on in an infinite regress, ending up in perplexity; it will always be looking yet again for what lies beyond that material body which gives the universe stability, since the argument can at no point stop [249] searching for what goes round the next container. **76**. Alternatively, according to the vain theory of the astronomers, a void is spread over the top of the sky, and because it slips on this the rotation of the universe revolves upon itself, meeting no solid corresponding structure which could cause resistance and reduce its circular motion. What then is that void, which they say is neither material not mental, how far does it extend, and what lies beyond it? What is the relation between the solid, resistant matter and that insubstantial void? What is the link between things of contrary nature?

77. And how can such an harmonious system of the universe consist of beings so diverse? What might one say the sky itself to be? – a mixture of the surrounding elements, or one of the whole range, or something distinct from them? what the stars themselves are, or whence their shining radiance? what that is, and how constituted? or what the reason is for their difference in beauty and magnitude? or the seven inner circles, which revolve contrary to the movement of the universe, what they are and by what force impelled? or that immaterial and ethereal empyrean and the air that is spread between, like a barrier separating the heat-making and consuming element from the soft and combustible? how the earth is set at the bottom of the whole? what it is that keeps it firmly in place? what prevents its downward fall? **78**. If some one were to examine us on these and similar questions, will there be any of such high intelligence as to guarantee knowledge of such things? No other answer can be given by right-minded people but this: he who made all things by wisdom, alone knows how to account for the [250] universe; and for our part, "By faith we perceive that the worlds were made by the word of God," as the Apostle says.[25]

79. If then the lower creation, which is within range of our perceptive faculties, lies beyond the limits of human knowledge, how can the one who by his mere will constituted the universe be within the grasp of our mind? It is mere "futility and delusion", in the Prophet's words,[26] to suppose it possible for any one to hold in thought the incomprehensible. It is like infants, who may be seen in the ignorance of childhood playing and quite serious at the same time. **80**. Often, when a sunbeam streams in upon them through a window, they are delighted by its beauty and pounce on what they see, and try to take the sunbeam in their hand, and compete with each other, and grasp the light, catching the ray, as they suppose, in clasped fingers; but when the clasped fingers are opened, the handful of sunbeam makes the children laugh and clap because it has slipped from their hands. **81**. So too the children of our generation, as the parable says,[27] play as they sit in the market place. They see the divine power illuminating their minds through the words of providence and the wonders in creation, like the radiance and warmth issuing from the physical sun; yet rather than marvelling at the divine generosity, and revering the one thereby made known, they overstep the mind's limitations and clutch with logical tricks at the intangible to catch it, and suppose that they can get hold of it with syllogisms, if they really do suppose so; when reason has disentangled and unwound the web of their sophistries, what they have caught appears to men of sense to be nothing at all. **82**. In this petty and infantile way they toy vainly with the impossible, and with childish hand [251] lock up the incomprehensible nature

[25] *Heb* 11,3.
[26] *Ps* 39/40,5.
[27] *Mt* 11,16.

of God in the few syllables of 'unbegottenness'; they advocate insanity, and think that the divine is of such size and kind that they could by human logic contain it in a single term. They pretend to follow the words of the saints, but are not afraid to elevate themselves above them; **83**. for things which none of those blessed men of whom there is even a mention recorded in the sacred books, can be shown to have said, these people, to quote the Apostle, "knowing not what they are saying",[28] nor what they are affirming, say they know those things, and claim to be able to direct others in that knowledge. On this ground they insist that they have concluded that the Only-begotten God is not truly what he is called: the logic of their syllogisms demands it.

84.–96. *The example of Abraham's faith*

84. What mean-minded pedantry! How disastrous and destructive to them their abstruse and exact philosophy! Who would ever so purposely side with Hell, as they have laboriously and deliberately dug themselves a pit of blasphemy? How far they have distanced themselves from Christian hope! By what a gap they have debarred themselves from saving faith! How far away they have settled from the bosom of Abraham, the father of faith! **85**. If we are to follow the great mind of the Apostle with his change of wording, and take the meaning of the story allegorically (though the historical truth of course remains), Abraham went out at God's command from his own land and his own kindred, on a journey appropriate for a prophetic man pressing on towards the apprehension of God. **86**. It is not, I think, a geographical move that [252] achieves the understanding of intelligible realities. Rather, Abraham left his own native land, I mean the lowly and earthly way of thinking, and so far as possible lifted his mind above its ordinary material limits, forsaking the soul's affinity with the physical senses, so that he might not, obstructed by any thing immediately apparent to sense, be impaired in his perception of invisible things. With no sound resonating, no vision distracting his mind with physical appearances, as the Apostle puts it, "walking by faith and not by sight",[29] he rose up so far in

[28] *1 Tim* 1,7.
[29] *2 Cor* 5,7.

his breadth of knowledge as to be reckoned the measure of human perfection, knowing God as far as was possible for this little, mortal power to reach out to and achieve. **87**. As a result the very Lord of all creation, as though discovered by the patriarch, is named personally, "The God of Abraham". Nevertheless, what does the Word say about him? – that he went forth "not knowing where he was going",[30] and even without being allowed to learn the name of the one he loved, yet neither resentful nor ashamed at such ignorance.

88. It was also a sure guide towards his goal, that in thinking about God he was not led to an understanding by anything material, nor did his thought ever get stuck in anything comprehensible and desist from the journey towards things beyond knowing. **89**. Having by the use of reason transcended the wisdom of his nation – I mean the Chaldean philosophy – which reaches only visible things, and rising above those known to sense, from the beauty of things observed and the harmony of the heavenly wonders [253] he yearned to see the original model of beauty. In just the same way, all the rest of what he grasped as his reasoning advanced – whether power, or goodness, or existence without beginning, or being bounded by no end, or whatever similar idea we may have for the divine nature – using all these as means and staircase for his upward journey, always standing on what he had discovered and reaching out to what lay ahead, "setting up in his heart", as the prophet says, the beautiful "rising stairs",[31] and rising above all that his own power could grasp, as being less than what he sought, when he had surpassed every verbal description of his nature which might be applied to God, having cleansed his mind of such notions, he resorted to faith, pure and unadulterated by any ratiocination, and he took as his indicator, infallible and manifest, of the knowledge of God just this – that he believed God to be greater and higher than any epistemological indicator.

90. This is in fact the reason why, after that ecstasy which came over him, from sublime visions Abraham resiled once more into human feebleness, and said, "But I am earth and ashes",[32] that is,

---

[30] Cf. *Heb* 11,8.
[31] *Ps* 83/84,6.
[32] *Gen* 18,27.

speechless and impotent when it comes to recounting the good he had mentally envisaged. **91**. Earth and cinders seem to me together to signify what is at once lifeless and sterile, and thus a law of faith is generated for subsequent history, using Abraham's story to teach those who approach God that there is no way to come near to God, unless faith interposes and of itself joins the enquiring mind to the incomprehensible nature. **92**. He gave up scientific investigation, and "Abraham believed God," it says, "and it was credited to him as righteousness."[33] Yet it was not [254] for his sake that it was written, the Apostle tells us, but for ours,[34] because it is faith, not knowledge, which God credits to men as righteousness. **93**. Knowledge adopts a sort of experiential[35] approach, assenting only to what is learnt, whereas Christian faith is different: its assurance is not of things learnt, but of things hoped for.[36] What is possessed is not hoped for: "Why should one hope," it says, "for what he has?"[37] What eludes our understanding, faith makes ours, by its own assurance guaranteeing the unseen. That is how the Apostle writes of the faithful one, that, "He endured as seeing the invisible."[38] It is therefore futile to claim that knowledge vainly puffed up[39] is able to know the divine Being. **94**. Neither is man so great as to equal the Lord in his power of comprehension – for "Who among the clouds shall be equal to the Lord?" says David[40] –, nor is the object of the quest so small as to be grasped by the reasonings of human littleness. Listen to the counsel of the Ecclesiast, not to utter a word in the presence of God, "For God," he says, "is in heaven above, and you on earth beneath."[41] **95**. He shows, I believe, from the relation of these elements to each other, or rather the distance between them, how far superior the divine nature is to being managed by human reason. As far above the touch of the fingers as the stars may be, so far, or rather much further, the nature which transcends mind

[33] *Gen* 15,6.
[34] *Rom* 4,23.
[35] ἐμπειρικὴν. It is perhaps better, following the majority of the manuscripts, to read ἐμπορικὴν, 'commercial'.
[36] *Heb* 11,1.
[37] *Rom* 8,24.
[38] *Heb* 11,27.
[39] Cf. *1 Cor* 8,1.
[40] *Ps* 88,7/89,6.
[41] *Eccles* 5,1/2.

rises above terrestrial reason. **96**. Having learnt, therefore, how great the difference of nature is, we should quietly stay within our proper limits. It is safer and at the same time more reverent to believe that the divine majesty is more than can be thought of, than to restrict his glory by certain ideas and think there is nothing beyond that.

97.–105. *Curiosity beyond what scripture says leads to error*

[255] **97**. In another way, too, one might argue that safety lies in leaving the divine nature unexplored, as being inexpressible and beyond the reach of human reasoning. Speculating about the obscure, and using the concepts of human reason to search for some kind of knowledge of things hidden, allows admission and currency also to false ideas, since speculation about the unknown accepts as true not only what is true, but often also what is false. **98**. The student of the Gospels and of Prophecy believes that the One who Is exists, from both what he has heard from the saints and from the harmony of visible things and from the works of Providence. By refraining from enquiry into what he is or how he exists, as being both unprofitable and unachievable, he will allow no entry of falsehood against the truth. **99**. By over-curiosity room is made also for false arguments, and if all curiosity is stilled, then surely the inevitability of error is excluded with it.

The truth of this argument may also be learned from this: how is it that the parties in the churches have wandered off into their manifold and varied ideas about God, each deceiving itself with some new current of opinion? How did these very people we are considering slither into this pit of iniquity? **100**. Would it not be safer for them all to follow the counsel of Wisdom, and not enquire into things too deep,[42] but calmly to take the simple deposit of faith as their sure refuge? But once insignificant human beings made a start on treading vainly among unthinkable things, and on mastering with propositions the inventions of their own empty mind, thence began the long [256] list of warriors against the truth; and these very dogmaticians of fraud, with whom our work is concerned, have appeared, those who want to bring divinity within a prescribed limit: all but openly they make an idol of their own theory, making this notion

[42] *Sir* 3,21.

expressed by 'unbegottenness' into a god, not as being by some rational process attributed to the divine nature, but as being itself God or the Being of God.

101. Perhaps they should have looked instead to the chorus of the saints – the prophets, I mean, and the patriarchs, in whose time the Word of truth spoke "in diverse parts and diverse ways",[43] and thereafter "those who became the eyewitnesses and servants of the Word";[44] – they should have respected the trustworthiness of those attested by the Spirit himself, and should have stayed within the limitations of those writers' learning and knowledge, and not have dared to tackle things which the intelligence of the saints did not attain. **102**. When God was yet unknown to the human race because of the idolatrous error which then prevailed, those saints made him manifest and known to men, both by the miracles which are revealed in the works done by him, and from the titles by which the various aspects of divine power are perceived. Thus they are guides towards the understanding of the divine nature by making known to mankind merely the grandeur of their thoughts about God; the account of his being they left undiscussed and unexamined, as impossible to approach and unrewarding to those who investigate it. **103**. Where everything else is concerned, they indeed explained that it came to be, heaven, earth, sea, times, ages, and the created order within them, but what each of them is, and how and whence, they did not say. So also with God, "that he is, and is a rewarder of those who seek him",[45] they urge us to believe, but his nature itself, [257] as being above every name, they neither named it nor were likely to. **104**. Whatever names we have learned to clarify the way we apprehend God, all such have something in common with and analogous to the kind of names which indicate the individuality of a particular man. Those who describe the unknown person by some recognisable characteristics say that he is (it may be) of noble birth and good breeding, famous for wealth, respected for his rank, in the bloom of youth and of such-and-such bodily stature. In saying such things they do not describe the inward nature of the one described, but some of the characteristics known about him; neither high birth nor riches nor notable status nor famous rank nor admirable youth

[43] *Heb* 1,1.
[44] *Lk* 1,2.
[45] *Heb* 11,6.

is humanity itself, but each of these is a feature of the particular person. **105**. Similarly, all the words found in holy scripture to indicate God's glory describe some feature of God, each providing its particular emphasis, whereby we learn that he is powerful, or not susceptible to evil, that he is without cause, or comes to no finite end, that he has control of the universe, or anything else about him. His being itself, however, scripture leaves uninvestigated, as beyond the reach of mind and inexpressible in word, decreeing that it should be honoured in silence by prohibiting enquiry into the deepest things and by saying that one ought not to "utter a word in the presence of God".[46]

106.–124. *We lack essential knowledge of soul, body and universe*

106. For this reason one may explore every divinely inspired word, and not find teaching about the divine nature, nor indeed about the essential existence of anything. Hence, we humans live in total ignorance, in the first place about ourselves, [258] and then about everything else. **107**. Who is in a position to understand his own soul? Who knows its inner being? – whether it is material or immaterial; whether it is to be seen as purely incorporeal or as having something of a corporeal kind about it; how it comes to be, how it is composed; whence it enters, how it departs; what bonding and interface it has with what constitutes the body; how the intangible and formless is confined in its own prescribed limit; what distinguishes its operations; how the same being both reaches up above the heaven in enquiring into invisible things, and also slides towards material passions, dragged down by the weight of the body, towards wrath and fear, pain and pleasure, pity and hardheartedness, expectation and memory, cowardice and daring, love and hatred, and all those things which produce contradiction in the soul's powers. **108**. Would not one who observes this reckon that he had a crowd of souls gathered within him, every one of those mentioned being quite different from the rest, and, insofar as any predominates, holding sway over all the rest, so that even reason itself may bend and submit to such dominant inclinations, and add its own cooperation to such impulses, like tribute to a tyrannical despot? **109**. This multiplicity and pluriformity of what is to be observed in the soul, does any word of

[46] *Eccles* 5,1.

inspired scripture tell us whether there is a single thing compounded from them all, and what is the mingling and conflation of opposites with each other, so that the many become a single entity? **110**. Yet each of these distinctly identified is confined in the soul as it were in a capacious jar. How is it we are not always aware of them as present within, feeling courage and cowardice at the same time, resenting and enjoying the same thing, [259] moved inwardly by the confusion and mixture of all the other emotions, though we recognize their partial dominance whenever one of them prevails and the rest are subdued? **111**. What in fact is this assembling and ordering, and the large vacant space within us, such that each has its own appointed place, kept apart by some sort of partitions from mixing with its neighbours? The question, too, whether wrath or fear or the rest of the feelings mentioned have substantial being, or are just insubstantial movements – what explanation is there of that? **112**. If they subsist, there is not one soul enclosed in us, as we have said, but a crowd of souls, with each of them distinguished as a proper and defined soul. Yet if we are to think of these as an insubstantial movement, how can the insubstantial control and dominate us, enslaving us like a tyrant, whichever of them happens to take control? **113**. Further, if the soul is in the intelligible order, how can multiplicity and composition be attributed to the intelligible, when such a notion applies specifically to these physical characteristics? The soul's capacity for growth, for appetite and nourishment and change, and the fact that every part of the body is nourished, while sensation does not penetrate every part, but some parts of us are as insensitive as lifeless things, since bones and cartilage, nails and hair, both grow and lack sensation, – **114**. who is there that understands even half the soul's function in these respects? You tell me!

115. Why speak of the soul? Not even in the physical being itself, in which the bodily qualities inhere, has so far been captured by clear comprehension; for if one mentally analyses the phenomenon into its constituent parts and attempts to envisage the subject by itself, stripping it of its qualities, what will be left to reflect upon, I fail to see. **116**. When you remove from the body its colour, shape, solidity, [260] weight, size, spatial location, movement, its passive and active capacity, its relation to other things, none of which is in itself the body, but all belong to the body, what will then be left to which the thought of a body applies? – that is something we can neither perceive by ourselves, nor do we learn it from scripture. **117**. Someone then who does not know himself, how is he to get to know any thing beyond himself? And the person who has got used to his own ignorance about himself, does he not plainly learn from this not to meddle with the hidden things which lie outside him? For the same reason we learn by the senses just enough about the elements of the world to be able to make use of each for our life, but as to a definition of their being, we have not understood it, nor do we regard our ignorance as a disadvantage. **118**. Why be concerned about the nature of fire, how it is kindled, how it flares up, how it takes hold on neighbouring fuel, and does not go out till it has burnt up and destroyed the material, how the spark lies hidden in the flint, how, though cold to the touch, the steel generates the flame, how sticks rubbed together produce fire, or how, brilliant with sunlight, water makes a flame? Leaving aside the reason for its upward surge and its power of continual movement and all such questions, we have learned to concern ourselves with and investigate only its useful effects for our life, knowing that one who accepts its benefits without such concern is no worse off than the concerned.

119. For this reason Scripture avoids dwelling on the being of created things as a pointless waste of time. It seems to me that the Son of Thunder, John, having loudly resounded with the preceding proclamations of the doctrines within him, had this in mind when at the end of his Gospel history [261] he said that these were many things done by the Lord, "which (in his words) if they were written one by one, the whole world could not contain the books that would be written".[47] He was not of course referring to those healing miracles; **120**. for of them the history left none unrecorded, even if it did not keep a record of all those healed by name. When it says that dead are raised, blind see again, deaf hear, lame walk, and again that every ill is healed,[48] by these words it leaves no tale of miracles untold, since it includes in the general terms every single event. Rather, with his deep knowledge the Evangelist perhaps means this: the majesty of the Son of God is to be learnt not only from his miracles done in the flesh, **121**. for these are small compared with the

[47] *Jn* 21,25.
[48] Cf. *Mt* 11,5; *Lk* 7,22.

rest of his mighty work. Look up at the sky, and see for yourself the beauty in it; apply your mind to the breadth of the earth, to the depths of the water, apprehending with your mind the whole world, observing by reason what exists beyond the world, and recognize these as the true works of him who visited you in the flesh, works which, he says, if they were written one by one, the what and the how and the whence and the how much of each, the quantity of information about the world would exceed the size of the world itself. **122**. Since God made the universe by wisdom, and the wisdom of God has no limit – "Of his understanding," it says, "there is no reckoning,"[49] the world which is contained in its own proper limits will not have room in itself for an account of the infinite wisdom. If then the whole world is too small to contain the information about the works of the Lord, how many worlds will contain an account of the God of the universe? **123**. Perhaps even the tongue of blasphemy will not deny the infinity of the [262] Maker of all things that were brought into being by his mere will! If then all creation cannot contain the account of itself, which is what great John testifies on our interpretation, how could little humanity possibly contain an account of the Sovereign Lord of creation? **124**. Let the bigmouths tell us, what is man, when compared with the universe? What geometric mark is so indivisibly small, what atom so refined and near to non-existence in that futile Epicurean theory, as the littleness of man is next to nothing compared with the universe? As great David also put it, having observed well our insignificance, "My substance is as nothing in your presence";[50] he does not say "nothing at all", but "like nothing", using the comparison with the non-existent to indicate extreme littleness.

IV. *Naming and conceiving God (125–195)*

125.–147. *Positive and negative words for God*

125. Nevertheless, beginning from such a negligible nature, they open their mouths against the ineffable Power, and measure the

[49] *Ps* 146/147,5.
[50] *Ps* 38,6/39,5.

infinite nature with a single title, squeezing the being of God into the word 'unbegottenness', intending thereby to advance their slander against the Only-begotten. When great Basil corrected their misguided idea, and gave some explanations about the words, as not derived from the natures, but applied conceptually to their subjects, so much do they avoid escaping back to the truth, that they stick, glued with lime, to what they said before, and do not shift from their sophistry, but decree that 'unbegotten' is not said conceptually, but expresses the nature. **126**. To go through the whole argument, [263] to present that silly, long-winded nonsense and to attempt a refutation point by point would involve long application, much time, and great difficulty, **127**. just as I hear that Eunomius himself spent a number of years, more than the Trojan War, laboriously hidden in silent retreat, in his deep sleep composing this long dream for himself. He was trying laboriously, not to interpret an idea, but to impose forced meanings on the texts, collecting fine-sounding words from certain writings. **128**. Just as the poor, for want of clothing, sew the edges of rags and stitch together tunics for themselves, so he gathers one expression here, another there, and thereby sews together his patchwork of a book, not without difficulty sticking together and reconciling the assemblage of words; his shabby, juvenile effort at competition is just as unsuitable for a man who aims at the truth, as the effeminacy of luxurious make-up would be for a tough, veteran athlete. **129**. I think it is better, after reviewing briefly the theme of the whole undertaking, to say "Goodbye" to the long chapters.

130. Our position therefore – I am adopting my master's teaching – is that we have a faint and slight apprehension of the divine Nature through reasoning, but we still gather knowledge enough for our slight capacity through the words which are reverently used of it. **131**. We claim that the meaning of all these names is not uniform, but some denote things that appertain to God, others those that are absent. So we call him just and indestructible,[51] [264] by 'just' indicating that justice appertains to him, and by 'indestructible', that destruction does not. It is also possible by reversing the terminology

[51] 'Indestructible' and 'indestructibility' are used to render ἄφθαρτος, ἀφθαρσία. There is no satisfactory term in English: alternatives might be 'incorruptible, -ility', 'imperishable, -ility', 'immortal, -ity'.

to attach epithets to God as appertaining, so as to express what is his by what is denied, and what is alien by what appertains. **132**. So, since injustice contradicts justice, and destructibility is the opposite of eternity, it is possible to apply the contradictions correctly to God, and to be in no error about what is fitting, when we say that he eternally is, and that he is not unjust, which is the same as saying that he is just and not liable to be destroyed. **133**. So we claim that the other titles also, by a reversal of meaning, may be suitably applied in each sense, as with 'good' and 'immortal' and all other expressions of the same kind. Each one of them can, in one or other of the alternative forms, indicate what applies, and what does not apply, to the divine nature; so that while the form of the name changes, the devout understanding of the Subject remains consistent. **134**. To say that God has no evil in him is the same as calling him good, to confess him as immortal as to say that he lives for ever. We perceive no difference of meaning between these, but mean the same thing by each expression, even though one appears to express a positive thing, the other a negative. **135**. Similarly, if we say that God is the beginning of all things, and if we also name him 'Unbegun', we are not in dispute about the thoughts, since by either expression we declare him Author and Cause of the universe. So whether we call him 'Unbegun' or 'Author of all things', we describe him first by what does not apply, secondly by what does apply, it being possible, as we said, by the exchange of descriptions to reverse the meaning of the words, and for what does apply, by a shift of form, to be [265] understood from the title that was formerly denied, and *vice versa*. **136**. It is legitimate, instead of saying he has no beginning, to define him as the Beginning of every thing, and instead of this again to confess that he alone exists unbegotten. Thus the words may seem, because of the change of form, to be different from one another, but the meaning of what is said remains one and the same. The purpose in speaking of God is not to think up resounding and harmonious verbal beauty, but to identify a reverent notion by which what befits the thought of God may be kept intact.

137. Since therefore it is reverent to reckon that the Cause of all has himself no transcendent cause, if we have this thought firmly fixed and established in us, what dispute still remains for the intelligent person over the terminology, when every word by which such an idea is expressed says the same thing? Whether you say that he is Beginning and Cause of all, whether you call him 'Unbegun', or 'Existing unbegotten', or 'Being from eternity', or 'Cause of all', or 'Alone without cause', all such are equivalent to each other where the meaning of the terms is concerned, and the words are of equal value; to quarrel about this kind of verbal sound is a waste if time, as if true religion lay not in the meaning, but in the syllables and sounds. **138**. Such then was the thought elaborated by our Teacher. It enables any one, whose vision is not obstructed by the screen of heresy, to perceive quite clearly that the manner of existence of the essential nature of the Divinity is intangible, inconceivable, and beyond all rational comprehension. Human thought, investigating and searching by such reasoning as is possible, reaches out and touches the unapproachable and sublime Nature, neither seeing so clearly as distinctly to [266] glimpse the Invisible, nor so totally debarred from approaching as to be unable to form any impression of what it seeks. **139**. By the reach of reason its goal is to discover what that is which it seeks, and in a sense it does understand it by the very fact that it cannot perceive it, inasmuch as it acquires clear knowledge that what it seeks is beyond all knowledge. **140**. It detects things which are incompatible with the divine nature, and is not unaware of those which it is proper to attribute to it; yet it cannot perceive what that nature itself is, to which these thoughts apply, but, from the knowledge of the things which are and are not attributed, it sees all that can be seen – that that which rests beyond every evil, and is perceived as possessing every good, must surely be such as is unutterable in word and inaccessible to thought. **141**. So when our Teacher has cleared away all unsuitable ideas in the way we understand the divine Being, and has urged and taught us to attribute to it everything fine and befitting divinity, because the First Cause is neither a destructible being nor one that came to be by generative process, but is deemed to be free of any such notion, and from the denial of what does not apply, and from the affirmation of what is reverently attributed to him comes the apprehension that he exists, – the constant battler against truth resists his words, and wants that verbal noise, I mean the word 'unbegottenness', to indicate unequivocally the being of God.

142. Yet it is obvious to any one with a slight training in the use of words, that indestructibility and unbegottenness by their privative prefix mean that neither of these things applies to God, that is, destruction and origin. There are many other synonymous words which [267] indicate the absence of what does not apply, rather than the statement of what is: innocent, unpained, harmless, undisturbed, and wrathless, unsleeping, immune to infection, impassible, inviolable, and so on. **143**. These are truly said and represent a kind of catalogue and listing of the bad ideas from which the Divinity is free, yet the statement does not by the words provide information about what is spoken of. What it is not, we learn from the sounds; what it is, the meaning of the words used does not show. **144**. It is as if one wanting to give a description of the nature of Man were to say he is not inanimate, nor insensible, nor winged, nor four-footed, nor aquatic; he would not indicate what is, but explain what is not, and would neither be lying in listing these features of Man nor would he plainly describe the subject. On exactly the same principle, though many such things are said of the divine Nature, by which we learn what we must understand God to be; but what in itself it essentially is, the words do not teach us. While avoiding every kind of concurrence with any wrong notion in our views about God, we make use of a great variety of names for him, adapting our terminology to various concepts. **145**. Since no one title has been discovered to embrace the divine Nature by applying directly to the subject itself, we therefore use many titles, each person in accordance with various interests achieving some particular idea about him, to name the Divinity, as we hunt amid the pluriform variety of terms applying to him for sparks to light up our understanding of the object of our quest. **146**. When we ask ourselves and enquire about what the Divinity is, we give various answers, such as, [268] that which transcends the constitution and ordering of things, that which has its existence from no prior cause, but constitutes the cause of being to all else, that to which generation and beginning, destruction and end do not apply, nor turning into its contrary, nor lessening of superiority, so that no evil finds place in it, and no good is lacking. **147**. If any one wants to put such thoughts into words, he must certainly describe what is immune to change for the worse as 'unchangeable and unalterable', and speak of the first Cause of the universe as 'unbegotten', of that which admits no destruction as 'indestructible', of that which declines to no end as 'immortal and unending', of him who governs the universe as 'almighty'; and thus, putting words to all the other reverent ideas, we use a variety of concepts to speak of him in one way and another, indicating by the names his power, his sovereignty, his goodness, his existing without prior cause or his everlasting continuance.

148.–158. *God is named for his actions, not for his being*

148. I claim therefore that people are entitled to use such nomenclature, adapting the appellations to their subject as each sees fit, and that what our author holds up as a terrible, scary bogey is no absurdity, that the application of names is more recent in every case than the actual thing, and also in the case of God. God is not a word, nor does his being consist of speech or sound. **149**. God is in himself whatever in faith he is deemed to be, but what is named by those who speak of him is not what he actually is, for the nature of him who Is is ineffable; but he gets his titles from the actions he is believed to perform for our lives. So in this particular case, the word just used: 'God', [269] we say, thinking as we give him the title of one who supervises, observes, and with his vision penetrates hidden things.[52] **150**. If however the Being exists prior to the actions, and we know the actions through the perceptions of sense, and if we describe these in such words as may be possible, what still remains so terrible about saying that the names are more recent than the things? If we cannot first explain what is being said about God before we think it, and if we think it by means of what we learn from his actions, and if before the act there exists the potency, and the potency depends on the divine will, and the will resides in the authority of the divine Nature – does that not make it clear to us that it is a matter of applying to the realities the terms we use to indicate what happens, and the words are a kind of shadow of the realities, matching the movements of things which exist?

151. That this is so, is clearly confirmed by divine scripture through great David, who refers to the divine Nature as it were by special and apt names which are suggested to him by the divine action: "Pitiful," he says, "and merciful is the Lord, patient and rich in mercies."[53] What do these words mean? Do they refer to action or to

[52] Gregory thinks of θεός, 'God', as derived from the verb θεᾶσθαι, 'gaze at', or 'view'. This false etymology was widely believed in ancient times.

[53] *Ps* 102/103,8.

nature? Every one will agree, it can only be to the action. **152**. When then did God perform his acts of pity and mercy and get the name from the action? Was it before mankind existed? But who then was in need of mercy? No, it surely came after sin, and sin after man. So after man came both the act of showing mercy and the title of mercy. **153**. Well, now, is our higher thinker than the prophets going to condemn even David, because he used his impressions of God to give him names? Or will he do battle with him on the pretext of that noble, quasi-tragic line, [270] "Do you glorify with words from conceptual thought the most blessed life of God, which glories in itself alone and before conceptual thinkers are born?" **154**. In defence of the prophet it will surely be said, that while it is true that the divine Nature is glorified in itself alone and before the birth of conceptual thinkers, yet the human mind utters only as much as it is able to learn from the activities. "From the greatness and beauty of created things, reasoning backwards," says Wisdom, "the generative Source of all things is perceived."[54] We utter such titles for the divine Being which transcends all thought, not to glorify it by the names we use, but to guide ourselves by what is said towards the understanding of hidden things.

155. "I have said to the Lord," says the prophet, "You are my God; for of my goods you have no need."[55] How then do we thus, as Eunomius puts it, "glorify the most blessed life of God", which the prophet declares to be in no need of human goods? Or does he suppose that 'glorify' stands for 'name'? **156**. We are indeed informed by those who use language correctly and are expertly trained in the use of words, that the word 'glorify' (ἀγάλλειν) is not used of mere denotation; that would be expressed with 'make known' (γνωρίζειν), 'denote' (δηλοῦν), 'indicate' (σημαίνειν), or some other such term, **157**. whereas 'glorify' is the same as 'glory in' (ἐπικαυχᾶσθαι) and 'rejoice in' (ἐπευφραίνεσθαι) and any other terms of the same meaning. He however alleges that we "glorify with words from conceptual thought the most blessed life". We do indeed reckon that to add any honour to the divine Nature, which transcends every honour, is more than human weakness can manage, but we do not

[54] *Wis* 13,5.
[55] *Ps* 15/16,2.

refuse to try to make something known about him through words and titles reverently conceived. **158**. For this reason, so far as we are able, [271] in pursuing what is reverent we apprehend that the first Cause has his existence from no superior cause. If any one accepts this, that is praiseworthy simply on grounds of truth. If however one judges such a statement to be more important than the rest of our notions of the divine Nature, and therefore says that God, exulting and rejoicing in this idea alone, glories in it as in something supremely excellent, that would be the work of the Muse of Eunomius, who says that Unbegottenness is glorified in itself alone, Unbegottenness which he says is Being and which he calls the blessed and divine Life.

159.–176. *God's being is prior to human conceptions of him*

159. Now, in accordance with "the manner to present use conformed, and the pattern by precedent informed"[56] (for so he again charms us with his play upon words!), let us hear how he thereby claims "to dissipate the opinion about him recently received, and to constrain the ignorance of those who are deceived;" – I shall use the very rhymes of our dithyrambic poet. "Having said," he tells us, "that conceptual statements by their nature dissolve along with their utterance, we have gone on to add: But God, when they are silent, and when they utter sound, when they have been made, and before the things which are were made, both was and is, Unbegotten." **160**. So let us find out what there is in common between the conceiving of words or the giving of names, and the actual things which we indicate through this or that utterance of names and words; so that if God exists unbegotten before mankind is constituted, we judge it wrong to put such an idea into intelligent speech, because it is dispersed together with the sound – if it is just by human conceptual thought that the name is given. **161**. To be spoken of is not the same as to be. In fact, [272] God is what he is by nature, but is spoken of by us, insofar as it is possible to speak of him, given the poverty of our nature, which keeps the workings of the mind undisclosed, unless they are brought into the open by voice and word.

[56] This is an attempt to suggest the word-play of Eunomius' Greek, which Gregory derides. τὸν ἐπιβάλλοντα τῇ χρείᾳ τρόπον καὶ τὸν προλαβόντα τύπον means more literally: "usage-fitting manner and previously existing form".

Consequently, when we perceive that he is from no prior cause, we express that perception by using a concept with the word 'unbegotten'. **162**. What harm is suffered by him who essentially Is, if we use a word to say how he exists? His unbegotten existence does not derive from his being called 'Unbegotten', but because he is such, he has the word attached to him. This is something our man of little brain has failed to observe, nor did he understand what he himself had proposed. Otherwise he would have stopped abusing those who conceptually create the term 'unbegotten'.

163. Look at what he says: "Conceptual statements dissolve along with their utterance; but God, both when they have been made, and before things which are were made, both was and is, Unbegotten." You can see that to be what he in fact is belongs to him before the existence of all things, being no less what he is, whether they are silent or whether they utter sound; while the use of words and names was first known when men were created, because they were endowed by God with the power of speech. **164**. If then creation is later than its Maker, and Man is last in the whole creation, and speech is a peculiarity of Man, and words and names are parts of speech, and 'unbegottenness' is a word – then why does he not realize that he is fighting against his own argument? Our assertion is that the names of existing things are invented for existing things by the human mind, and he himself concedes that those who use words are demonstrably later than the divine Life, and that the divine Nature exists, as it exists now and always existed, unbegotten. **165**. If therefore he himself concedes that the blessed Life precedes mankind (again [273] I go back and use the same argument), and we also do not dispute that it was later in time that men came into existence, and if we say that we have used words and names, from the moment we were created and received from our Maker articulate speech, and if 'unbegottenness' is a word denoting a particular idea, and every word is a part of human speech; – then one who concedes that the divine Nature exists before mankind must agree that the title invented for that Nature is of later origin. **166**. It was not likely that the use of the word operated before the creation of its users, just as farming did not operate before there were farmers, nor navigation before navigators, nor any other human activities before human life was constituted. Why then does he quarrel with us, when he cannot follow the logic of his own words?

"God was what he is," he says, "before Man came to be." We ourselves do not deny that. Every thing whatsoever that may be thought about God, existed before the world was constituted. **167**. But we assert that he is named after the one who names him was made. If the purpose of using names is that we should receive information from them about real things, and it is only ignorance that requires one to give information, and the divine Nature, because it is all-encompassing, is superior to all information, that proves that it is not for God's sake, but for ours, that names are applied to describe him who Is. **168**. It is not so that God may learn about himself, that the word 'unbegottenness' has become attached to his Nature. He who knows all things, and himself before all things, needs no syllables and words to learn what are his nature and rank; it is rather in order that we may ourselves get some understanding of what may be devoutly thought about him, that we have labelled our various thoughts with words and syllables, [274] stamping verbal shapes as signs and markers on our mental processes, so as to get clear and distinct pointers to our psychic processes by the sounds we attach to the ideas. **169**. So when we assert that the term 'unbegottenness' is a concept applied to indicate that God exists without beginning, what refutation is it of our argument, if it is said that, "when they are speaking and silent and thinking, and before any concept of created beings, God was and is unbegotten"? **170**. If however his existence before both word and thought is universally agreed, and if the giving of the name, by which our understanding is stated, is held to be invented by our conceiving it, and if his object in his dispute with us is to show that the title is not just conceived by human beings, but that it exists even before our creation, I do not understand what it is said about, and what it has to do with his set purpose of saying that God exists unbegotten before there are beings, and his struggle to affirm that a concept is a later existent than God.

171. Is there any one who asserts that God is a concept, that Eunomius should attack him with words such as these, and say, as he has said, "It is madness to reckon the concept older than those who conceive it"? Or as he goes on a little lower to add, "As if then their opinion were not this either, that human beings, although they are the latest of the creatures designed by God, precede their own concept." [275] The argument would have much force, if madness or folly led someone to say that God is a concept. **172**. If however this argument does not exist, nor ever has – for who would ever reach such a pitch of insanity as to say that he who truly Is, who brought into being all that exists, does not exist in a substantial being of his own, but would describe him as the conception of a title? – why this pointless shadow-boxing attack on assertions not made? **173**. Or is the reason for this mindless quarrelling obvious? – ashamed to face those who have been deceived by his logical trick over unbegottenness, once it was conclusively proved that the name is totally distinct from any meaning connected with being, he deliberately makes a muddle of what is being said, shifting the battle from the word to the things, so that he can easily knock down the unwary by this sort of muddle, if they think we have said that God is either a concept, or secondary to the invention of words by men; and that is why he leaves our position unrefuted and shifts the battle to other ground.

174. Our position was, as we have said, that the word 'unbegottenness' does not denote the Nature, but attaches to the Nature by being conceived, and that by it his existence without prior cause is indicated. The position they argued was that the word denotes the Being itself. Where then are the arguments that such is the meaning of the title? **175**. Yet while these things can certainly be dealt with in other words, all his effort is devoted to God's unbegotten existence; as though someone were to ask him plainly about this matter, what understanding he had of the word 'unbegottenness', whether as conceived to denote that the First Cause is without beginning, or whether it indicates the Being itself, and he were [276] solemnly and learnedly to answer that he has no doubt God is the maker of heaven and earth. **176**. Just as this word is irrelevant to the topic and not connected, in the same way you will find that in the case of his elegantly composed attack on us there is no connexion with his purpose. Let us look next at this.

177.–195a. *The power and limits of conceptual thought*

177. Eunomius says that God is unbegotten, with which we too agree; furthermore, that unbegottenness is Being, which we deny. We say that this is a name denoting God's unbegotten existence, not that unbegottenness is God. He promises to refute our argument; so what is his refutation? It is, he says, that before the creation of mankind he existed unbegotten. **178**. How does that affect the question? Eunomius promises to demonstrate that the name is the same as its bearer, since he defines 'unbegottenness' as Being. Where then is his proof? To demonstrate that God preexists the users of speech? What an incontrovertible and amazing proof! That is a refined piece of logic based on dialectical science, which none could envisage if he were not initiated in the abstruse skill. **179**. Yet in his enumeration to us of kinds of 'concept', he solemnly pokes fun at the word 'concept': "Of things thus said by way of concept," he says, "some have existence solely as uttered, as those meaning nothing, others have a proper meaning. Of these, some are for enlargement, as in the case of gigantic figures, others for diminution, as in the case of pygmies, some for attachment, as in the case of the many-headed, or for combination, as in the case of animals with mixed features." **180**. You see what our philosopher [277] chopped up our 'concept' into, before he would let its meaning get any further. 'Concept' is meaningless, he says, nonsensical, playing unnatural tricks, whether by foreshortening or by stretching the size prescribed by nature, by combining different beings or by making a monster with incongruous attachments. By these means he ridicules the word 'concept', and proves it is useless and of no benefit to any one. **181**. So where do we get the higher studies from? Where do we get the sciences of geometry and arithmetic, the disciplines of logic and natural philosophy, researches in mechanics, marvellous clocks of copper and water, the very philosophy of being itself, metaphysical speculation, and in sum the whole scholarly consideration of the great and sublime purusuits of the mind? What about agriculture? What about navigation? What about any of the business we do in life? **182**. How did the sea become passable to man? How was the airborne forced to serve the earth-bound? How is the wild beast tamed? How is the fearsome domesticated? Why does the stronger not refuse? Was it not through conceptual thought that all these discoveries were made for mankind? As I see it, mental conception is the way we find out things we do not know, using what is connected and consequent upon our first idea of a subject to discover what lies beyond. Having formed an idea about a matter in hand, we attach the next thing to our initial apprehension by adding new ideas, until we bring our research into the subject to its conclusion.

183. Why should I list the greater, more sublime achievements of conceptual thought? Any one not disposed to be contentious can see that every beneficial thing useful to mankind which time has invented, was not found out except by the use of conceptual thought. It seems to me that of all the [278] good things effected in us in this life, which are by divine providence present in our minds, to reckon conceptual thought the most precious would not contradict sound judgment.

184. This statement is something I have learned from Job, where in the story God is portrayed as making a pronouncement through storm and clouds, and among other things appropriate for God to say, he says that it is he who instructs mankind in crafts and who granted to women the art of weaving and embroidery.[57] That it is not by direct action that he taught us such skills, himself sitting over the exercise, as one may see in the case of those being taught in the physical world, is surely undeniable, except to the carnal and bestial person. **185**. Nevertheless, it says that instruction in such skills came to us from him. It was therefore by giving our race the ability of conceptual thought and invention that he himself brought us to the knowledge of these skills. In terms of causation, every discovery and achievement is to be referred to the Author of this ability: thus mankind has produced medical science, but it would not be wrong to say that medical science is a gift of God. **186**. Every single discovery in the course of human history, whatever it may be, which fulfils some useful purpose in peace or war, has never come to us from any other source than the intelligent thought which thinks up and discovers one thing after another; and intelligence is a work of God. From God therefore comes all that is produced for us by our intelligence.

187. If it is said by our opponents that mythical forms and unreal monsters are fictions imagined by conceptual thought, I do not deny it. [279] Even their argument fits our theme. We ourselves agree that the science of opposite things is just the same, of useful things and those which are not so, as in the case of medicine and navi-

[57] In the Greek Bible *Job* 38,36 reads: "Who gave to women the art of weaving or skill in embroidery?"

gation and any similar skill. One who knows how to help the sick with a drug would also be able, if he put his skill to evil use, to administer poison to the healthy. **188**. The one who steers the ship into harbour with the rudder could also steer it on to reefs and promontories, if he were minded to destroy those aboard by treachery. The painter uses the same skill to paint the most beautiful figure on a picture, and turns openly to copy the most disgusting. The physiotherapist uses his manipulation technique to correct the dislocated limb and, if so inclined, by the same skill puts the healthy one out of joint. **189**. There is no need to clutter up the argument by mentioning every case. In those described no one could deny that a person who has learned to exercise any skill for good ends could also use it for improper purposes; similarly we also say that the ability to think conceptually was implanted by God in human nature, but that some have misused the inventive power to make it serve and support undesirable fictions. **190**. So just because conceptual thought can plausibly invent falsehoods and non-existents, that does not mean it cannot investigate things that really are and truly exist; rather, to generous minds its suitability for such a purpose is evidence of its power in that regard. The fact that attempts to produce thrills or amusement in the spectators does not fail to find the conceptual thought necessary for the purpose, but that portraying people with many arms or many heads, breathing fire or miscegenated with serpents' coils, or increasing their size above normal or reducing [280] their natural proportions to make them ridiculous, relating how people were transformed into springs and trees and birds, whereby those who enjoy such things are able to find entertainment – this is, I would say, plain evidence that conceptual thought could by its inventive power apprehend higher aspects of learning too. **191**. It is not the case that perfect intelligence was fixed in us by the Giver for making up imaginary beings, while it is endowed with no power to produce things useful for the discovery of what enhances life. Rather, while the power of our soul to take initiatives and to choose is implanted in our nature to lead us on towards the attainment of beautiful and good things, some may also use such a drive for improper purposes; and yet no one would say that having sometimes the tendency to bad things demonstrates that the power to choose leads to no good. In just the same way, for conceptual thought to occupy itself with futile and unprofitable things does not condemn it as unable to be of use, but demonstrates that it is not ineffectual for life-enhancing and needful purposes. As in the one case it invents things for pleasure or thrills, so in the other it does not fail to provide means to approach the truth.

192. One question was, whether the First Cause, that is God, exists without beginning, or has his being dependent upon some beginning. Understanding with the intellect that what is perceived to derive from another cannot be First, we conceived a word denoting that idea, and say that the one who Is without superior cause exists unbegun, or if you like, without being begotten. We entitled the one who so exists 'Unbegun' and 'Unbegotten', indicating by the title not what he is, but what he is not. **193**. To make the thought as plain as possible, I will try to give a very clear illustration. Suppose the question is, whether a particular tree is planted or [281] self-sown. If it came about by planting, we shall of course say that the tree is planted, and if self-sown, unplanted. Such a title both states the truth (since the tree will certainly be the one or the other), and fails to indicate the tree's specific nature: we learn from 'unplanted' that the tree is self-sown, but whether it is a vine or a plane or some other such plant that is denoted, is not made known to us by the use of such a term. **194**. If the illustration is understood, we may now apply the principle to the subject which it illustrates. That the First Cause has his being from no superior cause, we understand. The God who exists without a begetter we name 'Unbegotten', converting the same idea into the form of a title. We make clear by the meaning of the title that he exists without being generated, but as to the Being that exists without begetting, what it is in its own nature, we are led to no insight by this designation. **195**. One would not expect conceptual thought to have such power as to overstep the limits of our nature, to attain the intangible, and to include in our knowledge things which there is no way to comprehend.

V. *Words spoken by God (195b–236)*

195b.–204. *Eunomius makes God speak physically*

Nevertheless Eunomius violently attacks our Master, and parades the argument which Basil puts about 'concept', and dances triumphantly on his words, as usual satirizing what is said with his own verbal jingles, and saying, "Their thought he takes over, their support he blushes over."[58] **196**. He reports some part of the ideas of the Master about conceptual thought, in which Basil claimed that the use of conceptual thought is not only effective for futile purposes, [282] but also has some potential for greater things. Then he brings in Basil's statements based on the consideration of corn and seed and food, accusing him of following secular philosophy, and alleges that Basil is restricting the providential care of God, because he will not concede that names are applied to realities by him. Basil is said to ally himself with the atheists by taking up arms against Providence; it is their opinion he admires above the laws, and to them he gives more credit for wisdom, because he does not observe those first words, which say that, when mankind had not yet been brought into being, the names of fruit and seed are used by scripture.[59,60] **197**. These are Eunomius' charges against us, though the ideas are not copied in his exact words, but with the phraseology slightly changed by us, enough to correct the harsh and disagreeable resonance of his verbal syntax. What is our answer? How do we respond to his concern for divine Providence? We are wrong, he says, because we do not deny that Man was made rational by God, yet we trace the invention of words to the rational power implanted in human nature by God. And that is the very grave charge on which the Teacher of true religion is accused of going over to the opinion of the atheists, and is called "inheritor and advocate of unlawful practices", and all the most terrible names!

198. Let this corrector of our faults tell us, then, was it God who attached titles to existing things? For what our new expounder of spiritual doctrines tells us is this: [283] before Man was formed, God gave names to bud and vegetation and grass and tree and the like, as he brought his creatures into being by his command. **199**. Now if he sticks to the mere letter, and to that extent follows the Jewish

[58] Literally, "those whose interpretation he appropriates, their testimony he is ashamed of". It is the use of secular Philosophy which Eunomius is alleging against Basil.

[59] Cf. *Gen* 1,11–12.

[60] Much of section 196 is printed in spread Greek text by Jaeger, indicating that the words are those of Eunomius. In view of Gregory's statement in 197 that he has compressed and selected from Eunomius and improved the style, it seems better to present it as indirect reportage, rather than direct quotation.

opinion, and has yet to learn that the Christian is not a disciple to the letter, but to the spirit (for "The letter," it says, "kills, but the Spirit gives life",)[61] and if he is offering us the bare, literal reading of the text, as though God had spoken these sentences, and if this is his belief, he will simply be arguing that God also uses just the same spoken sentences as people use, and spells out his thoughts in sound and speech.

200. If that is his view, then, he will surely not reject the consequences. Our speech is expressed through the organs of speech, windpipe, tongue, teeth, mouth, together operating to generate speech, and the pressure of air and the breath from within. Our windpipe resounds from underneath rather like a flute fitted inside the throat. Meanwhile the palate, by means of the cavity which opens through the nostrils, acts like the bridge on top of a stringed instrument and further increases the volume of the sound. **201**. The cheeks also make their contribution to speech, contracting and expanding as shapes are formed by various facial muscles, and further produce the voice through a narrow passage in accordance with the various twists and turns of the tongue, which it achieves with one part or another of itself by somehow roughening and compressing on the teeth or palate the breath that passes through it. **202**. The lips make a useful contribution too, as they manage the voice in various ways by their different movements and [284] play their part in completing the shape of the words. If therefore God applies names to things in the way our new exegete of the divine history stipulates, naming shoot and leaf and tree and fruit, he must certainly have spoken each name exactly as it is said, using, I mean, the concatenation of syllables, which are shaped either by lips or tongue or both together. **203**. If there is no other way for the name to be expressed than for the speech-generating bodily parts to produce the syllables and words by their various movements, they are surely attributing these things to God, and base their portrait of the divine on his need to speak. The kind of framing of bodily parts which generates speech surely constitutes shape; shape means bodily outline; and body cannot avoid being composite. **204**. But where composition is recognized, there surely dissolution of components is also implied; and

[61] *2 Cor* 3,6.

dissolution is the same in meaning as destruction. This then is the outcome of our wordsmith's triumph over us, that this private god of his, which he contrived by the use of the word 'unbegottenness', speaks so as not to be deprived of the invention of words, but is shaped by the vocalizing organs in order to speak the names, and is not without bodily nature because of his need for shapes – for surely no shape could be observed independently, unless it were imprinted upon a body – and will soon go on to suffering the effects implicit in corporeality, as he declines through composition to dissolution, and through that to destruction.

205.–218. *To whom does Eunomius think God speaks?*

205. Such is revealed to be the nature of the fresh god by the logic of what our new god-maker has said. But he takes up the cause of the scriptural words and claims that, "Moses explicitly proclaims that God said these things; and he adds the actual words, 'Let there be light,' and, 'Let there be a firmament,' [285] and, 'Let the waters be gathered,' and, 'Let the dry land appear,' and, 'Let earth bring forth plants,' and, 'Let the waters bring forth,' and all that is written thereafter."[62] So let us consider the meaning of the words. **206**. Even those quite naif are aware that there is a natural mutual connexion between listening and speaking: just as listening cannot function if no one speaks, so speaking cannot be effective unless it is directed to a listener. If therefore it says that God spoke, we need an indication also of the audience to which he spoke.

Will he tell us that he says these things to himself? Then in giving these orders, he is commanding himself. Who is going to accept this, that God sits giving himself instructions about what to do, and using himself as minister and agent in what he commands? **207**. Even if one were to allow the religious propriety of such a suggestion, would anybody, if he were by himself, need words and sentences, though he be merely human? It is enough for each that the stirring of the mind causes the intended action to begin.

Eunomius may of course say that it is a conversation with the Son. But what need was there of speech for that purpose? It is the mark of a corporeal nature to express the thoughts of the heart by

[62] Cf. *Gen* 1,3–20.

speech. That is why, as an equivalent to the use of the voice, communication through concepts expressed in writing was invented. **208**. We express our thoughts equally by the use of speech or in writing; for those not far away we approach within ear-shot, for those further off we make our thoughts plain by writing, while for those who are near we raise or lower the pitch of the voice. There are occasions when by simply nodding we make it clear to others what needs to be done, and even the eye glancing in a particular manner indicates the purpose we have in mind, and a hand moving in a certain way either forbids something or allows it to be done. **209**. If then those confined in the body [286] often make known to those around them the motions of the mind, even without voice or word or written message, and silence causes no impediment to the intended action, is there a need in the case of the immaterial and intangible "highest and first being", as Eunomius puts it,[63] for words to make clear the mind of the Father and to make known his purpose to the Only-begotten? – words which, as he himself says, "by their nature dissolve along with their utterance".[64]

I know not whether any person of intelligence will accept the truth of this, especially when every sound is certainly uttered into air; no speech is possible unless it consists of air. Even my opponents are bound to suppose some medium between the speaker and the person being addressed. **210**. If there were no such medium, how would the sound travel from the speaker to the hearer? What then will they call the medium by which they separate the Son from the Father? With bodies, aerial space lies between them, which is something in its proper nature distinct from the being of human bodies. God however, being intangible, having no shape, free from taint of composition, if, in communicating his purposes to the Only-begotten God in a similar, indeed the same, immaterial and incorporeal manner he did make the communication in speech, what medium had he, through which the word flowed and was carried to its home in the ears of the Only-begotten?

211. Perhaps we should not pass unnoticed the matter that the Divinity is not divided in its receptive activities, as in our case each

[63] Cf. 62 above.
[64] Cf. 48 and 159 above.

of the sense-organs deals separately with what is proper to it, sight with what is seen, but the faculty of hearing with what is heard; touch does not taste, nor has hearing any sense of smell or of flavour, but each abides by the one activity for which it was appointed by [287] nature, remaining somehow insensitive to what is not in its nature, unaware of the harvest enjoyed by the neighbouring sense. **212**. This case is however different: through and through, the Divinity is sight and hearing and knowledge. It would be quite wrong also to attach the more animal senses to the stainless Nature. Yet if we are going to suppose the Divinity a mean thing and reduce it to earthbound ideas, so as to think that the Father speaks words through a mouth, affecting the hearing of the Son, what is the medium that we suppose intervenes between the Father's voice and the Son's ear? **213**. This must be created or uncreated.[65] We cannot say it is created, for the word was uttered before the creation was constituted. Yet there is nothing uncreated except the divine Nature. If then there was no creation, and the word mentioned in the creation narrative was earlier, then when some one claims that speech and an audible voice are meant by the account, what will he suggest goes between the Son and the Father, on which the sound of speech is imprinted? If there is something between, it exists, surely, in its own proper nature, so as not to be identical with the Father nor to coincide in nature with the Son, but as something quite distinct it separates from each other the Father and the Son, pushing itself in between the two. **214**. What is the result? It is not created, for the creation is more recent than the word. We are taught that the Only-begotten is begotten; nothing is unbegotten except the Father. Therefore of necessity the word of truth compels us to hold that there is nothing between the Father and the Son. But where no separation is conceived, close conjunction is surely acknowledged; and what is totally conjoined is not mediated by voice and speech. By 'conjoined' I mean that which is totally inseparable; for the word [288] 'conjunction' (συνάφεια) does not imply a kind of bodily affinity in what is essentially intelligent, but the union and commingling of wills between one intelligent being and another.

[65] Jaeger punctuates as a question: "must this be created or uncreated?"

215. For indeed, there is no difference in will between the Son and the Father: as is the primary Beauty of goodness, so too is the Image of goodness. It is as when one looks in a mirror (there can be no objection to using physical models to present the idea); the image will reflect in every aspect the original object, so that the figure looking in is the cause of the figure in the mirror, and the image neither moves nor bends by itself, unless the original initiates the movement or inclination; only if the first figure moves, then of course the reflection in the mirror also moves with it. In just the same way, we would say, the "Image of the unseen God",[66] the Lord, is disposed immediately and directly like the Father in every movement. **216**. The Father wills something, and the Son who is in the Father has the Father's will – or rather becomes himself the Father's will. He who has in himself all that is the Father's[67] – there is nothing of the Father's he has not. If indeed he has in himself all that belongs to the Father, or rather the Father himself, then surely with the Father and all that the Father has, he also has in himself the whole will of the Father. **217**. He therefore needs no word to learn the Father's will, since he is himself the Father's Word according to the higher meaning of 'word'. What then is that word which is addressed to the real Word? And how does the real Word come to be in need of yet another word for instruction?

Perhaps someone will say that the voice of the Father came to the Holy Spirit. [289] **218**. But the Holy Spirit does not need verbal instruction either, since he is in God, as the Apostle says, and, "searches even the depths of God".[68]

If therefore God utters speech, and every word works on a hearer, then those who declare that God makes a speech in uttered words, must explain to us what is the audience for the divine words. He had no need to talk to himself, the Son was in no want of verbal instruction, the Holy Spirit, it says, searches out every thing, even the depths of God, and the creation did not yet exist: to whom is the word addressed?

---

[66] *Col* 1,15.
[67] Cf. *Jn* 16,15.
[68] *1 Cor* 2,10–11.

219.–232. *Speech without sound in a Psalm*

219. "But the text of Moses does not lie," he says, "where God is declared to have said something." Neither is great David a liar, when he clearly says in so many words, "The heavens tell God's glory, and the firmament proclaims his handiwork; day to day brings forth word, and night proclaims knowledge to night."[69] **220**. Having said that the heavens and the firmament tell a tale, and knowledge and words are announced by the day and the night, he goes on to add to his statements that these things are "not speech nor words", nor are "their voices heard".[70] How is it that tales and proclamations and words are not speech, nor a voice that enters through the sense of hearing? **221**. Is the prophet contradicting himself? Is he giving an impossible account, in telling of voiceless speech and unspoken tale and announcement without sound? Or is the prophecy above all true when by its words it teaches just this, that the celestial story and the word cried aloud by the day are not articulate speech or something spoken through the [290] mouth, but become a lesson in divine power to those who know how to understand when the voice is silent.

222. What conclusions can we draw about this? Perhaps if we understand that, we shall also have understood what Moses wrote. Sometimes the Scripture, to clarify the meaning of the subject under discussion, presents its account of intellectual matters in a somewhat physical way. For example, the doctrine which David seems to me to be setting out, what he taught by the words in question,[71] is this: nothing that is gets its existence from some spontaneous concurrence, as some have thought that our world and all that is in it was engineered by fortuitous and irrational combinations of primary elements with no providence penetrating existing things;[72] rather, there is a Cause of the whole system and structure, on which the whole nature of intelligible things depends, from which it gets its origins and causes, to which it looks and returns, and by which it abides. **223**. And because,

[69] *Ps* 18/19,2–3.
[70] *Ps* 18/19,4.
[71] See 219 above.
[72] Epicurean doctrine; cf. 410 below.

as the Apostle says, "His eternal power and divinity is seen, perceived from the creation of the world,"[73] therefore the whole creation, and above all the ordered display in the heavens, by the skill revealed in generated things demonstrates the wisdom of their Maker. What he seems to me to want to explain to us is the evidence of visible realities that what exists has been wisely and skilfully prepared and abides for ever by the power of the Governor of the universe. **224**. The very heavens themselves, he says, by displaying the wisdom of their Maker, all but utter sound as they cry out and proclaim the wisdom of their Designer, though without sound. One may hear them instructing us as if in speech, "As you look to us, you men, [291], to the beauty and the greatness in us, and to this perpetually revolving movement, the orderly and harmonious motion, always in the same paths and invariable, contemplate the one who presides over our design, and through the visible beauty let your mind rise to the original and invisible Beauty. For nothing in us is ungoverned or self-moving or self-sufficient, but every visible thing about us, every perceptible thing, depends upon the sublime and ineffable Power." **225**. This is not articulate speech, but through the visible things it imparts to our minds the knowledge of the divine power more than if speech proclaimed it in sound. The heaven, then, tells a tale but does not speak, and the firmament announces God's creation without the need of a voice, the day puts forth a word and there is no speech, and no one would say the prophecy is false;[74] in just the same way, since Moses and David have the same Instructor, I mean the Holy Spirit, the one who says that the command directed the act of creation is not suggesting to us that God is the Designer of words, but of things which are denoted by what the words mean. So that we might not think the creation to be something ungoverned and self-generating, he says that from the divine Nature it both originated and is constituted in an order and sequence.

226. It would be a large task to study closely the order of the doctrinal statements about the creation of the world made by Moses under the guise of narrative. To be sure, the error and futility of

[73] *Rom* 1,20.
[74] See 219 above.

our opponents' position would be ever more manifestly refuted by every thing he wrote. Any one interested may [292] examine in fuller detail our own and our opponents' arguments by looking at our works on Genesis.[75] **227**. We ought, however, to get back to discussing the topic before us, that in the case of God the verb 'say' does not of course connote voice and speech, but, by declaring the power of God coincident with his will, it indicates the intellectual notion in a manner more acceptable to our senses. **228**. The universe was constituted by the will of God, and it is the human habit to indicate our purpose first in a word, and thus to add the deed to match the purpose; the scriptural creation narrative, however, is a sort of introduction to theology for beginners, presenting the power of the divine Nature by things more easily understood, and easiest to take in for learning ideas is sense-perception. That is why, by putting first, "God said this should be," Moses presents the power of his initiating will, and by adding, "And it was so," he indicates that in the case of the divine Nature there is no difference between will and act. He is teaching that in God's case the thought leads straight to the act, and that the action does not follow after the thought, but the two are to be reckoned simultaneous and of a piece, the mental act and the power which completes the deed. **229**. The account allows no thought of anything between the purpose and the execution, but just as the light shines together with the kindling of the flame, coming from it and shining simultaneously with it, in the same way, while the existence of things created is the work of the divine will, yet it does not come after the decision in second place. [293] **230**. It is not like other beings whose nature includes the power to act, where one observes both the potential and the accomplished action. We say for instance that the one who is skilled in the science of shipbuilding is potentially a shipbuilder, but he is effective only when he displays his science in practice. It is not however like that with the blessed Life: rather, in that Life what is thought is in its entirety action and performance, the will passing instantly to its intended goal. **231**. As then the heavenly array attests the glory of its Designer and confesses its Maker, and needs no voice, so I think one might again go on to infer from the scripture of Moses that God, who gave being to the universe by his command,

[75] *Apologia in Hexaemeron* and *De opificio hominis*.

both says that the world is his own creation, and is in need of no words to express this thought. **232**. As therefore one who hears "heaven telling" does not look for articulate speech – to the man of intelligence the world speaks through the things that are made, without recourse to verbal expression –, so too if one hears Moses speaking as if God gives directions and orders about each part of the world distinctly named, he should neither assume that the prophet is lying, nor diminish his view of sublime things to small and earthbound thoughts, so as to reduce the Divinity in this way to human standards, supposing that he articulates his commands in speech as is our habit; rather, the command should represent the will, and the names of the created things should signify the coming into existence of things which are made. He will thereby learn two lessons from the text: that by merely willing it God constructed the universe, and that without trouble and effort the divine will became reality.

233. If any one interprets, "God said", more physically, so as [294] to argue on this ground that articulate speech was produced by him, that person will surely have to understand, "God saw",[76] along the lines of our sense-perception through the operation of his eyes, and, "The Lord heard and pitied me",[77] and, "smelled an odour of sweetness",[78] and all the stories which scripture relates in a physical fashion about God's head, foot, hand, nostril, eyelids, fingers or sandal, taking all these in a direct sense he will describe the Divinity to us in human shape just like the things apparent in ourselves. **234**. If, when one hears of the heavens as the works of his fingers,[79] and a mighty hand, uplifted arm, eye, eyelids, foot and sandals, one rises mentally by means of each expression to ideas proper to God, and does not spoil the account of the pure Nature by sullying it with corporeal notions, it would follow that one should consider the utterance of words also as representing the divine will. Yet one should not understand them as verbal utterances, but rather bear in mind that the Designer of intelligent nature has bestowed on us articulate speech in accordance to the limit imposed by nature, so that by it

[76] *Gen* 1,4.
[77] *Ps* 29,11/30,10.
[78] *Gen* 8,21.
[79] *Ps* 8,3.

we might be able to express the movements of the mind. **235**. The distinction of nature from nature, of the divine, I mean, from our own, is exactly matched by the difference which separates every thought of ours about the divine nature from what is far greater and more appropriate to God. As our power, compared with that of God, is as nothing, and our life compared with his life, and everything else about us with what is in him, is "as nothing [295] in his sight", as the prophecy says,[80] so our word compared with the Word that truly Is, is nothing. **236**. "In the beginning" it was not,[81] but was devised at the same time as our nature, nor is it seen as having an existence of its own, but as our Master says somewhere,[82] vanishes with the click of the tongue, nor is any effect of it to be observed, but it has its existence only in speech and writing. The Word from God, however, is God, a Word that in the beginning is and for ever abides, through whom all things are and consist, and he presides over the universe and wields all authority over things in heaven and things on earth, being Life and Truth and Righteousness and Light and every good thing, and upholding everything that is in being.

VI. *Human language (237–293)*

237.–246a. *God gives man the power to create words*

237. Such and so great, then, is the Word attributed to God; but Eunomius graciously allows God, as if it were something great, the word that is composed of nouns, verbs and conjunctions. He is not aware of the following comparison. The one who bestowed practical skill on our race is not credited with every single artefact, yet while it was he who gave our race the ability, it is by us that a house is produced, or a pedestal, a sword, a plough, or whatever else our life requires, and taken individually these are our works, but they point beyond to our own Cause, who designed our race to be receptive of every skill. In the same way the power of speech

[80] *Ps* 38,6/39,5.
[81] Cf. *Jn* 1,1.
[82] Cf. Basilius, *Adversus Eunomium* I 6 (PG 29, 524c).

is a work of him who made our race thus, but the invention of particular words for the purpose of describing objects was for us ourselves to contrive. **238**. Evidence of this is the fact that many things said are [296] generally thought to be thoroughly disgraceful and indecent, and no intelligent person would suppose God to be their inventor. So although some words familiar to us are in the divine scripture spoken personally by God, we should be aware that the Holy Spirit communicates with us in our own terms, just as in the story in Acts we learn that each person heard the teaching in his own native language, understanding the meaning of what was said in words he recognized.[83]

239. The truth of this may be more fully confirmed by a careful examination of the Levitical code. There baking pan and cake and wheat-flour and other such items are mentioned[84] as the Spirit uses the sacred rituals to suggest by symbols and riddles lessons beneficial to the soul, and he names certain measures in accordance with the custom of the time as '*hyphi*', '*nebel*' and '*in*'[85] and many such. **240**. Had he made these names and titles? Or did he so direct in the beginning that they should be made and named, so to call a certain seed 'wheat', to name its ground-up kernel 'flour', and to speak of the pastry in cooked dishes as 'topping', 'fillo' and 'pancake',[86] and to command the kind of vessel in which the moist dough is baked and hardened to be called a baking pan, and a certain quantity of liquid to be given the name '*in*' or '*nebel*', and the drier foods to be measured by the '*gomor*'.[87] **241**. It is nonsense and Jewish futility, falling far short of the splendour of Christianity, to suggest that the great, supreme God who transcends every title and thought, who upholds the universe by the mere power of his will, both bringing it to be and keeping it in being – that he [297] sits like some schoolmaster detailing the application of names. **242**. Rather, just as we

[83] *Acts* 2,6.

[84] *Lev* 2,4–5 etc.

[85] *1 Sam* 1,24 etc. and *Lev* 23,13 etc.

[86] These English words are meant to represent particular culinary items known to Gregory which we cannot with certainty identify. Literally, his terms mean 'superficial/top surface', 'membranaceous/membrane', and 'unfolded/flat'; fillo (or phyllo) is the very thin Greek pastry, which is popularly used for all kinds of savoury and sweet dishes.

[87] *Ex* 16,16 etc.

signal to deaf people what has to be done by using gestures and hand-signals, not because we ourselves have no voice of our own when we do this, but because it is quite useless to give verbal instructions to those who cannot hear, so, the human race being in a way deaf and unable to understand anything sublime, we hold that the grace of God, which speaks "in diverse parts and manners" in the prophets,[88] and frames the verbal expressions of the holy prophets to suit our mental grasp and habit, by these means leads us on to the apprehension of sublime things, not giving instructions in accordance with his own majesty – how should the great be confined in the little? – but in a form which comes down to the level of our small capacity. **243**. Just as God, in giving motive power to an animal does not go on to devise every single step (for once it has got its start from the Maker the creature moves itself, and goes off using its mobility as occasion offers, save that it is said of a man that his "steps are directed by the Lord"),[89] so also our race, having received from God the ability to talk and speak and announce our purpose, makes its way through things, applying signs to realities in the form of varieties of sound.

244. These then are the verbs and nouns which we use, and by which we indicate the meaning of things; and if before there are fruits, fruit is mentioned by Moses, and before there are seeds, seeds, [298] that does not refute our argument, nor is the intended meaning of the law-giver at variance with what we said about conceptual thought. **245**. That which as the end of past cultivation we call by the name of 'fruit', but which as the beginning of the future cultivation we call 'seed', that reality which underlies the names, whether it is wheat or some other crop that multiplies with sowing, tells us that it is not spontaneously generated, but that it grows up with this potential by the will of its Maker, so that the same becomes fruit, reproduces itself by becoming seed, and nourishes mankind with its superabundance. **246**. What springs up at God's will is the reality, not the name, so that the reality which substantively exists is the work of the Maker's power, but the sounds which identify things,

[88] *Heb* 1,1.
[89] *Ps* 36/37,23.

by which verbal reasoning[90] distinguishes things individually for accurate and distinct reference, these are the product and invention of the faculty of verbal reasoning, whereas this verbally rational faculty and nature itself is the work of God.

246b.–261. *The varieties of human language*

Furthermore, since rational speech belongs to all men, different words are inevitably used in accordance with differences between nations. **247**. If any one claims that light, heaven, earth or seeds were addressed by God in human fashion, he must surely go on to argue that it happened in one particular language. Which one it was, he must show us. If someone knows the first point, it is surely reasonable that he should know the second. **248**. At the Jordan after the descent of the Spirit,[91] and again in the hearing of the Jews,[92] and at the Transfiguration,[93] a voice is heard from above teaching mankind a certain lesson, not to set the mind on visible things alone, but also to believe that he is in truth the only-beloved Son of God. **249**. To enable the hearers to understand, such a voice [299] was imprinted by God upon the material air, couched in terms of the then prevailing linguistic practice. God, "who desires all to be saved and to come to the knowledge of the truth",[94] to the end that those who heard might reach salvation, articulated the word in air; as the Lord says also to the Jews – who thought, because the sound was physically in the air, that it had thundered – "It was not for my sake this voice came, but for yours."[95] **250**. Before the constitution of the universe, however, when there was nothing to receive the word, or any physical element capable of shaping articulate speech, how will the one who claims that God used words make sense of the account? He was incorporeal, the creation was not, the account allows no attribution of anything material to him, and those who might be

---

[90] λόγος, "word", in Greek means the rational faculty which is also the faculty of articulate speech, what distinguishes men from "dumb" animals (ἄλογα). Gregory in this passage uses both senses, speech and rationality, and we have chosen to cover this by doubling the translation as "rational speech".

[91] *Mt* 3,17 par.

[92] *Jn* 12,28.

[93] *Mt* 17,5 par.

[94] *1 Tim* 2,4.

[95] *Jn* 12,29–30.

helped by hearing had not yet been fashioned; and when men did not exist, neither, surely, had any language characteristic of a particular nation been formed. By what logic then does the one who looks to the mere letter, on this interpretation sustain such a view, as if God were uttering these verbs and nouns.

251. There is yet another way by which one might recognize the futility of this kind of claim. Just as the natures of the elements, being a work of their Maker, appear the same to all, and there is no difference as far as human perception is concerned in the part contributed by fire or air or water, but the nature is single and invariable in every case, operating in the same way and not affected by the differences between participating objects, so also the giving of names, if they had been applied to the realities by God, would be the same for all. **252**. As it is, the nature of things, being fixed by God, remains constant, whereas the words which denote them are divided into such a multitude of languages as [300] to make even counting them not easy. If any one brings up the confusion at the Tower as contradicting what has been said, not even there is it said that God made human languages, but that he confused the existing one, so that not all could understand every one else.[96] **253**. As long as life was the same for all, and was not yet divided into many different nations, the human population all lived with one language. But once by divine purpose the whole earth had to be occupied by human beings, they were pulled apart and scattered this way and that in accordance with their language-groups, and became adapted to this or that manner of speech and language, taking the common language as making a bond of common mind with each other; they were not at variance in their knowledge of realities, but they differed in the framing of words. **254**. Stone and wood do not appear different to different people, but the names used for wood do vary in each group; thus our argument holds firm, when it classes human words as inventions of our own conceptual thought. Neither in the beginning, while all mankind shared the same language, do we learn from scripture that any instruction about divine words was given to men, nor over those divided into various different languages does a divine law prescribe the way each person speaks. Rather,

[96] *Gen* 11,1–8.

having decided that men should speak in other tongues, God sent our race to make its way articulating sounds as each group pleased for the definition of names.

255. Moses therefore, born many generations after the Tower-building, uses one of the languages which arose thereafter in his historical account of the creation, and [301] attributes certain words to God, relating them in his own language which he had been reared in and was used to, not altering the words of God in some alien way and using a foreign form of speech, as if to argue by the foreign use and varied vocabulary that the words were God's own, but he uses his ordinary language to spell out his own words and those of God alike. **256**. Some of those who have studied the divine scriptures most carefully say that the Hebrew language is not even ancient in the way that the others are, but that after the other miracles this was the last performed for the Israelites, that this language was suddenly improvised for the nation after Egypt. There is a prophetic word which gives this credibility: "When he went out of Egypt," it says, "then he heard a language he did not know."[97] **257**. If then Moses was a Hebrew-speaker, and Hebrew is the latest of all languages, the one born so many thousand years after the creation of the world, who relates in his own language the speeches of God, is he not clearly teaching us not to ascribe to God any such language as is humanly formed, but to say these things because it is quite impossible to express one's thought otherwise than in human language, and to signify by what is said an understanding worthy of God and of a superior order? **258**. As to the notion that God used the Hebrew tongue when there was no one to understand such language, if one has thought seriously about it, I do not know how he can agree. In Acts we read that the reason why the divine power was divided into many languages, was so that no foreign-speaker should be deprived of its help.[98] But if God before creation conversed in human fashion, [302] whom did he intend to help with that language? **259**. To accommodate speech to the ability of the hearers in order to help them one might suppose to be not unworthy of the divine charity, when Paul too, the imitator of the Lord,

[97] *Ps* 80,6/81,5; the same story and Psalm-verse appear in Origenes, *Contra Celsum* III 7 (SC 136, 26).

[98] *Acts* 2,6.

knew how to adapt his speech appropriately to the capacity of his hearers, becoming milk to the infants and solid food for the adults.[99] But then to argue that, with no goal to be achieved by such a use of speech, God recites soliloquies with words of this sort, I cannot see how such a thought is not both ridiculous and blasphemous. **260**. The language of God is neither Hebrew nor spoken after any other fashion customary among the nations; but whatever words of God are recorded by Moses or the prophets, they are indications of the divine will, illuminating in one way and another the purity and intelligence of the saints with such share of the grace as their status merits. **261**. Thus Moses' speech accorded with his upbringing and education, but he attributes these words to God, as has often been said, because of the infancy of those recently brought to the knowledge of God, to present the divine will clearly, and in order to make the hearers readier to believe, once persuaded of the reliability of the account.

262.–268. *Eunomius falsely claims Moses in his support*

262. Eunomius does not agree, he who attacks us with such insults, "the heir and advocate of the lawful practice" – I shall turn abuse into courtesy and greet him in his own words – but [303] he affirms that "Moses himself gives evidence for him, that the use of things named and of names was bestowed upon men by the one who designed their nature, and that the entitling of the things given is older than the generation of their users." He says as much, word for word. **263**. If indeed he has acquired a private Moses, by whom these wise things are taught, and starting from there he boldly makes statements such as, "God appoints in detail" (these are Eunomius' words) "the vocabulary of mankind", here commanding, there forbidding, words to be applied to things, let him use the absurdities as he pleases, with the secret Moses as his ally. If however the only Moses is the one whose writing is the common knowledge of those trained in the divine word, then we shall accept our condemnation, should we be refuted by the words of Moses. **264**. Where then has he found the law of nouns and verbs? – let him quote from the

[99] Cf. *Heb* 5,12.

scriptures themselves. The creation story, the subsequent account of the origin of mankind, the history of certain events and the various legislation about observances religious and secular, these are the chief heads of Moses' book. If he says there is some legislation about words, let him show me the law, and I will be silent; but he cannot answer. **265**. Otherwise he would not leave out the more obvious proofs and then produce those statements which make him appear ridiculous rather than persuasive to his audience. To think that it is the cardinal point of true religion to attest God's invention of words, when to him the world [304] and the marvels in it are but slight praise, – is it not the ultimate idiocy, to set aside the great things and worship the Divinity for human things? A creative command took precedence, spoken in human words by Moses, but divinely done. **266**. So the creative will behind what was by divine power constructed is claimed by our shrewd biblical scholar to be instruction about words, and as if God had said, "Let there be word", or, "Let speech be constituted", or, "Let such-and-such be called so-and-so", this fellow puts forward in support of his own arguments the movement in the divine will which brought creation into existence.

For all his study and learning in the Bible he had not even realized that a mental impulse is often called by scripture a "voice". **267**. A witness of this is Moses himself, whom he often parades, but does not know in this respect. What person ever so slightly familiar with the book does not know that the people of Israel were often perplexed about their route through the Egyptian desert, when they had only just escaped from Egypt; with horrors threatening them on every side, the sea shutting off their advance in one direction, and behind them their foes trying to prevent their flight, they assembled and blamed that prophet himself for their plight.[100] As he comforted those stricken with terror and exhorted them to courage, there comes a voice from God addressing the prophet by name: "Why do you cry to me?"[101] **268**. Yet before those words the story mentions no word of Moses, but the God-ward thought of the prophet is called a voice, by implication uttered in the secret thinking of the heart.

[100] *Ex* 14,2–12.
[101] *Ex* 14,15.

If Moses then, on the testimony of him who hears "unspoken groanings",[102] cries out without a sound, what is so strange if the prophet too, knowing the divine will, insofar as [305] he was able to speak and we to hear, made it plain to us in known and familiar words, describing a discourse of God in somewhat physical terms, though it did not happen in spoken words, but was proclaimed by the works themselves.

269.–281a. *Evidence from the creation narrative in Genesis*

269. "In the beginning," he says, "God made," not, "the names for heaven and earth," but, "the heaven and the earth."[103] "And he said, 'Let there be light,'" not, "the word 'light'."[104] "And having divided the light from the darkness," he says, "God called the light 'Day', and the darkness he called 'Night'."[105] Our opponents will probably find support in this passage. I will present their case for them, and make good what they have omitted by logical extension of their position, so that our own doctrine may be firmly established by leaving no objection unconsidered. "God," he says, "called the firmament 'Heaven', and the dry land he called 'Earth', and the light, 'Day', and the darkness, 'Light'."[106] **270**. "How, then," they may say, "when the scripture testifies that the names were given to these things by God, do you say that the terms are of human conception?" How do we answer this? Once again we take refuge in the simple explanation, and say that he who brought all creation from not-being into being is the Designer of real things viewed in their substance, not of names without substance consisting of the sound of a voice and the clicking of a tongue. Real things get their names by some significant sound in accordance with the nature and potential inherent in each, in keeping with the local manner in each nation of attaching designations to objects.

271. Most of the things we see in the creation, however, have no simple nature, such that it might be possible to include the [306]

---

[102] *Rom* 8,26.
[103] *Gen* 1,1.
[104] *Gen* 1,3.
[105] *Gen* 1,5.
[106] Combining *Gen* 1,8; 1,10; 1,5.

object under one term, as in the case of fire there is by nature one underlying reality, whereas the name which denotes the reality is different: the one is luminous and burning, dry and hot and consuming the material it seizes, the name is a short sound pronounced in a single syllable. For this reason an account which distinguishes the potencies and properties observed in fire names each one separately, as we did just now; one could not say that a single term has been applied to fire, when one terms it bright or consuming or by some other of its observed features; such words are indicative of the potencies naturally inherent in it. **272**. It is just the same with the heaven and the firmament: one entity is denoted by each of the names, but the difference of the names indicates one feature of what is known in this creation, so that when we look at it we learn one thing from the term 'heaven', another from 'firmament'. **273**. When the account is outlining the limit of the visible creation, beyond which the mental and supernatural realm takes over, the beginning and end of all material existence is called, in contrast to the intangible, immaterial and invisible, the 'firmament'. When we study the circumference of existing things, by which all material existence is contained, we designate this, which is the boundary (ὅρος) of all visibles (ὁρατά), the heaven (οὐρανός).[107] **274**. The same applies to the earth and the dry land. When the heavy and dense stuff was divided into these two elements, the earth, I mean, and the waters, the designation 'dry land' [307] distinguishes it from the opposite property: dry land got its name in contrast to what is wet, when drained at the divine command of the encircling water it appeared in its own proper quality. **275**. The term 'earth', however, no longer connotes the designation of just one of its properties, but includes in its intrinsic meaning every feature of the element, such as solidity, compactness, gravity, resistance, suitability for nourishing all kinds of plants and animals. The dry land therefore in the account did not change its name into that finally given it, for it did not cease by the second name to be and to be called 'dry land'; but while each of the titles remains, a particular meaning underlies each of the terms,

[107] Gregory's dubious argument here depends upon a word-play which cannot be represented in English. Even in transliteration, the similarity of ὅρος and ὁρατά to οὐρανός is less obvious than it would be in Greek, where *h* is not written and hardly heard.

the one making a distinct contrast with the contrary nature and property, the other embracing all the potency observed in it.

276. So too in the case of light and day, and in that of night and darkness, we do not find the Maker of the universe manufacturing the sound of syllables in these cases. Rather, by these titles we recognize concrete realities. **277**. By the will of God the darkness is dissolved with the entrance of the light at the first act of creation. As the earth at the centre, enclosed on every hand by enveloping alien elements, held itself up (as Job says, "Suspending the earth upon nothing,")[108] it was inevitable that, with the light coming through on one side, because the earth facing it formed a barrier by its own mass, there should be left over some part of the darkness as the effect of shadow; and that, as the ever-moving revolution of the pole necessarily carried round with it the [308] gloom which accompanied the shadow, God should appoint this period of movement to be the measure of passing time. This measure is day and night. **278**. For this reason when Moses in his wisdom explained such doctrines to us in story-form, he referred to the gloom coming in as a result of the barrier of the earth as the separation of light from darkness, and spoke of the perpetual measurable succession of light and darkness around the circle of earth as day and night.[109] So the naming of the light as 'day' was not merely nominal, but just as the light came to be, and not just the name 'light', so too the measure of time came to be, and the name was consequent on the measure: it was not brought into being by its Maker as the sound of words, but the actual reality attracted to itself the indicating sign of the word.

279. If it had been plainly said by the lawgiver, that every visible and named thing is not self-generating or without a maker, but has its existence from God, we would have spontaneously agreed that the whole world, its parts, its observed order, and the power to recognize what is, are all made by God; in the same way he leads us, by what he has said, to this thought, that we should believe no existing thing to be without a beginning. Looking to this end he makes his way on an orderly path through events one by one, spelling out

[108] *Job* 26,7.
[109] *Gen* 1,4–5.

the sequence of things made. **280**. There was no other way to present this in his book, except by [309] adopting the meaning of specific names. Therefore, when it is written that "God called the light, 'Day'," [110] we are to understand that God made the day out of the light as something in its proper sense distinct. You would not give the same definition of light and of day, but light is thought of as the opposite of dark, while day is a quantitative measure of a period in the light. **281**. Similarly you will also understand night and darkness, using the same distinction of meaning, defining darkness as the opposite of what is thought of as light, and calling night the prescribed measure of darkness. Thus our explanation is valid in every respect, even if it is not set out strictly according to the formal premises of logic, demonstrating that God is the Designer of real things, not of mere words.

281b.–288. *Words are invented for man's benefit, not God's*

It was not for his benefit, either, that names are applied to things, but for our sake. **282**. Because we cannot all the time keep in view everything that is, while we acknowledge a thing that is always there, we consign another to memory. Our memory cannot be kept unconfused, unless the connotation of words distinguishes from each other the things stored in the mind. To God all things are present, and he has no need of memory, since all are embraced and observed by the power of his vision. **283**. What need has he then of verb or noun, when the wisdom and power within him embraces unconfused and distinct the nature of things that are? All that is and that exists is from God, and for our guidance there are attached to beings the names which denote real things. If one were to say that these came into existence to suit the habits of men, he [310] would be in no way infringing on the affirmation of Providence, for we do not say that the being of things that are comes from us, but just the names.

284. The Hebrew has one word for the sky, the Canaanite another, but both have the same idea, the difference of language causing no

[110] *Gen* 1,5.

doubt between them as to the understanding of the object. The ultra-pious, self-conscious reverence of these wise fellows, whereby, if it be conceded that the words for things are of human origin, that argues that men are "more primordial" than God, is confuted as being futile and insubstantial by the very example recorded of Moses himself. **285**. Who gave the name to Moses himself? Was it not Pharaoh's daughter, naming him after what happened? 'Moses' in the Egyptian language means 'Water'. At the tyrant's command, his parents put the baby in a box and committed him to the stream – so some historians have told his tale – and by God's will, after being swept off by the swirl of the waters it was deposited on the bank, and was there for the princess to find where she was washing her body by bathing; then, because the boy had been got for her from the water, it is said that she gave the boy the name as a reminder of what had happened,[111] a name which God himself did not decline to use for his servant,[112] nor did he judge it improper to let the name given to the prophet by the barbarian woman remain valid. **286**. So before him Jacob, having grasped the heel of his twin, because of the manner of his joint birth was called 'heelgrabber';[113] that is the meaning of 'Jacob' when it is translated into the Greek tongue according to the teaching of those informed about such things. **287**. In the case of [311] Phares too, again the midwife named him because of the circumstances of his birth, and no one has, Eunomius-like, asserted her claim to be more primordial than the authority of God.[114] The mothers gave names to the other patriarchs, too, Reuben, Symeon, Levi and all the rest alike, and no one arose at that time, like the present wordsmith, in "solicitous care" for the divine Providence, to stop the girls becoming more primordial than God by giving names. **288**. Why mention the examples one by one from the history? – 'Contradiction Water', 'Mourning Place', 'Foreskins Hill', 'Grape-bunch Cleft', 'Blood Field',[115] and all the similar names given by men, but often mentioned even with God as speaker, by which we may learn that it is neither beyond human competence to generate designations of real things through words, nor is the power of the divine Nature attested by these words.

---

[111] *Ex* 2,1–10.
[112] *Num* 12,7–8.
[113] *Gen* 25,26.
[114] *Gen* 38,29.
[115] *Num* 20,13; *Gen* 50,11 ("Mourning of Egypt"); *Josh* 5,3; *Num* 13,24; *Mt* 27,8.

289.–293a. *Human invention of words does not impugn divine providence*

289. The rest of the babblings of his wild attacks on the truth I shall pass over, as having no power to hurt its doctrines; I deem it superfluous to dwell upon futilities. Who is so unminding about more serious matters of mind as to waste effort on unintelligent statements, and to argue with those who say that we claim "the human mind to be more primordial and sovereign than the solicitous care of God", while we attribute "to his Providence a negligence that would disturb the most indifferent"? **290**. The voice of our accuser utters these exact words. For my part I reckon that putting effort into such things is like wasting time on old hags' dreams. [312] To imagine that one can by a form of words secure for the divine Nature its rank of primacy and sovereignty, and thereby demonstrate the great, solicitous care of God, while we in turn despise God and are indifferent to his proper providence, and to abuse us because, when men had received the power of speech from God, they used words on their own authority to designate things, – can such a thing be other than an old wives' tale or a drunkards' dream? **291**. The true power and authority, primacy and sovereignty of God, at least on our reckoning, do not consist of syllables, or all and every inventor of words would come to be equal with God, but endless ages, cosmic beauties, radiance of heavenly bodies, and the marvels on land and sea, hosts of angels and supermundane powers, and whatever else in the higher realm we hear hinted at by the scripture, these are what claim for God the power over all things; **292**. and to claim an audible voice for those naturally endowed with speech is no impiety against the Giver of the voice.

We do not regard this as a great matter, this discovering of indicators for things. He to whom the scripture gives the name 'Man' in the creation story,[116] the one formed like us, is named 'Mortal' by Job,[117] 'Human' by some secular writers,[118] and 'Vocal' by others,[119] not to mention the differences in the word used in various nations. **293**. Are we making their status also equal to God's, because they too have invented words of the same meaning as the title 'Man',

[116] *Gen* 1,26: ἄνθρωπος.
[117] *Job* 14,1: βροτός.
[118] A Homeric word: φώς.
[119] The poetic word μέροψ means 'articulate', hence 'human'.

by which they indicate the same subject? We ought to dismiss this futile discussion, as I said before; and the subsequent insults deserve no place, where he says that [313] we "tell lies against the divine oracles, and with utter audacity make problems about everything else, and God himself".

VII. *Conceptual thought and Christological titles (293b–366a)*

293b.–332. *Basil and Eunomius on names given to Christ*

Our discussion should now turn to the remaining topics. **294**. Eunomius again puts forward this quotation from our Master: "Similarly and with no alteration we have learned the usage of 'concept' from the divine word. Our Lord Jesus Christ, in revealing to mankind the nature of the Godhead, indicates it by various features to be observed in himself, calling himself 'Door', 'Bread', 'Way', 'Vine', 'Shepherd', and 'Light'."[120] **295**. As to the abusive words against us added by him (for so his dialectical art has taught him to argue with his opponents), I think we should overlook them, and not be disturbed by his juvenile follies. We should however deal with one sharp and unavoidable question which he puts forward in refutation of our argument. "Who," he asks, "is there among the holy ones who attests that these titles are applied to the Lord as concepts?" **296**. Which of them, I might reply to him, expressly condemns it, considering as blasphemous the view that the use of names is conceptual? If he claims that not having been mentioned is a sign of prohibition, then he must surely allow that not having been prohibited is an indication of permission. The Lord is called by these names; or do Eunomius' denials apply even to them? If he does deny that these words are used of Christ, we have won without a fight: **297**. what more obvious victory could there be than to show our opponent an open enemy of God by his prohibiting the divine titles of the Gospel? If however [314] he truly confesses that these names are applied to Christ, let him state the manner in which the titles are in reverence

[120] Jaeger notes that these words are apparently quoted from Eunomius' text, since they do not agree with the text of Basilius, *Adversus Eunomium* I 6–7 (PG 29, 524c–d) (cap. 7 init.). For the divine titles, cf. *Jn* 10,7; 6,35; 14,6; 15,1; 10,11; 8.12.

fitting for the Only-begotten. Does he designate stone[121] an indicator of his Nature? Has he perceived his Being by use of an axe?[122] Is the identity of the deity of the Only-begotten signalled by the door, or by each of the other titles, not to clutter up our argument by listing all of them? **298**. Each one of these titles is not the nature of the Only-begotten, not his deity, not the character of his being. Nevertheless he is so named, and the naming is valid; for it is right to consider that there is nothing idle or meaningless among the divine words. So let him give the explanation, if he rejects their being applied conceptually, how these names are fitting for God.

What we say is this: as the Lord in various ways provides for human life, each variety of benefit is identified in turn by one or other such title, the foresight and action therein observed becoming a particular kind of name; **299**. such a title is on our view applied 'conceptually'. If that does not please our gainsayers, let each have it as he likes. Only it is the one who is ignorant of the scriptural mysteries who will oppose what we say. **300**. If he were educated in the divine words, he would surely know that 'Curse', 'Sin', 'Frantic heifer', 'Lion cub', 'Robbed she-bear', 'Leopard' and similar names are applied to the Lord by the scriptures[123] in accordance with various concepts, as saints and divinely inspired men elucidated precisely with these titles the object at which their thinking aimed, even though at first sight these titles seem somewhat slanderous. If every one of these were not allowed to be correctly applied [315] to God in some conceptual way, the wording could not avoid suspicion of impiety. **301**. It would take a long time to argue and demonstrate how in every case these names are both slanderous in their ordinary understanding based on their first meaning, and that the conceptual explanation reconciles them with true reverence for God.

302. Let us proceed, however, in the logical order, and resume again our argument. Such names are used of the Lord, and no one familiar with the divinely inspired scriptures would deny that they are so used. What then? Does he assert that the words denote the Nature itself? – then he says that the divine Nature is manifold in form and

[121] The title 'stone' is given to Christ in such passages as *Mt* 21,42 and *1 Pet* 2,4, following *Ps* 117/118,22.
[122] Perhaps taking the 'axe' of *Mt* 3,10 / *Lk* 3,9 as referring to Jesus Christ.
[123] *Gal* 3,13; *2 Cor* 5,21; *Hos* 4,16; *Gen* 49,9; *Hos* 13,7–8.

in composition, declaring its complexity by the variety of meanings in the words. **303**. 'Bread' is not the same in connotation as 'Lion', nor 'Door' as 'Heifer', nor 'Axe' as 'Water', but for each title one may give a particular definition which has nothing in common with the others. Therefore they do not signify the Nature; but none would dare claim that the application of the titles is improper and meaningless. **304**. If then he is so called, yet not so by nature, and every thing said by the scripture is assuredly valid and is appropriately applied, what account remains to be given of such words being fittingly applied to the Only-begotten God, other than the conceptual way? It is clear that the Divinity is given names with various connotations in accordance with the variety of his activities, named in such a way as we may understand. What then is the damage done to devout thoughts by the cooperation of our own intelligence in interpreting the things that are done? We ourselves call this 'conceptual thought', but if someone wants to call it something else, we shall not object.

305. Nevertheless, as with fierce wrestlers, he will not release his unbreakable hold on us, but says in so many words, "That these [316] are names from conceptual thought, and are spoken through the conceptualization of certain persons, are things which none of the apostles or evangelists taught." After that invincible effort he raises that sanctimonious voice, using the tongue trained in such things to spit offensive vituperation at us again. **306**. "To put forward equivocity based on analogy," he says, "as the basis of human conceptualization, is the work of a mind which has discarded the valid, correct meaning, and considers the words of the Lord to have an invalid meaning and a sort of debased usage." Well, well! What a logical demonstration! How skilfully the argument draws towards its conclusion! **307**. Who would still stand by the argument for conceptualization with such a stench pouring from his mouth upon those who try to say anything? Then must even we on this ground give up our part in the pursuit of the argument with him, in case he launches this sour vituperation against us too? **308**. Or is it small-minded to be exasperated in reaction to such childish follies? We must therefore allow the abuser to use whatever style he likes.

We must however again take up his argument, in case there is even there some support for the truth. **309**. He mentions Analogy, and notes the Equivocity based on it. Where did he learn these words, and from whom? Moses did not say them; he has not heard them from prophets and apostles; evangelists do not use such expressions; these things are to be learned from no teaching of scripture. Where then does he get such talk? Is it not an invention of the mind, this kind of language, which uses the name 'analogy' to denote the specific meaning of the idea? How does he not realize that [317] he is using to support his attack the actual targets of his attack? **310**. He attacks the conceptual account, while himself using conceptual words to argue that one should not say anything conceptually.

"But none of the saints," he says, "taught this." But are you able to find a reference in any of the ancient writers to the word 'unbegottenness', or to its being used as the name of the actual Being of God, "or rather that the Unbegotten is itself the Being"? **311.** Or have you the right, whenever some wicked conclusion is not immediately reached, to innovate and invent whatever words you like, but if anything be said by someone else in order to demolish wickedness, to forbid your opponent the right? You will have seized a great tyranny, if you forcefully obtain for yourself this right, so that the very things you ban for others you yourself have the right to do, and the things you claim the right to attempt, you exclude other people from. **312**. You peremptorily reject the assumption that these titles are applied to Christ by conceptual thought, because none of the saints has declared that he should be so called. Why then do you decree that the divine Being should be identified by the name 'Unbegottenness', which none of the saints can be shown to have passed down to us? If this rule of verbal correctness, that only those words should be used which are taught by the divinely inspired text of scripture, then 'unbegotten' must be deleted from your own writings, since none of the saints has authorized it. **313**. Nevertheless you accept the word because of the meaning inherent in this term; and we in the same way have accepted the word 'concept' because of its inherent sense. Therefore we shall either take both out of use, or neither; and whichever of these is done, we shall win either way. Without any mention at all of 'unbegottenness', every word of our opponents against the truth is stifled, and the [318] glory that befits the Only-begotten God will outshine them all, no word being left which diminishes the majesty of the Lord by contradiction. **314**. If however both words stand, even so the truth will prevail, and we with it, since the word 'unbegottenness' will have shifted from the Being to the concept. But as long as he does not remove the word 'unbegotten' from his own writings, then our contemporary Pharisee would be well advised not to attend to our splinter till he has got rid of the log stuck in his own eyes.[124]

315. "God, on the other hand," he says, "has accorded a share of the most honourable names even to the most fragile of terrestrial beings without conferring on them equality of dignity, and of the meanest to the most potent without their naturally mean status being simultaneously removed by the names." He says these things word for word; it stands written by them, just as by us. If this has some deeply hidden meaning which escapes us, let those who have understood things beyond our ken tell us, those initiated by him into the inward and ineffable mystery. **316**. If however they offer no interpretation more than what can be immediately understood, I know not which of the two one would reckon the more pitiable, those who say such things, or those who give such things a hearing. "He has accorded," he says, "a share of the most honoured names even to the most fragile of terrestrial beings without conferring on them equality of dignity." Let us see therefore what these words mean. **317**. The most fragile things, he says, are granted the title belonging to the honourable, though they are not in their nature what they are called, and this, he claims, is God's doing, falsely to give [319] the inferior nature the more honourable designation. On the other hand he claims that God attaches words of low esteem to things naturally excellent, without their nature being simultaneously removed by the designation. **318**. To make our argument as clear as possible, the absurdity will be demonstrated with concrete examples. If someone were to call wicked the man famous for every virtue, or conversely were to say that the one with a reputation for equal evil is good and respectable, would such a person be considered by reasonable people to be in his right mind or to have any notion of the truth, when he exchanges contrary designations for each other, and the nature fails to attest what the names denote? I think not. **319**. These things this Eunomius says are done by God, which agrees neither with common sense nor with the testimony of scripture. In our everyday life it is the mark only of those out of their mind through drink or inflammation of the brain to be totally wrong about

124 *Mt* 7,3–5.

names, and to use words for things without regard to their meaning, to call a dog, for example, a human being, and to apply the title 'human' to a dog.

320. So far is divine scripture distant from concurring in such confusion, that one may hear prophecy manifestly in bitter complaint at these things: ". . . who calls the light darkness, and the darkness light," it says, "who treats the sour as sweet and the sweet as sour."[125] What then has he in mind when he thinks he ought to ascribe this absurdity to his God? Let those initiated into the mysteries by him tell us, which is in their judgment the "most fragile of terrestrial beings", which is adorned with "the most honourable" titles by God? **321**. The most fragile of beings are such animals as are constituted by birth from the rotting of damp things, the most honourable of beings [320] are virtue and holiness and whatever is dear to God. Are then flies and grubs and frogs, and things which originate in dung, honoured with the title of holiness and virtue, so that they are adorned with honourable names, but do not participate in "equality of dignity", as Eunomius puts it? **322**. We have never before heard such a thing, as that these fragile things have been called by the most magnificent titles, or that the naturally great and honourable has been insulted with the name of one of these. Noah was righteous, says the scripture, Abraham faithful, Moses meek, Daniel wise, Joseph chaste, Job blameless, and David perfect in patience. **323**. Let them tell us, then, whether somewhere each of these acquired titles from their opposites; or perhaps in the case of those with bad reports, like Nabal the Carmelite and Pharaoh the Egyptian and Abimelech the Philistine, and all those mentioned for their wickedness, whether they were honoured with more favourable names by the divine voice. These things are not so; but as they are in truth and nature, so are things judged and named by God, not named in contradiction to what they are, but described by their proper denotations in whatever way they may be most clearly displayed.

324. These are the things our mighty intellect, who alleges "debased usage", who cavils at those who "have discarded the valid, correct

[125] *Is* 5,20.

meaning", claims to know about the divine Nature, these are the glorious things he puts forward on the subject of God, who makes a mockery of real things by using false words, and "accords the most honourable titles even to the most fragile" things, where the nature contradicts titles, and [321] who insults the honourable with the same names as the meanest of beings. **325**. A man who makes virtue his goal may often be quite involuntarily diverted from the truth, and be oppressed with shame, but does he think that it befits the honour of God that he should appear to tell lies about the names given to things? That is not how the prophecies attest the divine Nature. "Longsuffering, plenteous in mercy and true," says David.[126] How is he true, who lies about realities and displaces the truth in the meanings given to names? "Straightforward is the Lord God", is another epithet applied by the same writer.[127] **326**. Is it straightforwardness to grace dishonourable things with the most honourable of titles, and by giving a bare name, void of the dignity indicated by the word, to deceive the recipient of the title? Such is the testimony of these theologians to their new god: the result of their much-vaunted logical precision is just this, to demonstrate that God himself both takes pleasure in deceitful tricks and is not free from feelings of jealousy. **327**. It is the effect of deceit to give names to fragile things which do not correspond to their nature and worth, but to bestow on them empty titles belonging to superior things, not conveying with the designation the real meaning the names given; and it is the effect of jealousy for one who is able to bestow the more honourable place on those given superior names to withhold that gift, as if he reckoned the promotion of fragile things were to his own hurt. **328**. My own advice to the intelligent would be, that even if the god of these Gnostics[128] were obliged to be such as that by the force of the syllogisms, they should still not think of the true God, the Only-begotten God, in that way, but look to the real truth of objects, to [322] attest the true worth of each, and to give names on the basis of facts. "Come," it says, "ye blessed," and "Go ye accursed,"[129]

[126] *Ps* 85/86.15.

[127] *Ps* 91,16/92,15.

[128] An abusive term assimilating Eunomius to the longstanding heresies dubbed 'Gnosticism' by orthodox critics. The only basis for such a comparison is the Eunomian claim to definite knowledge (γνῶσις) of the nature of God as 'unbegottenness'.

[129] *Mt* 25,34 and 41.

without honouring the one who deserves a curse with the word of blessing, nor conversely dismissing the one who has stored up the blessing for himself along with the utterly damned.

329. The purpose of our author's words, however, and the goal to which his argument points, what are they? No one should suppose that it is for want of words, so that he might be thought best able to extend the length of his book, that he extends his verbiage with unintelligible stutterings. Even his senseless words carry the suspicion of heresy. **330**. To say that "the most honourable names" are applied "even to the most fragile", even though by nature they do not happen to share in the dignity, is an argument which for him covertly facilitates the blasphemous conclusion: in order that those who learn his doctrine may know from him that, though the Only-begotten is called 'God',[130] 'Wisdom', 'Power',[131] 'Light',[132] 'Truth',[133] 'Judge'[134] and 'King',[135] 'God over all',[136] 'Great God, Prince of Peace, Father of the Age to Come'[137] and such-like, the honour extends only to the name, **331**. for the meaning of the names does not also include the dignity it describes. Consider what the wise Daniel did for the Babylonians: to correct their idolatrous error, so that they should not worship the bronze figure or the serpent, revering the title of 'god' which was ascribed to them by empty minds, he quite plainly demonstrated by his actions that the sublime name of God fits neither the reptile nor the shape on which the bronze was modelled.[138] That, in reverse, is what the enemy of God [323] endeavours to argue in the case of the Only-begotten God by his teaching, proclaiming this through every prepared statement: "Take no notice of the titles of the Lord which have been bestowed on him, as if from them you could deduce the ineffability and sublimity of his being; for many other very fragile things are honoured with superior names,

[130] *Jn* 1,18 etc.
[131] *1 Cor* 1,24.
[132] *Jn* 8,12 etc.
[133] *Jn* 14,6.
[134] *Acts* 10,42 etc.
[135] *Mt* 25,34 etc.
[136] *Rom* 9,5.
[137] *Is* 9,5/6 (*varia lectio*).
[138] Bel and the Dragon 3–26.

where the word may have a sublime meaning, but the nature is not affected by the majesty of the designation." **332**. The reason why he says that participation in honour extends only to mere names for things so classified, without any equality of dignity accompanying the title, is that when they learn all those things about the Son which are of sublime connotation, they may think that the honour attested of him by the words is titular only, and that he has no share in the equality of dignity, in accordance with the artificial logic in what has been written.

333.–342. *Contradictions and evasions in Eunomius*

333. Nevertheless, in delaying over absurdities I seem inadvertently to have favoured our adversaries. By setting the truth against futile propositions I think I may bore those who apply themselves to the argument before getting to grips with more relevant material. So we must leave these topics as they now stand to those of our audience more concerned with detail, and move the argument on to our intended ground. **334**. A statement which touches closely on the matters discussed should also be passed over in silence: "These things are however arranged in this way, because human conceptual thought enjoys no power over the giving of names." Who says this, that what is not deemed to have concrete subsistence could have power over any real thing? It is only those who manage matters by their own free choice who have the power actually to do anything, whereas conceptual thinking is an activity of our mind and is dependent upon the free choice of those who speak; it has no subsistence of its own, but [324] exists by the initiative of the speakers.

335. "But," he goes on, "God himself, who designed the universe, adjusts the designations of every named thing appropriately to the limits and rules of relation, action and analogy." This is either totally meaningless, or is contrary to his previous statements. If he now claims for God that he fits names appropriately to beings, why does he argue earlier that God bestows more sublime names on less honourable beings, without at the same time giving the dignity signified by the meaning of the names, and again that he insults things naturally great with words of dishonour, their nature not participating in the lowliness of the terms? **336**. Yet we may perhaps be wronging this unintelligible concatenation of words by subjecting it to these accusations. These things are far from making any sense, and I mean not only the right sense of true devotion, but they appear to be quite without intelligibility of any kind to people who know how to examine words correctly. **337**. So, as in the case of jelly-fish the appearance seems to have solid bulk, but its bulk is slime, disgusting to see and even more disgusting to handle, I deem silence over empty words the most decent thing, and pass over what he says, undiscussed. For this reason the question, by what law action, analogy and relation are determined, or who lays down for God the rules and principles of proportion and relation, it is perhaps better to leave unasked, rather than make our audience feel sick with our efforts to deal with these things and divert our argument from more important things.

338. I fear however that what we turn to from the writings of Eunomius are all alike lumps of slime and jelly-fish, so that inevitably our study [325] ends up as we have said, finding no solid material to work on in what he has written. Just as smoke or fog thickens and darkens the air, in which it has its consistency, stopping vision from working normally, but nevertheless does not have such density in itself that one who wishes to grasp it or hold it in his hands, or to resist an impact, so one might speak of this noble piece of writing and not be far from a true estimate. **339**. The prattle is plentiful, elaborated in an apparently weighty but inflated text, and to the not too perceptive mind, like a mist to one who sees it afar off, it appears to have some substance and shape; but if one gets close to it and applies the investigative mind to what is said, the ideas disperse like smoke as it is grasped, and scatter to nothing, and it does not offer any solidity or resistance to the impact of reasoned argument. **340**. What we should do is a problem. Either choice is exposed to criticism by the argumentative: whether we skip over the nonsense as if it were a crevasse and direct the argument towards flat and easy routes, engaging in our refutation those points which seem to have some force against the truth, or whether we extend the line of our battle against inanity to match the whole nonsense. In the latter case the effort will be a burden to those not disposed to hard work, and it will be useless as it stretches to many thousands of words to no purpose; **341**. if on the other hand we tackle only those points which seem to have some force against the truth, we shall give our opponents opportunity to accuse us of passing over matters which admit no refutation. Since therefore, of the two courses open to us, that of going through the whole work, and that of tackling only the most important points, the one is burdensome to the audience, the other liable to malicious misrepresentation, I would say that it is best to take a middle course, avoiding both [326] charges as far as possible. **342**. What way is this? By cutting down so far as possible the vast heap of all his futile efforts, we shall chiefly tackle the ideas, so as neither to plunge ineffectually into nonsense nor to leave uninvestigated any of what has been written.

343.–350a. *Words applied to the Lord by the Scriptures*

343. Eunomius' whole case, then, is dedicated to this one purpose, trying to prove that the Divinity speaks in human fashion, and that the words which denote real things are matched to entities by the Designer of the things himself. Therefore, in an attack on the one who said that such titles belong to the articulate rational nature which we received from God, he alleges that he is both mistaken as to the truth and does not hold to his own proposition; and in bringing this charge against him he uses as proof arguments like these: **344**. "Basil said," he tells us, "that, after our first idea is formed of the thing in question, the more refined and more precise consideration of what is in mind is called a 'concept'."[139] He supposedly refutes this statement with the following argument: "In cases where there is no 'first' or 'second' idea, none either 'more refined' or 'more precise' than another, there can be no room," he says, "for what is conceptual."

345. In the first place, this point too will be detected by attentive hearers as a fallacious argument. Our teacher did not propose this as the definition of every concept, but, having proposed a specific subdivision between objects of conceptual thought, in order not to admit a great deal of clutter into his argument, once he had stated this part clearly he left it to the intelligent to think out the whole from the part. **346**. Just as a person, having said that the animal is classified under many and varied species, [327] would not be convicted

[139] An inexact quotation by Eunomius of Basilius, *Adversus Eunomium* I 6 (PG 29, 524b).

of error if he put forward Man as a particular example, nor would any one correct him for getting his subject wrong, provided he did not offer the same account of birds and beasts and fish as he used to describe Man – in the same way, since much detailed division and diversity are involved in a rational account of the concept, it would not be an objection to say that one thing is not, strictly speaking, a concept because it is also something else; consequently, if some other kind of concept is perceived, the earlier definition is not mistaken. **347**. "If then," he says, "one of the apostles or prophets were shown to have used these names of Christ, falsehood would have something to commend it." So much industry in God's scriptures do the words quoted attest in our author! Did none of the prophets or apostles call the Lord 'Bread', 'Stone', 'Well', 'Axe', 'Light', or 'Shepherd'? **348**. What about David? Of whom then does he say, "The Lord shepherds me," or "Hear, thou who dost shepherd Israel"? – is there any difference between 'shepherd' as noun and 'shepherd' as verb?[140] – or "With thee is the Well of life"?[141] Does he accept that the Lord is called "Well", and "The Stone which the builders rejected"?[142] When John uses the word "Axe" to indicate the power of the Lord to destroy evil, and says, "Now is the Axe laid to the root of the trees",[143] does he not appear by his words to be a reliable witness to this? **349**. Moses, seeing the Lord in the light,[144] and John, calling him "the true Light",[145] and in the same way Paul, when at the first manifestation of God to him he was surrounded by light and afterwards he heard the words from the light, "I am Jesus whom you persecute"[146] – was he not sufficient as a witness? And as to Bread, let him read the [328] gospel, which says that the nourishment supplied to Israel from heaven by Moses was turned by the Lord himself into a figurative type of the Lord: **350**. "It was not Moses who gave you the bread, but my Father who gives the

---

[140] Jaeger's punctuation appears to be wrong here. The Psalm-verses are 22/23,1; 79,2/80,1.

[141] *Ps* 35,10/36,9.

[142] *Ps* 117/118,22; cf. *Mt* 21,42 par.

[143] Attributed to John the Baptist in *Mt* 3,10; *Lk* 3,9.

[144] Probably alluding to the pillar of fire, which is the presence of the Lord in *Ex* 13,21 etc., which gives light (*Ps* 104/105,39 etc.), rather than *Ex* 3,2 (the burning bush).

[145] *Jn* 1,9.

[146] *Acts* 9,5.

true Bread", referring to himself as the one "who came down from heaven and gives life to the world".[147] Yet our genuine hearer of the Law says that none of the prophets or apostles applied these titles to Christ.

350b.–358. *Words applied to the Lord by himself*

What follows next? "If the Lord himself used these names of himself, since the names of the Saviour cannot be either first or second, either more refined or more precise than one another, and he acknowledges all alike and with equal exactitude, it is impossible to reconcile the argument Basil uses about the concept[148] with any of them." **351**. I have admitted a flood of nonsense from this source into my book; I crave the indulgence of my readers, if we do not leave unconsidered even the most obvious nonsense. This is not to take delight in the discomfiture of the author – what do we gain if our opponents are convicted of absurdity? – but so that the truth may advance confirmed at every point. Since, he says, the Lord applied these appellations to himself without reckoning one first or second or more refined or more precise, it is not possible that these names should come from conceptual thought. **352**. What a memory for his own objective! Where is his knowledge of the words with which the dispute arose? Our Instructor referred to something generally familiar in order to explain 'concept', [329] and having clarified his meaning by the use of lowlier examples he then compares what he observes

[147] *Jn* 6,32–33.

[148] The Greek does not name Basil, but says, ". . . the argument spoken by him about the concept". There are difficulties in ordering the text here: (1) The rendering given in the middle of 350 (p. 328,8–9) agrees with Migne PG 45,1028bc and with William Moore, translating in *Nicene and Post-Nicene Fathers, Second Series*, V 285, against Jaeger, in putting the question mark after ἐφεξῆς, "follows next", rather than later, following "these names of himself". This also agrees with Jaeger's own punctuation of the parallel passage in 351 (pp. 328,21–22). (2) I have followed Moore in treating the last sentence of 350 (pp. 328,9–14) as a direct quotation of Eunomius by Gregory; this has the advantage that the word αὐτῷ, "by him", is more readily taken as Eunomius' reference to Basil, rather than as Gregory's to Eunomius. (3) Jaeger agrees with Migne and Moore in starting a new paragraph at 351. If the end of 350 is quotation, however, it can be seen as beginning a new discussion. (4) Unlike Moore and Jaeger, I have taken the second half of 351 (pp. 328,20–25) as Gregory's own paraphrase of the passage of Eunomius just quoted, rather than (as marked by both Moore and Jaeger) itself a direct quotation.

in the study to the things above.[149] What he said was that corn by itself appears to be essentially a single reality, but it changes its designations according to the various properties envisaged in it: as it becomes seed, fruit, food, and whatever else it becomes, so many are its names. **353**. In a similar way, he says, the Lord also is by himself whatever he is in nature, and when he is simultaneously named in accordance with his various activities, he does not possess a single title covering them all, but is accorded the name in accordance with each idea which arises in us from those activities. Why then should our argument be refuted by this statement, the argument which said it is possible to use fittingly many titles of the Son of God, who is single in his actual being, in accordance with the variety of actions and his relation to the things performed, in the same way that corn, though a single thing, enjoys various appellations derived from various ideas about it? **354**. How then are our words refuted if it is said that Christ uses these titles of himself? The question was not about who used the titles; our purpose was rather to consider what the titles mean, whether they denote the nature, or whether they are applied conceptually on the basis of action.

Acute and wide-ranging in his intelligence, however, Eunomius takes the published statement, to the effect that it is possible to discover many designations[150] to express the meaning of the activities, and apply them to a single being, and he uses it powerfully in the argument against us, saying that "such terms are not applied to the Lord by some one else". **355**. What has that got to do with our present purpose? Is it that, when the titles are spoken by the Lord, he will not allow these to be titles or designations or [330] words which indicate ideas? If he does not accept that these are titles, then the concept is indeed wiped out when the designations are wiped out. If on the other hand he does not deny that these words are titles, how is the case for the concept damaged by demonstrating that such names are applied, not by another person, but by the Lord himself? **356**. The argument was that, in the same way as in the example of corn, the Lord is one in his own substance, but has also the titles suitable to his actions. As the corn by common consent

[149] This passage refers to Basilius, *Adversus Eunomium*. I 6 (PG 29, 524b–c).

[150] "Many designations": a phrase from Basilius, *Adversus Eunomium* I 6 (PG 29, 524b).

has the appellations matching the conceptual thought applied to it, it was also argued that these words do not in the Lord's case denote the nature, but are constituted on the conceptual principle in our thoughts about him. **357**. Our opponent with great care avoids engaging in dispute with what was actually proposed, but says that he is given these titles by himself; it is as if one were investigating the meaning of the name given to Isaac, whether it means 'Laughter' as some say,[151] or something else, and some Eunomian were learnedly to reply that the name was given to the boy by his mother. But the question was not, one might say, by whom the appellation was produced, but what is the meaning of the name when translated into our language. **358**. Since then the subject of the debate is whether the various terms applied to the Lord are spoken as concepts, and not as indicating his nature, one who undertakes thus to demonstrate, from the fact that these titles are used of the Lord by himself, that they are not envisaged conceptually, how can one be counted sane, who both attacks the truth and [331] uses to support his attack such means as show the one he attacks to be superior?

359.–366a. *Eunomius alleges that applying concepts to God is blasphemous*

359. Next, as though the argument had reached the conclusion which he had intended, Eunomius goes on to put forward other charges against us, more serious, he claims, than those already stated. He expresses outrage and condemnation in advance about the book, and gets the audience very excited about the things he is going to say, in which he alleges that very wicked things are argued on our side, such that not only do we seize upon the titles bestowed by God as our own concepts (though he does not say what the bestowal of titles is, or when and how it came about), but that we also confuse every thing and treat as identical the being and the activity of the Only-begotten (though he does not discuss or give proofs about the question, how on our argument the activity is the same as the being). He brings the charges to their end and climax, using these words: **360**. "And now," he says, "turning from these topics he even inflicts on the supreme God outrageous blasphemies, using both fragmenting words and totally detached examples." For my part, even before

[151] Cf. *Gen* 21,3–6.

the topics discussed, I expected to be told what things our words are fragmenting from, and what our examples are detached from – not of course looking for an answer to these questions so much as to demonstrate how jumbled up and muddled our author's words are, in which he wins resonance from the old wives among virile humanity, and ingratiates himself by his bombastic vocabulary in the ears of those who admire such things, without realizing that for the educated reader he is setting up in this book a monument to his own discredit. **361**. [332] This however is not at all to our purpose. I wish the charges against him went no further than this, and that he were deemed to be not in error about the faith, but only at fault about the use of words, so that it were of no consequence for praise or blame whether it were expressed in this way or that.

362. At any event, the sequel in what he says against us continues as follows: "Having exposed the different use of concepts," he says, "applied in various ways to corn and to the Lord, Basil says that similarly the most holy Being of God is subject in various ways to concepts." This is the most serious of his charges, and on it are based those earlier dramatic speeches against us, as in his text he alleges wickedness and evil absurdity. What then is the evidence for impiety? **363**. Eunomius says some things about corn, carefully distinguishing these as general and immediately apparent, how it germinates, and how, when it is ripe, it nourishes with its harvest, shooting, growing and governed by certain natural powers. Having said that, it is reasonable, he says, to suppose that the Only-begotten God is in various ways subject to concepts because of the variety of his actions and certain analogies and relationships: he spells out at length these titles applied to him. "How," he nevertheless goes on, "is it not wrong, or rather wicked, to compare the Unbegotten with these things?" **364**. With what things? With corn, he says, and the Only-begotten God. Do you observe his devout reverence? He argues an equal separation from the dignity of Unbegotten God of humble corn and the Only-begotten God! And to show that we are not misrepresenting the case, one may learn his meaning from the very words he has written: "How," he says, "is it not wrong, or rather wicked, [333] to compare the Unbegotten with these?" By saying this he reduces to parity of esteem our ideas of corn and of the Lord, judging it equally absurd to compare God with either one of them. **365**. Every one must surely be aware that things which are equally distant from something else are themselves equal with each other. Thus, according to our wise theologian, the Maker of the ages, who also holds in his embrace the whole of natural existence, is shown to be of equal standing with the humblest of seeds, if in fact he and the humblest corn fall equally short of comparability with God. **366**. Yet so great is the wickedness of the book.

VIII. *Divine indestructibility (366b–386)*

366b.–377a. *Eunomius makes 'indestructible' part of God's Being, 'Father' a mere activity*

It is perhaps time however to consider the actual argumentation which leads to the blasphemy, in what respect it is consistent with itself in its logic. After saying that it is absurd to compare God with corn and with Christ, Eunomius says that God is not, like them, susceptible of change; where the Only-begotten is concerned however, having failed to say that he is not susceptible of change, thus clearly indicating his inferior dignity, he leaves the case in suspense at the point where, like the corn, he must not be compared with God. He offers no argument in this part to prove that the Son may not be set alongside the Father, as if his observations about the seed were enough to demonstrate at the same time the inferiority of the Son in relation to the Father.

367. Yet he speaks about the indestructibility[152] of the Father, belonging to him "not on the basis of activity".[153] For my part, if true Life acting is an activity, and if to live for ever, and never to suffer destruction, mean the same thing, for the time being I add nothing

[152] As indicated at *CE* II 131 (GNO I 263,29), 'indestructible' and 'indestructibility' are used to render ἄφθαρτος, ἀφθαρσία. There is no satisfactory term in English: alternatives might be 'incorruptible, -ility', 'imperishable, -ility', 'immortal, -ity'. At this point Jaeger prints the words, "indestructibility is not on the basis of his activity", as a quotation from Eunomius. It is better to see them as Gregory's paraphrase of the words quoted at *CE* II 371 (GNO I 334,23f), where see the note.

[153] In this passage and elsewhere 'activity, active, action, act' are used to render ἐνέργεια and its cognate terms; alternatives would be 'operate, operations', '(to) effect, effects'.

to the debate, but shall reserve it for its proper place. **368**. However, that the idea of indestructibility is single, being attributed alike to Father and Son, and for the Father to be indestructible [334] differs not at all from the indestructibility of the Son, since no difference is possible in indestructibility, whether by increase or diminution or by any other kind of distinction – that is something I would claim is timely said both now and always, so that his argument may thereby leave no room to assert that the Son does not participate with the Father in the idea of indestructibility. **369**. As indestructibility is understood of the Father, so it undoubtedly applies also to the Only-begotten. To be not liable to destruction – what both is, and is called, indestructibility – has the equivalent, or rather identical, meaning, whatever it is applied to. What then leads him to assert that only in the case of the Unbegotten God is his indestructibility not on the basis of his activity, as if to show by this the difference between the Father and the Only-begotten? **370**. If he suggests that his own created god is destructible, he can certainly demonstrate the difference of nature from the distinction between destructible and indestructible. If however both alike are not susceptible of destruction, and no thought of more or less is intelligible in indestructibility of nature, how does he prove that the Father is not comparable with the Only-begotten Son? Or what point is there in asserting that the Father's indestructibility is "not on the basis of activity".

371. He reveals his purpose, however, in the argument that follows. "Not on the basis of activities," he says, "is he indestructible and unbegotten, but as Father and Designer."[154] I ask the audience to pay particular attention to this. How does he suppose that the connotation of these two attributes is the same, creative design, I mean,

[154] Translating as though the Migne edition were right to read δὲ rather than τε. As the text stands, read "... unbegotten, as both Father and Designer". If Gregory's following argument is not totally false, the point Eunomius is making is precisely that 'indestructible' is an aspect of God's being, whereas 'Father' and 'Designer' relate to his actions and not to his essential being.

An alternative, with no support in manuscripts, would be to read ἐξ ἐνεργείας instead of ἀγέννητος ὡς, translating: "Not on the basis of activities is he indestructible, and on the basis of activity both Father and Creator." This would account for the fact that none of the following passage *CE* II 371–378 (GNO I 334–337) mentions 'unbegotten' until a further quotation is introduced at the end of 378 (GNO I 337,1–2); Gregory writes as though 'indestructible' stands alone in the text here.

and fatherhood? He designates each of these equally as an activity when he clearly explains in his book that he is not by activity indestructible, while he is named Father and Designer on the basis of activities. **372**. If then it is the same thing for him to be called Father and Designer, because [335] activity is the reason why he acquires both names, it is bound to follow that the effects of the actions should also be all of the same kind, inasmuch as they have the same basis in activity. The kind of blasphemy to which this logically leads is plain for any to see who knows how to observe the consequence. I would like however to add my personal thoughts on these matters while these words are under discussion. An activity that brings something into effect cannot subsist simply by itself, without any recipient of the movement which action causes, as when we say that the smith is active in some way, and that the material supplied is acted upon by his craft. **373**. These must therefore have a relation to each other, being the active and the passive potency, and if either of them is removed by the argument, the remaining one could not subsist by itself. If there is no passive, there will be no active. What follows from this? If the activity which produces some effect does not subsist by itself, unless the passive exists, and if the Father, as they tell us, is nothing but an activity, then the Only-begotten Son is shown thereby to be passive, shaped in accordance with the active motion which constitutes him. **374**. The Designer of all, we say, having laid out a passive and malleable stuff, put into action his own creative Being, in the case of perceptible things skilfully attaching the varied and manifold properties to his material in order to produce each of the things being made, and in the case of the intelligible beings shaping the [336] material in another way, not with properties, but with certain powers of choice; just so, if one defines the fatherhood as an activity, of necessity one may not describe the being of the Son except as a passive material thoroughly worked upon. **375**. If he is reckoned impassible, then impassibility will certainly be what responds to the active agent, and with action precluded there will surely be no product of action. So it is one of the two: either they will make the Being of the Only-begotten passible by these means, in order to be acted upon, or by shying away from that because of the manifest impiety, they will be arguing that it does not exist at all! **376**. What escapes passivity surely of itself admits no creative action upon it either. Therefore one who calls the Son the effect of some action also designates him as one of those passible things which had their origin in activity; or if he does deny the passibility, he will, with his passibility, deny also his existence. Since however with either horn of the dilemma we have described the impiety is apparent, whether saying he does not exist, or thinking him to be passible, the truth is apparent, exposed by the elimination of the absurdities. **377**. For if he truly is, and if he is not passible, then plainly he is not derived from an activity, but presumably he is true God, impassibly and eternally radiated and shining forth from the true God, the Father.

377b.–386. *Eunomius identifies God's indestructibility and unbegottenness with his being*

"It is in his very Being," he nevertheless says, "that God is indestructible." But which other divine attribute does not belong to the very Being of the Son – justice, goodness, eternity, absence of everything evil, boundless possession of every conceivable good? **378**. Would any one say that any thing fine[155] is an acquisition of the divine Nature, and not that whatever is fine begins there, and is to be considered as in it? The prophet says, "Whatever is fine is his, and [337] whatever is good is from him."[156]

Eunomius links with this the claim that he is unbegotten in his Nature. **379**. For my part, if he is saying this in the sense that the Father's Being exists unbegotten, I agree with what he says and do not oppose his assertion; no religious person at all would suggest that the Father of the Only-begotten is begotten. If however he makes this point in the light of the design of his book, and is arguing that unbegottenness itself is Being, I would say that this ought not to be passed by unquestioned, lest unobserved he inveigle the gullible into consenting to his blasphemy. **380**. That the idea of unbegottenness is one thing, and the meaning of the divine Being another, can be proved from what he has actually said himself: "It is in his very Being," he says, "that he is indestructible and unbegotten, a Being unmixed and free from any otherness and difference." He says this of God, whose Being is, he claims, Indestructibility and Unbegottenness. So three words apply to God: Being, Indestructible

[155] Rendering Greek καλός which can mean either "good" or "beautiful".
[156] *Zech* 9,17, reversing "fine" and "good".

and Unbegotten. **381**. If the sense of these three words applied to God is all one, then these three surely are Deity. It is as if someone wanted to define Man and called him articulate, apt to laugh and flat-clawed. Where these are concerned, because there is no difference of nature in each person, we say that the three words are all equally important, and as applied to their subject are a single thing, the humanity indicated by these words. **382**. If then Deity is just this, Unbegottenness, Indestructibility and Being, we say that[157] when any one of these is removed, by every necessity the Godhead is also removed with it. Just as one who is not rational nor apt to laugh would also not be called [338] human, so in the case of these three words, I mean 'Unbegotten', 'Indestructible', and 'Being', if Deity is so characterized, when one of the three is not present, then surely the idea of Deity must be removed from what remains.

383. Let him answer therefore, and say what view he takes of the Only-begotten God. Does he deem him begotten or unbegotten? He will of course say 'begotten', unless he is going to contradict his own words. If then 'the Being' and 'Indestructible', by which Deity is recognized, are the same as 'Unbegotten', the one who does not also have 'Unbegotten' will surely at the same time lose 'the Being' and 'Indestructible', and in their absence Deity also must necessarily be taken away. Thus the argument comes to a double conclusion to their blasphemous logic: **384**. if the words 'Being', 'Indestructibility' and 'Unbegotten' have the same meaning when applied to God, this new godmaker is plainly shown to acknowledge that the Son he has created is destructible, since he does not acknowledge him unbegotten; and not only that, he is also totally non-existent, since it is impossible to see him as possessing deity when 'Unbegotten' and 'Indestructible' are not to be envisaged, if it is really supposed that 'Unbegotten' and 'Indestructible' are the same as the Being.

385. Since however the disastrous effects of these arguments is obvious, someone should advise those who hesitate to change their mind towards the alternative, and not to resist the compulsion of the

[157] Jaeger marks an apparent anacoluthon here, and suggests the text might be amended to correct it. I have assumed that the sense of λέγομεν, "we say that", is carried over from a few lines above, and have repeated those words here for clarity. No emendation is therefore required.

obvious towards the truth, but to concede that each of these words has its proper meaning, which one may most readily identify by their contraries. **386**. The unbegotten we discover from its contradiction of the begotten, the indestructible is recognized by comparison with the destructible, and being is understood by contrast with the non-existent. Just as what has not been begotten is spoken of as 'unbegotten', and what is not destroyed is called 'indestructible', so too we call 'being' that which is not non-existent; and on the other hand, as [339] we say that the begotten is not unbegotten and the destructible we designate not indestructible, so too we do not say that being is non-existent. A being therefore is recognized by the existence of something, the destructible or indestructible by what sort of thing it is, the begotten or unbegotten by how it exists. The idea that it is, is one thing, the idea which by its meaning explains how or of what kind it is, is another.

IX. *Divine attributes and human concepts (387–402)*

387.–394. *The naming of God is a function of human corporeality*

387. It seems to me to be a good idea to skip over the nauseous intervening passage (that is how in my view we should speak of his senseless attacks on conceptual thought), and concentrate on our intended purpose. The many things spewed up like an issue of phlegm by our wordsmith to refute the Master's[158] views on conceptual thinking, are of such a kind that they cause no danger to those who come across them, however inexpert and gullible they may be. **388**. For who is so senseless as to take the things said by the Master, using corn as an illustration, by which he suggested to the hearer a certain method and approach to the thought of sublime things, and then to suppose that, when Eunomius attaches them exclusively to the words about the being of the God of the universe, he may be thought to be saying something and elaborating it with precision against the truth?

[158] I.e. Basil's.

389. For him to allege that the most fitting reason for God to beget the Son is his absolute authority and unsurpassable power (which in fact may be said not only of the world and the elements in it, but also of the reptiles and beasts), and for the grave theologian to propose this as the right way to understand the Only-begotten God; or to say that even before the creation of those who name things, God is addressed as Unbegotten or as Father or by his other titles, as if he were afraid that, should [340] his name not be uttered among those not yet created, he might not know himself, or lapse into forgetting himself, not knowing what he is if his name were not mentioned; and his mocking assault on our words, in its acute and astute extent: by all this he argues the case, that it is absurd to say that the Father, existing before all ages and times and every perceptible and intelligible being, was waiting for mankind, so that he could be named by their conceptual thinking. **390**. "Not named," as he himself says, "either by the Son, or by any of the intelligent beings made through him." No one, I believe, is so stuffed up with choking snivel as to be unaware that the Only-begotten Son, who is in the Father, and perceives the Father in himself,[159] has no need of noun or verb for the knowledge of the Subject, nor does the Holy Spirit, who searches the depths of God,[160] arrive at the knowledge sought by the pronunciation of names, nor does the disembodied race of the supernatural powers name the Divinity with voice and tongue; **391**. for where the immaterial and intelligent nature is concerned, the action of the mind is a word which has nothing to do with the physical use of organs. Even in the case of human nature we should have no need to use verbs and nouns, if it were possible to express clearly to each other the processes of the mind. As it is, since the thoughts which arise in us are unable to make themselves apparent because our nature is enclosed in its fleshly garment, we are obliged to attach various names to things as signs, and thereby to make the processes of the mind accessible to other people. **392**. If it were somehow possible to reveal the processes of the intellect in some other way, [341] we could do without the recurrent use of words, and we would more clearly and immediately deal with each other, exposing by intellectual impulses the very essence of the topics which the mind is engaged

[159] *Jn* 14,11 is nearer than the verses cited by Jaeger.
[160] *1 Cor* 2,10.

upon. As it is, the reason we give the name 'heaven' to one existent, 'earth' to another, and other names to other things, and that being related somehow to something and performing and suffering actions are all distinguished by us with particular words, is to prevent the mental process remaining in us uncommunicated and unknown. **393**. That supernatural and immaterial Nature, however, being free and unchecked by bodily confinement, needs no nouns or verbs either for itself or for the transcendent order; rather, if sometimes a word originating from the spiritual order of nature is recorded in the holy books, it is for our sake, for the hearers, that such a thing is said, because we are unable to understand what is meant in any other way, if it is not openly stated in names and verbs. **394**. If David by inspiration says that something is said to the Lord by the Lord,[161] it is David the speaker who could not otherwise express for us the doctrine he has in mind, unless he interpret in sounds and words that understanding of the mysteries which was put in him by God.

395.–402. *The power to name by conceptual thought is God's gift to Man*

395. It would be as well, therefore, in my opinion, to pass over all his philosophical talk against conceptual thought, even if he accuses of 'madness' those who suppose that the word for Deity is spoken conceptually by human beings to describe the Supreme Being. His purpose in thinking it necessary to disparage conceptual thought may be learnt from his own words by those who so wish. Our own understanding of the use of words we stated in what followed, that whereas [342] things have their own nature, whatever it is, it was the linguistic ability implanted in us by God that invented the interpretative sounds of their names.[162] **396**. If one were to attribute the cause of these things to the One who gave that ability, we ourselves do not disagree, just as we say that movement and sight and using our other senses also originate with him from whom we have been given such ability. So therefore the cause of our giving names to God,

---

[161] *Ps* 109/110,1 (cf. *Mk* 12,35–37 par.).

[162] See the whole discussion in *CE* II 177–293 (GNO I 276–313), especially *CE* II 189–195a (GNO I 279–281).

who is by his nature what he is, is by general consent attributable to God himself; but the power of giving names of one sort and another to all the things that come into our mind, lies in our nature, and whether one chooses to call it conceptual thought or something else, we shall not dissent.

397. We claim as evidence for this position the fact that the Divinity is not given the same titles among all, but the thought is interpreted differently as each group decides. We shall therefore ignore his cheap prattle about conceptual thought, and stick to the teachings, taking account of just one point which he put in the middle of his ramblings, where he thinks that God sat down with his first creatures like some schoolmaster or teacher of letters and gave them a lesson in nouns and verbs. **398**. There he says that those who were first created by God, or those immediately born from them, if they had not been taught how each thing is spoken of and named, would have lived together speechless and dumb, "And they would," he says, "have achieved nothing to help them survive, since the thought of each would be obscure for want of the signifiers, verbs, that is, and nouns." **399**. So great is the wild folly of the author, that he reckons the [343] ability implanted by God is not sufficient for every kind of verbal activity, but unless they learned things one by one, like people learning Hebrew or Latin word by word, they would not know what things are, recognizing neither fire, nor water, nor air, nor anything else that exists, unless they obtained the knowledge of these things through the names applied to them. **400**. Our own claim is that he who made all things by wisdom, and who gave living form to this rationally articulate creature, merely by bestowing reason on the species added the whole capacity to speak articulately.

401. To make a comparison: because we have in our nature the power of our senses from him that formed the eye and planted the ear, of ourselves we use each of our sensory organs for the purpose for which it exists, and have no need for any one to name the colours which our sight is able to grasp, for it is enough for the eye to become our teacher in such things; nor where things we perceive by hearing or taste or touch are concerned, have we need of other people to give us the information, since we possess in ourselves the power to judge each thing that arrives in our sense-organs. In the same way, we claim, the thinking power of the mind, having been made such by God, thereafter operates of itself and observes things, and to prevent the information falling into confusion, attaches signals in the form of words as labels to every thing. **402**. Such a doctrine was confirmed by great Moses when he said that names were attached to the dumb animals by Adam, writing in these words: "And God formed from the earth all the beasts of the field and all the birds of the air, and brought them to Adam to see what he would call them; and [344], whatever Adam called the living animal, that was its name; and Adam called out names for all the cattle and all the beasts of the field."[163]

X. *Further arguments on the alleged divine origin of words (403–444)*

403.–422. *Philosophical and literary aspects of the arguments about the origin of speech*

403. It appears however that the nonsensical attack Eunomius has composed against conceptual thought has held us back like sticky, glutinous mud, and will not let us get to grips with more useful topics. How could one pass over that earnest and carefully reasoned philosophy, where he says that "not only in the things made is the majesty of the Designer expressed, but also in their names is the wisdom of God displayed, he having fitted the appellations individually appropriately to each thing made". **404**. He may have read this himself, or learnt it from someone who had read it, in Plato's dialogue *Cratylus*,[164] and because of his dearth of ideas, I suppose, has stitched together his own nonsense with the rubbish he found there, doing the same as those who collect food by begging. **405**. Just as they get a little bit from each of their benefactors and gather their food of many different kinds, so Eunomius' book, for want of the true bread, laboriously gathers together scraps of verbs and nouns from all over the place, and for that reason, resonating with the literary beauty of the Platonic style, he thinks it right to adopt his philosophy as the Church's doctrine.

---

[163] *Gen* 2,19–20.

[164] Jaeger suggests *Cratylus* 390d–e as the passage in mind.

406. How many words, please tell me, are used to name the created firmament among different nations? We call it *ouranos*, the Hebrew *shamaim*, the Latin *caelum*, and other names the Syrian, the Mede, the Cappadocian, the Moor, the Thracian and the Egyptian, nor would it be easy to count [345] the different names which occur in use nation by nation for the sky and other things. **407**. Which of these, tell me, is the naturally fitting name, by which the magnificent wisdom of God is displayed? If you promote the Greek above the rest, the Egyptian may object and propose his own; if you give priority to the Hebrew, the Syrian will put forward his own word against it; the Roman will not yield priority to these, nor will the Mede accept that his own should not come first, and every one of the other nations will demand that his own should have priority over the rest. **408**. What follows? The theory will not convince, when it is divided between so many words by the disputants.[165]

"But from these things," he says, "as it were from laws publicly established, it is apparent that God appointed suitable and particular names for the natures." **409**. What a grand doctrine! What privileges the theologian bestows on the divine teachings! People would not begrudge them to the bath-men. In their case we let them make up words for the operations they are engaged in, and no one has dignified them with godlike honours, when they invent names for many things they produce, like foot-baths, hair-strippers, hand-towels, and many more of the same, names which by 'fitting naturally' reveal the object by the meaning of the words.

410. Nevertheless, I shall pass over these things, and also the immediately following account of Epicurean physics, which will there be claimed as having the same meaning as conceptual thought by one who says that the void, the atom, and the fortuitous generation of beings have a family likeness to what is meant by 'concept'. How well he has understood Epicurus! If [346] we attribute the words which denote things to the rational ability in our nature, we are thereby convicted of talking about indivisible particles and entanglements of atoms, collisions, repulsations and the like, as Epicurus

[165] Jaeger punctuates differently, giving a meaning something like, "What then will the theory not convince, when it is divided between so many words by the disputants?" This is very difficult to understand, and I have moved the question mark and made the main sentence a statement.

does.[166] **411**. Let us not discuss, either, his champion and ally in doctrines, Aristotle, whose view, he says in the subsequent discussion, agrees with the account of concept. The doctrine, he says, is his, that "Providence does not extend through all beings, nor reach as far as earthly things;"[167] and that is what Eunomius insists is "in harmony with the analysis of conceptual thought". Thus one may judge how carefully his doctrines are researched. He goes on, however, to say that "one must either not concede to God the making of beings, or else allow it and not take away the giving of names". **412**. And yet where the dumb beasts are concerned, as we have just said,[168] we learn the opposite from scripture: Adam did not make the animals, and God did not name them; rather, the creation was God's, the naming of the creatures Man's, just as the story is told by Moses.

413. Eunomius goes on to produce for us in his own words a praise of words, as though someone were trying to devalue the power of speech, and after this rash and bombastic assemblage of verbiage he claims that "on the principle of providence and in perfect measure he conjoins with the knowledge and use of necessities the distribution of [347] names". Many such things he babbles while fast asleep and then in his work brings them to invincible and irresistible logical certainty. **414**. I will quote not word for word, but setting out his case simply in terms of what he means: the invention of words, he says, is not to be attributed to poets who are deceived in their ideas about God. What credit the fine fellow gives God, attributing to God things invented by the skill of poets, so that thereby God may seem to men to be more revered, more exalted, when the disciples of Eunomius come to believe that *likriphis, karkaire, eurax, keraire, phy cheiri, size, doupese, arabese, kanachize, smerdaleon konabize, linxe, iache,*

[166] Jaeger refers to Epicurus, *Ep. ad Herodotum* 43–44 (Arrighetti 41–43), where atoms, collisions, repulsations appear in the identical, and entanglements with similar words (for the exact term, cf. Marcus Aurelius, *Meditationes* VII 50, Trannoy 77).

[167] This doctrine is compatible with Aristotle's general view that God does not concern himself with matters below himself. Jaeger notes that there is no exact parallel in Aristotle, but that the doxographic tradition attributes it to him, as Gregory does (cf. H. Diels, *Doxographi graeci*, Berlin ^{4}1976, 130f).

[168] See *CE* II 402 (GNO I 343f).

mermerixe,[169] and all such words are not through some skill recited by poets at their discretion, but they are mysteriously initiated in these words by God himself when they insert them in their verses.

415. This should be ignored, and so should that wise and irrefutable claim, that "we cannot point to the saints among men in the biblical history inventing further new words". If the human race had been unfinished before the appearance of those men, and not yet fully endowed with the gift of articulate speech, it would be right to expect from them the supply of what was lacking. **416**. If however, right at the beginning, the race existed entire and complete in its verbal and intellectual functioning, how could any one reasonably [348] require the saints to have initiated sounds or words in order to constitute conceptual thinking? – or, if we are unable to show this, judge that to be sufficient evidence that God himself gave us the rules for such syllables and words as these?

417. He says however, "Since God does not refuse conversation with his own servants, it is consistent to think that from the beginning he has appointed appellations fitting the reality". What then are we to say about that? We assert that the reason why God allows himself to converse with man is his kindness. **418**. Because it is not possible for our natural littleness to rise above its own limitations and to reach out to the exalted status of the Transcendent, he himself therefore brings down to the level of our weakness his kindly power, and in accordance with our capacity to receive it, he dispenses his generosity and aid. **419**. Compare the way in which by divine dispensation the sun, moderating the severity and directness of his rays by dilution with the intervening air, accommodates his brilliance and heat to the recipients, though in himself he is unapproachable by the feebleness of our nature; so the divine Power also, in the same way as in the illustration we have used, though it to an infinite degree transcends our nature and is unapproachable for immediate presence, like a compassionate mother joining in the baby-talk with the inarticulate whimperings of her babies, passes on to the human

[169] Jaeger supplies Homeric references for all these, mostly rare, poetic words. Translation does not seem helpful, but the list might read in English: *cross-wise, quaked, sideways, mingled, fie hand!, hissed, thudded, clashed, rang, resounded horrid, twanged, cry out, cogitated.*

race that which they are capable of receiving. Consequently, in the various divine manifestations to human beings he both appears in human form and speaks in human manner, and puts on the mask of wrath and pity and similar emotions, in order that by all the things suitable for us our childish life may be taken in hand, [349] coming into contact with the divine Being through providential words. **420**. That it is reverent to suppose that the Divinity is subject to no emotion corresponding to pleasure or pity or wrath, no one even modestly instructed in the truth of things would deny. Yet the Lord is said nevertheless to rejoice over his servants,[170] to be furiously angry with his fallen people,[171] and conversely, to show mercy to those to whom he shows mercy and likewise to pity them,[172] where the text informs us in every word of this kind, I believe, that the divine Providence deals with our feebleness by means of our own characteristics, so that those inclining to sin may restrain themselves from evils through fear of punishment, those convicted may not despair when they perceive the opportunity of gaining mercy by change of heart, and those who live rightly may by strictness of conduct take more delight in their virtues, as by their own way of life they give joy to the one who becomes the provider of good things.

421. Just as it is not possible, however, for a deaf mute to name one conversing with him in sign language such as he is able to understand, so it is not possible for human speech to encompass God, since he has used it towards human beings dispensationally. We ourselves habitually use clucking, lip-smacking or whistling to direct dumb animals, yet that by which we address the hearing of the animals is not to us speech: rather, to each other we behave naturally, while for the beasts the suitable noise and sign-language suffices for our needs. **422**. In his piety however Eunomius does not want God to use our words because of our propensity for evil, our good friend being unaware that for our sake God did not shrink from becoming either curse or sin;[173] [350] so far does God excel in kindness that he willingly took upon him the experience not only of our good things, but of our evils. One who accepted a share of

[170] *Is* 62,5; 65,19; etc.
[171] *Ps* 105/106,40; *Is* 5,25 etc.
[172] *Ex* 33,19 etc.
[173] *Gal* 3,13; *2 Cor* 5,21.

our evils, why should he avoid intercourse with our noblest part, I mean our rational speech?

423.–442. *A Psalm-verse about counting and naming*

423. However, Eunomius claims David as a supporter, and alleges that he says that names were given to things by God, "because it is written in this manner, 'Who counts the number of the stars, and calls them all by their names.' "[174] I myself think it is obvious to any reasonable person that the discussion of these words has nothing to do with the subject. But since some people might incautiously allow the argument, we shall deal briefly with them. **424**. The divine scripture often describes God in such terms as would seem to be not unsuitable for us, like, "The Lord was furiously angry",[175] and, "He repented of the evil against them",[176] "He changed his mind over having anointed Saul as king",[177] and, "The Lord arose like one asleep";[178] and furthermore it describes him as sitting, standing, moving and many such things, which do not naturally belong to God, but have their uses in meeting the needs of those being educated. **425**. In the loose living the threat of wrath induces fear; to those in need of the medicine of repentance it speaks of the Lord repenting of evil with them; for those swept towards pride by successes of some kind it uses the change of mind over Saul to warn that prosperity might not continue for them, even though it seem to come from God; and to those not plunged deep in sin, but who rise up from an empty way of life as if from sleep, it says that God rises up and wakes up with them, that he stands with those who walk undeviatingly towards the good, and sits with those who have settled upon the good, [351] and conversely moves and walks in the case of those removed from their steadfastness in the good. **426**. So in Adam's case the narrative depicts God walking in the evening in the garden,[179] indicating by the evening the inclination of the first-formed man towards dark things, and by the movement the unsteadiness and instability of mankind about what is good.

[174] *Ps* 146/147,4.
[175] *Ps* 105/106,40.
[176] *Jon* 3,10.
[177] *1 Sam* 15,35.
[178] *Ps* 77/78,65.
[179] *Gen* 3,8.

427. These matters may perhaps seem to be far removed from our intended topic. One thing however no one would say is irrelevant to our purpose: many people think that what they cannot grasp, God cannot grasp either, and if something eludes their own understanding, they imagine it is beyond the divine power too. **428**. We reckon number to be the measure of quantity, and number is nothing but the combination of units, the unit being increased in various ways into a multitude: thus the number ten is also a unit by the adding together of units to reach this number, and the hundred is in turn a unit composed of tens, the thousand is another unit and so is ten thousand by multiplication, the latter basing its sum on thousands, the former on hundreds. All these we distribute among objects, and use as signs of the quantity of the things being counted. **429**. It is therefore so that we may learn from the divine scripture that nothing is unknown to God, that the number of the stars is said to be counted by him, not as though the adding up were done literally – who would be so naive as to suppose that God manages reality with odd and even numbers, and calculates the number by adding units together to reach the sum of the grand total? – rather, because exact knowledge of quantity comes to us from number, it is in order that [352] we might learn that in God's case too all things are embraced by what his wisdom knows, and nothing escapes his exact reckoning, that it declares that God counts the stars. By these words it counsels us to believe, that God is not thought to be affected by the limitations of our own knowledge in managing reality, but that things incomprehensible and inconceivable to us are all embraced in knowledge by the divine wisdom. **430**. The stars are so many they are beyond number where human concepts are concerned, but the word of scripture, using the part to teach the whole, by saying that they have been counted by God, testifies that none of the things unknown to us is beyond the knowledge of God. That is why it says, "Who counts the number of the stars" – though manifestly not ignorant of the quantity of stars before he counted them; for how could he be ignorant of what he had made? **431**. The Governor of the universe could not be ignorant of what is embraced by his power to hold all things together. Then why ever should he count what he knows? It is for the ignorant to measure greatness by numbers, and he that knows all things before they exist needs no informant of the number in order to know objects. Nevertheless, he is said by David to count the number: it is obvious that for our instruction, as the word comes down to make things plain in accordance with our own capacity, David has declared by his use of words about number that God knows in detail things unknown to us.

432. So, just as he is said to count, though he needs no arithmetical survey to know the state of things, so too the prophecy speaks of his calling them all by names, but not thereby suggesting, I believe, calling with the voice; for surely the course of the argument would end up in something absurd and unworthy of the idea of God, if it really said that these names, [353] which are in regular use among us, were given to the stars by God. **433**. If any one allows that these were given by God, inevitably he must reckon that the names of Greek idols are attributed to them by the same source, and to suppose that all the mythic tales told about the naming of stars are true, since God validates the use of such terms for them. Thus the Seven who encircle the whole axis, which are shared out among the Greek idols,[180] will relieve from blame those in error in this regard, if indeed it is believed that this is appointed by God. **434**. So the myth of Orion and of Scorpio, and the stories of the Argo, become credible, so do the Swan, the Eagle, the Dog, and the legend about the Crown of Ariadne,[181] and he will be arguing that God is to be held to be the inventor of the names conceived to fit the pattern of constellations in the signs of the Zodiac, if Eunomius is really right in believing David to say that God attaches these names to them.

435. Since therefore it is absurd to think of God as the inventor of such names, so that the names of the idols may not appear to have got their origin from that source, it would be as well not to accept what is said without careful scrutiny, but to understand the same sense in this as we did in thinking about number. Because among us it is evidence of thorough knowledge if we are able to address the one known by name, it teaches us by these words that [354] the One who holds all things together nor only exercises knowledge upon the mass of the whole assembled total, but knows perfectly the

---

[180] The planets are all named after gods in the pantheon.

[181] Jaeger cites for Orion and these other stars and constellations Ps-Eratoshenes Catasterismi (Olivieri [= *Mythographi graeci* III/1] pp. 37, 9, 41, 30, 36, 39 and 5).

individual parts. **436**. That is why the word says, not only that he has counted up the numbers of the stars, but that he addresses each one by name, which shows that his perfect knowledge reaches the tiniest, and that he knows them one by one as perfectly as a man knows someone known to him by name.

If any one says that the names applied by God to the stars are different ones, names which human practice is unaware of, and supposes that David was referring to these, then such a person is mistaken and far from the truth. **437**. If there had been other names for the stars, the divine scripture would not have made reference to those names which are in regular use among the Greeks: Isaiah says, "He made the Pleiades and Hesperus and Arcturus and the Treasuries of the South;"[182] Job names Orion and Asheroth.[183] From this it is clear that divine scripture has used for our instruction the names in every-day use. Similarly we hear in Job of "Amalthea's horn", and in Isaiah of "Sirens", the former thus using the Greek idea to suggest the universal supply of good things,[184] and Isaiah using the name of the Sirens to indicate what is pleasing to the ear.[185] **438**. So just as in those cases the divinely inspired word has used names taken from mythological tales, with a view to benefiting the hearers, so in the other case the word has unashamedly spoken of the stars in terms conceived by human beings, teaching us that every [355] real thing whatsoever that is named by men has its being from God, the thing and not the name. **439**. It does not say that "he named", but that "he made the Pleiades and Hesperus and Arcturus". I think therefore that it has been sufficiently demonstrated in what has been said that David too is a supporter of our interpretation, since what he teaches in the prophecy is not that God names the stars, but that he knows perfectly, as is the way with men who know most perfectly those persons whom through frequent familiarity they can also address by name.

---

[182] Not *Is*, but *Job* 9,9.

[183] *Job* 38,31–32, where the text has *Mazuroth*, not *Asheroth* (which is a place-name, cf. *Num* 11,35).

[184] In the Greek of *Job* 32,14 this is the name of Job's third daughter. While originating in the myth of the goat Amalthea, which suckled the infant Zeus, the phrase was proverbial for a "horn of plenty". There is no astronomical connexion.

[185] *Is* 13,21 includes the mythical Sirens among the demonic occupants of the future ruins of Babylon. Gregory's interpretation is wide of the mark.

440. If one might also present the interpretation given by most people for these words from the Psalm, the absurdity of Eunomius' opinion about them would be much more convincingly proved. Those who have studied the sense of the divine scripture most thoroughly say that not every existing thing is worthy of being counted by God;[186] for in the shared meals of the Gospels, which took place in the desert, neither the children nor the women were thought worth counting, and in the exodus of the people of Israel only those already able to bear arms and do valiantly against the enemy were included in the list.[187] **441**. Not all the names of things are such as to be uttered by the divine mouth, but what is counted is the pure and heavenly, which because of its sublime conduct abiding uncontaminated with any mixture with the dark is called a star, while a name is given to whatever on the same principle is worthy of being inscribed on the divine tablets. Of things contrary in kind he says, "I will not mention their names with my lips."[188] **442**. The kind of names which the Lord gives to such stars, [356] we learn plainly from the prophecy of Isaiah, which says, "I have called you by name; you are mine;"[189] so if one makes himself God's possession, his work becomes his name. But the reader can decide that for himself.

443.–444. *Eunomius misuses Paul's interpretation of Adam*

443. As to his further argument, that the first events of the creation story are evidence that names were put on beings by God, these matters have been discussed enough already, and I reckon repetition would be superfluous. The name of Adam, which the Apostle says is prophetically applied to Christ and the church,[190] let Eunomius be free to interpret that as he will. **444**. No one would be so stupid, when Paul reveals to us hidden mysteries in the power of the Spirit, as to take as a more reliable interpreter Eunomius, the open enemy of the words of the divinely inspired testimony, who uses perverse exegesis of this passage to make a forced argument that the animal species were not named by Adam.

---

[186] Jaeger suggests a reference to Origenes, *In Matthaeum* XI 3 (GCS 38, 37,21ff).
[187] Cf. *Mt* 14,21; *Ex* 12,37.
[188] *Ps* 15/16,4.
[189] *Is* 43,1.
[190] *Eph* 5,31–32; cf. *1 Cor* 15,45.

XI. *Eunomius' charges against Basil (445–468)*

445.–454a. *The charge that Basil denies God is by nature indestructible*

445. Let us ignore Eunomius' insulting words, his mean uncultured style, and the stinking heap of vocal dung that with characteristic fluency emerges against our Master: "The sower of weeds and presence of the harvest,"[191] and "the corruption of Valentinus and the harvest from him," which he says is "heaped up in the soul" of our Master. Let the rest of his disgusting remarks be veiled in silence, just as we bury putrefying corpses in the ground, so that the stench may not become offensive to many people.

446. We must now move our argument on to the passage that follows. Once more he sets out a statement of the Master, which goes as follows: [357] "We call the God of the Universe indestructible and unbegotten, using these names according to different apprehensions: when we look at the ages[192] past, we find the life of God transcending every limit, and call him 'unbegotten'; but when we turn our mind to the coming ages, his infinity and boundlessness and his being constrained by no limit we designate 'indestructible'. **447**. So just as the endlessness of his Life is called 'indestructible', its lack of a beginning is called 'unbegotten', as we apply our conceptual thought to these things."[193] The verbal abuse, which he produces to preface his discussion of these words, we shall again pass over, 'substitute seed', 'sowing-instructor', 'the irrationality of his censure', and the other stuff he airily trots out with his insatiable tongue; but inasmuch as he tries deceitfully to misrepresent the argument, we too shall turn our attention to that. **448**. He promises to convict us of saying that it is not by nature that the Divinity is indestructible. In our view only those things are alien to the nature which

[191] Jaeger suggests the Greek text is here corrupt. If it is not, Eunomius perhaps used πρόσοψιν ('aspect') in the sense of 'presence', representing Basil as both the sower of evil weeds (ζιζάνια, 'darnel'), and himself the product of such sowing.

[192] Here and in what follows, the ambiguous Greek word αἰών,-ῶνος is invariably translated 'age, ages', because the discussion is about very long, but finite, periods of time. An alternative would be the transliteration *(a)eon(s)*. The same word is rightly rendered 'world' in some contexts, and 'to the age(s)' is a common biblical idiom for 'for ever' or even 'eternally'.

[193] Basilius, *Adversus Eunomium* I 7 (PG 29, 525b–c).

may be acquired or discarded; but as for those without which it is impossible to think of the underlying nature, how could any one be accused of separating the nature from them, itself from itself? If our argument gave the message that indestructibility were an additional growth upon God, as though it once did not belong to him or at some time will not, there would be occasion to bring these charges against us. **449**. If however our argument stipulates that the Divinity is always the same, and that what he is now he everlastingly is, and that nothing that he has not comes to be his by any sort of growth or addition, but that he exists everlastingly with every good that can be thought of or spoken, why are we accused of alleging that his indestructibility is not by nature?

[358] **450**. He pretends, however, to have based such a charge against our position on an exact reading of the Master's text: we supply God with indestructibility by adding 'the ages'. If it were we that produced our text for ourselves, the argument might perhaps be a proper subject for defence, as if we were now correcting and removing errors from the words in question; but since our words are quoted by our opponent, what stronger proof of their truth could there be than our adversary's testimony? **451**. How does our argument run, which Eunomius assembles to lay his charge against us? "When, he says,[194] we turn our mind to the coming ages, his infinity and boundlessness and never ceasing at an end we designate 'indestructible'." Does Eunomius think that 'designate' is the same as 'supply'? Who is so out of his mind that he does not know the proper meaning of these words? **452**. To supply is to get for him what does not belong, to designate is to give a name to denote what is. Why in these circumstances is our thinker of truth not ashamed to draw up his charge with open fraud? It is like those who because of some disability cannot see, and behave badly in the eyes of those who see, because they think that what is invisible to them is also unknown to those who are healthy; something similar has happened to our sharp-sighted Eunomius, and, quick of wit, he supposes his own impaired grasp of the truth is the same in his audience. **453**. Who is so stupid he will not put side by side the fraudulent text and the

[194] Apparently Basil is the speaker, quoted or summarized by Eunomius.

charge, and by reading the two convict our wordsmith of his crime? Our text designates indestructibility, he accuses one who supplies indestructibility. What [359] has supply to do with speech? Each person has the right to be tested by his own words; he is not liable to blame for those of others. As it is, he accuses us and looks daggers at us, but according to the truth of the matter he condemns none but himself. **454**. If supplying God with indestructibility is the charge, and that is said by no one but himself alone, then he himself becomes his own smart accuser, criticizing what is his, not what is ours.

454b.–461. *The charge that Basil denies that God is by nature unbegotten*

Where the word 'unbegotten' is concerned, we claim that just as infinity of existence is called indestructibility, so its being without beginning is called unbegottenness. Our opponent alleges that "on the basis of ages" we "advocate his prerogatives" in relation to all things begotten. **455**. I will not mention the slander whereby he classes the Only-begotten God with every begotten thing, reducing the Son of God by the inclusive term to the same level of esteem as everything that exists by creation. In my argument, however, I will present to my better-informed readers his senseless villainy: "On the basis of ages Basil advocates God's prerogatives in relation to all things begotten." What is this senseless empty talk? A man becomes an advocate of God, and claims his prerogatives on the basis of ages? What is the empty airy flight of these insubstantial words?[195] **456**. If the Master said that the divine Being's transcendence, in both directions, of the measurable extension of ages is signified by his having (as the Apostle put it) "neither beginning of days nor end of life",[196] so that the difference of idea is signified by the different words, and for that reason what precedes all beginning is called 'unbegun' and 'unbegotten', while what [360] is limited by no end is named 'immortal' and 'indestructible', is he not ashamed to write that these things are 'supply' and 'advocacy'.

457. He also says that the ages are 'cut into pieces' by us, as if he had not read what he had presented, or was composing his work

[195] Jaeger does not divide the sentence here, but defers the question mark till p. 360,1, following 'indestructible'.

[196] *Heb* 7,3.

without remembering what he was saying. What does the Master say? If we think about what was before creation, and, crossing over the ages with our mind, contemplate the infinity of everlasting life, we denote such a thought by using the word 'unbegotten', and if we turn our attention to the hereafter, and apprehend the life of God which exceeds the ages, then we explain this idea with the terminology of 'unending' and 'indestructible'. **458**. Where in the passage does the argument cut the ages, when to the best of our ability we proclaim in verbs and nouns the eternity of God revealed as in every respect constant, remaining the same from every point of view, and beyond any measure of time? **459**. Human life moves in measurable time, and proceeds by advancing from a beginning to an end, and our life here is divided into past and future, the latter being expected, the former remembered. For this reason, just as with our own condition we observe the past and future of temporal extension, so we speak of it also, by an improper usage, in the case of the transcendent Nature; not as though God in his own life has left behind him a period of time, and conversely moves on to what lies ahead in his life, but because our own understanding, observing the facts relating to our own nature, measures out the eternal in past and future, [361] when the past does not restrict the mind as it goes further back into the boundlessness of infinity, nor does the future promise any stop or limit to infinity.

460. If that is what we both hold and say, why all the noise about our cutting up ages? – unless Eunomius is going to say that the holy scripture also 'cuts into pieces' the ages, when it uses the same idea to denote the infinity of the divine Life: David praised the kingdom before the ages, and Moses showed the kingdom of God extending beyond the ages, so that we may learn from both of them that any thought of measure of time is enclosed within the divine Being, delimited by the infinity of the one who contains the universe on every side. **461**. Moses, looking to the hereafter, says that he reigns "for the age, the further age, and beyond".[197] Great David, leading the mind backwards, said, "God is our king before the age,"[198] and again, "God shall hear, who exists before the ages".[199]

[197] *Ex* 15,18.
[198] *Ps* 73/74,12.
[199] *Ps* 54,20/55,19.

462.–468. *The charge that Basil divides the being of God*

462. Yet our wise Eunomius has said Goodbye to teachers like those, and claims we speak of one life as 'unbegun', and another one as 'unending', and of differences and distinctions between certain ages, which by their differences tear apart even our picture of God. **463**. However, so that our quarrel with what he has said may not be over-long, we shall present untried and unexamined the actual laborious effort of Eunomius on these topics, since there is enough in his efforts at falsehood to make the truth quite clear to the intelligent. As his work proceeds he asks us what we think the ages are. Yet it would have been fairer for that sort of question to be put by us to him; for who is it that [362] says that he knows the being of God, who claims that things inaccessible to us are within the grasp of his own understanding? Let him therefore give us the natural history of the essence of the ages, since he boasts he has understood transcendent things, and not so badly scare us simple folk by threatening us with these twin precipices of alternative answers, making out that if we think the ages are one thing, one absurdity meets us, and if something else, another. **464**. "If you call them eternal," he says, "you will be Greeks and Valentinians and Barbarians; but if you call them begotten," he says, "you will no longer be confessing the unbegottenness of God." What an invincible and irresistible argument! Listen, Eunomius: if something is acknowledged as begotten, acknowledging it as unbegotten is ruled out. And what of the collapse of your own artful arguments, contrasting begotten with unbegotten, by which the unlikeness of the Son's being to his Begetter was being demonstrated? **465**. It appears from what we now learn that the Father is not unlike in being when compared with the begotten, but by the confession of his unbegottenness is utterly dissolved into non-being – if indeed calling the ages begotten means we are obliged no longer to confess the Unbegotten.

Let us consider the logical necessity by which he compels us to this combination of absurdities. **466**. "Whatever by their juxtaposition," he says "enables 'unbegun' to be attached to God, if they do not exist, there will be no attachment." What a strong and inescapable grip! He has got us out of the way, has strangled us like a wrestler in holds we cannot break. He says that by the juxtaposition of the ages 'unbegotten' is attached to God. By whom attached? Who says that 'unbegotten' is attached to the one who exists without beginning, by juxtaposition with certain things? Neither the words nor the thought of this absurdity can be proved to be in our own statements. **467**. The text [363] is its own advocate, since it contains nothing of the kind that he alleges against us; and as to the meaning of what has been said, who could be reckoned a more reliable exponent than those who fathered the book? We ourselves therefore have more right to say what we mean, when we stipulate that the life of God transcends the ages; and we say what we have said just now. **468**. Nevertheless he says that if there is no juxtaposition of ages, it is not possible to attach the results to God, and he tells us that unbegottenness is so attached. Let him also tell us by whom such a thing is attached to God. If it is his own doing, he would be ridiculously accusing our writings of his own folly; if it is ours, let him cite the passage, and we shall admit the charge.

XII. *Eunomius reduces all divine attributes to one (469–542)*

469.–479. *God is one, but has various attributes*

469. We ought, I think, nevertheless to pass over these matters and those which follow them. They are simply the games of children building castles in sand. He puts together one section of a paragraph, and barely reaches the end when he demonstrates that "the same Life is both unbegun and endless", fulfilling our own prayers by this effort. Nothing else is said by us than that the divine Life is one and self-consistent, infinite, eternal and unrestricted in its infinity by any limit on any side. **470**. So far our wordsmith bestows his labour and sweat on the truth, showing that the same Life is in no part limited, whether one considers what is before the ages, or thinks of the hereafter. In what follows, however, he reverts again to his own confusion. Having said that the same Life is both unbegun and endless, he removes the thought of life, compounds all the notions used to describe the divine life into a single idea, [364] and makes them all one: **471**. "If the Life," he says, "is unbegun and endless, indestructible and unbegotten, then indestructibility will be the same as unbegotten, unbegun as endless." To this he adds the support of syllogisms: "It is impossible," he says, "for the Life to be one, while the idea of indestructible is not the same as that of unbegotten." Well added by our noble friend! **472**. It appears that the idea of justice is not different from those stated either, nor that of wisdom, power, goodness, and every other divine title, and no word must have its specific meaning, but with the whole list of titles the underlying connotation will be one, and one defining notion must supply the standard meaning of every one of the expressions. If you are asked the meaning of 'Judge', you must answer with the interpretation 'unbegottenness'; if you are required to give a definition of 'justice', then 'incorporeal' should give you a convenient answer; and what does 'indestructibility' mean? – surely you will be able to say 'pity', or the meaning 'judgement' is to hand. **473**. Thus all the individual ideas may change places with each other, with no particular meaning separating one from another. If Eunomius decrees this, why do the scriptures waste time referring to the divine Nature by many names, giving God the titles 'judge', 'just', 'mighty', 'patient', 'true', 'pitiful', and many more of the same? **474**. If none of the words is taken in a specific sense, and all are mixed up with each other by the confusion of meaning, it will be pointless to use many titles for the same subject, when there is no difference of meaning to separate the names from each other. **475**. But who is so mentally paralysed he does not know that the divine [365] Nature, whatever it may be in essence, is one, understood as something simple, uniform, uncompounded, and by no means a manifold composite, whereas the human mind, prostrate on the ground, and buried deep in this earthly life, because it cannot see clearly what it seeks, reaches out to the ineffable Nature with many thoughts in many and varied ways, and does not hunt for what is hidden with any one idea? **476**. Understanding would be easy, if one single approach to the knowledge of God had been made distinct to us. As it is, we have perceived through the wisdom manifested in the universe that he who governs the universe is wise, and we have received an impression of power from the mighty works of wonder, and the belief that every thing depends upon that source becomes evidence that there is no prior cause of his existence.

477. Again, perceiving the abhorrence of evil, we apprehend his invariability and unmixed character where evil is concerned; and reckoning destruction by death to be the ultimate evil, we name immortal and indestructible the one who is alien to any such notion. We do not split up the Subject with these notions, but, whatever he may essentially be, believing it to be one, we assume that the object of our thinking is cognate with all such attributes. **478**. The titles do not conflict with each other as is the nature of opposites, so that if one exists, the other could not be attributed to him at the same time, as it is not possible for life and death to be attributed to the same person; but such is the meaning of each of the things we attribute to the divine Nature, that, though it may be distinctive in meaning, it in no way contradicts other names given at the same time. **479**. What contradiction is there between 'just' and 'incorporeal', even though the words do not coincide with each other in meaning? [366] How does goodness clash with 'invisible'? No more is the eternity of the divine Life, though known by two words and two thoughts, 'endless' and 'unbegun', cut apart by the difference of the words. Neither is the one the same in meaning as the other (for the one points to the absence of beginning, the other to the absence of end), nor does the difference between the properties attributed to him produce any division in the Subject.

480.–485. *The claim that different attributes divide God's being*

480. Such then are our views. Those of our opponent, however, according to the actual way he compiles the text, are such that they get no support from the arguments, since he otherwise spits out at random such pompous and senseless verbiage under the guise of sentences and paragraphs; but the purpose of his words is this, that there be no difference in meaning between the various names. **481**. It seems that we are obliged to present his statement word for word, to avoid any appearance of fraudulently attributing to him something which does not belong. He says: "Since true words derive their designation from the real subjects denoted, and where they are different they fit different realities, and conversely the same fit the same, one or the other must be the case: either the reality denoted is quite different, or the denoting word is not different either."[200] **482**. These things and many more like them he produces to argue his intended case, excluding from his consideration certain relations, comparisons, shape, size, part, time and place, as if by their removal unbegottenness would come to denote the Being. The [367] argument goes like this (I shall express the thought in my own words):

---

[200] This obscure passage is more fully quoted at *CE* II 487 (GNO I 368,6–18).

483. The Life, he says, is nothing but the Being, or else some element of composition might be attributed to the simple Nature, which would thus be divided into the attribute and the subject of the attribution. Rather, he says, what the Life is, the Being is. He does well to philosophize in this way; no reasonable person would deny that these things are so.

484. Yet how does he bring the argument to its conclusion? "If in denoting the unbegun," he says, "we denote the Life, and if true reason requires that we call that Life 'Being', the divine Being itself is," he says, "denoted by 'unbegotten'." We ourselves agree that the divine Life is not begotten by something else, which is indeed the meaning of the idea of 'unbegun'; but that the Being is what is meant by the words about not being begotten is in our view the thinking only of raving lunatics. **485**. For who is so mad as to claim that the definition of 'being' is 'non-begetting'? Just as 'begetting' is cognate with 'begotten', so obviously 'non-begetting' is closely connected to 'unbegotten'. Since unbegottenness indicates what is *not* true about the Father, how can we construe the indication of what does *not* belong as 'being'?[201] Yet he awards himself something which agrees neither with our view nor with the logic of his own premises, and concludes that what denotes the divine Life is the unbegottenness of God.

486.–491. *Eunomius' arguments apply equally to the Son*

486. So that [368] his nonsense on this subject may be thoroughly exposed, let us consider the text in this way: by means of the arguments about the Father by which he turns the definition of being into that of unbegottenness, let us inquire whether we can equally, using the same arguments, bring the being of the Son also to unbegottenness. **487**. "There must be," he says, "one and the same idea for the same Life, which is absolutely one, even if in titles and man-

[201] Wilamowitz suspected some words are missing here. Our rendering is in keeping with Jaeger's own interpretation: Unbegottenness has just been shown to have a negative import, i.e. the Father has no prior generative agent; how can we then take this negation, "He has no prior generative cause", as defining his essential Being?

ner and order it appear diverse. Since true words derive their designation from the real subjects denoted, and where they are different they fit different realities, as conversely the same fit the same, one or the other must be the case: either the reality denoted is quite different, or the denoting word is not different either, since there is no underlying reality beside the Life of the Son,[202] on which one might either stamp the thought or impose the other word." **488**. Is there any incoherence in that text, so that such things should not be said or written of the Only-begotten? Is not the Son also "life absolutely one"? Is it not appropriate that "one and the same idea" should apply to him, "even if in titles and manner and order it appear diverse?" Will it not be established where he is concerned, that "one or the other must be the case: either the reality denoted is quite different, or the denoting word is not different either, since there is no underlying reality besides" his Life, "on which one might either [369] stamp the thought or impose the other word". **489**. Nothing of our own has been added to Eunomius' words about the Father, but we have adopted his actual premise and logic, only substituting the name 'Son'. If then he too is one absolute Life devoid of all composition and reduplication, and there is no underlying reality beside the life of the Son (for how could any admixture of alien reality be suspected in what is simple? what is perceived as so associated would no longer be simple), and if the being of the Father is also a simple life, and according to the principle of life and simplicity there is no diversity in the simple life, no addition, no subtraction, no variation of quantity or quality generating change, it must follow that those things which coincide in the same thoughts should also be named with the same appellations. **490**. If then the reality evincing the simplicity of life in Father and Son is understood as one, and since, as has been said, the principle of simplicity admits no variation, it necessarily follows that the title which fits one belongs naturally to the other. If therefore the simplicity of the Father's life is signified by the appellation 'unbegottenness', that word will not be unsuitably applied to the Son as well. **491**. As man is referred to as that which is rational, mortal, and receptive of thought and knowledge in the same way in the case of Adam as in that of Abel, and in no way is the name given to the nature changed by

[202] Eunomius wrote 'Father'; see *CE* II 489 (GNO I 369,2–5).

coming to life whether by being begotten in the case of Abel, or not by being begotten in the case of Adam, so, if the designation of the Father's life as 'simple' and 'uncompounded' implies unbegottenness, so also in the case of the life of the Son the same thought must of necessity be attached to the same word; if it is true, as Eunomius asserts, that "one or the other must be the case: either the reality denoted [370] is quite different, or the denoting word is not different either".

492.–503. *The absurdity of making divine attributes all identical*

492. Why, however, do we waste time dwelling on futile matters, when we ought to offer Eunomius' book itself to those keen on hard work to expose the folly of his arguments, and, without any one correcting him on that score, to demonstrate to the educated not only the blasphemy of the doctrine, but also the spineless morality. In many ways he misinterprets the word 'concept' not in accordance with our thinking, but as he chooses, and as in a night-battle when no one can discern friend from foe, with weapons he thinks he is directing against us he stabs his own doctrine unawares. **493**. The point at which he thinks he ought to separate himself furthest from the devout members of the church is this, the argument that later on God became a Father, and the title of fatherhood is more recent than his other titles which are attributed to him: he has been called Father ever since he decided to become a Father, and did so.[203] **494**. Now in this present book he argues that all the appellations attributed to the divine Nature coincide with each other in meaning and there is no difference between them;[204] but one of the names attributed is 'Father', for he is called 'Father' in the same way as he is called 'indestructible' and 'everlasting'. He may therefore confirm in the case of this word too his view about the other titles, and drop his earlier opinion, if indeed the idea of fatherhood is also to be included with all the other appellations; **495**. for it is clear that if the meaning of 'indestructible' and 'Father' are the same, then, as

[203] Jaeger prints this description of Eunomius' past views in spread type as if it were a quotation. In the absence of direct evidence to the contrary, it is better to see it as Gregory's own summary of Eunomian teaching.

[204] Again, against Jaeger, I regard this as Gregory's summary, not Eunomius' words.

he is confessed as for ever indestructible, so he must be as for ever Father, since, so he says, all the names have one meaning. Alternatively [371] if he is scared of acknowledging God's fatherhood as eternal, he must necessarily destroy his present case, and confess that a particular meaning inheres in each title, and all his great nonsense about the titles has burst like a bubble and vanishes.

496. He may defend himself from this dilemma on the ground that only the titles of 'Father' and 'Designer' are attached to God as additional developments, because "on the basis of activity", as he himself says,[205] both these words are applied to God. If he does, that will cut down the great trouble we have in achieving our goal, admitting things which would need a good deal of work from us to prove conclusively. If the meaning of the words for 'Father' and 'Designer' is one – for each is 'on the basis of activity' – then what is meant by the words must surely be the same in both cases; for where what is meant is the same, the subject can surely not be different either. **497**. So if it is on the basis of activity that he is called both 'Father' and 'Designer', then it is surely possible also to use the names the other way round, and say that God is Designer of the Son and Father of the stone, if the title 'Father' plays no part in the permanent description of his nature. That what is argued by this means is absurd can no longer be doubted by men of sense. **498**. Just as it is absurd to think of a stone as God, or any other thing that exists by creation, so it will be conceded that one ought not to affirm the godhead of the Only-begotten God, if one and the same description affirms both names for God in accordance with his activity, as Eunomius argues, the description by which he is named both Father and Designer.

499. Let us stick to our task, however. In his criticism of our argument, which says that the knowledge of God is acquired by us through various apprehensions, he says that [372] as presented by us he is no longer simple, since he participates in the notions indicated by each title, and by participation in those finally achieves his perfection of being. I write this in my own words, abbreviating his

[205] See the quotation at *CE* II 371 (GNO I 334,23f).

long ramble. **500**. Faced with this empty-headed and feeble splurge I do not think that any sane person would acquit even the response to it of folly. If there were anything like it in what we have said, we would certainly either have to retract the errors, or else bring to the obscurity of the thought the corrective of interpretation. Since however nothing of the kind has been said by us, nor does the logic of what we have said force the mind to such a necessary conclusion, what need is there to dwell on matters generally agreed, and bore the reader with the length of our discourse? **501**. Who is so far out of his mind that, having heard that devout notions of God are gathered by us through many ideas, he supposes that the Divinity is composed of diverse elements, or that he assembles his own perfection by acquiring things? Someone, for instance, discovered geometry, and let it be assumed that this same person is the inventor also of astronomy, as well as medicine, grammar and geometry and some other such skills: because the names of the skills attributed to the one mind are many and varied, is his mind for that reason to be regarded as composite? **502**. Yet what is meant by medicine differs widely from astronomical science, and grammar has nothing in common with geometry as far as meaning is concerned, nor again navigation with agriculture. Nevertheless it is possible to combine the idea of each of these in a single mind, without the mind as a result becoming a manifold synthesis, or [373] all the names of the skills being amalgamated in a single meaning. **503**. If therefore the human intellect suffers no loss of simplicity through having so many names applied to it, why should one think that, if God is called wise, just, good, eternal, and all the divine epithets, unless a single connotation is envisaged for all the names, he either becomes manifold, or else by participation in these accumulates the perfection of his nature?

504.–523a. *The syllogism: indestructibility and unbegottenness are incompatible unless identical*

504. We must now consider also his gravest charge against us. It is as follows: "To put the argument at its most concise," he says, "he does not even preserve the Being itself uncontaminated and pure of things evil and alien." So great is the charge; but what is the proof? Let us examine his vehement oratorical argument against us. "If it is by endlessness of life alone," he says, "that he is indestructible, and by absence of beginning alone that he is unbegotten, insofar as he is not indestructible, he will be destructible, and insofar as he is not unbegotten, he will be begotten." **505**. He repeats the same thing and again says: "So he will be in respect of having no beginning unbegotten and also destructible, and in respect of his endlessness indestructible and also begotten." That then is his "most concise argument," which he threatens to produce against us to prove that we say the being of God is contaminated with alien and evil things! I would think it would be obvious to those who have in them a healthy ability to judge the truth, that, because the Master has given no handle in his actual words for misrepresentation, Eunomius has twisted those words to his liking and concluded with this childish game of logic-chopping. [374] **506**. However, to make it as clear as possible to every reader, I will spell it out again word for word,[206] and set beside it the words of Eunomius. "We claim," our Master says, "that the God of the Universe is indestructible and unbegotten, using these terms with distinct notions. When we look back to past ages, we find the life of God surpassing every limit and call him unbegotten; when we turn our minds to the future ages, then what is boundless and infinite and stops at no end we name indestructible. **507**. Thus as the endlessness of life is called 'indestructible', so its want of a beginning is called 'unbegotten', as we envisage these things by conceptual thought." That is the argument of the Master. He teaches us by his words that the divine Life, being by nature one and self-consistent, neither begins from any beginning nor is restricted by any end, and that it is possible to affirm clearly by certain words the properties envisaged in this Life. **508**. We assert that something derives from no prior cause by using the words 'unbegun' and 'unbegotten', and that it is limited by no ending, nor dissolves into destruction, is indicated by the terms 'indestructible' and 'endless'. By this it is established that, in the case of the divine Life, we ought to say that what has no beginning exists unbegotten, and that unending existence we ought to call 'indestructible', because everything that ceases to exist vanishes utterly, and when we hear of the vanishing of what is, we understand the destruction of what

[206] To be taken with a pinch of salt, as Jaeger notes; cf. *CE* II 527–528 (GNO I 380,15–23). The text derives from Basilius, *Adversus Eunomium* I 7 (PG 29, 525b–c).

existed before. He says therefore that the one who never ceases to be, and is immune to destructive dissolution is called 'indestructible'.

509. [375] What does Eunomius make of this? "If it is by endlessness of life alone," he says, "that he is indestructible, and by absence of beginning alone that he is unbegotten, insofar as he is not indestructible, he will be destructible, and insofar as he is not unbegotten, he will be begotten." Who gave you this notion, Eunomius, that indestructibility is not envisaged as within the whole life of God? Who cut the divine life in two, and gave particular names to each half, so as to say that whichever part one adjective belongs to, the other does not belong to it? **510**. This is the acuity of your own logic, to say that the Life which exists unbegun is destructible, and that the unbegun cannot be combined in thought with the indestructible Life. It is the same as if someone said that Man is articulate and receptive of understanding and knowledge, attaching both these designations together to the subject with distinct intention and meaning, and then he were ridiculed by someone like this saying the same sort of thing: "If Man is receptive of thought and knowledge, for that reason he cannot be articulate, but inasmuch as he is receptive of knowledge, he will be only that, and his nature has no room for the other; conversely, if he decides that Man is articulate, it will no longer be possible for him to be receptive of understanding, **511**. for inasmuch as he is articulate, he will be proven to have no part in intelligence." If the folly and absurdity in this case is obvious to all, there can surely be no doubt about the other. When you read what the Master said, you will find that the logical game is a phantom: in the human illustration being receptive of knowledge is not ruled out by being articulate, nor being articulate by being receptive of understanding; nor does the eternity of the divine Life either lack indestructibility, if it is unbegun, nor, if indestructibility is attributed to it, will it forfeit its status as unbegun. **512**. The one who with the [376] precision of exact logic looks for the truth, having interpolated what he liked from his own material into our text, contradicts himself and refutes himself, without touching our case. Our position was nothing other than this: to claim that the Life which exists unbegun is named 'unbegotten' conceptually – named, not made –, and to designate that which extends into infinity by the term 'indestructible', not to make it indestructible, but to signify that it is such; **513**. hence it is a property of the Subject that the divine Life is infinite in both directions, but whether this or that attribute is applied to the Subject in speech concerns only the word used to indicate the attribute designated. It is one feature of the divine Life that it exists without prior cause: this is indicated by the term 'unbegotten'. It is another feature of the divine Life that it is infinite and has no end: this is stated by the use of the word 'indestructible'; hence what the Subject actually is, is above every name and thought; but that it has no prior cause, and never turns into the non-existent, those are the meanings of the conceptual thought behind these words.

514. What then is it in our views that drives him to this senseless game, so that he reverts to the topic and says the same thing again? These are his words: "So in respect of having no beginning he will be unbegotten and also destructible, and in respect of his endlessness indestructible and also begotten."[207] Though this may not be dealt with in detail in our book, for the person who has any kind of intelligence it is obvious how ridiculous and nonsensical it is, or rather wicked and damnable. **515**. The argument by which he deduces the link between 'corruptible' and 'unbegun', in the same way [377] makes a mockery of every orthodox divine title. These are not the only two applied to the divine Life, unbegun existence and immunity from destruction, but it is called immaterial and wrathless, changeless and incorporeal, invisible and unconfigured, true and just, and there are ten thousand other attributes of the divine Life, every one of which by itself is described in some particular sense by the words which indicate it. **516**. With every one of these words – every one, I mean, which indicates an idea appropriate to God – it is possible to tie up the alien linkage conceived by Eunomius. Thus 'immaterial' and 'wrathless' are both applied to the divine Life, but not both with the same meaning. We understand by the term 'immaterial' that the Divinity is free from contamination with matter, while 'wrathless' means that the passion of anger is alien to him. **517**. Eunomius will presumably attack these too, and dance to the same tune as in the quotation. He will say, tying up the absurdity in the same knot, "If he is called immaterial inasmuch as he is untouched by contamination of matter, to that extent he will not be

[207] Cf. *CE* II 504 (GNO I 373,21–23).

wrathless, and if he is wrathless inasmuch as anger is absent, it is not possible for 'immaterial' to be confessed of him, but of necessity by being free from matter he will be shown to be immaterial and also wrathful, and by the absence of anger he will be found to be wrathless and material at the same time." So he will also do with all the other words.

518. If we may, we would propose another similar pair of words: I refer to 'changeless' and 'incorporeal'. Since these two words are used of the divine Life each with its own particular meaning, the wisdom of Eunomius will again argue absurdity in their case too: if [378] what is always the same is what is meant by the term 'unchanging', and the adjective 'incorporeal' refers to intellectual being, Eunomius will surely say the same in their case too, that the attributes envisaged in the words are incompatible with each other, alien and incommunicable. **519**. In being for ever the same the divine will be only changeless, and not incorporeal, while because it is an intellectual being with no bodily figure it possesses incorporeality, but is removed from changelessness. Thus it comes about, that when immutability is attributed to the divine Life, that proves it is not only changeless but corporeal, but when its intellectual state is considered, it is firmly ruled to be at once incorporeal and changeable. **520**. These are Eunomius' clever contrivances against the truth! What need is there to extend the argument with verbiage by going into everything?

One can see how this illogicality can be argued similarly in every case. Certainly 'true' and 'just' will, according to the preceding logical nexus, in the same way conflict with each other: one thing is meant by truth, another by justice. **521**. So Eunomius might logically say of these too, that the true is incompatible with the just, justice is lacking in truth, and as a result when any one considers the freedom from injustice in God, the Divinity will be shown to be at the same time just and false, while if we consider his freedom from falsehood, we argue that the Divinity is at once true and unjust. **522**. It is the same with 'invisible' and 'unconfigured'. It would be possible[208] using the same ingenuity as already explained to say that

[208] Omitting διὰ τῶν, which is Jaeger's alternative to supposing some words to have fallen out.

there is no invisibility in what is unconfigured, and no absence of figuration in the invisible, but that [379] figure is involved in invisibility and visibility conversely will argue absence of figure, applying the same syllogistic skill to these matters as he did with 'indestructible' and 'unbegun': that when we consider the uncompounded state of the divine Life, we speak of its being without figure, not however invisibility; and when we observe that it is not possible to see God with bodily eyes, while allowing invisibility we shall not also concede that he exists unconfigured. **523**. If these things seem alike ridiculous and senseless to everybody, how much more will the intelligent person condemn the absurdity of those statements on which the argument was based, when it logically produced the absurdity in these cases!

523b.–536. *Logical games with the endless and the unbegun*

However, he attacks the saying of the Master, as improperly seeing indestructibility in the endless and perceiving endlessness in the indestructible. So let us have the same sort of fun with Eunomius' meticulousness too. Let us consider his own judgment in the same way about these words, and find out what it is. **524**. Will he say that the endless is something different in meaning from the indestructible, or conclude that they are one?[209] If he says they are both one, he will be agreeing with our argument; if he says that the meaning of 'indestructible' is one thing, that of 'endless' another, it follows that where things are different from one another they are not the same as one another in meaning. **525**. Therefore if the sense of 'indestructible' is one and that of 'endless' quite another, and each of these is what the other is not, the conclusion follows that the indestructible is not endless, nor is the endless indestructible, but the endless will be destructible, the indestructible liable to end. I implore my readers not to turn their scorn for this absurdity against us.

526. This is the game we ourselves have been compelled to play against the buffoon, in order to disentangle by a like childishness his infantile web of syllogism. If however it [380] does not seem too ponderous and irritating to my readers, it might not be a bad time

[209] Jaeger punctuates as a statement: "He will either . . .".

to quote again word for word what Eunomius says: "If it is by endlessness of life alone," he says, "that he is indestructible, and by absence of beginning alone that he is unbegotten, insofar as he is not indestructible, he will be destructible, and insofar as he is not unbegotten, he will be begotten." He repeats the same thing, and again says: "So in respect of having no beginning he will be unbegotten and also destructible, and in respect of his endlessness, indestructible and also begotten." **527**. The irrelevant and superfluous material inserted in between I pass over, as making no further contribution to the course of the argument; but that the meaning of our own writings, from which he himself has quoted, has nothing to do with the charges urged against us by him, is in my view easy for everyone to observe. "We claim," our Master says, "that the God of the Universe is indestructible and unbegotten, using these terms with distinct connotations. **528**. By his surpassing the boundary of the ages by any measure of temporal extension," he says, "whether we consider what is from the beginning or what lies ahead, that either aspect of the everlasting Life is infinite and unbounded, we indicate the one by the word 'indestructibility', the other by 'unbegottenness'."[210] Eunomius however asserts that we say that the unbegun is being and the endless another being, as if to combine two sections of beings spoken of in contradiction. And so he argues the absurdity, posing his own premises, and tying them together with his own logic; having pressed his own conclusions to the point of absurdity he nowhere touches our position. **529**. The idea that only with regard to endlessness of life is God indestructible is his, and not ours. Similarly, that the indestructible [381] is not unbegun is also the invention of his strict logic, which places what does not belong in the category of essential being. We ourselves would allow nothing as essential being which does not belong. **530**. It is not proper to God for his life either to end in destruction, or to have begun with a generative act: this is what is expressed by the two words 'indestructibility' and 'unbegottenness'.

He however makes a great fuss about our doctrines with his own nonsense, and by his accusation against us condemns himself unawares. **531**. By stipulating that unbegottenness is being, he ends up logically in the very absurdity which he alleges against our doctrines.

[210] Very loosely repeating the loose quotation in *CE* II 506–507 (GNO I 374,3–13).

Since it is held that in measuring time beginning is one thing and end another, if anyone were to claim that absence of the one was essential being, he would suppose that his Life, being bisected, existed only as unbegun, and that it did not by nature extend further towards endlessness, if unbegottenness really is to be reckoned the Nature. **532**. If however one insists that both are Being, then it necessarily follows, according to the argument produced by Eunomius, that each of the designations with its own connotation also has its existence in the notion of the Being, existing only to the extent declared by the meaning of the term. Eunomius' reasoning will prevail, precisely if neither the unbegun possesses endlessness, nor is the endless without beginning, because on his reasoning each of the things stated is Being, and the two are incompatible in sense with each other: neither does beginning have the same meaning as end, nor can the words for these, which negate each other, come together in what they denote.

533. So that he may himself acknowledge his own folly, the proof will be taken from his own words. He says in his attack on us that God by being endless [382] is unbegotten, and by being unbegotten is endless, the connotation of the two words being one. If then in endlessness he is unbegotten, and endlessness and unbegottenness are the same in meaning, and if he allows that the Son is endless, on this logic he will be obliged to allow that the Son is also unbegotten, if indeed the endless is, as he has said, the same as the unbegun. **534**. Just as he sees the endless in the unbegotten, so he professes also to have observed the unbegun in the endless. He would not regard the interchangeability of names as in doubt, but, "By nature and not by addition of ages," he says, "God is unbegotten." Who is going to quarrel with saying that God is by nature all that is attributed to him? **535**. It is not by juxtaposition of the ages that we say God is just, mighty, Father and indestructible, nor with reference to anything else that exists, but we apply every piously conceived attribute to the Subject itself, whatever that may by nature be. So if we suppose neither age nor any other conceivable work of creation had been devised, God would still be no less than he is now believed to be, in need of no ages to make him what he is. **536**. "But he has a life," says Eunomius, "not externally derived, nor composite, nor diverse: he himself is the everlasting Life, immortal because of his very life, indestructible because of his very immortality."

These things we also learn about the Only-begotten, which no one will deny, unless he will openly contradict the words of John. Life is not externally derived for the Son, for, "I am the life," he says;[211] nor [383] is his life composite, nor diverse, but he is because of his very life immortal, – for where else could one acknowledge immortality if not in life? – and indestructible because of his very immortality. What is stronger than death and destruction is surely not externally derived.

537.–542. *Eunomius nonsensically identifies 'unbegotten' with 'endless'*

537. Our own understanding has followed so far; but the puzzle composed in what he says is for those trained in the art of stenography[212] to interpret. From that art the words seem to me to have originated. What does he say? "Being indestructible without beginning he is unbegotten without end, being so called in no other respect, for no other reason, to no other end."[213] One with a refined ear and a perceptive mind knows already before I comment that, apart from the din of the words, which hammer out their dissonant juxtaposition, there is no trace of intelligible meaning in the sentence. **538**. If even a shadow of sense should turn up amid the verbal clatter, what turns up is sure to be wicked or ridiculous. What have you in mind, do tell me, when you say that he is indestructible without beginning and unbegotten without end? Do you suppose that the beginning is the same as the end, and that the two words apply to the one idea, as the names 'Peter' and 'Simon' both point to the one subject? And for this reason, as you reckon the beginning is the same as the end, have you similarly linked in one connotation the two mutually contradictory words, 'beginning', I mean, and 'end', and conversely you thought 'endless' the same as 'unbegun' and made the two words one by blending them together?

---

211 *Jn* 11,25.

212 Literally "the wisdom of Prunicos". The allusion is obscure, but Gregory uses the phrase in the same sense at *CE* I 50 (GNO I 39,17). According to Lampe in *PGL*, προύνικος, normally meaning 'bath-attendant', is (jocularly?) applied to stenographers.

213 This sentence, which Gregory professes to find unintelligible, could be otherwise translated. The last word, here rendered 'so called', might equally well be rendered 'spoken of' or 'named'.

[384] Is that the purpose of the mixing of the words when you say that he is endlessly unbegotten and unbegottenly endless?

539. And how is it you do not see the wickedness in what you say as well as the absurdity? If because of this novel mixture the reversal of names makes no difference, so that the unbegotten is endlessly unbegotten and the endless unbegottenly endless, then it must follow that everything endless cannot exist without being unbegotten; and so you will find, dear Sir, that the much vaunted unbegottenness, which alone, according to you, characterizes the Father's being, becomes the common property of every immortal thing, and makes them all consubstantial with the Father,[214] because it denotes in the same way all things whose life through immortality goes on indefinitely, archangels, angels, human souls, and perhaps even the rebellious Power itself, the devil and the demons. **540**. If the endless and the indestructible on your argument certainly exists unbegotten, the unbegottenness must certainly be attributed to every unending and indestructible thing. Such is the fate of those who, before they have learnt what they ought to learn, by what they try to teach expose to public gaze their own want of learning. **541**. If he had any critical judgment, he would not have failed to recognize the specific sense inhering in 'unbegun' and 'endless', and that, while endlessness is common to all things that are held to continue in life to infinity, 'unbegun' applies only to that which has no prior cause. **542**. How then is it possible to think of what is common to them all as having that same meaning for them, as is universally held to be the singular property of God alone, and thereby either to make unbegottenness common property of all things that possess immortality, or else to allow that none is immortal, if endless existence belongs only to the unbegotten, and conversely unbegotten existence belongs only to the endless. This way, all things endless might be thought to be unbegotten.

[214] One cannot avoid the regular translation 'consubstantial', but it obscures slightly the argument about being: immortals all become the-same-in-being as the Father.

XIII. *Eunomius' claim that words for God originate in God (543–560)*

543.–553. *The claim that words for God are prior to man's concepts*

543. [385] Let us set aside this topic, and thereafter also keep silent about the usual vituperation, which he pours generously into his text, and let us go on to read what follows next. I think that it might be right to leave most of the subsequent passage too without comment. In all this material he is just the same, not engaging with what we wrote, but providing his own occasions for refutation from what is ostensibly ours. One trained in criticism might say detailed rebuttal is a waste of time, when every intelligent person reading his[215] book can convict him of deceit from his very words. **544**. "The dignity of God," he says, "is older that the conceptual thought" of our Teacher. We do not deny it. The dignity of God, whatever one ought to consider that to be, is not only prior to our race, but also transcends the whole creation and the ages themselves. How then does this affect the argument, if the dignity of God is acknowledged not only older than Basil, but older than all that is?

"Yes," he says, "but the name is the dignity." **545**. And who has demonstrated that the appellation is the same thing as the dignity, so that we too may agree with his proposition? "A solemn law of a nature," he says, "tells us that with named things the dignity of the name does not lie within the power of those who name." What is this law of the nature, and why is it not universally valid? If a nature[216] in fact decreed such a thing, it must have had the power over all those who share the nature, as with all other things that are proper to their own nature. **546**. If then the law of our nature made the names spring up for us from things, like plants from seeds or bulbs, and did not [386] leave the imposition of significant designations to the discretion of those who point the things out, all of us men would have had the same language as each other. If the words applied to things were not diverse, we presumably would not differ from each other about the form of speech. He says that it is

[215] Reading αὐτοῦ, as in *Lexicon gregorianum* III 274 at ἐντυγχάνω A,5,b. Jaeger's αὐτὸν is apparently a misprint.

[216] Jaeger's proposed addition of the definite article <ἡ> obscures Gregory's allusion to Eunomius' own wording just above at p. 385,21, and is here ignored.

"holy and very fitting to the law of Providence that words are applied to things from on high." **547**. Why then did not the prophets know what is holy, and had not learned the law of Providence, when they never on your principles made a god of 'unbegottenness'? Why does even God himself not know this kind of holiness, when he does not from on high attach the names to the animals shaped by him, but grants to Adam the right of name-giving? If it is appropriate to the law of Providence and holy, as Eunomius says, for words to be applied to things from on high, it is surely unholy and unfitting that names should be attached to things by those below.

548. "But the Minder of all things," he says, "by a law of creative design saw fit to sow seeds in our souls." Even if these things were sown in the souls of men, how is it that from Adam until you stepped forward[217] no crop grew from this vacuity (though planted, so you say, in the souls of men), so that 'unbegottenness' should be the title given to the Father's being? It would have been spoken by Adam and all his descendants, if God had really planted such a seed in his nature. **549**. Just as things which now grow out of the ground persist from the first creation for ever in their seminal succession, and there is no departure from their nature in the present seed, so this word, according to what you say, sown in their nature by God, would have germinated at the same time as the first speech in the first-formed pair, and [387] would have continued alongside the succession of their descendants. Since however that was not there at the first, for none of the earlier people, down to the present, uttered such a thing before you, clearly a rogue and deviant seed has sprung up of a kind of darnel, not one of those good seeds which, as the Gospel says, God cast into the field of our nature.[218] **550**. Whatever is entirely in the common nature cannot have its origin of existence now, but made its appearance with the nature at its first constitution, such as the activity of the senses, the relation of desire or rejection towards various human concerns, and whatever else of this kind is recognized as a common part of their nature; history has changed none of these in those who have come after, but humanity has been

[217] παράβασις is apparently a metaphor from the theatre, where an actor or chorus steps forward to address the audience.
[218] *Mt* 13,24–30.

preserved continuously with the same features from the first people to the most recent, the nature having lost nothing of what belonged to it at the start, nor acquiring what did not belong. **551**. To make a comparison, seeing is recognized as common to the nature, but specialist seeing is acquired with practice by those who study sciences; for not everybody can understand what is learned by use of mathematical instruments, or appreciate the demonstrations of geometrical diagrams, and other such things, where it is not vision, but the use of vision for a purpose that is discovered by the science. Similarly one might say that rational speech is common to human nature, and is a property brought into existence at the same time as the nature, but that inventing terms to indicate realities comes from human beings who have acquired the power of speech in themselves from God, and who always, as seems to them best for the [388] identification of things being pointed out, invent words which denote the realities.

552. "But if these prevail," he says, "one of the two is logically implied: either the concept is older than its conceiver, or the titles naturally proper to God and preexisting the universe are later than the creation of men." Must we really do battle with this kind of thing, and engage in rational debate with such obvious nonsense? Who is so naive as to be stung by such things, and to suppose, if he believes that the words come from the rational faculty, that he must either allow that spoken words are older than those who speak them, or must think he offends the Deity, because men name the Deity as best they can manage after they come to be. **553**. That the transcendent Nature has no need of words resounding from voice and tongue has already been said, and it would be superfluous to clutter up our argument by repetition. What is by nature both complete and without excess neither lacks anything it needs nor possesses anything it does not need. Since therefore it has been demonstrated in the words already written, and it is agreed by the general consensus of intelligent persons, that he has no need to call things by name, no one is likely to deny that claiming for God things he does not need is utterly wicked.

554.–560. *A dilemma for Eunomius, who identifies God's attributes with his being*

554. I do not believe however that we should spend time on these and similar topics, nor refute in detail the passage which follows. For those better informed the work composed by our opponent will itself appear advocate enough of the doctrines of true religion. He says that "the Being is itself indestructibility and likewise immortality." **555**. For my part, whether these belong to the divine Nature or whether [389] the Being is by connotation these very things, I do not think it is anything I need quarrel with him about. Whichever of the propositions prevails, it will certainly strengthen our case. If it is a property of the essential being that it is not destroyed, so it is certainly a property of it that it does not originate from being begotten; and thus the idea of unbegottenness will be placed outside the connotation of 'Being'. **556**. If however, because God is not destroyed, one were to say his Being is indestructibility, and because he is stronger than death, were to stipulate that for this reason his very Nature is immortality, and the Son is indestructible and immortal, then the being of the Only-begotten will be indestructibility and immortality. If then the Father is indestructibility, and the Son is indestructibility, and each of these is a being, and no difference is conceived in the meaning of indestructibility, then one being will surely be in no way different from the other, if the nature is in both cases equally free from destructibility.

557. Although by repeating the same arguments he binds us, or so he thinks, in inexorable dilemmas, saying that if we decide for what is a property of the Being, the Deity is proved to be composite, but if the simplicity is allowed, then indestructibility and unbegottenness will surely be proved to connote the essential being itself, once more we shall demonstrate that he himself supports our own claims. **558**. If he makes the divine Being utterly composite by attributing any property to it, then surely he will remove not even fatherhood from outside the essential being, but will concede that he is Father by nature as he is indestructible and immortal, and thus even unwillingly will accept the Son into communion with his Nature. It will not be possible, if the other is by nature Father, to separate the Son from a relationship of essential nature with him. **559**. If however he says that fatherhood is a property of God outside his nature, he must also surely allow us the right to attribute a property to the Father, [390] so that his simplicity is in no way negated if the property of unbegottenness is identified as outside his essential being. But if he says that 'indestructible' and 'unbegotten' connote the being itself, and insists that both the words have the same meaning as each other, there being no difference between them, because the connotation inherent in both is the same, and claims that the meaning of 'indestructible' and 'unbegotten' is one, he who is one of these is surely also the other. **560**. Yet that the Son is indestructible even they do not dispute; so on Eunomius' argument he too is unbegotten, if indestructibility really has the same meaning as unbegottenness. So it is one thing or the other: he must either agree that 'unbegotten' signifies something other than indestructibility, or he will stick to his opinions and utter many blasphemies about the Only-begotten, either making him destructible to avoid saying he is unbegotten, or arguing he is unbegotten to avoid proving him not destructible.

XIV. *Privative and negative words for God (561–610)*

561.–570. *On abbreviating a response to nonsense, especially that about 'privation'*

561. I do not know what I should now do, whether to proceed step by step through all the material, or whether here too to rule out debate with empty words. One might compare the case of traders in poisons, where the experiment with a small dose guarantees to the buyers the deadly effect of the whole drug, and no one doubts, once having learnt the poisonous effect from the part, that the whole thing offered for sale is a deadly drug. In the same way I think, now that this poisonous dosage in his book has been displayed by our scrutiny, reasonable people will no longer be in doubt that the whole thing is the same kind of drug as has been already demonstrated, and for this reason I reckon it undesirable to go to any lengths in devoting time to vanities. **562**. Nevertheless, because the champions of deceit find something persuasive from any source, and there is a fear that not to cast an eye over some of their labours might become a specious excuse for attacking us, on the grounds that their strongest arguments are left out, [391] for this reason we beg those who support our effort, without condemning any idle chatter, to follow seriously our argument which everywhere of necessity extends itself in opposition to the endeavours of falsehood. **563**. When he had scarcely finished dreaming up in deep sleep his fantasy about conceptual thought, equipping himself with those feeble and senseless endeavours he moves his work on to another illusion far more witless than his earlier fantasy. One may learn the futility of his effort by looking carefully at his analysis of 'privation'. **564**. Getting involved with all his rubbish I would leave to Eunomius and those like him who have no experience of reflecting on the most important subjects. We shall tackle briefly the main headings of what he has said, so that none of the charges made may be left out, nor any nonsense extend our work to unprofitable length.

565. When he is about to include his analysis of privative words, he promises that he will "demonstrate the incurable absurdity," as he himself puts it, of our doctrines, and an "affected and culpable piety." Such is his promise. What is his proof of the allegations? "When they say," he replies, "that God is unbegotten by being deprived of begottenness, we refute this by saying that neither this word nor this thought are at all fitting for God." **566**. Let him tell us who is the champion of this argument, whether anyone from the time mankind came into existence until now, whether among Barbarians or Greeks, can be shown to have uttered such a thing, and we shall shut up. Of all human beings ever born there is none could be proved to have said such a thing, unless he were mad. For who is so far [392] beside himself with liquor, who so far out of his mind with insanity or brain-fever, as to put this thought into words, that begottenness is natural to the unbegotten God, and that, deprived of his natural former state of being begotten, he afterwards became unbegotten? **567**. These things are devices of rhetoric, when they are proved wrong, to evade the disgrace of being proved wrong by bringing forward other persons. Just such is his defence of that *Defence* of his, attributing the reason for his title[219] to judges and accusers, but able to point to no accusers, no seat of judgment, no court. Now too, as if he were correcting the stupidity of others, he says he has "come to the necessity of speaking like this." **568**. This is his

[219] Eunomius is quoted to this effect in *CE* I 65 (GNO I 44,15–45,1).

proof of our "incurable absurdity and affected and culpable piety." "But," he says, we are "at a loss as to how to deal with the situation, and try to hide our perplexity by attacking him for his worldly philosophy, and claiming personal communication with the Holy Spirit." **569**. This is another illusion, to suppose that he possesses so much secular philosophy as to frighten Basil because of it. That is the way some people often imagine they are enthroned among kings and enjoy the supreme dignity, the deceitful visions seen in dreams inducing this illusion as a result of their waking desire. **570**. Basil, he says, not being able to deal with the written text, attacks Eunomius for his worldly philosophy. Mind you, he would have taken such a charge seriously, that he was thought to have alarmed some of his readers through the surfeit of words, not to mention Basil or any of those like [393] him (if there is or ever has been any one quite like him).

571.–580. *Words, ideas, and the transcendence of God*

571. The argument in between – if indeed it is an argument, his servile abuse and the tasteless jibes with which he thinks he can run down our own argument – all that I leave out, regarding it as offensive and disgusting to contaminate our book with so many blemishes, like those who are disgusted by swollen, stinking boils, and scarce can bear the sight of those who from plethoric thickening of the bodily humours have their appearance altered by warts and pimples. His opinion I shall briefly set out, while avoiding the great stench made by his words. The argument will in the first instance be freely presented by me, with no falling back into insolent distortion of what is said. **572**. Every word, or every word properly so called, is a sound which denotes some movement of thought; and every activity and motion of the healthy mind aims, so far as it is able, at the knowledge and consideration of existent things. The nature of existents is twofold, being divided into what is intelligible and what is sensible. The knowledge of things apparent to sensation, however, because they are readily observable, is available commonly to all, since identification by the senses engenders no ambiguity about the object. **573**. Differences of colours and of the other qualities which we identify by hearing, smell, or the sense of touch or taste, all of us who share the same nature recognize them and name them with one voice, as we do also those remaining ones which seem to have a more superficial relevance to the affairs which occupy our life, those which deal with the political and moral sphere of life. **574**. On the other hand, in contemplating intelligible nature, because it transcends sense-perception, as the mind [394] reaches out speculatively towards things which elude sensation, we behave in various ways about the object of our quest, and in accordance with the impression made on the mind of each of us about the subject, we express our understanding as best we can, approximating as nearly as possible to the meaning of our thoughts through the connotation of the words. **575**. In these matters it is often possible to succeed in one's goal on both counts, the mind not missing the mark and the voice directly expressing the thought through the correct interpretation. But it can also happen that one is wrong on both counts, or on one or other of them, with either the apprehending mind or the interpretative faculty missing the mark.

576. There are thus two ways in which every word is made correct, the certainty of the idea and the verbal expression, and it would be best to pass the examination on both counts; but it is none the less good not to be mistaken about the correct understanding, even if the word falls short of the idea. Therefore when the mind is exercised upon high and invisible subjects, which the senses cannot reach – and I am speaking about the divine and ineffable Nature, on which it is rash to seize on anything hastily with the mind, and still rasher to commit the interpretation of the idea engendered in us to casual words –, then we dismiss the sound of words, which is expressed in this way or that, according to the meaning of the sounds uttered, and we take into account only the idea expressed in the words, in accordance with its soundness or otherwise, leaving these details of verbal and linguistic questions to the scholarship of grammarians. **577**. Since then we denote through the application of names only things that are known, and it is not possible to deal with things beyond knowledge by calling them by names – for how could anyone denote the unknowable? –, no suitable appellations being available for these which [395] might adequately represent the subject, we are obliged to reveal the idea of the Deity engendered in us by many and various titles, in whatever way we can.

578. However, the things which come into our comprehension are surely such that the realities either are observed within measurable time, or produce the notion of extension in space, in which each particular is apprehended, or else come within our purview as delimited by beginning and end, being limited at either end by non-being; for every thing that has beginning and end of existence begins from non-being and ends in non-being. Or else, we understand the end of all things by combining physical characteristics as what appears when destruction and passion and change and transformation and such things are compounded together. **579**. For this reason, so that the transcendent Nature may not appear to have anything in common with lowly things, we use of the divine Nature words and ideas which negate such things, calling what is beyond the origin of the ages 'preeternal', what is beyond origination 'unbegun', what does not end 'endless', and what exists without body 'incorporeal', what is not destroyed 'indestructible', and what is not liable to change, passion or variation 'impassible', 'changeless', and 'invariable'. **580**. Those who wish may make what linguistic analysis they please of such words, and may add other words to these, calling them 'privative' or 'negative' words or what they please; for our part let us leave such things to those anxious to teach or learn, and let us apply ourselves solely to the sense, whether it falls within a devout understanding worthy of God, or outside it.

581.–587. *Titles of God based on his activities*

581. If then God once was not, or at some time will not be, he would not properly be called either unending or unbegun. Similarly he would not be immutable, incorporeal or [396] indestructible, if there were any suspicion about him of material body, destructibility, change or anything like that. If however it is reverent to attribute none of these to him, then it would surely be religiously correct to use of him words which separate from incongruities, and to say those things which we have mentioned many times already, that he is indestructible, endless, unbegotten and so forth, the meaning inherent in each of these titles informing us only of his separation from the things immediately observed, not explaining the actual nature which is separated from the incongruities.

582. What the Divinity is not, the connotation of all these titles first makes plain, while what that is by nature, which is not those things, remains obscure. The rest of the terms too, the connotation of which indicates something positive and real, give an indication not of the actual divine Nature, but of what can in true reverence be thought about it. **583**. When we perceive that no existing thing, whether visible or intelligible, is constituted by self-generation and chance, but that everything which is understood as existing depends upon the Nature which transcends the whole universe, and has its cause of existence in that source, and when we observe the beauty and greatness of the wonders in creation, from all these things and their like we get other ideas about the Divinity, and explain each of the ideas generated in us by particular words, following the counsel of Wisdom, who says that we should "from the greatness and beauty of the creatures contemplate by analogy the Originator of all".[220] **584**. We call 'Designer' the Maker of all, and 'Mighty' the one who controls so great a creation, whose might sufficed to bring what he willed into being. Considering the good in our life [397] we are logical in naming the source of that life with the designation 'Good', and having learnt from the divine scripture the impartiality of the coming judgment, we thereby name him 'Judge' and 'Righteous'. To sum up briefly, the ideas which arise in us about the divine Nature we carry over into the form of names, such that no epithet is used of the divine Nature without some specific idea. **585**. Even the word 'God' (θεός) we understand to have become prevalent because of the activity of oversight. Because we believe that the Divinity (θεῖον) is present to all things and watches (θεᾶσθαι) all things and penetrates all things, we indicate such an idea with this title,[221] led in this direction by the word of scripture. The one who says, "My God, look at me,"[222] and, "See, O God,"[223] and "God knows the secrets of the heart,"[224] is plainly interpreting the sense inherent in this title, that God (θεός) is so called from his watching (θεᾶσθαι). **586**. It makes no difference whether you say, "Look," or "See," or "Watch". Therefore, because he who watches (θεώμενος) sees what is watched (τὸ θεατόν), he who watches is rightly called the 'God' (θεός) of what is seen. So again, having by this means learnt some partial activity

[220] *Wis* 13,5.
[221] This false etymology of θεός already appears in Irenaeus and Clement, according to *PGL*, *s.v.*
[222] *Ps* 21,2 LXX (rather than 54/55,3 indicated by Jaeger).
[223] *Ps* 83/84,10(9); this phrase is not frequent in scripture, as Jaeger suggests.
[224] *Ps* 43,22/44,21.

of the divine Nature, we have not by this word come to hold in mind the divine Being itself. Yet we do not, because we are at a loss for the proper word, reckon that the Divinity forfeits any of his glory. **587**. The inability to express unutterable things, while convicting us of the poverty of our nature, has more power to demonstrate the glory of God, when it teaches us, as the Apostle says, that to believe him to be above every name is the only fitting way to name God.[225] That he transcends every effort of thought, and is found to be beyond the reach of naming, stands as a testimony to mankind of his ineffable majesty.

588.–595. *Eunomius' claim that privative titles demean God*

[398] **588**. As far as the titles applied to God are concerned and the mode in which they are expressed, these are the principles we recognize. We have presented them to the more kindly of our hearers in a form lacking elaboration and simple, having judged it both indecent and improper for us ourselves to oppose vigorously the feeble attacks of Eunomius about these subjects. What is one to say to one who claims that we "make the form of names superior to the dignity of those named, bestowing on the names precedence over the realities, and equality on things unequal"? **589**. This is quoted in his own words. Let him who is qualified to judge decide whether there is anything near the mark, for which a defence would be merited, in the vehement allegation of the slanderer that we "bestow on the names precedence over the realities", when it is obvious to all that no name has of itself a substantial existence, but that every name is a sign and indicator of some substantial being and idea, by itself existing neither in being nor in thought. **590**. How it is possible to bestow gifts on what does not exist, let him tell the disciples of his fraud, since he claims to use nouns and verbs properly! I would not have mentioned these matters at all, if it had not been necessary through them to provide a demonstration of the weakness of our wordsmith on the subject of meaning and verbal expression.

As to what he drags in, incompatible with inspired scripture and not to the point, artificially arguing a difference in immortality between angels and men, I do not know what his purpose is or what he is

[225] *Phil* 2,9.

trying to prove by this, so I shall leave that out also. What is immortal, *qua* immortal, admits no comparison of more or less.[226] **591**. For if in comparison one member of the pair falls short where immortality is concerned, inevitably [399] that one will not be called immortal at all: how could something be correctly termed 'immortal' if comparison with another proved it mortal? I also pass over his subtle suggestion, "that one should not bid the idea of privation to be indifferent or neutral, but should call privation the removal of what is good, and that one ought not to denote distance from evil things by this word" – as if, should these views prevail, the word of the Apostle about him were no longer true, when it says that he alone possesses immortality and gives it to others.[227] **592**. What the statement now introduced by him has to do with the preceding argument, is impossible either for us or for any other intelligent person to understand, and because we cannot penetrate these clever subtleties he calls us "unskilled both in discernment of realities and conferment of verbalities".[228] These are his actual written words. **593**. All such things are powerless against the truth, and I pass them by without detailed consideration.

So too with his attacks on the interpretation we have proposed of 'indestructible' and 'incorporeal', that these two epithets denote in the one case that he is non-dimensional, whereby the three-fold measurement of physical bodies does not apply, and in the other immunity to destruction. So too with his statement, in these terms, "We do not approve of the form of names diverting to unsuitable ideas", and his supposition that these two terms refer, not to not being or not belonging, but to the actual being, these too we deem to deserve silence and deep oblivion, and I shall leave it to readers to detect for themselves [400] the combination of wickedness with nonsense. He claims that the destructible is not the opposite of indestructible, and that privative denotation does not denote removal of evil, but that being itself is denoted by the subject. **594**. If it is

[226] Jaeger compares Aristotle, *Categories* 3b33, "It seems that being does not admit of more or less."

[227] *1 Tim* 6,16.

[228] This is a clumsy attempt to represent a play on words, which Gregory perhaps remarks on in the next few words. Eunomius writes more literally, ". . . discernment of realities and usage of words" (τῶν πραγμάτων κρίσεως καὶ τῶν ὀνομάτων χρήσεως).

reckoned by the one who puts these empty arguments together that the term 'indestructible' does not rule out destruction, it must surely follow that such a form of title indicates the opposite. If indestructibility is not freedom from destruction, there is surely the simultaneous assertion of what is negated, for it is the nature of opposites that when one is negated the statement of its contrary replaces it.

595. That other acute argument we also dismiss, that God is by nature immune to death, as though there were any one who held the contrary opinion on the subject. Our view is that where opposites are concerned it makes no difference whether you say that the one is, or that the other is not: so in the present discussion, when we say that God is Life, it means that by this confession we refuse to envisage his death, though that may not be expressly said; and when we confess him immune to death, by its very wording our statement implies that he is Life.

596.–604. *Negative terms make divine attributes distinct*

596. "But I do not see," he says, "how on the basis of what is missing God could transcend his own creatures;" and on the basis of this shrewd argument he calls great Basil "silly, and wicked with it", because he is brave enough to use such words. I would advise him not to be too generous in using insults against those who say these things, or he may find himself insulting himself too with the same words unawares. For perhaps he would not himself deny that the majesty of the divine Nature is made known in the fact that it has nothing in common with those things in which the lower nature is shown to participate. **597**. If he possessed any of these, he would not be superior, but would surely be the same as everything that participates in the characteristic. If [401] however he is above these things, it is exactly by not having these qualities that he excels those who have them, just as we say the sinless is superior to those with sins. Separation from evil is proof of being rich in the best things.

Let the offensive person live according to his nature, but for ourselves, having briefly noted what is said in this part, we shall apply the argument to our present task. **598**. He says that "he likewise surpasses mortal things as immortal, destructible things as indestructible, and begotten things as unbegotten." Is the logic of impiety in God's enemy obvious to all, or must we expose it by what we say? Who does not know that things which are surpassed in equal measure must be equal to each other? If then the destructible and the begotten are likewise surpassed by God, and the Lord is begotten, let Eunomius draw the impious conclusion which emerges from his statement. **599**. It is clear that he considers being begotten is the same as destruction and death, just as in his earlier words he declared the unbegotten to be the same as the indestructible. If then he sees destruction and being begotten as equal, and says that God is likewise distant from both, and if the Lord is begotten, no one should demand that we add what follows from the logic, but let him work out the conclusion by himself, if equally and in the same degree the divine Nature is distant from the begotten and the destructible.

"But it is impossible," he says, "to call him indestructible and immortal by the absence of death and destruction." **600**. Let those who are dragged by the nose be convinced by the words, and those who are led about as each pleases, and let them say that destruction and death are present in God so that he may be called immortal and indestructible. For if it is not the absence of death and destruction, as [402] Eunomius says, that the titles negating these things indicate, then surely it is their antitheses and opposites that are argued by this refined logic. **601**. Each one of the ideas, surely, is either absent or not absent, as with light and darkness, life and death, health and sickness, and so on. In these cases, if the one idea were said to be absent, the presence of the other would certainly be implied. So if he says that it is not by absence of death that God is called immortal, he would appear to be clearly arguing that death is present with him, and thereby denying the immortality of the God of the universe. **602**. For how could one still be truly immortal and indestructible, of whom he says that destruction and death are not absent from him? But perhaps someone will say that we are seizing too malignantly on the argument, for no one would be so mad as to argue that God is not immortal. No person however knows what goes on secretly in anyone's mind, and our guess as to what lies hidden is derived from what is actually said. **603**. Let us therefore repeat the statement: "It is not by absence of death," he says, "that God is called immortal." How are we to take this claim, that death is not absent from God, though he be called immortal? If therefore he bids us think this, then surely Eunomius' god is mortal and subject to destruction. Where death is not absent from someone, it is not his nature to be immortal. Yet if the terms do not connote the absence of either death or destruction, they are either applied pointlessly to the God over all, or they contain within them some other sense. **604**. What that might be, is for our subtle logician to explain. We, however, who are, as Eunomius says, "unskilled both in discernment of realities and conferment of verbalities",[229] have learnt to call 'undiseased' not the one who is free from power, but the one who is free from disease, and 'unmaimed' not the one removed from [403] drinking parties, but the one who has no maiming injury in him; and we use names for everything in the same way, manly and unmanly, sleepy and sleepless, and whenever this practice applies.

605.–610. *If immortality is being, that applies also to the Son*

605. What benefit there is, however, in allowing the serious study of this nonsense, I do not know. For a man of grey-haired age who looks to the truth it is no small cause for blame if he allows himself to utter with his mouth the ridiculous and frivolous words of his adversary's contentiousness. I shall therefore pass over those remarks, and those which follow immediately upon them, which are these: "Neither does the truth attest anything," he says, "co-natured with God . . . ."[230] **606**. (If he had not said this, who would have said that God is double-natured, except you who say that every named attribute is co-natured with the essential being of the Father, and nothing attaches to him from without, but you embed every divine title in the being of God?) He goes on, ". . . nor indeed enshrining in the laws of true religion such an attribute from without and formed by us." I again crave pardon for the words: it is not to make a joke that I have set these ridiculous words before my readers, but so as to persuade my audience what sort of verbal equipment he starts from, this man who besmirches our simplemindedness and then launches himself against the truth. **607**. What he is as a writer, and what sort of things he utters as he plumes himself and parades before insensitive hearers, who acclaim him ill-composedly advancing through these bombastic rhetorical aridities, as though he had conquered all by the power of his words.[231]

---

[229] Repeated from *CE* II 592 (GNO I 399,14–16), where see note.

[230] This is an incomplete sentence. Even when *CE* II 606 (GNO I 403,17–19) is added, it remains a genitive absolute without a main clause.

[231] Gregory appears to be ironically imitating the verbosity he criticizes.

But, he says, the being itself is immortality. I would say to him, "What then do you say about the being of the Only-begotten? Immortality or not? For in this case too, 'Simplicity,' as you put it, [404] 'admits no co-naturing'." **608**. If he denies that the being of the Son is immortality, then his purpose is obvious. The opposite of 'immortal' does not need a subtle intellect to understand it. Just as the logic of dichotomy proves what is nor indestructible to be destructible, and what is not immutable to be mutable, so surely what is not immortal is mortal. What then will our exponent of new doctrines decide about the being of the Only-begotten? **609**. Again I will put the same question to our wordsmith. Will he grant that this too is immortality, or will he not agree? If he will not accept that the being of the Son is immortality, he will be obliged to concede the opposite, proving that by the negation of the positive it is actually death. **610**. If on the other hand he avoids the absurdity by giving the name 'immortality' also to the being of the Only-begotten, he must because of this necessarily concede that there is no difference in essential being. For if the nature of the Father and that of the Son is equally immortality, and immortality is by no conceivable difference divided against itself, then even our adversaries themselves confess that no conceivable difference is to be found between the being of the Father and that of the Son.

XV. *Eunomius' final fraud, and Gregory's response (611–627)*

611.–624. *Is the Father from non-being? A misrepresentation exposed*

611. Now it is time to describe the grave charge, which he makes at the end of his work, alleging that we say that "the Father is from total non-being." Stealing an expression from its context, and dragging it stripped and disconnected from the remaining body of text, he tries to bite into it, tearing at it with his ineffectual teeth, or rather slobbering over the book. I will first state the meaning of the careful judgments made on the subject by the Master, then I will set out the argument itself word for word, so that the one who introduces damaging corruptions into the works of the truly religious may be exposed for all to see. **612**. Introducing us to the [405] connotation of 'unbegotten' in his own words, our Master suggested an approach to understanding the problem by showing that the connotation of 'unbegotten' is different from the meaning of 'being'. When, he says, the evangelist began his genealogy of our Lord with Joseph, and then went back always to the earlier person and made Adam the end of the genealogy,[232] and because it was not possible for a physical father to precede the first-formed, called him son of God, it is obvious for every one to accept with the mind, he says, this point about God: God, whose son is Adam, does not himself have his existence from another in the same way as those listed in the human genealogy. **613**. When, having gone through them all, we accept God into our thought after all the rest, we are thinking of the beginning of all. Every beginning, if it depends upon something else, is not the beginning. Therefore, if God is the beginning of all, there can be nothing whatever preceding the beginning of all things. This is the Master's account of the meaning of 'unbegotten'.

To show that nothing untrue has been attributed to him by us, I will quote *verbatim* his statement on the subject: **614**. "The Evangelist Luke," he says, "in giving his account of the fleshly genealogy of our God and Saviour Jesus Christ, and working his way backwards from the last to the first, began with Joseph, saying that he was the son of Eli, and he of Mattath, and thus going backwards he traced his account as far as Adam; coming to the earliest, and saying that Seth was from Adam and Adam from God, there he stopped going backwards. In the same way as the Evangelist said that Adam is from God, we are to ask ourselves, 'From whom is God?' **615**. Is it not obvious [406] to the understanding of all that he is from no one? Clearly, what is from no one is unbegun, and what is unbegun is the unbegotten. Just as in the case of men it is not their essential being to be from someone, so also in the case of the God of the universe one may not say that to be unbegotten is his essential being."[233] With what eyes now do you look to your captain? – I address you, the flock of those who are perishing. Why do you still give ear to one who has by his words put up such a monument to his own villainy? Are you not ashamed, at least now if not before, to use such a guide to the truth? **616**. Will you not take this as a sign of his lunacy about doctrines, when he so shamelessly goes

[232] *Lk* 3,23–37.
[233] Jaeger cites this passage as Basilius, *Adversus Eunomium* I 15 (PG 29, 545b–548a).

against the truth of what is actually written? Is this how he also interprets to you the words of Scripture? Is this how he champions the truth of his doctrines, in order to convict Basil of tracing the genealogy of the God over all from total non-being?

617. Am I to utter what he has said? Am I to quote his shameless words? I pass over the insults, I complain not at the vituperation; I do not blame one with bad breath because he stinks, nor the one with a crippled body because he is crippled. Such things are natural misfortunes which are not liable to blame by reasonable people. The urge to insult is a weakness of mind, a misfortune of the soul with its healthy intelligence crippled. I have no discussion of his vituperation. But that vehement and irresistible web of syllogism, with which he brings his allegation against us to his own conclusion, that I will write down expressly, word for word: **618**. "So that he may not be prevented," he says, "from saying that the Son derives from participation in him who is, he has inadvertently said that the God over all is from total non-being. For if 'nothing' is the same [407] in meaning as total non-being, and the substitution of synonyms is unavoidable, one who says that God is from no one is saying that God is from total non-being."

Which of these words shall we consider first? That he thinks the Son derives from participation in God,[234] and spreads the foul smell from his mouth on those who do not accept this? Or shall we recount in full the feeble illusion of his sophistic syllogism? That the thought of sons belonging to the divine being by participation comes from poets and myth-makers, is something everyone knows who has even the slightest good sense. **619**. So it is that those who string together myths in verse depict people such as Dionysus, Heracles, Minos and others like them from the bonding of spirits with human bodies, and elevate such people above the rest of men by reason of the superiority which comes from participation in the higher nature. This word

[234] This formula, that the Son is "from μετουσία of" the being of God, is misleadingly attributed to Basil by Eunomius. μετουσία is a word for the participation of particular instances in universal ideas. It is used by the Fathers of the participation of believers in the life of God, but generally rejected as too weak and subordinate a relation of the Son to the Father, which is regarded as essential: the one being of God is possessed by the Son as well as the Father, and he is not just one instance of some higher idea of godhead. Gregory's critique here is typical. See *PGL*, *s.v.* μετουσία.

therefore should be passed over in silence, as originally a proof of folly and impiety, and we should rather put forward that irresistible syllogism, so that the simple-minded among us may learn what is lost by those not trained in logical method.

620. "For if 'nothing'," he says, "is the same in meaning as total non-being, and the substitution of synonyms is unavoidable, one who says that God is from no one is saying that God is from total non-being." Who agreed with the one threatening us with the Aristotelian spear,[235] that to say someone has no father is the same as saying that he has come to exist from total non-being? Any one who counts those listed by the scripture in the genealogy one by one can obviously see always a father preceding the person mentioned. **621**. What was Eli of Joseph? What was Mattath of Eli? What was Adam of Seth? [408] Is it not quite clear even to the most naive that the list of these names that are mentioned is a catalogue of fathers? If Seth is Adam's son, then surely Adam is the father of the one begotten by him. So tell me, who then is the father of the God over all? Answer the question, say something, give a reply, put all your logical skill into operation to deal with this enquiry. Can you find an explanation which escapes the grip of your syllogism? **622**. Who is the father of the Unbegotten? Can you say who? Is he after all not unbegotten? If pressed, you will surely say, what indeed absolutely must be said, 'No one'. Why then, my friend, is that soggy web of your syllogism not yet invalidated? Do you realize you have dribbled all over your own chest? What did great Basil say? – that the Unbegotten is from no father, for from the fathers listed in the genealogy the sequence permits the addition of 'father' to be understood unexpressed. **623**. You turned 'from no father' into 'nothing', and again by changing 'nothing' into 'total non-being' you reached the conclusion of that invalid syllogism. These ingenuities of your logical precision will therefore be turned against you. Who is the father of the Unbegotten, I ask? No one, you will be obliged to say. The Unbegotten certainly has no father. **624**. If then no one is father of the Unbegotten, and 'nothing' is substituted for 'no one' by you, and 'nothing' on your account is the same in meaning as

[235] A jocular reference to Aristotle's logical prowess.

'total non-being', and the substitution of synonyms is unavoidable, as you claim, then the one who says that no one is the father of the Unbegotten is saying that the God over all is from total non-being.

625.–627. *Conclusion: Eunomius himself exposed by Basil and Gregory*

625. "Such an evil it is" apparently, Eunomius – I shall quote your own words – not, [409] "to honour seeming above being wise," for that is perhaps a minor misfortune, but to be ignorant of yourself and not to know how great is the difference between the height-seeking Basil and the earth-bound beast. **626**. If that sharp, divine eye were to survey our life, if it were to traverse human history on the wing of wisdom, it would swoop down on you and show with his sweep of words what a pot full of folly you have turned into, and who it is against whom you have raised yourself up with lying deceit, using insults and abuse against him in your efforts to look important to old crones and *castrati*. **627**. Nevertheless, you should not stop expecting his talons. Compared with him, our work may be judged a small part of a big claw, but against you it is so big that it will be enough to tear apart your shell of deceit and reveal the muck hidden inside the jar.

PART III

COMMENTARY

GREGORS ZUSAMMENFASSUNG DER EUNOMIANISCHEN POSITION IM VERGLEICH ZUM ANSATZ DES EUNOMIUS (*CE* II 1–66)

Thomas Böhm

I. *Einleitung*

Die Kirche ist umgeben von den Belagerungsmaschinen der Häresie, so dass die Notwendigkeit besteht, in den Kampf einzugreifen.[1] In der Eingangspassage zum zweiten Buch seiner Schrift gegen Eunomius wendet sich Gregor von Nyssa aus seiner Perspektive einer der Hauptthesen des Eunomius zu, wonach die Ungezeugtheit oder Agennesie (ἀγεννησία) mit der οὐσία bzw. dem Sein Gottes gleichgesetzt ist, wie dies Eunomius in seiner Apologie entfaltet hatte.[2] Dabei geht Gregor so vor, dass er in einem Proömium den Leser auf die Bedeutung des Sachverhaltes hinweisen will, indem er – wie dies Basilius in *Adversus Eunomium* I 1–2 entsprechend ausgeführt hatte[3] – dem Leser vor Augen hält, dass Eunomius von der wahren Gottesverehrung abweicht[4] und sich als Feind der Wahrheit, worunter meist der Teufel verstanden wird, in Gegensatz zur Überlieferung der Kirche setzt. Damit wird Gregor der rhetorischen Aufgabe des *attentum parare* gerecht. Die Aufmerksamkeit des Lesers erreicht Gregor auch dadurch, dass die Kirche durch die Häresie des Eunomius bedroht ist wie in einem Kampf durch die Belagerung.[5] Wohlwollend gestimmt werden die Leser dadurch, dass Eunomius in der Gestalt des Goliath auftritt, der sich als kopflos erweist[6] und der mit *1 Kor* 11,3 das Haupt, nämlich Christus, bereits verloren hat,[7] während

[1] Vgl. *CE* II 8 (GNO I 228,12–24).
[2] Vgl. Eunomius, *Apologia* 7–8 (Vaggione 40–42).
[3] Vgl. Basilius von Caesarea, *Adversus Eunomium* I 1–2 (SC 299, 140–156); zu *Adversus Eunomium* des Basilius bereite ich eine eigene *editio maior* vor, die bei GCS erscheinen wird, sowie eine deutsche Übersetzung bei BGL.
[4] Vgl. *CE* II 3 (GNO I 226,18–21).
[5] Vgl. *CE* II 8 (GNO I 228,12–24).
[6] Vgl. *CE* II 5–6 (GNO I 227,13–228,5).
[7] Vgl. *CE* II 6 (GNO I 227,27–228,5).

Gregor den Kampf gegen den übermächtigen Goliath (nämlich Eunomius) wie David aufnimmt[8] in der Hoffnung auf die göttliche Macht, die sich gnädig zuwendet.[9] Mit diesem ersten Anlauf hat es Gregor entsprechend der proömialen Topoi erreicht, die Aufmerksamkeit und das Wohlwollen der Leser hervorzurufen. Das *docilem parare* gelingt Gregor dadurch, dass er darauf verweist, sein Bruder Basilius habe sich bereits damit auseinandergesetzt, wie der Begriff des Ungezeugtseins zu verwenden sei, worauf aber Eunomius nicht weiter eingegangen sei.[10]

Die folgenden Ausführungen behandeln zunächst die Grundthese des Eunomius, um von hier aus die Reaktion Gregors darzustellen.

II. *Die Position des Eunomius*

Eunomius zufolge gibt es entsprechend der allgemeinen Überzeugung und der Lehre der Väter nur einen Gott, der weder durch sich selbst noch durch einen anderen geworden ist. Wenn er also weder früher als er selbst noch etwas anderes früher sein kann, so folge daraus das 'unerzeugt' (ἀγέννητος) oder besser: er ist unerzeugte οὐσία, ein Begriff, der weder der menschlichen Erfindung entspringt noch als Privation verstehbar ist. Dies bedeutet für Eunomius, dass das Sein Gottes notwendig als unerzeugt bestimmt werden muss. Weil demgegenüber der Einziggeborene gezeugt ist und diese Bestimmung seine οὐσία betrifft, besteht zwischen dem Unerzeugten und dem Erzeugten keine Gemeinsamkeit; folglich sind sie seins- oder wesensmäßig different.[11]

Diese Bestimmung Gottes ergibt sich für Eunomius zunächst aus dem Argument, dass das Erste (Gott) nicht früher oder später als es selbst sein kann und dass nichts anderes das Erste vor dem Ersten sein könne.[12] Mit der Frage nach dem Vorher- oder Später-Sein

[8] Vgl. *CE* II 5 (GNO I 227,22–26).

[9] Vgl. *CE* II 9 (GNO I 229,2–9).

[10] Vgl. *CE* II 10–11 (GNO I 229,18–230,14).

[11] Vgl. Eunomius, *Apologia* 7–8 (Vaggione 40–42); zum Ansatz des Eunomius vgl. z.B. Th. Böhm, *Theoria Unendlichkeit Aufstieg. Philosophische Implikationen zu* De vita Moysis *von Gregor von Nyssa*, Leiden – New York – Köln 1996, 108–122 (dort weitere Lit.); R. M. Hübner, "Zur Genese der trinitarischen Formel bei Basilius von Caesarea", in: M. Weitlauff – P. Neuner (Hrsg.), *Für euch Bischof, mit euch Christ. FS für Friedrich Kardinal Wetter zum siebzigsten Geburtstag*, St. Ottilien 1998, 150f.

[12] Vgl. Eunomius, *Apologia* 7 (Vaggione 40).

Gottes in seiner Einheit greift Eunomius auf eine Diskussion zurück, die sich aus der ersten Hypothesis des platonischen *Parmenides* ergibt, nämlich die Frage, ob das Eine gleichaltrig mit sich selbst, jünger und/oder älter als es selbst und das andere als es selbst sein könne, und zwar unter dem Gesichtspunkt der ersten Hypothesis des platonischen *Parmenides*: "wenn Eines ist".[13] Nähme man an, dass das Eine das gleiche Alter wie es selbst oder wie anderes hätte, müsste es auch an der Zeit hinsichtlich der Gleichheit oder Ähnlichkeit teilhaben, Prädikate, die nach Platon aber *nicht* auf das Eine zutreffen.[14] Im Sinne Platons würde dies implizieren, dass das Eine an der Zeit teilhaben müsste. Daraus ergäbe sich jedoch, dass aufgrund der Teilhabe dem Einen etwas hinzukäme, woran es teilhat, so dass das Eine *qua* Eines nicht mehr es selbst wäre, sondern zusammengesetzt, also nicht mehr Eines als Eines an und für sich selbst.[15]

Diese Ausführungen Platons (*Parm.* 140e) wurden in den antiken Kommentaren prinzipientheoretisch gedeutet. Speziell für die Frage nach dem Älter- und Jüngersein bzw. dem Gleichaltrig-Sein berichtet Proklos von Ansichten der Neuplatoniker, die das 'Älter' und 'Jünger' als eine Folgeordnung deuteten.[16] Nach deren Interpretation, allen voran derjenigen des Jamblich, sei 'älter' die einfachere und allgemeinere Bestimmung, wodurch ein ontologischer Status ausgedrückt werde.[17] Zudem behauptet Aristoteles, Platon habe die Begriffe 'früher' und 'später' in dem Sinne verstanden, dass etwas, das früher ist, ohne anderes existieren könne.[18] Das Allgemeinere und in der gedanklichen Ableitung Ursprünglichere kann somit einerseits als das ontologisch Vorgeordnete gedacht werden, dieses Ursprüngliche aber zugleich nicht-reziprok bestimmt werden, weil das Vorgeordnete ohne das ihm Folgende sein kann. Einheit bzw. das Eine kann folglich als von der Vielheit unabhängig und zugleich als Grund der Vielheit gedacht, somit hinsichtlich einer verursachenden und begründenden

---

[13] Platon, *Parm.* 137c und 140e.

[14] Platon, *Parm.* 139e–140b.

[15] Diese Ausführungen sind hier modifiziert entnommen aus Th. Böhm, *Theoria*, 110f.

[16] Vgl. Proklos, *In Parm.* (Cousin 1216,37–1217,13).

[17] Vgl. B. Dalsgaard Larsen, *Jamblique de Chalcis. Exégète et philosophe*, Aarhus 1972, 423–428; E. Sonderegger, *Simplikios: Über die Zeit. Ein Kommentar zum Corollarium de tempore*, Göttingen 1982, 124; zu Proklos vgl. W. Beierwaltes, *Proklos: Grundzüge seiner Metaphysik*, Frankfurt [2]1979, 227–229.

[18] Vgl. Aristoteles, *Met.* 1019a2–4; ferner Alexander von Aphrodisias, *In Met.* (CAG I 55,22–23); Plotin, *Enn.* V 5 [32] 4,13–16.

Priorität verstanden werden. Weil das Eine (Gott) weder früher noch später als es selbst ist, ist es selbst *vor* allem und dementsprechend auch nicht durch etwas anderes erzeugt.[19] In diesem Sinne kann es Grund von allem sein, folglich – im Kontext der eunomianischen Theologie – auch die Ursache des Sohnes, sofern dieser einzigerzeugt ist.[20]

In einem weiteren Schritt muss Eunomius aufweisen, wie der Begriff ἀγέννητος im Hinblick auf die οὐσία verstanden werden kann, d.h. wie die Form der Negation zu deuten ist, wenn ausgeschlossen ist, dass die Aussagen epinoetisch zu deuten sind, also u.a. von der menschlichen Aussprache unabhängig sein sollen. Dabei wehrt sich Eunomius dagegen, diese Negation im Sinne einer Privation zu verstehen. Denn Privationen sind nur dann Privationen, wenn eine zugrundeliegende Natur als positive Bestimmung angenommen wird, auf die hin die Abwesenheit dieser Bestimmung ausgesagt wird; in diesem Fall ist die Privation eine sekundäre Aussage.[21] Dies hieße: Wäre der Begriff ἀγέννητος privativ zu verstehen, müsste auch angenommen werden, dass Gott zunächst eine γένεσις zukäme, so dass er erst unerzeugt geworden wäre. Daraus ergibt sich, dass dem Begriff ἀγέννητος zwar sprachlich ein negativer Charakter zukommt, der aber nicht pejorativ gedacht sein soll.[22] Ein solches Verständnis verweist auf den Diskussionszusammenhang von 'Negation' und 'Privation', wie sich dies etwa bei Alexander von Aphrodisias zeigt: "Die Privation unterscheidet sich nämlich von der Negation (. . .), dass die Negation für das Seiende und Nichtseiende prädiziert wird, die Privation aber für eine zugrundeliegende Natur."[23] Eine Privation wird von etwas prädiziert, was prinzipiell die von Natur aus vorhandene Möglichkeit zu einer Leistung besitzt, die im Falle der Privation aktuell nicht vorhanden ist, wie etwa bei der Blindheit oder Taubheit. Eunomius könnte demnach den Begriff ἀγέννητος so verstehen, dass er ihn im Sinne einer Negation gebraucht, die selbst keine Privation impliziert.

---

[19] Zu diesen Ausführungen vgl. grundlegend J. Halfwassen, *Der Aufstieg zum Einen. Untersuchungen zu Platon und Plotin*, Stuttgart 1991, 374–376.

[20] Vgl. dazu Th. Böhm, *Theoria*, 112f.

[21] Vgl. Eunomius, *Apologia* 8 (Vaggione 40–42).

[22] Dazu Th. Böhm, *Theoria*, 114.

[23] Alexander von Aphrodisias, *In Met.* (CAG I 327,22–24); vgl. auch Proklos, *Theol. Plat.* II 5 (Saffrey-Westerink 37–39); dazu R. Mortley, *From Word to Silence I: The Rise and Fall of Logos*, Bonn 1986, 137–139.

Eunomius kann also den Begriff ἀγέννητος als strikte Negation im Sinne des Ausschlusses von Endlichem aus dem Unendlichen (d.h. Gott) ausweisen und dies in einem weiteren Schritt auf die οὐσία Gottes anwenden.[24]

Dies stellt jedoch ein Problem dar, das sich im Anschluss an Plotin ergibt und bei Dexipp diskutiert wird.[25] Denn Plotin betont, dass man von der οὐσία sagen könne: οὐκ ἔστιν.[26] Man könne – so Seleukos, der Gesprächspartner des Dexipp – also nur behaupten, was die οὐσία nicht ist, aber das gebe keine Information darüber, was die οὐσία sei. Dexipp hebt in seiner Antwort hervor, dass man in diesem Falle keine strikte Definition liefere, sondern eine Beschreibung (ὑπογραφή). Aber auch im Falle von Definitionen verwende man Negationen, so z.B., wenn man das Indifferente zwischen gut und schlecht bestimmen wolle. In diesem Fall sage man, es sei weder gut noch schlecht. So könne man in positivem Sinne für die οὐσία die Negation verwenden, um die οὐσία im eigentlichsten Sinn (κυριωτάτη) anzuzeigen. Es sei folglich möglich, die Affirmation durch die Negation (ἀπόφασις) zu erkennen.[27] Diese Weiterführung durch Dexipp kann also zeigen, dass die Negation in neuplatonischen Gedankengängen nicht nur von der Privation getrennt wurde, sondern die Negation auf die Affirmation verweisen kann, wie im Falle der οὐσία. In diesem Sinne kann Eunomius m.E. auch betonen, dass man bei Gott von der unerzeugten οὐσία sprechen könne, die sich von derjenigen des Sohnes wesentlich unterscheidet.[28]

Daraus ergibt sich, dass im Hinblick auf Gott das 'unerzeugt' im Zusammenhang mit Gottes Einheit als Bestimmung der οὐσία prädiziert wird, so dass – wie Eunomius am Ende von *Apol.* 8 betont – das 'unerzeugt' auch nicht auf einen Teil Gottes angewandt werden, nicht in ihm als Getrenntes existieren und auch nicht als von ihm different gedacht werden könne.[29] Damit ist die οὐσία dahingehend 'bestimmt', dass sie eins, unzusammengesetzt und unerzeugt ist. Auffällig ist an der Argumentation des Eunomius, dass er Gott (nicht den Vater) in diesem Kontext als die Ursache, die selbst nicht verursacht

[24] Vgl. Th. Böhm, *Theoria*, 115–117.
[25] Vgl. Dexipp, *In Cat.* (CAG IV/2 44).
[26] Plotin, *Enn.* VI 1 [42] 2,15.
[27] Vgl. Dexipp, *In Cat.* (CAG IV/2 44).
[28] So Th. Böhm, *Theoria*, 117 mit leichten Modifikationen.
[29] Vgl. Eunomius, *Apologia* 8 (Vaggione 42).

ist, versteht, die aufgrund ihrer Einheit nicht zusammengesetzt und nicht erzeugt sein kann. Diese 'Bestimmungen' betreffen das Sein (die οὐσία) Gottes, sind also als wesenhafte Prädikationen aufzufassen, die trotz ihrer Negation auf die Position verweisen. Dabei spricht Eunomius in der *Apologie* jedoch nicht davon, dass die οὐσία Gottes die Unerzeugtheit (ἀγεννησία) sei.

III. *Die Argumentation des Gregor von Nyssa*

Um die Position des Eunomius zu widerlegen, geht Gregor von Nyssa zunächst auf den Zusammenhang von ἀγεννησία und οὐσία ein.[30] Dabei wählt Gregor einen Weg, der ganz pointiert *nicht* mit der gegnerischen Argumentation einsetzt, sondern auf der biblischen Grundlage Aussagen über den einzigerzeugten Gott (den Sohn) anführt: Er sei Wahrheit, wahres Licht, Kraft Gottes und Leben.[31] Damit greift Gregor bereits seine Sicht der ἐπίνοια-Lehre auf, dass nämlich die unterschiedlichen Begriffsbestimmungen nicht die οὐσία betreffen, um damit die eunomianische Position, wie Gregor sie versteht, eines *flatus vocis* außer Kraft zu setzen.[32] Dem dient auch das zusätzliche Argument Gregors, das seiner Erkenntnis- und Sprachtheorie entstammt, dass die menschlichen Möglichkeiten einer konzeptuellen Bildung das Sein selbst (die οὐσία) nicht erreichen,[33] weil einerseits entsprechend der stoischen Sprachtheorie die semantische Repräsentation (Laut und Bedeutung) vom im Zeichen repräsentierten Objekt unterschieden sind[34] und weil andererseits diskursives Denken und Sprache durch Abständigkeit (διάστημα, διάστασις) charakteriert sind und stets Etwas, nämlich etwas Bestimmtes im Verhältnis zum Anderen, benennen und so die in sich nicht differenzierte οὐσία (Gottes) nicht gedacht und ausgesagt werden kann.[35] Man erreicht also ein Wissen, *dass* etwas ist, nicht *was* es ist hinsichtlich der οὐσία,[36] ein Thema, das

[30] Vgl. *CE* II 12–22 (GNO I 230,15–233,10).

[31] Vgl. *CE* II 12 (GNO I 230,19–21).

[32] Zur Position des Eunomius vgl. Th. Böhm, *Theoria*, 176–178; zur Problematik des *flatus vocis* vgl. ebd., bes. 177; zu Gregor ebd., 187–198, jeweils mit den entsprechenden Nachweisen.

[33] Vgl. *CE* II 12 (GNO I 230,22–26).

[34] Vgl. Th. Böhm, *Theoria*, 189–190 mit Nachweisen.

[35] Vgl. Th. Böhm, *Theoria*, 193–197 mit den entsprechenden Hinweisen sowie den neuplatonischen Konnotationen dieser Theorie.

[36] Vgl. *CE* II 13 (GNO I 230,26–30).

seit Philo von Alexandrien breit erörtert ist – u.a. auch bei Basilius in *Adversus Eunomium* –, das aber bereits in der zweiten Analytik des Aristoteles vorbereitet ist.[37]

Immer wieder kontrastiert Gregor in dieser Eingangspassage die Lehre der Schrift und den orthodoxen Glauben mit der Position des Eunomius: Während nach der Schrift dem Vater und dem Sohn die gleiche Ehre zukommen,[38] weicht Eunomius davon durch die Konzeption der Ungezeugtheit (ἀγεννησία) ab.[39] Dies spitzt Gregor dann auch in *CE* II 18–19 dahingehend zu: Die Wahrheit lehre, dass der *Vater* nicht von einer höheren Ursache stamme; die Eunomianer nennen dies Ungezeugtheit. Dem Einziggezeugten komme das Gezeugtsein zu; beides stehe im Widerspruch. Dies bedeute eine Differenz im Sein (οὐσία), so dass die eine οὐσία gezeugt, die andere ungezeugt sei.[40]

Mit dieser Zusammenfassung der eunomianischen Lehre, nämlich dass die ἀγεννησία die οὐσία sei und sich daraus eine Differenz der Natur von Vater und Sohn ergebe,[41] ist die Grundlage der weiteren Diskussion geschaffen. Gegenüber der Position des Eunomius ist jedoch ein Wandel eingetreten: Dieser hatte nämlich als Ausgangspunkt *Gott* gewählt, sofern er *einer* ist. Für Eunomius ist die Prädikationsstruktur von Gott und Vater different. Die Aussage 'Vater' – außer bei Schriftzitaten wie *Joh* 14,28 (der Vater ist größer als der Sohn) – setzt er beim willentlichen und energetischen Hervorgang des Sohnes an.[42] Ferner hatte Eunomius in der ersten Apologie den Begriff ἀγέννητος, nicht den Abstraktbegriff ἀγεννησία eingeführt, um einerseits die Ursprungslosigkeit Gottes zu betonen, andererseits – wie sich dies aus dem zuvor erwähnten philosophischen Diskussionszusammenhang nahelegt – damit die Nicht-Reziprozität für Gott aussagen zu können. Aufgrund der *Einheit* kann Gott die unverursachte Ursache sein, so dass die nähere Bestimmung durch eine Prädikation (nämlich das Adjektiv ἀγέννητος) keinerlei Differenz in Gott impliziert.

[37] Vgl. Philo von Alexandrien, *De mutatione nominum* 11–38 (Wendland III 158–163); Basilius, *Adversus Eunomium* I 14 (SC 299, 224); Aristoteles, *Anal. Post.* 71a11–17; dazu Th. Böhm, *Theoria*, 135, Anm. 73 mit weiteren Belegen.

[38] Vgl. *CE* II 16–17 (GNO I 231,27–232,1).

[39] Vgl. *CE* II 15–17 (GNO I 231,8–232,1).

[40] Vgl. *CE* II 18–19 (GNO I 232,1–19).

[41] Vgl. *CE* II 21 (GNO I 232,26–233,1).

[42] Vgl. Eunomius, *Apologia* 12,11–12 (Vaggione 48); dazu besonders K.-H. Uthemann, "Die Sprache der Theologie nach Eunomius von Cyzicus", *ZKG* 104 (1993) 143–175, hier 151f.

Somit muss eine *notwendige* Koextensivität bestehen, die in dem *einen* Gott keinen Unterschied setzt. Erst aufgrund der Tatsache, dass Gregor wie zuvor schon Basilius z.B. in *Adversus Eunomium* I 5 die ἀγεννησία aus dem Begriff ἀγέννητος ableitet und diese wiederum mit der οὐσία gleichsetzt (als interpretative Darstellung der Position des Eunomius),[43] werden die folgenden Überlegungen Gregors auch nachvollziehbar.

Denn Gregor wiederholt in *CE* II 23 genau noch einmal die eunomianische Position in dieser Form, indem er betont, dass *sie*, d.h. die Eunomianer, folgendes lehren: Gott wird ungezeugt genannt; das Göttliche ist seiner Natur nach einfach; was einfach ist, ist unzusammengesetzt. Folglich ist Gott der *Natur* nach unzusammengesetzt und ungezeugt, beides gehört zu seiner Natur, die selbst die *Ungezeugtheit* ist.[44] Werner Jaeger gibt diese Passage zwar als Zitat aus der zweiten Apologie des Eunomius aus.[45] Da Gregor allerdings offensichtlich eine zusammenfassende Pointierung der eunomianischen Position liefern will, dieser Abschnitt auch durch die Pluralform ("sie sagen . . .") eingeleitet wird und die folgenden Passagen lediglich Paraphrasen sind, scheint es besonders aufgrund der sonstigen Ausführungen des Eunomius plausibler zu sein, hier eher von einem zugespitzten Referat der gegnerischen Meinung auszugehen als von einem Zitat.[46] Dementsprechend wäre es auch nicht zwingend, dass Eunomius das Sein Gottes als Ungezeugtheit bezeichnet hätte, was dann auch mit den Ausführungen der ersten Apologie kompatibel wäre.

Im Gegensatz dazu überdecken sich aber für Gregor diese Prädikate nicht, weil das Unzusammengesetzte auf die Einheit bezogen ist, der Begriff ἀγέννητος jedoch auf das Unverursachtsein. Obwohl beides von einem Subjekt ausgesagt wird, werden *unterschiedliche* (epinoetische) Bestimmungen vorgenommen. Daraus ergibt sich für Gregor – gerade weil diese Differenz in der Bezogenheit der Bestimmung besteht –, dass aus dem Begriff der *Einheit* gerade die *Ungezeugtheit* nicht abgeleitet werden kann.[47]

---

[43] Vgl. Basilius, *Adversus Eunomium* I 5,132 (SC 299, 180).

[44] Vgl. *CE* II 23 (GNO I 233,11–17).

[45] Vgl. den Kursivdruck in *CE* II 23 (GNO I 233,11–17).

[46] Vorsichtig in dieser Richtung auch R. P. Vaggione, *Eunomius. The Extant Works*, Oxford 1987, 105, Anm. 3.

[47] Vgl. *CE* II 24–25 (GNO I 233,17–234,3).

Aus der Ineinssetzung von Einheit und Ungezeugtheit versucht Gregor das Argument *ad absurdum* zu führen: sollten 'einfach' und 'ungezeugt' ein und dasselbe meinen und folglich ungezeugt auch nicht bedeuten, ohne Ursache zu sein, sondern dass Gott deshalb ungezeugt genannt wird, weil er einfach und unzusammengesetzt ist, müsste daraus folgen: Weil der Sohn einfach ist – was Eunomius zugestehe[48] – müsste der Sohn aufgrund der Einheit Ungezeugtheit sein. Oder sie müssten sonst seine Gottheit leugnen. Dieses Argument ergibt sich daraus: Wenn die Gottheit notwendig bestimmt ist durch die Einheit, die Einheit jedoch Ungezeugtheit bedeuten soll, dann müsste der Einziggezeugte (d.h. der Sohn), weil er gezeugt ist, nicht eines sein und folglich zusammengesetzt. Ist er jedoch zusammengesetzt, ist er nicht Gott, weil Gott notwendig einer ist.[49]

Nach einem Zwischenargument, auf das hier nicht eingegangen werden soll,[50] fasst Gregor seine eigene Sicht zusammen: Das Sein des Vaters ist einfach und nicht Einfachheit, seine οὐσία ist ungezeugt und nicht Ungezeugtheit. Gleiches gelte für den Sohn hinsichtlich der Begriffe 'einfach' und 'gezeugt'.[51] Genau dies würde sich jedoch mit dem *Ansatz* des Eunomius decken, nicht aber mit den Konsequenzen, die daraus gezogen werden.

Eunomius hatte aus der Bestimmung εἷς im Zusammenhang mit dem ὕστερον -πρότερον-Argument abgeleitet, dass Gott auch ἀγέννητος ist – das sieht Gregor zurecht. Eunomius hatte dies auf die οὐσία bezogen und betont, Gott müsse als ἀγέννητος οὐσία bestimmt werden, d.h. οὐσία und 'ungezeugt' korrelieren notwendig miteinander – auch das sieht Gregor zurecht. Aber Eunomius hatte daraus *nicht* gefolgert, dass dann die οὐσία auch ἀγεννησία sei. Das ist die *conclusio* Gregors. Die Differenz ergibt sich m.E. u.a. aus der unterschiedlichen Einschätzung der ἐπίνοια: Eunomius wollte offensichtlich verhindern, dass Prädikationen beim Transzendenten von der menschlichen Sprachleistung abhängen, während Gregor den inventiven Charakter der Sprache betont, dann aber eine klare Differenz von absolutem Bereich und Sprache setzen muss, die ihren Ausdruck in der *Unerkennbarkeit* und *Unsagbarkeit* der οὐσία an und für sich selbst findet.

---

48 Vgl. *CE* II 26 (GNO I 234,3–4).
49 Vgl. *CE* II 26–27 (GNO I 234,3–18).
50 Vgl. *CE* II 28–29 (GNO I 234,19–235,8).
51 Vgl. *CE* II 30 (GNO I 235,8–18).

Aus demselben Grundduktus heraus, dass aus der Einheit die Unerzeugtheit abgeleitet wird, müsste laut Gregor auch angenommen werden, dass der *Vater*, weil er Schöpfer ist, in seiner οὐσία ferner so bestimmt wird, dass er Schöpfung ist.[52] Resümierend ergibt sich für Gregor, dass der Begriff ἀγέννητος nicht auf die οὐσία bezogen werden kann, sondern lediglich die Differenz zwischen 'ungezeugt' und 'gezeugt', also von Vater und Sohn anzeigt.

Dasselbe lässt sich im folgenden Abschnitt zeigen (*CE* II 35–41):[53] Nach Eunomius bezeichnet der Begriff ἀγέννητος die οὐσία, folglich werde für Gregor auch nicht der Existenzmodus ausgesagt, wonach der Begriff 'ungezeugt' besage, dass eine frühere Ursache ausgeschlossen sei. Denn – so Gregor – die ἀγεννησία *sei* die οὐσία.[54] Darum gebe es keine Möglichkeit, diesen Sachverhalt auszudrücken,[55] wenn die Ungezeugtheit *nicht* die Abwesenheit einer hervorbringenden Ursache meint, sondern das Sein selbst. Folglich bezeichne 'ungezeugt' gar nicht mehr 'ungezeugt', sondern dass Vater und Sohn dasselbe sind, wenn die Differenz von 'gezeugt' und 'ungezeugt' entfällt.[56] Daraus folge, dass ἀγέννητος nicht die οὐσία bezeichne.

Eunomius hatte jedoch argumentativ genau zu zeigen versucht, dass aus der Einheit die Ursachelosigkeit folge, somit Gott als unerzeugt zu betrachten sei. Lediglich aus der Aussage, Gott sei ungezeugte οὐσία, um eine Differenz in Gott zu vermeiden, lässt sich der Schluss Gregors für die eunomianische Theologie nicht ziehen, somit auch nicht der Sabellianismusvorwurf.[57]

Aus der von ihm zugespitzten eunomianischen Position zieht Gregor – aus seiner Sicht zurecht – den Schluss, dass Vater und Sohn nicht denselben Rang haben, wenn angenommen wird, dass die οὐσία oder Natur des Vaters in der Ungezeugtheit besteht, die des Sohnes jedoch in der Gezeugtheit.[58] Dies ergibt sich aus der

---

[52] Vgl. *CE* II 31–33 (GNO I 235,18–236,14).
[53] Vgl. *CE* II 35–41 (GNO I 236,21–238,8).
[54] Vgl. *CE* II 35 (GNO I 236,21–25).
[55] Vgl. *CE* II 36 (GNO I 236,25–237,4).
[56] Vgl. *CE* II 37–39 (GNO I 237,4–27).
[57] Vgl. *CE* II 37–39 (GNO I 237,4–27). Zur ἐπίνοια (*CE* II 42–50, GNO I 238,12–240,20) vgl. die Beiträge von Theo Kobusch und Basil Studer in diesem Band. Auf eine Analyse sei hier verzichtet, zumal dieses Thema an dieser Stelle von Gregor nicht umfassend erörtert wird. Die Passage zeigt jedoch, dass gerade die Frage der ἐπίνοια offensichtlich für Gregor zentral ist.
[58] Vgl. *CE* II 52 (GNO I 241,3–13).

Restriktion des Lebens des Sohnes, weil dieser in seiner Gezeugtheit einen Anfang hat und nicht ewig ist wie der Vater[59] und der Titel Geschöpf zudem den des Sohnes ersetzt.[60] Demnach ergibt sich eine Unterordnung des Sohnes/Geschöpfes unter Gott.[61] Folglich könne er auch nicht verehrt werden,[62] was jedoch der Schrift widerspreche.[63] Wenn Ungezeugtheit die wahre Gottheit ausdrücke und diese dem Sohn nicht zukomme, können andere Eigentümlichkeiten Gottes auch nicht vom Sohn ausgesagt werden, wenn diese nicht dem gehören, der nicht Ungezeugtheit ist.[64] Dies ist aufgrund der Annahme des Eunomius, dass οὐσία und ἀγέννητος korrelieren, durchaus schlüssig. Es zeigt sich, dass Eunomius gerade hier zum Stachel im Fleisch wurde, nämlich bei der Rolle des Sohnes hinsichtlich der Gottesverehrung. Die Lösung durch Basilius und Gregor bestand jedoch nicht nur in ihrer auch unterschiedlichen ἐπίνοια-Lehre mit dem origenistischen und biblischen Hintergrund[65] und den philosophischen Konnotationen,[66] mit der Erkenntnis- und Sprachrestriktion im Hinblick auf die göttliche οὐσία, sondern die eunomianische Position war auch der Anlass für die Dissoziierung von οὐσία und der Weise der Realisierung (τρόπος τῆς ὑπάρξεως bzw. ὑποστάσεως), die sich bei Basilius und den pseudo-basilianischen Büchern *Adversus Eunomium* IV–V zeigt, Texte, die – selbst wenn dies umstritten ist – von Apolinarius stammen könnten.[67] Ein Textvergleich zwischen Basilius, *Adversus Eunomium* I–II und Pseudo-Basilius, *Adversus Eunomium* IV–V zeigt m.E., dass die pseudo-basilianischen Bücher IV–V *vor Adversus Eunomium* I–II geschrieben sind.[68] Eine nochmalige Überprüfung der Chronologie hat in diesem Zusammenhang ergeben, dass die *Apologie* des Eunomius vermutlich erst Ende 360 vorgetragen und Mitte 361 publiziert wurde, dass also die ursprüngliche Diskussion in den Jahren 361 bis 364

[59] Vgl. *CE* II 52 (GNO I 241,11–13).
[60] Vgl. *CE* II 53 (GNO I 241,17–19).
[61] Vgl. *CE* II 54 (GNO I 241,19–24); dazu auch *CE* II 57 (GNO I 242,14–24).
[62] Vgl. *CE* II 59 (GNO I 243,4–13).
[63] Vgl. *CE* II 50–51 (GNO I 240,10–241,3).
[64] Vgl. *CE* II 63 (GNO I 244,10–18).
[65] Vgl. dazu den Beitrag von B. Studer.
[66] Dazu die Ausführungen von Th. Kobusch in diesem Band.
[67] Vgl. R. M. Hübner, "Zur Genese", 148f. 153.
[68] Vgl. Th. Böhm, *Basilius von Caesarea, Adversus Eunomium I–III*. Edition, Übersetzung, Textgeschichte, Chronologie (Habilitationsschrift), München 2003, 52–76; ferner Th. Böhm, "Basil of Caesarea, *Adversus Eunomium* I–III, and Ps. Basil, *Adversus Eunomium* IV–V", *StPatr* 37 (2001) 20–26.

stattfand.[69] Meines Erachtens gab Eunomius den Anstoß für zahlreiche theologische, aber auch philosophische Reaktionen, die – wie der Fall Gregors zeigt – zu Formulierungen geführt haben, die dem Anliegen des Eunomius nicht immer gerecht werden.

[69] Vgl. Th. Böhm, *Basilius*, 7–96.

DIVINE INFINITY AND ESCHATOLOGY: THE LIMITS AND DYNAMICS OF HUMAN KNOWLEDGE, ACCORDING TO GREGORY OF NYSSA (*CE* II 67–170)

Morwenna Ludlow

I. *Introduction*

In paragraphs 67–170 of the second book of Gregory of Nyssa's treatise against Eunomius, one finds several theological themes, philosophical ideas and literary images which are typical of Gregory's writing. Indeed, one might almost argue that this extract encapsulates some of his most central ideas. In it Gregory states that we cannot fully know God. He justifies this by arguing that finite human reason cannot comprehend the infinite God; this argument is reinforced by analogies which emphasise how difficult it is to know things even within the created realm (even our own selves). Gregory uses Abraham as an example of a man who exemplifies the correct attitude to God – that is, faith, rather than knowledge – and he emphasises that one should not stray beyond the bounds of Scripture. This is both a warning to his readers and an attack on his Arian opponents, whom he accuses of being thoroughly unscriptural in their theology. Gregory then develops his arguments about knowledge in a specifically linguistic direction, which brings him to the main preoccupations of the *CE* II as a whole: Eunomius' definition of God as ἀγέννητος, the proper character of theological language and the role of ἐπίνοια.

This paper will not focus on these last three themes, which are treated expertly and in detail by other contributions to this volume. Rather, I wish to examine Gregory's ideas about human knowledge of God by focussing on his use of imagery – in particular, the symbol of the ladder which occurs briefly in the middle of Gregory's interpretation of the Abraham story. By looking at some of the forbears of this image, and by examining how ladder imagery functions both in this extract and in some other of Gregory's works, I wish to demonstrate how Gregory has developed a very sophisticated literary technique, which combines and alludes to symbols from several different sources, whilst weaving them together into an original literary creation. However, I want to argue further that this is not just a literary technique, but is also a theological method. That is, although the *origins* of the image of the ladder may lie both in the Old Testament and in Plato, the key to Gregory's *interpretation* and *use* of the image lies in the New Testament. He takes his method from the writer of *Hebrews* who takes Abraham's journey to the promised land to mean a journey to "the city . . . whose architect and builder is God".[1] Thus, Gregory takes on images from both Hebrew and Greek thinkers and sees them as anticipating a meaning which is only fully realised in Christ.

To a certain extent, of course, this is merely to re-examine Gregory's use of allegorical interpretation. As he says in *CE* II 85, we should "follow the great mind of the Apostle . . . and take the meaning of the story [of Abraham] allegorically". Many scholars have already examined how Gregory chooses images and stories from the Old Testament and reads them in the light of the New Testament, and there have been debates over to what extent Gregory depends on, or goes beyond, or differs from Origen in this respect. However, this paper will attempt to move the discussion of allegory and images beyond a discussion of Gregory's biblical hermeneutics into a discussion of how he reads other, secular, texts.

Again, much work has been done on Gregory's philosophical influences; most, however, has concentrated on asking which *ideas* or *arguments* Gregory takes from his classical forbears, rather than on seeking out also the *symbols* or *images* which he borrows from them. Whilst it is undoubtedly true that Gregory is influenced by the arguments of Greek philosophy, his work also draws on images (especially visual ones), in an extremely imaginative way. It is precisely because Gregory sometimes leans on the imagery and symbolism of, for example, Plato, and not always on Plato's arguments or ideas, that the exact nature of Gregory's influence by Plato is so hard to pin down.

In this way, then, I am hoping to bring together two areas of discussion in studies of Gregory that are so often held apart: that is, the allegorical interpretation of the Old Testament and the influence of Greek philosophy. It is through the mingling of images from both

[1] *Heb* 11,10.

Hebrew and Greek cultures in the creative womb of Gregory's Christian mind that we come to what one might call a "rebirth of images".[2] My point is that the reborn image does not merely echo or mirror previous uses of the same image; rather it is something new and one should attend carefully to the changes the author has made in its use. This paper will also emphasise the fact that Gregory's 'literary' reappropriation of images occurs even in texts like the *CE* which have tended to be studied from a more philosophical angle.

Thus, besides attempting to demonstrate Gregory's method in action, this paper will also propose that an understanding of this method can help our understanding of his text. As a consequence of this analysis, it will also suggest a development in Gregory's use of one particular image – a development which may perhaps parallel a more profound theological development. First, however, the next part of this paper will discuss the structure and context of *CE* II 67–170, in order to set the scene for the analysis of the image of the ladder.

II. *Context and structure*

In both his first and his second books against Eunomius, Gregory's arguments alternate between discussion of the wider theological issues and discussion of Eunomius' precise terminology – particularly, of course, his use of the words ἀγέννητος and ἐπίνοια. From a theological point-of-view, this enables Gregory to use his attack on Eunomius to make some wide-ranging theological claims, whilst always returning to the very words of Eunomius' text. In doing so, Gregory tacitly claims for himself a scholarly precision which contrasts with the false precision which Eunomius himself asserts.[3] Furthermore, in claiming that Eunomius reduces all the divine attributes to one (i.e. ἀγέννητος), as Gregory does in *CE* II 62, for example, Gregory is not only making a theological point, but is also making a rhetorical move, contrasting Eunomius' allegedly mealy-mouthed approach to talking about God, with Gregory's own more expansive, imaginative

[2] To borrow an expression from Austin Farrer: see his *Rebirth of Images: the Making of St. John's Apocalypse*, Westminster 1949.

[3] Gregory attacks this precision in e.g. *CE* II 61 and 84.

approach.[4] In other parts of the text, however, this perspective is shifted: Eunomius is the one with too broad an outlook; he is the one who wanders beyond the straight and narrow range of description justified by Scripture, while Gregory sticks within the limits of the language of the biblical canon.[5] Eunomius' language is all over the place: and the result of this indiscipline is a false confidence in the ability of his purportedly precise language to define God. On the other hand, Gregory paradoxically asserts both that his own language is *limited* by Scripture, but draws attention to what he sees as the *limitless* nature of Scriptural language.[6]

This switch in focus from the large scale to the small and back again, can be somewhat bewildering for the reader, and means that Gregory's arguments are not constructed with the sort of rigour one would demand of a modern philosopher. But it would be foolish to claim that there is no reason behind Gregory's method. Whatever one may feel at times about the success of either Gregory's arguments or his rhetorical strategy, one can certainly be confident in asserting that this is a highly-crafted work by an author who is extremely self-conscious of his art. Whenever Gregory criticises his opponents for their artifice and over-rhetorical approach, one cannot help feeling that he is being disingenuous. Although the structure of the *CE* is loose, in the sense that there is no systematic building-up of a cumulative argument, it can be argued that the work as a whole does have other, less obvious, structures, one of which is the use of a shifting focus as a conscious literary or rhetorical strategy.

The work is perhaps more obviously structured within each of its parts. (These are indicated by Roman numerals in Prof. Hall's translation.) Usually Gregory will begin with an idea from Eunomius, often quoted in his opponent's own words. Sometimes (particularly in the latter half of *CE* II) this will be followed by an opposing quotation from Basil. Gregory will then proceed to refute Eunomius' claim, with a mixture of logical argument, analogy, illustration, and *reductio ad absurdum*. Frequently, a passage will conclude with an insult directed at his opponent, which will recall the original idea which

---

[4] See also *CE* II 125 (all quotations from *CE* II are from the translation by S. G. Hall): "[our opponents] measure the infinite nature with a single title, squeezing the being of God into 'unbegottenness'"; cf. *CE* II 82.472ff.

[5] E.g. *CE* II 96–105.

[6] *CE* II 101.

began the section. This is sometimes coupled with a warning to his audience not to repeat the same errors. Within each passage there is much repetition for emphasis and sometimes a slightly more formal circular form of composition in which Gregory successively returns to various themes and ideas with which he started.

In the section under consideration by this paper (*CE* II 67–170), Gregory is countering the accusation that is found in the preceding part:

> Whereas all men of sense reckon it is impossible for the ineffable nature to be expressed in the meaning of any words, and our knowledge cannot extend so far as to reach things transcending knowledge, and our competence with words has not been endowed with such power as to describe what is being thought of when something utterly sublime and divine comes to mind, then these sophisticates condemn the rest for stupidity and ignorance in the science of logic, and claim that they themselves know these things and are able to impart that knowledge to whomsoever they please.[7]

Consequently, Gregory begins the next part with his claim against Eunomius: "human nature has not the capacity in it to understand precisely the being of God" (*CE* II 67). He then goes on to explain the reason for this: the gap between the infinite creator and the finite creation. The explanation proceeds in various ways: first, with an analogy from the respective natures of earthbound animals, birds, humans and angels (*CE* II 68–69); next with a philosophical argument from the nature of finite and infinite (*CE* II 69–70); and then with a further illustration from the natural world, this time focussing on astronomical phenomena (*CE* II 71–78). These last paragraphs result in the conclusion that only the maker, God, can know the mysteries of the heavens, and that (quoting *Heb* 11,3), it is "by faith [that] we perceive that the worlds were made by the word of God". Next follows the analogy of children who think they can catch a sun-beam (*CE* II 79–81), which functions both as a warning to his audience not to think that they can know God, and as a useful way to draw attention to the childishness of his opponents (a common tactic in the *CE*).[8] The image of light, which frequently symbolises

[7] *CE* II 61.

[8] See, e.g. *CE* I 675 (tr. Hall 133): "Now I broach these ridiculously childish suggestions as to children sitting in the market-place and playing; for when one looks into the grovelling earthliness of their heretical teaching it is impossible to

revelation in both Christian and pagan writings, is used in such a way as to emphasise that the light descends to or is given to those on earth. The Arians' error is then summarised as going beyond or misusing the text of Scripture and as restricting God by applying to him terms which cannot hope properly to describe him (*CE* II 82–83).

Thus, in these sections, Gregory proceeds by alternating plain statement and argument with imaginative illustration. Moreover, his illustrations themselves echo one another (moving 'upwards' from the birds of the air to astronomical phenomena in the heavens themselves and then returning just as the beams of the sun descend to earth). Finally, he uses a quotation from Hebrews about faith which not only anticipates his use of Hebrews, and in particular the notion of faith, to interpret Abraham's journey, but also demonstrates his own loyalty to Scripture in contrast to the attitude of his opponents.

In the next few sections (*CE* II 84–89) Gregory brings in the example of Abraham. The illustration is introduced by an explanation of the cause of Gregory's opponents' error: they have separated knowledge from faith. By contrast, Gregory refers to *Hebrews* 11 and argues that if one takes the story of Abraham allegorically as a journey towards God, it is clear that Abraham knew God so far as is humanly possible, but then transcended this by faith, which brought him to the realisation that God was above all human knowledge. Within the Abraham example is embedded the further illustration of the ladder, which will be analysed further in a moment. Gregory concludes his use of the Abraham story and *Hebrews* 11, by stressing that it was faith, not knowledge which was credited to Abraham as righteousness.

This leads us to a passage in which the faith/knowledge contrast is further elaborated, again with reference to *Hebrews* 11 (*CE* II 90–94). Finally, in *CE* II 95–96 Gregory brings several of his themes together: he recapitulates the idea of the gap between creator and created, but expressing it in terms of 'heaven and earth' which recalls his earlier heavenly analogies. He repeats the content of the statement with which he started in *CE* II 67 – that human nature cannot understand God – but subtly recasts it in the light of his discussion

help falling into a sort of sportive childishness"; and *CE* II 469: "They are simply children's games, building castles in the sand."

of faith (πίστις), as a statement which we are instructed not to *know*, but to *believe* (πιστεύειν).[9]

In the next few sections (*CE* II 97–105) Gregory further elaborates the idea that one should keep human knowledge within limits by adding to it the idea that speculation leads to error (*CE* II 97). He sets off against each other the positive example of Scripture and the negative example of Eunomius and his supporters, and it is here that Gregory elaborates the paradoxes which separate him from these opponents. They "have wandered off into their manifold and varied ideas about God"; yet their error is that they "want to bring the divinity within a prescribed limit".[10] Contrasted with this double fault of undisciplined plenitude and overly-rigorous exactitude is Scripture (and, by implication, Gregory's own method):

> Perhaps they should have looked to the choir of the saints, – the prophets, I mean, and the patriarchs, in whose time the Word of truth spoke "in diverse parts and in diverse ways" . . . – they should have respected the reliability of those attested by the Spirit himself, and should have stayed *within the limitations* of those writers' learning and knowledge.[11]

This comment is typical of Gregory's hermeneutics which sees Scripture both as having immense (perhaps infinite) depth and as limiting excessive readings.[12] In paragraphs 104–105 the general principle of the unity and diversity of Scripture is applied specifically to the names of God (they apply to the one God, but their multiplicity is explained in terms of the fact that they apply not to his being but to his attributes). These two paragraphs thus anticipate the more linguistic focus of *CE* II 125–170.

In *CE* II 106–124 Gregory argues that humans are ignorant not only about God, but also of the created world – even of themselves. This proposition is examined from the point-of-view of knowledge of body and soul, and Gregory's obvious display of erudition (recounting different theories about the passions and about the nature of

---

[9] *CE* II 96: "It is safer and more reverent to believe [πιστεύειν] that the divine majesty is more than can be thought of . . . [οἴεσθαι]."

[10] *CE* II 99–100.

[11] *CE* II 101 (my emphasis).

[12] For a more thorough treatment of this, see M. Ludlow, "Origen and Gregory of Nyssa on the Unity and Diversity of Scripture", *International Journal of Systematic Theology* 4, 1 (2002) 63ff.

body and soul) echoes his similar display in *CE* II 71ff. The passages are also clearly linked by their common theme – how can one know the infinite God if one does not know the finite world?[13] – yet their message is subtly different. Whereas one might expect not to be able to understand the wonders of the heavens, one might at least expect to be able to know oneself – indeed, famously, many Greek philosophers commanded it. In a clever move, then, Gregory brings together a large section of the *CE* II (paragraphs 67–124), framing them with these two discussions of our knowledge of the created world, the second not so much repeating the first as being its mirror-image, the focus on the earthly individual contrasting with the earlier focus on the distant heavens.

In paragraphs 125–170 the themes of *CE* II 67–124 are repeated with a specific linguistic focus. The error of Eunomius is stated in *CE* II 82 and 100 as falsely claiming to *know* that God is 'unbegottenness' (ἀγεννησία). In *CE* II 125 this error is expressed in more linguistic terms: Eunomius' false claim is about the *title* 'unbegotten' (αγέννητος). Gregory repeats the idea that reasoning is not completely inappropriate in respect of God[14] – it gives a "faint and slight apprehension (ἀντίληψις) of the divine nature" – but adds to this the claim that such 'knowledge' (γνῶσις) of God as humans have comes through the *names* used of him (*CE* II 130). Similarly, the claim that the goal of human reasoning is to understand "that what it seeks is beyond all knowledge" (*CE* II 139) echoes the claim made earlier about Abraham (*CE* II 89), but is supplemented by a comment about which *names* are therefore appropriate and which are inappropriate to apply to God (*CE* II 140). Eunomius' error is then satirised using the symbolism of noise – in contrast with the light/sunbeam metaphor used for the same purpose earlier on (*CE* II 141). Corrections of Eunomius' errors are then set out clearly: negative words applied to God say what he is not (not what he is); words for God refer to his actions (not his being); by allowing a plethora of words to be applied to God the Cappadocians are not seeking to glorify him, but to guide the reader/speaker to what is hidden (*CE* II 142–158). The treatise then moves to the more technical discussion of ἐπίνοια.

[13] Compare, for example, *CE* II 69–70 and *CE* II 122–124.
[14] Cf. *CE* II 89.98.100.

Throughout *CE* II 67–170, there is evidence of Gregory's careful composition. The studied return to various ideas, their recapitulation and elaboration may owe something to Gregory's rhetorical training – not in the sense that he is here producing a formal speech rigidly structured according to the principles of the Second Sophistic, but in the more general sense that Gregory has learnt how to speak well: how to emphasise his main themes with constant repetition, how to recapture drifting attention with vivid analogies, familiar images and the occasional bout of vituperative insult. Like a jazz pianist improvising, Gregory wanders: sometimes he appears to have lost the plot, but he always returns to the same key. This does not always make for an argument which is systematically presented and easy to follow: it is more impressionistic than systematic, more poetic than scientific.[15] One may question its effectiveness, but one should have sympathy for the effects Gregory was *trying* to achieve, even if one finds the style ultimately rather unsatisfying or confusing.

However, it is the first two parts of *CE* II 67–170 – that is the statement and explanation of the claim that we cannot know God, and its illustration by the character of Abraham – that are the primary focus of this paper. These illustrate the way in which Gregory's composition can sometimes be extraordinarily detailed, with its circling back to certain themes (faith and *Hebrews* 11) and ranges of imagery (analogies concerning the heavens). This technique highlights several key themes: first, the idea of the 'gap' between God/heaven and earth; secondly, the importance of *Hebrews* 11, and thirdly the ambiguity of human knowledge and language. All of these will play a part in my interpretation of Gregory's ladder image, to which the next part of this paper now turns.

III. *The ladder*

> Having by the use of reason transcended the wisdom of his nation – I mean the Chaldean philosophy – which reaches only visible things, and rising above those known to sense, from the beauty of things observed and the harmony of the heavenly wonders he yearned to see the original model of beauty. In the same manner, all the rest of what he grasped as his reasoning advanced, – whether power or goodness,

[15] Remember that Gregory criticises Eunomius' pseudo-scientific rigour.

> or existence without beginning, or being bounded by no end, or whatever similar idea we may have for the divine nature, – *using all these as means and staircase for his upward journey, always stepping upon what he had discovered and reaching out to what lay ahead, 'setting up in his heart', as the prophet says, the beautiful 'rising stairs', and rising above all that his own power could grasp,* as being less than what he sought, when he had surpassed every verbal description of his nature which might be applied to God, having cleansed his mind of such notions, he resorted to faith, pure and unadulterated by any ratiocination, and he took as his indicator, infallible and manifest, of the knowledge of God just this, – that he believed God to be greater and higher than any epistemological indicator.[16]

The image of the ladder, or steps, or staircase, does not occupy much space in Gregory's interpretation of the Abraham story. However, it is one important focal point for his argument about divine infinity and the pursuit of God. Particularly as it is elaborated in Gregory's later works, the ladder becomes an eschatological as well as an epistemological image. But this paper will argue that the seeds of this use of ladder imagery are apparent, even in this passage from *CE*, particularly if one pays attention to its immediate context and the themes highlighted above.

Firstly, Gregory seems to be alluding not just to any staircase, but specifically to Jacob's ladder. This is, admittedly, an implicit reference which Gregory does not make explicit, but elsewhere in his works (as will be shown below) he connects talk of staircases and steps specifically with Jacob's ladder. Furthermore, the stories of Abraham and Jacob have much that connect them: Jacob's vision of the staircase took place at Bethel; Bethel was the first place Abram is said to have pitched his tent after having left Ur.[17] Both patriarchs were on a journey from home; both have a vision of or from God; both receive a promise from God about their offspring and land. The fact that Abraham is moving on from the Chaldean study of heavenly wonders, not only recalls the astronomical illustrations earlier on, but perhaps reminds us that Jacob's ladder reached between the earth and the true heavens.

Indeed, it is perhaps not too far-fetched to suggest that Gregory has in a sense collapsed the stories of all three patriarchs into that of Abraham. This may have been encouraged by the recollection of

---

[16] *CE* II 89 (my emphasis).
[17] *Gen* 28,19; *Gen* 12,8.

Hebrews 11, which is constantly running through Gregory's mind here, and which closely binds the three patriarchs together. According to *Hebrews*, Isaac and Jacob "were heirs with [Abraham] of the same promise", that is the promise of the city of God (*Heb* 11,9). Furthermore, all died without having received the physical land they were promised, which indicates to the author that their real desire for "a better country, that is a heavenly one" (*Heb* 11,13–16). Furthermore, there are signs that Gregory has melded together the signification of Abraham, Isaac and Jacob in Alexandrian theology. In Origen, for example, we find Abraham as the symbol of faith, Isaac of science and Jacob of contemplation.[18] In our passage from Gregory, the overall theme is obviously faith, but it is also Abraham who "transcends the wisdom of his nation", Chaldean philosophy being seen as the science of observing the stars. There is good reason to see this natural philosophy as one of the steps Abraham ascended, not something he merely turned his back on: in the passage quoted above, reason leads him from the things "known to sense", that is, "from the beauty of things observed and the harmony of the heavenly wonders" to "the original model of beauty". The clear implication is that without the earthly beauty he would not have been led by reason to the idea of beauty; thus it is reasonable to assume that earthly beauties, as well as the abstract ideas of "power or goodness", etc. are "resources and [a] staircase for his upward journey". Finally, of course Abraham is a man of vision, who through faith received the wisdom that God is higher than all knowledge. The significance of *Jacob's* ladder, rather than a set of merely epistemological steps, is that it stretches from earth to heaven, and that, in the Septuagint version, "the Lord stood on it".[19] Thus the steps traversed by Abraham, Isaac and Jacob respectively in Origen's reading, are taken in succession by the one person of Abraham, in Gregory's.

Of course, while the image in this passage might recall Jacob's ladder, it is also clearly calling to mind another most famous set of steps – that is those in Plato's *Symposium*. At the climax of Diotima's speech she says:

> This is the right way of approaching or being initiated into the mysteries of love, to begin with examples of beauty in the world, and

---

[18] Origen, *Commentary on the Song of Songs*, Preface 3,18–19 (tr. Greer 235).

[19] *Gen* 28,13 (LXX): ὁ δὲ κύριος ἐπεστήρικτο ἐπ' αὐτῆς.

> using them as steps (ἐπαναβασμοῖς) to ascend continually with that absolute beauty as one's aim, from one instance of physical beauty to two and from two to all, then from physical beauty to moral beauty, and from moral beauty to the beauty of knowledge, until from knowledge of various kinds one arrives at the supreme knowledge whose sole object is that absolute beauty, and knows at last what absolute beauty is.[20]

This idea (both as it is expressed here and as it is expressed elsewhere in Plato's works) is echoed fairly closely by Gregory's comment that Abraham moved from "the beauty of things observed" but yearned to see "the original model of beauty" (*CE* II 89).[21] It is also clear that Abraham, like Diotima's ideal soul, moves from the particular to the general. However, beyond this initial immediate resemblance there are several differences: Abraham's movement is impelled by faith, not love, for example. But most importantly, Abraham moves *beyond* general ideas of absolute power or goodness to a state in which he believes that God himself cannot be known. This contrasts with Diotima's "supreme knowledge".[22]

It seems likely, then, that Gregory has in mind both the Platonic image of steps and the *Genesis* story of Jacob's ladder. The fact that he does not refer to either very closely is not the point: he is refracting the original image, not copying it. (His allusive and sometimes vague method of referring to earlier texts is illustrated nicely by the fact that his recollection of *Psalm* 83/84 – the reference to "beautiful

---

[20] Plato, *Symp.* 211b ff (tr. Hamilton 94).

[21] *Gen* 28,12 uses the word κλίμαξ (LXX), and Plato ἐπαναβασμός but Gregory is not consistent in the Greek words he uses for steps, or ladder (this point is illustrated in the quotations cited below). My point is that one should look for the images or ideas underlying the words and not become too dependent on the precise coincidences of vocabulary in which Gregory himself appears not to be interested.

[22] It is possible that Gregory also has in mind a passage from Plotinus' treatise on beauty *Enneads* I 6 [1] 1,8–20 which uses the step image in a recapitulation of several themes from Plato. "What is it which makes us imagine that bodies are beautiful and attracts our hearing to sounds because of their beauty?. . . . What is this principle then which is present in bodies? We ought to consider this first. What is it that attracts the gaze of those who look at something, and turns and draws them to it and makes them enjoy the sight? If we can find this perhaps we can use it as a stepping-stone and get a sight of the rest" (tr. Armstrong 233–4). However, I think it most likely that it is the general Platonic image of steps, or the original image in the *Symposium* that Gregory is recalling. That is not to say that Gregory might not be influenced by other imagery in Plotinus' treatise on beauty, particularly his use of light symbolism and an interesting analogy with journeying home – an interesting contrast with the patriarch's being called *away* from home. See Plotinus, *Enneads* I 6 [1] 8,22–23 (tr. Armstrong 257).

'rising stairs' [ἀναβάσεις]" – is itself only a very approximate quotation of the Septuagint.)

Let us turn now to the way in which Gregory uses the image of the ladder in some of his other works. In his treatise *De virginitate*, one finds the image used in perhaps its most closely Platonic sense.[23] Here Gregory advocates an ascent from outer to inner beauty, using the material as a step (ὑποβάθρα) to the intellectual. Although the emphasis seems in some places to be on an intellectual or epistemological ascent, nevertheless, Gregory does stress that the Beauty which is invisible and formless is an object of our love, not just of knowledge.[24] Although there are hints that the archetype is ultimately unknowable, in this treatise Gregory tends to evade the issue, talking of participation but not analysing what that participation consists in.

Gregory's homilies *De beatitudinibus* use the image of steps and the ladder several times, in parallel with the motif of an ascent of a mountain. Both are used to convey to the reader the idea that the text of the Beatitudes in Scripture indicates a spiritual ascent: that is, the text – if read allegorically – *describes* an ascent of the soul from material to heavenly things, but furthermore it will *facilitate* such an ascent for the soul of its reader if it is interpreted in such a way. Thus the text of Scripture is in itself a metaphorical ladder for the soul.

Gregory begins by describing this ladder-like quality of the Beatitudes in *Homily* II 1. Even if they do not appear to be written in a sequence, Gregory argues that:

> I think the arrangement of the Beatitudes is like a series of rungs (βαθμίδων), and it makes it possible for the mind to ascend by climbing from one to another . . . If our thought could take wing, and we could stand above the vaults of heaven, we should find there the supercelestial land which is in store as the inheritance for those who have lived virtuous lives. . . . The phenomenal world, insofar as it relates to physical perception, is wholly akin to itself. Even though one thing may seem to be high in terms of location in space, yet it is below the level of intelligible being, which it is impossible for the mind to scale, unless it first transcends by thought those things which the senses can reach.[25]

[23] *De virginitate* (GNO VIII/1 291,15–292,15).
[24] E.g. *De virginitate* (GNO VIII/1 293,23–294,1; 296,14–15).
[25] *De beatitudinibus* II 1 (tr. Hall 32).

Here we find some familiar themes: the ascent by steps; the use of knowledge by sense perception to rise higher; the idea that the goal of such knowledge is, or dwells in, a heavenly realm. (This last is even emphasised by an allusion to the soul in Plato's *Phaedrus* rising on wings to heaven for a God's eye view.) Interesting is Gregory's mention of the 'gap' between even the highest things in the material world and the intellectual realm – a theme very prominent in *CE* II. Another important development lies in Gregory's claim that the ladder is not only a philosophical process (carried out, for example, by the process of epistemological abstraction) but is also a theological one, undertaken by and in the reading of Scripture.

In subsequent *Homilies* the theme of the ladder is recapitulated: for example, in IV 1 the Word of God leads us by the hand up the ladder (κλῖμαξ).[26] This reminds us that the Beatitudes are the words of Jesus Christ, and anticipates the declaration in *Homily* V 1 that the ladder is indeed like Jacob's ladder (κλῖμαξ), "with God standing firmly on it".[27] This explicit connection of the ladder theme with Jacob asserts that just as the ladder vision was intended to teach Jacob about the way to God, so the text of Scripture performs the same function for its readers. Furthermore, Gregory makes an ontological point: the fact that God stands on, or at the top of Jacob's ladder, is read together with the idea that the Beatitudes are an ascending study of blessedness. Consequently, what is at the top of the ladder is the summit of blessedness, the archetype of blessedness, the origin from which all other blessedness flows.[28] Most importantly, however, in *Homily* V on the Beatitudes, Gregory establishes the idea that the ascent of the ladder is not purely towards knowledge of, but also towards *participation in* God: "To participate in the Beatitudes is nothing less than sharing in deity, towards which the Lord leads us up by his words."[29]

The treatise *De virginitate* and *De beatitudinibus* are both probably earlier than *CE*; by contrast, the next two instances of ladder imagery

[26] *De beatitudinibus* IV 1 (tr. Hall 47–48). As in *CE* II 89, Gregory quotes *Ps* 83/84,6.

[27] See also *De beatitudinibus* VI 5 (tr. Hall 71–72) for another reference to Jacob's ladder raising the soul up (compared also to Elijah's fiery chariot).

[28] *De beatitudinibus* V 1 (tr. Hall 57): "The elevation of the Beatitudes, one above another, prepares us to approach God himself, the truly blessed one who stands firmly above all blessedness."

[29] *De beatitudinibus* V 1 (tr. Hall 57).

to be examined come from the two famous works written towards the end of Gregory's life: *De vita Moysis* and *In Canticum canticorum.* In the latter, the ladder image comes in the context of an exegesis of the verse: "Arise, come my companion, my fair one, my dove!" On this, Gregory writes that "we now see the bride being led up by the Word up a staircase (ἐν βαθμῶν ἀναβάσει) by the steps (ἄνοδοι) of virtue to the heights of perfection".[30] In this sentence and the passage surrounding it, Gregory conveys several ideas which have already become familiar: the Word leading the soul up the staircase, the ascent being associated with beauty (in this case the bride becomes more beautiful), and the summit being participation in God/Beauty. The staircase itself is partly composed of Scripture (the Word "sends her a ray of light through the windows of the prophets and the lattices of the Law"),[31] but Gregory also says that the steps are those of virtue – just as he does throughout the Beatitudes. But there are two vital novelties in the use of the ladder motif here. First, Gregory is more willing to connect the ascent of the soul to beauty with the idea of desire.[32] Secondly, he explicitly connects the idea of God being at the summit of the ladder with the idea of divine infinity and this then leads him to the conclusion that the ascent of the soul up the ladder – that is the participation of the soul in God – must be a *perpetual* progress.[33]

A similar development in the use of the ladder image is observable in *De vita Moysis* (II 220–239, tr. Ferguson-Malherbe 112–116). Again we have some standard elements from Gregory's earlier writings: a rise towards beauty, a rise from image to archetype, the idea that God attracts the soul and the connection of ladder with mountain imagery. But there are also the new elements we saw in the work *In Canticum canticorum*: a willingness to express the impetus of the soul in terms of desire (albeit in combination with the virtue of hope), and the idea of divine infinity leading directly to the idea that the ascent of the soul is perpetual.[34] In addition to these, Gregory

[30] *In Canticum canticorum* V (GNO VI 158,19–21).

[31] *In Canticum canticorum* V (GNO VI 158,21–159,2).

[32] *In Canticum canticorum* V (GNO VI 159,8): ἐπιθυμία.

[33] *In Canticum canticorum* V (tr. McCambley 119): "The soul continually grows through participation in what is beyond it and never stops growing."

[34] *De vita Moysis* II 238–239 (tr. Ferguson-Malherbe 116): "But every desire (ἐπιθυμία) for the Good which is attracted to that ascent constantly expands as one progresses in pressing on to the Good. This truly is the vision of God: never to be satisfied in the desire to see him. But one must always, by looking at what he can

connects his ladder image to his much-quoted verse from *Philippians* which describes the believer as "straining ahead (ἐπεκτεινόμενος) for things to come" (*Phil* 3,13). Thus we read:

> The soul rises ever higher and will always make its flight yet higher – by its desire of the heavenly things straining ahead (συνεπεκτεινομένη) for what is still to come, as the Apostle says. . . . For this reason we also say that the great Moses, as he was becoming ever greater, at no time stopped in his ascent, nor did he set a limit for himself in his upward course. Once, having set foot on the ladder (κλῖμαξ) which God set up (as Jacob says), he continually climbed to the step (βαθμίς) above and never ceased to reach higher, because he always found a step higher than the one he had attained.[35]

IV. *Conclusions: perpetual progress and eschatology*

One can, therefore, see a development in Gregory's use of the ladder image. He moves from a fairly basic epistemological use in *De virginitate*, to the connection of Plato's epistemological steps with Jacob's ladder in the *De beatitudinibus*. It is in these homilies that the image first begins to be reborn as a symbol new to Gregory. In them, the ladder symbolises not merely an epistemological ascent, nor merely a journey in faith (or virtue), but the fusing of these two climbs upwards into one ascent which involves every aspect of the soul, moral and intellectual. Crucially, Gregory also connects the ladder with Scripture's role in facilitating – almost embodying – that ascent. In the works *In Canticum canticorum* and *De vita Moysis*, Gregory's ladder image is further amplified to include the notions of desire (adding to the moral and intellectual dimensions of the soul's ascent) and of a perpetual progress.

The latter is justified not only by the idea of divine infinity, which according to Gregory's logical argument must mean that the soul can never fully grasp God, but also by the general eschatological impetus of the two works in which the ladder image is found. *In Canticum canticorum* ends with an eschatological vision in which all rational creation joins together in the eternal praise of God. *De vita*

see, rekindle his desire to see more. Thus no limit would interrupt growth in the ascent to God, since no limit to the Good can be found nor is the increasing of desire for the Good brought to an end because it is satisfied."

[35] *De vita Moysis* II 225.227 (tr. Ferguson-Malherbe 113–114).

Moysis ends with Moses seeing, but not reaching the promised land: this leads to a slightly odd ending to *De vita Moysis* from a dramatic point-of-view – a gentle *diminuendo* rather than a grand finale – however, it fits with Gregory's belief that knowing and loving God is a journey to be travelled eternally. In both cases, this eschatological dimension perhaps indicates that when Gregory talks of the ascent of the soul to God, he is not just meaning the 'vertical' relation of the soul to God as experienced timelessly, for example, in a moment of prayer. Rather, he also means (perhaps he mainly means) the temporal pilgrimage of a soul to God, a pilgrimage which finishes not in the *possession of* God (just as Moses never possessed the promised land), but in the eternally growing *participation in* God (the language of participation is found associated with the ladder image in Gregory's works *De beatitudinibus, In Canticum canticorum* and *De vita Moysis*).[36]

On first sight, given the wider subject-matter of the treatise as a whole, and given that the echo of Plato's steps is rather more obvious than the connection with Jacob's ladder, one might think that in *CE* II Gregory is using the ladder image in a straightforwardly epistemological way. The lesson appears to be that one must, like Abraham, move on from our intellectual attachment to material things and, by faith, come to the realisation that God is beyond comprehension. In this case, one might assume that Gregory is more concerned with the vertical, epistemological relation between soul and God and that the temporal eschatological aspect to the image has not yet appeared as it does in his later works.

However, is there more to it than that? – especially if one grants the connection with Jacob's ladder and allows for the possibility that Gregory is creating a *new* ladder image out of its Platonic and Old Testamental forbears? In particular there is the underlying influence of *Hebrews* 11. In vv. 13–16, the biblical writer declares:

> All of these [Abraham, Isaac and Jacob] died in faith without having received the promises, but from a distance they saw and greeted them. They confessed that they were strangers and foreigners on the earth, for people who speak in this way make it clear that they are seeking a homeland. If they had been thinking of the land that they had left behind, they would have had opportunity to return. But, as it is, they desire a better country, that is, a heavenly one. Therefore God is not

[36] *De beatitudinibus* V 1 (tr. Hall 57); *In Canticum canticorum* V (GNO VI 158,12–19); *De vita Moysis* II 230 (tr. Ferguson-Malherbe 114).

> ashamed to be called their God; indeed, he has prepared a city for them.

At the end of chapter 11 and the beginning of chapter 12, the author of *Hebrews* then draws a conclusion for his readers:

> All these, though they were commended for their faith, did not receive what was promised, since God had provided something better so that they would not, apart from us, be made perfect. Therefore . . . let us . . . run with perseverance the race that has been set before us, looking to Jesus the pioneer and perfecter of our faith.

The idea of the race recalls the *Philippians* passage much beloved by Gregory; the image of the patriarchs seeing but not reaching the promised land chimes in with the way in which Gregory closes *De vita Moysis*.

When Origen read the story of the patriarchs through the lens of *Hebrews* 11, he observed that the patriarchs lived in tents "so that through this they might make it clear that whoever is eager for the divine philosophy must not have any place of his own on earth and must always move on, not so much from place to place as from the knowledge of lower things to the knowledge of higher things".[37] Gregory develops this by reference to his doctrine of divine infinity, to come to the conclusion that Abraham moved from lower to higher things, but ultimately came to the realisation that he could *never* know God.

However, in this passage in the *CE* Gregory does not apparently draw the further, *eschatological* conclusion of the soul's *perpetual progress* in God which we find in later works. This is surely because Gregory in *CE* II is naturally interested more in epistemological questions and not in the fate of the soul. From the premise of divine infinity he draws the conclusion that one can never know God, but he is not concerned to answer the theological and spiritual questions: what does that mean for the fate of the soul after the resurrection? what does that mean for our concept of beatitude?

Nevertheless, two important theological aspects of Gregory's use of the Abraham story in the *CE* should be noted. Firstly, it is I think possible to show that there are in this passage of *CE* II the seeds of this later, eschatological, development of the ladder metaphor. These

[37] Origen, *Commentary on the Song of Songs*, Preface 3,20 (tr. Geer 235).

seeds consist in several things: first, the idea of divine infinity is highlighted; secondly, Abraham's story is focussed around the idea of a journey, that is, a pilgrimage. This journey is understood in both a literal and a spiritual sense. The faithful realisation that God is unknowable is revealed to Abraham (God names himself), but Abraham has had to make himself ready for it through a gradual progress in faith. This progress took time – a fact which is emphasised in the account by the fact that the historical Abraham had to progress in a spatial sense too. It is this idea of pilgrimage which the stories of Abraham and Jacob's ladder add to the otherwise Platonic imagery of the steps. By combining the two, Gregory has added to the vertical image of the epistemological ascent a horizontal dimension which gives the ascent to God in Gregory its characteristic dynamic. Gregory seems to be pointing not towards a timeless moment of ecstatic contemplation, but towards an earthly life of faith. Implicitly, another attack on Eunomius lies beneath the surface here: on the one hand, Eunomius works too hard on his philosophy; on the other, he does not work hard enough at faith.

Secondly, this idea of pilgrimage helps Gregory to emphasise the positive aspects of the earlier parts of the journey. One of the problems with the Platonic epistemological ascent is that it leaves the status of the material very ambiguous: on the one hand, the ascent must start with material examples of beautiful things; on the other, the soul must rise above them in order to grasp true Beauty. Beautiful things should be steps in the ascent, but to the unwary they can become traps, holding the soul back. Very quickly, then, the ascent tends to be portrayed not so much as transcending the material as rejecting it. The idea of pilgrimage, on the other hand, has the advantage of suggesting that the earlier stages are important and necessary stages through which one must travel. Indeed, the idea of a three-fold journey of faith, science and contemplation suggests that the ascent for Gregory is cumulative: faith is not left behind in the quest for knowledge and contemplation of God (just as in Origen's threefold scheme for reading Scripture, the spiritual reading is dependent on and does not replace the literal and moral readings). This is not to say that the ambiguity of the first material stages of the journey is entirely absent in Gregory: particularly in *De virginitate*, where the emphasis is epistemological, there is a strong sense that the soul is being asked to leave material things behind. This is much less the case in the later, more eschatological works, where the focus is on the transformation, not the rejection, of the material. By contrast, in *CE* II we find the ambiguity expressed almost bluntly: on the one hand, Gregory writes, "in thinking about God [Abraham] was led to an understanding by nothing material" and "by the use of reason he transcended the wisdom of his nation"; on the other hand, he did use his earthly power of reasoning (which is presumably dependent on material perception) to grasp various ideas (such as power or goodness) which were the very steps of his ascent.[38] This ambiguity runs throughout Gregory's theology: he seems more fully aware of it towards the end of his life, where the ascent to God is described in ever more lusciously material ways; here in the *CE* II it is perhaps – in the marrying of Plato's steps with Jacob's ladder – in the process of being resolved.

What we find, then, in the *CE* II is indeed an image which has been reborn, but one which is still in a process of growth in Gregory's mind. However, one must avoid the temptation to read back into the *CE* II (and, indeed, the *De virginitate*) eschatological themes that are not yet present. This study of Gregory's use of the image of the ladder thus has some useful implications for the study of his writings. Firstly, it has stressed that Gregory uses similar images in different ways in different contexts. Sometimes the differences can be explained in terms of a development in his thought; but this is not necessarily always the case. Consequently, as new images are reborn from the fertile womb of Gregory's mind, one should *neither* expect these images to have the same meaning as their pagan, Jewish and Christian forbears, *nor* should one expect each of these similar images to have exactly the same meaning or function as the other. They have a family resemblance; they are not twins. Secondly, in drawing attention to the varied way in which Gregory uses these images, this paper suggests that in order to assess Gregory the theologian, one needs to look not only at Gregory the philosopher and Gregory the Scriptural exegete, but also at Gregory the writer: to what effect and with what aim is he using the images in these varied ways?

My conclusion, with regard to *CE* II 84–96, then, is that although Gregory has not ruled out a temporal dimension to our progress

[38] For other positive references to reasoning (λογισμός) in the ascent see *CE* II 89.100; even sense-perception is given a positive role: *CE* II 82.

through knowledge to a faithful recognition of divine incomprehensibility, his interpretation of the story of Abraham does not have so strong an eschatological dimension as his later uses of the ladder image. This is not to say that his use of the image here is unskilled – as we have seen his composition of this part shows much effort, and the image of the ladder is both evocative and conveys well what Gregory has to say. Nevertheless, one must confess that it is in his later works, that the combination of Platonic and biblical associations is fused with ever greater confidence into an image of the soul's eschatological destiny which becomes truly and unforgettably Gregory's own.

DIE ROLLE DER EPINOIA NACH EUNOMIUS UND GREGOR UND DIE THEOLOGISCH-PHILOSOPHISCHEN HINTERGRÜNDE (*CE* II 171–195)

Charalambos Apostolopoulos

I. *Einleitung: Die verschiedenen sprachphilosophischen Thesen der beiden Autoren (CE II 171–178)*

In diesem Passus tritt die sprachphilosophische Gewissensfrage der Zeit explizit auf, ob der Name das wirkliche Wesen der Dinge selbst bezeichnet oder nicht.[1] Diese Frage, die bekanntlich auf Platons *Kratylos* zurückgeführt werden kann,[2] stellt Gregor in unserem Text folgendermaßen dar: "Was verbindet das Ersinnen der Wörter (ῥημάτων ἐπίνοια) bzw. das Setzen der Namen mit den Dingen selbst, die wir durch den einen oder anderen Klang der Namen und Wörter bezeichnen?"[3] Im Abschnitt, den ich vorzustellen habe, gibt es einen deutlichen Hinweis auf die Hauptthese des Eunomius im Bereich der Gotteserkenntnis, dass der Name 'Ungezeugtsein' (ἀγεννησία) das Wesen Gottes bezeichnet sowie die Gegenthese Gregors, dass dieser Name sich nicht in eigentlicher Weise auf das Wesen bezieht, sondern lediglich auf die Anfangslosigkeit und Unendlichkeit des "ersten Grundes" hinweist.

Den verschiedenen sprachphilosophischen Thesen der beiden Autoren können wir näherkommen, wenn wir nur darauf bedacht sind, die polemisch bedingten gegenseitigen Parodien ihrer Behauptungen einigermaßen zur Seite zu schieben. Wenn Gregor etwa gleich am Anfang[4] sich über die einmalige Verzerrung seiner These beschwert, er habe angeblich Gott mit ἐπίνοια gleichgesetzt, sollte man ernstlich

[1] Vgl. vor allem *CE* II 173 (GNO I 275).

[2] Vgl. Platon, *Crat.* 390de: καὶ Κρατύλος ἀληθῆ λέγει λέγων φύσει τὰ ὀνόματα εἶναι τοῖς πράγμασι, καὶ οὐ πάντα δημιουργὸν ὀνομάτων εἶναι, ἀλλὰ μόνον ἐκεῖνον τὸν ἀποβλέποντα εἰς τὸ τῇ φύσει ὄνομα ὂν ἑκάστῳ καὶ δυνάμενον αὐτοῦ τὸ εἶδος τιθέναι εἴς τε τὰ γράμματα καὶ τὰς συλλαβάς.

[3] *CE* II 160 (GNO I 271).

[4] Vgl. *CE* II 171f (GNO I 274f).

versuchen, den ursprünglichen Vorwurf des Eunomius bzw. dessen eigenen Epinoia-Begriff zu rekonstruieren. Denn es sieht tatsächlich wie ein Wahnsinn aus, Gott, dem "seiend-seienden" (ὄντως ὄντα), dem Urgrund alles Existierens, das eigene wirkliche Wesen (ὑπόστασις) absprechen zu wollen, ja ihn mit einem bloßen Namen in unserem Kopf gleichzusetzen.[5]

Und wenn Eunomius darauf beharrt, dass das Wort ('Ungezeugtsein') das Wesen selbst offenbart, woher schöpft diese Behauptung ihre Überzeugungskraft? Gregor stellt selbst die Frage auf,[6] doch sehr bequem wirft er gleich seinem Gegner vor, er spreche Unsinn, verwirrendes, zusammenhangsloses Zeug (πρὸς τὸν σκοπὸν ἀσυνάρτητον).[7] Und zum Thema 'Ungezeugtsein' fügt er hinzu: "Wir behaupten dies sei ein Name, der lediglich darauf hinweist, dass Gott *ist* ohne jeglichen vorausgegangenen Geburtsakt (ἀγεννήτως τὸν θεὸν ὑφεστάναι), [wir behaupten] nicht, das 'Ungezeugtsein' sei selbst Gott".[8] Hat aber Eunomius das so gemeint? Hat er überhaupt jemals das 'Selbstbewusstsein' Gottes für sich beansprucht, wie seine Gegner es ihm vorzuwerfen scheinen? Mit seiner Emphase auf der ἀγεννησία als dem Hauptmerkmal Gottes wollte er vielleicht lediglich dessen Wesen in seiner Einfachheit denken und bewahren, dass Er *ist* was er *ist*: Ὁ Ὤν (*Exodus* 3,14).[9]

II. *Der Epinoia-Begriff des Eunomius nach der Darstellung Gregors (CE II 179–180)*

Von dem durch die menschliche Vernunft (i.e. ἐπίνοια) Gesagten gilt, dass es entweder nur in der lautlichen Äußerung (κατὰ τὴν προφοράν) Existenz besitze – wie z.B. Wörter, die nichts bezeichnen, d.h. die *voces non significativae* – oder in einem eigenen Denkakt (κατ' ἰδίαν διάνοιαν). Und davon ist das eine durch Vergrößerung entstanden, wie z.B. alles Kolossale, anderes durch Verkleinerung, z.B. die Pygmäen, oder durch Hinzufügung, wie die Polykephalen, oder

[5] Vgl. *CE* II 172f (GNO I 275).
[6] Vgl. *CE* II 175 (GNO I 275f).
[7] *CE* II 176 (GNO I 276).
[8] *CE* II 177 (GNO I 276).
[9] Vgl. M. Wiles, "Eunomius: hair-splitting dialectician or defender of the accessibility of salvation?", in: R. Williams (Hrsg.), *The making of orthodoxy. Essays in honour of Henry Chadwick*, Cambridge ²2002, 157–172, bes. 164ff.

durch Zusammensetzung, wie z.B. die Mischtiere.[10] Diese in epikureischer Sicht dargelegte Auffassung der ἐπίνοια als einer bedeutungslosen, gedankenlosen, bloß das Widernatürliche sich ausdenkenden Tätigkeit oder als eines bloß phantasierenden Vermögens, degradiert offenbar die Vernunfttätigkeit zu etwas Nutzlosem für das Leben.

Über die theologisch-philosophischen Hintergründe der eunomianischen Deutung der ἐπίνοια hat bereits Theo Kobusch bei seiner Analyse der sprachphilosophischen Grundlagen unserer Schrift auf dem VI. Kongress in Pamplona (1986) Erleuchtendes berichtet.[11]

III. *Gregor von Nyssa: Das Hohelied auf die (als menschliche Vernunft konzipierte) Epinoia (CE II 181–191)*

Wenn aber die ἐπίνοια wie von Eunomius als etwas für das Leben Nutzloses abgetan wird, ist – so wendet Gregor ein – das spezifisch Menschliche am menschlichen Leben gar nicht zu begreifen. Woher haben wir denn die Errungenschaften der Geometrie, der Arithmetik, der Logik und Physik, aber auch die Erfindungen der Maschinen und schließlich die Metaphysik in Form der Ontologie und der philosophischen Theologie? Sie alle beruhen auf der Tätigkeit menschlicher Vernunft ebenso wie auch die 'Künste' Ackerbau und Schiffahrt. "Ist das alles nicht durch die 'Epinoia' zugunsten des menschlichen Lebens erfunden worden?" stellt Gregor die rhetorische Frage, um gleich zur Definition der ἐπίνοια überzugehen:

> Denn nach meiner Definition ist die ἐπίνοια Zugriff auf das Unbekannte mit dem Zweck es zu erfassen (ἔφοδος εὑρετικὴ τῶν ἀγνοουμένων), der von einem ersten (intuitiven) Verständnis des Forschungsobjekts ausgeht und das daraus Folgende schrittweise entwickelt (bzw. entdeckt). Denn indem wir etwas vom Objekt unserer Untersuchung (im voraus) verstehen und zu dieser Art des Vorgreifens – über die νοήματα die wir mittlerweile entdecken – das Nachfolgende zusammenpassen, führen wir das Unternehmen unserer (diesbezüglichen) Forschung zu seinem Ziel (Ende).[12]

---

[10] Vgl. SVF II 87; 88; Epicurus, *Fr.* 36 (Usener 105–106).

[11] Vgl. Th. Kobusch, "Name und Sein. Zu den sprachphilosophischen Grundlagen in der Schrift *Contra Eunomium* des Gregor von Nyssa", in: L. F. Mateo-Seco – J. L. Bastero (Hrsg.), *El "Contra Eunomium I" en la produccion literaria de Gregorio de Nisa. VI. Coloquio Internacional sobre Gregorio de Nisa*, Pamplona 1988, 247–267, bes. 253ff.

[12] *CE* II 182 (GNO I 277). Die Übersetzung von Theo Kobusch, "Name und

Die in diesem Sinne definierte ἐπίνοια erscheint also als Stifterin der Kultur überhaupt.[13] Diese Fähigkeit des Verstehens und Erfindens, die Vernunft im weitesten Sinne, die von Gott dem Menschen nicht bloß gegeben, sondern – wie es auch in der Rede von der Erschaffung des Menschen (Περὶ κατασκευῆς ἀνθρώπου) ganz ausdrücklich gesagt wird – *übergeben* worden ist (vom Seinigen – als Eigentum – gegeben, [μετέδωκεν]),[14] hat dennoch einen durchaus ambivalenten Charakter. Denn sie kann sich verfehlen. Wie Theo Kobusch bei seiner erwähnten Analyse des Epinoia-Begriffs Gregors zu Recht betont hat, macht Gregor sich hier die These des Eunomius von der Nichtigkeit menschlicher Vernunft zunutze: Gerade die Fähigkeit, das Wider- und Unnatürliche, das Phantastische und Unwahre auszusinnen, zeigt, dass die ἐπίνοια uns eigentlich zu einem guten Zweck von Gott gegeben wurde. Sie ist wie die Entscheidungsfreiheit des Menschen (προαίρεσις) selbst:[15] der jeweilige Missbrauch ist ein Beweis dafür, dass sie beide, die Vernunft wie die Freiheit, eigentlich notwendig

Sein", 255, ἐπίνοια sei das "inventive methodisch gesicherte Wissen des Unbekannten" halte ich für nicht richtig. Ἔφοδος bedeutet doch Angriff, Anrücken, höchstens 'Fortschritt' und diese Bedeutung hat der Terminus auch bei Aristoteles, *Topik* I 12, 105a13–14, wenn er in technischem Sinne in der Definition des induktiven Schlusses begegnet: ἐπαγωγὴ (sc. die Induktion) δὲ ἡ ἀπὸ τῶν καθ' ἕκαστον ἐπὶ τὰ καθόλου ἔφοδος . . . Auch die englische Übersetzung der Epinoia-Definition von Stuart George Hall ("As I see it, mental conception is the way we find out things we do not know, using what is connected and consequent upon our first idea of a subject to discover what lies beyond") halte ich für nicht ganz geglückt.

[13] Ganz ähnlich preist schon Isokrates in seiner *Andidosisrede* (Περὶ ἀντιδόσεως) (*Or.* 15,253–257, Mandilaras III 130–131), den Logos als Kulturmacht. Im Logos sieht Isokrates den Inbegriff des Menschseins: Die Redegabe, so heißt es da, unterscheidet den Menschen vom Tier. Die Fähigkeit zu überzeugen und mitzuteilen (πείθειν καὶ δηλοῦν), also die Kommunikation, hat Gemeinschaftsleben und Zivilisation möglich gemacht. Auf dem Logos beruhen die sittlichen Normen und die Möglichkeit der Erziehung. Die Redeweise ist ein Abbild (εἴδωλον) der Sinnesart der Seele. Auch das Denken und Überlegen ist ein Sprechen mit sich selbst. So ist der Logos unser Führer bei jedem Tun und Denken. Dieser Text ist feierlich-sakral stilisiert. Er ist ein Manifest und eine Gründungsurkunde dessen, was man in einem bestimmten Sinne 'Humanismus' nennt: nämlich der Vorstellung dass das Sprachvermögen im Zentrum der menschlichen Existenz stehe und deshalb die Ausbildung der sprachlichen Ausdrucks- und Kommunikationsfähigkeit in die Mitte des Bildungsprozesses gestellt werden müsse. Die ursprüngliche Bedeutung der Rhetorik, für das öffentliche Leben einer Demokratie handlungsfähig zu machen, ist damit weit überschritten.

[14] Gregor von Nyssa, *De hominis opificio* (PG 44, 149b–c).

[15] Siehe dazu Ch. Apostolopoulos, *Phaedo Christianus. Studien zur Verbindung und Abwägung des Verhältnisses zwischen dem platonischen 'Phaidon' und dem Dialog Gregors von Nyssa 'Über die Seele und die Auferstehung'*, Frankfurt a.M. – Bern – New York 1986, 257ff.

und von unendlichem Nutzen für die Seele sind. Die Bewegung der ἐπίνοια auf das Vergebliche und Nutzlose kann ihre Fähigkeit zum Guten und Nützlichen kaum in Zweifel ziehen: "So wie sie dort dasjenige erfand, was Lust oder Überraschung hervorbringt, so wird sie auch hier ihren Angriff auf das Wahre nicht verfehlen."

IV. *Das 'Ungezeugtsein' Gottes als Beispiel negativer Theologie (CE II 192–195)*

Das 'Ungezeugtsein' (ἀγέννητον) bzw. das 'Anfanglose' (ἄναρχον) ist ein Name, der lediglich die Tatsache bezeichnet, dass der 'erste Grund', d.h. Gott, ohne Anfang *ist.*[16] Dieser Name verweist nur auf das, was Gott *nicht* ist, nämlich abhängig – durch die Geburt – von einem anderen. Er sagt nichts darüber, was Gott *ist.* Das unbestimmt-unendliche (ἀόριστον) göttliche Wesen entzieht sich schlechterdings allen Benennungen durch die menschliche ἐπίνοια.[17] Wie schon oft hervorgehoben wurde (E. von Ivánka, Paul Tillich), ist Gott für Gregor jenseits aller Namen und aller Begriffe, unerreichbar, undenkbar und unaussprechbar. Er ist nicht gut, sondern jenseits des Guten, ja sogar – ein ganz kühner Gedanke – nicht Gott, sondern jenseits Gottes, sofern der Name 'Gott' schon irgendeinen Begriff, einen Gedanken, eine Bestimmung bedeutet. Diese radikale Auffassung der Unendlichkeit Gottes, welche Gott im Unbestimmbaren und Unaussprechbaren verschwinden lässt, wird freilich auch Eunomius' Reaktion hervorrufen, der seinen Gegnern polemisierend vorwirft, sie wissen

[16] Die Lehre von der Anfangslosigkeit Gottes tritt im allgemein christlichen und jüdischen Denken gelegentlich in der Polemik gegen heidnische Götter auf. Erst in der Christologie treten Probleme auf, sofern die biblische Redeweise von der Zeugung des Sohnes an mythische Theogonien erinnern konnte. Zu einer Kontroverse über *die 'Agennesie'* des Sohnes kam es aber erst durch Arius und seine Nachfolger wie Eunomius. Sie beschränkten bekanntlich das Prädikat streng auf Gott den Vater und folgerten, dass der Sohn einen zeitlichen Anfang haben müsse: ἦν ποτε ὅτε οὐκ ἦν (bei Athanasius *Or. contra Arianos* I 5, PG 26, 21a). Siehe hiezu den informativen Artikel 'Anfang' von Herwig Görgemanns, in *RAC Suppl.*, Bd. I (2001), Sp. 401–448, bes. Teil *E. Anfang oder Anfangslosigkeit Gottes (der Götter),* 442ff (mit weiterführender Literatur).

[17] Das griechische Wort ἀόριστον hat bei Gregor eine Bedeutung, die sich nicht mit einem deutschen Wort angemessen wiedergeben lässt. Sie changiert zwischen 'unendlich', 'unbestimmt' und 'unbegrenzt'. Der Einfachheit halber steht hier immer: 'unbestimmt-unendlich'.

eigentlich nicht, was sie anbeten, wie die Samariter der alten Zeiten (*Joh* 4,22).[18]

Dennoch scheint Gregor von Nyssa mit seiner Vorstellung vom Unbestimmt-Unendlichen der 'göttlichen Natur' es philosophisch ernst zu meinen. Wie ich bei anderer Gelegenheit gezeigt habe, gelangt der späte Gregor, in seinem Versuch, beide Aspekte, das In- und zugleich Über-Sein des göttlichen Wesens als eine paradoxe Einheit zu denken, zu einer merkwürdigen Konzeption des Göttlichen als eines Unbestimmt-Unendlichen, einer Konzeption, die sich weder mit der griechisch-philosophischen noch mit der christlichen Tradition deckt.[19] Das Wesen des Göttlichen, das für Gregor im Grunde das 'wahrhaft Seiende', den als Realität erfahrenen Bestand des seinsmächtigeren Geistigen bedeutet, ist hier so radikal negativ formuliert, dass es sich tatsächlich nicht bloß als das 'unbegreifbare Geheimnis' hinstellt, das, sich gegen jede weitere Aussage über sein Wesen sperrend, jegliche Konturen, auch die des Guten oder Gottes oder die des 'Etwas' zersprengt, sondern auch, ganz überraschend ins Positive schlagend, ein sich selbst transzendierendes Unbestimmt-Unendliches (ἀόριστον) suggeriert: Das göttliche Wesen übersteigt dauernd sich selbst![20] Dieser kühne Gedanke, der das Erkenntnis- und Lebensziel im Unerkennbaren und Unbestimmbaren, ja Unberechenbaren verschwinden lässt, verträgt sich offenbar kaum mit der auf Berechenbarkeit, 'Umfassbarkeit', Beständigkeit und Maß angelegten Seinsordnung der griechischen Metaphysik.

Auch der Christ aber dürfte – ohne unausgewiesene Hypothesen – mit den Unendlichkeits*begriffen* des Kirchenvaters wenig anfangen können! Meine Interpretationsthese, dass der Unendlichkeitsbegriff bei Gregor tendenziell auf das Unbegrenzt-Unbestimmte Gottes abzielt, habe ich ja in der Auseinandersetzung gerade mit der christlich-theologischen Deutung des gregorianischen Unendlichkeitsbegriffes gewonnen. Dieser zufolge bezeichnet dieser Begriff die spezifische Differenz des Schöpfers gegenüber dem Geschöpf. Nach meinem Urteil jedoch ist 'die' Unendlichkeit keine eigentümliche christliche Aussage. Selbst

[18] Gregor von Nyssa, *CE* III/I 105 (GNO II 39,13–14); Basilius, *Ep.* 234,1 (Courtonne III 41).

[19] Siehe dazu Ch. Apostolopoulos, "ΑΟΡΙΣΤΟΝ. Anmerkungen zur Vorstellung vom Unbestimmten-Unendlichen der 'göttlichen Natur' bei Gregor von Nyssa", *StPatr* 37 (2001) 3–11.

[20] Ch. Apostolopoulos, "ΑΟΡΙΣΤΟΝ", 5f, Anm. 3.

in seinem früher verfassten Dialog Περὶ ψυχῆς καὶ ἀναστάσεως, diesem "*Phaedo Christianus*" aus dem vierten nachchristlichen Jahrhundert – wo unser Thema als Problem der Ewigkeit und insbesondere der Göttlichkeit des gewordenen bzw. gezeugten Geistes wiederkehrt und das ἀόριστον sich bereits als ein hervorragender Begriff des Göttlichen erweist – liegt der Schwerpunkt der Darstellung nicht auf der "radikalen Unterscheidung" zwischen Erschaffenem und Unerschaffenem, vielmehr auf ihrer wesenhaften (origenistisch anmutenden) Gemeinschaft, wie sie sich aus der der Welt transzendenten – nicht ganz bestimmbaren – Natur des Logos (νοῦς τις) ergibt, an dem beide, Gott[21] und Mensch, teilhaben.[22]

[21] Vgl. bes. *De anima et resurrectione* (PG 46, 57b).
[22] Siehe dazu Ch. Apostolopoulos, *Phaedo Christianus*, 306f, Anm. 15.

THE LANGUAGE OF GOD AND HUMAN LANGUAGE (*CE* II 195–293)

Anthony Meredith

Overview

With the help of Stuart Hall's translation and the discussion concerning the difficulty of offering a totally satisfactory account of the structure of the piece before us it may still be helpful to isolate certain basic issues from the text before us.

Gregory spends sections 198–204 (GNO I 282–284) in attacking the absurdity of the literalism of Eunomius' approach to scripture which leads him to argue that God has vocal chords. 205–214 (GNO I 284–288) God has no need to use language anyway, above all in communicating with his Son, 215–221 (GNO I 288–290).

Scripture has more than a merely literal meaning (222–226, GNO I 290–292), it has also a deeper θεωρία. Gregory's own allegorical method is here under defence. Then from 227–238 (GNO I 292–296) Gregory attacks any physicalist view of God. Instead, 239–250 (GNO I 296–299) God gave us the power to name things for ourselves with the help of our rational intelligences (269, GNO I 305). At 261 (GNO I 302) God did not speak Hebrew. Words differ, things do not; there never was a primitive language, even before Babel. Again and again Gregory insists at 269–275 (GNO I 305–307) that God created things not names . . . a point repeated at 276–281 (GNO I 307–309). 282–293 (GNO I 309–313) God does not need names, we do. This is not a denial of providence as Eunomius suggests. Our ability to name things is a divine gift and far below the wonder of the things that God created.

Preliminary observations

The central issue Gregory faces throughout the whole of this section 195–293 (GNO I 281–313) is in effect a defence of Basil – as indeed is the whole of the *Contra Eunomium* – and by implication of

Gregory himself against the accusation made by Eunomius that their understanding of the nature of language and of God's relationship to it amounted in effect to a denial of divine providence and indeed of the divine availability as a result of an excessive insistence on the divine unknowability. For if God is in and of himself inaccessible to the human mind what is the point or the possibility of intelligible discourse about God? This is very clear from the extract of Eunomius cited in section 196, where reads as follows: "He accuses him [that is Basil] of following pagan (ἔξωθεν) philosophy and so of circumcising the divine providence (κηδεμονία)."[1]

I. *The secular nature of Eunomius' approach*

Gregory begins by offering what he himself admits is less a straight statement than a paraphrase of the Eunomian position. Eunomius had accused Basil of following secular philosophy, ἔξωθεν φιλοσοφία,[2] and consequently of limiting or denying any sense of divine providence. Both sides can use this type of argument. Later in this book (sections 405, 410 and 411, GNO I 344–346) Gregory accuses Eunomius in turn of allowing himself to be misled by Plato, Epicurus and Aristotle. Similarly Origen in *Contra Celsum* had sought to discredit the position of Celsus by suggesting he was an Epicurean because of his supposed denial of providence.[3] In the field of controversy it was quite possible for 'orthodox' and 'heretics' alike to accuse each other of being too dependent on the arguments of secular philosophy. So, too, Tertullian "the zealous African", as Gibbon terms him, despite his opposition to "secular philosophy" towards the close of his *Apology*, is capable of describing the Stoic Seneca, as "our Seneca".

---

[1] *CE* II 196 (GNO I 282,3–7). It is instructive to see that Eunomius was as capable as were both Basil and Gregory of attributing the errors, as they saw them, of the Cappadocians to the mischievous influence of alien philosophy, above all the atheistic followers of Aristotle and Epicurus. Basil at *Adversus Eunomium* I 9 (SC 299, 198) accuses Eunomius of deriving his views ἐκ τῆς κόσμου σοφίας. Likewise Gregory at *CE* I 88 (GNO I 52). Again both sides were quite capable of accusing the other of a denial of divine providence. Eunomius does this at *CE* II 196 (GNO I 282); Gregory does the same and associates Eunomius in so doing with the teaching of Epicurus at *CE* II 410 (GNO I 345–346). Origen levels a like accusation against Celsus at *Contra Celsum* I 8; I 9; I 20 (SC 132, 94–96; 96–100; 126–128).

[2] Cf. Basil, *Adversus Eunomium* I 7 (SC 299, 188–192).

[3] Cf. Origen, *Contra Celsum* IV 99 (SC 136, 430–434).

II. *Theories of the origin and nature of language*

Basil in his *Adversus Eunomium* I 6 had given attention to the precise meaning of the central expression ἐπίνοια, which was his preferred way of categorising the language we employ in our attempts to understand and define the divine nature.[4] For Basil the word expresses, as it does for Gregory, a human expression or rather invention, enabled in us by the power of God. It is not, therefore, as Eunomius supposes, a fanciful expression, but rather our own reflection on the concepts we form through the reflective power we have from God. To use more modern terminology, for Gregory and Basil language is neither purely conventional, nor natural – the Anomoean position – but in between. As has been pointed out the difficulty with the Cappadocian position is that it lacks the idea of analogy. For Eunomius the position of Basil makes all language purely human and therefore both arbitrary and fictional.

It is perhaps worth remarking that although in this treatise Gregory, following Basil assigns to the expression ἐπίνοια a precise linguistic sense, it is by no means the case that this is the only sense the word bears. It is worth noting that it appears on several occasions in *De vita Moysis* II 95 and 113, and it simply means device or stratagem for dealing with a difficulty.[5] The use of the expression is also to be found in *Oratio catechetica* on at least five occasions.[6] It is this way, meaning faculty rather than meaning, that Gregory defines his usage of the expression at *CE* II 182 (GNO I 277,21) as a ἔφοδος εὑρετική, a way of finding things out rather than the actual result, not unlike Basil in *Adversus Eunomium* I 6.[7]

This being so, there is a marked difference between the Cappadocian usage and that of Origen, where in the *Commentary on John* I 28,200 and in *Contra Celsum* II 64, as we have seen, the word is applied to aspects of Christ, like word, wisdom and shepherd and so on, rather than either to the divine nature itself or to the way we discover

[4] Cf. Basil, *Adversus Eunomium* I 6 (SC 299, 182–188).

[5] Cf. Gregory, *De vita Moysis* II 95; 113 (GNO VII/1 62,6; 68,1).

[6] *Oratio catechetica* (GNO III/4 7,7; 26,2; 60,22; 66,4; 87,15). On the first two of these occurrences Srawley (*Oratio catechetica magna. The Catechetical Oration of Gregory of Nyssa*, Cambridge 1903, 4) compares Gregory's usage with that to be found in the *Contra Eunomium*, "In his view," he writes, "it is an inventive faculty and at the same time more trustworthy than fancy."

[7] Cf. Basil, *Adversus Eunomium* I 6 (SC 299, 182–188).

truth.[8] So also in *Contra Celsum* II 64, Origen can write: "Although Jesus was one he had many aspects."[9]

Eunomius indicts Basil for reducing, if not denying altogether, the notion of divine providence, by an unwillingness to accept the divine origin of language. This, so Eunomius urges, results from a refusal to take seriously the words of *Genesis*, which insist that the naming of plants took place before the creation of mankind. In other words Eunomius' accusation is both that Basil is anti-providential and that he denies the clear sense of *Genesis* 1,5: "And called the light day and the darkness he called (ἐκάλεσεν) night."

The philosophical provenance of Eunomius' theory is almost certainly Plato's *Cratylus* 391d–e, as is suggested by Gregory at *CE* II 404 (GNO I 344). In that passage Socrates is reported as saying: "He [that is Homer] distinguishes between the names by which gods and men call the same things. Do you not think that he gives in those passages great and wonderful information about the correctness of names? For clearly the gods call things by names that are naturally right (θεοὶ αὐτὰ καλοῦσιν πρὸς ὀρθότητα ἅπερ ἔστι *φύσει ὀνόματα*)" (my emphasis). As far as I am aware this discussion of the nature of language above all of the language we apply to God, or to anything else, is quite new in Christian circles. Marcion had indeed adopted a literal approach to the bible, but not in deference to a philosophical view of the nature of language. Origen seems nowhere to discuss the issue of the nature of language as such, and defends the biblical texts impugned by Marcion by the use of allegory and by appeal in *De principiis* IV 2,6,[10] to the practice of Saint Paul in *1 Corinthians* 9–10 and in *Galatians* 4. If indeed Gregory is correct in attributing Eunomius' ideas to Plato's *Cratylus*, Eunomius was the first to do so.

What is not altogether clear is whether the Eunomian adoption of Plato's theory of language proceeded solely from controversial motives or rose independently, from a genuine interest in philosophy. Was he a sophistic logician or a genuine philosopher? For our purposes it hardly matters.[11] The immediate motive for Eunomius'

---

[8] Cf. Origen, *Commentary on John* I 28,200 (GCS 10, 37); *Contra Celsum* II 64 (SC 132, 434–436).

[9] Origen, *Contra Celsum* II 64 (SC 132, 434–436).

[10] Origen, *De principiis* IV 2,6 (Görgemanns-Karpp 714–720).

[11] Jean Daniélou in two celebrated articles both in *Revue des études grecques* –

insistence on the sacred character of language, is clear enough. Eunomius wishes to argue that God has a name given by God to himself and that name is ἀγέννητος. If this argument is accepted it would automatically exclude the Son from the divine nature. The central argument, therefore, of Eunomius is dual. He hopes to disprove the deity of the Son, by defining the divine nature in such a way as to exclude from it the idea of derivation; the definition of God does this by the single expression ἀγέννητος. No son *can* be unbegotten.

The Cappadocian position that the attribution of names belongs to our own human intelligences to our λογικὴ δύναμις[12] by means of human conceptions, ἐπίνοιαι, labours according to Eunomius, under two serious defects. (1) It is against the ψιλὸν γράμμα of scripture,[13] which expressly asserts at several points the fact that God himself named things. At *Genesis* 1,5 we read "God called the light day" – the LXX reads ἐκάλεσε at this point – similarly at verses 8 and 10 – a point insisted upon by Eunomius at sections 269, 280 and 281 (GNO I 305; 308–309). The attribution of the power of naming things to merely human agency is taken by Eunomius, as we have seen, to be a denial of divine providence. At section 197 Gregory refers somewhat ironically to Eunomius as the "great protector of divine providence".[14] Such an argument assumes an understanding of providence of a strongly Stoic/Platonic kind. It is perhaps worth noting that Gregory of Nazianzus deplores the Aristotelian/Epicurean denial of providence in section 10 of his *First Theological Oration* and invites Eunomius to attack that rather than Christian doctrine.[15]

"Eunome l'Arien et l'exégèse néo-platonicenne du Cratyle", *REG* 69 (1956) 412–432, and "Grégoire de Nysse et le néo-platonisme de l'école d'Athènes", *REG* 80 (1967) 395–401 – argued that Eunomius' linguistic ideas derived from the Neoplatonism of Iamblichus. But the actual commitment of Eunomius to any sort of philosophy has been hotly disputed by other scholars and even Gregory accuses him of devotion to Aristotle, as at *CE* II 411 and 620 (GNO I 346; 407), and Epicurus, as in note 1, as well as to Plato. It is doubtful whether we should treat Eunomius as a philosopher at all.

12 Cf. *CE* II 246; 270; 290 (GNO I 298,15; 305,24; 312,5).

13 Cf. *CE* II 250 (GNO I 299,16).

14 Cf. *CE* II 197 (GNO I 282,19).

15 Gregory of Nazianzus, *Or.* 27,10,6–9 (SC 250, 94–96).

III. *Defence of Basil*

Gregory's initial reply to this attack on his 'master' Basil,[16] is to insist that the argument he and his brother use, that God handed over to men the power to name things does not in practice amount to a denial or diminution of the providence of God. Indeed both here and elsewhere it is a constant argument of Gregory that the language we employ with the help of ἐπίνοιαι with which to discourse is God's gift to us which enables us to understand and as it were label the universe. This has already emerged at *CE* II 182 and 185 (GNO I 277–278). In the latter passage he terms it an ἐπινοητικὴ καὶ εὑρετικὴ δύναμις (so also 228, GNO I 292). In an important passage, 243 (GNO I 297), Gregory argues that once God's initial work was at an end, God gave mankind the power to think and express thoughts by speech and so to confer words on things in order to designate them.

IV. *The 'language' of God*

A. *Gregory attacks the implied literalism of Eunomius' treatment of scripture*

This second and more extensive argument is, that to claim that God himself uses language is to adopt a literal approach to Holy Scripture and to avoid going deeper in a search for the spiritual truths that lie concealed under the bare letter (222, GNO I 290). Such a manner of argument is not unlike that employed by Origen in book 4 of *De principiis* in order to deal with Marcion's attack on scripture, which attack, so Origen argued, rested upon an ignorance of or refusal to go deeper in understanding the meaning of scripture on the pattern of Saint Paul. It is worth mentioning at this juncture the interesting fact that Marcion, Arius and Eunomius all appeal in their

[16] Gregory often terms his brother Basil διδάσκαλος – a term he also applies to his sister Macrina, though less frequently – both here in sections 195, 196, 197 (GNO I 281–282), where he is termed "master of piety", and 236 (GNO I 295) and above all in his funeral oration on Basil. Mann *Lexicon Gregorianum* II 398 lists 30 examples from the *Contra Eunomium* I and II alone. The expression "our teacher" can be found at *CE* I 61, 81, 126, 144, 535, 601, 653, 655 (GNO I 43,6; 50,14–15; 65,6; 70,11; 181,16–17; 199,13; 214,11; 214,22–23), and *CE* II 66, 141, 345, 445 (GNO I 245,6; 266,16; 326,25; 356,20).

differing ways to a literal understanding, the ψιλὸν γράμμα of scripture as Gregory twice terms it (at 199 and 250, GNO I 283; 299), in order to further their views. By contrast the approaches of Origen and Gregory are far from being literal.

B. *God does not need language to communicate, He has no body*

But Gregory offers another argument. To assume that God actually uses language implies on the part of God certain physical ideas that are quite absurd. First of all God has no vocal chords, simply because he is without a body (200–202, GNO I 283–284) – indeed he is also eyeless, for the same reason. This is made very clear at 233 (GNO I 293–294), where Gregory also ridicules the notion of God either hearing or smelling despite the apparent witness of in turn *Genesis* 1,4, *Psalm* 29,11, "The Lord heard and had pity" and *Genesis* 8,21, "When the Lord smelled the pleasing odour of Noah's sacrifice". There Gregory argues that if you insist on understanding 'said' in a bodily manner, why not seeing and hearing and smelling as well, with reference to the words of *Genesis* 1,4, "God saw that it was good". Any suggestion that God has a body or parts offends the spiritual idea of God.

C. *The Father needs no language to communicate with the Son*

He goes on to argue that before the creation of the universe whom would God have to address anyway. At 207 (GNO I 285) Gregory argues that only bodily natures require either ἐπίνοιαι or language with which to communicate their ideas. The divine nature, Father and Son being bodiless require neither. The precise sense in which Gregory (and Basil) understand the term ἐπίνοια will be addressed in the passage following directly on this one, beginning at section 294 (GNO I 313). The only person(s) He could have addressed were the Son and Spirit; but the divine nature is shared by all three, principally by the Father and the Son and they need no language to communicate, so close are they to each other (213, GNO I 287) there is no διάστασις between them. The Son is aware of the designs of the Father without needing the medium of speech with which to discover them.

In section 214 (GNO I 287–288) Gregory insists on the close connexion existing between Father and Son by means of the use of the language of συνάφεια and its various sources, all derived from the root of συνάπτω. Slightly earlier in the same section he argues that where no διάστασις is envisaged, there all is closely related συνημμένον. Such language is no stranger in Gregory, as witness *CE* I 224 and 279 (GNO I 92; 108) and also appears not infrequently in Basil, for example in *On the Holy Spirit* 24, 40, 60 and 63.[17] In his *Theological Orations*, interestingly, Gregory of Nazianzus appears not to use the word or its relatives, except for συναφές at 4,20.[18]

But not only do they share the same nature, they also share the same θέλημα (216, GNO I 288). The former point is insisted upon by Gregory in his treatment of *John* 10,30, "The Father and I are one" at *CE* I 498–503 (GNO I 170–172) where Gregory defines his position against Arius and Sabellius alike. For the identity of wills Gregory appeals in section 216 (GNO I 288,19–21) to *John* 16,15, "All that the Father has is mine". Unity of both nature and will preclude the need for any form of external verbal communication.

But the most powerful positive argument urged by Gregory against Eunomius is the strong relationship he insists upon between word and action in God. So at 229 (GNO I 292–293) he urges that in the divine nature there is no distinction between will and activity, (228, GNO I 292), between choice (προαίρεσις) and action (πρᾶξις). They are as closely connected as the flame and the shining that comes from it. At 246 (GNO I 298) he writes that the consequence of the divine will is not a name (ὄνομα) but a reality (πρᾶγμα). A little later (251–254, GNO I 299–300) he argues that although things do indeed depend for their existence upon God's design and will, the differing names are the discoveries of human intelligence, ἀνθρώπιναι φωναὶ τῆς ἡμετέρας διανοίας. This is a frequent refrain, as we have already seen. God, by contrast, as we have also seen, needs no language with which to communicate; his words are actions. On several occasions at 225, 270, 278 and 281 (GNO I 291; 305; 308; 309) he repeats the aphorism that God is the immediate author not of ῥήματα or ὀνόματα but of πράγματα. Eunomius, by contrast, Gregory insists in a forceful passage in section 290 (GNO I 311–312), is really being exceedingly childish in arguing that Basil's proposal

[17] Basil, *De spiritu sancto* 24, 40, 60, 63 (FC 12, 142–144; 194–198; 256–258; 266–268).
[18] Gregory of Nazianzus, *Or.* 30,20,7 (SC 250, 266).

to attribute the discovery of language to our λογικὴ δύναμις is in effect to deny or seriously to diminish the divine πρόνοια. The true power of God is to be found not in words but in action.

Conclusions

The following issues therefore emerge as the primary theses of Gregory, in his defence of the power of the God-given human mind to name things and so by implication of the wrongness of defining the divine nature by the solitary title of the unbegotten only one.

1. God has provided all rational beings with the power of thought and language (λογικὴ δύναμις) with the help of which we are enabled to give names to things (237, 246, 290, GNO I 295; 298; 311–312). This power we possess does not mean a denial or diminution of the providence of God.
2. God is a spiritual being and has no need of human or indeed any sort of language with which to communicate his thoughts and wishes, either absolutely or by way of communication with the Son, between whom and the Father there exists the closest possible συνάφεια. In him, as is often repeated, word and action coincide. This means that there is no gap between design and performance, nor is there any distance between ὀνόματα and πράγματα. Whatever he has in his mind takes place (281, 283, GNO I 309–310).
3. Gregory protests against the literal interpretation of scripture invoked by Eunomius and expressed by the phrase ψιλὸν γράμμα at 199, 250 (GNO I 283; 299). The general point seems to be that a literal approach to scripture goes hand in hand with a materialistic view of the nature of God.
4. It ought to be stressed that in his whole approach, above all in his attitude to the term ἐπίνοια, Gregory is on the one hand remarkably free from the usages from Hellenistic philosophy outlined by Theo Kobusch. Further there is little to connect him with the particular sense given to the word with reference to the nature of Christ, and outlined by Origen in his *Commentary on John* I 28,200 (GCS 10, 37). Gregory's dependence on Basil is the most salient feature of his whole approach.
5. How might or did Eunomius reply to the critique of his *Apology*? In a later passage of his *Apology* Gregory at *CE* III/I 105 (GNO

II 39) reports that he was accused along with Basil of advocating agnosticism on the basis of *John* 4,22, "You worship what you know not" a jibe Basil had already dealt with in his *Letter* 234[19] with the help of a distinction between οὐσία and ἐνέργεια.

6. One simple conclusion to be drawn tentatively from this whole discussion is that neither Eunomius nor the two brothers can be discovered at least within the context of their disagreement to be under the influence of any particular philosophical system, though as we have seen both were happy to accuse the other of being seduced by secular philosophy.

[19] Basil, *Ep.* 234 (Courtonne III 41–44).

CHRISTOLOGICAL TITLES – CONCEPTUALLY APPLIED? (*CE* II 294–358)

Johannes Zachhuber

Gregory of Nyssa entered the Eunomian controversy late. In his *Contra Eunomium* he rebuts a lengthy writing by Eunomius which in its turn was an answer to a book Basil had written some twenty years earlier against a (yet again) previous book by the sometime bishop of Cyzicus. In many ways, Gregory's *Contra Eunomium* is, more than anything else, an apology for his elder brother against the attacks levelled against him by his anomoian foe. For us this means that reconstructing Gregory's argument is impossible without some glance at what Basil had said. Eunomius had, in his second book, largely confined himself to a refusal of Basil's position pointing out mistaken assumptions, wrong conclusions and weak demonstrations in the *Adversus Eunomium*. Gregory's primary task is it to counter this attack by showing that, far from being mistaken, wrong and weak, Basil's arguments were valid refutations of Eunomius' heretical distortions of the Christian faith and powerful demonstrations of the orthodox truths of the Church.

After some preliminary remarks about relevance and difficulty of the problem broached here (1) I shall, therefore, start from a consideration of some relevant passages in Basil's *Adversus Eunomium* (2) to proceed with a tentative reconstruction of Eunomius' counterarguments (3). This will be followed in turn by a discussion of Gregory's apology for his brother (4). Some concluding remarks bring this paper to an end (5).

I. *Eunomius' challenge and the problem of divine attributes: some preliminary remarks*

The passage in Gregory's *Contra Eunomium* II that is under discussion in this article takes its starting point essentially from one section of Basil's *Adversus Eunomium* the main idea of which is to urge that the titles applied to Christ by scripture have their origin in human conception.[1] Why would that be so? The answer is not as straightforward as one may expect.

The immediately apparent reason, of course, is that Eunomius, in his *Apology*, had claimed that the name 'unbegotten' was God's 'real' name, not one applied "according to human conception" but "according to truth":

> When we say 'Unbegotten', then, we do not imagine that we ought to honour God only in name, according to human conception; rather according to truth, we ought to repay him the debt which above all others is most due to God: the acknowledgement that he is what he is.[2]

What Eunomius means to say here is fairly obvious: God *is* unbegotten whether human beings think of him in this way or not, whether they employ this term or not, whether they exist or not:

> Expressions based on conception have their existence in name and utterance only, and by their nature are dissolved along with the sounds [which make them up]; but God, whether these sounds are silent, sounding or have even come into existence, and before anything was created, both was and is unbegotten.[3]

It appears that Eunomius does not here wish to enunciate a specific theory of ἐπίνοια disregarding the possibilities of the human mind. He seems to take it for granted that there is a difference between what later thinkers would call *in intellectu* and *in re*. The ascription of 'unbegotten' to God expresses what God really is and not only what people think of him. Is this objectionable from an Orthodox point of view? I doubt it.[4] It seems evident that, when church fathers

---

[1] Basil, *Adversus Eunomium* I 5,124–7,49 (SC 229, 180–192).

[2] Eunomius, *Apologia* 8 (Vaggione 40,16–42,1): ἀγέννητον δὲ λέγοντες, οὐκ ὀνόματι μόνον, κατ' ἐπίνοιαν ἀνθρωπίνην, σεμνύνειν οἰόμεθα δεῖν, ἀποτιννύναι δὲ κατ' ἀλήθειαν τὸ πάντων ἀναγκαιότατον ὄφλημα τῷ θεῷ τὴν τοῦ εἶναι ὅ ἐστιν ὁμολογίαν. ET: Vaggione (with changes). In the following, translations are mine unless otherwise indicated.

[3] Eunomius, *Apologia* 8 (Vaggione 42,1–7): τὰ κατ' ἐπίνοιαν λεγόμενα ἐν ὀνόμασι μόνοις καὶ προφορᾷ τὸ εἶναι ἔχοντα ταῖς φωναῖς συνδιαλύεσθαι πέφυκεν. ὁ δὲ θεὸς καὶ σιωπώντων καὶ φθεγγομένων καὶ γεγονότων καὶ πρὸ τοῦ γενέσθαι τὰ ὄντα, ἦν τε καὶ ἔστιν ἀγέννητος. ET: Vaggione.

[4] Gregory, in fact, confirms it at *CE* II 161–163 (GNO I 271f). Eunomius' wording evokes the frequent claim in early Christian thought that, what in the human mind is transitory, in God is real. Historically this is one of the roots of the use of *hypostasis*-terminology with regard to God. Cf. e.g. Basil, *De spiritu sancto* 17,41,17–21 (SC 17bis, 394): ἀλλ' οὐκ ἂν πιστεύσαιμι εἰς τοσοῦτον αὐτοὺς παραπληξίας ἐλαύνειν, ὥστε φάναι τὸν θεὸν τῶν ὅλων, ὥσπερ κοινότητά τινα, λόγῳ μόνῳ θεωρητήν, ἐν οὐδεμιᾷ δὲ ὑποστάσει τὸ εἶναι ἔχουσαν, εἰς τὰ ὑποκείμενα διαιρεῖσθαι.

as well as later theologians speak of God's attributes, they normally assume that those predicates correspond with real properties of God.

Eunomius' position on divine names becomes more problematic as he goes on to argue that, as God's being is absolutely simple, every name said of God either means 'unbegotten' too or is wrongly applied to the Supreme Being:

> . . . every word used to signify the essence of the Father is equivalent in force of meaning to 'the Unbegotten' because the Father is without parts and uncomposed.[5]

Intuitively this contention seems implausible enough. To find the right argument against it is less easy. God's simplicity in itself was universally acknowledged. It is equally clear that this makes the assumption of divine properties as such problematic. Speaking of properties appears to imply necessarily some kind of multiplicity which, by definition, must be absent from divine substance. Eunomius' doctrine of God as 'the unbegotten' (ἀγέννητος) is his characteristically sweeping solution to that problem: there is one and only one attribute of God. Saying that God is unbegotten substance tells us everything about him; other attributes would then add no extra information about his being. If we use them, we do so on precisely that understanding: they mean exactly the same as 'unbegotten'.

The question, then, is not whether human usage, employing a variety of concepts for the description of divine substance, is as such ultimately accurate. It cannot be. The question is whether it is acceptable that all attributes customarily employed are reduced to just one, which is thought to capture the true essence of God. Eunomius apparently thinks this works for 'unbegotten'. The alternative would be to argue that all attributes used by human beings are not exhausting the fullness of divine being and that, therefore, their multiplicity expresses the limits of human cognition more than the actual being of God. One might also urge that there is, within divinity, a level that is not pure simplicity, and that it is this level to which our thoughts about God refer.

These are, in fact, two strategies: one, aiming at epistemology and philosophy of language, addresses the question of how our thoughts

[5] Eunomius, *Apologia* 19 (Vaggione 58,16–8): εἰ τοίνυν πᾶν ὅπερ λέγεται τῆς τοῦ πατρὸς οὐσίας σημαντικόν, ἴσον ἐστί κατὰ τῆς σημασίας δύναμιν τῷ ἀγεννήτῳ διὰ τὸ ἀμερὲς καὶ ἀσύνθετον . . . ET: Vaggione.

and words are formed and applied. The other, directed ultimately at metaphysics, asks what those thoughts and words are applied to. These strategies are not, of course, totally different. Both to some extent aim at explaining how human beings can know something of God without 'knowing' him as they know things within the created world. Basil and Gregory probed both approaches: we find them arguing that human cognition never reaches divine substance as such but remains in the sphere of properties expressing God's activities. They also claim, in particular in their anti-Eunomian polemic, that due to the origin of human language in human ἐπίνοια the Eunomian assumptions are excluded.

It is not difficult to understand why they did so. The problem posed by Eunomius is a difficult one to tackle. In fact, the question of whether there is any ultimately successful strategy against Eunomius' position must be regarded as open, and this paper, which shall leave it to one side, certainly does not presume otherwise.[6] The problem with Basil's and Gregory's argument is not, then, that they used both strategies, the problem is, or so I shall argue, that they were not careful holding them apart. There is a subtle but vital distinction to be made between the *object* of which names are significant and the *capacity* by means of which they are imposed. They may be indicative of (δηλωτικά) substance or nature (οὐσίας/φύσεως), of activity or properties (ἐνεργείας/ἰδιωμάτων); they are said (λέγονται) by nature (φύσει) or by conception (ἐπινοίᾳ). It seems that both, Basil and Gregory have more, and more interesting, things to say about the former, but they do it often under the disguise of the latter, which makes their argument less convincing than it might otherwise have been.

II. *Basil on the 'epinoetic' character of Christological titles*

As is well known the elaboration about ἐπίνοια and its consequences for divine names fills large parts of Basils *Adversus Eunomium* and

[6] One only has to recall the more modern argument of rationalists like Spinoza or Hegel to realise the difficulties inherent in the epistemic claims of 'negative theology'. What do we mean by saying we know that we do not know the divine essence? How is it to be understood, e.g., that we 'know' that it is simple but then pretend not to know it as such?

almost the entirety of Gregory's *Contra Eunomium* II. For practical reasons my comments are largely restricted to those sections prescribed for this paper. Basil takes the remarks from Eunomius' *Apology* for an all-out assault on the human capacity of discursive reasoning. He therefore proposes a closer look at this capacity: "What ἐπίνοια as such is, this I would like to investigate."[7]

The reason why Basil takes this approach becomes clear as he goes along. Eunomius, he charges, reduces ἐπίνοια to cases of misapprehension, of empty fantasy, in brief, of 'paranoia'. What other uses are there of ἐπίνοια which Eunomis ignores? Basil sees ἐπίνοια primarily and most properly as the analytical capacity so vital for human cognition. We perceive something as simple when we first become aware of it. It is then the work of ἐπίνοια to further differentiate this initial impression by an act of analytical division. This division, we say, is done "by conception only".[8] Thus we may perceive something first only as a body. It then is reason (λόγος) by means of ἐπίνοια which subsequently analyses it into the constituents of which it is made up: colour, shape, size etc. Similarly with corn: while as such a simple reality we find that we employ a variety of terms for its more accurate description: fruit if we look at its end; seed if we consider it as the origin of what is to come; food insofar as it is appropriated to the body that is to consume it.[9] What we thus perceive to be simple by substance is conceptualised as being quite complex.

These examples should be sufficient to show the general drift of Basil's interest in ἐπίνοια. His precise understanding of ἐπίνοια, however, remains as shadowy as the problems of his approach are apparent. Does Basil wish to draw a distinction between a reality that as

[7] Basil, *Adversus Eunomium* I 6,1–2 (SC 299, 182): αὐτὸ δὲ τοῦτο, τί ποτέ ἐστιν ἡ ἐπίνοια, ἡδέως ἂν ἐρωτήσαιμι.

[8] Basil, *Adversus Eunomium* I 6,21–25 (SC 299, 184): ὁρῶμεν τοίνυν, ὅτι ἐν μὲν τῇ κοινῇ χρήσει τὰ ταῖς ἀθρόαις ἐπιβολαῖς τοῦ νοῦ ἁπλᾶ δοκοῦντα εἶναι καὶ μοναχά, ταῖς δὲ κατὰ λεπτὸν ἐξετάσεσι ποικίλα φαινόμενα, καὶ πολλὰ ταῦτα τῷ νῷ διαιρούμενα, ἐπινοίᾳ μόνῃ διαιρετὰ λέγεται.

[9] Basil, *Adversus Eunomium* I 6,44–51 (SC 299, 186): Οἷον τοῦ σίτου νόημα μὲν ἁπλοῦν ἐνυπάρχει πᾶσι, καθὸ φανέντα γνωρίζομεν· ἐν δὲ τῇ ἀκριβεῖ περὶ αὐτοῦ ἐξετάσει, θεωρία τε πλειόνων προσέρχεται, καὶ προσηγορίαι διάφοροι τῶν νοηθέντων σημαντικαί. τὸν γὰρ αὐτὸν σῖτον νῦν μὲν καρπὸν λέγομεν, νῦν δὲ σπέρμα, καὶ πάλιν τροφήν· καρπὸν μέν, ὡς τέλος τῆς παρελθούσης γεωργίας· σπέρμα δέ, ὡς ἀρχὴν τῆς μελλούσης· τροφὴν δέ, ὡς κατάλληλον εἰς προσθήκην τῷ τοῦ προσφερομένου σώματι.

such is simple and only becomes multiple on account of our mental operations? If we remember that his eventual interest is to defend conceptual thought of God, we may be inclined to understand him so. Such an argument would do little, however, to allay Eunomius' confrontation of 'by conception' and 'in truth'. In fact it would confirm it. Alternatively one might propose that Basil's intent is to rehabilitate ἐπίνοια by arguing that it discovers the more complex structure inherent in being and therefore is not as empty as Eunomius had charged. Such a reading would be supported by the impression in some formulations that the first notion of a single and simple thing is somehow rough and unrefined and for this reason in need of the work of ἐπίνοια. But while such a reading would help explain Basil's interest in salvaging ἐπίνοια from Eunomius' disdain for it, it would at the same time inevitably lead to disastrous consequences once the object under investigation is neither body nor corn, but God, a being which is assumed to be pure simplicity.

Problems abound, then, whichever way we look at Basil's argument. If anything they become even more obvious once we consider the central example with which he illustrates his theory, Christological titles. Basil takes the various designations Jesus gives to himself such as 'door', 'vine', 'way' and 'shepherd' as expressive of varying conceptions (ἐπίνοιαι) of what is evidently and essentially one single reality (ἓν κατὰ τὸ ὑποκείμενον, μία οὐσία).[10] These titles, he says, indicate to human beings God's love of men and the grace of divine dispensation (τὴν φιλανθρωπίαν τῆς θεότητος καὶ τὴν ἐξ οἰκονομίας χάριν)[11] by means of 'some properties that are seen around' the saviour (ἰδιώμασί τισι τοῖς θεωρουμένοις περὶ αὐτόν).[12] This example may appear to tilt the balance between the two possible interpretations, which have been suggested above, in favour of the former: what *is* one (by nature or substance) appears to be manifold from the perspective of human beings. In spite of his protestations, Basil would, then, seem to be not so far away from Eunomius' position on ἐπίνοια.

It appears most unlikely, however, that Basil takes the ἐπίνοιαι of Christ to be subjective constructions of the human mind. In fact, the example of the Christological titles shows, I think, that Basil's

[10] Basil, *Adversus Eunomium* I 7,12–5 (SC 299, 188–90).
[11] Basil, *Adversus Eunomium* I 7,5–6 (SC 299, 188).
[12] Basil, *Adversus Eunomium* I 7,7 (SC 299, 188).

understanding of ἐπίνοια differs from both readings that were suggested initially. Basil must assume that Christ is both one (in substance, that is) and many – the latter with regard to his soteriological activity. Ἐπίνοια then relates to this aspect of him, it refers to the saviour in so far as he is or better *becomes* multiple as part of the divine dispensation.

If this is accepted, as I think it must, then this has two not quite negligible consequences for Basil's argument. The first is that it clearly is not concerned with anything like a conceptualist theory of language. Basil may doubt that we know and are able to express precisely that and how Christ is one (although he does not here dwell on this point).[13] He does certainly not doubt that we know and express ourselves, due to our conceptual capacity, with some precision about his ἐνέργειαι. His point, then is not by what capacity we apply names, but what names apply to. Ἐπίνοια teaches us about the various aspects of a body or the multiple notions we have of corn: in both cases it helps us distinguish between their several properties which exist. The titles of Christ are equally said of his soteriological functions. They are not applied to his single and simple nature. Whether or not those titles, or any other names, are applied *by* nature or *by* conception seems rather irrelevant for the present issue.

The other consequence is this: in all the examples Basil has considered so far, it appears that the force of his argument depends heavily on the co-existence of unity and diversity in the same object of cognition. It is not difficult to predict that this line of argument creates tremendous difficulties once it is applied to God. Basil has entirely forsaken the opportunity to argue for disanalogies between created being and God, disanalogies that may be the central cause of our inability to grasp divine substance in its essential simplicity.

If Basil shows anything then it is this: that our knowledge of Christ extends only to his dispensational properties, not to his nature. Why, then, would he have thought that those titles are applied conceptually? What is more, why would he have assumed that such a fact

[13] He elsewhere expresses his conviction that any thing's substance is inscrutable because human cognition always knows properties that are 'around' the substance (Basil, *Adversus Eunomium* I 12,30–48, SC 299, 214–216; cf. my: "Stoic substance, non-existent matter? Some passages in Basil of Caesarea reconsidered", in: *StPatr* forthcoming).

(if true) would have a bearing on the dispute with Eunomius? I would suggest two influences that may help explain why he expected to find here an answer to the anomoian challenge.

a) Basil probably knew the usage – encountered frequently in the commentary literature of late ancient philosophy – that something is 'one in reality/substance' (ὑποστάσει) but many 'by conception' (ἐπινοίᾳ).[14] Its intention is to mark a distinction in the way our mind divides being. It is one thing to divide a forest into single trees or humankind into its individuals, quite another to divide a tree into root, stem and leaves, or to speak of the outer end of one of its twigs. The forest is divided into things that continue to exist separately (ὑποστάσει), the tree is divided *only* in our thought.[15] The point was not either to say or to deny that all division is done conceptually, but to mark a distinction with regard to the kind of parts resulting from such a division.

We can perceive, I think, why Basil thought it useful to apply this distinction to the problem he was facing but also why it could not work for that purpose. Basil's premise is this: God is one, single being and yet we employ legitimately a variety of terms for him. So he too is 'one in substance' but many 'according to our conception' of him. Eunomius' argument, however, had been that one specific term, 'unbegotten', was used of God properly denoting him in his singularity and simplicity. What Basil needs to counter this contention is a theory explaining that *all* names have their origin in human conception, that no exception can be made for any term, such as Eunomius requests for 'unbegotten'. But from the fact that what is one in substance, is many according to our conception, this does not follow. The force of the juxtaposition Basil employs thus leads him into quite a different direction from the one intended.

b) Next to this philosophical I would suggest a theological influence. Origen, in the second book of his *Contra Celsum*, advanced a theory according to which Christological titles were applied conceptually. His wording resembles closely that of Basil when he writes that "Jesus

---

[14] Cf. Alexander of Aphrodisias, *In Met.* B 5 (CAG I 229,31–230,1): Surface, line and point can be without a liquid by conception, but not *hypostasei*. R. E. Witt has argued that the origin of that juxtaposition lies with Posidonius: 'ΥΠΟΣΤΑΣΙΣ', in: H. G. Wood (ed.), *Amicitiae Corolla for J. R. Harris*, London 1933, 319–343, here 325.

[15] From Basil's wording at *Adversus Eunomium* I 6,25 (SC 299, 184) (. . . ἐπινοίᾳ μόνῃ διαιρετὰ λέγεται) it appears that he was aware precisely of this usage.

being one was many things by conception".[16] Origen clearly means what he says for the point of his elaboration is that Jesus is different things to various kinds of people. In this way he seeks to counter Celsus' charge that Jesus ought to have appeared to all men universally if he were God, a charge Origen takes seriously. He argues that Jesus, in his earthly life and after, appeared to people according to their capacity of recognising the divine.

There is no place here to enter into a thorough investigation of this theory, but it ought to be instantly clear what 'many by conception' means for Origen and that it is plausible for him to employ this terminology. There actually is a 'subjective' element to the kind of cognition envisaged here. The varying degree of perfection amongst human beings is the reason that, what is essentially one, appears in various ways.

It is generally accepted that Origen's theory of the ἐπίνοιαι of Christ has influenced Basil's elaboration in his *Adversus Eunomium* whether directly or via some mediator, such as Eusebius of Caesarea.[17] Any of those authors, however, would have had a theological justification for this kind of theory which for Basil did no longer exist. Origen, in the first book of his *Commentary on the Gospel of John*, makes it quite certain what the ontological background of the many and various titles of Christ is:

> Now God is altogether one and simple; but our Saviour, for many reasons, since God 'set him forth a propitiation' (cf. *Rom* 3,25) and 'a first fruits of the whole creation' (cf. *Col* 1,15), is made many things, or perhaps all these things, the whole creation, so far as capable of redemption, stands in need of him.[18]

This is the ultimate reason for the existence of the many titles which Origen in the same passage calls ἐπίνοιαι.[19] His intention here is to

[16] Origen, *Contra Celsum* II 64 (GCS 3, 185,26): Ὁ Ἰησοῦς εἷς ὢν πλείονα τῇ ἐπινοίᾳ ἦν.

[17] Cf. Basil Studer, "Der theologiegeschichtliche Hintergrund der Epinoiai-Lehre Gregors von Nyssa" in this volume, esp. section III. Die origenische Herkunft der Epinoiai-Lehre and the references given there.

[18] Origen, *In Iohannem* I 20,119 (GCS 10, 24,23–6): ὁ θεὸς μὲν οὖν πάντη ἕν ἐστι καὶ ἁπλοῦν· ὁ δὲ σωτὴρ ἡμῶν διὰ τὰ πολλὰ, ἐπεὶ « προέθετο » αὐτὸν « ὁ θεὸς ἱλαστήριον » καὶ ἀπαρχὴν πάσης τῆς κτίσεως, πολλὰ γίνεται ἢ καὶ τάχα πάντα ταῦτα, καθὰ χρῄζει αὐτοῦ ἡ ἐλευθεροῦσθαι δυναμένη πᾶσα κτίσις. English translation: ANF.

[19] Origen, *In Iohannem* I 19,118 (GCS 10, 24,17–22).

offer a vision in which Christ mediates between the absolute simplicity of God and the utter multiplicity of the created world. The fact that he is the redeemer is inextricably intertwined with this mediating role. He *is* one, but becomes many in his soteriological activity. Again, he *can* become many because he is not as simple as God is. For Origen, Christ is the first in a world characterised by unity-in-multiplicity. The variety of epinoetic names applied to Christ mirrors that fact as much as the differing ontological position of those contemplating him.

Both, Basil and Eunomius reject this kind of reasoning, and yet one may perceive an echo of Origen's theory where Basil mentions specifically Christ's love of men and the divine dispensation in connection with his various titles. Christ is 'one in substance', but his various activities and the relation (σχέσις) towards his soteriological benevolence make him receptive of many names. Whatever Basil's precise position in the *Adversus Eunomium* is towards the Christological problem,[20] fundamentally it seems indubitable that the theological background, once again, may help explain, but hardly justifies, the use Basil makes here of ἐπίνοια. For Origen, the application of titles to Christ is based precisely on his difference from the father in ontological rank.

It is beyond the scope of this paper to subject Basil's argument to minute scrutiny, but what has been said should have sufficed to clarify the main outlines of my initial thesis. Basil rightly aims at the central and most controversial point of Eunomius' theory, which is the assumption that the simplicity of God means that all predicates are to mean 'unbegotten' or be falsely said of God. While he pretends to counter it with a theory of ἐπίνοια, his actual illustrations demonstrate more his awareness that the differentiation of οὐσία and ἐνέργεια is what really provides an answer to Eunomius' challenge. As far as I can see for most of what Basil says the required conceptual framework is marked by what names signify, not how they

[20] Generally, the Cappadocian position is to transfer to Christ's humanity what Origen and others had said of his divine nature. How this works with the doctrine of Christ's ἐπίνοιαι is shown by H.-J. Sieben. Cf. id. "Vom Heil in den vielen 'Namen Christ' zur 'Nachahmung' derselben. Zur Rezeption der Epinoia-Lehre des Origenes durch die kappadokischen Väter", *ThPh* 73 (1998), 1–28. While this removes one problem it creates another: those ἐπίνοιαι can not help solve the difficulty of different divine attributes.

are applied, by distinctions like 'one in substance – many in activity'; or again: 'one in nature – many in properties'. Gregory too, as we shall see, is using them, but they are not the same as the distinction between natural and conceptual imposition of names.

III. *Eunomius' reply – attempt of a reconstruction*

Given this situation we need not be surprised that Eunomius was not immediately silenced by Basil's reply to his *Apology*. What exactly his arguments were against Basil's theory of Christological titles we cannot fully ascertain. Gregory's rendering of Eunomius' words in this passage is so selective and – to all appearance – distorting that their reasonable reconstruction seems all but impossible.[21] Gregory hardly ever quotes more than a single statement at a time. Sometimes, therefore, even its literal meaning is far from clear in the rendering we have. But even where we may be reasonably certain about this we lack crucial information with regard to context, information that would be necessary for a satisfactory interpretation. Eunomius' intent regularly remains as unclear as the precise status of a particular argument: was it meant to be directed against a specific statement of Basil's? Was it meant as a general truth? Was it meant as a *reductio ad absurdum*? Was it ironic? From the evidence we have we often can only guess. Consequently, what is offered here remains to some extent fraught with speculation.

Essentially, I take it, Eunomius offers four arguments against Basil's contentions in the passage under investigation. The first seems straightforward enough: there is no evidence that any biblical author ('any of the saints';[22] 'the apostles and evangelists')[23] ever claimed that these titles were applied conceptually. We know that it was a staple of fourth-century polemical literature that whatever your opponent said was first submitted to the 'tradition test' which of course it regularly failed. Strangely though, all those writers quite freely admitted non-biblical, non-traditional vocabulary to their own language. Gregory

[21] Cf. R. P. Vaggione (ed.), *Eunomius. The Extant Works*, Oxford 1987, 89–94 on Gregory's citations from Eunomius' second apology.
[22] *CE* II 295 (GNO I 313,16).
[23] *CE* II 305 (GNO I 316,2–3).

was not without a point retorting: if ἐπίνοια is not used by the saints, what about ἀγεννησία?[24]

It is less easy to reconstruct the second argument. Gregory quotes it as saying that

> to cite [a case of] homonymy based on analogy as 'human conceptualization', is the work of a mind which has discarded what is valid, correct meaning, and considers the words of the Lord in an invalid sense and a sort of debased usage.[25]

For Eunomius, the analogous application of names is a case of equivocation (ὁμωνυμία). This is in line with the standard distinction as, for example, in Porphyry's *Commentary on the Categories*.[26] Eunomius simply applies this general principle here arguing that the analogical application of words like 'vine' to Christ is a case of homonymy: the two things have nothing in common, except the predicate said of them. According to Eunomius, such use of terms for Christ is not, however, a good example for a general theory of naming. Why not?[27] The use of a metaphor always presupposes a primary understanding of both terms' meaning. We must know what 'vine' as well as 'Jesus Christ' normally signify in order to appreciate the force of the word 'I am the vine'. In other words, while it might be granted that metaphorical use of terms is conceptional (actually Eunomius appears not to grant it at all),[28] the primary signification on which it rests is an entirely different matter. Eunomius, then, accuses Basil of discarding this primary signification, the 'valid, correct' understanding where he takes metaphorical usage as evidence for the notional application of names.

---

[24] *CE* II 310 (GNO I 317,4–7). Eunomius apparently does not speak of ἀγεννησία, but of God as οὐσία ἀγέννητος. He deduces this term, as we have seen, from *Ex* 3,14.

[25] *CE* II 306 (GNO I 316,6–11): τὸ γάρ τοι, φησί, τὴν ἐξ ἀναλογίας ὁμωνυμίαν προφέρειν εἰς ἀνθρωπίνην ἐπίνοιαν, ψυχῆς ἔργον τὸν μὲν ἐρρωμένον νοῦν κατὰ δίκην παρῃρημένης, ἀρρώστῳ δὲ διανοίᾳ καὶ πεφωρημένῃ τινὶ συνηθείᾳ τοὺς τοῦ κυρίου λόγους ἐπισκοπούσης. ET: Hall (with changes).

[26] Porphyry, *In Cat.* (CAG IV/1 65,18–20.31–66,2). I leave aside the problem posed by Porphyry's sharp distinction of analogy and metaphor according to which Christological titles would probably not be allowed to be counted as *homonyma*. Others, like Atticus, lumped the two together, and so does Eunomius (*op. cit.*, CAG IV/1 66,29–67,32).

[27] I take it that Eunomius understands 'analogy' broadly in the sense of Aristotle's definition of 'metaphor' as the "application of an alien name by transference" (*Poetics* 21, 1457b6f: μεταφορὰ δέ ἐστιν ὀνόματος ἀλλοτρίου ἐπιφορά).

[28] See below at n. 32.

Eunomius' third argument runs like this:

> God on the other hand has accorded a share of the most honourable names even to the most fragile of terrestrial beings without bestowing on them equality of dignity, and of the meanest to the most potent without the naturally mean status being simultaneously conferred by the names.[29]

On the face of it this statement seems quite clear. While Gregory rages against it pretending that Eunomius thinks of virtue and holiness being said mendaciously of bad things,[30] it would appear that Eunomius thought of a term like οὐσία which at once denotes most properly the supreme being and is said of any, even the most modest part of God's creation. He might also have thought of goodness which the creator himself applied to his handiwork in its entirety (*Gen* 1,31). The converse, then, seems to apply in the case of the Christological titles which apply to the Only-Begotten words from the terrestrial sphere. In both cases, Eunomius seems to urge, the use of those names teaches us nothing about what these things are. So why are they employed?

Their use, apparently, is not a human fancy: God is expressly said to be its originator. But why would God bestow on a thing a name that does not express its being? Leaving to one side Gregory's charge that God is thus made lying,[31] the question of what Eunomius thinks remains open. Is this part of a more complex theory of naming, or is Eunomius just pointing to the obvious fact that names do not always fully reflect a thing's ontological status to dismiss Basil's musings about Christological titles? The answer may lie in a fragment which appears to continue the present argument and is adduced by Gregory somewhat further down in his refutation:

> It has been *arranged* in this way, however; human conception enjoys no power over the giving of names. But God himself, who designed the universe, adjusts the designations of every named thing appropriately to the limits and rules of relation, activity and analogy.[32]

[29] *CE* II 315 (GNO I 318,10–15): Ἀλλ' ὁ θεός, φησί, καὶ τοῖς ἀσθενεστάτοις τῶν περὶ γῆν τῶν τιμιωτάτων μεταδέδωκεν ὀνομάτων, μὴ συμμεταδοὺς τῆς τῶν ἀξιωμάτων ἰσομοιρίαις, καὶ τοῖς κυριωτάτοις τῶν εὐτελεστάτων, μὴ συμμεταφερομένης ὑπὸ τῶν ὀνομάτων τῆς φυσικῆς εὐτελείας. ET: Hall (with changes).

[30] *CE* II 321 (GNO I 319,28–320,6).

[31] Vgl. *CE* II 317 (GNO I 318,30–319,1): καὶ τοῦτο ἔργον εἶναι λέγει θεοῦ, τὸ διαψεύδεσθαι τῇ τιμιωτέρᾳ κλήσει τὴν χειρόνα φύσιν.

[32] *CE* II 334–335 (GNO I 323,23–26; 324,1–5): ταῦτα μέντοι τοῦτον διατέτακται

Eunomius thus affirms that naming originates with God. This naming activity of God, however, knows of more rules than the conformity of name and substance. There are names accorded by God to apply to a thing's activity. Even for the metaphorical use of names God, in this reading, would have provided.

This is still a far shot from a satisfactory theory, but due to our lack of further information I leave this claim here to move on to the fourth and last argument Gregory ascribes to Eunomius in the present context. He quotes it as follows:

> Since, he says, the Lord applied these appellations to himself without reckoning one first or second or more refined or more precise, it is not possible that these names should come from conceptual thought.[33]

Here at last we have a train of thought that seems straightforward enough. Eunomius' line of reasoning starts from Basil's declaration that ἐπίνοια is the human faculty that refines our cognition by analysing the cruder impressions produced by sense perception. But if the titles of Christ are used by himself, this model is not applicable. It is crucial to see that Eunomius here refers back to Basil's own statement. The author of the *Apologia Apologiae* would not have been ignorant of the fact that Paul, John and other biblical writers used those titles of Christ, but Basil himself had pointed out that Jesus employed them first.[34] In whatever way, then, these names apply to divine, soteriological activities, whatever analogies they produce, they are not due to the inventive nature of any theologian as long as we believe what the Bible tells us.

* * *

τὸν τρόπον, οὐ τῆς ἐπινοίας τῶν ἀνθρώπων λαχούσης τὴν ἐξουσίαν τῶν ὀνομάτων [. . .] ἀλλ' αὐτοῦ, φησί, τοῦ τὰ πάντα δημιουργήσαντος θεοῦ σχέσεως τε καὶ ἐνεργείας καὶ ἀναλογίας μέτροις καὶ νόμοις προσφυῶς ἑκάστῳ τῶν ὀνομαζομένων τὰς προσηγορίας συναρμόζοντος. ET: Hall (with changes).

[33] *CE* II 351 (GNO I 328,21–25): ἐπειδή, φησίν, ἑαυτῷ ταύτας ἐπέθηκε τὰς προσηγορίας ὁ κύριος οὔτε τι πρῶτον νοῶν οὔτε δεύτερον οὔτε λεπτότερόν τι ἢ ἀκριβέστερον, οὐκ ἔστιν ἐξ ἐπινοίας εἶναι ταῦτα εἰπεῖν τὰ ὀνόματα. ET: Hall. It is not altogether clear whether this is the actual quotation from Eunomius and how it relates to a similar statement in II 350. For the present argument this philological detail is irrelevant.

[34] Basil, *Adversus Eunomium* I 7,4–6 (SC 299, 188): Ὁ κύριος ἡμῶν Ἰησοῦς Χριστὸς ἐν τοῖς περὶ ἑαυτοῦ λόγοις, τὴν φιλανθρωπίαν τῆς θεότητος καὶ τὴν ἐξ οἰκονομίας χάριν τοῖς ἀνθρώποις παραδηλῶν . . .

Overall, Eunomius appears to have largely restricted himself in this section to a refutation of Basil's elaboration in *Adversus Eunomium* I 7. Thus, not much of excitement is produced by an analysis of his statements. There are indications though that he extended his 'linguistic theory' to the remarkable claim that God provides for any legitimate use of language, including even the use of metaphors.

IV. *Gregory's apology for Basil*

Gregory, in the section prescribed for this paper, chiefly seeks to refute the aforesaid arguments adduced by Eunomius and thus to defend Basil's original contentions against the heresiarch. The more polemical replies that cover great parts of Gregory's text I propose to gloss over. They hardly seem to give an answer to Eunomius' objections, presenting instead much rhetorical tit for tat. More interesting is the way Gregory positions himself vis-à-vis the principal question Basil had raised. Basil, while claiming to argue for a conceptual theory of naming had, in fact, sought to establish that names refer to activities or properties, certainly not to substances. We shall presently see that the same tendency in Gregory is even more apparent. While keeping up the claim of an epinoetic theory of naming in principle, his actual argument draws crucially on the distinction of what is signified.

Near the outset of our section, having quoted both Basil's original contention[35] and Eunomius' first counterargument, Gregory finds himself prompted to lay out his position in principle:

---

[35] Gregory's rendering of Basil's argument poses a riddle. Apart from more negligible changes, which I here ignore, it differs substantially from the original by saying that Christ revealed to men through his titles τὴν φύσιν τῆς θεότητος instead of τὴν φιλανθρωπίαν τῆς θεότητος καὶ τὴν ἐξ οἰκονομίας χάριν, the reading we find in Basil's book (I 7,5–6, SC 299, 188). Jaeger takes this as evidence that Gregory quotes from Eunomius' text (note *ad locum*; GNO I 313). One might imagine that Eunomius changed the wording, as the stronger claim (the titles denote divine nature) might appear to facilitate his criticism. From what is left in Gregory's treatise, however, there is little evidence that he in any way drew on this supposed reading. Gregory, on the other hand, should have been alerted by this distortion of Basil's text (whether or not he had a chance to check its accuracy at once). Only a little later he states explicitly that those titles cannot refer to the nature of the Only-begotten, but must indicate his activities (II 298, GNO I 314). This corresponds well enough to Basil's original text, but contradicts the version he quotes. As far as I see, an explanation is not forthcoming.

> What we say is this: As the Lord in various ways provides for human life, each variety of benefit is identified in turn by one or other such title, the foresight and action therein observed becoming a particular kind of name. Such a title is in our view applied by concept (ἐπίνοια).[36]

The argument continues thus: Evidently all these titles are used by scripture. They therefore must be accepted as valid predicates of Christ and cannot be empty notions. On the other hand, they do not denote Christ's divine nature. Gregory concludes:

> If then he is so called, yet not by nature, and every thing said of the Lord by the scripture he assuredly is and is properly so designated, what principle remains for such words being fittingly applied to the Only-begotten God, other than the conceptual way?[37]

Why do the titles not refer to the nature? The reason given is this: as divine nature is absolutely simple it cannot be receptive of a variety of names. Or, to put it the other way around, if those titles were indicative of divine nature or substance, this would make the latter multiple (πολυειδής) and composite (πολυσύνθετος).[38]

Gregory here argues very much along the lines of Origen and Basil. He does not dispute that various names can only be applied to an object which itself is manifold. This, clearly, is not the case for divine nature. Consequently, Christological titles refer to him in so far as he is part of the history of salvation. Gregory, it may be observed, is more careful than Basil to mark out the difference to Origen: in his divine nature, Christ is as little receptive of various names as the Father. The difference, then, is no longer primarily that between 'God' who is absolutely simple and the Son who is not (as had been the case with Origen),[39] but between divine substance or nature, which is absolutely simple and therefore not the object of reference for human predication, and divine activity (ἐνέργεια).

---

[36] *CE* II 298–299 (GNO I 314,14–19): ἡμεῖς μὲν γὰρ τοῦτό φαμεν, ὅτι πολυειδῶς τοῦ κυρίου τῆς ἀνθρωπίνης προνοοῦντος ζωῆς ἕκαστον εὐεργεσίας εἶδος δι' ἑκάστου τῶν τοιούτων ὀνομάτων καταλλήλως γνωρίζεται, τῆς ἐνθεωρουμένης αὐτῷ προνοίας τε καὶ ἐνεργείας εἰς ὀνόματος τύπον μεταβαινούσης. τὸ δὲ τοιοῦτον ὄνομα παρ' ἡμῶν « ἐπινοίᾳ » λέγεται ὀνομάζεσθαι. ET: Hall.

[37] *CE* II 304 (GNO I 315,19–23): εἰ τοίνυν λέγεται μέν, οὐ κατὰ φύσιν δέ, πᾶν δὲ τὸ παρὰ τῆς γραφῆς λεγόμενον κύριον πάντως ἐστὶ καὶ προσφυῶς ἐπιλέγεται, τίς ἕτερος ὑπολείπεται λόγος τοῦ ἁρμοζόντως τῷ μονογενεῖ θεῷ τὰς τοιαύτας τετάχθαι φωνὰς πλὴν τοῦ κατ' ἐπίνοιαν τρόπου; ET: Hall (with changes).

[38] *CE* II 302 (GNO I 315,10–3).

[39] Cf. Origen, *In Iohannem* I 20,119 (see n. 18 above).

Everything in this chain of thought seems more plausible than the claim that it leads to conceptual application of names. Gregory clearly uses the juxtaposition of nature and energy to urge that Christological titles are said of the latter, not the former. Needless to say, this is not implying anything about the way they are imposed. On the contrary, his contention that a variety of names would violate divine simplicity (incidentally, quite in agreement with Eunomius on this particular point) would seem to make more sense on the basis of a realistic theory.

Gregory's tacitly realistic credentials come out even more distinctly in his reply to what I counted above as Eunomius' third argument.[40] Against the claim that exalted names may signify things and *vice versa*, Gregory stresses as unequivocally as one would wish the correspondence of names and things. He all but subscribes to Eunomius' theory of divine imposition of names where he claims:

> As they are in truth and nature, so are things judged and named by God, not named in contradiction to what they are, but described by their proper denotations in whatever way they may be most clearly displayed.[41]

Is this a statement by Eunomius putting forth his notorious 'naturalistic' theory of language? No, it is a verbatim quotation from Gregory of Nyssa, the great champion of later conventionalist theories,[42] replying to Eunomius' claim that God has apportioned a share of honourable names to ordinary things and similarly allocates more modest terms to Christ. Gregory does not here take exception to the assertion that God gives names. The idea, however, that those names might not correspond to a thing's substance seems outrageous to him: "It is the work of deceit to give names to fragile things which do not correspond to their nature and worth."[43] But the true

---

[40] Cf. at n. 29 above.

[41] *CE* II 323 (GNO I 320,19–22): ὡς ἔχει φύσεως τε καὶ ἀληθείας, οὕτω τὰ ὄντα παρὰ τοῦ θεοῦ κρίνεταί τε καὶ λέγεται, οὐκ ἐναντίως τοῖς οὖσιν ὀνομαζόμενα, ἀλλ' ὡς ἂν μάλιστα καταφανῆ γένοιτο τὰ σημαινόμενα ταῖς οἰκείαις προσηγορίαις ἐξαγγελλόμενα. ET: Hall.

[42] Cf. Th. Kobusch, "Zu den sprachphilosophischen Grundlagen in der Schrift *Contra Eunomium* des Gregor von Nyssa", in: L. F. Mateo-Seco – J. L. Bastero (eds.), *El 'Contra Eunomium I' en la producción literaria de Grigorio de Nisa*, Pamplona 1988, 247–68.

[43] *CE* II 327 (GNO I 320,18–9): ἀπάτης μὲν γάρ ἐστι τὸ μὴ ὡς ἔχει φύσεώς τε καὶ ἀξίας τὰ ἀσθενῆ τῶν πραγμάτων κατονομάζειν ... ET: Hall (with changes).

God is free from deceit and jealousy and therefore "looks to the real truth of objects, attests the true worth of each and gives names on the basis of facts".[44]

Later, while dealing with what I counted as Eunomius' fourth argument,[45] Gregory returns to the subject proper of Christological titles. In his view, the question of whether Christ employed these titles of himself or not is irrelevant. Why would that be so? Gregory summarises Basil's position as follows:

> The Lord is by himself whatever he is by nature, and when he is simultaneously named after his various activities (ἐνέργειαι), he does not possess a single title which is applied to them all, but is accorded the name in accordance with the idea which arises in us from that activity. . . .
>
> How then are our words refuted if it is said that Christ uses these titles of himself? The question was not about who uses these titles; our purpose was rather to consider what these titles mean, whether they denote the nature, or whether they are applied conceptually (ἐπινοητικῶς) on the basis of activities.[46]

To be sure, Gregory does not forget to mention that our mind plays a role in the application of those titles, but the general tendency of his argument, once again, goes in a different direction. The Christological titles, this is the bottom line of what Gregory tells us, are applied not to his divine nature, but to his providential and redeeming function. While this is in line with what Basil had said, it is in no way a rebuttal of Eunomius' contention by means of conceptual semantics. Gregory here continues precisely with the wavering and the confusion that we had observed in Basil with regard to this distinction. Like his elder brother, Gregory confounds the issue of the object of a name's signification with that of the mode or origin of signification.

---

[44] *CE* II 328 (GNO I 321,28–322,1): ἀλλὰ πρὸς τὴν ἀλήθειαν τῶν ὑποκειμένων ὁρᾶν καὶ τὸ κατ' ἀξίαν ἑκάστῳ προσμαρτυρεῖν καὶ ἐκ τῶν πραγμάτων κατονομάζειν. ET: Hall (with changes).

[45] Cf. at n. 33 above.

[46] *CE* II 353–354 (GNO I 329,8–12.17–23): ὁ κύριος ἐστί μὲν καθ' ἑαυτὸν ὅ τι ποτὲ κατὰ τὴν φύσιν ἐστί, ταῖς δὲ τῶν ἐνεργείων διαφοραῖς συνονομαζόμενος οὐ μίαν ἐπὶ πάντων ἴσχει προσηγορίαν, ἀλλὰ καθ' ἑκάστην ἔννοιαν τὴν ἐξ ἐνεργείας ἐγγινομένην ἡμῖν μεταλαμβάνει τὸ ὄνομα . . . πῶς οὖν ἀνατρέπει τὰ εἰρημένα ὁ λέγων περὶ ἑαυτοῦ ταῦτα τὸν Χριστὸν τὰ ὀνόματα λέγειν; οὐ γὰρ ὅστις ὁ κατονομάσας τὸ ζητούμενον ἦν, ἀλλὰ περὶ τῆς τῶν ὀνομάτων ἐννοίας ἡ θεωρία προέκειτο πότερον φύσιν ἐνδείκνυται ἢ ἐπινοητικῶς ἐκ τῶν ἐνεργειῶν ὀνομάζεται. ET: Hall (with changes).

That Gregory pretends not to understand (or actually does not understand) the relevance of Eunomius' hint to Christ's application of these titles to himself is perhaps the best evidence for the general direction of his mind on this particular question. The issue is not, for him, who has made up those titles, but whether they apply to divine nature or to properties, energies or whatever is *around* (περί) it. This, indubitably, is an important point, but clearly distinct from the question of whether these names are provided for by God himself or whether they are produced by our conceptual capacity. For the latter question the fact that the god-man uses them of himself would perhaps at least demand an explanation.

V. *Conclusion*

Three final considerations bring this communication to a close:

a) In what sense can Gregory be said to have offered a successful apology for his brother Basil? Gregory, as has been seen, in the particular question under enquiry here quite faithfully follows the path trodden by Basil. He answers Eunomius' criticism by reaffirming the arguments his brother had used. To some extent he improves on them. It appears that the more prevalent, as well as more promising, line of argument in Basil is given even more prominence in Gregory, who appears to draw primarily on the distinction between cognition of nature and cognition of energy. One may thus read his elaboration as a slight emendation of Basil's argument, but this is perhaps too strong a statement given Gregory's full-scale identification with his brother's authority. It must not be forgotten, however, that Gregory's self-assigned task in the *Contra Eunomium* gave him practically no room for even modest, explicit criticism of Basil.

That Gregory himself found the οὐσία-ἐνέργεια distinction more helpful for the theological problem he was facing becomes clearer from other writings of his. Without the specific task of defending an early book by Basil he almost inevitably approached the problem of divine names by means of that distinction the classic example being the *Ad Ablabium*, where Gregory is more conspicuous and at the same time more consistent with regard to that question.[47] The

[47] Cf. G. Maspero, *La Trinità e l'uomo*, Rom 2004, 114–47.

crucial passage there[48] draws a distinction between the way our mind deals with created being and the way it approaches God. In the former case, Gregory says, we can normally see with ease how the names we employ fit a thing's being. In the latter case this is different. While every term tells us something that is 'around' divine nature, they do so by means of properties which are indicative of the specific, providential activities of God towards men.

Against too much enthusiasm, however, we should guard ourselves: Gregory's argument in the *Ad Ablabium* leads to the conclusion that divine ἐνέργεια too is unified.[49] A satisfactory clarification of the relation of this unity on the one hand, and the multiple divine attributes that we employ on the other, is not an achievement with which either of the Cappadocians should be credited.

b) The comparison of the *Ad Ablabium* at the same time brings out what is in my view the main deficiency of the present argument while proving as well that Gregory could do better. Not only is Gregory there focussing on the juxtaposition of essence and energies, he also constructs his argument as a disanalogy between the created and the uncreated realm, an element that is almost entirely lacking from Basil's line of reasoning in the *Adversus Eunomium* and consequently from Gregory's *Contra Eunomium*. Failure to emphasise the difference between cognition within the created world and cognition of God, however, invites quite unwelcome conclusions.

This can be seen from a text which admittedly is remote, but nevertheless fascinatingly similar. In his work *Christianity not mysterious* (1696) John Toland employs an argument that is (with all its Lockean overtones) into its very wording strikingly close in particular to Basil's line of thought.[50] Toland there bashes the claim that God would be a mystery because we cannot fully comprehend his being. If this were so, he argues, everything around us would be a mystery as well: we know

> nothing of Bodies but their Properties; God has wisely provided we should understand no more of these than are useful and necessary for us. [. . .] Thus our Eyes are not given us to see all Quantities, nor perhaps any thing as it is in it self, but it bears from Relation to us.[51]

---

[48] Gregory of Nyssa, *Ad Ablabium* (GNO III/1 42,13– 44,16).
[49] *Op. cit.* (GNO III/1 44,7–16).
[50] J. Toland, *Christianity not Mysterious*, London ^{2}1696 (repr. London 1995).
[51] *Op. cit.*, 75–6.

We understand the things around us in so far as we comprehend their properties which make an impact on us. Similarly we understand God sufficiently if we know his activities towards man. Toland concludes:

> That [. . .] when we do as familiarly explain such Doctrines, as what is known of natural things, (which I pretend we can) we may then be as properly said to comprehend the one as the other.[52]

If knowledge of God is as mysterious as any knowledge, then it is only a matter of taste or perspective whether all, or none, cognition is seen as being beyond reason. Toland is quite right to press home this point. It is not, of course, a necessary conclusion that, in fact, the latter of the two options is right, and neither Basil nor Gregory would be obliged to subscribe to Toland's view. It is, however, a possible conclusion demonstrating that Basil's reasoning is dangerous in so far as it could be used for results quite different from the ones he had intended.

c) On a final note I return to the concept of ἐπίνοια. The analysis offered here has led to the conclusion that the topic of conceptual application of names is much less important for the Cappadocian argument against Eunomius than is often claimed. In particular, it is doubtful that in Basil's and Gregory's version it is a successful argument against Eunomius. Why is this so? Basil's argument about ἐπίνοια, I think, went off to a wrong start with his insistence on the theological relevance specifically of its analytic capacity. Thinking, however, and in particular thinking of God, the human mind inevitably proceeds synthetically. Attributes like 'good' or 'life' do not impose a mental division on some object which, apart from this intellectual act appears to us as simple and unified. They rather bring conceptions the mind has of the world into as comprehensive a unity as possible, but still fall short of the absolute simplicity thought to be encountered in God.

The epistemic approach, which, if my argument is accepted, is rather unsuccessful in the Cappadocians, is not of course devoid of theological significance. The example of Thomas Aquinas should suffice to evidence the opposite.[53] At the same time it is interesting

---

[52] *Op. cit.*, 79.

[53] Thomas Aquinas, *Summa Theologiae* I[a], qu. XIII, art. 2, resp.: *Et ideo aliter dicendum est quod huiusmodi quidem nomina significant substantiam divinam, et praedicantur de Deo substantialiter, – sed deficiunt a repraesentatione ipsius.* The eventual upshot of this line of argument is, of course, the theory of analogy.

to observe that Thomas follows the epistemic line of thought not least to fend off the assumption that no name is significant of God's essence. Of the two approaches found in the Cappadocians he thus employs one while criticising the other. This may at least be an indication that a decision must be made between the two. The choice need not be Aquinas' one, but to pursue this question would be the task of a further paper.

DER URSPRUNG DER SPRACHE NACH EUNOMIUS UND GREGOR VOR DEM HINTERGRUND DER ANTIKEN SPRACHTHEORIEN (*CE* II 387–444; 543–553)

Lenka Karfíková

In diesem Beitrag soll ein Aspekt der Sprachauffassung bei Eunomius und Gregor dargelegt werden, und zwar die Vorstellungen der beiden Gegner vom Ursprung der Sprache.[1] Ich gehe dabei von der Passage *CE* II 387–444 (GNO I 339,8–356,16) und 543–553 (GNO I 385,1–388,24) aus,[2] die sich mit dieser Problematik beschäftigt. Zugleich sind in diesen Paragraphen (als ein ironisches Mittel) mehrere Berufungen auf die antiken Sprachtheorien konzentriert, denen ich den abschließenden Teil meiner Ausführungen widme.

I. *Eunomius*

Unsere Passage – die die Reaktionen des Eunomius auf Basilius' Polemik *Adversus Eunomium* I 5–8 (=PG 29, 520c–529c),[3] höchstwahrscheinlich v.a. an I 8 (=PG 29, 528ab), enthält – bringt mehrere sprachtheoretisch interessante Eunomius-Zitate. Über den Ursprung der Sprache lesen wir da:

> Hätte (Gott) den ersten Menschen oder ihren unmittelbaren Nachkommen nicht beigebracht, wie die einzelnen Dinge genannt werden und heißen, müssten sie ganz verstand- und sprachlos zusammen leben. Und sie

[1] Zu der Sprachproblematik in der ganzen Polemik vgl. B. Pottier, *Dieu et le Christ selon Grégoire de Nysse. Etude systématique du 'Contre Eunome' avec traduction inédite des extraits d'Eunome*, Paris – Turnhout 1994, 143–206; M. S. Troiano, "I Cappadoci e la questione dell'origine dei nomi nella polemica contro Eunomio", *Vetera Christianorum* 17 (1980) 313–346.

[2] Die Passage wird durch Gregors Erörterung der Ungezeugtheit und Unsterblichkeit als verschiedener Gottesattribute in *CE* II 445–542 (GNO I 356,17–384,32) unterbrochen.

[3] Vgl. die Rekonstruktion durch R. P. Vaggione, *Eunomius. The Extant Works*, Oxford 1987, 106–113.

> könnten auch nichts von dem, was sie zum Leben nötig haben, verwirklichen, da ihr Denken ohne Kenntnis der bezeichnenden Worte, d.h. der Verben und Namen, ganz dunkel wäre.[4]

Die 'bezeichnenden Worte' (σημαίνοντα), so entnehmen wir dieser Stelle, haben für das Denken des Menschen und sogar für sein Leben eine konstitutive Bedeutung. Ohne diese Worte wäre das Denken (διάνοια) 'dunkel' (ἄδηλος) und könnte keineswegs eine Grundlage der Handlung sein. Die 'bezeichnenden Worte' sind dabei nach Eunomius die 'Verben und Namen' (ῥήματα καὶ ὀνόματα),[5] es handelt sich also nicht so sehr um die Sprache in ihrer syntaktischen Struktur, sondern vielmehr um eine Nomenklatur, die bestimmt, "wie die einzelnen Dinge genannt werden (λέγεται) und heißen (ὀνομάζεται)". Gott selber musste diese Nomenklatur dem Menschen gleich am Anfang des Menschengeschlechts bekannt machen, d.h. bevor der Mensch zu sprechen begann, war schon klar, "wie die einzelnen Dinge genannt werden und heißen".

Diese Auskunft scheint für das Verstehen der Sprachauffassung nach Eunomius eine entscheidende Bedeutung zu haben. Wir erfahren drei Grundeinsichten, die durch andere Eunomius-Zitate in unserer Passage nur weiter erhellt werden: (1) die Benennungen (die Namen) gehören zu den Dingen selbst, (2) der Mensch kann sie mit göttlicher Hilfe ablesen, (3) sie werden im Menschengeschlecht tradiert.

[4] *CE* II 398 (GNO I 342,22–29).

[5] Die Kategorien ὄνομα (für die πράττοντες = die Handelnden) und ῥῆμα (für die πράξεις = Handlungen) gehen auf Platon zurück (*Soph.* 262a; vgl. auch *Crat.* 399ab; 425a; 431b), von dem sie auch Aristoteles übernahm (*Int.* 16a1. 19ff; *Poet.* 1457a10–18). Es handelte sich jedoch weder eindeutig um die Bezeichnungen der Wortarten 'Name' und 'Verb', noch der Satzteile 'Subjekt' und 'Prädikat'; vgl. T. Borsche, "Platon", in: P. Schmitter (Hrsg.), *Sprachtheorien der abendländischen Antike*, Tübingen 1991, 140–169, bes. 153ff. Erst die Stoa mit ihrem Interesse für die Grammatik benutzte diese Begriffe für die Wortarten, deren sie ursprünglich wahrscheinlich vier, später fünf bzw. sechs unterschied: Name (später differenziert in allgemeinen Name, προσηγορία, und Eigenname, ὄνομα), Verb (ῥῆμα), Konjunktion (σύνδεσμος), Artikel (ἄρθρον) (bzw. noch Adverb, μεσότης), vgl. Diogenes Laërtius VII 58 (Marcovich 479); s. dazu A. C. Lloyd, "Grammar and Metaphysics in the Stoa", in: A. A. Long (Hrsg.), *Problems in Stoicism*, London 1971, 58–74; M. Baratin, "Aperçu de la linguistique stoïcienne", in: P. Schmitter (Hrsg.), *Sprachtheorien*, 193–216, bes. 196f.

I.1. *Die Namen gehören zu den Dingen selbst*

Die Namen, so Eunomius, sind nicht nur eine menschliche Zutat, der für die Dinge keine Bedeutung hätte, sondern gehören konstitutiv zu den Dingen selbst und sind ursprünglich Gott allein bekannt. Die Benennungen (könnte man vielleicht paraphrasieren) sagen eine intelligible Struktur aus, die den Dingen bei ihrer Schöpfung auferlegt wurde. Gott hat "jedem der erschaffenen Dinge seinen eigenen und angemessenen Namen angepasst".[6] Schöpfung und Namensgebung stellen für Eunomius eine untrennbare Einheit dar: "Entweder sollen wir Gott nicht einmal die Entstehung der Dinge zuschreiben, oder – wenn wir das tun – dürfen wir ihm auch die Namensgebung (τὴν τῶν ὀνομάτων θέσιν) nicht absprechen."[7]

Für diese Vorstellung beruft sich Eunomius auf die biblische Erzählung in *Gen* 1,[8] nach der Gott die Welt durch sein Wort erschuf und selbst dem Licht und der Dunkelheit ihre Namen gab, sowie auf eine andere biblische Stelle (*Ps* 146/147,4), wo es von Gott heißt, dass er "die Menge der Sterne zählt und einen jeden mit seinem Namen ruft".[9] Durch eine typologische Deutung versucht er umgekehrt zu zeigen, dass der biblische Bericht von der Benennung der Tiere, die Adam anvertraut wurde (*Gen* 2,19–20), keine Auskunft über die Namensgebung, sondern eine Botschaft über Christus und die Kirche enthält.[10] Für Eunomius ist es sogar "nach dem Gesetz der Vorsehung und göttlich festgelegt (ὅσιον)", dass die Dinge 'von oben' (ἄνωθεν) benannt werden.[11]

I.2. *In die Seele des Menschen wurden Keime der Namen eingegeben*

Die Namen der Dinge sind jedoch für den Menschen nicht ganz unlesbar. Die Nomenklatur des Schöpfers stellt eine "öffentlich bekannte Gesetzgebung" (νόμοι ἐμφανῶς κείμενοι)[12] dar, die der Mensch, dank

[6] *CE* II 403 (GNO I 344,11–13).
[7] *CE* II 411 (GNO I 346,13–15).
[8] Vgl. *CE* II 443 (GNO I 356,4–7) mit Hinweis auf *CE* II 262 (GNO I 303, 1–6) und 269 (GNO I 305,13–15).
[9] *CE* II 423 (GNO I 350,8–9).
[10] Vgl. *CE* II 443–444 (GNO I 356,7–16). Gregor lässt die Interpretation von *Gen* 2,19–20 durch Eunomius wahrscheinlich absichtlich aus (vgl. B. Pottier, *Dieu et le Christ*, 169).
[11] *CE* II 546 (GNO I 386,5–7).
[12] *CE* II 408 (GNO I 345,13–14).

einer göttlichen Belehrung, ablesen kann. Es geht wahrscheinlich nicht so sehr darum, wie Gregor spottet, "dass sich Gott wie ein Erzieher oder Schulmeister zu den ersten Menschen niedergesetzt hätte, um ihnen einen Unterricht über die Verben und Namen zu geben".[13] Gott hat, so Eunomius, "in die Seele des Menschen Samen eingepflanzt" (ταῖς ἡμετέραις ἐγκατασπεῖραι ψυχαῖς),[14] dank derer die wesensbestimmenden Namen (und mit ihnen die Struktur der Dinge) erkennbar sind. Der Mensch erhielt also etwas diesen Namen Entsprechendes oder mit ihnen Kompatibles, vielleicht eine Art ihrer Keime. Aus den Eunomius-Stellen geht nicht eindeutig hervor, ob die göttliche 'Saat' in den menschlichen Seelen mit dem 'Unterricht' durch Gott identisch ist. Aus seiner Bemerkung, nach der die göttliche 'Belehrung' nur den ersten Menschen galt, dürfen wir jedoch deduzieren, dass Eunomius neben der keimhaften Nomenklatur in den menschlichen Seelen auch noch ihre Aktivierung durch ein Eingreifen Gottes am Anfang des Menschengeschlechts voraussetzt.

Das menschliche 'Nachbilden' oder 'Ablesen' der Namen hat jedenfalls, so Eunomius, eine grundsätzliche Bedeutung für die Orientierung und Handlungsfähigkeit des Menschen. Ohne die Namen zu kennen, wären die Menschen unfähig die Dinge zu identifizieren und zu gebrauchen.[15] Auch könnten sie sich nichts einander mitteilen und die menschliche Gemeinschaft würde auf ein tierisches Niveau sinken: die Menschen müssten 'vernunft- und sprachlos zusammen leben' (ἀλογίᾳ καὶ ἀφωνίᾳ συζῆν).[16]

I.3. *Die Namen der Dinge werden tradiert*

Die göttliche Belehrung über die Namen der Dinge war, wie gesagt, nur für die ersten Menschen (oder ihre unmittelbare Nachkommen) notwendig,[17] in den späteren Generationen werden die Namen schon tradiert. Sobald also die Menschen die Namen der Dinge abgelesen haben, geben sie diese Kenntnis weiter, ohne jedoch die Benennungen spontan zu erdenken. Wir erfahren ja nirgendwo in der Bibel, argumentiert Eunomius, dass die heiligen Menschen die Namen aus-

---

13 *CE* II 397 (GNO I 342,19–21).
14 *CE* II 548 (GNO I 386,19–20).
15 Vgl. *CE* II 413 (GNO I 346,23–347,1).
16 *CE* II 398 (GNO I 342,25–26).
17 Vgl. *CE* II 398 (GNO I 342,22–23).

denken würden.[18] Die Namen werden 'von oben' gegeben, wie wir schon wissen,[19] und sie gründen "in den benannten Dingen selbst, nicht in der Autorität derjenigen, welche die Namen aussprechen".[20]

Nicht einmal die heidnischen Dichter erfinden die Namen, meint Eunomius. Einerseits haben die Dinge schon ihre Namen, andererseits lesen sie die Dichter nicht einmal richtig ab, sondern produzieren vielmehr ihre eigenen Fiktionen (sie 'lügen', διαψεῦσθαι).[21] Eunomius kennt also auch eine menschliche Sprache, die nicht in den Dingen selbst, sondern nur in der Phantasie, Denkkraft oder Begriffsbildung (ἐπίνοια) des Menschen gründet, und daher ein bloßer *flatus vocis* ist.[22]

---

[18] Vgl. *CE* II 415 (GNO I 347,18–21).

[19] Vgl. *CE* II 546 (GNO I 386,6–7).

[20] *CE* II 545 (GNO I 385,22–24); ähnlich auch Eunomius, *Apol.* 18 (Vaggione 54ff).

[21] *CE* II 414 (GNO I 347,4–6).

[22] Vgl. *CE* II 179 (GNO I 276,22–30); ähnlich auch Eunomius, *Apol.* 8 (Vaggione 42). Es wäre jedoch vorschnell daraus zu schließen, dass Eunomius die menschliche Begriffsbildung *nur* in diesem Sinne versteht, wie ihm die Kappadokier (*CE* II 179–180, GNO I 276,20–277,7; ähnlich schon Basilius *AE* I 6; SC 299, 182) und nach ihnen einige der modernen Interpreten vorwerfen, als wäre er eine Art 'Nominalist' *avant la lettre* (vgl. E. Cavalcanti, *Studi eunomiani*, Roma 1976, 117; auch Th. Kobusch findet in der Epinoia-Auffassung des Eunomius ein nominalistisches Element, da hier dem Bezeichneten – oder dem Gedachten, mit dem es Kobusch identifiziert – kein selbständiger ontologischer Status eignet, vgl. Th. Kobusch, *Sein und Sprache. Historische Begründung einer Ontologie der Sprache*, Leiden 1987, 53). In seiner ersten *Apologie* führt Eunomius an, man müsse "die Begriffe der benannten Dinge beachten (ταῖς τῶν ὑποκειμένων ἐννοίαις) und ihnen die Benennungen folgen lassen (ἀκολούθως ἐφαρμόττειν τὰς προσηγορίας)" (*Apol.* 18; Vaggione 54). Eunomius scheint damit einerseits die Begriffe (ἔννοιαι) der Dinge zu unterscheiden, deren keimhafte Kenntnis dem Menschen eingeboren ist und nach denen die Benennungen gebildet werden sollen, andererseits scheint er jedoch auch solche Namen zu kennen, die *nur* durch die menschliche ἐπίνοια gebildet, nicht die Dinge selbst, sondern lediglich eine Fiktion zum Ausdruck bringen. B. Pottier unterscheidet daher zwischen der ἐπίνοια als der Quelle reiner Fiktionen und der ἔννοια als einer in der Natur der Dinge verwurzelten Vorstellung (vgl. B. Pottier, *Dieu et le Christ*, 152). K.-H. Uthemann versucht dagegen die Epinoia-Auffassung des Eunomius zu rehabilitieren: die Fiktionen werden zwar *nur* durch die ἐπίνοια gebildet, dies heißt jedoch nicht, dass die ἐπίνοια *immer* nur die Fiktionen produziert und sich nie nach den Dingen selbst orientieren kann (vgl. K.-H. Uthemann, "Die Sprache der Theologie nach Eunomius von Cyzicus", *ZKG* 104 (1993) 143–175, bes. 151–154; ähnlich ders., "Die Sprachtheorie des Eunomios von Kyzikos und Severianos von Gabala. Theologie im Reflex kirchlicher Predigt", *StPatr* 24 (1993) 336–344, bes. 339; in einem ähnlichen Sinne auch Th. Böhm, *Theoria Unendlichkeit Aufstieg. Philosophische Implikationen zu De vita Moysis von Gregor von Nyssa*, Leiden 1996, 179, Anm. 52). Eunomius scheint tatsächlich auch eine andere Begriffsbildung als das Produzieren von Fiktionen zu kennen, es lässt sich jedoch aus den bestehenden Texten nicht

I.4. *Die Benennung Gottes geht dem Menschen voraus*

In der Sprachauffassung des Eunomius, wie in unserer Passage dargelegt, kommt eine entscheidende Bedeutung der Benennung Gottes zu. Eunomius' Lehre über die Namen, die dem Menschen vorausgehen, gründet vor allem in seiner Überzeugung, dass ein solcher Name, der dem Menschen vorausgeht und den der Mensch aufgrund einer von Gott geschenkten Fähigkeit ablesen kann, die Benennung Gottes als 'ungezeugt' = 'ungeschaffen' (ἀγέν[ν]ητος) ist.[23] Diese Bezeichnung gehört ja Gott früher, als er mit ihr vom Menschen bezeichnet wird. Seine 'Ungezeugtheit' hängt ja nicht davon ab, ob er so vom Menschen genannt wird.[24] Die Würde Gottes (ἀξία) kommt nämlich nach Eunomius gerade in seinem Namen zum Ausdruck oder ist sogar mit ihm identisch: "Der Name ist (das Gleiche wie) die Würde."[25] Und da diese Würde natürlich 'älter' ist als die menschliche ἐπίνοια (die Begriffsbildung oder ein durch sie gebildeter Begriff), muss auch der göttliche Name 'älter' sein als diese Fähigkeit. Das Gegenteil vorauszusetzen müsste absurde Folgerungen mit sich bringen, meint Eunomius: "Dann ist entweder die ἐπίνοια älter als ihre Benutzer (τῶν ἐπινοούντων), oder die Benennungen (προσηγορίαι), die Gott nach seiner Natur gehören und die allem vorausgehen, sind später als die Erschaffung des Menschen."[26]

Den Namen Gottes zu benutzen (auszusprechen) kommt dabei ausschließlich dem Menschen zu, nicht den 'geistigen Wesen' oder sogar dem Sohn: "Weder der Sohn," meint Eunomius, "noch die durch ihn geschaffenen geistigen Wesen sprechen Gott mit Namen an (ὀνομάζεσθαι)."[27]

Nur den Menschen ist es vorbehalten, dass sie dank der von Gott geschenkten Fähigkeit die Struktur der Dinge (in der göttlichen Nomenklatur ausgesprochen) ablesen und durch die Sprache nachsagen können. Diese 'Kompatibilität' zwischen der menschlichen Sprache und der Struktur der Dinge (wie in der göttlichen Nomenklatur ausgedrückt) macht es auch möglich, dass Gott zu seinen Dienern

---

beweisen, ob er sie auch ἐπίνοια nennen würde (dies gibt auch Th. Böhm, *Theoria*, 176, zu).

[23] Vgl. *CE* II 44 (GNO I 238,26–29); ähnlich Eunomius, *Apol.* 8 (Vaggione 40–42).

[24] Vgl. *CE* II 389 (GNO I 339,28–340,4).

[25] *CE* II 544 (GNO I 385,19).

[26] *CE* II 552 (GNO I 388,3–7).

[27] *CE* II 390 (GNO I 340,9–11).

spricht, wie in der Bibel berichtet. Diese Rede (ὁμιλία) Gottes ist für Eunomius sogar ein Beweis der Kompatibilität zwischen der göttlichen Nomenklatur und der menschlichen Sprache: "Lehnt es Gott nicht ab zu seinen Dienern zu reden, dann müssen wir daraus schließen, dass er auch von Anfang an den Dingen entsprechende Bezeichnungen gab."[28]

Eunomius unterscheidet damit eigentlich drei Arten der Sprache (wie wir deduzieren können): (a) Die göttliche Nomenklatur, die unmittelbar zu Gottes Schöpfung gehört, (b) die Fähigkeit des Menschen diese Nomenklatur dank der Samen in seiner Seele abzulesen und sich dadurch in den erschaffenen Dingen zu orientieren, (c) die Lüge der Dichter, d.h. eine menschliche Sprache, die nicht die Struktur der Dinge selbst wiedergibt, sondern in der Phantasie des Menschen wurzelt.

II. *Gregor*

Warum ist nun Gregor mit dieser Lehre des Eunomius nicht zufrieden?

II.1. *Die Namen gehören nicht zu den Dingen selbst*

Ähnlich wie vor ihm schon Basilius,[29] ist Gregor vor allem überzeugt, dass die Namensgebung nicht ein Teil der schöpferischen Aktivität Gottes ist, sondern erst einen nachträglichen Versuch des Menschen darstellt, die erschaffenen Dinge zu erkennen. Diese Sprachfähigkeit (ἡ λογικὴ δύναμις = die Fähigkeit des Denkens und der Sprache), nicht die Namen, wurde dem Menschen von Gott geschenkt: "Die Dinge sind geordnet, wie es ihrer Natur entspricht, jedoch die Namen, durch die sie ausgedrückt werden, wurden durch die Sprachfähigkeit erfunden, die Gott in unsere Natur eingegeben hat."[30]

---

[28] *CE* II 417 (GNO I 348,6–10).

[29] Basilius befasste sich mit der Begriffsbildung bzw. Namensgebung in *AE* I 5–6 (SC 299, 180–188); bzw. *AE* II 4 (SC 305, 18–22); II 9 (SC 305, 36–38). Zu seiner originellen Auffassung der Eigennamen, die nicht das Wesen, sondern eine einmalige Verbindung der charakteristischen Züge zum Ausdruck bringen, vgl. P. Kalligas, "Basil of Caesarea on the Semantics of Proper Names", in: K. Ierodiakonou (Hrsg.), *Byzantine Philosophy and its Ancient Sources*, Oxford 2002, 31–48.

[30] *CE* II 395 (GNO I 341,29–342,3).

Einen eindeutigen biblischen Beleg für diese Vorstellung findet Gregor in der Rollenteilung zwischen Gott und Adam bei der Erschaffung und Benennung der Tiere (*Gen* 2,19–20):[31] "Weder hat Adam die Tiere geschaffen, noch ihnen Gott die Namen gegeben, sondern nach der Erzählung des Mose geht ihre Entstehung auf Gott zurück, die Benennung des Entstandenen jedoch auf den Menschen."[32] Gott übertritt also die 'heilige Satzung' des Eunomius, nach der die Namen 'von oben' verteilt werden müssen:

> Wie kommt es, dass Gott selber diese heilige Satzung nicht kennt, und dass er die Tiere, die er schuf, nicht von oben benannte, sondern die Macht (ἐξουσία) der Namensgebung dem Menschen anvertraute? Entspricht es dem Gesetz der Vorsehung und ist es göttlich gesetzt, dass die Namen von oben gegeben werden, wie Eunomius behauptet, dann widerspricht es der heiligen Satzung und ist völlig unangemessen, dass jemand von unten die Benennungen gibt.[33]

Wie nach Gregors Überzeugung die kosmogenetische Rede Gottes in *Gen* 1 zu interpretieren ist, wurde an einer anderen Stelle der ganzen Polemik geklärt[34] – nämlich als die Konstitution der Dinge selbst und die Festlegung ihrer Funktion (das Licht *als* Tag, die Dunkelheit *als* Nacht). In unserer Passage konzentriert sich Gregor daher auf die Deutung eines anderen biblischen Arguments des Eunomius (*Ps* 146/147,4), wo es von Gott heißt, dass er "die Menge der Sterne zählt und einen jeden mit seinem Namen nennt".[35] Gottes 'Zählen' der unzählbar vielen Sterne deutet nämlich an, so Gregor, dass Gott auch das für den Menschen Unbegreifliche kennt. Es ziemt sich ja nicht von Gott vorauszusetzen, dass er die Sterne durch das Verbinden der Einheiten in eine Summe zählt, um festzustellen, wie viele sie sind. Durch dieses Bild bringt die Heilige Schrift zum Ausdruck, dass Gott die Sterne gut kennt – da ja die Anführung der Zahl für den Menschen eine genaue Kenntnis bedeutet.[36] Und ähnlich, wenn die Schrift sagt, dass Gott die Sterne "mit den Namen

---

[31] Auf diese Szene hat sich mehrmals auch Philo berufen, der jedoch den ersten, mit einer besonderen Kraft ausgestatteten Menschen für die Namensgebung verantwortlich machte (vgl. z.B. *De opificio mundi* 148, Cohn I 51–52; *Legum allegoriarum* II 14–15, Cohn I 93–94; *De mutatione nominum* 63–64, Wendland III 168; anders jedoch *De decalogo* 23, Cohn IV 273–274).

[32] *CE* II 412 (GNO I 346,17–20).

[33] *CE* II 547 (GNO I 386,10–17).

[34] Vgl. *CE* II 263–281 (GNO I 303,7–309,15).

[35] Vgl. *CE* II 423–440 (GNO I 350,5–355,21), hier *CE* II 423 (GNO I 350,8–9).

[36] Vgl. *CE* II 429 (GNO I 351,29–352,3).

ruft", wird nicht gemeint, dass er den Sternen ihre Bezeichnungen zuteilte, wie sie uns bekannt sind, und dass er sie laut hervorriefe[37] – diese Vorstellung ist für Gregor schon deswegen ganz unakzeptabel, weil die Bezeichnungen der Sterne mit den Namen der heidnischen Götter zusammenhängen.[38] Es wird vielmehr angedeutet, dass Gott auch die Einzelheiten der ganzen Schöpfung kennt – mit dem Namen anzusprechen gilt ja unter den Menschen als ein Zeichen einer näheren Bekanntschaft.[39]

II.2. *Dem Menschen wurde die Sprachfähigkeit, nicht die Namen geschenkt*

Wie Eunomius, ist auch Gregor überzeugt, dass die Sprache dem Menschen von Gott geschenkt wurde. Er stellt sich jedoch nicht vor, dass der Mensch dank der 'Samen in seiner Seele' die Namen der göttlichen Nomenklatur ablese, sondern dass er selber aufgrund seiner Sprachfähigkeit die Namen ausdenkt. Nur in einem abgeleiteten Sinne lässt sich sagen, dass die Namen von Gott stammen – da nämlich die Fähigkeit der Namensbildung von ihm stammt. Der Ursprung oder die Ursache (αἰτία) der Namen ist also in Gott, die Vollmacht oder Ausübung (ἐξουσία) der Namensgebung wurde jedoch dem Menschen anvertraut, und zwar seiner Sprachfähigkeit (ἡ λογικὴ δύναμις) oder Begriffsbildung (ἐπίνοια).[40]

Gott, so Gregor, gab in die menschliche Seele nicht die Samen der einzelnen Worte ein, die "aus den Dingen erwachsen würden wie die Sprosse aus den Samen oder Wurzeln",[41] sondern lediglich die formale Sprachfähigkeit, die schon selbst die Namen erfindet.[42] Wie Gott dem Menschen die Augen gab, die schon von sich aus die Farben unterscheiden, hat er auch "die Verstandeskraft (ἡ διανοητικὴ δύναμις) so geschaffen, dass sie sich selbst in Bewegung setzt und den Dingen zuwendet, und damit die Erkenntnis keine Konfusion erleidet (ὡς ἂν μηδεμίαν σύγχυσιν ἡ γνῶσις πάθοι), gibt sie jeder Sache ihre eigene sprachliche Bezeichnung wie ein unterscheidendes Zeichen".[43]

---

[37] Vgl. *CE* II 432 (GNO I 352,24–28).
[38] Vgl. *CE* II 433 (GNO I 353,1–10).
[39] Vgl. *CE* II 435–436 (GNO I 353,23–354,7).
[40] Vgl. *CE* II 396 (GNO I 342,3–12).
[41] *CE* II 546 (GNO I 385,29–31).
[42] Vgl. *CE* II 400 (GNO I 343,7–10).
[43] *CE* II 401 (GNO I 343,20–25).

Die Verstandeskraft des Menschen hat also nach Gregor ihre eigene Spontaneität, die sich den Dingen zuwendet und das Chaos der Erfahrungen durch 'sprachliche Bezeichnungen' (αἱ διὰ τῶν φωνῶν ἐπισημειώσεις) wie 'unterscheidende Zeichen' (σήμαντρα) ordnet. In diesen beiden Aspekten besteht nach dieser Stelle die Erkenntnis (γνῶσις) des Menschen.[44]

An einer anderen Stelle unserer Passage erfahren wir jedoch, dass die Worte unsere Gedanken (νοήματα) zum Ausdruck bringen, d.h. die Bewegungen unseres Denkens (τὰς τοῦ νοῦ κινήσεις), die der Mensch als ein körperliches Wesen den anderen nicht direkt, sondern nur durch Vermittlung der Namen (ὀνόματα) als Zeichen (σημεῖα) der Dinge zeigen kann.[45]

Die Notwendigkeit Worte zu benutzen wird an den beiden Stellen jeweils anders begründet: Einerseits soll ein Chaos in der Erkenntnis beseitigt und jede Sache durch ihre Bezeichnung bestimmt werden, andererseits ist es nur durch die Worte möglich eigene Gedanken den anderen mitzuteilen. Sollen wir versuchen, die beiden Aussagen zu verbinden, dann würde die Sprachfähigkeit des Menschen wie folgt vorgehen: Die Verstandeskraft (ἡ διανοητικὴ δύναμις) wendet sich spontan den Dingen zu und organisiert die Erfahrungen durch sprachliche Bezeichnungen (αἱ διὰ τῶν φωνῶν ἐπισημειώσεις); die so entstandenen Gedanken (νοήματα) oder Geistesbewegungen (αἱ τοῦ νοῦ κινήσεις) teilt sie den anderen mit dank der Sprachfähigkeit (ἡ λογικὴ δύναμις), nämlich durch Vertretung der Dinge durch Namen (ὀνόματα) als sprachliche Zeichen (σημεῖα).

In seinen Ausführungen über die unkörperlichen Wesen nennt Gregor die 'geistige Aktivität' (ἡ κατὰ τὸν νοῦν ἐνέργεια) dieser reinen Geister auch 'Sprache' (λόγος), die keine körperlichen Organe gebraucht. Er bemerkt jedoch zugleich, dass die Sprache eigentlich mit der Körperlichkeit zusammenhängt: Wären die Menschen nicht körperlich, könnten sie sich die Bewegungen ihres Denkens (τὰ τῆς διανοίας κινήματα) direkt, ohne die ausführliche Vermittlung der Worte (ῥήματα) einander mitteilen. Stattdessen müssen sie nicht nur die Namen der einzelnen Dinge (wie 'der Himmel' oder 'die Erde'),

[44] *Ibid.* An einer anderen Stelle schildert Gregor den heuristischen Vorgang der ἐπίνοια, in dem das Denken durch die Worte eine Sache immer präziser zu fassen versucht (vgl. *CE* II 181–182, GNO I 277,7–26). Ähnlich auch Basilius, *AE* I 6 (SC 299, 184–188).

[45] Vgl. *CE* II 391 (GNO I 340,24–28).

sondern auch die sprachlichen Bezeichnungen für die anderen Kategorien einführen, wie für die Relation (τὸ πρός τί πως ἔχειν), das Wirken (τὸ ἐνεργεῖν) und das Erfahren des Wirkens (τὸ πάσχειν).[46]

Gregor setzt damit wahrscheinlich einerseits die 'Bewegungen des Denkens' voraus, die dem Geist angehören, andererseits das Organisieren der Erfahrungen in die Worte und die sprachliche Mitteilung der Gedanken. Die Worte hängen jedenfalls mit der Sinnlichkeit zusammen: sie organisieren die (Sinnes)erfahrungen und durch die sinnliche Vermittlung machen sie die Geistesbewegungen bekannt. Die 'geistige Aktivität' der unkörperlichen Wesen kann nur in einem übertragenen Sinne als 'Sprache' bezeichnet werden (da diese Wesen miteinander kommunizieren), und nicht einmal das menschliche Denken versteht Gregor als eine innere 'Rede', sondern als 'Geistesbewegungen'.[47] Schon deswegen ist es für ihn völlig unvorstellbar, dass der unkörperliche Gott Sprache benutzen oder die Namen geben sollte. Der innergöttliche Austausch zwischen den einzelnen göttlichen Personen darf keineswegs als eine 'Sprache' verstanden werden.[48]

II.3. *Der Mensch denkt die Namen aus, und die Namen der gleichen Dinge sind verschieden*

Die Namensgebung ist nun nach Gregor kein Ablesen der göttlich auferlegten Struktur der Dinge und keine Entwicklung einer keimhaften Nomenklatur, die in die Seele des Menschen eingegeben würde, sondern sie ist der menschlichen Wahl (προαίρεσις) vorbehalten.[49] Anders wären ja – und dies ist ein wichtiges Argument Gregors gegen die Konzeption seines Gegners – die Namen der gleichen Dinge in den einzelnen Sprachen nicht unterschiedlich, sondern alle Menschen müssten eine gemeinsame, aus der Natur selbst hervorgegangene Sprache sprechen.[50] Ein solches 'Naturgesetz' (ὁ τῆς φύσεως νόμος) gibt es jedoch nach Gregor nicht: Was sich nämlich in der Zeit ändert und nicht dem Menschengeschlecht als ganzem zukommt,

---

[46] Vgl. *CE* II 391–392 (GNO I 340,19–341,9).

[47] Vgl. *CE* II 207 (GNO I 285,13–19). In der Schrift wird manchmal als eine 'Benennung' (φωνή) das 'Denken', d.h. 'ein Impuls des Denkens' (ὁρμὴ διανοίας) Gottes bezeichnet, dies darf jedoch, so Gregor, nicht zu einer anthropomorphen Gottesvorstellung verführen (*CE* II 266–268, GNO I 304,12–305,4).

[48] Vgl. *CE* II 212–218 (GNO I 287,6–289,10).

[49] Vgl. *CE* II 546 (GNO I 385,28–386,2).

[50] Vgl. *CE* II 546 (GNO I 385,2–5).

kann nicht ein Teil der Natur sein.[51] Die Namen gehören also nicht zur Natur. Zur Natur gehört jedoch die Sprachfähigkeit, die die Namen bildet, ähnlich wie zu ihr das Sehen gehört, nicht jedoch seine spezialisierte Form (z.B. das Sehen durch optische Geräte oder das Einsehen der geometrischen Beweise), die zur Natur dank der Mühe des Menschen 'hinzutritt' (προσγίνεται).[52]

Die Namensgebung, die zur Natur 'hinzutritt', richtet sich jedoch danach, so Gregor in unserer Passage, wie es dem Menschen 'geeignet' (ἀρέσκον) scheint "für die Deutlichkeit des zu erklärenden Gegenstandes" (πρὸς τὴν τῶν δηλουμέμων σαφήνειαν).[53]

Die Sprache orientiert sich damit zwar an den auszusprechenden Dingen, sie folgt jedoch auch (oder vor allem) den Kommunikationsbedürfnissen. Daher, fährt Gregor fort, lässt sich auch die Pluralität der Sprachen erklären, die der Pluralität der Nationen entspricht. Welche dieser Sprachen, so fragt Gregor, würde die göttliche Nomenklatur zum Ausdruck bringen, wie sie Eunomius voraussetzt? Die Theorie des Eunomius scheint durch diese Pluralität allein schon 'zerrissen' zu sein.[54]

---

[51] Vgl. *CE* II 545 (GNO I 385,24–28); *CE* II 550 (GNO I 387,6–16).

[52] Vgl. *CE* II 551 (GNO I 387,16–19).

[53] *CE* II 551 (GNO I 387,28–388,2). An einer anderen Stelle erfahren wir zwar, dass die Namen der 'Natur und Macht' der Dinge entsprechen (κατὰ τὴν ἐγκειμένην ἑκάστῳ φύσιν καὶ δύναμιν), diese Namen werden jedoch den Dingen von einzelnen Nationen gegeben 'nach ihren gewohnten Bräuchen' (κατὰ τὴν ἐπιχωριάζουσαν ἐν ἑκάστῳ ἔθνει συνήθειαν, *CE* II 270, GNO I 305,23–26). Diese Namen bringen dabei immer nur einen Aspekt der Dinge zum Ausdruck (z.B. 'Erde' und 'trockenes Land', *CE* II 274–275, GNO I 306,25–307,16), nämlich die Art und Weise, wie die Dinge in ihren Verhältnissen untereinander und in ihrer 'Macht' (δύναμις, *CE* II 275, GNO I 307,15–16) dem Menschen erscheinen (κατὰ τὸ φανέν, *CE* II 148, GNO I 268,19). Ähnlich lesen wir, dass "die Benennungen (φωναί) wie Schatten der Dinge (σκιαὶ τῶν πραγμάτων) seien, nach den Bewegungen dessen, worüber sie sprechen, gebildet". Dies heißt jedoch nach Gregor kein Ablesen einer göttlichen Nomenklatur, die mit den Dingen verbunden wäre, sondern eben eine Wiedergabe der *Bewegungen* der Dinge, d.h. eine Beschreibung dessen, was geschieht: "den Ereignissen (τοῖς πράγμασιν) werden die Aussagen hinzugefügt, die beschreiben, was passiert (αἱ σημαντικαὶ τῶν γινομένων προσηγορίαι)" (*CE* II 150, GNO I 269,11–14). Zum stoischen Hintergrund dieser letzten Vorstellung vgl. G. C. Stead, "Logic and the Application of Names to God", in: L. F. Mateo-Seco – J. L. Bastero (Hrsg.), *El "Contra Eunomium I" en la produccion literaria de Gregorio de Nisa. VI. Coloquio internacional sobre Gregorio de Nisa*, Pamplona 1988, 303–320, bes. 309.

[54] Vgl. *CE* II 406–408 (GNO I 344,25–345,12). Die Erzählung vom Turm in Babylon (*Gen* 11) sagt ja nicht, meint Gregor, dass Gott verschiedene Sprachen

Dazu tritt noch der Umstand, dass die Menschen stets (ἀεί) neue Bezeichnungen erfinden.[55] Die Namen wurden nicht am Anfang des Menschengeschlechts bekannt gemacht, sondern werden alle Zeit neu gegeben, sobald neue Dinge erscheinen. Passende Namen für sie einzuführen ist keineswegs Gott allein vorbehalten, sondern so machen es, wie Gregor spottet, auch die Bader:

> Auch ihnen steht es ja frei die Namen für die Tätigkeiten auszudenken, die sie ausüben. Und niemand hat sie göttlich gepriesen, wenn sie ihre Erfindungen 'Fußwaschbecken', 'Enthaarungsmittel', 'Handtücher' usw. nennen, obwohl diese Namen durch ihre Bedeutung angemessen die Dinge bekannt machen, denen sie gegeben werden.[56]

II.4. *Auch die Gottesnamen gehen auf den Menschen zurück*

Die Menschen geben jedoch nicht nur den neu konstruierten Fußwaschbecken ihre Namen, sondern suchen auch eine Benennung für Gott. Es ist zwar unmöglich sein Wesen auszudrücken, jeder kann aber 'nach seiner Vermutung' (κατὰ τὸ δοκοῦν) sagen, was er eingesehen hat (τὸ νοηθέν). Deswegen sind auch die Gottesnamen unterschiedlich.[57] Die Ehre Gottes geht bestimmt dem Menschen und seiner Sprache voraus, ohne vom Menschen abhängig zu sein. Diese Ehre ist jedoch nicht mit der Benennung (προσηγορία) Gottes identisch, wie Eunomius behauptet.[58] Die Menschen versuchen von Anfang des Menschengeschlechts an Gott zu benennen, ohne ihn je fassen zu können. Die Unangemessenheit dieser Versuche ist jedoch keine Lästerung, da von der Sprache gar nicht zu erwarten ist mehr als die Gedanken des Menschen zu fassen.[59]

---

gründete, sondern dass er die Menschheit zur Strafe verstreute. Jede Nation hat dann ihre eigene Sprache entwickelt, ähnlich wie die noch ungeteilte Menschheit ihre ursprüngliche Sprache gebildet hatte. Keine dieser Sprachen stammt jedoch in ihren konkreten Namensgebungen von Gott (*CE* II 252–254, GNO I 299,28–300,26). Diese Theorie bezeichnet A. Borst im Rahmen seiner Untersuchung der patristischen Sprachvorstellungen als 'revolutionär' (vgl. A. Borst, *Der Turmbau von Babel. Geschichte der Meinungen über Ursprung und Vielfalt der Sprachen und Völker*, Bd. I, Stuttgart 1957, 244).

[55] Vgl. *CE* II 551 (GNO I 387,27–388,2).

[56] *CE* II 409 (GNO I 345,18–24).

[57] Vgl. *CE* II 397 (GNO I 342,13–15).

[58] Vgl. *CE* II 545 (GNO I 385,19–21).

[59] Vgl. *CE* II 552 (GNO I 388,9–14). An einer anderen Stelle führt Gregor an,

Dies gilt, so Gregor, auch für den Gottesnamen 'Ungezeugtheit'. Nicht einmal dieser Name wurde von Gott in die Menschennatur keimhaft eingegeben, wie Eunomius glaubt – wäre dem so, dann müsste ja dieser Name von Anfang an im Gebrauch sein, was offensichtlich nicht der Fall ist.[60]

Es ist nach Gregor überhaupt völlig abwegig die menschliche Sprache Gott zuzuschreiben. Er braucht sie nicht, wie sie die unkörperlichen Wesen allgemein nicht brauchen.[61] Und es wäre unangemessen zu glauben, Gott habe etwas Überflüssiges, da dadurch seine Vollkommenheit vermindert wäre.[62] Nur um der Menschen willen, die ihn anders nicht verstehen könnten, gebraucht Gott manchmal die menschliche Sprache, wie in der Schrift belegt. Das ist jedoch ein Zeugnis seiner Menschenliebe (φιλανθρωπία), die auf das Niveau des Menschen herabsteigt, nicht ein Beweis seiner Sprachbedürftigkeit.[63] Wie die Sonne nach der göttlichen Ökonomie ihre Strahlen mit der Luft vermischt sendet, damit wir ihr Licht und ihre Wärme genießen können, während die Sonne selbst uns unerreichbar bleibt, so offenbart sich auch der unzugängliche Gott den Menschen in ihnen angemessenen Gestalten (θεοφάνειαι), nimmt menschliche Emotionen des Mitleids oder Zornes an und spricht die menschliche Sprache.[64] Es sind jedoch Akte seiner Kondeszendenz, nicht Äußerungen seiner Natur selbst, ähnlich wie sich die Mutter dem Lallen ihrer Kinder anpasst,[65] wie die Menschen im Umgang mit den Tieren ihre Stimmen nachahmen oder wie sich jemand mit dem Taubstummen in seinen Zeichen verständigt. Wie jedoch nicht zu erwarten ist, dass uns der Taubstumme anders als mit seinen Zeichen anspricht, so ist

dass die Namen, die Gott von den Menschen gegeben werden, nicht sein unaussprechliches Wesen (wie es Eunomius für den Namen 'Ungezeugtheit' beansprucht), sondern nur sein Wirken (ἐνεργεῖν) fassen können (*CE* II 149, GNO I 268, 25–30; ähnlich Basilius, *AE* I 8, SC 299, 194–196). Gregor will damit in seiner Theologie nicht vom Wesen, sondern vom Wirken Gottes ausgehen. Dadurch bekennt er sich zu einer anderen theologischen Methode als Eunomius, die Eunomius zwar auch kennt (*Apol.* 20, Vaggione 58; vgl. dazu K.-H. Uthemann, "Die Sprache", 145–149), jedoch für weniger zuverlässig hält (vgl. *Apol.* 23, Vaggione 62ff).

[60] Vgl. *CE* II 548–549 (GNO I 386,18–387,6).

[61] Vgl. *CE* II 390 (GNO I 340,11–18); *CE* II 393–394 (GNO I 341,9–21).

[62] Vgl. *CE* II 553 (GNO I 388,17–24).

[63] Vgl. *CE* II 417–418 (GNO I 348,10–17).

[64] Vgl. *CE* II 419 (GNO I 348,17–349,1); vgl. auch *CE* II 424–426 (GNO I 350,13–351,6) über die anthropomorphen biblischen Stellen, wo von Gott die Emotionen des Zornes, Mitleids usw. ausgesagt werden.

[65] Vgl. *CE* II 419 (GNO I 348,24–25).

auch nicht zu erwarten, dass die menschliche Sprache Gott nennen kann. Nach seiner 'Ökonomie' benutzt daher Gott die Sprache des Menschen:[66]

> Die Menschenliebe (φιλανθρωπία) Gottes ist so groß, dass er freiwillig nicht nur unsere guten Dinge, sondern auch die schlechten erfahren wollte. Nahm er jedoch sogar an den schlechten teil, warum sollte er sich weigern an dem Besten, was wir haben, teilzunehmen, nämlich an der Sprache?[67]

* * *

Gregor und Eunomius unterscheiden sich damit nicht so sehr in ihrer Meinung vom Ursprung der Sprache, die für beide eine göttliche Gabe ist. Unterschiedlich sind jedoch ihre Vorstellungen von der Form dieser Gabe. Während nach Eunomius Gott selber den Dingen ihre Namen als einen konstitutiven Teil gab und dem Menschen eine Fähigkeit diese Namen aufgrund der Samen in seiner Seele abzulesen schenkte, versteht Gregor die Gabe der Sprache als eine formale Fähigkeit die Namen zu bilden und zu gebrauchen nach eigener Erwägung und eigenem Nutzen. In beiden Fällen erscheint die Sprache als eine unentbehrliche Voraussetzung der Orientierung des Menschen unter den Dingen und der menschlichen Gemeinschaft; für Gregor ist sie jedoch rein eine Funktion dieser Zwecke, nicht ein Ablesen der göttlichen Benennungen, die mit den Dingen verbunden wären. Die Namen der Dinge wurden daher nach Gregor nicht am Anfang des Menschengeschlechts entdeckt, wie Eunomius behauptet, sondern werden immer wieder neu gebildet für die neu erscheinenden Dinge. Diese Namen sind in verschiedenen Sprachen unterschiedlich nach dem Belieben der Benutzer, die vor allem ihre Gedanken einander mitteilen und sich mit anderen verständigen wollen. Nicht einmal die Namen, die von den Menschen Gott gegeben werden, können als ein adäquater Ausdruck seiner Ehre gelten, wie Eunomius das für den Namen 'Ungezeugtheit' beansprucht, sondern sie stellen einen menschlichen Versuch dar eigene Gotteserkenntnis zum Ausdruck zu bringen.

---

[66] Vgl. *CE* II 421 (GNO I 349,17–26).
[67] *CE* II 422 (GNO I 350,1–5).

III. *Zwischen Platonismus und Aristotelismus, Epikureismus und Stoa*

Unsere Passage, wie schon erwähnt, ist besonders reich an verspottenden und abschätzigen Urteilen über eine antike philosophische Inspiration der beiden Gegner. Einen Höhepunkt erreicht diese Ironie in Gregors Vorwurf, dass sich Eunomius vom platonischen Dialog *Kratylos* beeinflussen ließ:

> Vielleicht hat er das im platonischen Dialog *Kratylos* gelesen oder von einem gehört, der das dort las, und wegen einer ungeheueren Armut an eigenen Gedanken hat er diesen Quatsch an sein eigenes Geschwätz genäht, gleich wie die Menschen, die sich ihre Nahrung durch Betteln besorgen. Wie nämlich die Bettler aus den kleinen Mengen von den einzelnen Wohltätern ein buntes und verschiedenartiges Essen zusammenstellen, so treiben auch die Ausführungen des Eunomius, unter einem Mangel an wirklicher Speise leidend, von allen Seiten Brosamen der Verben und Namen zusammen. Und daher, wenn er sich die Schönheit der platonischen Sprache aneignete, hält er es für gut, seine Philosophie zur Lehre der Kirche zu machen.[68]

Durch diese Invektiven reagiert Gregor auf die Behauptung des Eunomius, dass sich "in den Namen die Weisheit Gottes zeigt, da Gott jedem geschaffenen Ding seine eigene und angemessene Benennung anpasste" (οἰκείως καὶ προσφυῶς ἑκάστῳ τῶν γενομένων τὰς προσηγορίας ἁρμόσαντος).[69] Diese Vorstellung kommt tatsächlich der im *Kratylos* erörterten Meinung nahe, dass die Namen (z.B. durch ihre Etymologie, 393d) die Dinge nachahmen.[70]

Im zitierten Absatz erwägt Gregor auch die Möglichkeit, Eunomius schöpfe nicht direkt aus dem Dialog des Platon, sondern aus seinen Interpreten, und er fügt zugleich ironisch hinzu, dass er sich "die Schönheit der platonischen Sprache aneignete" (περικτυπηθεὶς τῇ καλλιφωνίᾳ τῆς Πλατωνικῆς λέξεως).[71] Dieses letzte Schmeicheln betrifft wahrscheinlich die erhabene Ausdruckweise des Eunomius, die Gregor an einer anderen Stelle als 'arrogant und bombastisch' (ἀσύφηλον καὶ στομφώδη) verspottet.[72]

---

[68] *CE* II 404–405 (GNO I 344,13–25).

[69] *CE* II 403 (GNO I 344,10–13).

[70] Wir haben jedoch keinen Beleg dafür, dass Eunomius die 'Angemessenheit der Benennungen' nach ihrer Etymologie suchte. Dies treibt eher Gregor selber, wenn er einige hebräische Eigennahmen erklärt (vgl. *CE* II 285–288, GNO I 310,11–311,17).

[71] Vgl. *CE* II 405 (GNO I 344,22–23).

[72] Vgl. *CE* II 413 (GNO I 346,22–23).

Diese Auskünfte führten Jean Daniélou zu seiner interessanten Hypothese, dass Eunomius – wahrscheinlich durch seinen Lehrer Aëtius – mit dem mysterienfreundlichen Neuplatonismus der Schüler des Jamblichos (und mit ihrer erhabenen Sprache) bekannt gemacht wurde und von ihnen (höchstwahrscheinlich aus ihren *Kratylos*-Kommentaren) auch seine Vorstellung vom göttlichen Ursprung der Sprache übernahm.[73] Auch die *Chaldäischen Orakel*, diese Bibel einiger Neuplatoniker, sprechen ja vom heiligen Charakter der barbarischen Namen.[74] Daniélou zitiert als seinen Hauptbeleg einen Kommentar des Jamblichos (nach Daniélou Ps.-Jamblichos) zu diesem Werk, wo es heißt, dass die Namen nicht auf eine menschliche Konvention zurückgehen (κατὰ συνθήκην), sondern der Natur der Dinge selbst entsprechen (τῇ φύσει συνήρτηται τῶν ὄντων) und tradiert werden. Die göttlichen Namen dürfen nämlich nicht als menschliche Begriffe (ἐπίνοιαι) ausgedacht oder kraft des Verstandes gesucht (λογικαὶ διέξοδοι), sondern nur aus einer göttlichen Gabe verstanden werden.[75] Eine ähnliche Theorie vom göttlichen Ursprung der Namen finden wir auch im späteren *Kratylos*-Kommentar von Proklos,[76] der sicherlich, so Daniélou, auf die Kommentare seiner Vorgänger zurückgeht, aus denen auch Eunomius schöpfte.

Diese Hypothese, die sich auch auf die subordinationistische, 'neuplatonisierende' Theologie des Eunomius beruft,[77] hat u.a. J. M. Rist einer Kritik unterworfen. Er sucht einen möglichen Ursprung der Sprachvorstellungen des Eunomius eher im *Kratylos* selbst und in den Grammatikmanualen stoischer Prägung als in den angeblichen von Jamblichos abhängenden *Kratylos*-Kommentaren, deren Existenz sogar unsicher erscheint.[78]

---

[73] Vgl. J. Daniélou, "Eunome l'Arien et l'exégèse néoplatonicienne du Cratyle", *REG* 69 (1956) 412–432.

[74] Vgl. *Oratia Chaldaica* 150 (Des Places 103).

[75] Vgl. Jamblichos, *De oraculis* VII 4–5 (Des Places 191,12–195,3).

[76] Vgl. Proklos Diadochos, *In Platonis Cratylum* 51 (Pasquali 18–20). Im Zusammenhang mit der Sprachauffassung des Eunomius untersuchte diesen Kommentar Th. Böhm, *Theoria*, 181ff.

[77] Gegen die Vorstellung des J. Daniélou von Eunomius als einem Neuplatoniker polemisierte schon im Jahr 1964 Alfred Schindler, ohne jedoch einen neuplatonischen Einfluss an seine Sprachauffassung zu leugnen (vgl. A. Schindler, *Die Begründung der Trinitätslehre in der eunomianischen Kontroverse. Eine Untersuchung zu den Apologien des Eunomius, zu Basilius' des Grossen Schrift gegen Eunomius und zu Gregors von Nyssa trinitarischen Schriften*, unpublizierte Dissertation, Zurüch 1964, 137–150).

[78] Vgl. J. M. Rist, "Basil's 'Neoplatonism': Its Background and Nature", in: P. J. Fedwick (Hrsg.), *Basil of Caesarea: Christian, Humanist, Ascetic. A Sixteen-Hundreth Anniversary Symposium*, Bd. I, Toronto 1981, 137–220, bes. 185–188.

Es besteht tatsächlich keine überzeugende Ähnlichkeit zwischen den magischen Namen der *Chaldäischen Orakel* und dem syllogistischen Verfahren des Eunomius, der traditionell einer sophistischen oder aristotelischen 'Technologie' verdächtig war.[79] Seine Position enthält trotzdem platonische 'Implikationen',[80] vor allem in seiner Überzeugung von der eingeborenen Fähigkeit der menschlichen Seele die Strukturen der Dinge zu erkennen. Nach dem platonischen *Kratylos* darf jedoch die Sprache nicht automatisch als ein treues Abbild der Dinge gelten, sondern muss als das Werk eines 'Gesetzgebers' (νομοθέτης) der Sprache immer wieder nach den Verhältnissen zwischen den Ideen überprüft werden, zu denen die Worte ausgerichtet sind. Und gerade die 'Verhältnisse zwischen den Ideen' (ἡ ἀλλήλων τῶν εἰδῶν συμπλοκή), die die Sprache begründen (*Soph.* 259e), kann der Mensch in seinem Denken und seiner Sprache (λόγος) als ein 'Dialektiker' untersuchen und dadurch am Werk des Gesetzgebers der Sprache eine Kritik üben.[81]

Diese Vorstellung enthält jedoch ein Paradox, das die Position Platons prekär macht oder ihr ihre Dynamik verleiht: die Verhältnisse zwischen den Ideen, die für die Sprache normativ sein sollen, werden zugleich durch die Sprache selbst untersucht. Vielleicht ist es gerade diese Paradoxie, die in der Sprachtheorie des Eunomius zu kurz kommt. Die göttliche Nomenklatur spricht nach seiner Überzeugung ganz treu die Dinge aus und die Sprache des Menschen kann diese Nomenklatur entweder ablesen, oder an ihr vorbeigehen,

---

[79] Vgl. z.B. *CE* II 604 (GNO I 402,28). Zu dieser Anklage s. E. Vandenbussche, "La part de la dialectique dans la théologie d'Eunomius 'le technologue'", *RHE* 40 (1944/45) 47–72. Nach der Überzeugung des Verfassers war jedoch Eunomius nicht nur ein 'Technologe' (ein aristotelisch inspirierter Sophist), sondern in seiner hierarchischen Metaphysik kam er eher dem Platonismus nahe (vgl. E. Vandenbussche, *La part*, 70–72). Eunomius als einen 'logic chopper' zeigt auch R. P. Vaggione, *Eunomius of Cyzicus and the Nicene Revolution*, Oxford 2000, 93ff.

[80] Vgl. Th. Böhm, *Theoria*, 185. Auch R. P. Vaggione (*Eunomius of Cyzicus*, 239, Anm. 262) hält es 'in einem breiteren Sinne' für richtig, die Inspiration der Sprachauffassung des Eunomius im platonischen *Kratylos* zu sehen. Die Überzeugung des Eunomius, dass das Denken die Struktur der Realität wiederspiegelt, bezeichnet er als eine *contentual logic* (vgl. R. P. Vaggione, *Eunomius of Cyzicus*, 245). P. Kalligas vermutet als eine mögliche Quelle die verschollene Abhandlung *Über die Namen* des Theodor von Asine (vgl. P. Kalligas, "Basil of Caesarea", 41, Anm. 35).

[81] Vgl. Ch. Kahn, "Les mots et les formes dans le 'Cratyle' de Platon", in: *Philosophie du language et grammaire dans l'antiquité* (*Cahiers de Philosophie Ancienne*, N. 5; *Cahiers du Groupe de Recherches sur la Philosophie et le Langage*, N. 6–7), Bruxelles 1986, 91–103. Im Zusammenhang mit unserer Polemik befassten sich mit dem Dialog G. C. Stead, "Logic", 303–305; Th. Böhm, *Theoria*, 179f.

sie ist jedoch nicht ein deklariertes ständiges Überprüfen dieser Nomenklatur.

Trotzdem übt Eunomius selber ein solches Überprüfen der Sprache, wie ich an einem Beispiel zeigen möchte. In seiner ersten *Apologie* heißt es, dass die gleichen Benennungen (προσηγορία) die gleichen Wesen (οὐσία) und die unterschiedlichen Namen (ὀνόματα) dagegen unterschiedliche Wesen bezeichnen.[82] Die Sprache scheint also ein treuer Spiegel der Dinge selbst zu sein. Zugleich entwickelt da jedoch Eunomius einerseits seine Lehre von der Konvertibilität der göttlichen Prädikate (die alle, obwohl einander unterschiedlich, die gleiche Bedeutung haben, z.B. 'der Seiende' und 'der einzig wahre Gott'), andererseits seine Vorstellung vom metaphorischen Gebrauch der gleichen Worte, die anders von Gott, anders vom Menschen ausgesagt werden (z.B. 'das Auge' oder 'die Vaterschaft').[83] Wie diese Fälle bezeugen, müssen die gleichen Worte nicht immer die gleichen Dinge und die unterschiedlichen Worte die unterschiedlichen Dinge bezeichnen. Für den Gebrauch und für das Verstehen der Sprache ist also die Kenntnis der Verhältnisse zwischen den Dingen entscheidend und nicht umgekehrt, obwohl zugleich auch die Anwendung der gleichen, bzw. unterschiedlichen Worte etwas Wichtiges von den Dingen andeutet und zu einem Ausgangspunkt ihrer Erkenntnis werden kann. Wenn Eunomius selber mit dieser Dialektik auch arbeitet, hat er sie nicht (soweit wir wissen) zu einem Teil seiner Sprachtheorie gemacht, wodurch sein 'Platonismus' etwas rigid erscheint.

Seine Überzeugung vom göttlichen Ursprung der Namen, die Eunomius in die Nähe einiger Neuplatoniker führt, muss jedoch nicht seine Abhängigkeit von ihnen in diesem Punkt beweisen. Wie Daniélou selbst anführt, finden wir auch bei Klemens von Alexandrien und Origenes Passagen vom göttlichen Ursprung (oder auch der Macht) der Namen, bei Origenes sogar eine Klassifizierung der antiken Sprachvorstellungen nach dem Kriterium des Ursprungs der Namen φύσει oder θέσει.[84] Origenes glaubt jedoch, dass die einzelnen Sprachen

---

[82] Vgl. Eunomius, *Apol.* 9 (Vaggione 44); *Apol.* 18 (Vaggione 56).

[83] Vgl. Eunomius, *Apol.* 16–17 (Vaggione 52–54); *Apol.* 18 (Vaggione 56).

[84] Vgl. Klemens von Alexandrien unter Berufung auf *Kratylos* (*Strom.* I 143,6–7, GCS 15, 89); Origenes, *C. Cels.* I 24–25 (SC 132, 136–144; zu dieser Passage, die teilweise in die *Philokalie* eingenommen wurde, vgl. M. Harl, in: SC 302, 447–457); *C. Cels.* V 45–46 (SC 147, 130–134). Origenes erwähnt die aristotelische Vorstellung der konventionalen Namensgebung (θέσει), die stoische Überzeugung, dass die Namen

nicht durch menschliche Konvention entstanden, sondern von Gott geschenkt wurden, und daher sind auch die Namen (besonders die göttlichen Namen) unwechselbar und unübertragbar.[85]

Wie die Analysen des Antonio Orbe zeigten, war Origenes sehr wahrscheinlich eine entscheidende Inspiration für die beiden Gegner unserer Polemik in ihrer Lehre von den Benennungen Gottes und den christologischen Titeln (ἐπίνοιαι, d.h. verschiedene Namen, die die Einzelaspekte des göttlichen Logos und seines Wirkens zum Ausdruck bringen).[86] Während jedoch Eunomius aus dieser Christologie eine Regel beibehielt, dass nur der Logos als vom Vater abgeleitet und als der Mittler der Schöpfung mehrere epinoetische Bezeichnungen trägt, haben die Kappadokier die epinoetischen Benennungen auch auf Gott angewendet.[87] Ich halte es für sehr wahrscheinlich, dass Origenes auch für die Vorstellungen der beiden Gegner vom Ursprung der Sprache eine wichtige Rolle spielte. Während jedoch Eunomius seinen Glauben an die göttliche Herkunft der Namen übernahm,

der Natur (φύσει) entsprechen, da sie nach den ersten die Dinge nachahmenden Lauten gebildet werden, und die epikureische Anschauung, dass die Namen sogar diese Laute selbst sind (srv. Origenes, *C. Cels.* I 24, SC 132, 136). Zur Vorstellung des Origenes, dass die Namen das Wesen der Dinge künden, vgl. R. Gögler, *Zur Theologie des biblischen Wortes bei Origenes*, Düsseldorf 1963, 217–211.

[85] Der Einfluss des Origenes auf die Sprachvorstellungen des Eunomius mag direkt wie auch indirekt, durch die Bibelexegese des Lukian von Antiochien vermittelt wirken, die für Aëtius maßgebend erscheint. Vgl. A. Schindler, *Die Begründung*, 150–153. Zu Aëtius s. auch L. R. Wickham, "The Syntagmation of Aetius the Anomoean", *JThS* 19 (1968) 532–569, bes. 558, Anm. 1. Zu der Formation des Aëtius, die wahrscheinlich das Studium der aristotelischen *Kategorien* mit dem Kommentar des Porphyrius und die lukianische Exegese umfasste, vgl. R. P. Vaggione, *Eunomius of Cyzicus*, 16–23; zu seinem Einfluss auf Eunomius vgl. 35.

[86] Vgl. Origenes, *C. Cels.* II 64 (SC 132, 434); *In Ioh.* I 21,125 – I 39,292 (SC 120, 126–206); *In Ioh.* II 18,125–128 (SC 120, 290–292); *Hom. Gen.* 14,1 (SC 7bis, 334); *De princ.* IV 4,1 (SC 268, 402–404); s. dazu H. Crouzel, "Le contenu spirituel des dénominations du Christ selon le livre I du Commentaire sur Jean d'Origène", in: ders. – A. Quacquarelli (Hrsg.), *Origeniana Secunda*, Roma 1980, 131–150; zur Theorie der ἐπίνοιαι als den gedachten Bedeutungen in ihrem Zusammenhang mit dem Freiheitsgedanken bei Origenes s. Th. Kobusch, "Die philosophische Bedeutung des Kirchenvaters Origenes. Zur christlichen Kritik an der Einseitigkeit der griechischen Wesensphilosophie", *ThQ* 165 (1985) 94–105.

[87] Vgl. A. Orbe, *La epinoia. Algunos preliminares históricos de la distinción kat'epinoian. En torno a la Filosofía de Leoncio Bizantino*, Roma 1955, 17–22 und 42–45). Von den Ausführungen des Origenes über die verschiedenen biblischen Aussagen von Gott bzw. Christus (ἐπίνοιαι), die nicht das Wesen, sondern nur die Einzelaspekte fassen, behielt Eunomius besonders die Anwendung der Bezeichnung ἐπίνοια für diejenigen Benennungen, die nicht das Wesen Gottes fassen (vgl. R. P. Vaggione, *Eunomius of Cyzicus*, 242f).

haben die Kappadokier seine *Epinoia*-Lehre in eine ganze Sprachtheorie entwickelt, in der mehrere parallele Ausdrücke nach der Möglichkeit der menschlichen Erkenntnis die unterschiedlichen Aspekte der erkannten Dinge bezeichnen.

Diese Theorie der Kappadokier gründet höchstwahrscheinlich letztlich auf der stoischen Unterscheidung von ἐπινοίᾳ und κατὰ τὴν ὑπόστασιν (die auch Origenes kannte).[88] So sind z.B. (nach Poseidonios) οὐσία und ὕλη das Gleiche κατὰ τὴν ὑπόστασιν und unterscheiden sich ἐπινοίᾳ μόνον, d.h. ihre Referenz ist die gleiche, die bezeichneten Aspekte jedoch unterschiedlich.[89] Die *Epinoia*, ein Begriff, der in unserer Polemik so wichtig war, bedeutete dabei für die Stoiker so viel wie ein Sediment des Denkens (ἐναποκειμένη νόησις),[90] das weitere Kombinationen der aus der Sinneserfahrung abgeleiteten Vorstellungen ermöglichte und dadurch für die Bildung der neuen, in der Sinneserfahrung nicht direkt verankerten Begriffe verantwortlich war.[91] Diese Erzeugnisse der 'logischen Phantasie' haben jedoch als immateriell keine Existenz im eigentlichen Sinne (ὑπάρχειν), sondern nur eine Subsistenz im Denken (ὑφεστάναι).[92] Dieser Status gehört damit nach den Stoikern der immateriellen Bedeutung der Worte an, d.h. dem 'Bezeichneten' oder dem 'durch die Sprache Gemeinten' (τὸ λεκτόν oder τὸ σημαινόμενον), das sie einerseits von dem bezeichnenden Laut (τὸ σημαῖνον), andererseits von der außersprachlichen Referenz (τὸ τυγχάνον) unterschieden, die beide materiell sind.[93] Dieses 'durch die Sprache Gemeinte' (σημαινόμενον) spielt bekanntlich auch in der kappadokischen Sprachauffassung einen wichtigen Part, wo es jedoch manchmal mit dem aristotelischen Begriff

---

[88] Zur Unterscheidung des einen ὑποκείμενον in Christus und den mehreren Namen (ὀνόματα), die sich auf ihn ταῖς ἐπινοίαις (als gedachte Unterscheidung der einzelnen Aspekte) beziehen vgl. Origenes, *Hom. Jerem.* VIII 2 (SC 232, 358).

[89] Vgl. Poseidonios, *Fr.* 92 (Edelstein-Kidd 99). S. dazu G. C. Stead, "Logic", 309–311.

[90] Vgl. Galenus, *Defin. medicae* 126 (SVF II 89).

[91] Vgl. Sextus Empiricus, *Adv. math.* VIII 56 (SVF II 88).

[92] Vgl. Diogenes Laërtius VII 63 (SVF II 181). Zur Unterscheidung zwischen der Existenz des Materiellen (ὑπάρχειν) und der Subsistenz im Denken (ὑφεστάναι) vgl. Chrysippus, *Phys.*, Fr. 26 aus Arius Didymus (SVF II 509), wo zwar als subsistent die künftige und vergangene Zeit bezeichnet wird; die Zeit als immateriell hat jedoch den gleichen Status wie die λεκτά (vgl. Sextus Empiricus, *Adv. math.* X,218 = SVF II 331).

[93] Vgl. Sextus Empiricus, *Adv. math.* VIII 11 (SVF II 166). S. dazu A. A. Long, "Language and Thought in Stoicism", in: ders. (Hrsg.), *Problems*, 75–113; Th. Kobusch, *Sein und Sprache*, 25–35.

(νόημα) des Denkens als der Bedeutung (ἔμφασις) der Worte in eins fällt,[94] was in der stoischen Auffassung eigentlich nicht möglich wäre.[95]

Die Position Gregors in unserer Passage erscheint überhaupt am ehesten der Auffassung des Aristoteles ähnlich, nach der die Sprache (λόγος) ihre Bedeutung nicht 'von Natur aus' (φύσει) oder 'organisch' (ὡς ὄργανον), sondern aufgrund einer Vereinbarung (κατὰ συνθήκην) trägt. Die Sprache ist also für Aristoteles nicht ein natürliches Organ des Menschen, sondern ein Ergebnis seiner Überlegung, dazu noch einer gemeinsamen, zwischenmenschlichen Vereinbarung. Der phonetische Ausdruck (τὰ ἐν τῇ φωνῇ) sind dabei Symbole (σύμβολα) oder Zeichen (σημεῖα) des in der Seele Erfahrenen (τῶν ἐν τῇ ψυχῇ παθημάτων), nämlich der Gleichnisse (ὁμοιώματα) von Dingen selbst. Während die Dinge für alle Menschen dieselben (ταὐτα) sind, und sogar ihre Abbilder oder Erfahrungen in der Seele dieselben (ταὐτα) sind, ist ihr phonetischer (und von ihm abgeleiteter schriftlicher) Ausdruck unterschiedlich (*Int.* 16a1–17a7).[96]

Dieser Vorstellung kommt Gregor in seiner Sprachauffassung sehr nahe, obwohl er sie nicht ganz übernimmt (es wäre verführerisch seine Inspirationsquelle im verschollenen Kommentar zu *De interpretatione* des Porphyrius zu suchen, wie einige Forscher die Inspiration für Basilius' Theorie der Eigennamen im *Kategorienkommentar* des Porphyrius finden).[97] Auch für ihn ist die Sprache sicherlich keine

[94] Vgl. Th. Kobusch, "Name und Sein. Zu den sprachlichphilosophischen Grundlagen in der Schrift Contra Eunomium des Gregor von Nyssa", in: L. F. Mateo-Seco – J. L. Bastero (Hrsg.), *El "Contra Eunomium I"*, 256–258.

[95] Vgl. A. C. Lloyd, "Grammar", 65.

[96] Es ist nicht völlig klar, was hier Aristoteles mit den παθήματα ἐν τῇ ψυχῇ meint, die er als Abbilder der Dinge darstellt. Vielleicht geht es um Abdrücke der Dinge in der Seele, aus denen durch die Abstraktion die Begriffe (νοήματα) gebildet werden: Diese Abdrücke sind in allen Seelen gleich, da sie von den gleichen Dingen abgeleitet werden, und daher sind auch die von ihnen abstrahierten Begriffe einerseits eine adäquate Auffassung der Dinge selbst, andererseits für alle Menschen gemeinsam, obwohl in verschiedenen Sprachen mit unterschiedlichen Worten ausgedrückt (so interpretiert die Passage H. Arens, *Aristotle's Theory of Language and Its Tradition. Texts from 500–1750*, Amsterdam – Philadelphia 1984, 24–57). Oder meint hier Aristoteles mit den παθήματα gleich die Begriffe, wie die Mehrheit der Interpreten meint (vgl. schon Ammonios Hermiou, *In Int.*, CAG IV/5 22,9f; 22,19f; 24,11; vielleicht auch Boethius, *Comm. Int.* I 1, Meiser II 43; gegen Arens in diesem Sinne H. Weidemann, "Grundzüge der Aristotelischen Sprachtheorie", in: P. Schmitter (Hrsg.), *Sprachtheorien*, 170–192; ders., in: Aristoteles, *Peri hermeneias*, Berlin 1994, 140f; ähnlich auch A. A. Long, "Language", 79).

[97] Vgl. P. Kalligas, "Basil of Caesarea", 46f.

natürliche Funktion, sondern eine gesellschaftliche Konvention.[98] Er würde wahrscheinlich auch zustimmen, dass die Sprache die Abbilder der Dinge in der Seele zum Ausdruck bringt und dass diese Ausdrücke unterschiedlich, während die Dinge dieselben sind. Sogar die Abdrücke der Dinge in der Seele oder die Begriffe von ihnen sind für Gregor teilweise die gleichen,[99] diese Vorstellungen oder Begriffe entsprechen jedoch nicht den Dingen selbst als ihre treuen Abbilder, weil die Dinge für den Menschen teilweise unerkennbar bleiben.[100] Wie wir in unserer Passage erfahren, bleibt auch (und vor allem) die Gottheit für den Menschen in ihrem Wesen unbegreiflich und unerreichbar, und ein jeder kann nur dasjenige, 'was es ihm scheint' und 'was er einsah' zum Ausdruck bringen.[101]

Die Sprache bringt damit auf verschiedene Art und Weise die menschliche Erkenntnis von den Dingen zum Ausdruck, die zum Teil gemeinsam, nach den Aspekten jedoch unterschiedlich ist und die nicht ganz den Dingen selbst, sondern ihrem Erscheinen entspricht. Die Sprache enthält dazu für Gregor einen kommunikativen und pragmatischen Aspekt: Jeder Sprechende bringt zum Ausdruck, was er einsehen konnte, durch ein Interesse geführt seine Gedanken den anderen mitzuteilen, und nach dieser Absicht wird auch seine Sprache gestaltet.

Die Position Gregors könnte daher als eine Art Aristotelismus charakterisiert werden, zu dem jedoch die Unerkennbarkeit der Dinge selbst hinzutritt. Eunomius macht auch auf eine Ähnlichkeit der kappadokischen Vorstellung mit dem Aristotelismus aufmerksam, den er in dieser Hinsicht als gottlos tadelt. Er macht es jedoch sehr ungeschickt, weil er sich (soweit wir wissen) nicht auf die konventionale

---

[98] Auf die 'konventionalistische' Sprachvorstellung des Gregor macht auch A. Viciano aufmerksam, vgl. A. Viciano, "Algunas leyes lógicas del lenguaje, según Gregorio de Nisa: A próposito de dos pasajes de 'Contra Eunomium I'", in: L. F. Mateo-Seco – J. L. Bastero (Hrsg.), *El "Contra Eunomium I"*, 321–327.

[99] Die Elemente erscheinen, so Gregor, allen Menschen gleich (ὡσαύτως φαίνονται) (*CE* II 251, GNO I 299,21). Ähnlich der Stein oder das Holz scheinen (δοκεῖ) nicht als etwas je anderes, obwohl sie von den verschiedenen Nationen unterschiedlich bezeichnet werden (*CE* II 254, GNO I 300,15–18). An einer anderen Stelle erfahren wir, dass die verschiedenen Nationen den Himmel zwar unterschiedlich nennen (ὀνομάζειν), sie verstehen (νοεῖν) ihn jedoch alle gleich (*CE* II 284, GNO I 310,2–5).

[100] Vgl. *CE* II 79 (GNO I 250,3–10); *CE* II 106–118 (GNO I 257,26–260,25); ähnlich schon Basilius, *AE* I 12–13 (SC 299, 214–218).

[101] CE II 397 (GNO I 342,14–15).

Namenauffassung beruft, sondern die Vorstellung des Basilius direkt mit einer Ablehnung der Vorsehung in der sublunaren Sphäre gleichsetzt: "Es ist nämlich seine Lehre (*scil.* des Aristoteles)," schreibt Eunomius, "dass die Vorsehung nicht alles Seiende umgreift und dass sie die irdischen Angelegenheiten nicht betrifft."[102]

In dieser Form kann Gregor den 'Aristotelismus'-Verdacht schnell ablehnen (er leugnet ja die Vorsehung nicht für die Dinge, sondern für ihre Namen) und ihn auf Eunomius selber fallen lassen.[103] Was genau Gregor durch diese Anklage meint, leuchtet von dem ganzen Kontext nicht eindeutig ein, vielleicht verspottet er den Anspruch des Eunomius die Dinge mit den Begriffen fassen zu können oder einfach seinen Gebrauch des syllogistischen Verfahrens. Soviel ist jedoch klar, dass Gregor den Vergleich der kappadokischen Position mit dem Aristotelismus in der Frage der Vorsehung als unangemessen und unbegründet abweist.[104] Die Vorstellung vom konventionalen Ursprung der Namen bleibt dabei (leider) ganz beiseite.

Neben dem Vorwurf des Aristotelismus parodiert Eunomius die *Epinoia*-Vorstellung des Basilius auch durch ihren Vergleich zur epikureischen Physik mit ihrer Lehre von der zufälligen Entstehung der Dinge (αἱ τύχαιαι τῶν ὄντων γενέσεις). Die Begriffsbildung, die nicht das Wesen der Dinge zum Ausdruck bringt, erscheint nämlich Eunomius gleich 'zufällig' wie die Entstehung der Dinge durch die zufällige Gruppierungen der Atome.[105]

Diese Anklage der kappadokischen Position erscheint zuerst paradox, besonders wenn man bedenkt, dass die epikureische Sprachvorstellung die Worte als einen natürlichen Widerhall der Dinge verstand. Auch diese Lehre rechnete jedoch mit einer gedanklichen Durchdringung der ersten spontanen Laute und einer allmählichen Beseitigung der Mehrdeutigkeiten, einer wachsenden Prägnanz sowie

[102] CE II 411 (GNO I 346,6–9). W. Jaeger, *ad loc.*, findet diese aristotelische Vorstellung in der doxographischen Tradition bezeugt, die sich auf die verlorengegangenen Dialoge des Aristoteles stützte (vgl. H. Diels, *Doxographi graeci*, Berlin – Leipzig 1929, 130f).

[103] Schon Basilius hat die aristotelischen Neigungen des Eunomius getadelt, besonders den unkritischen Gebrauch, den er von den aristotelisch-stoischen Syllogismen und der *Kategorien*-Schrift macht. Vgl. Basilius, *AE* I 5,43–45 (SC 299, 172–174); *AE* I 9 (SC 299, 200).

[104] Vgl. CE II 411 (GNO I 346,4–12).

[105] Vgl. CE II 410 (GNO I 345,25–346,4); vgl. Epikur, *Ep. ad Herodotum* (Arrighetti §43–44); Marcus Aurelius, *Meditationes* VII 50 (Trannoy 77).

einer Bereicherung um Fachausdrücke für das neu Entdeckte.[106] Die Worte bringen zuerst spontan die Erlebnisse (πάθη) und Wahrnehmungen (αἰσθήσεις) zum Ausdruck, die allmählich in die 'antizipierenden Vorstellungen' (προλήψεις) sedimentieren, aufgrund derer die Dinge benannt werden.[107] Zwischen dem bezeichneten Ding und dem bezeichnenden Wort steht damit für die Epikureer in dieser zweiten Phase der Sprache eine 'antizipierende Vorstellung' wie eine Art 'Universalie', die (wieder auf einem natürlichen Weg) die Benennungen der Dinge durch die Lautorgane hervorruft.

Wie bekannt, wurden die Epikureer schon in der Antike angeklagt, dass sie ein selbständiges Bestehen der Bedeutung (λεκτά) leugnen und nur den bezeichnenden Laut (φωνή oder σημαῖνον) und das bezeichnete Ding (τὸ τυγχάνον) in Betracht ziehen.[108] Dieser Vorwurf gilt jedoch im strengen Sinne nur für die erste Phase der Sprache nach den Epikureern, oder es spiegelt sich in ihm vielleicht ihre Verweigerung für die 'antizipierenden Vorstellungen' (als eine Art konstant gewordener Abdrücke der Dinge in der materiellen Seele) einen besonderen immaterialen Status einzuführen, wie es die Stoiker für ihre λεκτά taten (die anders in dem materiellen Universum der Stoa keinen Platz hätten).[109]

Unter dem Eindruck dieser Anklagen verstehen jedenfalls einige Forscher die Position des Eunomius als in diesem Punkt dem Epikureismus nahekommend.[110] Um eine wirkliche Ähnlichkeit der beiden Sprachtheorien kann es sich jedoch natürlich nicht handeln.[111]

---

[106] Vgl. Epikur, *Ep. ad Herodotum* (Arrighetti §75–76).

[107] Vgl. Diogenes Laërtius, X 33 (Arrighetti §33).

[108] Vgl. Plutarchos, *Adv. Colotem* 22, 1119f (Arrighetti §146), Sextus Empiricus, *Adv. dogm.* II 13 (Arrighetti §147).

[109] In diesem Sinne interpretieren die Anklage A. A. Long, "Aisthesis, Prolepsis and Linguistic Theory in Epicurus", *Bulletin of the Institute of Classical Studies of the University of London*, 1971, 114–133 (bes. 120–121) und nach ihm M. Hossenfelder, "Epikureer", in: P. Schmitter (Hrsg.), *Sprachtheorien*, 217–237 (bes. 232–233).

[110] Vgl. Th. Kobusch, "Name und Sein", 253–254; zum Epikureismus auch ders., *Sein und Sprache*, 32–33.

[111] Die Epikureer wollen um jeden Preis vermeiden, dass ein Gott die Worte ausdenken müsse (und dadurch in seiner Seligkeit verkürzt wäre). Die Worte entstehen nach ihrer Vorstellung durch eine Kombination der natürlichen vokalen Reaktion und ihrer Präzisierung durch das Denken, sie sprechen nicht die Struktur der Dinge aus, sondern die unmittelbaren menschlichen Eindrücke, bzw. die antizipierenden Vorstellungen von den Dingen. Die Sprache ist damit in ihrer ersten Phase ein spontaner Ausdruck der menschlichen Reaktionen, in ihrer zweiten Phase enthält sie ein konventionalistisches Element (die ursprüngliche Sprachvorstellung Epikurs

Durch die Überzeugung, dass die Sprache die menschlichen Eindrücke von den Dingen aussagt und allmählich zur Präzisierung gelangt, kommt die epikureische Sprachvorstellung tatsächlich eher den Kappadokiern nahe, ein wesentlicher Unterschied liegt jedoch darin, dass für die Kappadokier die Worte ursprünglich nicht eine natürliche vokale Reaktion, sondern eine durchdachte Konvention darstellen, die sich an der Beschaffenheit und Wirkung der Dinge orientiert.

Die Polemik zwischen den Kappadokiern und Eunomius ist damit nicht ein bloßer Widerhall der Divergenzen zwischen den Stoikern und Epikureern oder der aristotelischen und der platonischen Sprachauffassung oder letztlich zwischen Kratylos und Hermogenes im platonischen Dialog selbst, sondern erscheint auf beiden Seiten als ein kompliziertes Gewebe der antiken Elemente. Eunomius setzt eine göttliche Nomenklatur voraus, in der die Struktur der Dinge selbst zum Ausdruck kommt, und diese Überzeugung unterscheidet ihn deutlich von den Epikureern und rückt ihn in die Nähe der Schüler des Platon. Mit einigen Neuplatonikern teilt er – gegen Platon selbst – den Glauben an einen göttlichen Ursprung der Worte. Daher versteht er die ständige kritische Selbstüberprüfung aufgrund der Verhältnisse zwischen den Dingen selbst nicht als eine wichtige Funktion der Sprache (obwohl er solche kritische Überprüfung durchführt). In seiner Überzeugung, dass die Dinge durch ihre Begriffe aufgefasst werden können, kommt Eunomius Aristoteles nahe.

Gregor versteht die Worte als eine Struktur, durch welche die Erkenntnisse des Menschen organisiert und seine Gedanken mitgeteilt werden, was an die stoische Auffassung denken lässt. Die stellvertretenden Benennungen sprechen die Eindrücke und Erkenntnisse des Menschen von den Dingen unter verschiedenen Aspekten aus. Diese Benennungen richten sich dabei nach dem Willen des Menschen die Dinge so zu beschreiben, wie sie ihm erscheinen, und sie dienen der Verständigung und der Kommunikation. Dadurch tritt in die Sprachvorstellung Gregors ein konventionalistisches oder pragmatisches Element ein, das sich den Konventionalismus des Aristoteles

soll sogar durchaus konventionalistisch gewesen sein und mit der Sprache als einer künstlich eingeführten Fachterminologie gerechnet haben – diese letzte Hypothese entwickelt A. A. Long, "Aisthesis", 125–126, aufgrund der Fragmente aus der Schrift *De natura*, XXVIII von Epikur; ähnlich auch M. Hossenfelder, "Epikureer", 234–235). Alle diese Motive sind Eunomius ganz fremd.

nicht nur zu eigen macht, sondern ihn durch seine Skepsis gegenüber der Erkenntnis der Dinge selbst sogar überbietet.

Eine wichtige Inspirationsquelle scheint für beide Seiten der Polemik auch die Sprachvorstellung des Origenes zu sein. Während jedoch für Eunomius der Glaube an die göttliche Herkunft der Worte entscheidend war, wurde für die kappadokischen Brüder die Pluralität der christologischen Titel bei Origenes zu einem Musterbeispiel, wie sich die Mehrheit der verschiedenen Bedeutungen zu einem einzigen Referenten verhält, wobei diese Bedeutungen die menschliche Erkenntnis von den Dingen, nicht die Dinge selbst zum Ausdruck bringen.

DIVINE SIMPLICITY AND THE PLURALITY OF ATTRIBUTES (*CE* II 359–386; 445–560)

Joseph S. O'Leary

In *CE* II 67–358 and again in 387–444 Gregory clarifies the status of human knowledge, conceptuality and language in regard to the divine. In the sections I shall study here, he turns to a defence of Basil's account of the attributes 'unbegotten' and 'imperishable', which Eunomius had impugned. Tracking this phase of the discussion, I hope to gain a more precise understanding of Gregory's thought on the nature of divine attributes and perhaps to sight some significant weaknesses and blind spots in his argumentation. The wider questions of how Gregory's argumentation is to be placed in regard to later reflection on these issues, notably in Augustine and the Scholastics, or how a critique of it can contribute to an 'overcoming of metaphysics' in theology, in the wake of Harnack and Heidegger, can only be lightly touched on here.

I. *Inconclusive anti-Arian arguments in* CE *II 359–378*

At *CE* II 362 Eunomius accuses Basil of teaching that "the most holy essence of God receives ἐπίνοιαι in various ways".[1] It is implied that Basil compromises the divine unity by introducing diversity, undermines the divine simplicity, and subjects the divine to human conceptualization. Aetius had claimed that "if 'unbegotten' does not present the ὑπόστασις of God, but the incomparable name is of human conceiving (ἐπινοίας), God is obliged to the conceivers, because of the conception 'unbegotten', not bearing the excellence of the name in essence" (prop. 12). If 'unbegotten' is merely a name, then the human utterance is greater than the divine being (prop. 26).[2]

[1] *CE* II 362 (GNO I 332).

[2] See L. R. Wickham, "The *Syntagmation* of Aetius the Anomean", *JThS* 19 (1968) 532–569.

These objections are not sudden innovations. Long before, Justin had said: "No name is to be ascribed to the Father of all, since he is unbegotten (ἀγεννήτῳ ὄντι). To whatever a name is ascribed the one ascribing the name is elder. So 'Father' and 'God' and 'Creator' and 'Lord' and 'Master' are not names, but are applied from the benefits and works."[3] It may be that in this case, as in others, those branded as 'heretics' are simply persisting too rigidly in an older orthodoxy.

For Basil: "after the first idea coming to us from sensation, the subtler and more exact consideration of the object of thought is called ἐπίνοια".[4] His view, as illustrated by the example of the corn

[3] Justin Martyr, *Apologia secunda* 6,1–2 (Wartelle 204).

[4] Basil, *Adversus Eunomium* I 6 (PG 29, 524b). Petavius calls this "*quasi secunda et repetita notio vel cogitatio*" (Dionysius Petavius, *Opus de theologicis dogmatibus* I 9,2, Thomas 120). Sesboüé calls it "le temps second de la connaissance intellectuelle" (B. Sesboüé, *Saint Basile et la Trinité*, Paris 1998, 71), a reflective ἐπιλογισμός supervening on the first global and spontaneous apprehension (ἐπιβολή). The terminology is Stoic (cf. B. Pottier, *Dieu et le Christ selon Grégoire de Nysse*, Namur 1994, 159). Gregory concedes to Eunomius that Basil's definition was incomplete (see *CE* II 345f, GNO I 326f); his own ἐπίνοια is less analytical, more dynamic and heuristic; he has less faith in the reliability of ἐπίνοιαι, except as pedagogical devices leading us on the spiritual path to God (*CE* II 154.242, GNO I 270.297). Even in the case of Basil, Pottier speaks of a 'linguistic quasi-Kantianism': "For Basil, the names designate with a certain precision all that *surrounds* the substance, but they never penetrate to the hard metaphysical core" (B. Pottier, *Dieu et le Christ*, 164). In sharpening the opposition between κατ' ἐπίνοιαν and κατὰ φύσιν (*CE* II 304, GNO I 315), Gregory tends to make ἐπίνοιαι more flimsy and conjectural than they were in Basil. He sees naming God as a kind of game or hunt. His theology is so dominated by a sense of the unknowability of the divine essence that the attributes might seem to be no more than human guesswork, leaving the divine essence utterly elusive (while the trinitarian differentiations as well are condemned to epiphenomenal status or imperfectly integrated with the conception of the essence). "The substance of God is not to be touched and known; it is an abstraction and, in a sense, a fantasy; there is no core of the divine being to be grasped as the final, 'essential' quality of God, only the divine works, God willing to relate to the world in love" (R. Williams, *The Wound of Knowledge*, London 1990, 62). A similar objection is voiced in Karl Barth, *Kirchliche Dogmatik*, II/1, Zollikon – Zürich 1940, 364ff. Holl had pointed out that Gregory seeks a derivation of the Trinity from the one activity of God as ζωοποιὸς δύναμις, expressed in λόγος and πνεῦμα: "But if Gregory thereby attained a more vivid presentation of the threefold ordering in the divinity, the leap from this initial deployment to a doctrine of the hypostases is all the greater for him. So far Gregory has produced in reality only modes of the one divinity" (K. Holl, *Amphilochius von Ikonium in seinem Verhältnis zu den grossen Kappadoziern*, Tübingen 1904, 210). For Stead, likewise: "the undivided Godhead which they share is not so much manifested in three personal beings or modes as contradicted by the imposed characteristics by which they are distinguished" (Ch. Stead, "Divine Simplicity as a problem for orthodoxy", in R. Williams, ed., *The Making of Orthodoxy*, Cambridge 1989, 267). Bergjan thinks that "Gregory presupposes the trinitarian persons, but

in its different stages of growth, is robustly realistic. For the theological usage of ἐπίνοια, he cites first the ἐπίνοιαι of Christ, thus linking his thought to the famous use of ἐπίνοια in Origen's *Commentary on John*, and only then turns to the divine attributes as such, placing ἀφθαρσία alongside Eunomius's favoured ἀγεννησία. Origen generally confined ἐπίνοιαι to the Son, whom he regarded as compound, and was wary of multiplying attributes of the ultimate, simple God. Basil corrects this by stressing that the Son, too, is ἓν ὑποκείμενον, μία οὐσία.[5] This Christological point of departure creates confusion about the strictly theological use of ἐπίνοια, which itself, as we shall see, harbours ambiguities.[6]

Following Origen, Eunomius agrees that Christ, unlike the unbegotten God, can receive ἐπίνοιαι, in virtue of "the diversity of the activities and certain analogies and relations".[7] Gregory is indignant that here Eunomius puts the Son on the same level as corn, over against the unbegotten God. He points out that Eunomius fails to mention that the Son, too, is incapable of change.[8] Eunomius wants to see the imperishability of the Son as different from that of the Father, since "it is not on the basis of activities, as Father and

then defines the deity in such a way that no possibility of differentiation in God can be named" (S.-P. Bergjan, *Theoderet von Cyrus und der Neunizänismus*, Berlin 1994, 83). For Drecoll, "the Neo-Nicene distinction of μία οὐσία and τρεῖς ὑποστάσεις does not surreptitiously solve the problem that the notion of God is inaccessible to human reason, but upholds two basic coordinates of the Christian confession, namely, that one must speak of the existence of *one God*, yet can only speak of this God as Father, Son or Spirit" (V. H. Drecoll, *Die Entwicklung der Trinitätslehre des Basilius von Cäsarea*, Göttingen 1996, 285f). Maspero attempts to find a nexus between the ineffability of the divine essence and the positive revelatory function of the divine persons (G. Maspero, *La Trinità e l'uomo*, Rome 2004, 220).

[5] Cf. B. Pottier, *Dieu et le Christ*, 160.

[6] Basil's Christological illustration of ἐπίνοια continues to create confusion in modern scholarship. Bergjan refers to "the simple ὑποκείμενον to which different names are related as their object of reference" (S.-P. Bergjan, *Theoderet von Cyrus*, 39), speaking of Christ in a way that suggests confusion with the simple divine essence. Drecoll point out that "there is no polynymy here, since the different designations correspond to the different *energeiai* of Christ" (V. H. Drecoll, *Die Entwicklung der Trinitätslehre*, 78). Pottier contrasts the plurality based on ἐνέργειαι in the names of Christ with a plurality based on "a variety of finite intellectual considerations reaching toward the contemplation of God' in the divine attributes" (B. Pottier, *Dieu et le Christ*, 163). He admires Basil's strategy of coupling imperishability and unbegottenness, in order to "prove the subjectivity of these two negative concepts, and thus bring them close to the names of Christ" (*ibid.*, 162), but does not bring into view the lurking theological difficulty.

[7] *CE* II 363 (GNO I 332).

[8] *CE* II 366 (GNO I 333).

Creator, that he is imperishable and unbegotten, but it is according to the essence that God is imperishable and unbegotten, being unmixed and pure of every otherness and difference".[9] The meaning is that 'Father' and 'Creator' are names given on the basis of activities, whereas 'imperishable' and 'unbegotten' are the names of the essence, eternally valid. Gregory offers a provisional demurral, which is something of a red herring: "the true Life acting (ἑαυτὴν ἐνεργοῦσα) is an activity, and to live for ever and never to suffer perishing mean the same thing".[10] He then argues that there is no greater or less in imperishability, so that the Son too should be recognized to share divine imperishability.[11] This is a question-begging argument when addressed to an Arian. Both premises, that there is no greater or less in the concept of imperishability, and that the Son, being immune to corruption, is just as imperishable as the Father, would be rejected by Eunomius. He would say that the name 'imperishable' can be used as a synonym of 'unbegotten' when applied to God, but that as applied the Son it is merely a homonym; the Son's imperishability is not even analogous to the Father's, but is a created or merely titular quality. The pattern of Gregory's argument here recurs in regard to the attributes of 'eternity' at the end of *CE* I and 'simplicity' earlier in *CE* II. His claim at *CE* II 29 that simplicity is the same for Father and Son connects with his commonsense scepticism about talk of greater and lesser degrees of being: a thing either is or is not[12] – and with the idea that the divine nature, being infinite, cannot receive addition.[13] Eunomius probably made a slip when he wrote: "If, then, all expressions used to signify the essence of the Father are equivalent in force of meaning to 'the unbegotten', because he is without parts and uncomposed, following the same reasoning, also in the case of the Only-begotten, all names are identical with 'the begotten'."[14] If the Son is not absolutely simple, there is no need to posit such a synonymity among his attributes.[15]

---

[9] *CE* II 371.377.380 (GNO I 334.336.337).
[10] *CE* II 367 (GNO I 333).
[11] Cf. *CE* II 368–370 (GNO I 333f).
[12] Cf. *CE* I 162.180–182 (GNO I 75.79f). See Aristotle, *Categories* 5, 3b33–4a9; J. Zachhuber, *Human Nature in Gregory of Nyssa*, Leiden 2000, 97.
[13] Cf. *CE* I 169 (GNO I 77).
[14] Eunomius, *Apol.* 19 (Vaggione 56–58).
[15] A similar mistake is his talk of three simple essences (*CE* I 151–154, GNO I 71–73); see B. Pottier, *Dieu et le Christ*, 125–128, who unnecessarily supposes Plotinian

Finally, Gregory comes to a crucial point, Eunomius's equiparation of fatherhood and creatorhood. He vamps up the implications: "An activity that brings something into effect cannot subsist simply by itself... If the Father, as they tell us, is nothing but an activity, then the only-begotten Son is shown thereby to be passive, shaped in accordance with the active motion which constitutes him."[16] The σχέσις of Father and Son (in contrast to how the term is used in trinitarian theory) becomes that of maker and thing made, which Gregory, playing on the anti-Arian convictions of the faithful, makes sound monstrous in this context. "If one defines the fatherhood as an activity, of necessity one may not describe the being of the Son except as a passive material thoroughly worked upon."[17] If the opponents still want to call the Son impassible, shying away from the impiety of denying it, that would make it impossible for the Father to exert his activity, so they would end up saying that the Son does not exist at all![18] Again a question-begging argument, since Arians would no doubt admit the Son to be passible. In fact, Gregory has

influence. In the argument from divine simplicity, Eunomius has said that "if God is by nature uncompounded, and the epithet 'unbegotten' applies to him, then to be unbegotten must belong to his nature, and his nature is nothing else than unbegottenness" (*CE* II 23; see also 22; 31, GNO I 233; 233; 235). Gregory replies by attacking a straw man, the idea that simplicity in itself must be unbegottenness (*CE* II 25. 29. 42, GNO I 233–234. 234–235. 238). He argues that if simplicity and unbegottenness are the same, the Son would either have to be called unbegotten because of the simplicity of his essence or one would have to deny his simplicity and therefore his divinity. Petavius objects that this argument "*non satis ad rem pertinet, neque Eunomii argumentationi satisfacit. Non enim ille ex eo quod* agennêtos *esset et* innascibilis *Deus, etiam* haploun *et* asyntheton, *incompositum esse pugnabat et* simplicem, *neque ut dialectici loquuntur,* in formali sensu *id esse verum asserebat. Sed cum et innascibilis sit Deus, et idem, quamlibet diversa notione, sit simplex, eumdem concludebat non solum innascibiliem et simplicem esse, sed innascibilitatem ipsam et simplicitatem*" (Dionysius Petavius, *Opus de theologicis dogmatibus* I 7,5, Thomas 111). Also problematic is Gregory's statement that "the essence is simple but not simplicity and in the same way it is unbegotten and not unbegottenness" (*CE* II 30, GNO I 235). Later logic would say that absolute attributes of God do indeed name the essence; thus God is not just good but Goodness, not just simple but Simplicity, as opposed to relative attributes like Creator, which Gregory conflates with the absolute ones (*CE* II 31, GNO I 235): "*non solum simplex est, sed etiam simplicitas, sicut non tantum bonus et justus et verus est, set etiam bonitas et justitia et veritas et quidquid aliud secundum essentiae proprietatem dicitur*", and if the divine nature could be called unbegotten it could also be called unbegottenness (Dionysius Petavius, *Opus de theologicis dogmatibus* I 7,6, Thomas 112; see F. Diekamp, *Die Gotteslehre des heiligen Gregor von Nyssa*, Münster 1896, 167f).

[16] *CE* II 372f (GNO I 334f).

[17] *CE* II 374 (GNO I 335f).

[18] Cf. *CE* II 375 (GNO I 336).

dismissed, not refuted, the idea of a passible Son, in order to affirm the Son in Nicene style as "true God, impassibly and eternally radiated and shining forth from the true God, the Father".[19]

"Which other of the conceptions fitting to God does not belong to the very essence of the Son: justice, goodness, eternity, absence of all evil, boundlessness in every conceivable good?"[20] This would make better sense if he wrote 'God' instead of 'the Son'. All the divine attributes have the status Eunomius claims for imperishability and unbegottenness. In the next sentence Gregory indeed returns to speaking of the divine nature: "The prophet says that 'Every fine thing is his, and every good thing, from him' (*Zech* 9,17). He [Eunomius] appends to this the claim that he is unbegotten according to essence."[21] Gregory agrees that the Father is unbegotten, denies that unbegottenness is the divine essence.

Like Basil, Gregory muddies the argument by equiparating the ἐπίνοιαι applied to the Son in his incarnate mission with the attributes of God: "Every one of these titles is not the nature of the Only-begotten, not his deity, not the character of his being. Nevertheless he is so named, and the naming is valid; for it is right to consider that there is nothing idle or meaningless among the divine words. So let him give the explanation, if he rejects their being applied conceptually, how these names are fitting for God."[22] Eunomius would not accept the premise that the Son is truly God. But Gregory assumes throughout that his opponents will not dare deny the divinity of the Son, and produces these question-begging arguments at every turn.[23] Yet he also points out that the Eunomians believe the Son to be God in a merely titular sense.[24] He plays on an apparent weakness in Eunomius's system, the necessity of admitting two senses to such titles as 'light' as applied to Father and Son, one sense in which 'light' is synonymous with 'unbegotten' and a lesser sense fitted to the Son: "as great as the difference is between unbegotten and begotten, so great must be that between light and light, life and

[19] *CE* II 377 (GNO I 336).
[20] *CE* II 377 (GNO I 336).
[21] *CE* II 378 (GNO I 336f).
[22] *CE* II 298 (GNO I 314).
[23] Cf. *CE* II 26f. 29f. 33. 37–39. 42. 294–298. 368–377. 383–385. 455. 464f. 486–490. 497f. 533. 536. 556. 560 (GNO I 234. 234f. 236. 237. 238. 313f. 333–336. 338. 359. 362. 367–369. 371. 381f. 382f. 389. 390).
[24] Cf. *CE* II 51–59. 331f (GNO I 240–243. 322f).

life, power and power".[25] There is an interesting psychology here: one argues against heretics, but the authority of the Church can be invoked at any point as a self-evident premise preempting their arguments and consigning them to futility. This is primarily a lesson in belief to the already converted faithful. The gap between the heresy and truth is glaringly revealed, arousing horror and wrath.[26] But the appeal to authority can intimidate the heterodox as well, convicting their quibblings of baselessness by dashing them against the rock of truth. This gesture lies beneath the surface of the detailed refutations and gives them their fundamental orientation. Neither Basil nor Gregory take seriously the fact that Eunomius thinks in a radically different framework, for they keep speaking as if he really agrees with their own linguistic presuppositions (for instance, their use of commonsense analogy between human and divine names,[27] or their application of divine names to the Son).

II. *The logic of 'unbegotten'*

The substantive identity of any divine attribute with the divine essence itself will be accepted in later theology, and Basil and Gregory occasionally recognize that they are not at odds with Eunomius on this point. Aquinas reconciled the diversity of divine attributes with the unity, and the simplicity, of the divine subject by seeing God as the

[25] *Apol.* 19 (Vaggione 56–58). See B. Sesboüé, *Saint Basile et la Trinité*, 42f; J. Zachhuber, *Human Nature*, 46f. Eunomius thus immunizes the properly divine attributes from contamination by their lower, merely homonymous senses. I do not quite see how this "involves him in a series of increasingly inextricable contradictions" or "is a confession of weakness, for the gap is no longer located between the language of substances and that of the sensible world, but insinuates itself into the consideration of the substances itself" (B. Sesboüé, *Saint Basile et la Trinité*, 43). Pottier believes that in conceding that one cannot have unbegottenness without imperishability, Eunomius jeopardized his own system "by softening the fixed idea that ἀγέννητος alone expresses the entire substance of God?" (B. Pottier, *Dieu et le Christ*, 162, followed by B. Sesboüé, *Saint Basile et la Trinité*, 74), but this concession, if it is such, is perfectly consistent with his premises; predicates properly applying to the divine nature are synonymous. It is Basil who runs into difficulty by treating the two attributes as names of the divine essence; he does feel that 'unbegotten' belongs more to the register of the personal properties but "the discourse is not yet at the height of the insight" (B. Sesboüé, *Saint Basile et la Trinité*, 75).

[26] *CE* II 56 (GNO I 242).

[27] See B. Sesboüé, *Saint Basile et la Trinité*, 80.

pure act of being. There is no place for potentiality or any kind of composition in the divine nature. His attributes are identical with his essence, in the sense that already for Augustine God is his goodness, his justice etc., and these attributes are identical with one another in God: "*quae iustitia ipsa bonitas, et quae bonitas ipsa beatitudo*".[28] Furthermore, God is his own essence, and his own being, and there is no room in God for a differentiation of essence and existence, such as underlies *causa sui* theories that would ground God's existence in his essence.

How much of this later clarity is already present in Gregory? His understanding of divine simplicity can sound rather rough and ready, without the refinements of Plotinus or Aquinas: "How could anyone take that to be pluriform and composite which has neither form nor shape, and to which no concepts of size and magnitude apply?"[29] However, he does grasp the identity of the divine essence and its attributes: "life and truth and justice and goodness and light and power – these the only-begotten God both is and is said to be, under different apprehensions (κατὰ διαφόρους ἐπιβολάς), being simple, without parts or composition".[30] The divine essence, being simple, is not one thing through its own nature and another through the possession of its attributes.[31]

The agreement between Eunomius and the Cappadocians would have been more evident if Eunomius had chosen to illustrate his view of theological language with an attribute that applied less problematically to the divine essence. Unfortunately, 'unbegottenness' has a confusing amphibolous status. It names the divine essence if taken in the sense of uncausedness (ἀγένητος) – though its negative character makes this difficult to grasp, and Gregory sometimes errs through the commonsense reaction of saying "how can something merely negative name the divine essence" – whereas in its trinitarian sense (ἀγέννητος) as signifying the unbegottenness of the Father, it has a special status which Basil and Gregory do not always sufficiently distinguish. The debate with Eunomius may have set off on the wrong foot. When Eunomius undertook to demonstrate what seemed this

[28] Augustinus, *De Trinitate* XV 7 (CCL 50a, 469f).

[29] *CE* I 231 (GNO I 94); cf. Gregory of Nyssa, *De mortuis* 3 (PG 46, 509c).

[30] Gregory of Nyssa, *Adv. Apollinar.* 5 (GNO III/1 136,27–30); see *CE* II 483 (GNO I 367).

[31] Cf. Gregory of Nyssa, *Adv. Macedonianos* 5 (PG 45, 1305d).

obvious truth of divine ἀγεννησία, Basil taunted him as one that would prove the sun's brightness at midday. For Basil, the ἐπίνοια 'unbegotten' tells us not *what* God is, but *how* he is – without beginning.[32] No one, Basil exclaims, has ever contended "that the unbegotten has been begotten of himself or of another"; no one has been so mentally unsound as to question "the unbegottenness of the unbegotten".[33] In his confident precipitation, Basil is misled by the residual confusion between ἀγένητος, not being brought into being, not caused, and ἀγέννητος, not begotten. It will become clear that the Son is ἀγένητος, but not ἀγέννητος, and that ἀγένητος is an absolute predicate, so that ἀγενησία is identical with the divine essence. This result is quite counter-intuitive. That God is his own goodness has a certain plausibility, that he is supreme imperishability is rather less convincing, for the term imperishable seems merely negative and rather abstract, and that God is supreme uncausedness hardly seems to refer to any substantial reality. But ἀγένητος should be understood as a negation of a negation, denying a limit proper to becoming or to caused being: "The negative modality of language conceals a positivity, and the particularity of the attribution says something essential about God. Since the attributes in God are identical with the substance, the concepts expressing them effectively envisage the substance",[34] as Basil only dimly senses.

Eunomius's αὐτό ἐστιν οὐσία ἀγέννητος could have been dealt with by a simple clarification: the Father alone is unbegotten, the divine essence is not unbegotten, but uncreated. Basil instead argued: "If unbegottenness follows God, then it clearly comes to God from outside, and what is external to God is not his essence."[35] He constructed a specious contradiction: "How can unbegottenness follow God and again not follow him but be embraced in the definition of his substance?"[36] The implication that the names we attribute to God come from outside and do not constitute God's essence gives a basis to Eunomius's accusation of a subjection of God to human notions.

[32] This Stoic distinction is taken up by Gregory, *Ad Ablabium* (PG 45, 133c) and *CE* II 386 (GNO I 338f).
[33] Basil, *Adversus Eunomium* I 5 (PG 29, 516b).
[34] B. Sesboüé, *Saint Basile et la Trinité*, 78.
[35] Basil, *Adversus Eunomium* I 5 (PG 29, 517bc).
[36] Basil, *Adversus Eunomium* I 5 (PG 29, 517c–520a).

Instead of keeping the distinction between divine uncausednesss and the unbegottenness of the Father firmly in focus, Basil tackles Eunomius on the status of divine attributes in general, launching an immense quarrel that is tangential to the anti-Arian battle. The real question was not whether unbegottenness is predicated κατ' ἐπίνοιαν or κατὰ φύσιν of God, but what unbegottenness means and how it is properly used in speaking of God. Basil wants to keep unbegottenness outside God, as a human ἐπίνοια about God, and he fails to clarify exactly how the term applies to God.

Eunomius thought that 'unbegotten' was a divinely given name; his attitude is perhaps comparable to that of Judaism toward the inscrutable Tetragrammaton: "When we say 'unbegotten', we do not think to give honour by a name or according to human ἐπίνοια only, but to accomplish according to truth the most necessary of duties, the ascription to God of his being what he is. For what is said according to ἐπίνοια has its being only in names and enunciation, and its nature is to be dissolved with the sounds of the voice."[37] This passage merely 'suggests' that unbegottenness was the *only* name of God.[38] In stressing the simplicity of the divine essence, Eunomius gives the plurality of the attributes a merely nominal status. They serve only to express the divine essence over and over again, and the variety of their significations is illusory. For Basil and Gregory, erring in the other direction, the attributes do not name the essence, but represent our human conceptions concerning it. Later theology would correct them by stressing the *fundamentum in re* of the attributes: their objective reality is grounded in the divine essence where they are one.

If Eunomius really claimed to understand God's essence as well as God himself understands it,[39] he might have meant that it is an unnameable mystery to both God and us. The Cappadocians play the apophatic card against Eunomius, but perhaps Eunomius himself is close to the apophatic. All the names of the divine essence are synonymous, and if a name, such as 'light', is shared by God and creatures (including the Son, first of creatures and creator of all the rest), it is in a purely equivocal sense. To confess God as 'unbe-

[37] Eunomius, *Apol.* 8 (Vaggione 40–42); see Basil, *Adversus Eunomium* I 6 (PG 29, 521ab; 524a); Gregory, *CE* II 44; 159; 209 (GNO I 238f; 271; 285f).

[38] R. Williams, *The Wound of Knowledge*, 53.

[39] Cf. Socrates Scholasticus, *Historia ecclesiastica* IV 7 (PG 67, 472b–475c).

gotten' could be to put a fence around the divine transcendence, in a naming that lies beyond any ordinary naming. Origen (*De orat.* 4,2) also "argues that since God is unchanging, so must his name be. He allows that there might be more than one name, provided that they all carry the same signification, but the one name that he selects to give (recalling its scriptural source) is ὤν – being or being-itself . . . For Eunomius, insistence on ἀγέννητος as characterizing the divine οὐσία is a way of spelling out what is implicit in the fact that God's name is ὤν."[40] We may read the Eunomian watchword ἀγέννητος οὐσία differently if we place the accent on οὐσία.

The unclarified status of 'unbegotten' generates murkiness. Eunomius set up a tricky target in identifying God's unbegottenness with his essence, and this was compounded when Basil added imperishability as an attribute enjoying the same status as unbegottenness; but as an absolute predicate imperishability is indeed one with the divine essence, whereas as a relative predicate unbegottenness is not. Basil offered an initial clarification: "The term 'Father' has the same significance as 'unbegotten', in addition to introducing as well the conception of the Son which it implied by the relation. For the true Father alone is from no other, and 'from no other' is the same as 'unbegotten'."[41] Eunomius, in response, points to three paradoxes arising from treating fatherhood and unbegottenness as synonymous. Gregory replies that Basil claims no such synonymity;[42] 'Father' denotes both the Father's unbegottenness and his begetting of another; no contradiction arises in this clear situation. He glides from this trinitarian sense of unbegottenness to the divine transcendence of any beginning, treating 'Father' as a relative name and 'unbegotten' as an absolute one.[43] Later he isolates the specifically trinitarian sense more clearly: "If we do not learn from the word 'unbegotten' the difference which distinguishes the ὑποστάσεις, but are to understand that this word indicates the nature itself . . . then it must follow that God is either not unbegotten, or not so described, there being no

[40] M. Wiles, "Eunomius: hair-splitting dialectician or defender of the accessibility of salvation?", in R. Williams (ed.), *The Making of Orthodoxy*, Cambridge 1989, 166. In his student years in Alexandria, Eunomius must have absorbed Origenian thought; see R. P. Vaggione, *Eunomius of Cyzicus and the Nicene Revolution*, Oxford 2000, 35.

[41] Basil, *Adversus Eunomium* I 5 (PG 29, 517a).

[42] Cf. *CE* I 549–611 (GNO I 386–404).

[43] *CE* I 575f (GNO I 394).

word specifically to provide that kind of connotation."[44] He challenges Eunomius to distinguish the different senses of 'unbegotten' if he wishes to apply it both to the divine nature and to the difference of the hypostases.[45] On the negative point, that unbegottenness is not a name of essence, Gregory is right. Petavius supplies him with the answer he needed: When Eunomius says "God is unbegotten", he may refer to the divine nature or to one of the Persons; only in the latter application is the statement true.[46] Gregory speaks of relative predicates (τὰ σχετικά), both trinitarian and in reference to creation, but does not consistently define ἀγεννησία as a relative predicate.

Confusion about the status of 'unbegotten' is particularly evident in *CE* II 379–386. Gregory writes: "If he is saying this in the sense that the Father's essence (οὐσία) exists unbegotten, I agree with what he says." What he rejects is the idea that "unbegottenness itself is the essence (αὐτὴν τὴν ἀγεννησίαν οὐσίαν εἶναι)".[47] Gregory wants to keep ἀγεννησία κατ' ἐπίνοιαν but not κατ' οὐσίαν (see 314), but in practice has he not just slipped into using the word κατ' οὐσίαν? If he argues that the Father exists unbegottenly, but is not unbegottenness, he is heading for trouble with the logic of divine attributes.

"The notion of unbegottenness is one thing, the definition of the divine essence another."[48] Gregory intends to show this from Eunomius's own words. Quoting Eunomius, "He is unbegotten and imperishable according to the essence itself, since it is unmixed and pure of every otherness and difference", Gregory notes that Eunomius uses three words in speaking of God: 'essence', 'imperishable' and

---

[44] *CE* II 36 (GNO I 236f).

[45] Cf. *CE* II 40.43 (GNO I 237f).

[46] "*Quocirca eunomianam istam calumniam hoc modo licet refellere. Deum cum ait innascibilem esse, id ambiguum est ac distinctione opus habet. Aut enim divinitatem ipsam naturamque Dei vox significant hoc sensu, ut ejus proprietas ista sit quae in divinitatis consortes omnes transeat: aut Dei vocabulum certam de tribus personam exprimit, cujus id sit proprium. Atque hoc posteriore modo verum illud est quod dicitur, innascibilem esse Deum, qui sit Pater; priore, falsum*" (Dionysius Petavius, *Opus de theologicis dogmatibus* I 7,5, Thomas 111). Unbegottenness, *innascibilitas*, in Thomist Trinitarian theology is not one of the two processions, the three persons, or the four relations, but one of the five 'notions' or 'notional acts' in God, alongside paternity, filiation, active and passive spiration. The phrase 'notional act' is intended perhaps to exclude the idea that these are notions applied to God from the outside. Everything in God is itself God, so like the processions and relations, the notions must be identical in being with the divine essence.

[47] *CE* II 379 (GNO I 337).

[48] *CE* II 380 (GNO I 337).

'unbegotten'[49] – which already implies a certain otherness and difference. "If the conception of God these three words convey is one, then the deity is identical with these three",[50] and if any is lacking its absence destroys the definition of divinity.[51] Then an anti-Arian twist: if Eunomius calls the Son 'begotten', then the Son loses by the same token his imperishability, his being and his divinity.[52] Again, it is hard to see why this should be a problem for Eunomius. The problem would rather seem to be Gregory's, who has not yet established clearly why 'unbegotten' is not an essential divine attribute, unlike imperishability. Since the co-essentiality of the three terms has such disastrous Christological consequences, he undertakes to show Eunomius that they have distinct significances: "The unbegotten we discover from its opposition to the begotten, the imperishable is recognized by comparison with the perishable, and the essence is understood by contrast with the non-existent (τὸ ἀνυπόστατον)."[53] The terms to which the three words are opposed – what is begotten, what perishes, what is non-existent – are clearly distinct, so presumably this, for Gregory, clarifies the distinctness of the three words themselves. As he continues, he seems to turn in circles: "Just as what has not been begotten is spoken of as 'unbegotten', and what is not destroyed is called 'imperishable', so too we call being what is not non-existent; and on the other hand, as we say that the begotten is not unbegotten and the perishable we designate not imperishable, so too we do not say that the essence is non-existent." Then the distinction between a thing's existence and its mode of existence comes into play, without reflection on the possible non-applicability of this logic to the divine: "Essence therefore is recognized by the existence of something, the perishable or imperishable by *what sort* of thing it is, the begotten or unbegotten by *how* it exists. The account (λόγος) of being is one thing, another that which indicates the manner or the quality."[54] Here Gregory is trying to put a distance between attributes like imperishability and unbegottenness on the one hand and the divine essence on the other. The former have to do with

[49] *CE* II 380 (GNO I 337).
[50] *CE* II 381 (GNO I 337).
[51] *CE* II 382 (GNO I 337f).
[52] *CE* II 383 (GNO I 338).
[53] *CE* II 386 (GNO I 338f).
[54] *CE* II 386 (GNO I 338f).

modes of being, the latter with being itself. But he misses the special quality of divine attributes here, and he fails to differentiate the attribute of imperishability, which applies to the divine essence as such, and the attribute of unbegottenness which applies only to the Father.

III. *Defending Basil's approach to divine attributes* (CE *II 445–468*)

In *CE* II 387–444 we have a general discussion of ἐπίνοιαι, going back to Basil's illustration of the corn. Then Gregory returns to the question of the attributes at *CE* II 446, as he undertakes to defend a passage of Basil impugned by Eunomius: "We call the God of the Universe imperishable and unbegotten, using these names according to different apprehensions (ἐπιβολάς): when we look at the ages past, finding the life of God transcending every limit, we call him 'unbegotten'; but when we cast (ἐπιβάλωμεν) our mind to the coming ages, the infinity and boundlessness and never being comprehended by any end we designate 'imperishable'. So just as the endlessness of the life is called 'imperishable', its lack of a beginning is called 'unbegotten', as we apply our conceptual thought to these things."[55] This discussion is anticipated in *CE* II 130–147.

The polemic context of this discussion does not make for clarity. Today we can regret that Basil and Gregory did not interpret Eunomius more generously. He had, after all, posed a reasonable objection: if it is of the essence of God to be unbegotten, how can a begotten Son be truly God? We can suspect that the heat of their indignation is in proportion to their inability to answer the objection clearly. The current phenomenon of 'flamers' and 'ranters' on rowdy internet forums sheds an unflattering light on the history of theological disputation, and makes us prize the level-headed rationality of the more scholastic writers. Even if Eunomius at times was guilty of what Gregory describes as a 'stinking heap of vocal dung', all this should have been set aside in the interests of clarifying the basic issues.[56]

---

[55] *CE* II 446f (GNO I 356f), quoting Basil, *Adversus Eunomium* I 7 (PG 29, 525b).

[56] Cf. *CE* II 445 (GNO I 356). B. Pottier (*Dieu et le Christ*, 39) thinks that the 'aridity' of *CE* II 390–560 is due to its being a 'reprise' of Eunomius's major

III.1. *The charge that Basil supplied imperishability from outside, on the basis of ages, and not as of the essence* (CE *II 445–456*)

Eunomius objects that Basil grounds the meaning of the divine attributes in a temporal perspective rather than in a logical necessity based on the very nature of the divine. It associates imperishability with mere endlessness and unbegottenness with beginninglessness in a way that suggests that we can think of God only in temporal categories. Such thought would have little logical or ontological force, being chiefly an exercise in imagination, issuing in the discovery that temporal categories fail to grasp the divine infinity and boundlessness.

Eunomius "promises to convict us of saying that not by nature is the divinity imperishable".[57] Gregory might have conceded that Basil's utterance as it stands fails to locate the necessity of this attribute, and tends to reduce imperishability to the phenomenological realization that we cannot imagine divine life coming to an end. But Eunomius had pounced on an interpretation of Basil's language that is belied by the wider theological vision of both Basil and Gregory. Since of course they see imperishability as an attribute "without which it is impossible to think of the underlying nature", and as a quality God never lacks, never suggesting "that imperishability is an additional growth (ἐπιγεννηματικήν) upon God",[58] there is no basis for Eunomius's allegation. Still, Eunomius may have sensed a weak point in the Cappadocians' attitude to divine attributes, their readiness to distinguish qualities of the essence from the inconceivable essence itself, failing to think through the implications of the identity of God's attributes with God's essence.

Gregory also sees Eunomius as captious in objecting that "we supply God with imperishability by adding 'the ages'".[59] Eunomius is perhaps objecting not to an addition but to a subtraction – to make imperishability a matter of 'ages' falls short of its full sense as a necessary attribute of the divine nature. Gregory in turn pounces on an inaccuracy in Eunomius's characterization of Basil's view. There is no need to defend Basil's text against the accusation of 'supplying'

theses (a reprise he sees, unconvincingly, as announced in 387–389). But most of this section is a tit-for-tat defence of Basil's statement, which Eunomius had impugned. Such discussion is almost bound to be arid.

[57] *CE* II 448 (GNO I 357).

[58] *CE* II 448 (GNO I 357).

[59] *CE* II 450 (GNO I 357f).

qualities on God, since he did not use that word at all. Basil wrote: "When we turn our mind to the coming ages, his infinity and boundlessness and never ceasing at an end we *designate* 'imperishable'." Gregory asks: "Does Eunomius think that 'designate' is the same as 'supply' (πορίσαι)?"[60] "To supply is to give someone what he has not, to designate is to give a name to what he already has."[61] Eunomius probably took the word 'supply' from Aetius: "if God is envisaged from outside as 'unbegotten', the ones envisaging (ἐπιθεωρηθέντες) are superior to what is envisaged, supplying (πορισάμενοι) him a name greater than his nature" (prop. 13). The word implies that something is added to God from outside. Gregory waxes indignant at Eunomius's misrepresentation and portrays him as condemning only an invention of his own.[62]

Gregory makes Basil's language his own: "We claim that just as the endlessness of life is named imperishable, so its beginninglessness is named unbegotten",[63] and points out its biblical warrant: "neither beginning of days nor end of life" (*Heb* 7,3; quoted *CE* II 456). Basil was loth to move beyond biblical language, which could make his representations of the divine rather simplistic. While defending him against Eunomius, Gregory tends to add subtle touches to Basil's language that nudge it in a more metaphysical direction.[64]

III.2. *The charge that Basil divides the divine being* (CE *II 457–468*)

Eunomius further claimed that Basil divides the ages into two parts, placing God in an endless future or endless past. Gregory resumes Basil *Adversus Eunomium* I 7 (PG 29, 525c): "If we think about what was before creation, and, transcending the ages with our thought, apply our minds (λογισώμεθα) to the infinity (τὸ ἀπερίγραπτον) of

---

[60] *CE* II 451 (GNO I 358).

[61] *CE* II 452 (GNO I 358).

[62] *CE* II 452–454 (GNO I 358f).

[63] *CE* II 454 (GNO I 359).

[64] Basil sometimes connects ἀγέννητος with absence of cause: "When our mind (νοῦς) inquires if the God above all has a cause superior to him (αἰτίαν ὑπερκειμένην), and can conceive (ἐπινοεῖν) of none, it calls the beginningless (τὸ ἄναρχον) of his life ἀγέννητον" (Basil, *Adversus Eunomium* I 15, PG 29, 545b). Gregory regularly paraphrases ἀγέννητος as 'without a cause' (see *CE* I 557–580, GNO I 187–193; *CE* II 18. 24f. 28. 35. 37. 136f. 146f. 158. 161. 175. 192ff, GNO I 232. 233. 234. 236. 237. 265. 267f. 270f. 271f. 275f. 280f). On Gregory's metaphysical correction of Basil's 'rigid biblicism', see K. Holl, *Amphilochius von Ikonium*, 197ff.

everlasting life, we denote such a notion (νόημα) by using the word 'unbegotten'; if we turn our attention to the hereafter, and apprehend the life of God which exceeds the ages, then we explain this idea with the terminology of 'unending' and 'imperishable'."[65] A single phenomenon of everlasting divine life is the terminus at which both projections arrive. "We proclaim the eternity of God emerging the same under every apprehension (κατὰ πᾶσαν ἐπιβολήν)."[66] He admits that a licence of language is involved: "just as with our own condition we observe the past and future of temporal extension, so we speak of it also, by an improper usage (ἐκ καταχρήσεως), in the case of the transcendent nature".[67] But our human temporal condition means that we can approach eternity only through projections of endless past or future, as Scripture does (*Ps* 44,4; 48,14; 74,12), and what we discover in the process is that "any thought of measure of time (διαστηματικὸν νόημα) is enclosed within the divine nature, delimited by the infinity (τῇ ἀπειρίᾳ) of the one who contains the universe on every side".[68]

The charge of cutting up the ages implies the charge of cutting up the divine being itself: "we speak of one life as 'unbegun', and another one as 'unending', and of differences and distinctions between certain ages, which by their differences tear apart even our picture of God".[69] Eunomius wants to abolish the diversity of pictures of God that a diversity of attributes entails; his single naming of the divine essence would no doubt exclude any imagining of God at all. A reference to past and future makes language about God far too complex and colourful. Eunomius "asks us what we think the ages are. Yet it would have been fairer for that sort of question to be put by us to him; for who is it who says that he knows the being of God, who claims that things inaccessible to us are within the grasp of his own understanding?"[70] The apophatic note makes a strength out of Basil's and Gregory's apparent weakness, a weakness shared by the biblical teachers to whom Eunomius has blithely said 'Begone!'.[71] Eunomius poses a dilemma: if the ages are eternal, then

[65] *CE* II 457 (GNO I 360).
[66] *CE* II 458 (GNO I 360).
[67] *CE* II 459 (GNO I 360).
[68] *CE* II 460 (GNO I 361).
[69] *CE* II 462 (GNO I 361).
[70] *CE* II 463 (GNO I 361f).
[71] *CE* II 462 (GNO I 361).

Basil is subscribing to something like the Valentinian aeons, but if they are begotten, he is no longer confessing God as unbegotten. Gregory mocks this non-sequitur: "If we hold something to be begotten, we no longer uphold divine unbegottenness!"[72] The argument of Eunomius is that if we confess the Father as unbegotten, on the basis of ages, we dissolve him into non-being. How so? The addition of 'ages' compromises divine unbegottenness, making it contingent on something created; if the ages cease to exist, so does the beginninglessness predicated of God by reference to them.[73] Gregory asks who talks of 'adding' unbegottenness to God by reference to the ages; this is a quibble, for Eunomius may be using the verb προσγίγνομαι in the innocuous sense of 'to predicate'. "He says that if there is no addition of ages, it is not possible to attribute what results therefrom to God, and he tells us that unbegottenness is so added. Let him also tell us by whom such an addition is made. If by himself, he would be ridiculously accusing our writings of his own folly."[74] But as in the case of the quarrel about πορίσαι above, the real target of Eunomius's objection is less the attribution as such than its inadequate basis. Eunomius seeks to apprehend the divine nature on its own terms, with no reference to creatures; he thinks that to characterize God by reference to the created realm is to make God dependent on the latter.

III.3. *Divine unity and the plurality of attributes* (CE *II 469–479*)

Gregory rejoices that Eunomius agrees that "the same Life is both unbegun and endless",[75] but deplores his further remark that "if the life is unbegun and endless, imperishable and unbegotten, then imperishability will be the same as unbegottenness, unbegun as endless."[76] The life of God is one, but, Gregory insists, the two attributes in question cannot be treated as synonyms. Gregory easily draws an absurd consequence: all the scriptural names of God would then have the same meaning, so that if asked to define 'imperishability' you can reply 'compassion' or 'judgment'.[77] How does Gregory rec-

[72] *CE* II 464 (GNO I 362).
[73] Cf. *CE* II 466 (GNO I 362).
[74] Cf. *CE* II 468 (GNO I 363).
[75] Cf. *CE* II 469 (GNO I 363).
[76] Cf. *CE* II 471 (GNO I 364).
[77] Cf. *CE* II 473 (GNO I 364).

oncile the unity and simplicity of the divine nature with a variety of distinct attributes? (a) Does he see the attributes as merely negative, removing various unsuitable attributes from the divine? (b) Or does he see them as subjective apprehensions of our minds, while the divine remains intrinsically ungraspable by our minds? (c) Or does he see the divine as precontaining all perfections in a supreme degree, where they are entirely one, whereas they exist only in a dispersed and partial form in creatures, so that our language can attribute them to God in an analogical way? Gregory's view is that "the divine nature, whatever it may be κατ' οὐσίαν, is one, understood as simple, uniform, uncompounded, and by no means a manifold composite, whereas the human mind, prostrate on the ground, and buried deep in this earthly life, because it cannot see clearly what it seeks, reaches out to the ineffable nature with many thoughts in many and varied ways, and does not hunt for what is hidden with just one idea".[78] This is closest to (b) above. Our conceptions do not amount to a firm analogical discourse about God, but are rather a hit and miss affair; but insofar as they can sometimes hit the mark, they are not merely subjective. The idea of hunting, reminiscent of the *Sophist*, suggests that the concepts used are a net to be deployed skilfully, and that there is no standard, systematic set of concepts that could determine the divine. Unbegottenness means: "the belief that everything depends on him becomes our evidence that there is no prior cause of his existence".[79] Creation also tells us of God's wisdom and power. Moreover, "we apprehend his invariability and unmixed character where evil is concerned, and considering the corruption of death the last of evils, we call immortal and imperishable the one who is alien to any such notion. We do not split up the subject (τὸ ὑποκείμενον) with these conceptions, but,

[78] *CE* II 475 (GNO I 364f). Citing this text, Petavius notes: "*Affirmabat Eunomius proprietatum divinarum notiones sic implicatas invicem involutasque esse, ut cum unam intelligimus, necessario intelligamus et alteram. Hoc Gregorius Nyssenus absurdum, imo nefarium judicat ac plenissima disputatione confutat: negat, inquam, hoc quod Eunomius putabat verum esse, in unius consideratione ac notione proprietatis contineri involvique notionem alterius*" (Dionysius Petavius, *Opus de theologicis dogmatibus* I 9,8, Thomas 125). Compare: "Since not one title has been discovered to embrace the divine nature by applying directly to the subject itself, we therefore use many titles, each person in accordance with various apprehensions (ἐπιβολάς) achieving some particular idea about him, to name the divinity, as we hunt amid the pluriform variety of terms applying to him for sparks to light up our understanding of the object of our quest" (*CE* II 145, GNO I 267).

[79] Cf. *CE* II 476 (GNO I 365).

whatever it is κατ'οὐσίαν, believing it to be one, we assume that the object of our thinking has an affinity with all such attributes",[80] attributes which are in no contradiction with one another.

III.4. *The claim that different attributes divide God's essence* (CE *II 480–491*)

Eunomius supposes that the unity of the divine nature implies the synonymity of the words referring to it: "either the reality denoted is quite different, or the denoting word is not different either".[81] Gregory approves of the following Eunomian statement: "The life is not other than the essence, so that nothing of composition may be conceived of the simple nature, divided into the attribute and the subject of the attribution. Rather, what the life is, the essence is."[82] But when Eunomius adds that "the divine essence itself is denoted by 'unbegotten'",[83] Gregory objects: "Who is so mad as to claim that non-generation is a definition of essence? . . . Since unbegottenness indicates what is *not* true about the Father, how can we construe the indication of what does *not* belong as 'being'?"[84] But this is not sufficiently reflected. One cannot class only positive attributes as essential while leaving negative ones accidental or extrinsic. For Basil, there are a variety of valid names of God, some pointing to what is present in him, others to what is not present.[85] Gregory also distinguishes two sets of divine attributes, the negative (*CE* II 579–581) and the positive, which "give an indication not of the actual divine nature but of what can in true reverence be thought about it".[86] However, he admits that the same attribute may take both a positive and a negative form, e.g. 'good' and 'absence of evil'; 'author (ἀρχή) of all things' and 'unbegun' (ἄναρχος).[87]

Gregory offers a question-begging *reductio*: "By means of the very arguments by which, for the Father, he has brought the definition of the essence around to unbegottenness, let us investigate whether

[80] Cf. *CE* II 477 (GNO I 365).
[81] Cf. *CE* II 481 (GNO I 366).
[82] Cf. *CE* II 483 (GNO I 367).
[83] Cf. *CE* II 484 (GNO I 367).
[84] Cf. *CE* II 485 (GNO I 367).
[85] Cf. Basil, *Adversus Eunomium* I 10 (PG 29, 533c).
[86] Cf. *CE* II 582 (GNO I 396).
[87] *CE* II 134ff (GNO I 264ff).

we can equally, using the same arguments, refer the essence of the Son too to unbegottenness."[88] The application of Eunomius's argument to the Son hardly helps the anti-Arian cause, because the premise of the argument, the idea that different attributes naming the same thing must be identical, is so clearly wrong; so the argument merely serves to expose the absurdity of the premise. Eunomius's linguistic theory distinguishes clearly between the properly divine attributes, all synonymous with unbegottenness, and other attributes, so any transference of the argument to the Son falls flat. "If then he too is one absolute life devoid of all composition and reduplication, and there is no underlying reality beside the life of the Son, – how could any admixture of alien reality be suspected in what is simple?"[89] This sentence seems to lose its way, as if conscious of its strained, question-begging quality. Gregory argues that if the Son is true God, he too will be unbegotten, according to Eunomius's logic. Ironically, Eunomius himself had argued that the orthodox doctrine of consubstantiality would force its adherents to maintain that the Son too is unbegotten.[90] But Eunomius by no means holds that the Son is true God or has the simplicity of the divine nature (despite what he says at *CE* I 231). Moreover, Gregory risks proving too much in proving the Son to be unbegotten.

III.5. *Against the synonymity of divine attributes* (CE *II 492–503*)

He drops the argument quickly, referring to it as 'futility'[91] as he returns to the absurdity of making divine attributes all identical. Eunomius holds that God "has been called Father ever since he decided to become a Father".[92] But on his own theory all the divine attributes are identical, so that "as he is confessed as for ever imperishable, so he must be as for ever Father".[93] This is not really an anti-Arian argument, but merely another piece of jousting to overturn the theory that all titles of God are synonymous and make Eunomius admit that "a particular meaning inheres in each title".[94]

[88] Cf. *CE* II 486 (GNO I 367f).
[89] Cf. *CE* II 489 (GNO I 369).
[90] Eunomius, *Apol.* 14 (Vaggione 50). See B. Sesboüé, *Saint Basile et la Trinité*, 37.
[91] Cf. *CE* II 492 (GNO I 370).
[92] Cf. *CE* II 493 (GNO I 370).
[93] Cf. *CE* II 495 (GNO I 370f).
[94] Cf. *CE* II 495 (GNO I 370f).

It is again question-begging, since Eunomius has another set of titles for God that are on the basis of activity – in other words, he gives 'Father' a status similar to 'Creator', as Gregory belatedly notices.[95] It is hard to see that Gregory's argumentation does anything to invalidate this choice.[96] Arguing now from the claims Eunomius actually makes for the terms 'Father' and 'Designer', he again draws absurd consequences: "If the connotation of the words for 'Father' and 'Designer' is one . . . it is surely possible also to use the names the other way round, and say that God is Designer of the Son and Father of the stone."[97] So Eunomius must deny the divinity of the Son or assert the divinity of a stone, a point that would hardly embarrass him, since he does deny the former.[98] Again Gregory seems to sense a flimsiness in his argumentation for he proceeds: "Let us stick to our purpose, however",[99] as if the preceding were nothing to the purpose. He reasserts that a diversity of attributes does not impugn divine simplicity. If one mind can retain a variety of sciences, with no loss of simplicity, what is to prevent God having many attributes?[100] But he glosses over the problem of the absolute simplicity of the divine essence.[101] We may see him gesturing here toward Leonard Hodgson's idea of organic unity: "approximation to the ideal of organic unity is measured by a scale of intensity of unifying power".[102]

---

[95] Cf. *CE* II 496 (GNO I 371).

[96] Pottier sees the status given to 'Father' and 'demiurge' as a glaring exception to Eunomius's theory of synonyms, and notes that Gregory seizes on this incoherence, "revelatory of a deeper malaise" (B. Pottier, *Dieu et le Christ*, 174). The alleged malaise consists in the way the theory of synonymity flattens the sense of individual attributes, "doing violence to language", and forcing Eunomius to make an exception for 'Father' and 'demiurge' because "they resist the flattening better than the other attributes, and are thus excluded from their family" (*ibid.*, 175). This is unconvincing: since Eunomius never counted these two terms among the absolute divine attributes there is no incoherence in his theory.

[97] *CE* II 496f (GNO I 371).

[98] *CE* II 498 (GNO I 371). "*Sed neque multum hoc argumentum moveretur Eunomius, et opificem creatoremve Filii non minus quam Patrem appellari Deum pateretur ut et lapidis*". He might have rejected the locution 'Father of the stone', but only because fatherhood implies "*imitationem quamdam rationis et intelligentiae ac virtutis*" (Dionysius Petavius, *Opus de theologicis dogmatibus* I 7,7, Thomas 112).

[99] *CE* II 499 (GNO I 371f).

[100] Cf. *CE* II 503 (GNO I 373).

[101] "*Sed hoc exemplum minus in Deo valet, siquidem hoc omne quod in Deo est, Deus est ac divina ipsa substantia, nec est in eo accidens ullum*" (Dionysius Petavius, *Opus de theologicis dogmatibus* I 7,9, Thomas 113).

[102] Cited, Ch. Stead, "Divine Simplicity", 265.

III.6. *The claim that imperishability and unbegottenness are incompatible unless identical* (CE *II 504–523a*)

Eunomius charges that Basil "does not even preserve the essence itself uncontaminated and pure of things evil and alien", for in making unbegottenness a matter of absence of beginning, he leaves an aspect of God that is not unbegotten. "'If it is by endlessness of life alone', he says, 'that he is imperishable, and by absence of beginning alone that he is unbegotten, insofar as he is not imperishable, he will be perishable, and insofar as he is not unbegotten, he will be begotten'."[103] Gregory replies that just as man is both articulate and receptive of knowledge, and it would be absurd to say that he is not one insofar as he is the other, so "neither does the eternity of the divine life lack imperishability, if it is unbegun, nor, if imperishability is attributed to it, will it forfeit its status as unbegun".[104] Petavius finds the root of Eunomius's mistake in a confusion between conceiving or naming something, and being that thing. To conceive or name imperishability is not to conceive or name unbegottenness, yet to be imperishable is to be unbegotten. Eunomius transfers the separations that are intrinsic to our thoughts and notions to the thing itself that is known and reflected on.[105] The earlier quarrel about whether language 'supplies' or 'designates'[106] also turned on this confusion, which Gregory clears up when he writes: "Our position was nothing other than this: to claim that the life which exists unbegun is named 'unbegotten' conceptually, – named, not made, – and to designate that which extends into infinity by the term 'imperishable', not to make it imperishable, but to signify that it is such."[107] Both

[103] *CE* II 504 (GNO I 373).

[104] *CE* II 511 (GNO I 375).

[105] "*Huic sophisticae calumniae Gregorius accurate respondet, qua ex ejus disputatione istud efficitur, in eo sitam esse fallaciam, quod haec invicem permiscet, concipi animo vel appellari rem aliquam, et in se ac reipsa quippiam esse. Ac verum id quidem est, quatenus immortalis a nobis Deus intelligitur, eo ipso conceptu non intelligi principii expertem. At Eunomius non de intelligentia conceptuque loquitur, sed esse ipsum assumit . . . Quoniam diversa illa Dei attributa re unum idemque sunt, sed variis notionibus intelligentiisque subjici possunt, quarum una non est altera. Quod discrimen non in ipsa re, sed in cognitione nostra consistit. Nam subjectum ipsum totum, quantum est, ingenitum pariter et incorruptum est, etsi alia sit atque alia* ἐπίνοια *sive notio quae diversis itidem vocabulis explicatur. Neque ut in mente nostra, sic in re cognita, divisio ac separatio proprietatum est ulla*" (Dionysius Petavius, *Opus de theologicis dogmatibus* I 7,8, Thomas 113).

[106] *CE* II 450–454 (GNO I 357ff).

[107] *CE* II 512 (GNO I 376).

words denote divine infinity; their diversity resides in the finite perspectives of the subject who uses them. "It is one idea about the divine life that it is without cause; this is indicated by the term 'unbegotten'. It is another idea about the divine life that it is boundless (ἀόριστον) and endless; this the designation 'imperishable' presents. Hence whereas the subject (ὑποκείμενον), whatever it may be, is above every name and thought, that it neither is from a cause, nor ever comes round to non-existence, those are the ἐπίνοιαι signified by these words."[108] Again it is implied that the words have a merely negative meaning, not providing a grasp of the unknowable divine essence. Eunomius's effort to make out that diverse attributes imply a division in God, who cannot be one insofar as he is the other – "So in respect of having no beginning he will be unbegotten and also destructible, and in respect of his endlessness imperishable and also begotten"[109] – is again dispatched in a long series of reductions *ad absurdum*: "In respect of being immaterial he will not be wrathless", etc.

III.7. *Imperishability and endlessness* (CE *II 523b–542*)

Eunomius accuses Basil of "improperly seeing imperishability in the endless and endlessness in the imperishable",[110] no doubt in the sense that imperishability is an attribute of the divine essence whereas endlessness is merely a human ἐπίνοια based on experience of time. Gregory finds Eunomius to contradict his claim that all divine attributes are synonymous, since he refuses to identify endlessness and imperishability. But Eunomius would distinguish between the attributes of the essence and attributes derived from God's ἐνέργειαι, such as 'Father' and 'Creator' or from human ἐπίνοιαι, such as 'beginningless' and 'endless', so that Gregory's argument again misses its target.

Basil's statement on the ἐπίνοιαι of unbegottenness and imperishability[111] was quoted almost verbatim in 446f and 506f, although 'transcending every beginning' became 'transcending every limit', thus orienting the statement more toward a unitary concept of divine

[108] *CE* II 513 (GNO I 376).
[109] *CE* II 514 (GNO I 376).
[110] *CE* II 523 (GNO I 377).
[111] Cf. Basil, *Adversus Eunomium* I 7 (PG 29, 525bc).

infinity that could be reached both by the forward and the backward searching of the mind. Now the statement is refashioned in a more unitary style: "By his surpassing the boundary of the ages according to every measure of temporal extension, whether we consider what is from the beginning or what lies ahead, we indicate the infinity and unboundedness of the everlasting life according to either conception, now by the word 'imperishability', now by 'unbegottenness'."[112] The different ἐπιβολαί toward past and future are united in the idea of transcending τῆς τῶν αἰώνων περιγραφῆς κατὰ πᾶν διάστημα τῆς χρονικῆς παρατάσεως. Beginningless and endless fade from view, sublated into the concept of infinity. Both attributes are required to bring out the full notion of eternity, as we know from *CE* I 666–684, and if either were preferred, why should it not be the one that looks to the future rather than the one that looks to the past? "If, however, they are determined thus to divide the thought of eternity, and to make the one fall within the realm of that being, and to reckon the other with the non-realities of deity . . . I would advise them to reverse their teaching, and to count the unending as being, overlooking the unoriginate rather, and assigning the palm to that which is future and excites hope, rather than to that which is past and stale."[113] The issue is the unity and simplicity of God, which Eunomius sees as compromised by the contrasting ἐπίνοιαι. Gregory resolves it by recalling the two, ἀφθαρσία and ἀγεννησία, to the same underlying reality of divine infinity. This answer would not work so well for the other divine attributes, and thus fails to address thoroughly the question of how the plurality of attributes are united in the divine essence.

"The idea that only with regard to endlessness of life is God imperishable is his, and not ours" – this clears away a misunderstanding that Basil's language courted. "Similarly that the imperishable is not unbegun is the invention of his strict logic, which inserts in the definition of essence what does not belong. We ourselves shall ascribe to the essence nothing that does not belong."[114] That is, it is Eunomius only who confines the divine essence to the most limited sense of the conceptions we bring into play, whereas we use them to point

[112] *CE* II 528 (GNO I 380).
[113] *CE* I 672 (GNO I 219f).
[114] *CE* II 529 (GNO I 380f).

to a single, simple, infinite essence. 'Unbegottenness' signifies that "it is not proper to God for his life . . . to have begun in a generative act".[115] Gregory holds to the representations of beginning and end, as if to stress a necessary supplementarity between the two notions, unbegottenness and imperishability, thus dislodging the former from the supreme position conferred on it in Eunomius's theology.

Is it the fetishism about unbegottenness that leads Eunomius into his baseless quibbles? He suspects that in adding endlessness to unbegottenness, Basil misses the full sense of unbegotten, and leaves the divine nature partly unbegotten. Gregory argues that it is Eunomius's own logic that leads to this absurd idea: "Since it is held that in measurement of time beginning is one thing and end another, if anyone were to claim that lack of the former is the essence, he would suppose that its life, being bisected, exists only as unbegun, and that it does not by nature extend any longer towards endlessness, if unbegottenness is to be deemed the nature."[116] But this seems to be an incorrect argument, for Eunomius refuses to connect unbegottenness to any notion of temporal beginning. More reduction follows: "If, however, one insists that both [privation of beginning and of end] are essence, then it necessarily follows according to the argument produced by Eunomius, that each of the designations with its own connotation has its existence in the notion of the essence (ἐν τῷ τῆς οὐσίας λόγῳ), existing only to the extent declared by the meaning of the term."[117] If the attributes are the essence, rather than mere designations, then different attributes, especially if regarded as contradictory, split the essence in two. But this is not entailed by Basil's more modest theory of language. Note Gregory's shyness about giving his ἐπίνοιαι the status of names of the essence, even as he upholds their valid application, as far as they go, to the essence.

Eunomius had distinguished between imperishability as a name of essence and endlessness as a mere ἐπίνοια. But he spoils that potential riposte when he says that "God in his endlessness is unbegotten and in his unbegottenness endless, the connotation of the two words being one".[118] This would be more tenable if he had written 'imperishability' instead of 'endlessness'. Gregory again brings in the Son:

[115] *CE* II 530 (GNO I 381).
[116] *CE* II 531 (GNO I 381).
[117] *CE* II 532 (GNO I 381).
[118] *CE* II 533 (GNO I 381f).

it would follow that if the Son is endless he is unbegotten. This is not an anti-Arian argument, since the unbegottenness of the Son is not an orthodox tenet. A further consequence, that the immortality of angels would also assure their unbegottenness,[119] confirms that the argument has no bearing on Arian issues. Meanwhile, Gregory fully agrees with Eunomius on the status of the divine attributes: "Who is going to quarrel with saying that God is by nature all that is attributed to him? . . . Concerning the underlying reality (ὑποκείμενον), whatever that may be by nature, we entertain every piously conceived notion."[120]

Eunomius has one further statement, which Gregory mocks as nonsensical: "Being imperishable without beginning he is unbegotten without end, and is said to be so neither according to something else, nor because of something else, nor in regard to something else."[121] The last phrases here I take to mean that God's essence is not defined with reference to temporal realities. The statement seeks to make the synonymity of the attributes vivid, which is rather counter-productive and should have been unnecessary. Gregory presents Eunomius as saying the beginningless and endless are the same thing, or even that beginning and end are the same thing.[122] He attempts to convict Eunomius of impiety and absurdity, first by foisting on him the conclusion that "what is endless cannot exist without being unbegotten" – ignoring that the synonymity of attributes applies only to God; then by arguing that if imperishability and unbegottenness are synonymous, imperishable beings such as angels, the human soul and even demons are unbegotten and consequently consubstantial with the Father, whose defining trait is unbegottenness.[123] Needless to say, Eunomius would reject such an equiparation of divine imperishability with mere immortality. He would not be impressed by Gregory's offer to clarify his thinking for him: "While endlessness is common to all things that are held to continue in life to infinity, 'unbegun' applies only to that which is without cause."[124] Note that in breaking the Eunomian identity of unbegottenness and

[119] Cf. *CE* II 539 (GNO I 384).
[120] *CE* II 534f (GNO I 382).
[121] *CE* II 537 (GNO I 383).
[122] Cf. *CE* II 538 (GNO I 383f).
[123] *CE* II 539 (GNO I 384).
[124] *CE* II 541 (GNO I 384).

imperishability, and in ascribing only the former exclusively to God, Gregory also undermines the Basilian symmetry between beginningless and endless.

III.8. *A dilemma for Eunomius* (CE *II 554–560*)

After another discussion of the status of language (543–553), Gregory takes up Eunomius's statement that "the essence itself is imperishability and, by the same token, immortality".[125] He sees no need to quarrel about "whether (a) these belong to the divine essence or whether (b) in virtue of what they signify, they are the essence".[126] He is ready to admit that the attributes not only belong to God by nature but are identical with the divine nature. "Whichever of these utterances prevails, it will completely support our argument."[127] The idea that the attributes accrue to the essence without being identical with them seems to reflect the general tenour of Gregory's commonsense thinking on the ἐπίνοιαι. But even if he adopts wholeheartedly Eunomius's stress on the identity of attributes and essence – a view that would prevail in later orthodox theology – it only strengthens the case he is making. For, if (a) is right, then the attribute of 'unbegottenness' merely belongs to the essence and does not signify the essence.[128] If (b) is accepted, Eunomius's claim that unbegottenness is identical with the divine essence, is granted; since Gregory is ready to accept (b) it is rather pointless to celebrate an advantage granted by (a) that (b) undoes.

If (b) is right, incorruptibility and immortality are the very essence of God, and it follows that since the Son enjoys these attributes they will be his very essence.[129] For Eunomius, however, the convertibility of attributes with essence applies only to God, so that to apply it to the Son is to beg the question, by presuming that the Son is God. Gregory does not quite do this here. Instead he claims to find a divine attribute in the Son, and uses Eunomius's logic to identify that attribute with the Son's essence, thereby proving the Son's divinity. Eunomius would reject this argument, for he would see the Son

[125] *CE* II 554 (GNO I 388).
[126] *CE* II 555 (GNO I 388f).
[127] *CE* II 555 (GNO I 388f).
[128] *CE* II 556 (GNO I 389).
[129] Cf. *CE* II 556 (GNO I 389).

as immortal and imperishable only in a homonymous, titular sense. Gregory says that God is said to be imperishable since he is 'not subject to perishing' and to be immortal because he is 'stronger than death'. Eunomius would find this commonsense account inadequate, claiming a far stronger sense for these statements when based in the divine essence than when applied to Christ. Concluding the argument from (b), Gregory says that since both the Father and the Son are imperishability, which in both cases is their essence, and since no difference can be found between the two imperishabilities, there is no difference between the two essences (556). This is close to the argument of 368–370; Eunomius would deny the identity and the claim that there can be no greater and less in imperishability.

Gregory imagines Eunomius presenting him with a dilemma: "if we distinguish that which accrues from that which is, we make the deity composite, whereas if we acknowledge his simplicity, then the imperishability and unbegottenness are seen at once to signify his very essence".[130] In other words, the doctrine of divine simplicity obliges the rejection of (a) and the adoption of (b). Instead of saying which of the two he subscribes to, Gregory claims that such a dilemma again helps his argument. First Gregory argues from (b): "For if he will have it that God is made composite by our saying that anything accrues to him, then he certainly cannot eject the fatherhood either from the essence, but will confess 'Father' by nature, as in the case of 'imperishable' and 'unbegotten', and thus albeit unwillingly receive the Son into the proper realm of the nature."[131] This is weak, since Eunomius would not accept 'Father' as one of the essential names of God, consigning it rather to the status of a name based on divine activity, like 'Creator'. Moreover, as he echoes Athanasius's arguments that the Sonship of the Logos is natural and not merely titular, Gregory risks equiparating 'Father' with the attributes of the divine essence (further compounding the confusion caused when 'unbegottenness' is treated as an attribute of the essence). Then Gregory argues from (a): "If however he says that fatherhood appertains to God outside the nature, he will allow us the right to say that things appertain to the Father, in such wise that the simplicity is not at all negated if predication according to unbegottenness is

[130] *CE* II 557 (GNO I 389).
[131] *CE* II 558 (GNO I 389).

located outside the essence."[132] Here Gregory seems to refer to unbegottenness as a specific attribute of the Father. If so, his argument no longer directly engages Eunomius on the question whether attributes of the divine essence as such are ἐπίνοιαι from the outside or identical with the essence. Returning to (b), Gregory says that if the attributes are identical with the essence and with one another, then in the Son's case, since he is imperishable he will be unbegotten as well. Thus Eunomius must either admit that unbegottenness signifies something other than incorruptibility or else say that the Son is unbegotten, or else, in order to avoid this, say that the Son is corruptible.[133] Eunomius would deny that the Son has any divine attribute or that the logic of divine attributes applies to him, so Gregory's argument again falls flat. In reducing Eunomius's view of the identity of attributes to absurdity (an unbegotten Son) or blasphemy (a perishable Son), Gregory seeks to prove that the attributes are not synonymous, in their *modus significandi*; this does not necessarily exclude their ultimate identity in the divine essence itself.

IV. *Envoi*

To espouse the mobile contours of Gregory's rhetoric and logic, and to bring out the overall shape of his thought, whether as translator or commentator, is no easy task. The profile I have sketched is no doubt, as in dealing with any complex text, infinitely revisable. I retain the impression that there is an oscillation in his thought between a commonsense view that treats the divine attributes as if they were items of ordinary language and a more reflective awareness of their peculiar character. The status of 'endlessness', the least glamourous of the attributes dealt with, perhaps best indicates this. "God is by nature all that is attributed to him",[134] so he is by nature endless, yet his imperishability is more than mere endlessness,[135] and endlessness is a quality shared by all things that will live for ever.[136] Commonsense application of 'endless' to God is justifiable only at the basis of imaginative groping, and indeed Gregory is ever ready

132 *CE* II 559 (GNO I 389f).
133 Cf. *CE* II 560 (GNO I 390).
134 *CE* II 524 (GNO I 379).
135 Cf. *CE* II 529 (GNO I 380f).
136 Cf. *CE* II 541 (GNO I 384).

to admit that the divine essence lies far beyond the grasp of any concepts. But there is a specific inadequacy in Basil's language which he fails to correct. There was a need to fashion an attribute for God that could unhesitatingly be applied as a name of the divine essence. Neverendingness was not such an attribute. Infinity or eternity was what was required. Gregory does provide this, but he keeps neverendingness going alongside it, instead of sublating it without remainder in the idea of infinity. The basic flaw is that both Basil and Gregory are too fond of simple, biblically warranted ways of referring to God and too suspicious of Eunomius's technology, and this impedes them in striving forward to integral lucidity. Their elaborate development of apophatic ideas is largely tangential to the problem Eunomius raised and seems to compensate for the instability inherent in their treatment of the attributes as human notions of an inconceivable divine essence.

Reading the Fathers in the spirit of metaphysical consolidation, one attempts to assess the Cappadocian project in light of the trinitarian discourses of Origen and Athanasius, which it corrects or completes, and in light of later theology that pushed for a firmer grounding of theological language in objective ontological reference. A counter-metaphysical reading, questioning back to the original events of which patristic theology offers a Hellenistic systematization, will treasure in Gregory his keen sense of the straw-like character of his argumentation, measured not against some hyper-essential transcendence in the manner of Pseudo-Dionysius, but against the reality of the revealed God of Scripture.[137] The inconsistency we detected in Basil's and Gregory's entire argumentative strategy could indeed be read as a symptom of their sense of being torn between opposing currents – between the irresistible onward march of metaphysical reason, on the one hand, and on the other their conviction that the biblical realities remained irreducible to any metaphysics, and that even the most orthodox dogmatic clarifications had chiefly a negative role, to keep our limited human thinking within its proper bounds. The extent to which their grasp of the biblical realities is itself already infiltrated with metaphysical, Platonist habits of thought and perception is a further topic for deconstructive analysis.

[137] See J. S. O'Leary, *Questioning Back: The Overcoming of Metaphysics in Christian Tradition*, Minneapolis 1985; *ibid.*, "'Where all the ladders start': Apophasis as Awareness", *Archivio di Filosofia* 70 (2002) 375–405.

GOTTESBEZEICHNUNGEN UND UNSTERBLICHKEIT IN GREGOR VON NYSSA (*CE* II 561–627)

Volker Henning Drecoll

I. *Gliederung von CE II 561–627*[1]

CE II 561–590a	I)	Eunomius' Ablehnung von στέρησις auf die Gotteslehre (390,17–398,24)
CE II 561–564	Ia:	Polemischer Abschnitt (390,17–391,17)
CE II 565–571	Ib:	Referat bzw. Darstellung der eunomianischen Position und vorläufige Bekämpfung (391,18–393,13)
CE II 572–576a	Ic:	Dihärese der τῶν ὄντων γνῶσίς τε καὶ θεωρία (Ankündigung 393,11–13, Dihärese 393,14–394,17)
CE II 576b–587	Id:	Anwendung auf die Gotteslehre, und zwar a) allg. (394,17–395,3), b) auf die ἀποχωριστικά (395,3–396,13) und c) auf die positiven Bezeichnungen (396,13–397,31)
CE II 588–590a	Ie:	Eunomius' Argument, Basilius mache die Namen wichtiger als die zugehörige ἀξία bzw. die πράγματα (398,1–24)
CE II 590b–610	II)	Das Beispiel der ἀθανασία (398,24–404,20)
CE II 590b–595	IIa:	Eunomius' Beispiel der ἀθανασία bei Engeln, Menschen und Gott zur Verdeutlichung des Unterschieds von στέρησις und ἀπόστασις (398,24–400,21)
CE II 596–599a	IIb:	Eunomius' Auffassung von ἀθανασία als Bezeichnung der ὑπεροχή Gottes (400,22–401,25)
CE II 599a–604	IIc:	Eunomius' Verständnis von ἀθανασία ≠ ἀπουσία θανάτου (401,25–403,4)

[1] Vgl. die abweichende Gliederung von Stuart Hall (in diesem Band).

CE II 605–610	IId: Eunomius' Argument, es bestehe keine συμφυΐα zwischen Gott und den Geschöpfen (403,5–404,20)
CE II 611–624	III) Eunomius' Argument, aus Basilius' Gotteslehre folge, dass Gott gänzlich aus Nichtseiendem sei (404,21–408,30)
CE II 611	IIIa: Ankündigung des Vorgehens (404,21–32)
CE II 612–613	IIIb: Paraphrase von Basilius' Argument und seiner Intention (404,32–405,20)
CE II 614–617	IIIc: Basilius' Argument als wörtliches Zitat (405,21–406,5) und Polemik (406,5–27)
CE II 618–624	IIId: Eunomius' Argument als wörtliches Zitat (406,27–407,4) und Widerlegung: Ablehnung des μετουσία-Konzepts (407,4–21), Unerlaubtheit der Gleichsetzung von τινὰ πατέρα μὴ ἔχειν und ἐκ τοῦ πάντη μὴ ὄντος γεγενῆσθαι (407,21–408,30)
CE II 625–627	IV) Abschluss (408,31–409,15)

II. *Der Streit um die Angemessenheit des στέρησις-Konzepts*

zu Ia: Gregor nutzt in *Contra Eunomium* verschiedene polemische Techniken, gegen Ende des 2. Buches begegnet mit zunehmender Häufigkeit die polemische Technik, die besagt, dass man die Meinung des Gegners eigentlich gar nicht anzuführen oder zu widerlegen braucht – und dann *quasi* im Sinne einer *praeteritio* doch auf zentrale Themen und Argumente eingeht.

So erwägt Gregor in *CE* II 561 zunächst, ob man dem Ablauf der *Apologia apologiae* noch weiter folgen soll (Möglichkeit A: 390,17f)[2] oder den Kampf (μάχη) hiermit beenden (Möglichkeit B: 309,18f). Letzteres wird zunächst scheinbar befürwortet, indem ein ausführlicher Vergleich (καθάπερ – οὕτως) zeigt, dass die bisherige Widerlegung die verderbliche Wirkung der eunomianischen Theologie zur Genüge ans Licht gebracht hat. Dies wird verglichen mit dem Verkauf von

[2] Im Folgenden beziehen sich Zahlen mit Komma (z.B. 391,15–18) auf GNO I und geben Seite(n) – Komma – Zeile(n) an.

Giften, wobei bereits das Versuchen einer kleinen Menge die verderbliche Wirkung zweifelsfrei erweist. Vergleichspunkt ist die Evidenz der verderblichen Wirkung, die sich bereits in einem Teil (des Gifts bzw. der bislang widerlegten Aussagen aus der *Apologia apologiae*) zeigt (390,19–30). Daraus folgt, dass eigentlich für die, die Verstand haben (νοῦς), eine Fortführung der Widerlegung überflüssig ist (390,26–30).

Trotzdem fährt Gregor mit der Widerlegung fort, greift also zu Möglichkeit A (signalisiert durch ἀλλά), und zwar mit dem Argument, man müsse dem Vorwurf entgehen, die wichtigeren Argumente (τὸ ἰσχυρότερον) in der *Apologia apologiae* ausgelassen zu haben, schließlich finden[3] die Gegner πολλαχόθεν Aussagen, die überzeugen sollen (τὸ πιθανόν) (390,30–391,4). Daher bittet Gregor seine Leser, die mit seinem Eifer nun schon vertraut sind und ihn dabei nicht der Redseligkeit bezichtigen,[4] bereitwillig der Widerlegung zu folgen. Es folgt die polemische Kennzeichnung der eunomianischen Theologie als eine Abfolge von Träumen (ὄνειρος – ἕτερος ὄνειρος) (391,4–9) und die Nennung des Themas des begonnenen Abschnitts (Abschnitt I = 390,17–398,24), nämlich: περὶ τῆς στερήσεως (391,9–11). Dabei soll die Argumentation nicht in Gänze (πάσῃ τῇ φλυαρίᾳ) vorgeführt und widerlegt werden, sondern zusammengefasst: διὰ συντομίας (391,11–17).

zu Ib: Die Auseinandersetzung mit der τεχνολογία (Begriff in 391,10.19) des Eunomius beginnt mit der Wiedergabe eines eunomianischen Arguments (391,18–27).[5] Eunomius lehnt es ab, Gott aufgrund einer στέρησις als ἀγέννητος zu bezeichnen, und zwar scheidet die Anwendung des Konzepts στέρησις vom Begriff her (φωνή) ebenso aus wie vom Inhalt her (ἔννοια) (391,23–27).[6] Das Referat wird

---

[3] εὑρίσκουσι ἑαυτοῖς nimmt hier fast die Bedeutung von "sie verschaffen sich" an (im *Lexicon Gregorianum* III 590, s.v. εὑρίσκω aufgeführt unter B.1.d "etw. finden, antreffen, entdecken, auf etw. stoßen", doch scheint der Gebrauch mit dem Reflexivpronomen selten zu sein).

[4] Zu μηδεμίαν καταγνόντας ἀδολεσχίαν (*scil.* ἡμῶν) vgl. *Lexicon Gregorianum* V 176: "auch (mit aus d. Zush. zu erg.) Gen.-Ausdr."

[5] Die Meinung des Eunomius wird zunächst in der indirekten Rede wiedergegeben: ὡς αὐτός φησιν (391,19–22), dann wörtlich (391,23–27, Zitatformel: φησίν 391,23), als Übergang zwischen indirekter Rede im AcI und direktem Zitat fungiert: ἡ μὲν οὖν ὑπόσχεσις αὕτη. ὁ δὲ τῶν ἐγκλημάτων ἔλεγχος τίς; (391,22f).

[6] Eunomius verteidigt damit die Ablehnung des στέρησις-Begriffs aus *Apologia* 8,9f (SC 305, 248), die Basilius in *Adversus Eunomium* I 9,4f (SC 299, 198) angeführt und anschließend bekämpft hatte, vgl. R. P. Vaggione, *Eunomius. The Extant Works*, Oxford 1987, 114 mit Anm. 35.

aufgenommen wenige Zeilen später (392,11–14).[7] Der Vorwurf des Eunomius an Basilius lautet: Basilius verleumde ihn, Eunomius, wegen seines Gebrauches der paganen Philosophie, weil er nicht wisse, was er als Argumente gegen Eunomius gebrauchen solle, und stelle dem die eigene Berufung auf die Lehre des heiligen Geistes gegenüber (392,14–19).[8]

Gregor widerlegt Eunomius zunächst polemisch in zwei Schritten, bevor er (ab 393,14) in die inhaltliche Auseinandersetzung einsteigt (= Ic). Zunächst (391,27–392,11) weist er Eunomius' Argument als eine vorgeschobene Abwehr gegen eine von niemandem vertretene Ansicht zurück (391,27–32, vgl. 392,10f: ὡς ἀλλοτρίαν μωρίαν ἐπανορθούμενος). Dabei setzt er ein bestimmtes Verständnis von Eunomius' Gebrauch von στέρησις voraus, nämlich quasi ein prozessuales Verständnis: στέρησις als zur φύσις erst sekundär hinzutretende Beraubung. Angewandt auf die Gottesvorstellung würde dies bedeuten, dass Gott von seiner φύσις her über γέννησις verfügte, und dieser natürlichen Eigenschaft dann aber beraubt würde und so erst ἀγέννητος würde.[9] Diese (als wahnsinnige Raserei gekennzeichnete) Meinung wird von niemandem vertreten, also ist Eunomius' Abwehr dieses Gedankens vorgeschoben (391,32–392,7) – genauso wie der Titel *Apologia* vorgeschoben sei, weil Eunomius in der Abfassungssituation weder ein Gerichtsverfahren noch Ankläger oder Richter konkret nennen konnte (392,7–10).[10]

---

[7] Die Fortsetzung des Eunomiuszitats 392,14–19 gehört wohl zwischen die indirekte Wiedergabe in 391,19–22 (vgl. die in der GNO-Edition gesperrt gedruckten Wörter, die im Zitat 392,12–14 wieder begegnen) und das Zitat in 391,23–27. R. P. Vaggione, *Eunomius*, 114 bleibt für die Frage, wie 391,19–27 und 392,11–19 zusammengehören, ohne Auskunft. Seine Paraphrase vernachlässigt, dass Eunomius das στέρησις-Konzept für den Begriff der Ungezeugtheit begrifflich wie inhaltlich ablehnt.

[8] Vgl. Basilius, *Adversus Eunomium* I 9,6–14 (SC 299, 198–200); vgl. R. P. Vaggione, *Eunomius*, 114 mit Anm. 36.

[9] Schon in der Apologie hatte Eunomius die Kategorisierung von ἀγέννητος als στέρησις mit dem Verweis darauf abgelehnt, dass eine στέρησις gegenüber der ἕξις sekundär ist. Basilius hatte dies als Übernahme der aristotelischen Kategorienschrift gegeißelt (*Adversus Eunomium* I 9,8–11, SC 299, 200), gemeint sind wohl Stellen wie *Kat.* 10, 13a32–34 (wo jedoch der Begriff δεύτερος nicht fällt). Dazu, dass dieses Verständnis von στέρησις u.a. bei Syrian und Alexander von Aphrodisias belegt ist, vgl. Th. Böhm, *Theoria – Unendlichkeit – Aufstieg. Philosophische Implikationen zu De vita Moysis von Gregor von Nyssa*, Leiden 1996, 115f mit Anm. 53f.

[10] Diesen Gedanken hatte schon Basilius an den Anfang seiner Widerlegung von Eunomius' *Apologie* gestellt, vgl. Verf., *Die Entwicklung der Trinitätslehre des Basilius von Cäsarea. Sein Weg vom Homöusianer zum Neonizäner*, Göttingen 1996, 60–62. Vgl. zu *CE* I 65–71 (GNO I 44,15–47,2) J.-A. Röder, *Gregor von Nyssa. Contra Eunomium I 1–146*. Frankfurt a.M. 1993, 214f.

Sodann (392,19–393,1) beschäftigt er sich mit dem Vorwurf, Basilius habe ihn, Eunomius, wegen des Gebrauches der paganen Philosophie angegriffen, weil er keine Argumente zur Hand hatte. Dies stuft er zunächst als Traum ein (Aufgriff des Motivs ὄνειρος aus 391,4–9) und verdeutlicht das mit einem Vergleich (οὕτω), wonach einige sich im Traum als Königskollegen wähnen und entsprechend überschätzen (392,21–25). Entsprechend ist Eunomius' Vorwurf als Selbstüberschätzung anzusehen, besonders die Meinung, dass er, Eunomius, dem Basilius aufgrund seiner Philosophiekenntnisse als φοβερός erschienen sei (392,20f.25–393,1).

Eine weitere *praeteritio* bezieht sich auf die Argumentation διὰ μέσου (393,2, die laut Gregor eigentlich kaum als λόγος angesehen werden kann) (393,1–6) und vergleicht (ὥσπερ) dies mit der Abscheu gegenüber eiternden Geschwüren und der damit verbundenen Entstellung (393,6–9). Stattdessen will Gregor den Sinn (νοῦς) kurz (δι' ὀλίγων) erläutern und dazu etwas weiter ausholen (393,9–13).

zu Ic: Gregor beginnt mit einer Definition, derzufolge ein λόγος im eigentlichen Sinne des Wortes (ὅ γε ἀληθῶς λόγος) der lautliche Ausdruck einer gedanklichen Bewegung ist (τῶν κατ' ἔννοιαν κινημάτων φωνή). Und diese gedankliche Tätigkeit (ἐνέργειά τε καὶ κίνησις) richtet sich, wenn sie gesund ist (als Gegensatz wären denkbar u.a. μανία, ὄνειρος und φαντάζειν) auf die Erkenntnis und Betrachtung des Seienden (πρὸς τὴν τῶν ὄντων γνῶσίν τε καὶ θεωρίαν), und zwar so sehr sie kann (393,14–17).

Dies ist die Voraussetzung dafür, dass Gregor die φύσις der τὰ ὄντα in einer Dihärese näher beschreibt, und zwar unterteilt er sie zunächst in τὸ νοητόν und τὸ αἰσθητόν (393,17–19).[11] In dem letzteren Bereich, bei den sinnlich wahrnehmbaren Dingen, entsteht eine allen gemeinsame Erkenntnis (κοινὴ ἡ γνῶσις), weil die fünf Sinne zu unumstrittenen Erkenntnissen führen, die sich in gleicher Weise artikulieren lassen (ὁμοφώνως) (393,19–26), gemeinsamer Bezugspunkt ist die identische φύσις derer, die über diese Sinne verfügen (393,25f). Zu diesem Bereich, bei dem es keine ἀμφιβολία gibt, gehört auch alle Erkenntnis πρός τε τὸν πολιτικὸν καὶ τὸν ἠθικὸν τοῦ

[11] Ähnliche Dihäresen gebraucht Gregor z.B. in *Or. Cat.* (GNO III/4 21,7–10); *In Eccl.* VI (GNO V 373,21–374,2); *In Cant. Cant.* VI (GNO VI 173,7–11); vgl. *Lexicon Gregorianum* I 113. Vgl. D. L. Balás, ΜΕΤΟΥΣΙΑ ΘΕΟΥ. *Man's Participation in God's Perfections according to Saint Gregory of Nyssa*, Rom 1966, 43.

βίου σκοπόν (393,26–29).[12] Hiervon unterscheidet sich die Betrachtung der νοερὰ φύσις grundlegend. Gregor legt dabei eine Unterscheidung der Philosophie in drei Bereiche zugrunde, nämlich in a) Physik, b) Ethik, c) Metaphysik.[13]

In dem letzteren Bereich, der Metaphysik stellt sich das Problem, dass der Erkenntnisgegenstand oberhalb der sinnlichen Wahrnehmung liegt und daher das Denken (διάνοια) sich nur vermutungsweise (στοχαστικῶς) nach dem Erkenntnisobjekt (vgl. τὸ ὑποκείμενον 394,3) ausstrecken (ἐπορέγομαι) kann und nach bestem Vermögen das, was dabei als Gedanke (διάνοια) entsteht, auszudrücken sich bemüht – ein Prozess der Annäherung (ἐγγίζοντες), quasi der Optimierung, der die Begriffe zunehmend an das Gedachte angleicht (393,29–394,5). Hierbei gibt es nun zwei Möglichkeiten (μέν – δέ), nämlich entweder gelingt es dem Denken, das Ziel zu erreichen und außerdem lässt sich das Gedachte auch noch entsprechend ausdrücken (394,6–9), oder es verfehlt entweder beides oder eines von beiden. Zwar dürfte das, was beides umfasst (Erkenntnis und begriffliches Ausdrücken), besser sein; nicht weniger gut aber ist es, gedanklich-inhaltlich richtig zu liegen (τῆς προσηκούσης μὴ διαμαρτεῖν ὑπολήψεως), selbst wenn die sprachliche Formulierung (λόγος) hinter dem Gedachten (διάνοια) zurückbleibt (394,9–17).

zu Id: Für die Gotteslehre[14] ergibt sich aus Ic als Konsequenz, dass Gregor sich nur mit dem Sinn der Worte auseinandersetzen will, nicht mit den Genauigkeiten des Wortlautes und der Bezeichnungen, die er den τέχναι der Grammatiker überlassen möchte (394,17–27). Gregor möchte seine Untersuchung darauf beschränken, ob der Sinn

---

[12] Die Verbindung von ἠθικός und πολιτικός ist bei Gregor singulär, vgl. *Lexicon Gregorianum* IV 96.

[13] *In Inscr.* II 3 (GNO V 75,29–76,12) basiert Gregors Argumentation auf der Zweiteilung von θεωρητική und ἠθικὴ φιλοσοφία, in *Vita Moysis* II (GNO VII/1 43,23) spricht Gregor von der ἠθικὴ καὶ φυσικὴ φιλοσοφία, ähnlich auch ebd. 68,11–13, an letzterer Stelle nennt er dann Geometrie und Astronomie und nennt dann als dritten Punkt die λογικὴ πραγματεία (vgl. *Lexicon Gregorianum* IV 96). Damit entspricht er der klassischen platonischen Dreiteilung der Philosophie in Logik/Dialektik, Physik (incl. Betrachtung des Seins und der Theologie) und Ethik, vgl. z.B. Alkinoos, *Didaskalikos* III (Whittaker – Louis 153,26–30, hier bes. die Note complémentaire 28 p. 78f). Hiervon weicht die in *CE* gebotene Einteilung in Physik, Ethik und Metaphysik ab, der die Unterscheidung in αἰσθητά und νοερά zugrundeliegt.

[14] Der Übergang von der allgemeinen Überlegung zur Anwendung in der Gotteslehre ab p. 394,17 wird durch den Ausdruck περὶ τῶν ὑψηλῶν καὶ ἀθεάτων und die anschließende Parenthese λέγω δὲ περὶ τῆς θείας καὶ ἀφράστου φύσεως ausgedrückt.

gesund ist oder nicht (394,25f). Er sieht es als verwegen an, anzunehmen, dass man bei der göttlichen Natur zu einem auf der Hand liegenden geistigen Erfassen kommen kann, aber für noch verwegener, den einmal verwandten Bezeichnungen die Aufgabe zu übertragen, auch den Inhalt (die ἐγγινομένη ὑπόληψις) sprachlich auszudrücken (ἑρμηνεία) (394,18–22). Entsprechend kann das, was oberhalb der Erkenntnis liegt, nicht mit Begriffsbezeichnungen erfasst werden (keine προσηγορία erweist sich als προσφυής und drückt das ὑποκείμενον hinreichend aus), und dies begründet wiederum, dass man gezwungen ist, in der Gotteslehre eine Vielzahl von Bezeichnungen zu verwenden, um die Annahme (ὑπόνοια parallel zu ὑπόληψις in 394,16.22) über Gott auszudrücken (394,27–395,3).

Diese Vielzahl von Bezeichnungen erläutert Gregor jetzt in zwei Abschnitten weiter, und zwar zunächst die negativen Bezeichnungen (395,3–396,13), dann (ἀλλά) die positiven (396,13–397,31).

Voraussetzung für die negativen Bezeichnungen ist, dass alles, was in den Bereich menschlichen Erfassens fällt (= τὰ κάτω πράγματα 395,15),[15] unter eine von vier Fällen (viermaliges ἤ in 395,4.5.7.11) fällt: i) zeitliche Erstreckung (διαστηματικὴ παράτασις),[16] ii) räumliche Ausdehnung (τοπικὸν χώρημα), iii) Begrenztheit (περιγραφή) der Existenz durch Anfang und Ende und iv) Veränderlichkeit der Eigenschaften (*scil.* es geht mit φθορὰ καὶ πάθος καὶ τροπὴ καὶ ἀλλοίωσις einher), begründet in der Zusammengesetztheit von allem Körperlichen (395,3–14). Da die göttliche Natur mit den Dingen, die unter diese vier Fälle fallen, keine οἰκειότης hat, werden für sie sog. ἀποχωριστικὰ νοήματά τε καὶ ῥήματα gebraucht (395,14–17).[17] Dies verdeutlicht Gregor mit Beispielen: προαιώνιος, ἄναρχος, ἀτελεύτητος, ἀσώματος, ἄφθαρτος, ἀπαθής, ἄτρεπτος, ἀναλλοίωτος (395,18–23).

Von dieser Argumentation aus lehnt er das Argument des Eunomius, das auf der Anwendbarkeit des Konzepts στέρησις beruht, ab, es sei egal, ob man von στερητικά oder ἀφαιρετικά oder noch etwas anderem spreche – es gehe nur um den Sinn (νοῦς) (395,23–29). Die Annahme,

[15] Der Ausdruck ist bei Gregor singulär, entspricht aber dem häufig vorkommenden ἡ κάτω φύσις, vgl. *Lexicon Gregorianum* V 312 (unter B.2.) und 313 (unter B.4.c).

[16] Dass διαστηματικός hier eine zeitliche Erstreckung meint, legt die Differenzierung zur räumlichen Perspektive (τοπικός 395,5f) nahe, vgl. *Lexicon Gregorianum* III 370.

[17] Das Adjektiv ἀποχωριστικός begegnet bei Gregor nur hier (vgl. *Lexicon Gregorianum* I 512), vgl. aber χωριστικός 396,3, χωρισμός 396,8.

dass Gott früher oder irgendwann einmal nicht war (Anspielung auf den Anathematismus von 325: ἦν ποτε ὅτε οὐκ ἦν), würde bedeuten, dass Gott weder ἀτελεύτητος noch ἄναρχος wäre (395,30–32). Ebenso würde man die Bezeichnungen ἀναλλοίωτος, ἀσώματος und ἄφθαρτος ablehnen, wenn man einen Körper, Vergänglichkeit oder Veränderlichkeit bei Gott annehmen würde (395,32–396,2). Weil dies aber nicht der Fall ist, ist der Gebrauch der χωριστικὰ ῥήματα angemessen, der jedoch nur den χωρισμός von dem ausdrückt, was vordergründig bei uns existiert, der jedoch nichts über die φύσις aussagt (396,2–10). Fazit: wenn die Bedeutung dieser (*scil.* negativen) Bezeichnungen zeigt, was das Göttliche nicht ist, bleibt im Undeutlichen, was jenes gemäß seiner Natur ist, was diese (Bezeichnungen) nicht sind (396,10–13).

Die Erläuterung der Namen, die auf eine θέσις bzw. ὕπαρξις[18] verweisen, also die positiven Bezeichnungen, verweisen ebenfalls nicht auf die φύσις selbst, sondern auf den Bereich der τὰ περὶ αὐτὴν εὐσεβῶς θεωρούμενα (396,13–16). Dabei verweist das Adverb εὐσεβῶς bereits auf einen bestimmten Modus, zu den Betrachtungen "um die göttliche Natur herum" zu kommen, der im Folgenden durch die Bezugnahme auf die Schrift und ihre "Unterweisung" mehrfach aufgegriffen wird. Voraussetzung für die positiven Bezeichnungen ist die These, dass im Bereich des Seienden (und zwar des materiell erscheinenden wie des gedachten) nichts zufällig existiert, sondern an der göttlichen Natur 'hängt' (ἐξῆπται) und von dort her die αἰτία seiner Existenz hat (396,16–20). Dies bildet die Voraussetzung dafür, dass man aus der Schönheit und Größe der θαύματα in der Schöpfung einzelne Aspekte mit jeweils eigenen Bezeichnungen ausdrückt, eine Art 'Analogieverfahren', das biblisch mit *Weish* 13,5 belegt wird (396,21–27).[19]

---

[18] Auch Basilius, *Adversus Eunomium* I 10,28–44 (SC 299, 206), hatte die negativen von den positiven Bezeichnungen (θέσιν καὶ ὕπαρξιν . . . ἀποσημαίνουσιν) unterschieden und eine Diskussion darüber abgelehnt, welches philosophische Konzept (ἀφαίρεσις etc.) man für die negativen Bezeichnungen zugrundelegen könne (vgl. *CE* II 580, GNO I 395,25f), vgl. Verf., *Die Entwicklung der Trinitätslehre*, 70.

[19] Das Adverb ἀναλόγως entstammt *Weish* 13,5. Gregor passt den Wortlaut von *Weish* 13,5 der Syntax seines Satzes an, man kann daher besser von "enger Aufnahme" sprechen, unverändert aus *Weish* 13,5 stammt ἐκ (LXX add. γὰρ) μεγέθους καὶ καλλονῆς κτισμάτων ἀναλόγως, das finite Verb θεωρεῖται wird umformuliert: φησιν . . . δεῖν . . . θεωρεῖσθαι, entsprechend wird aus dem Nominativsubjekt ein Akkusativ, zusätzlich wird das Pronomen αὐτῶν durch das nicht in *Weish* 13 stehende

Dies erläutert Gregor nun durch verschiedene Begriffe, die als Beispiele dienen: δημιουργός, δυνατός, ἀγαθός, κριτής und vor allem θεός. Diese Bezeichnungen gehen auf das menschliche Denken zurück,[20] doch wird das Denken seinerseits wieder von der Schrift erzogen (παιδευθέντες 397,3, vgl. διδαχθέντες 397,20). Dies verdeutlicht Gregor besonders an der Bezeichnung θεός, deren mutmaßliche etymologische Bedeutung dessen, der auf alles schaut,[21] durch eine Reihe von Bibelzitaten belegt wird (397,8–19).[22] Auch diese Bezeichnung führt nicht zur Erkenntnis der οὐσία Gottes (397,19f), sondern zeigt vielmehr die Schwäche der menschlichen Natur auf und verweist darauf, dass Gott über jedem Namen (Anspielung auf *Phil* 2,9) ist, ist also ein Beleg der ἄφραστος μεγαλειότης Gottes (397,23–31).

Die Einteilung der Gottesbezeichnungen bei Gregor in ἀποχωριστικά und ἀναλόγως gebildete Begriffe ist zu vergleichen mit den Möglichkeiten zur geistigen Betrachtung Gottes im Platonismus. So werden im *Didaskalikos* des Alkinoos drei Arten der νόησις hinsichtlich Gott genannt, i) κατ' ἀφαίρεσιν ἀπὸ τοῦ αἰσθητοῦ, ii) κατ' ἀναλογίαν (womit hier der direkte Vergleich gemeint ist, etwa zwischen Sehen und Denken), iii) ein gedanklicher Aufstieg, ausgehend von der Betrachtung körperlicher Schönheit (κάλλος), Wechsel zur Betrachtung der Schönheit der Seele usw. bis hin zur Betrachtung des ersten Guten.[23] Gregors ἀποχωριστικά entsprechen sachlich der ersten Art,

τῶν πάντων aufgelöst: δεῖν τὸν τῶν πάντων γενεσιουργὸν θεωρεῖσθαι, ähnlich wird *Weish* 13,5 von Gregor gebraucht in *CE* II 154 (GNO I 270,8f; ohne δεῖν) und *In Eccl.* I (GNO V 285,2–4; ebenfalls ohne δεῖν, statt θεωρεῖσθαι: καθορᾶσθαι), ἀναλόγως begegnet nur als Adverb (Langerbecks Konjektur zu *In Cant. Cant.* I, GNO VI 18,5 ist zu verwerfen), vgl. *Lexicon Gregorianum* I 283.

[20] Vgl. bereits νοήσαντες 396,16, κατανοήσαντες 396,22, ἐννοήσαντες 396,30, νοήματα 396,23.24; 397,6, θεωρεῖσθαι in 396,27 entstammt *Weish* 13,5.

[21] Zum Zusammenhang mit θεᾶσθαι und der daraus abgeleitenen Etymologie, θεός meine die ἐποπτικὴ ἐνέργεια Gottes, vgl. *Lexicon Gregorianum* III 757.

[22] Zitiert werden *Ps* 54,3 LXX (hierher stammt als Zitat nur πρόσχες μοι, die Anrede ὁ θεός stammt aus *Ps* 54,2 LXX, das indef. Possessivum μου ist in Anklang zu *Ps* 54,2–3 LXX ergänzt), *Ps* 83,10 LXX (unverändert: ἴδε ὁ θεός) und *Ps* 43,21 LXX (wörtlich, unter Auslassung einiger Wörter in der ersten Vershälfte), vgl. *Lexicon Gregorianum* IV 243. Gregor betont die Synonymie der in diesen Zitaten verwandten Verben προσέχω, βλέπω (bzw. Aor. ἰδεῖν) und θεάω (397,16f).

[23] Alkinoos, *Didaskalikos* X (Whittaker – Louis 165,16–34). Weniger vergleichbar sind die drei Wege Synthese, Analyse und Analogie bei Kelsos, vgl. Origenes, *Contra Celsum* VII 44 (SC 150, 116–120). Vgl. Whittaker, Note Complémentaire 203, in: Alkinoos [wie Anm. 13], 106f.

die positiven Begriffe stellen eine Mischform aus der zweiten und dritten Art dar, und zwar insofern, als es sich einerseits um als Vergleiche analogiehaft gebrauchte Begriffe handelt (= ii), andererseits um Übertragungen, die auf Rückschlüssen aus der sinnlich wahrnehmbaren Welt beruhen (= iii).

zu Ie (398,1–24): Der Abschnitt setzt das Ausgeführte (vgl. 398,1f) in Beziehung zu dem Vorwurf des Eunomius, Basilius mache die Namen wichtiger als die ἀξία/πράγματα.[24] Zweimal wird Eunomius referiert (398,7–11 und 398,14f), wobei nicht klar wird, ob die Eunomius-Zitate vom Ablauf der *Apologia apologiae* her hierher gehören (und zu einem längeren, übergangenen Abschnitt gehören) oder einen früheren Abschnitt heranziehen, der übergangen worden war und aus dem Gregor jetzt noch zwei Notizen bringt.[25] Inhaltlich weist Gregor den eunomianischen Vorwurf mit dem Hinweis auf die in Ic-d erläuterte Einordnung der Gottesbezeichnungen zurück, weil Gregor zufolge kein Name die Existenz (ὑπόστασις) als οὐσιώδης hat (398,16f), sondern lediglich ein γνώρισμά τι καὶ σημεῖον οὐσίας τινὸς καὶ διανοίας, das jedoch für sich genommen nicht über Existenz verfügt (398,17–19). Darin erweist sich die ἀτονία der eunomianischen Polemik (vgl. ἄτονος 398,4).[26]

III. *Die ἀθανασία Gottes als Testfall für negative Gottesprädikate*

zu IIa:[27] Inwiefern das στέρησις-Konzept bei Gott nicht angemessen ist, scheint Eunomius anschließend am Begriff der ἀθανασία verdeut-

---

[24] Vgl. R. P. Vaggione, *Eunomius*, 114. Der Begriff τύπος (398,7) legt es nahe, dass Eunomius hier auf Basilius, *Adversus Eunomium* I 9,26–31 (SC 299, 200–202; evtl. auch *Adversus Eunomium* I 9,40–46, SC 299, 202) reagiert.

[25] Zu beiden Möglichkeiten würde 398,22–24 passen, eventuell spricht 399,11f eher für die erstere Möglichkeit, wenn damit gemeint ist, dass das jetzt gemeinte Argument mit dem vorangegangenen (= Ia–Id) nichts zu tun hat.

[26] Dazu, dass der Begriff ἄτονος bzw. ἀτονία als Bezeichnung der 'Schwäche' eines gegnerischen Arguments vorkommt und dementsprechend nur in der Auseinandersetzung mit Eunomius und Apollinarius auftaucht, vgl. *Lexicon Gregorianum* I 604f.

[27] Der Neuansatz ist in der GNO-Ausgabe nicht durch einen Absatz o.ä. markiert und wird auch von R. P. Vaggione, *Eunomius*, 114 nicht berücksichtigt (Vaggione teilt die *Apologia apologiae* nach der sicherlich nicht ursprünglichen Kapitelzählung von Basilius, *Adversus Eunomium* I ein, was weder der zu vermutenden Argumentation des Eunomius noch der Gregors entspricht), doch geht es ab 398,26 um ein neues Argument des Eunomius (ἐπισύρεται) und zugleich um ein neues Thema, das in

licht zu haben.[28] Dabei scheint er zunächst anhand biblischer Belege (398,24f) einen Unterschied der ἀθανασία beim Menschen und bei den Engeln geltend gemacht zu haben. Leider lässt die *praeteritio* Gregors (398,27f) nicht erkennen, wie dieses Argument genau aussah.[29] Gregor macht hiergegen unmittelbar geltend, dass der Begriff des ἀθάνατον keine Abstufung als μᾶλλον – ἧττον zulasse, weil dies bedeuten würde, neben dem Element des ἀθάνατον auch einen gewissen Anteil am Gegenteil anzusetzen, dann aber würde der betreffende Gegenstand nicht mehr unsterblich sein (398,28–399,3). Das anschließende Eunomiuszitat differenziert zwischen στέρησις und ἀπόστασις, στέρησις beziehe sich auf die Trennung (χωρισμός) vom Besseren, ἀπόστασις meine die Distanz vom Schlechteren (399,3–8).[30] Es lässt sich überlegen, in welchem Bezug der Unterschied zwischen ἀπόστασις und στέρησις zu der Behauptung eines Unterschieds der Unsterblichkeit bei Engeln und Menschen steht. Zwei Möglichkeiten der Interpretation sind zu erwägen:

i) Eunomius hat dazu aufgefordert, das στέρησις-Konzept als μὴ ἀδιάφορος καὶ μέση anzusehen: also einerseits als nicht unterschiedslos, andererseits als 'mittlere Größe' (*scil.* die eben Abstufungen erlaubt). Das würde dann bedeuten, dass der Unterschied der Unsterblichkeit bei den Engeln und den Menschen in Verbindung mit dem στέρησις-Konzept zu verstehen wäre, also als eine Eigenschaft, die in Abgrenzung zum Besseren besteht (nämlich als abgestufte und nicht [*scil.* wie bei Gott] absolute), während die Unsterblichkeit bei Gott eher als eine ἀπόστασις zu beschreiben wäre, als ein Enthobensein über dem Bereich des Schlechteren, der Sphäre des Sterblichen.

ii) Der Unterschied zwischen ἀπόστασις und στέρησις wurde mit dem Unterschied der Unsterblichkeit bei Engeln und Menschen in Verbindung gebracht, etwa dergestalt, dass die Unsterblichkeit der

---

CE II 561–589 (GNO I 390–398) nicht genannt worden war (vgl. lediglich *CE* II 556, GNO I 389,7–11 in Entgegnung auf das Eunomiuszitat *CE* II 536, GNO I 382,24–26, vgl. die Aufnahmen in 383,1–4 und 388,29f, vgl. sodann 384,12.28f).

[28] Auf welche Textstelle bei Basilius, *Adversus Eunomium* I 9 oder 10 Eunomius damit reagiert, ist unsicher, der von Vaggione, *Eunomius*, hergestellte Bezug zum Anfang von *Adversus Eunomium* I 10 ist terminologisch nicht eindeutig, da die Begriffe ἀθάνατος und στέρησις auch in *Adversus Eunomium* I 9,27f.48f (SC 299, 200–202) fallen.

[29] Ohne Auskunft bleibt auch R. P. Vaggione, *Eunomius*, 114, Anm. 37.

[30] Die Differenz zwischen στέρησις und ἀπόστασις wird nicht berücksichtigt von R. P. Vaggione, *Eunomius*, 114 mit Anm. 39, vgl. zu dieser Unterscheidung bei Syrian und Alexander von Aphrodisias Th. Böhm, *Theoria*, 115f mit Anm. 53f.

Engel als eine ἀπόστασις zu verstehen sei, die der Menschen jedoch aufgrund eines στέρησις-Konzepts. Nach dieser Interpretation sind die Engel dem Bereich des Sterblichen ebenso entzogen wie Gott. Das würde erklären, wieso Gregor in Eunomius' Argumentation einen Widerspruch zu *1 Tim* 6,16 sieht, wonach nur Gott unsterblich sei und allen anderen die Unsterblichkeit erst verleihe (399,8–11). Denn wenn die Unsterblichkeit der Engel als ἀπόστασις zu verstehen ist, sind neben Gott auch die Engel quasi von Natur aus unsterblich, eben der Sphäre des Schlechteren, der Sterblichkeit enthoben. Gleichzeitig würde es bedeuten, dass die Differenz zwischen Unsterblichkeit bei Engeln und Menschen keine graduelle (μᾶλλον – ἧττον) Abstufung, sondern eine kategoriale (eben zwischen στέρησις und ἀπόστασις) wäre. Die Qualifikation des στέρησις-Konzeptes bei den Menschen als μὴ ἀδιάφορος καὶ μέση ist dann entweder dahingehend zu verstehen, dass nicht alle Menschen diese Unsterblichkeit erlangen, oder dahingehend, dass bei den Menschen unterschiedliche Formen bzw. Abstufungen von Unsterblichkeit anzunehmen sind. (z.B. analog zur Auferstehung zum Gericht und der Auferstehung zum ewigen Leben).

Leider geht Gregor so über Eunomius' Argumentation hinweg, dass sich zwischen diesen beiden Interpretationsmöglichkeiten nicht mit letzter Sicherheit entscheiden lässt. Die erste Interpretationsmöglichkeit steht vor dem Problem, Gregors Anführung von *1 Tim* 6,16 nicht erklären zu können. Außerdem bemerkt Gregor wenige Zeilen später, dass Eunomius es ablehne, die Gottesbezeichnung ἄφθαρτος als Gegensatz zu φθαρτός zu verstehen und somit die negative Bezeichnung als eine ἀπόστασις τοῦ χείρονος aufzufassen, vielmehr gehe es um ein Gottesprädikat, das sich unmittelbar auf das Sein Gottes beziehe (also nicht in Relation zu besser – schlechter stehe) (400,1–4). Dies spricht relativ deutlich für Interpretationsmöglichkeit ii).

Ebenfalls für diese letztere Interpretationsmöglichkeit spricht die Überlegung, welche Bibelverse Eunomius in seiner Argumentation benutzt haben könnte. Das Wort ἀθανασία ist in der LXX sowie im NT selten, von den wenigen Stellen[31] kommen im Grunde nur zwei in Frage, nämlich *Weish* 8,17, wonach die συγγένεια σοφίας

[31] Belege für ἀθανασία: *Weish* 3,4; 4,1; 8,13.17; 15,3; *4 Makk* 14,5; 16,13; [Aq. *Ps* 47,15 LXX], *1 Kor* 15,53f; *1 Tim* 6,16; für ἀθάνατος *Weish* 1,15; *Sir* 17,30; 51,9; *4 Makk* 7,3; 14,6; 18,23.

(von Eunomius als die Engel interpretiert?) über ἀθανασία verfügt, und *1 Kor* 15,53f, wonach die Menschen ἀθανασία 'anziehen'. Eine Gegenüberstellung dieser beiden Zitate könnte von Eunomius dahingehend gedeutet worden sein, dass die Engel eine stetige Unsterblichkeit haben, eben als συγγένεια σοφίας, wohingegen die Menschen die Unsterblichkeit erst im Eschaton 'anziehen'. Für eine Verwendung von *1 Kor* 15,53f spricht auch die parallele Behandlung von ἀθάνατος und ἄφθαρτος (401,7–9).[32]

Polemisch bemerkt Gregor, dass dieser, auf den Unterschied der ἀθανασία bei Engeln und Menschen bezogene Gedankengang nichts mit dem vorangegangenen zu tun habe, und dass Eunomius, sich dessen bewusst, seine Gegner als unverständig bei der Beurteilung von Dingen und dem Gebrauch von Namen bezeichne (399,11–16).

Im Stile einer *praeteritio* verweist Gregor auf einen weiteren Abschnitt, in dem Eunomius sich mit der Erläuterung von ἄφθαρτος und ἀσώματος (*scil.* als Verneinung einer körperlichen διάστασις bzw. als Bezeichnung als τῆς φθορᾶς ἀνεπίδεκτον) beschäftigt haben muss. Wahrscheinlich hat Eunomius auch für diese Begriffe geltend gemacht, dass sie sich in der Gotteslehre nicht als στέρησις verstehen lassen, sondern als Aussagen über das Sein Gottes selbst, quasi in einem absoluten Sinne[33] (399,16–400,1, vgl. 400,3f: ἀλλ' αὐτὸ τὸ εἶναι διὰ τοῦ ὑποκειμένου σημαίνεσθαι). Hierzu passt das von Gregor aufgegriffene Argument, dass es nicht richtig sei, dass die äußere Gestalt bzw. Prägung (τύπος)[34] von ὀνόματα zu unsachgemäßen Konzepten führt (399,23–25).

Der Weigerung des Eunomius, das Gottesprädikat ἄφθαρτος auf den Gegensatz zu φθαρτός zu beziehen (400,1f), stellt Gregor eine *reductio ad absurdum* gegenüber: Dann müsste für Gott gerade das Gegenteil erfüllt sein, der Begriff ἄφθαρτος also gerade auf die Veränderlichkeit Gottes verweisen (keine ἀλλοτρίωσις φθορᾶς, sondern eine

[32] Allerdings hatte schon Basilius, *Adversus Eunomium* I 9,27f (SC 299, 200), mit der Beispielreihe ὁ ἄφθαρτος, ὁ ἀθάνατος, ὁ ἀόρατος argumentiert, aber der Begriff ἀόρατος scheint in Eunomius' Argumentation keine Rolle gespielt zu haben, vielleicht eben wegen der Verwendung von *1 Kor* 15,53f.

[33] Jaegers Konjektur add. τὸ μὴ (399,25) ist wohl richtig, weil die Konstruktion die Infinitivreihung τὸ διαβάλλειν . . . καὶ τὸ λέγειν . . . καὶ τὸ . . . ὑπολαμβάνειν verlangt und zusätzlich der Gegensatz ἀλλὰ τοῦ εἶναι die Negation verlangt, der Fehler zudem als Haplographie verständlich zu machen ist.

[34] Der Begriff τύπος entstammt Basilius, *Adversus Eunomium* I 9,27.28.61 (SC 299, 200–204), vgl. oben Anm. 24, vgl. zu 399,23–25 auch Basilius, *Adversus Eunomium* I 10,21f (SC 299, 204–206).

συγκατάθεσις) (400,4–11). Demgegenüber setze er, Gregor, die Abwesenheit von θάνατος bei Gott als gleichbedeutend mit der Affirmation von Leben bei Gott an, dies sei in der φύσις der ἀντίθετα begründet, die besagt, dass die Aufhebung/ἀφαίρεσις des einen Elements das Vorhandensein (die Setzung: θέσις) des Gegenteils (ἀντικείμενον) bedeutet[35] (400,11–21).

zu IIb: Eunomius hat die Ablehnung des στέρησις-Konzepts u.a. damit begründet, dass das ὑπερέχειν Gottes sich gar nicht durch Negativbezeichnungen ausdrücken lasse (solange diese im Sinne einer στέρησις, also als Aussagen bloßen Mangels an etwas, zu verstehen seien)[36] (400,22f). Nachdem Gregor die polemische Kennzeichnung des Basilius als ἠλίθιος ebenso polemisch zurückgegeben hat (400, 24–28), sucht er Eunomius von einer mutmaßlichen gemeinsamen Denkvoraussetzung her zu widerlegen, nämlich der These, dass sich die Besonderheit der göttlichen Natur darin erkennen lasse, dass sie keine κοινωνία mit dem hat, woran die Welt (ἡ κάτω φύσις) teilhat, denn dann wäre sie mit diesem eher identisch, ihr Überragen (ὑπερανίσταμαι) drückt sich gerade dadurch aus, dass es das (*scil.* woran die Welt teilhat) nicht hat, Beispiel: der Sündlose ist besser als die Sündenbeladenen, die Trennung von Bösem erweist einen Reichtum an Gutem (400,28–401,4).

Im Sinne einer *praeteritio* (401,5–7) bricht Gregor diesen Gedankengang ab und greift auf das nächste Eunomiuszitat zurück, das ebenfalls das Thema ὑπερέχειν betrifft.[37] Hiernach bezeichnen die Gottesprädikate ἀθάνατος, ἄφθαρτος und ἀγέννητος in gleicher Weise (ὁμοίως) das ὑπερέχειν Gottes (401,7–10). Gregor hält mit einer rhetorischen Frage zunächst die Widerlegung für überflüssig, weil die ἀσέβεια dieser Aussage auf der Hand liege (401,10–12), skizziert dann aber doch, worin er das Problem dieser Aussage sieht. Aus Eunomius' Aussage leitet Gregor ab, dass das Gottesprädikat ἀγέννητος (ebenso wie ἀθάνατος und ἄφθαρτος) als absolute Aussage über das

---

[35] Vgl. Aristoteles, *Kat.* 10, 11b35–12a2.

[36] Damit hat Eunomius wohl auf Basilius, *Adversus Eunomium* I 10,42–48 (SC 299, 206–208), reagiert, vgl. R. P. Vaggione, *Eunomius*, 115 mit Anm. 41.

[37] Der Begriff ὑπεροχή begegnete schon bei Eunomius, *Apologia* 10,4 (SC 305, 252; vgl. dann Basilius, *Adversus Eunomium* I 20,34–41, SC 299, 246), das Verb ὑπερέχω steht bereits in Basilius, *Adversus Eunomium* I 13,42 (SC 299, 220), daher ist es wahrscheinlich, dass Eunomius hier auf Basilius, *Adversus Eunomium* I 13,36–14,3 (SC 299, 218–220) reagiert hat, vgl. ähnlich R. P. Vaggione, *Eunomius*, 115 mit Anm. 42.

Überragen Gottes verstanden werden muss, also als Aussage über die Differenz zwischen der φύσις Gottes und dem Bereich des Vergänglichen (401,24f). Weil die genannten drei negativen Prädikate in gleicher Weise (ὁμοίως) zu verstehen sind, gilt für den Bereich, der als Gegensatz zu Gott zu denken ist, dass er nicht nur φθορά und θάνατος unterliegt, sondern auch der γέννησις (401,13–21). Wenn aber Christus als γεννητός beschrieben wird (401,15.20f), ergibt sich daraus als Konsequenz (die zu ziehen Gregor wieder dem Leser überlässt; 401,22f), dass Christus nicht Gott ist, dass also das, was durch das gleiche Maß (ὁμοίως = τῷ αὐτῷ μέτρῳ) überragt wird, miteinander gleich (ἴσα) ist (401,12f). Bleibt also als zu erschließende Konsequenz der eunomianischen Theologie, dass Christus nicht als Gott zu charakterisieren ist.

zu IIc: Die Ablehnung der στέρησις für die negativen Gottesprädikate bedeutet für Eunomius, dass auch das Prädikat ἀθάνατος nicht als ἀπουσία θανάτου zu verstehen ist (sondern als quasi absolut zu nehmende Bezeichnung von Gottes Natur). Gregor zitiert diese eunomianische Aussage dreimal (401,25–27; 402,8f.19f), ohne auf ihre Intention näher einzugehen. Nach dem ersten Zitieren betont er die Widersinnigkeit der Aussage, indem er die Verneinung von ἀπουσία θανάτου unmittelbar als Vorhandensein von θάνατος (und φθορά) bei Gott deutet. Hieran anknüpfend beharrt er auf der logischen Konsequenz, dass bei Gegensatzpaaren die Verneinung des einen die Affirmation des anderen Begriffs nach sich zieht (Beispiele: Licht – Finsternis, Leben – Tod, Gesundheit – Krankheit)[38] (401,30–402,8). Nach dem zweiten Zitieren wiederholt Gregor diese Konsequenz, dass Eunomius damit die Unsterblichkeit Gottes im Grunde leugne, und verwahrt sich gegen den Vorwurf, er gehe ἐπηρεαστικώτερον (ziemlich bzw. zu verleumderisch)[39] mit Eunomius um, denn so wahnsinnig sei niemand, die Unsterblichkeit Gottes zu leugnen. Doch möchte Gregor Eunomius beim Wortlaut seiner Aussage behaften (nicht auf einen verborgenen Nebensinn eingehen) (402,9–19). Auch nach dem dritten Zitieren wiederholt Gregor die von ihm gesehene

[38] Das Gegensatzpaar ὑγιεία – νόσος verwendet Gregor entsprechend zu Aristoteles, *Kat.* 10, 12a2–20, wo jedoch der Gegensatz von Tod und Leben nicht begegnet und der Gegensatz zwischen Weiß und Schwarz gerade als Gegensatz fungiert, zwischen dem es Zwischenstufen gibt (eben die Grautöne).

[39] Diese Stelle ist der einzige Beleg bei Gregor für den Komparativ zum nur als Adverb gebrauchten ἐπηρεαστικῶς, vgl. *Lexicon Gregorianum* III 376.

Konsequenz, dass Gott dann sterblich und Tod und Vergänglichkeit (φθορά) unterworfen sei, und überlässt es dann Eunomius, den verborgenen Sinn der Aussage zu erläutern (402,20–27), und stellt dem das eigene Verharren[40] bei dem normalen Sprachgebrauch (συνήθεια 403,4) gegenüber (402,28–31), das bei Gegensatzpaaren eben die Negation des einen die Affirmation des anderen bedeute, Beispiele ἄνοσος, ἄπηρος, ἄνανδρος, ἄϋπνος (402,31–403,4).

zu IId: Mit einer *praeteritio* (403,5f.9f) und der polemischen Aussage, dass die Ausführung des Lächerlichen des Gegenspielers einen selbst in Verruf bringt (403,6–9) beginnt Gregor den letzten Abschnitt zum Thema ἀθανασία. Dabei enthält das zugrundegelegte Eunomiuszitat diesen Begriff gar nicht, sondern stellt nur einen (bei Eunomius wohl das vorangehende Argument begründenden) *Genitivus absolutus* dar, der von Gregor in zwei Hälften zitiert wird: in ihm verneint Eunomius, dass die Wahrheit eine συμφυΐα bezeugt bzw. die Frömmigkeit ein solches Konzept vorschreibt (403,10–12.16–18).[41] Gemeint ist wohl, dass für die Beschreibung Gottes selbst von einer völligen kategorialen Verschiedenheit ausgegangen werden muss, sich also weder von der Sache her noch von der gedanklichen Konzeption her (sei es mit philosophischem Hintergrund [ἔξωθεν] oder von Eunomius selbst [παρ' ἡμῶν] her) eine Relationalität Gottes zur Schöpfung nahelegt (die für Eunomius in der Anwendung des στέρησις-Konzepts auf Gott gegeben wäre).

Hiergegen macht Gregor geltend, dass gerade Eunomius einen Bezug zwischen den Bezeichnungen (bzw. ihrer ἔννοια) und der οὐσία des Vaters herstellt (συμφύω) und die Namen gerade an zentraler Stelle mit der οὐσία Gottes verbindet bzw. derselben aufpfropft (ἐγκεντρίζω).[42] Nach einer weiteren polemischen Ausführung (403,19–28) stellt Gregor seinerseits Eunomius vor die Alternative, entweder auch

[40] Dies kennzeichnet Gregor mit einem ironischen Rückgriff auf das Eunomiuszitat 399,14–16, das er so gerade umdreht.

[41] Vgl. R. P. Vaggione, *Eunomius*, 115, der ebd. Anm. 42 bemerkt: "Gregory passed over a good deal at this point."

[42] Bei Gregor wird das Verb ἐγκεντρίζω außer an dieser Stelle nur in *In Cant. Cant.* (GNO VI 117,20) gebraucht (abgesehen vom Stichwort κλάδος deutet an dieser Stelle nichts auf eine Rezeption von *Röm* 11,17–24), *Lexicon Gregorianum* III 12f zieht in Erwägung, ob in der Bedeutung des Verbs in *CE* II 606 (GNO I 403,16) die Bedeutung von κέντρον als 'Mitte' bestimmend ist, so dass das Verb hier heißt: "konzentrieren auf, vollständig ausrichten auf, (wie in einem Mittelpunkt) in eins setzen mit". Die Frage lässt sich deswegen kaum entscheiden, weil jegliche 'Pflanzenmetaphorik' fehlt (es sei denn, man wollte diese aus διφυής 403,12 und συμφύω 403,14 ableiten).

die οὐσία Christi als ἀθανασία zu beschreiben oder nicht (403,28–30). Letzteres läuft darauf hinaus, Christus dem Vergehen und dem Tod zu unterwerfen (404,1–8), ja ihn selbst als Tod zu beschreiben (404,10–13), ersteres läuft darauf hinaus, gerade hinsichtlich der οὐσία eine Identität zwischen Vater und Sohn anzunehmen (wobei vorausgesetzt wird, dass der Begriff ἀθανασία nicht aufgespalten werden, also keine διαφορά beinhalten kann) (404,13–20).

Der gesamte Abschnitt II lässt die tiefe Differenz zwischen den theologischen Systemen Gregors und des Eunomius erkennen. Für Eunomius haben die Gottesprädikate, auch die mit *α-privativum* gebildeten,[43] etwas mit der οὐσία Gottes zu tun. Daraus folgt, dass sie nicht als Verhältnisbegriffe in Verbindung mit anderem, besonders der Welt, zu begreifen sind (daher auch nicht aufgrund einer στέρησις, einer ἀπουσία oder überhaupt als Ausdruck einer συμφυΐα gebildet werden können), sondern quasi Ausdrücke *sui generis* sind, absolut zu nehmende Ausdrücke, die auf das Wesen Gottes verweisen. Die Transzendenz Gottes würde für Eunomius dadurch gestört, dass Gott einem Gegensatzpaar zugeordnet würde, bei dem das andere Element weltlich-geschöpflich wäre. Das Gegensatzpaar würde dann die Differenz zwischen Gott und der Schöpfung überbrücken, gerade weil die Gottesprädikate die οὐσία Gottes angeben.

Genau dies lehnt Gregor ab. Für ihn grenzen die negativen Bezeichnungen Gott lediglich als transzendent ab, sie sind ἀποχωριστικά, die über die φύσις bzw. οὐσία Gottes nichts aussagen. Sie umfassen deswegen auch nicht als eine Metastruktur Gott und die Schöpfung, sondern verweisen nur auf die Differenz zwischen beidem. Dies ermöglicht es Gregor, die logische Struktur von Gegensatzpaaren gerade auch in der Gotteslehre anzuwenden, eben weil damit die οὐσία Gottes selbst nicht erfasst ist.

IV. *Der Streit um die Bedeutung der negativen Gottesprädikate für die Ontologie der Gotteslehre*

zu IIIa: Das letzte Argument des Eunomius aus Buch I der *Apologia apologiae* (vgl. 404,22: ἐπὶ τέλει τοῦ λόγου) behauptet, dass Basilius' (= ἡμᾶς 404,23) Gotteslehre darauf hinauslaufe, Gott-Vater "aus dem

[43] Vgl. hierzu Th. Böhm, *Theoria*, 117.173–174.

gänzlich Nichtseienden" sein zu lassen. Gregor erwidert zunächst polemisch, dass Eunomius' Argument darauf basiere, dass er eine Aussage des Basilius aus dem Kontext reiße (404,24–27). Dann kündigt er sein eigenes Vorgehen an, nämlich zunächst den Grundgedanken (διάνοια) des von Eunomius ausgewerteten Basiliuszitates zu erläutern und dann das Basiliuszitat als Beweis wörtlich anzuführen (404,27–32).

zu IIIb: Der Kontext des umstrittenen Basiliuszitates ist die Bedeutung des Attributs ἀγέννητος (vgl. 405,17f), wobei Basilius zeigen will, dass die Bedeutung von ἀγέννητος nichts mit dem Konzept (ἔννοια) der οὐσία zu tun habe (404,32–405,4). Es folgt eine Paraphrase (vgl. φησί 405,4.9) von Basilius' Argument. Er habe anhand der Genealogie des *Lukasevangeliums* von Joseph rückwärts jeweils nach der ἀρχή gefragt, wobei er bei Adam aufgehört habe, der als Protoplast keinen körperlichen Vater gehabt habe, sondern eben Gott (405,4–9; Adam hat keinen körperlichen Vater, sondern wird von dem Evangelisten als (ἐκ) τοῦ θεοῦ = 'Gottes'/'von Gott stammend' bezeichnet 405,9, vgl. 405,27–29). Dabei ist evident, dass Gott wiederum seine Existenz (ὑπόστασις) nicht einer anderen Instanz verdankt (*scil.* also als die eigentliche ἀρχή anzusehen ist) (405,9–14). Denn eine ἀρχή hängt nicht von etwas anderem ab, sonst ist es keine ἀρχή. Wenn Gott als die ἀρχὴ τοῦ παντός anzusehen ist, gibt es also kein ὑποκείμενον (405,14–17).

zu IIIc: Es folgt das wörtliche Basiliuszitat.[44] Für Basilius ist die Tatsache entscheidend, dass die Lukasgenealogie dabei aufhört, Adam als ἐκ τοῦ θεοῦ anzusehen. Das bedeutet, dass man bei Gott sagen muss, dass er ἐξ οὐδενός ist, eben τὸ ἄναρχον, was mit τὸ ἀγέννητον identisch sei. Ebensowenig wie bei den Menschen τὸ ἔκ τινος die οὐσία bezeichnet, ebensowenig bezeichnet das ἀγέννητον (= τὸ ἄναρχον = ἐξ οὐδενός) die οὐσία Gottes (405,21–406,5).[45]

[44] Von dem bei Sesboüé gebotenen Text (Basilius, *Adversus Eunomium* I 15,12–19.22–28, SC 299, 224–226) weicht das Zitat bei Gregor wie folgt ab (nicht vermerkt im Apparat von Sesboüé oder Jaeger): Basilius I 15,17 ἀνάλυσιν – Gregor 405,25 ἀνάβασιν (Gregors Lesart ist wahrscheinlich richtig), Basilius I 15,17 ἐπανάγων – Gregor 405,26: ἐπαναγαγών (vgl. aber app. crit.) (unentscheidbar), Basilius I 15,20–22 οὐχι . . . ἐκτιθέμενος – Gregor om. (wahrscheinlich Kürzung durch Gregor), Basilius I 15,24 ἐστιν ἐν – Gregor 405,30: ἐστι (unentscheidbar); Basilius I 15,27 ἐπὶ ἀνθρώπων – Gregor 406,3: ἐπὶ τῶν ἀνθρώπων (unentscheidbar).

[45] Vgl. Verf., *Die Entwicklung der Trinitätslehre*, 70f.

Im Anschluß an dieses Zitat wendet sich Gregor zunächst an die Anhänger des Eunomius (= ὑμεῖς), die er als Herde der Zugrundegehenden bezeichnet (ἡ τῶν ἀπολλυμένων ἀγέλη) (406,5f). Er fragt polemisch, ob sie sich nicht schämen, sich auf einen solchen χειραγωγός zu berufen, der solchermaßen die Zitate verdreht, und bezeichnet Eunomius' Vorgehensweise als 'schamlos'[46] (406,7–12). Entscheidend ist, dass Eunomius genauso, wie er mit dem Basiliuszitat umgeht, auch die Bibelzitate auslegt (13–16).[47] Gregor fragt sich selbst, ob er die Freveleien anführen oder nicht eher übergehen soll. Schließlich bezichtigt man auch nicht jemanden seiner körperlichen Defekte (φύσεως ἀτυχήματα, etwa Mundgeruch oder körperliche Verletzungen) (406,15–21). Die Bemühung, frevelhaft zu sein, ist als Krankheit der λογισμοί und unglückliche Verletzung der Seele anzusehen (406,21–23). Deswegen führt Gregor nur unmittelbar die Aussage an, mit der Eunomius das Basiliuszitat gegen "uns" (die von Gregor vertretene Basiliuspartei) verdreht (406,23–27).

zu IIId: Das Eunomiuszitat setzt bei der Intention des Basilius an, den Sohn ja nicht ἐκ μετουσίας τοῦ ὄντος sein zu lassen. Dafür nehme Basilius sogar in Kauf, Gott-Vater aus dem gänzlich Nicht-Seienden (ἐκ τοῦ πάντη μὴ ὄντος) sein zu lassen. Dies ergibt sich, weil Basilius ja behauptet, dass Gott-Vater ἐξ οὐδενός sei, οὐδέν bzw. μηδέν aber mit μὴ ὄν identisch (ταὐτόν) sei und man gleichwertige Aussagen (ἰσοδυναμοῦντα) durch einander ersetzen könne. Also behauptet der, der sagt, Gott-Vater sei ἐξ οὐδενός, dass Gott ἐκ τοῦ πάντη μὴ ὄντος sei (406,28–407,4).

Rhetorisch fragt Gregor, wogegen er als erstes vorgehen soll, gegen die Meinung, dass der Sohn im Sinne der Teilhabe an Gott teilhat (ἐκ μετουσίας τοῦ θεοῦ), oder gegen die Zusammenstellung des gesamten Arguments (407,4–8). Anschließend geht er auf beide Punkte ein.

Aufgrund von μετουσία bei der göttlichen Natur Söhne anzusetzen, gehört ins Reich der Dichter und Mythenbildner, die irgendwelche Dionysos-, Heraklesfiguren etc. erfinden, die eine Verbindung mit menschlichen Körpern haben, aber gleichzeitig durch die Teilhabe an der stärkeren Natur über die übrigen Menschen erhaben sind (407,8–16). Dieses Konzept (*scil.* den Sohn analog hierzu an Gott

[46] Vgl. ἀναιδεία 406,8 (abgesehen von einer Ausnahme nur im Zusammenhang mit Eunomius, vgl. *Lexicon Gregorianum* I 266), ἀναισχύντως 406,12 (als Adverb nur hier, häufiger ist ἀνεπαισχύντως, vgl. *Lexicon Gregorianum* I 269.318), ἀναισχυντία 406,16f.

[47] Das Fragezeichen in 406,16 ist nicht zwingend.

lediglich teilhaben zu lassen) zeigt von sich aus so viel Unvernunft (ἄνοια) und Frevelei (ἀσέβεια),[48] dass man es nicht zu widerlegen braucht (407,16–21).

Ausführlicher geht Gregor auf den zweiten Punkt ein. Dazu wiederholt er den entscheidenden Teil des Eunomiuszitats noch einmal (407,21–25). Er kennzeichnet die Argumentationsweise des Eunomius als Schwingen der 'Aristotelischen Lanze',[49] und zwar genauer den Punkt, dass das τινὰ πατέρα μὴ ἔχειν mit dem τὸ ἐκ τοῦ πάντη μὴ ὄντος γεγενῆσθαι identisch (ταὐτόν) sei (407,25–28).

Die Lukasgenealogie ist eine Aufzählung (ἀπαρίθμησις) der Väter (407,28–408,4). Analog ist bei Gott-Vater nach dem Vater zu fragen. Die ironische Aufforderung Gregors an Eunomius zu sagen, wer als Vater von Gott-Vater zu nennen ist, hierfür die gesamte τέχνη aufzuwenden, zwingt Eunomius zu der Alternative, entweder das Attribut ἀγέννητον fallen zu lassen oder zu sagen, dass es keinen Vater von Gott-Vater gibt, dass die Antwort lautet: οὐδείς (408,4–11). Dadurch bricht die Argumentation des Eunomius zusammen (408,11–13). Eunomius hat nicht beachtet, dass in Basilius' Argumentation die Bedeutung des ἀγέννητος beschrieben wird als ἐξ οὐδενὸς πατρός, selbst wo das Wort 'Vater' nicht ausdrücklich hinzugefügt ist. Stattdessen hat er aus dem ἐξ οὐδενὸς πατρός ein μηδέν gemacht und dies mit dem ἐκ τοῦ πάντη μὴ ὄντος gleichgesetzt (408,1–20). Also lässt sich das Argument des Eunomius gegen ihn umdrehen. Eunomius muss zugeben, dass der ἀγέννητος keinen Vater haben kann, also οὐδείς der Vater Gottes ist, dies wird dann mit μηδέν gleichgesetzt, was als identisch mit dem τὸ πάντη μὴ ὄν angesehen wird, also ergibt sich gerade aus Eunomius' Argumentation, dass ihm zufolge Gott-Vater eigentlich aus dem Nicht-Seienden ist (408,20–30). Damit hat Gregor sein Argumentationsziel erreicht. Eunomius ist dadurch widerlegt, dass der Vorwurf, den er gegen Basilius erhebt, gerade gegen ihn selbst zu erheben ist.

[48] Zur Verbindung von ἄνοια und ἀσέβεια vgl. *Lexicon Gregorianum* I 386.

[49] Vgl. hierzu den Beitrag von Ladislav Chvátal in diesem Band.

V. *Der Abschluss*

Das Ende von *CE* II ist polemischer Art. Gregor greift Worte des Eunomius auf (dass es schlimm sei, weise zu scheinen und nicht zu sein), und führt dies fort. Noch schlimmer sei es, sich selbst zu verkennen und nicht den Unterschied zwischen dem hochfliegenden Basilius und dem am Lande lebenden Tier (*scil.* also Eunomius selbst) zu kennen (408,31–409,4). Das Bild des 'hochfliegenden' (ὑψιπετής) Basilius führt Gregor noch fort: Wenn das scharfe und göttliche Auge des Basilius (*scil.* wie bei einem Greifvogel aus der Höhe) Gregor sähe, wenn er mit dem Flügel der Weisheit (τὸ τῆς σοφίας πτερόν) lebte, wäre er herabgeflogen und hätte gezeigt, gegen wen sich Eunomius erhoben hat, mit welcher Scherbe der Unvernunft er verknüpft ist (συμφύω), wobei er danach jagt, jemand zu sein zu scheinen, und zwar bei den alten Frauen und den Kastraten (ἐκτομίαι)[50] (409,4–10). Trotzdem ist die Hoffnung noch nicht aufzugeben, weder hinsichtlich Eunomius noch hinsichtlich der Krallen des Basilius. Seine eigene Aufgabe beschreibt Gregor darin, quasi als ein Teil einer Kralle (ὄνυχος μοῖρα) angesehen zu werden, als das, was für Eunomius ansteht, bezeichnet er es, dass die Schale zerbrochen und so die durch die Scherbe verborgene Gestaltlosigkeit gezeigt wird (409,10–15).

[50] Bei Gregor nur hier (vgl. *Lexicon Gregorianum* III 134), γραΐδιον taucht bei Gregor nur in der Polemik mit Eunomius auf, vgl. *Lexicon Gregorianum* II 224.

PART IV

SUPPORTING STUDIES

IV.1. PHILOSOPHICAL QUESTIONS

ÉPINOIA ET IMAGINAIRE CHEZ GRÉGOIRE DE NYSSE (*CE* II 172–195)

Evanghélos Moutsopoulos

Presque tous les philosophes grecs s'accordent pour voir dans la pensée humaine le produit de la collaboration de l'ensemble des facultés de l'esprit : sensation (αἴσθησις), imagination (φαντασία), opinion (δόξα), intellection (νόησις), entendement (διάνοια), raison (λόγος). Or, plus son activité se trouve affranchie de l'intervention des facultés dites inférieures, plus la raison agit seule, et plus son activité se voit épurée de toute intervention falsificatrice de la rectitude de son cheminement, partant délivrée de tout danger de jugement erroné. À ce propos, Aristote distingue avec rigueur les sophismes, syllogismes volontairement mensongers, des paralogismes, syllogismes involontairement erronés, les uns et les autres résultant de l'altération d'un des éléments de leurs prémisses, dont le plus fréquent serait le double sens attribué au moyen terme (ὅρων τετράς) ou encore le choix d'une argumentation fautive (*argumentum ad hominem ; ad verecundiam*).[1]

Aucune de ces démarches n'est exempte de fausseté ; mais c'est surtout le recours à l'imagination, qui, depuis Platon, fut rendu responsable de l'aberration de la pensée.[2] Le néoplatonisme tenta de réhabiliter l'imaginaire en renversant le rôle fondamental de l'imagination par rapport à l'image, donnée première, sans toutefois aller

[1] Cf. E. Moutsopoulos, "Vers un élargissement du concept de vérité : le presque-vrai", *Annales de la Faculté des Lettres et Sciences Humaines d'Aix* 40 (1966) 189–196.

[2] Cf. Platon, entre autres, *Phédon* 110d : συνεχὲς ποικίλον φαντάζεσθαι ; *Rép.* II 380d : φαντάζεσθαι ἄλλοτε ἐν ἄλλαις ; IV 476a : πανταχοῦ φανταζόμενα ; *Soph.* 216c : παντοῖοι φανταζόμενοι ; *Tim.* 43e : ἑκατέροις τὰ ἑκατέρων φαντάζεται ; 49e : οὐδέποτε τῶν αὐτῶν ἑκάστων φανταζομένων ; 54b : οὐκ ὀρθῶς φανταζόμενα ; 60a : φανταζόμενον ἐλαιηρὸν εἶδος ; Aristote, quant à lui, *De anima* 431a16–17 : οὐδέποτε νοεῖ ἄνευ φαντάσματος ἡ ψυχή ; *De mem. et reminisc.* 449b33–450a1 : νοεῖν οὐκ ἔστιν ἄνευ φαντάσματος, semble exclure l'existence d'une raison pure ; cf. cependant *De anima* 428a25 : οὐκ ἔστι συμπλοκὴ δόξης καὶ αἰσθήσεως, ainsi qu'on serait tenté de l'envisager et tenant compte du rôle intermédiaire de l'imagination. Cf. Épicure, *Rat. sent.* XXIV 3 (Arrighetti 129) : πᾶσαν φανταστικὴν ἐπιβολὴν τῆς διανοίας ... τὸ δοξαζόμενον καὶ τὸ προσμένον ... τῇ ματαίῳ δόξῃ ; *Lettre à Hérod.* 51,5–7 (Arrighetti 47) : τὸ διημαρτημένον οὐκ ἂν ὑπῆρχεν, εἰ μὴ ... τῇ φανταστικῇ

jusqu'à soutenir une thèse contraire à la tradition.[3] Les Pères suivirent, dans l'ensemble, cette tradition qui leur permettait, entre autres, et au-delà de leur effort de fonder la foi sur la raison, de combattre les hérésies, n'hésitant pas à adopter à cet effet les 'tropes', ces arguments que les Sceptiques avaient utilisés pour démontrer l'impossibilité de la connaissance. Grégoire de Nysse, pour sa part, on le verra, use de la notion d'*épinoia* pour indiquer le résultat de l'activité d'une faculté supplémentaire qui intervient dans le processus de la pensée rationnelle qu'elle renforce ou qu'elle altère selon qu'elle dessert une intention bonne ou mauvaise, grâce au concours de l'imagination, entendue comme formatrice,[4] mais aussi comme déformante.

Le sens de la notion d'*épinoia* a varié au cours des siècles : il désigna à l'origine, et conformément à son étymologie, une pensée seconde venant confirmer, infirmer, corriger ou compléter une pensée première ;[5] puis, une simple représentation[6] ou même la finalité d'un dessein mental ;[7] enfin, la faculté d'inventer autant que son produit, l'invention.[8] C'est dans cette acception que Grégoire de Nysse emploie le terme d'*épinoia* et ses dérivés[9] dans le livre II du traité *Contre*

ἐπιβολῇ ; [2] 75,10 (Arrighetti 67) : τῶν παθῶν καὶ τῶν φαντασμάτων. Pour les Stoïciens, cf. Némésius (Morani 55,20–22) : φανταστικὸν διάκενον ἑλκυσμόν, ὡς ἐπὶ τῶν μεμηνότων ; Plut., *Placit. philos.* IV 12 (Diels 401) : φανταστικὸν . . . διάκενος ἑλκυσμός ; Cf. E. Moutsopoulos, *Le problème de l'imaginaire chez Plotin*, 2e éd., Paris 2000, 14–39.

[3] Cf. E. Moutsopoulos, *Le problème de l'imaginaire*, 40–68. cf. Idem, *Les structures de l'imaginaire dans la philosophie de Proclus*, Paris 1985, 97–176.

[4] Cf. E. Moutsopoulos, "L'imagination formatrice", *Annales d'Esthétique* 2 (1963) 64–71 ; cf. Idem, *Les structures*, 25 et la n. 57 ; 29 et la n. 2 ; 33 et la n. 23 ; 83 et la n. 67 ; 234.

[5] Cf. Soph. *Antig.* 389 : ψεύδει γὰρ ἡ ἐπίνοια τὴν γνώμην, Platon, *Phéd.* 99d : δεύτερον πλοῦν, *Polit.* 300b : δεύτερος πλοῦς, *Philèbe* 19c ; Cf. E. Moutsopoulos, "*Deuteros ploûs*, la mise en valeur d'une expression proverbiale", *Nautica Chronica* 5 (1998) 26.

[6] Cf. Thucid. III 16 ; Polybe I 20,12 ; V 110,10, où on rencontre déjà une allusion au rôle de l'imagination.

[7] Cf. Eurip., *Phén.* 408 : τίν' ἐπίνοιαν ἔσχεθες ; *Médée* 760 ; Aristoph., *Thesm.* 766 ; *Oiseaux* 405 ; 1073 ; *Plout.* 45.

[8] Cf. Aristoph., *Cav.* 90 : οἶνον σὺ τολμᾷς εἰς ἐπίνοιαν λοιδορεῖν ; ibid., 539 : ἐπίνοια ἀστειοτάτη ; 1202 : πῶς ἐπενόησας ἁρπάσαι ; 1322 : ὦ θαυμαστὰς ἐξευρίσκων ἐπινοίας ; *Guêpes* 346 : καινὴν ἐπίνοιαν ζητεῖν ; Xénoph., *Cyr.* 2, 3, 19 ; Théophr., *Des odeurs* 7.

[9] Grég. Nys., PG 45, 334c : τὸ ἐπινοεῖν ('inventer') auquel s'ajoutent ἐπινόησις ('invention' – acte d'inventer), ἐπινόημα ('invention' – résultat de l'acte d'inventer),

Eunomius, qui est une réponse aux objections du destinataire au livre I ; objections rejetées parce que provenant d'un esprit mal intentionné, et destinées à occulter la vérité du dogme. L'accusation fondamentale qu'il adresse à Eunomius, c'est d'avoir osé lui reprocher de soutenir que le nom de Dieu, qui désigne son essence, est une invention humaine.[10] Vraisemblablement, Eunomius a pu s'inspirer à ce sujet d'une source antérieure.[11] Néanmoins, la critique de Grégoire à la critique d'Eunomius constitue en soi la réfutation d'une invention au second degré, c'est-à-dire d'une invention déformante opposée à une invention explicative initiale. En traduction libre, l'argument de Grégoire est le suivant : "on ne saurait refuser l'être en soi à celui qui *est* par excellence et qui a su porter à l'existence tout ce qui existe".[12]

Grégoire accuse tout particulièrement Eunomius de recourir en l'occurrence à un sophisme du type connu comme "changement de critère" ; notamment, de faire dévier son propos à partir d'un adjectif (ἀγέννητος) qui désigne un état, vers un substantif (ἀγεννησία) dont le sens n'est même pas en cause.[13] En fait, Grégoire estime qu'Eunomius, voyant son enseignement anéanti, se réfugie dans une argumentation sophistique sans fondement, semant par là le doute et créant une confusion des termes,[14] dont il résulterait une confusion dans les esprits non versés dans la question.[15] Par un véritable artifice de raisonnement qui frôle la supercherie, il aurait tenté de

---

ἐπινοηματικός ('inventif'), ἐπινοήμων, ἐπινοητέον, ἐπινοητής, ἐπίνοια désignerait la 'pensée seconde, complémentaire'. Grégoire utilise également le terme d'ἐπίνοια dans un sens tout différent pour marquer une cohérence logique.

[10] En fait, ce qui est reproché à Eunomius, c'est une inconséquence logique qui frôle l'aberration (παραπληξία).

[11] Cf. déjà Lucien, *Assemblées des dieux* 13 : ὀνόματα ὑπὸ τῶν φιλοσόφων ἐπινοηθέντα.

[12] Cf. *CE* II 172 (GNO I 275,5–7) : τὸν ὄντως ὄντα καὶ τὰ ἄλλα πάντα ὅσα ἔστιν εἰς γένεσιν ἀγαγόντα, τοῦτον μὴ καθ' ὑπόστασιν ἰδίαν εἶναι λέγειν, ἀλλ' ἐπίνοιαν ὀνόματος αὐτὸν ἀποφαίνεσθαι ; Cf. E. Moutsopoulos, "Une archéologie chrétienne de l'être est-elle possible?", *Diotima* 9 (1981) 184–186.

[13] Cf. *CE* II 172–173 (GNO I 275,7–8) : τί μάτην σκιαμαχεῖ τοῖς οὐ τεθεῖσι μαχόμενος ; cf. *CE* II 176 (GNO I 276,4–5) : τῆς . . . καθ' ἡμῶν μάχης.

[14] Cf. *CE* II 173 (GNO I 275,8–14, notamment 13–14) : ἑκὼν ποιεῖται τῶν λεγομένων τὴν σύγχυσιν, ἀπὸ τοῦ ὀνόματος ἐπὶ τὰ πράγματα μεταβιβάζων τὴν μάχην, cf. *CE* II 173–174 (GNO I 275,17–18) : καταλιπὼν ἀνέλεγκτον τὸ ἡμέτερον (argument qui portait sur la qualité d' 'incréé' attribuée à Dieu) πρὸς ἕτερα μεταφέρει τὴν μάχην. Cf. Aristote, *Sec. anal.* III 7, 75a38 : μετάβασις εἰς ἄλλο γένος.

[15] *CE* II 173 (GNO I 275,14–15) : ὡς τοὺς ἀνεπιστάτους εὐκόλως διὰ τῆς τοιαύτης παρακρουσθῆναι συγχύσεως.

déformer le sens d'un simple artifice du langage. Selon la thèse constante de Grégoire, l'idée de Dieu est une donnée première, alors que l'attribut ἀγέννητος, 'non créé', auquel il renvoie, en est la conséquence logique[16] qui désigne une existence indépendante de toute cause,[17] étant elle-même cause première.[18] Le terme d'*épinoia* acquiert ici une signification nouvelle : il désigne le résultat d'une dérivation logique rigoureuse et non point l'invention sophistique d'un esprit qui fait appel à l'activité incontrôlée de l'imaginaire.[19]

Grégoire poursuit son interrogatoire contre les allégations répétées d'Eunomius qui aurait indûment inventé, tout en le lui imputant, le terme ἀγεννησία, dérivé du terme ἀγέννητος. En effet, cause première, Dieu est et demeure increé. Ce terme est appliqué à un fait indiscutable.[20] Or le terme ἀγεννησία, lui, non seulement ne se rapporte pas à un fait, dans la mesure où il ne désigne nullement une essence et une qualité,[21] mais, de plus, il est faussement attribué à Grégoire en tant que synonyme du terme de divinité. La différence sémantique subtile à saisir, est énorme, et l'objection de Grégoire se voit ainsi justifiée.[22] Son attitude implique qu'il se conforme (i) à une conception partiellement inspirée de la théologie négative en formation à son époque ; et (ii) à une tendance nominaliste, elle aussi en train de se former de son temps.[23] Dans cet ordre d'idées, le terme ἀγεννησία, inventé par Eunomius, n'indiquerait pas le fait que Dieu existe sans avoir été créé, mais se substituerait à son existence et le remplacerait au niveau du langage, s'identifiant ainsi avec lui,[24] ce qui serait absurde. L'emploi du terme ἀγεννησία serait simplement (et sans plus) un moyen de désigner *après coup* (ἐπίνοια au second degré) ce que désigne déjà ἀγέννητος (ἐπίνοια au premier degré) : le

[16] Cf. *CE* II 174 (GNO I 275,20) : ἐξ ἐπινοίας ἐφαρμόζειν τῇ φύσει, *CE* II 175 (GNO I 275,28–29) : ὡς ἐπινοουμένου.

[17] Cf. *CE* II 174 (GNO I 275,21) : τὸ ἄνευ αἰτίας αὐτὸν ὑφεστάναι σημαίνεται.

[18] Cf. *CE* II 175 (GNO I 275,29) : πρὸς ἔνδειξιν τοῦ ἀνάρχως εἶναι τὸ πρῶτον αἴτιον.

[19] Cf. E. Moutsopoulos, *Les structures*, 73–92 ; cf. idem, *Le problème de l'imagination*, 40–68.

[20] Cf. *CE* II 177 (GNO I 276,7–8) : τούτῳ καὶ ἡμεῖς συντιθέμεθα.

[21] Cf. *CE* II 177 (GNO I 276,7–8) : φασι . . . καὶ τὴν ἀγεννησίαν οὐσίαν εἶναι.

[22] Cf. *CE* II 177 (GNO I 276,9) : πρὸς τοῦτο παρ' ἡμῶν ἀντίρρησις.

[23] Le ps.-Denys, *Des noms divins*, s'en inspirera ouvertement. Cf. E. Moutsopoulos, "La fonction catalytique de l'ἐξαίφνης chez Denys", *Diotima* 23 (1995) 9–16.

[24] Cf. *CE* II 177 (GNO I 276,9–11) : ὄνομα γὰρ τοῦτό φαμεν ἐνδεικτικὸν εἶναι τοῦ ἀγεννήτως τὸν θεὸν ὑφεστάναι, οὐ τὴν ἀγεννησίαν εἶναι θεόν.

fait que Dieu existe par soi-même. L'argumentation vicieuse d'Eunomius aurait altéré (διακωμῳδεῖ) la signification 'normale' du terme d'ἐπίνοια, en se servant de sa propre *épinoia* (au sens d' 'invention') en donnant libre cours à son imagination inventive dans le but de déformer la portée du discours de Grégoire.[25] L'influence positive de l'imaginaire est rendue franchement négative dès lors que son intervention cesse d'être formatrice pour devenir déformante de pensées et de paroles.[26]

C'est pourtant cette acception d'une *épinoia* déformante qu'Eunomius est précisément censé reconnaître à ce terme que Grégoire fut, il est vrai, le premier à utiliser dans son texte précédent.[27] Lui-même accuse d'ailleurs, à son tour, Eunomius de dévaloriser l'importance de la signification positive de l'*épinoia*, en substituant frauduleusement au terme ἀγέννητος, simple désignation de convenance,[28] le terme ἀγεννησία. Le statut de l'*épinoia* en tant que cohérence logique se voit dégradé au point de devenir celui d'une vile altération découlant d'un procédé utilisé selon les circonstances. Une telle falsification du sens de l'*épinoia* serait elle-même aberrante. Et Grégoire de reprendre, d'énumérer et de formuler à son tour et à sa manière les vices reconnus à l'*épinoia* par Eunomius dont l'argumentation constitue une parfaite illustration des possibilités mises à la disposition d'une pensée perverse par ce mécanisme : analyse trop poussée, évaluation contre nature, allongement, compression ou intensification des mesures et assemblage excessif de données par ailleurs incompatibles, au point de s'avérer inutile et dépourvu de sens, sinon dangereux. . . .[29]

---

[25] Cf. *CE* II 179 (GNO I 276,21–22) : ἐν ταῖς περὶ τῆς ἐπινοίας διαστολαῖς αὐτὸ διακωμῳδεῖ τῆς ἐπινοίας τὸ ὄνομα.

[26] Cf. E. Moutsopoulos, "L'imagination formatrice", *loc. cit.* (cf. *supra* et la n. 4) ; cf. Idem, *La pensée et l'erreur*, Athènes 1961, 37–52 ; cf. Idem, *La connaissance et la science*, Athènes 1972, 134–141.

[27] Grégoire (*CE* II 179, GNO I 276,22–29) cite Eunomius textuellement : τῶν γὰρ οὕτω κατ' ἐπίνοιαν λεγομένων φησὶ τὰ μὲν κατὰ τὴν προφορὰν ἔχειν μόνην τὴν ὕπαρξιν ὡς τὰ μηδὲν σημαίνοντα, τὰ δὲ κατ' ἰδίαν διάνοιαν· καὶ τούτων τὰ μὲν κατὰ αὔξησιν ὡς ἐπὶ τῶν κολοσσιαίων, τὰ δὲ κατὰ μείωσιν ὡς ἐπὶ τῶν πυγμαίων, τὰ δὲ κατὰ πρόσθεσιν ὡς ἐπὶ τῶν πολυκεφάλων ἢ κατὰ σύνθεσιν ὡς ἐπὶ τῶν μιξοθήρων. L'énumération de ces procédés de falsification de la réalité, loin d'être exhaustive, n'est qu'indicative.

[28] Cf. *supra* et les nn. 6 et 17.

[29] Cf. *CE* II 180 (GNO I 276,29–277,7) : ὁρᾷς εἰς τί τὴν ἐπίνοιαν ἡμῖν ὁ σοφὸς διακερματίσας περαιτέρω τὴν δύναμιν αὐτῆς προελθεῖν οὐκ ἠξίωσεν. ἀσήμαντον εἶναί φησι τὴν ἐπίνοιαν, ἀδιανόητον, τὰ παρὰ φύσιν σοφιζομένην ἢ διακολοβοῦ-

Il s'agit, cela va de soi, d'une critique subjective à deux volets réunis tant qu'ils désignent deux attitudes de répulsion communes aux deux esprits, mais opposées lorsque Eunomius envisage la notion d'*épinoia* dans une acception uniquement négative, alors que Grégoire la considère comme positive ou négative selon l'intention qu'elle véhicule et qu'elle exprime. Chacun des points de vue fait partie d'une stratégie distincte : Eunomius a attaqué le premier en dénonçant les effets d'une *épinoia* néfaste ; Grégoire contre-attaque en reprenant d'abord à son compte les dénonciations d'Eunomius avant de signaler les avantages d'une *épinoia* envisagée selon un point de vue positif. Effectivement, souligne-t-il, l'inventivité de la raison assistée par l'imagination, et dont l'*épinoia* fait preuve, est rendue flagrante dans le domaine des sciences et des pratiques. L'*épinoia* serait notamment à l'origine de tout progrès en mathématiques, en géométrie, dans la science et la philosophie des nombres, en logique, en physique théorique, en météorologie, en philosophie (ontologie et théorie des idées) dans le domaine de la technologie (invention de machines) et, en général, dans tous les domaines supérieurs qui se rapportent au psychisme humain. La même *épinoia* serait à l'origine de tout progrès dans l'agriculture, la navigation, l'économie. Bref, c'est à l'*épinoia* de l'esprit que serait due la maîtrise de la nature, par ailleurs indomptable,[30] au profit de la vie humaine.[31]

À ce point, Grégoire estime avoir assez préparé le terrain pour être en mesure d'avancer une définition de la notion d'*épinoia* qui, d'après lui,[32] serait "un processus conduisant à partir d'une pensée première. . . , à la découverte de ce qui est encore inconnu, et préfigurant la connaissance de ce qui se situe au-delà" ;[33] définition pléthorique, certes, qui est loin de présenter la concision et l'élégance

σαν ἢ ὑπερτείνουσαν τὰ ὡρισμένα μέτρα τῆς φύσεως ἢ ἐξ ἑτεροφυῶν συντιθεῖσαν ἢ τερατευομένην ταῖς ἀλλοκότοις προσθήκαις. ἐν τούτοις καταπαίξας τοῦ τῆς ἐπινοίας ὀνόματος ἄχρηστον αὐτὴν καὶ ἀνόνητον τῷ βίῳ τὸ κατ' αὐτὸν ἀποδείκνυσιν. Proclus dissertera longuement sur les relations de la raison et de la νόησις en tant que sa lumière et que son instrument. Cf. *Comm. sur le Timée* (Diehl I 255,6–7), notamment à propos du long passage de Sévère (philosophe du IIe siècle de notre ère, éclectique qui se laissa influencer par le stoïcisme), *Commentaire sur le Timée*, conservé par Eusèbe, *Praepar. Evang.* XIII 17 (PG 21, 700–701), sous le titre d'"Extraits des livres de Sévère le platonicien sur l'âme".

30 Cf. *CE* II 180–181 (GNO I 277,7–19).

31 Cf. *CE* II 182 (GNO I 277,19–20).

32 Cf. *CE* II 182 (GNO I 277,20) : κατά γε τὸν ἐμὸν λόγον.

33 *CE* II 182 (GNO I 277,21–23) : ἔφοδος εὑρετικὴ τῶν ἀγνοουμένων, διὰ τῶν προσεχῶν τε καὶ ἀκολούθων τῇ πρώτῃ περὶ τὸ σπουδαζόμενον νοήσει τὸ ἐφεξῆς ἐξευρίσκουσα.

des définitions aristotéliciennes,[34] strictement élaborées sur le principe ἐκ γένους καὶ διαφορῶν,[35] mais qui présente l'avantage de mettre en valeur le caractère à la fois complémentaire et "supératif" de l'*épinoia* par rapport à la pensée principale à laquelle elle s'associe. Grégoire poursuit son argumentation en explicitant le contenu de sa définition, dans l'intention, bien entendu, de montrer l'importance du rôle de l'*épinoia* au cours du processus de l'intellection. Inconsciemment, selon toute vraisemblance, il décrit alors, un peu naïvement, il est vrai, la structure du syllogisme classique[36] que l'*épinoia* est supposée compléter.

À la suite de cette parenthèse d'ordre technique dans le déroulement de l'argumentation, l'auteur poursuit son éloge de l'*épinoia* et de son utilité pour l'humanité en postulant que toute conscience bienveillante conviendra des bienfaits de cette activité, promue, pour la cause, en faculté de l'esprit.[37] Commence alors une nouvelle énumération de ces bienfaits.[38] C'est l'occasion, pour l'auteur, de reconnaître à l'*épinoia* une dimension d'inventivité tout en lui accordant le mérite, très généralement formulé, d'être à tous égards utile à l'homme.[39] L'humanité devrait lui être reconnaissante de l'ensemble des innovations réalisées au cours des âges grâce à son impulsion et au déploiement de ses possibilités.[40]

---

[34] Cf. par exemple la définition de l'induction (ἐπαγωγή), Arist., *Top.* I 12, 105a13 : ἡ ἀπὸ τῶν καθ' ἕκαστα ἐπὶ τὸ καθόλου ἔφοδος, dont la définition grégorienne reflète, à n'en pas douter, le souvenir. En effet outre le terme ἔφοδος, commun aux deux définitions, le terme προσεχῶν renvoie directement à l'expression προσεχὲς γένος, appliquée à l'un des éléments structuraux de la définition, telle qu'Aristote la conçoit.

[35] Cf. Arist., *Top.* I 8, 103b15 : ὁ ὁρισμὸς ἐκ γένους καὶ διαφορῶν ἐστιν, cf. *ibid.*, VI 3, 141a28 ; VI 4, 141b.

[36] Cf. *CE* II 182 (GNO I 277,23–26) : νοήσαντες γάρ τι περὶ τοῦ ζητουμένου τῇ ἀρχῇ τοῦ ληφθέντος (prémisses, majeure), διὰ τῶν ἐφευρισκομένων νοημάτων συναρμόζοντες τὸ ἀκόλουθον εἰς τὸ πέρας τῶν σπουδαζομένων τὴν ἐγχείρησιν ἄγομεν (conclusion).

[37] Cf. *CE* II 183 (GNO I 277,28–29) : ἔξεστι . . . τῷ μὴ φιλονείκως ἔχοντι πρὸς τὴν ἀλήθειαν κατιδεῖν . . .

[38] Cf. *CE* II 183 (GNO I 277,25–26) : καὶ τί μοι τὰ μείζω καὶ ὑψηλότερα τῶν τῆς ἐπινοίας κατορθωμάτων ἀπαριθμεῖσθαι.

[39] Cf. *CE* II 183 (GNO I 277,29–30) : τὰ ἄλλα πάντα, ὅσα βιωφελῆ τε καὶ χρήσιμα τῇ ζωῇ τῶν ἀνθρώπων.

[40] Cf. *CE* II 183 (GNO I 277,31) : ὁ χρόνος ἐφεῦρεν. Cette expression est manifestement inadéquate. En réalité, ce n'est pas le temps qui invente, mais bien l'esprit humain. On serait tenté de reconnaître ici un souvenir de Xénophane, fr. B18 (Diels – Kranz I 133,14 = Stobée, *Ecl.* I 8,2 ; *Flor.* 29,41) : χρόνωι ζητοῦντες ἐφευρίσκουσιν ἄμεινον.

Grégoire frôle ici le domaine de la philosophie de l'histoire dont il adopte cependant un modèle totalement différent des modèles classiques hérités aussi bien de l'antiquité grecque que de la tradition paléotestamentaire : le premier, de structure cyclique ;[41] le second, comme ligne droite descendante que le christianisme transformera en ligne brisée.[42] De toute évidence, il se rend à la conception xénophanienne du progrès, qui, vers la fin du Moyen Âge, sera reprise et mise en valeur successivement par Joachim de Flores et Gerardo di Borgo San Donnino.[43] Pour eux, l'histoire ne serait qu'un progrès discontinu à trois étapes : celles du Père (Ancien Testament), du Fils (Nouveau Testament) et de l'Esprit, dont le point de départ se situerait en l'an 1260. Ce progressisme sera plus tard rénové par Condorcet[44] et, finalement, par Auguste Comte (règle 'des trois états').[45] Le progressisme grégorien semble n'attribuer la marche de l'histoire ni à l'humanité elle-même ni à la providence divine, mais à la dynamique du temps qu'il personnifie en quelque sorte, et ce dans un cadre plutôt continuiste, à l'encontre du cadre kairique discontinuiste envisagé par les penseurs médiévaux et modernes qui viennent d'être cités.[46]

Si la providence divine doit nécessairement apparaître dans ce contexte, elle le fait moyennant la faculté de l'*épinoia* dont le genre humain a été gratifié (χαρισάμενος).[47] À ce point, se rendant compte du danger qui le guette, de dévier du dogme plus ou moins constitué de son temps, Grégoire se rachète en s'appuyant sur un passage de l'Écriture,[48] où Dieu révèle aux hommes qu'il aurait (εἴη) enseigné (ἐπιστήσας), spécialement aux femmes, le savoir du tissage et de la décoration.[49] On conviendra, bien entendu, et à condition de

[41] Cf. V. Goldschmidt, *Le système stoïcien et l'idée de temps*, Paris 1953, 135 et suiv.

[42] Cf. E. Moutsopoulos, *L'itinéraire de l'esprit*, t. 3, *Les valeurs*, Athènes 1977, 268–292.

[43] Cf. *ibid.*, 285–287.

[44] Cf. *ibid.*, 286.

[45] Cf. A. Comte, *Cours de philosophie positive*, 6 vols, Paris 1830–1836. Cf. G. Vlachos, "Des prophéties anciennes aux prophéties modernes", in : *L'avenir, Actes du XXIe Congrès de l'ASPLF (Athènes 1986)*, Paris 1987, 55–72.

[46] Cf. E. Moutsopoulos, *Philosophie de la kairicité*, Athènes 1985, 188–189 ; Idem, "Kairos et histoire", *Actes de l'Adacémie d'Athènes* 59 (1984) 532–553.

[47] Cf. *CE* II 183 (GNO I 277,32–278,3) : καί μοι δοκεῖ πάντων τῶν κατὰ τὴν ζωὴν ταύτην ἐνεργουμένων ἐν ἡμῖν ἀγαθῶν τῶν ταῖς ψυχαῖς ἡμῶν παρὰ τῆς θείας προμηθείας ἐνυπαρχόντων τὴν ἐπίνοιάν τις προτιμοτέραν κρίνων μὴ ἂν τῆς πρεπούσης κρίσεως διαψευσθῆναι.

[48] Cf. *Jb* 38,36 (LXX) : τίς δὲ ἔδωκεν γυναιξὶν ὑφάσματος σοφίαν ἢ ποικιλτικὴν ἐπιστήμην, cf. *CE* II 184 (GNO I 278,4–7). Cf. *infra*, et la note suivante 49.

[49] Cf. *CE* II 184 (GNO I 278,7–9) : ὅτι αὐτὸς εἴη ὁ ταῖς τέχναις ἐπιστήσας τὸν ἄνθρωπον καὶ γυναιξὶ χαρισάμενος ὑφαντικήν τε καὶ ποικιλτικὴν ἐπιστήμην.

faire preuve de bonne foi,[50] qu'un tel enseignement ne fut pas réalisé sur le terrain, comme cela se passe au niveau de la scolarité, c'est-à-dire en présence du maître.[51] Néanmoins, étant donné que Dieu affirme avoir transmis aux hommes ces compétences,[52] on en conclura que ce qu'ils tiennent surtout de lui, c'est la faculté d'inventer[53] et que par conséquent, c'est à lui que toute invention et tout exploit sont raisonnablement attribuables.[54]

Il faut tenir compte du caractère polémique du texte grégorien pour comprendre le cheminement irrégulier et discontinu de sa pensée : il s'agit d'une réponse à une accusation injuste, et il est plus ou moins naturel que la rédaction du texte ait été accomplie en état de verve. Donc, soit l'auteur se laisse momentanément 'égarer', quitte à se reprendre, comme dans le cas déjà mentionné où il attribue le progrès de l'humanité au temps, alors qu'il s'agit de le situer *dans* le temps,[55] soit il procède par à-coups, comme dans l'énumération des bienfaits de l'*épinoia*. C'est donc pour la troisième fois qu'après une mise au point de la question de la paternité de l'*épinoia*, se rendant compte de ses omissions, il reprend cette énumération pour l'étendre à la médecine[56] à laquelle il attribue le reste des bienfaits dont jouit l'humanité, considérés à présent dans leur ensemble, pour que le compte soit exhaustif au possible.[57] Afin de relier cette adjonction

---

Faire remonter les origines de l'art du tissage à une inspiration divine est une tradition bien ancienne. Cf. E. Moutsopoulos, "Un instrument divin : la navette, de Platon à Proclus", *Kernos* 10 (1997) 241–247.

[50] Cf. *CE* II 184 (GNO I 278,12–13).

[51] Cf. *CE* II 184 (GNO I 278,9–12) : οὐκ ἐνεργείᾳ τινὶ τὰς τοιαύτας τέχνας ἡμᾶς ἐδιδάξατο αὐτὸς προκαθήμενος τῆς ἐργασίας, καθάπερ ἐν τοῖς σωματικῶς διδασκομένοις ἔστιν ἰδεῖν, cf. *CE* II 185 (GNO I 278,16) : αὐτὸς ἡμᾶς πρὸς τὰς τέχνας προήγαγε.

[52] Cf. *CE* II 185 (GNO I 278,13–14) : ἀλλὰ μὴν εἴρηται παρ' αὐτοῦ γεγενῆσθαι ἡμῖν τῶν τοιούτων τεχνῶν ἡ καθήγησις. Cf. *supra*, et la n. 49.

[53] Cf. *CE* II 185 (GNO I 278,15–16) : ὁ δοὺς τῇ φύσει (humaine) τὴν ἐπινοητικὴν καὶ εὑρετικὴν τῶν ζητουμένων δύναμιν.

[54] Cf. *CE* II 185 (GNO I 278,17–18) : τῷ τῆς αἰτίας λόγῳ πᾶν τὸ εὑρισκόμενόν τε καὶ κατορθούμενον εἰς τὸν ἀρχηγὸν (donateur) τῆς δυνάμεως ταύτης ἐπαναφέρεται.

[55] Cf. *supra*, et la note 46.

[56] Cf. *CE* II 185 (GNO I 278,19) : οὕτω καὶ τὴν ἰατρικὴν ὁ βίος εὕρατο. On notera ici le passage (provisoire) de l'*esprit* humain à la *vie* humaine.

[57] Cf. *CE* II 186 (GNO I 278,20–23) : καὶ πᾶν ὅτιπέρ ἐστι κατὰ τὴν ἀνθρωπίνην ζωὴν ἐξευρημένον κατ' εἰρήνην καὶ πόλεμον πρός τι τῶν χρησίμων ἐπιτηδείως ἔχον.

à ce qui précède, Grégoire affirme, une fois de plus, que l'*épinoia* procède du divin.[58]

La partie démonstrative de l'argumentation se termine ici. Ce qui suit n'est que l'application des conclusions tirées de l'effort de l'auteur de combattre et d'invalider l'idée avancée par Eunomius selon qui, rappelons-le, il est faux d'attribuer à Dieu la qualité d'ἀγεννησία, qualité pourtant littéralement inventée *ad hoc* par lui-même en vue de réfuter la thèse initiale de Grégoire qui n'avait utilisé que le terme ἀγέννητος en le considérant comme une *épinoia*, une invention après coup, au sens d'une qualification noétique complétant l'idée de Dieu. Grégoire passe alors à l'attaque. On se rappellera qu'il accorde au terme d'*épinoia* deux acceptions : une positive, applicable à sa propre thèse, et qu'il défend tout au long de son argumentation ; et une négative, qu'il applique, à titre d'exemple, à l'usage trompeur du terme d'ἀγεννησία, produit de l'inventivité d'un esprit malveillant, celui de son adversaire.

D'entrée de jeu, la stratégie[59] de Grégoire consistait, dans l'ensemble, à discréditer Eunomius et sa thèse. Désormais, il se propose de le confondre en l'attaquant dans les détails et commence par feindre d'accepter en principe que l'*épinoia* contribue à formuler et à rationaliser des créations fabuleuses (μυθώδη) et des monstruosités mensongères.[60] Ses ressources, affirme-t-il toutefois, sont susceptibles d'être utilisées en bien et en mal, comme dans le cas de la médecine où un médicament peut être également administré comme poison ; de la navigation où le capitaine, au lieu de sauver son navire, le fait échouer pour que périssent les passagers ; en peinture où l'artiste est capable de reproduire les formes les plus belles aussi bien que les plus laides ;[61] en orthopédie enfin, où le rebouteux qui remet en place un membre désarticulé peut tout aussi bien en tordre un

---

[58] Cf. *CE* II 186 (GNO I 278,23–26) : οὐδαμόθεν ἡμῖν ἔσχε τὴν πάροδον, ἀλλὰ τοῦ νοῦ τὰ καθ' ἕκαστον ἡμῖν καταλλήλως νοοῦντος καὶ ἐφευρίσκοντος· νοῦς δὲ, (tout comme l') ἐπίνοια, ἔργον θεοῦ· οὐκοῦν ἐκ θεοῦ πάντα ὅσα διὰ τοῦ νοῦ ἡμῖν πεπόρισται.

[59] Cf. *CE* II 187 (GNO I 278,29–279,1) : τὸν ἡμέτερον σκοπόν.

[60] Cf. *CE* II 187 (GNO I 278,27–28): . . . τὰ μυθώδη πλάσματα καὶ τὰ ψευδῆ τερατεύματα παρὰ τῆς ἐπινοίας λογοποιεῖσθαι καὶ πλάσσεσθαι . . .

[61] Cf. toutefois E. Moutsopoulos, *Les catégories esthétiques. Introduction à une axiologie de l'objet esthétique*, 2e éd., Athènes 1996, 27–28, *à propos* de la laideur. Cf. Idem, "La laideur et ses droits dans le domaine des arts", in : V. Cauchy (éd.), *Philosophie et Culture, Actes du XVIIe Congrès Mondial de Philosophie (1983)*, Montréal 1988, 705–709.

autre encore valide.[62] Bref,[63] tout le monde serait d'accord sur le fait qu'un art se prête à un bon et à un mauvais usage.[64]

Il en serait de même de l'*épinoia*, faculté dont Dieu nous aurait armés pour faire le bien, mais qui, souvent, et par abus, dessert des machinations condamnables, si elle ne les crée.[65] Ce n'est donc pas parce qu'elle est susceptible d'inventer des faussetés (ψευδῆ) et des données inexistantes (ἀνύπαρκτα) qu'elle sera jugée incapable de scruter et de proposer des vérités.[66] C'est pourquoi on doit lui être reconnaissant de l'éventualité même de son bon usage.[67] Tout au plus, les distortions de la régularité et de la symétrie qu'elle occasionne, si elles ne visent pas au mal, sont-elles propres à provoquer le rire et le plaisir esthétique,[68] tout en confirmant ses potentialités en direction du bien.[69] Ce n'est que par abus qu'une faculté destinée à servir les bonnes intentions (προαιρετική, προαίρεσις) s'écarte du droit chemin.[70] Par conséquent, son usage vicieux ne suffit pas à la condamner dans l'ensemble.[71]

Grégoire entame enfin la conclusion générale de son argumentation en en rappelant le point de départ : cause première, Dieu, est-il soumis à quelque principe ou non (ἄναρχος)?[72] L'entendement s'opposant à concevoir une cause première dépendante, force était d'inventer (ἐπενοήσαμεν) un attribut qualifiant cette cause, cet être (ὄντα), qui existe par lui-même (ἀνάρχως) et sans avoir été créé (ἀγεννήτως), en considérant non ce que cet être est, mais ce qu'il n'est pas,[73] ainsi qu'on le ferait à propos d'une plante dont on se

---

[62] Cf. *CE* II 187–188 (GNO I 279,4–11).

[63] Cf. *CE* II 189 (GNO I 279,15–16).

[64] Cf. *CE* II 189 (GNO I 279,16–19).

[65] Cf. *CE* II 189 (GNO I 279,21–23) : κατακεχρημένων δέ τινων τῇ ἐφευρετικῇ δυνάμει διάκονον πολλάκις καὶ συνεργὸν γίνεσθαι τῶν ἀνωφελῶν εὑρημάτων.

[66] Cf. *CE* II 190 (GNO I 279,23–25).

[67] Cf. *CE* II 190 (GNO I 279).

[68] Cf. *CE* II 190 (GNO I 279,26–280,4). Grégoire se réfère ici à Aristote, *Poét.* 5, 1449a33 (à propos du risible) : ἁμάρτημά τι καὶ αἶσχος ἀνώδυνον καὶ οὐ φθαρτικόν. Cf. E. Moutsopoulos, "D'une application de la catégorie esthétique du visible : la catégorie du comique d'après Aristote", in : *IVth International Conference on Aristotle's Poetics and Rhetoric (2001)*, Athens 2004, 230–239.

[69] Cf. *CE* II 191 (GNO I 280,4–6).

[70] Cf. *CE* II 191 (GNO I 280,6–16).

[71] Cf. *CE* II 191 (GNO I 280,16–21).

[72] Cf. *CE* II 192 (GNO I 280,23–25).

[73] Cf. *CE* II 192 (GNO I 280,28–29) : οὐ τί ἐστιν, ἀλλὰ τί οὐκ ἔστι διὰ τοῦ ὀνόματος ἐνδεικνύμενοι. Sur la théologie négative, cf. J. Whittaker, "Ἄρρητος καὶ ἀκατονόμαστος, in : H.-D. Blume – F. Mann (eds.), *Platonismus und Christentum. FS Heinrich Dörrie*, Münster 1983, 109–125.

demanderait si elle a été plantée ou si elle a poussé d'elle-même (αὐτοφυές, ἀφύτευτον). On conçoit le mode d'existence de la plante αὐτοφυής en évoquant le fait qu'elle ne fut pas plantée. En la désignant d'une manière plutôt que d'une autre on demeure dans le vrai ; mais, ce faisant, on n'est pas plus avancé quant à son essence (platane ou vigne). Ayant saisi le sens de l'exemple, on peut passer à la réalité qu'il figure : Dieu. Ce passage est censé critique voire *kairique* (καιρός).[74] Désigner la cause première (τὸ πρῶτον αἴτιον), Dieu, d'être non créé (ἀγεννήτως ὄντα Θεόν) revient à lui attribuer une qualité sous forme de nom 'inventé',[75] sans réussir pour autant à concevoir ce qu'est cette essence qui existe sans avoir été créée.[76] Notre raison demeure limitée pour pouvoir saisir l'insaisissable, même en se servant de son inventivité.[77] Tout au plus, l'artifice inventé permet-il une consolidation de nos connaissances déjà acquises.

Faculté à double tranchant, l'*épinoia* est utile quand elle sert une bonne intention dans la vie pratique ; mais, s'agissant de choses divines, elle est impuissante à fournir quoi que ce soit d'autre que des moyens appropriés en vue d'une meilleure compréhension de ce que l'on en sait déjà. Eunomius aurait déformé (σφετερίζεται) sans vergogne (ἐπαισχύνεται)[78] l'utilisation du terme d'*épinoia* par Grégoire, en inventant littéralement, à partir de l'adjectif ἀγέννητος, le substantif ἀγεννησία,[79] et en insinuant par là que Grégoire aurait identifié le sens de ce terme avec la divinité. Par un détour astucieusement accompli, Grégoire arrive à ses fins : confondre et discréditer Eunomius. En même temps il élabore une théorie de l'*épinoia*, dont le bien-fondé et l'originalité sont évidents. L'analyse de son texte correspondant permet de constater son rationalisme qu'on qualifiera de critique dans la mesure où il ne saurait s'apparenter à quelque dogmatisme : le suprarationnel qui caractérise le divin ne peut être atteint par la

[74] Cf. *CE* II 194 (GNO I 281,8–10) : εἰ δὴ νενόηται τὸ ὑπόδειγμα, *καιρὸς* (nous soulignons) ἂν εἴη μεταβιβάσαι τὸν λόγον ἐπὶ τὸ πρᾶγμα οὗ τὸ ὑπόδειγμα. Cf. E. Moutsopoulos, "Sur une connotation spatiale de la notion de kairos chez Platon, Aristote et Proclus", *Philosophia* 31 (2001) 135–138.

[75] Cf. *CE* II 194 (GNO I 281,11–12) : τὸν οὖν ἀγεννήτως ὄντα θεὸν εἰς ὀνόματος τύπον τὴν ἔννοιαν ταύτην παράγοντες ἀγέννητον ὠνομάσαμεν.

[76] Cf. *CE* II 194 (GNO I 281,15–17) : αὐτὴ δὲ ἡ οὐσία ἡ ἀγεννήτως οὖσα τίς κατὰ τὴν ἰδίαν φύσιν ἐστίν, οὐδὲν ἐκ τῆς ἐπωνυμίας ταύτης πρὸς τὸ κατιδεῖν ὡδηγήθημεν.

[77] Cf. *CE* II 195 (GNO I 281,17–21).

[78] Cf. *CE* II 196 (GNO I 281,25–26).

[79] Cf. *supra*, et la n. 24.

raison qui ne fait alors que déployer ses possibilités non pour en savoir davantage sur lui, mais pour le mieux comprendre. En en appelant à des données de l'imaginaire, l'*épinoia*, faculté auxiliaire mobilisée dans de tels cas difficiles, se concrétise alors *en* ces données ; autrement dit, *en* images nominatives, toujours négativement formulées, qui, en l'occurrence, se présentent sous l'aspect de "noms divins".

LIMITES DU LANGAGE, LIMITES DU MONDE DANS LE *CONTRE EUNOME* II DE GRÉGOIRE DE NYSSE

Georges Arabatzis

Avant de passer à l'analyse du *CE* II, citons ce passage du IIIe livre où Grégoire s'interroge sur ce qu'Eunome dit à propos du Fils Unique, qu' "Il n'habite pas (οἰκειοῦται) cette valeur, c'est-à-dire la valeur de s'appeler l'être". Grégoire s'indigne :

> Quelle philosophie est celle-ci, bien à côté du Logos ! . . . Qui parmi les hommes du passé, soit des Grecs soit des philosophes barbares,[1] qui parmi les nôtres qui, à travers le temps, ont-ils dénommé valeur ce qui est ? Il est habituel à ceux qui s'occupent du Logos de parler de ce qu'ils voient comme ce qui se-dresse-en-soi-même (ὑποστάσει)[2] en utilisant le nom de l'être ; c'est par l'être qu'on nomme ce qui est . . . Si l'on admet le nom de valeur pour l'être, alors Celui-qui-est n'habite-t-Il pas l'être ? . . . Pourquoi tu dis qu'Il n'habite pas l'être ? Dire qu'Il n'est pas chez Lui dans l'être signifie qu'Il est étranger à l'être. Dire pour quelqu'un qu'il n'est pas chez lui cela veut dire qu'il est autre et, ainsi, l'entreprise métaphysique [d'Eunome] (ἡ τῶν σημαινομένων ἀντιδιαίρεσις) devient visible : le demeurant chez lui n'est pas autre et l'autre n'est pas chez lui. Celui qui ne demeure pas dans l'être est tout autre que l'être. Et celui qui est autre que l'être n'est pas demeurant de l'être. Ce déterminisme du non-lieu vient de son induction (ἐπήγαγεν) selon laquelle l'essence qui s'empare aussi de cette demeure attire dans l'en-soi le concept de l'être.[3]

[1] Cf. Diogène Laërce, *Vie et doctrines des philosophes illustres*, Prologue 1 (Marcovich I 5); cf., aussi, Clément d'Alexandrie, *Strom.* I 71 (GCS 76, 45–46).

[2] Cf. M. Heidegger, "Comment se détermine la φύσις", in: M. Heidegger, *Questions I et II*, Paris 1968, 517 : "Si les Grecs saisissent l'être tantôt comme se-dresser-en-soi-même, ὑπόστασις-*substantia*, tantôt comme s'étendre-devant, ὑποκείμενον-*subjectum*, les deux ont tout autant de poids parce que dans les deux cas leur regard envisage l'Un et Unique : le venir depuis soi-même à l'être, l'entrée dans la présence."

[3] *CE* III/VIII 59–62 (GNO II 261,5–262,3): ὅτι οὐκ οἰκειοῦται ταύτην τὴν ἀξίαν. ἀξίαν γὰρ ὀνομάζει τὴν τοῦ ὄντος προσηγορίαν. ὢ παραλόγου φιλοσοφίας. τίς τῶν πώποτε γεγονότων ἀνθρώπων εἴτε παρ' Ἕλλησιν εἴτε παρὰ τῇ βαρβαρικῇ φιλοσοφίᾳ, τίς τῶν καθ' ἡμᾶς, τίς τῶν ἐν παντὶ τῷ χρόνῳ ἀξίαν ὄνομα τῷ ὄντι ἔθετο; πᾶν γὰρ

Ce passage, traduit de telle manière, présente des similitudes frappantes avec la pensée de Heidegger. L'être n'est pas une valeur pour Grégoire comme le pensera aussi Heidegger contre le Néokantisme. Pour Heidegger, l'être se comprend par rapport à une demeure ou, autrement dit, on ne comprend pas l'être, on l'habite. Très proche semble être ici l'intuition de Grégoire. L'affinité entre les deux pensées nous a même conduit à adopter la manière 'barbare' de Heidegger dans ses propres traductions des textes grecs.[4] Ainsi, on associe Grégoire aux préoccupations ontologiques de notre temps,[5] où le langage joue un rôle de première importance.

La théorie grégorienne du langage est construite sur la base de la réfutation d'Eunome. Il est vrai que la théorie du langage d'Eunome, si l'on juge d'après ce que Grégoire dit, semble être de nature profondément métaphysique : dans le *CE* II, on voit qu'Eunome avance sans ambiguïté la thèse de la dépendance directe des noms de la volonté divine. Suivant ce principe, il poursuit son entreprise de clarification catégorielle des attributs divins et surtout du concept d'inengendré (ἀγέννητον). Aristote voyait dans la génération de père en fils un paradigme de continuité d'existence singulière, évitant, ainsi, tout recours à quelconque participation à une idée, thèse soutenue par Platon. Aristote niait encore toute notion de contradiction directe sans la médiation d'un sujet qui soutiendrait le passage d'un

τὸ ἐν ὑποστάσει θεωρούμενον ἡ κοινὴ τῶν λόγῳ κεχρημένων συνήθεια *εἶναι* λέγει. παρὰ δὲ τὸ εἶναι ἡ τοῦ ὄντος ἐπωνυμία παρεσχημάτισται. (. . .) δεδόσθω τὸ ὂν ἀξίαν κατονομάζεσθαι. τί οὖν ὁ ὢν οὐκ οἰκειοῦται τὸ εἶναι; (. . .) οὐκοῦν μὴ εἶναι λέγεις τὸν τὸ εἶναι μὴ οἰκειούμενον; τὸ γὰρ μὴ οἰκειοῦσθαι τῷ ἀλλοτριοῦσθαι ταὐτὸν σημαίνει, καὶ πρόδηλος ἡ τῶν σημαινομένων ἀντιδιαίρεσις. τό τε γὰρ οἰκεῖον οὐκ ἀλλότριον καὶ τὸ ἀλλότριον οὐκ οἰκεῖον. ὁ οὖν μὴ οἰκειούμενος τὸ εἶναι ἠλλοτρίωται πάντως τοῦ εἶναι. ὁ δὲ τοῦ εἶναι ἀλλότριος ἐν τῷ εἶναι οὐκ ἔστιν. ἀλλὰ τὴν ἀνάγκην τῆς ἀτοπίας ταύτης ἐπήγαγεν εἰπὼν τῆς καὶ τούτου κυριευούσης οὐσίας πρὸς ἑαυτὴν ἑλκούσης τὴν τοῦ ὄντος ἔννοιαν.

[4] Cf. *ibid*, la note du traducteur sur le style heideggerien de traduire (490–491, note 1): "la traduction en français de la traduction par Heidegger . . . présente un côté abrupt et pour tout dire *barbare* [c'est moi qui souligne]. Comme le dit Heidegger, ce type de traduction est en fait le contraire de ce qu'on entend habituellement par traduire. Il ne se justifie que s'il permet d'aller jusqu'à ce qui est dit dans l'autre langue". Cf. également, Th. W. Adorno, *Jargon der Eigentlichkeit. Zur deutschen Ideologie*, Frankfurt am Main 1964.

[5] Cf. Jean Daniélou, *L'être et le temps chez Grégoire de Nysse*, Leiden 1970, Introduction, VIII–IX: "A côté d'une philosophie de l'être, la pensée de Grégoire est une philosophie du temps. Et c'est peut-être l'union de ces deux traits, *Zeit und Sein*, qui est le trait fondamental de sa synthèse".

attribut à son contraire.[6] La combinaison de ces deux présuppositions autour de l'attribut d'inengendré servait de cadre conceptuel aux ambitions ariennes d'Eunome. À plusieurs reprises Grégoire blâme l'aristotélisme d'Eunome. On devrait, pourtant, clarifier ce qu' 'aristotélisme' veut dire dans ce contexte. Il semblerait que c'est au parallélisme logico-grammatical d'Aristote[7] – très contesté par la logique moderne – que répond le parallélisme théologico-grammatical promu par Eunome ; dans le langage philosophique moderne on parlerait d' 'onto-théologie'.[8] Et comme dans le cas d'Aristote on essaie de faire à partir des noms des valeurs logiques, de même chez Eunome on essaie de faire à partir des noms des valeurs théologiques. Dans cette perspective, la réfutation grégorienne pourrait même prendre une allure déconstructive.[9]

Contre ce parallélisme se dresse la critique grégorienne de la métaphysique eunoméenne. Il faudrait, pourtant, essayer de voir plus clairement les étapes de la réflexion de Grégoire. Pour ce dernier, les limites du langage humain sont fixées par les limites du monde que l'intellect humain peut concevoir. Si ce monde inférieur qui est objet de nos sens se trouve, déjà, au-delà des limites de notre compréhension, comment alors pourra-t-on comprendre Celui qui, par sa volonté, a composé le tout ?[10] Les noms ne sont qu'une sorte d'ombres des choses ;[11] en étudiant les mots et les noms, on ne fait que quêter les traces de la piété ;[12] il n'y a pas de lien direct entre les mots et Dieu. Les noms sont inventés par nous, pour saisir l'être ;[13] la réalité est là, avant l'invention des noms. Eunome a essayé de montrer que le nom illustre l'essence ; cela est selon lui le pouvoir du nom.[14] Pour Grégoire, le langage est en rapport avec le divin

[6] Cf. J.-P. Dumont, *Introduction à la méthode d'Aristote*, Paris 1986, chap. II: Ce quelque chose qui est sujet, 27–39.

[7] Cf. S. M. Th. Larkin, C.S.J., *Language in the Philosophy of Aristotle*, The Hague – Paris 1971, 21ss.

[8] C'est sur ce point que l'effort d'Eunome peut se dire métaphysique: "la métaphysique est une onto-théologie", M. Heidegger, "Identité et différence", in : M. Heidegger, *Questions* I et II, 289.

[9] Cf. M. Laird, "Whereof We Speak: Gregory of Nyssa, Jean-Luc Marion and the Current Apophatic Rage", *Heythrop Journal* 42 (2001) 1–12, où plus de références bibliographiques.

[10] Cf. *CE* II 79 (GNO I 250,3–6).

[11] Cf. *CE* II 150 (GNO I 269,13).

[12] Cf. *CE* II 158 (GNO I 270,31–271,1).

[13] Cf. *CE* II 167 (GNO I 273,25f).

[14] Cf. *CE* II 174 (GNO I 275,23f).

dans la mesure où l'intellect d'invention langagière est une œuvre de Dieu.[15] Le pouvoir de l'intellect à produire des fictions est un indice de la grandeur du pouvoir inventif au sujet des noms.[16] La physiologie même du discours parlé chez l'homme prouve l'impossibilité de l'attribuer à Dieu et de dire que le Très Haut s'exprime en parlant.[17] Dire que la création raconte la grandeur divine n'est qu'une métaphore ;[18] le discours humain, tout autre que le Logos véritable, n'existait pas dès le commencement mais il fut créé en même temps que la nature humaine.[19] Parler apophatiquement, quand, par exemple, on profère le terme 'inengendré', est une façon de se taire à propos des choses dont on ne peut pas se prononcer. La négation d'une affirmation n'est pas une affirmation, c'est la réfutation de se prononcer affirmativement. Les attributs de Dieu, même s'ils sont singuliers, ne peuvent être contradictoires entre eux.[20] L'effort de mettre de l'ordre catégoriel aux attributs négatifs de Dieu est, par conséquent, une entreprise dénuée d'importance.

Le monde d'ici-bas, le monde naturel, à la différence du monde intelligible et supra-cosmique, est le monde des contradictions d'où sont nés les noms pour signifier les différences des éléments comme, par exemple, la terre, la ξηρά, est le contraire de l'eau.[21] Ici, Grégoire se montre également ou, peut-être, aristotélicien encore plus fin qu'Eunome ; de même, quand il résume avec justesse la théorie d'Aristote sur le bonheur lequel ne connaît pas de distinction entre actuel et potentiel.[22] Les divers noms, selon Grégoire, ne sont que les expressions du mouvement de notre intellect.[23] Le monde naturel, finalement, est la limite de notre usage des noms qui ne sont que les inventions de la faculté discursive, mise à notre disposition par Dieu ;[24] la faculté onomatopoétique des hommes n'est pas étrangère à leur faculté cognitive. Très importante est, ici, la distinction faite par Grégoire entre πορίζειν et προσαγορεύειν, c'est-à-dire entre suppléer

---

[15] Cf. *CE* II 185 (GNO I 278,14f).
[16] Cf. *CE* II 190 (GNO I 279,23–280,6).
[17] Cf. *CE* II 200 (GNO I 283,13f).
[18] Cf. *CE* II 223 (GNO I 290,16–22).
[19] Cf. *CE* II 236 (GNO I 295,3f).
[20] Cf. *CE* II 478f (GNO I 365,22–366,8).
[21] Cf. *CE* II 274 (GNO I 307,1–4).
[22] Cf. *CE* II 230 (GNO I 293,1–6).
[23] Cf. *CE* II 391 (GNO I 340,21f).
[24] Cf. *CE* II 395 (GNO I 341,22–342,3).

à une aporie et se prononcer à propos de l'être.[25] Le terme même de πορίζειν est d'origine platonico-aristotélicienne, élaboré notamment dans le *Banquet*[26] et dans la méthodologie aristotélicienne qui distingue entre méthode scientifique qui doit répondre à une aporie, méthode dialectique qui traite d'une problématique et méthode rhétorique qui concerne les questions de croyance. On connaît, par ailleurs, que les pensées hellénistique et romaine ont évacué l'aspect purement scientifique de l'aristotélisme et ont tenté d'effectuer la superposition entre dialectique et rhétorique.[27]

Pour Eunome, les noms ont de la valeur et leur valeur est celle des choses qu'ils dénomment ; elle n'est aucunement la valeur du pouvoir des fabricants de noms.[28] Au niveau de l'analyse de la langue, cela voulait dire qu'Eunome est partisan d'une théorie de dénomination rigide, opposé à l'idée que les noms ne sont que des descriptions abrégées comme c'est la position de Grégoire. Ainsi, d'après ce dernier, le nom de Dieu, Θεός, est créé pour désigner le divin qui est partout visible, θεατόν. D'ailleurs, cette description abrégée qu'est le nom Θεός ne nous rapproche pas davantage de l'essence divine, pas plus que tout autre nom que les hommes auraient pu concevoir. Le fait que Dieu dépasse ce résumé nominal est preuve de sa grandeur indicible.[29] En ce qui concerne l'erreur dans la dénomination, le paradoxe est qu'Eunome pense que Dieu a attribué aux êtres les plus faibles les noms les plus dignes (τιμιώτατον) sans leur faire partager la part correspondante des dignités, et aux êtres suprêmes les noms les plus triviaux sans leur communiquer, en même temps, la trivialité naturelle.[30] On pourrait, peut-être, ici, apercevoir une sorte de critique de la part d'Eunome adressée à la hiérarchie ecclésiastique ; en tout cas, on se trouve devant une contradiction au sein de la pensée eunoméenne. Pour Grégoire, cet argument eunoméen veut montrer que la dignité concerne les noms seuls tandis que le pouvoir des noms ne participe pas à la valeur qui n'est que phénoménale.[31]

---

[25] Cf. *CE* II 451 (GNO I 358,12f).
[26] Cf. S. Kofman, *Comment s'en sortir?*, Paris 1983, 113.
[27] Cf. R. McKeon, "The Hellenistic and Roman Foundations of the Tradition of Aristotle in the West", *The Review of Metaphysics*, 32/4, 128 (1979) 700ss.
[28] Cf. *CE* II 541 (GNO I 384,21–24).
[29] Cf. *CE* II 585f (GNO I 396f).
[30] Cf. *CE* II 315 (GNO I 318,10–15).
[31] Cf. *CE* II 331 (GNO I 322,21–23).

Sur ce point, la question des valeurs nous introduit à celle des normes qui régissent le développement de l'opposition entre les deux pensées. Il est évident que, malgré toutes leurs différences dogmatiques, Eunome et Grégoire se réfèrent à un fond de culture grecque classique qui leur est commun. Quelle serait, alors, la portée réelle de la controverse entre Grégoire et Eunome ? Pour Jean Daniélou, "cette discussion constitue un chaînon précieux de l'histoire des discussions sur l'origine des langues dans l'antiquité et nous ouvre des horizons sur l'histoire du néo-platonisme entre Jamblique et Proclus".[32] Il vaudrait mieux s'attarder ici sur les positions de Daniélou à propos des théories du langage chez les deux penseurs. "Eunome", écrit-il, "défend une théorie curieuse, selon laquelle les mots sont révélés par Dieu. Grégoire lui oppose une doctrine de l'origine humaine du langage."[33] Pour Daniélou, les dites théories ne se situent pas exactement dans le prolongement direct des théories antiques mais sont significatives d'une opposition intérieure au néoplatonisme. Daniélou rattache Grégoire au courant néoplatonicien exprimé notamment par Hiéroclès – une tradition autre que celle de Plotin, de Porphyre et de Jamblique – malgré le fait qu'Hiéroclès est postérieur au Père grec. Les similitudes seraient dues à une source commune, la philosophie d'Ammonius Sakkas.[34] Le nom d'Ammonius Sakkas évoque, bien-sûr, d'importantes interrogations sur l'origine de la philosophie chrétienne,[35] auxquelles Daniélou n'aurait pas pu rester indifférent. Malgré les problèmes généraux que les thèses exposées ci-dessus causent à l'historien des idées, nous avons décelé un passage d'Hiéroclès qui rappelle fortement les positions de Grégoire sur l'arbitraire des mots et leur dépendance des opérations de la faculté intellectuelle.[36]

---

[32] J. Daniélou, "Eunome l'Arien et l'exégèse néo-platonicienne du Cratyle", *REG* 69 (1956) 412.

[33] *Ibid.*

[34] Cf. *ibid.* et J. Daniélou, "Grégoire de Nysse et le néo-platonisme de l'École d'Athènes", *REG* 80 (1967) 395–401. Les mêmes positions se trouvent également dans son livre tardif sur *L'être et le temps chez Grégoire de Nysse*, 13: "Hiéroclès est postérieur à Grégoire, mais ils paraissent se rattacher à une même forme de néo-platonisme." Ici, les préoccupations ontologiques de Daniélou indiquent un tournant par rapport à l'existentialisme de son *Platonisme et théologie mystique. Doctrine spirituelle de saint Grégoire de Nysse*, Paris ²1953.

[35] Cf. H. Langerbeck, "The Philosophy of Ammonius Saccas and the Connection of Aristotelian and Christian Elements Therein", *The Journal of Hellenic Studies* 57 (1957) 67–74.

[36] Le texte grec d'Hiéroclès est le suivant : τὰ γὰρ τοιαῦτα [sc. ὀνόματα] οὐδὲν μετέχει τῆς τῶν ὀνομάτων ὀρθότητος, ὅτι μηδὲν τῆς οὐσίας ἢ τῆς ἐνεργείας παρίστησι

Or, quelles sont, plus précisément, les prérogatives du courant auquel Grégoire semble-t-il s'attacher ? Il paraît bien qu'il s'agit de faire le point sur l'originel autrement que dans les limites de l'onto-théologie. Le statut 'barbare' de la langue se trouve lié à la condition même de l'homme. Pour les uns, la langue provient directement de Dieu – c'est notamment, selon Daniélou, la position d'Origène – et l'homme parcourt l'échelle des hypostases. Pour les autres, les langues font preuve du génie des peuples et l'homme est une limite (μεθόριος) dans le monde. C'est ainsi qu'à travers la théorisation du langage on vient à repenser le concept même de l'homme. Est-ce le même chemin parcouru par Grégoire ? Référons-nous, ici, brièvement, à Basile le Grand, non pas pour étudier sa propre argumentation contre Eunome mais pour se pencher sur son évaluation célèbre de la culture hellénique. Il s'agit du traité *Aux jeunes gens sur la manière de tirer profit des lettres helléniques*.[37] Là, et à propos de la notion de valeur, Basile fait une distinction entre la valeur de la vie présente et celle de la vie future parallèle à la distinction entre âme et corps. Cette dernière distinction, dit-il, est un paradigme des plus habituels (οἰκειωτέρῳ) chez les Chrétiens. Elle est, ainsi, une distinction avancée pour servir de signe de démarcation entre culture hellénique et culture chrétienne. L'âme, dit Basile, est τιμιωτέρα à tout aspect du corps ; similaire à cette distinction est la différence entre les deux vies et les deux cultures ; le superlatif de τιμιωτέρα veut à la fois dire 'la plus digne' et 'la plus honnête'. Pour résumer le noyau gnoséologique de l'approche basilienne, la distinction entre âme et corps ne signifie pas, seulement ou littéralement, que l'hellénisme est le corps et le christianisme l'âme mais il s'agit plutôt d'un paradigme

---

τῶν πραγμάτων ἐκείνων, οἷς κεῖται ὀνόματα. τὴν οὖν ὄντως ὀρθότητα τῶν ὀνομάτων ἐν τοῖς ἀϊδίοις τῶν πραγμάτων προσήκει ζητεῖν καὶ τούτων ἐν τοῖς θείοις καὶ τῶν θείων ἐν τοῖς ἀρίστοις. ὅθεν καὶ τὸ τοῦ Διὸς ὄνομα σύμβολόν ἐστι καὶ εἰκὼν ἐν φωνῇ δημιουργικῆς οὐσίας τῷ τοὺς πρώτους θεμένους τοῖς πράγμασι τὰ ὀνόματα διὰ σοφίας ὑπερβολὴν ὥσπερ τινὰς ἀγαλματοποιοὺς ἀρίστους διὰ τῶν ὀνομάτων ὡς δι' εἰκόνων ἐμφανίσαι αὐτῶν τὰς δυνάμεις. τὰ γὰρ ἐν τῇ φωνῇ ὀνόματα σύμβολα τῶν ἐν τῇ ψυχῇ νοήσεων ἀπειργάζοντο, τὰς δὲ νοήσεις αὐτὰς γνωστικὰς εἰκόνας τῶν νοηθέντων πραγμάτων ἐποιοῦντο . . . οἱ πολλοὶ οὐχ ὁρῶσι διὰ τὸ χρῆσθαι ὀρθῶς ταῖς κοιναῖς ἐννοίαις, ἃς προσέφυσεν ὁ δημιουργὸς τῷ λογικῷ γένει πρὸς ἐπίγνωσιν ἑαυτοῦ. Hiéroclès, *In Aureum Pythagoreorum Carmen Commentarius* (Koehler 105,14–26; 108,15–19).

[37] Cf. Basil le Grand, *Aux jeunes gens sur la manière de tirer profit des lettres helléniques* 2,20f (Boulenger 43).

sur le fait que la différence entre les deux cultures est aussi claire pour 'nous' que la distinction entre âme et corps ; le 'nous' de Basile veut dire, nous les Chrétiens, mais, aussi, nous qui sommes dans le vrai ou, autrement, dans la droiture (ὀρθότης) de pensée. La droiture de pensée, donc, consiste à bien faire les distinctions, à posséder l' 'habitus' de la droiture, à savoir demeurer dans la droiture.

Pour Grégoire, la pureté de raisonnement n'est moins imprégnée de philosophie grecque. Il est vrai qu'il accuse Eunome, comme on l'a déjà souligné, d'aristotélisme. Toutefois, il n'est pas, lui-même, étranger à la philosophie du Stagirite comme on l'a montré plus haut. Grégoire attribue également à Eunome l'influence du *Cratyle* de Platon. Le platonisme de Grégoire est tout aussi évident et les références, par exemple, au *Phèdre* ne sont pas moins importantes, malgré le fait que la source n'est jamais mentionnée par son nom. À un moment, Grégoire se permet la liberté d'ironiser sur l'éducation philosophique de son adversaire quand il réfute l'accusation d'Eunome que l'ἐπίνοια est d'origine épicurienne et que la conception des mots selon l'ἐπίνοια correspond à un atomisme linguistique : selon Eunome, si Grégoire dit que les noms viennent de la faculté intellectuelle de l'homme alors le sens est né de l'entrelacement de ces unités significatives,[38] entrelacement qui serait analogue au *clinamen* épicurien. "Oh, comme Eunome a compris Épicure !", s'exclame ironiquement Grégoire.[39] Bien-sûr, l'effort de la part d'Eunome de lier l'ἐπίνοια à l'épicurisme n'est aucunement innocent car en utilisant le nom d'Épicure, c'est comme s'il accusait le parti grégorien d'impiété. Ce bref débat autour de l'épicurisme fait taire d'autres influences probablement exercées sur la pensée grégorienne : on pense au scepticisme à propos de la faculté intellectuelle de l'homme ou à l'apologie stoïcienne de la nature. Le comble est que, selon les dires de Grégoire, juste après la référence à Épicure, Eunome accuse la notion d'ἐπίνοια d'être d'origine aristotélicienne. Décidément, on a le sentiment d'être pris dans un jeu de miroirs par rapport aux références philosophiques des deux hommes.

Or, il semble que le texte de Grégoire comprend deux types de discours. Le premier est la critique de la métaphysique eunoméenne où Grégoire affirme, avant toute autre chose, que les mots dépendent

[38] Cf. *CE* II 410 (GNO I 345,25–346,4).
[39] *CE* II 410 (GNO I 345,29).

de l'intellect humain. Est-ce pour cette raison que Grégoire serait un idéaliste comme le prétend, par ailleurs, R. Sorabji ?[40] Nous ne le croyons pas en ce qui concerne la théorie grégorienne du langage car, ici, la limite de l'usage du langage est, comme on l'a répété, le monde naturel. Or, ce premier type du discours de Grégoire est transcendé par un deuxième, une sorte de 'jeu de langage' auto-référentiel des deux opposants. Un indice qui pourrait nous orienter est la distinction grégorienne suivante : à plusieurs reprises Grégoire accuse Eunome en utilisant le terme péjoratif de λογογράφος ou de τεχνολόγος. Par contre, quand il parle de Basile, il fait état d' "auditeur prudent" (συνετὸς ἀκροατής),[41] empruntant le terme à Ésaïe. Affirmer ainsi une telle différence c'est rester en plein champ platonicien ; on pense à l'apologie du discours parlé fait par Platon dans son *Phèdre*, contre la λογογραφία de Lysis.

On devrait insister, ici, sur les points suivants : il est évident qu'aussi bien Grégoire qu'Eunome construisent leurs propos sur un fond commun de tradition philosophique ; or, Grégoire se dresse avec un zèle particulier contre les efforts eunoméens de substantialisation du langage. La manière dont Eunome intègre les mots au sein de la Création ressemble fort à des 'absoluités' du langage qui fournissent le matériel à certains des plus brillants récits de Jorge Luis Borges. Grégoire n'est pas seulement schématique quand il accuse Eunome d'être un 'sophiste' ; il distingue d'une façon claire chez ce dernier un réductionnisme du tout au langage ; d'où probablement l'attachement de Grégoire à des formulations contenues dans le *Phèdre* de Platon, où est défendue l'idée d'une saine rhétorique. Par ailleurs, les thèses de Grégoire sont d'un réel intérêt en ce qui concerne les interrogations modernes à propos de la différence ontologique ; sur cette question le passage du *CE* III qui a ouvert notre texte est profondément significatif. En vérité, l'aperception d'un pareil différence entre le langage et le monde n'est pas caractéristique de l'ontologie seule.[42] La mise en rapport avec la modernité prouve que Grégoire, sur la

---

[40] R. Sorabji, *Time, Creation and the Continuum. Theories in Antiquity and the Early Middle Ages*, London 1983, 287ss.

[41] *CE* II 49 (GNO I 240,4).

[42] "L'étonnement devant l'existence du monde dont parle encore Wittgenstein . . . pouvait même autoriser un rapprochement avec Heidegger ou, du moins, une comparaison"; J. Lacoste, *La philosophie au XXe siècle*, Paris, 1988, 38. Cf. également ce fameux passage de Wittgenstein: "la proposition est capable de représenter la réalité, mais elle n'est pas capable de représenter ce qu'elle doit avoir de commun avec

base des outils fournis par la philosophie classique, a su restructurer les données conceptuelles à sa disposition.

Pour Daniélou, dans le champ du langage, "la conception réelle de Grégoire et de Basile est la conception commune des grammairiens, celle que nous appellerons scientifique".[43] Par ailleurs, "ce que nous voyons revivre en Grégoire de Nysse", écrit-il, "c'est l'esprit scientifique de la Grèce classique, celui des présocratiques et des aristotéliciens".[44] Plus précisément, le fait de lier le langage à la nature de l'homme et de penser l'homme comme limite laisse ouverte la possibilité, pour un chrétien comme Grégoire, de se prouver homme de science ou, autrement, d'explorer le champ scientifique délimité par Basile dans son traité sur les lettres helléniques, celui des sciences littéraires. C'est peut-être cela que les spécialistes de la déconstruction en matière de religion appellent *logophasis* au sein de l'*apophasis* grégorienne, pour distinguer la positivité du discours de la théologie mystique de toute sorte d'hyper-essentialité.[45] En s'opposant à Eunome, Grégoire, à la suite de Basile, garantit les potentialités du discours poétique (au sens aristotélicien du terme) de l'âge chrétien.

---

la réalité pour pouvoir représenter la réalité, à savoir la forme logique. Pour pouvoir représenter la forme logique, il nous faudrait, avec la proposition nous situer à l'extérieur de la logique, c'est-à-dire à l'extérieur du monde"; L. Wittgenstein, *Tractatus logico-philosophicus*, trad. fr., Paris 1961, prop. 4.12, cité notamment in P. Hadot, *Exercices spirituels et philosophie antique*, nouvelle édition revue et augmentée, Paris 2002, chap. La théologie négative, 249.

[43] J. Daniélou, "Eunome l'Arien", 416.

[44] *Ibid.*, p. 432.

[45] Cf. M. Laird, "Whereof We Speak".

GLOSSOGONY OR EPISTEMOLOGY? EUNOMIUS OF CYZICUS' AND BASIL OF CAESAREA'S STOIC CONCEPT OF ΕΠΙΝΟΙΑ AND ITS MISREPRESENTATION BY GREGORY OF NYSSA

John A. Demetracopoulos

My intention[1] is to shed more light on Gregory of Nyssa's attempt at justifying Basil of Caesarea's views of ἐπίνοια and show that in so doing he misrepresented Basil's (as well as Eunomius') views. Before, however, examining the most relevant passages from Gregory's *Contra Eunomium* II, some crucial notes on what ἐπίνοια means in Eunomius' and Basil's texts are naturally in order.

'Επίνοια was placed in the context of the Trinitarian quarrels of the 4th century by Eunomius. Unfortunately, Eunomius' usage of this term in his first piece, the 'Απολογία, is rather obscure. Nowhere does he define it; he just uses it thrice in the 8th chapter:

> 'Αγέννητον δὲ λέγοντες, οὐκ ὀνόματι μόνον κατ' ἐπίνοιαν ἀνθρωπίνην σεμνύνειν οἰόμεθα δεῖν, ἀποτιννύναι δὲ κατ' ἀλήθειαν τὸ πάντων ἀναγκαιότατον ὄφλημα τῷ Θεῷ, τὴν τοῦ εἶναι ὅ ἐστιν ὁμολογίαν. Τὰ γάρ τοι κατ' ἐπίνοιαν λεγόμενα, ἐν ὀνόμασι μόνον καὶ προφορᾷ τὸ εἶναι

[1] Let a double note be made in advance. This paper is a highly selective abridgment of a forthcoming monograph of mine on *The Philosophical Theology of Eunomius of Cyzicus: a Restoration*, Athens, forthcoming in 2007. For more documentation and full secondary literature one should refer to the monograph. Secondly, its point happens to clash with the established admiration of Gregory of Nyssa and match with the critical approach to his thought inaugurated by H. F. Cherniss and followed recently by C. G. Stead and others. The former, in his old well-known study, *The Platonism of Gregory of Nyssa*, Berkeley 1930, concluded that Gregory, in his attempt at submitting philosophy to theology, "contradicted himself at every point" (H. F. Cherniss, *The Platonism*, 57; 63) and that in his "polemic against Eunomius . . . every weapon is used that is suited to hurt the enemy" (27), regardless of the inconsistencies in which he was involved. The latter, in his "Ontology and Terminology in Gregory of Nyssa" (in: H. Dörrie – M. Altenburger – U. Schramm, eds., *Gregor von Nyssa und die Philosophie. Zweites internationales Kolloquium über Gregor von Nyssa, Freckenhorst bei Münster 18.–23. September 1972*, Leiden 1976, 107–127, esp. 107) concluded from his research into special topics that Gregory "lacks the essential attributes of the philosopher – the concern for consistency and the respect for truth". "Provided [his conclusions] seem reasonably persuasive, he is satisfied; and

ἔχοντα, ταῖς φωναῖς συνδιαλύεσθαι πέφυκεν, ὁ δὲ Θεὸς καὶ σιωπώντων καὶ φθεγγομένων καὶ γεγενημένων καὶ πρὸ τοῦ γενέσθαι τὰ ὄντα ἦν τε καὶ ἔστιν ἀγέννητος.[2]

Surprisingly enough, no scholar has thus far paid due attention to the μόνον of the first sentence.[3] Contrary to what Basil and Gregory say of Eunomius' ἐπίνοια, this μόνον shows that Eunomius does not discard ἐπίνοια *en bloc*; what he says is just that conceiving God through ἐπίνοια is not sufficient (οὐ . . . μόνον), since there is a way of a closer approach to His 'being' (τὸ εἶναι, οὐσία or ὑπόστασις). Eunomius, when saying ἀποτιννύναι . . . κατ' ἀλήθειαν (not just κατ' ἐπίνοιαν), used the Stoic distinction between ἀληθές and ἀλήθεια.[4] 'Αληθές is a truth which can be possessed even by a non-sage, who does not know why what he believes is true and, for that reason, may wrongly change his mind and fall into falsehood. That is why Eunomius says that τὰ . . . κατ' ἐπίνοιαν λεγόμενα . . . ταῖς φωναῖς συνδιαλύεσθαι πέφυκεν.[5] 'Αλήθεια, in contrast with ἀληθές, is the firmly

this [is] characteristic of his . . . opportunistic use of philosophical themes" (C. G. Stead, "Ontology and Terminology", 116; cf. id., "Why Not Three Gods? The Logic of Gregory of Nyssa's Trinitarian Doctrine", in: H. R. Drobner – C. Klock, eds., *Studien zu Gregor von Nyssa und der christlichen Spätantike*, Leiden – New York – København – Köln 1990, 149–163, esp. 149). This is the spirit of my monograph *Philosophy and Faith. The Demonstrability of Christian Dogmas according to Gregory of Nyssa or Fides deprecans intellectum*, Athens 1996, where Cherniss' main point was enriched and systematized by a list of Gregory's plain contradictions in matters regarding ontology, epistemology, logic, ethics, and apologetics.

[2] Eunomius, *Apologia* 8 (Vaggione 40–42; SC 305, 246–248).

[3] Even desperate 'corrections' of this passage (in full despise of the manuscript evidence) have been suggested, so as to make it match somehow with the standard interpretation (see e.g. K.-H. Uthemann, "Die Sprache der Theologie nach Eunomius von Cyzicus", *ZKG* 104 [1993] 143–175, esp. 153).

[4] See Sextus Empiricus' *Adversus Mathematicos* VIII 81–83 (Mutchmann II 120–121) (VIII 80–84, Mutchmann II 120–121: Περὶ ἀληθοῦς καὶ ἀληθείας). Cf. A. A. Long, "Language and Thought in Stoicism", in: A. A. Long (ed.), *Problems in Stoicism*, London 1971, 75–113 (esp. 98–112). An ethical statement in chapter 13 of the 'Απολογία is very close to the main ethical corollary drawn by the Stoics from their distinction between ἀληθές and ἀλήθεια. This distinction taken for granted the Stoics said that falsehood does not consist in uttering something contrary to an ἀληθές but in clashing with ἀλήθεια, "ψευδές or ἀληθές are words which fix the truth or falsity of statements made at a particular time" (A. A. Long, "Language and Thought", 101). Likewise, Eunomius declares that speaking the truth is good not in principle but only under conditions: μηδὲν τῶν ἀληθῶν [*nota bene* the careful use of ἀληθές, not ἀλήθεια] ἐν καιρῷ καὶ μέτρῳ λεγομένων ὑπαίτιον (Eunomius, *Apologia* 13,3–4, Vaggione 48; SC 305, 258).

[5] Let us also recall the Biblical *dictum*: Λογισμοὶ γὰρ θνητῶν δειλοί, καὶ ἐπισφαλεῖς αἱ ἐπίνοιαι ἡμῶν (*Sap* 9,14).

established edification of all the particular truths by the sage, who always knows fully what he talks about.[6]

Let us go back to ἐπίνοια. Eunomius' 'Απολογία offers us some important information with regard to the logical status of ἐπίνοια. In chapters 16–18, a distinction is drawn between two classes of 'divine names'. Under the first one fall various names which regard God *per se* – for example, 'being', 'not-generate', 'incorruptible', 'immortal', 'eternal', 'life' and 'light'. Since, however, God is simple, they all have the same 'reference' *and* 'meaning' when applied to Him. In terms of ancient Logic, they are πολυώνυμα, that is synonyms. On the other hand, the second (and lower) class of 'divine names', which are the various ἐπίνοιαι, comprises ἑτερώνυμα, which describe God *ad extra*, that is His various relations with the world ('protector', 'saviour' etc.).

Let us now turn to Basil's response to Eunomius. As I have argued elsewhere,[7] Basil's *Adversus Eunomium* (363–366) I 6–7 (SC 299, 182–192) should be regarded our principal source for the Stoic ἐπίνοια. Basil's aim was to reconcile the multiplicity of God's names with His substantial simplicity. And he drew upon Plotinus' *Enneads* VI 2 [43] 3,20–25:

> Ὅλως δὲ ἴσως οὐδὲ τὸ Ἓν [i.e. the Second One] φατέον αἴτιον τοῖς ἄλλοις εἶναι, ἀλλ' οἷον μέρη αὐτοῦ καὶ οἷον στοιχεῖα αὐτοῦ καὶ πάντα μίαν φύσιν μεριζομένην ταῖς ἡμῶν ἐπινοίαις, αὐτὸ δὲ εἶναι . . . ἓν εἰς πάντα καὶ φαινόμενον πολλὰ καὶ γινόμενον πολλά.

Plotinus (VI 2 [43] 4,1–9; 14) brings forth the simile of body, which, albeit one, is composed of a *substratum* and its various properties

[6] By the way, grasping God's "essence" does not mean for Eunomius knowing God's '*quid est*', as he is constantly accused from his time, e.g. by Basil of Caesarea (*Adversus Eunomium* I 12,9, SC 299, 212; cf. Gregory of Nyssa's *Contra Eunomium* II 67–129; GNO I 245,19–263,20) up to-day; for, according to Eunomius, God is ἀσύγκριτος (*Apologia* 9; 11; 26; Vaggione 42,3, 46,7–9 and 68,3–7; SC 305, 250,3, 256,7 and 288,4–9), that is radically different from anything else. Rather, grasping God's 'essence' means just realizing the unbridgeable gap between Him and His creatures, that is realizing His uniqueness. Thus, Eunomius' statement that ἀγέν(ν)ητον or ἀγεν(ν)ησία is God's 'essence' is no rationalistic in tenor; as a matter of fact, this statement is just a reproduction of a passage from Dionysius of Alexandria's writing Περὶ τοῦ μὴ ἀγέννητον εἶναι τὴν ὕλην, which is partially preserved in Eusebius' *Praeparatio evangelica* VII 19,3 (GCS 43/1, 401,12–13): Αὐτοαγένητόν ἐστιν ὁ Θεὸς καὶ οὐσία ἐστὶν αὐτοῦ, ὡς ἂν εἴποι τις, ἡ ἀγενησία.

[7] "The Sources of Content and Use of ἐπίνοια in Basil of Caesarea's *Adversus Eunomium I*: Stoicism and Plotinus" (in Modern Greek with an English summary), Βυζαντινά (Salonica) 20 (1999) 7–42.

(magnitude, colour, shape etc.), which are "divided by our reasoning" (λόγῳ). Basil states a similar view and puts forward the same simile, in order to describe God's simplicity and multiplicity.

Basil insisted on the exact significance of Plotinus' ἐπίνοια. Drawing, in all probability, upon the (lost) logical part of Arius Didymus' *Epitome*,[8] he produced three definitions. 'Επίνοια is an epistemological process through which our mind discerns the various (past, present and future) aspects of a thing perceived through a κοινὴ ἔννοια as one and simple. Through this 'afterthought' one divides a being into: *i)* its parts (1st definition); *ii)* its categorical properties (instances of substance, quality, quantity etc.) (1st definition); *iii)* its previous and next states or acts, relying on its present state (2nd definition). The third case falls under what the Stoics called ἐπιλογισμός, which uncovers τὰ πρόσκαιρα ἄδηλα, namely, what cannot be grasped, for a given moment, directly through the senses. The 3rd definition includes the properties of the two previous ones: as ἐπίνοια can be defined any speculative analysis of a being *prima facie* perceived as one.

As one can see in the Appendix, Basil's doctrine is almost identical with the epistemological process described in a text contemporary to him, namely, pseudo-Augustine's *Categoriae decem* (ca. 350/380), which in fact comes from Themistius' (317–*ca.* 388) circle.[9]

Needless to say, Basil's restriction[10] of Eunomius' ἐπίνοιαι to imaginary things, such as mythological monsters, or to senseless words,[11] is false. As we saw, Eunomius regarded ἐπίνοια as a preliminary stage of grasping God, not as mere babbling. And in this point

---

[8] See my forthcoming monograph: *The Philosophical Theology of Eunomius of Cyzicus: a Restoration,* Excursus II ("The Source of Eunomius' Stoic Epistemological and Logical Ideas: *Arius Didymus* [or *Arius Augusti*] *deperditus*").

[9] See my paper "Alcuin and the Realm of Application of Aristotle's Categories", in J. Merinhós – A. Pacheco (eds.), *Actes du XIe Congrès International de Philosophie Médiévale: "Intellect and Imagination in the Middle Ages", Porto (Portugal), 25–30/8/2002,* Vol. I, Porto 2004, 950–959. Cf. also id., "Stoic Epistemology in the Early Middle Ages. 'Επίνοια in Basil of Caesarea's *Adversus Eunomium*, 'Intentio' in Pseudo-Augustine's *Categoriae decem*, and Alcuin's Aspectual Theory of Aristotle's Categories" (forthcoming in the *Archiv für mittelalterliche Philosophie und Kultur* 13, 2007). Let it be noted that in the Latin text ἐπίνοια is called 'intentio'. As we will see (cf. *infra*, pp. 392–393), a similar process is described by the verb 'intendere' in Cicero's *Academica*.

[10] Basil of Caesarea, *Adversus Eunomium* I 6,34–35 (SC 299, 186).

[11] I.e. the so-called ἄσημοι φωναί (βλίτυρι, σκινδαψός etc. mentioned by Gregory of Nyssa in *CE* III/V 44, GNO II 176,6–7). Cf. Basil's *Adversus Eunomium* I 6,2–3 (SC 299, 182).

Eunomius and Basil are in fact in accord with each other, regardless of what the latter said of the former.

Let it be added that Basil's ἐπίνοιαι, like the Eunomian ones, correspond to the logical status of ἑτερώνυμα. For example, Basil's example of the various aspects of σῖτος (seed, fruit, bread) had been produced two centuries earlier by Alexander of Aphrodisias,[12] who had explicitly called these aspects ἑτερώνυμα.

Let us now see how Gregory of Nyssa presents and defends Basil's ἐπίνοια against Eunomius. First, Gregory reproduces, just as unfairly, Basil's misinterpretation of Eunomius' ἐπίνοια. This can be seen, for example, in the following passage from Eunomius' Ὑπὲρ τῆς Ἀπολογίας ἀπολογία as preserved and bitterly commented upon by Gregory:

> . . . αὐτὸ διακωμῳδεῖ τῆς ἐπινοίας τὸ ὄνομα. "Τῶν γὰρ οὕτω κατ' ἐπίνοιαν λεγομένων," φησὶ, τὰ μὲν κατὰ τὴν προφορὰν ἔχειν μόνην τὴν ὕπαρξιν, ὡς τὰ μηδὲν σημαίνοντα, τὰ δὲ κατ' ἰδίαν διάνοιαν· καὶ τούτων τὰ μὲν κατὰ αὔξησιν, ὡς ἐπὶ τῶν κολοσσιαίων, τὰ δὲ κατὰ μείωσιν, ὡς ἐπὶ τῶν πυγμαίων, τὰ δὲ κατὰ πρόσθεσιν, ὡς ἐπὶ τῶν πολυκεφάλων, ἢ κατὰ σύνθεσιν, ὡς ἐπὶ τῶν μιξοθήρων." . . . Ὁρᾷς εἰς τί τὴν ἐπίνοιαν ἡμῖν ὁ σοφὸς διακερματίσας περαιτέρω τὴν δύναμιν αὐτῆς προελθεῖν οὐκ ἠξίωσεν. Ἀσήμαντον εἶναί φησι τὴν ἐπίνοιαν, ἀδιανόητον, τὰ παρὰ φύσιν σοφιζομένην, ἢ διακολοβοῦσαν ἢ ὑπερτείνουσαν τὰ ὡρισμένα μέτρα τῆς φύσεως, ἢ ἐξ ἑτεροφυῶν συντιθεῖσαν ἢ τερατευομένην ταῖς ἀλλοκότοις προσθήκαις. Ἐν τούτοις καταπαίξας τοῦ τῆς ἐπινοίας ὀνόματος, ἄχρηστον αὐτὴν καὶ ἀνόνητον τῷ βίῳ . . . ἀποδείκνυσιν.[13]

Eunomius lists the Stoic ways of producing imaginary ideas as preserved in Sextus Empiricus.[14] As a matter of fact, however, he does not reduce ἐπίνοια to these sorts of beings. This is indicated by the usually discarded opening word of his passage: οὕτω. Imaginary things and words without sense are τὰ *οὕτω* κατ' ἐπίνοιαν λεγόμενα, not *all* τὰ κατ' ἐπίνοιαν λεγόμενα. And yet, Gregory in his interpretation passes οὕτω over in silence.

Anyway, that Gregory would not treat Eunomius better than his brother did would be all too expected; to mention Ammianus

---

[12] Alexander of Aphrodisias, *In Metaphysica* (CAG I 247,18–29).

[13] *CE* II 179–180 (GNO I 276,21–277,7).

[14] Sextus Empiricus, *Adversus Mathematicos* VIII 58–60 (Mutschmann II 115–116); III 40–50 (Mau III 115–117). Cf. Diogenes Laertius, *Vitae philosophorum* VII 52–53 (Marcovich I 475–476). The mode κατὰ πρόσθεσιν does not occur in Sextus or Laertius; this means that Eunomius had used a Stoic source unknown to us.

Marcellinus,[15] *nullas infestas hominibus bestias, ut sunt sibi ferales plerique Christianorum expertus*... What, however, is rather unexpected is that Gregory fails to describe correctly even his own brother's views. Let us recall his definition of ἐπίνοια:

> Ἔστι γὰρ κατά γε τὸν ἐμὸν λόγον ἡ ἐπίνοια ἔφοδος εὑρετικὴ τῶν ἀγνοουμένων, διὰ τῶν προσεχῶν τε καὶ ἀκολούθων τῇ πρώτῃ περὶ τὸ σπουδαζόμενον νοήσει τὸ ἐφεξῆς ἐξευρίσκουσα. Νοήσαντες γάρ τι περὶ τοῦ ζητουμένου, τῇ ἀρχῇ τοῦ ληφθέντος διὰ τῶν ἐφευρισκομένων νοημάτων συναρμόζοντες τὸ ἀκόλουθον, εἰς τὸ πέρας τῶν σπουδαζομένων τὴν ἐγχείρησιν ἄγομεν.[16]

Gregory accompanies this definition by a set of examples taken from the various arts, liberal and illiberal, which show that, in contrast to Basil's conception of ἐπίνοια, his own conception was not epistemological. Whereas Basil speaks of *discovering* more truths about reality, Gregory speaks of *inventing* things and adding them up to reality for the benefit of humankind. In so doing, Gregory seems not to draw upon any logical work, as Basil did, but upon Philo of Alexandria's doctrine of the origins of civilization from ἀνθρωπίνη ἐπίνοια.[17]

Philo's description of ἐπίνοια seems to be Stoic. In a passage from Cicero's *Academica*, where the general Stoic idea of philosophy is expounded and defended against radical Scepticism, *intendere*, which, as we saw, in pseudo-Augustine's *Categoriae decem* (*Paraphrasis Themistiana*)

---

[15] Ammianus Marcellinus, *Historia* XXII 5,4 (Fontaine 99).

[16] *CE* II 182 (GNO I 277,20–26).

[17] Philo of Alexandria, *De praemiis* 145,7 (Cohn V 370); *De fuga* 168,2–5 (Wendland III 146–147); *De mutatione* 249,2 (Wendland III 200); *De specialibus legibus* I 334,1–3; 335,3; 345,3; 336,1 (Cohn V 81; 81; 84; 81); *De migratione* 142 (Wendland II 295); *De somniis* I 204,2–3; I 40,1–2; II 212,6 (Wendland III 249; 213; 251). Cf. Clement of Alexandria, *Stromata* I 16,74,1–80,6 (GCS 15, 47,20–52,23). On Gregory's reading of Philo's writings see J. Daniélou, *Platonisme et théologie mystique. Doctrine spirituelle de saint Grégoire de Nysse*, Paris 1944, 74–77; 262–266; 274–276; id., *L'être et le temps chez Grégoire de Nysse*, Leiden 1970, 31; 85–93; 107; 117–132; D. T. Runia, *Philo and the Church Fathers. A Collection of Papers*, Leiden – New York – Köln 1995, 18–19; 129; 145–151; 257–258. *Occasione data* I cannot resist the temptation to suggest (even though without documentation) in brief a new parallel between Philo and Gregory; the latter's famous identification of the everlasting search for God (*In Ecclesiasten* VII, GNO V 400,20–401,2) with the very finding of Him sounds as an echo of Philo's strikingly similar idea in *Legum allegoriae* I 32–50 (Cohn I 69–73), esp. 36 and 40, where the fundamental tenet of the "ephectic Sceptics" that they ἔτι ζητοῦσιν (Sextus Empiricus, *Pyrrhoniae hypotyposes* I 2, Bury I 4) seems to be assimilated into the Platonic framework of Philo's doctrine of the transcendence of God and the

corresponds to Basil of Caesarea's ἐπίνοια (cf. Appendix, p. 395) is used in both epistemological and cultural senses:

> *Mens enim ipsa, quae sensuum fons est atque etiam ipsa sensus est, naturalem vim habet, quam* intendit *ad ea quibus movetur. Itaque alia visa sic arripit, ut iis statim utatur, alia quasi recondit, e quibus memoria oritur; cetera autem similitudinibus construit, ex quibus efficiuntur notitiae rerum, quas Graeci tum* ἐννοίας *tum* προλήψεις *vocant; eo cum accessit ratio argumentique conclusio rerumque innumerabilium multitudo, tum et perceptio eorum omnium apparet et eadem ratio perfecta is gradibus ad sapientiam pervenit.*
>
> *Ad rerum igitur scientiam vitaeque constantiam aptissima cum sit, mens hominis amplectitur maxime cognitionem et istam* κατάληψιν, *quam, ut dixi, verbum e verbo exprimentes 'conprensionem' dicemus, cum ipsam per se amat. Nihil enim est ei veritatis luce dulcius tum etiam propter usum. Quocirca et sensibus utitur et artes efficit quasi sensus alteros et usque eo philosophiam ipsam corroborat, ut virtutem efficiat, ex qua re una vita omnis apta sit.*
>
> *Ergo i qui negant quicquam posse conprendi, haec ipsa eripiunt vel instrumenta vel ornamenta vitae, vel potius etiam totam vitam evertunt funditus ipsumque animal orbant animo, ut difficile sit de temeritate eorum perinde ut causa postulat dicere.*

The anti-Sceptical conclusion of this passage reminds us strongly of Gregory's bitter attack on Eunomius' alleged 'nihilistic' views of human mind.[18]

True, Gregory distinguishes between discovering and inventing. Yet, this releases him neither from wrongly ascribing to Basil's ἐπίνοια the sense of invention nor from another fundamental confusion, which has to do with another misrepresentation of Eunomian thought. The reason why Gregory refers to ἐπίνοια in the Philonic sense of the term is that he wants to combat Eunomius' alleged doctrine of the 'natural' character (φύσει) of the 'names' and explain language in terms of man's own mental ability and inventiveness, that is in terms of ἐπίνοια. This strategy led him to transfer Basil's ἐπίνοια from the field of epistemology, to which it plainly and exclusively belongs, to the field of glossogony. Gregory refers to Basil's 2nd definition of ἐπίνοια as follows:

---

correlate idea that the very seeking of God, even without finding, is felicity itself. This is, I think, one of the roots of Gregory's concept of "perpetual progress". Let it be also added that the ascription of the multifarious sects of civilization to ἐπίνοια in *CE* II 181–183 (GNO I 277,7–278,4) may share a common Greek source with the theory of the origins of civilization based on *inventio atque excogitatio* as expounded in Cicero's *Tusculanae disputationes* I 25–27, § 62–67 (Pohlenz 248–251).

[18] *CE* II 180–191 (GNO I 276,29–280,21).

> Τοῦ δὲ μεγάλου Βασιλείου διορθωσαμένου τὴν ἠπατημένην ὑπόνοιαν καί τινα περὶ τῶν *ὀνομάτων* διεξελθόντος ὡς *οὐκ ἐκ φύσεως* ὄντων, ἀλλὰ *κατ' ἐπίνοιαν* ἐπικειμένων τοῖς πράγμασι . . .[19]
>
> . . . Περὶ τῆς *τῶν ὀνομάτων* ἐννοίας ἡ θεωρία προέκειτο, πότερον *φύσιν* ἐνδείκνυται ἢ *ἐπινοητικῶς* ἐκ τῶν ἐνεργειῶν ὀνομάζεται.[20]

That in so doing he does not do justice to Basil's ἐπίνοια is obvious. What is more, the reason why he led himself to this 'lateral loss' rests on shaky foundations, too. For, if we remember what we said of Eunomius' doctrine of the 'divine names' in the Ἀπολογία, we shall realize that Eunomius accepted a 'conventional' (θέσει) doctrine of human language. He accepted the existence of πολυώνυμα, that is of various names standing for one and the same thing: μηδὲ ταῖς φωναῖς πέφυκεν ἀκολουθεῖν τῶν πραγμάτων ἡ φύσις, τοῖς δὲ πράγμασιν ἐφαρμόζεσθαι κατὰ τὴν ἀξίαν ἡ τῶν ὀνομάτων δύναμις.[21]

As of the passages from the Ὑπὲρ τῆς Ἀπολογίας ἀπολογία produced by Gregory in order to show that Eunomius regarded some names, such as ἀγέν(ν)ητος, as 'natural', they all admit of an interpretation compatible with the plain 'conventional' doctrine of Ἀπολογία. According to Eunomius, some 'names' are 'natural' only in the sense that their 'signifié' (*not* their 'signifiant') denotes the essential properties of the things they stand for.

Rebus sic stantibus, Gregory's long argumentation for the conventional character of human speech[22] is just an *ignoratio elenchi*, since it misses the point of Eunomius' theonymy and epistemology,[23] whose conception of ἐπίνοια actually does not differ from Basil of Caesarea's ἐπίνοια and the *intentio* of the heavily Stoicizing *Paraphrasis Themistiana* of Aristotle's *Categories*.

---

[19] *CE* II 125 (GNO I 262,21–24). Cf. *ibid.* (GNO I 262,27–28): κατ' ἐπίνοιαν λέγεσθαι *vs.* τὴν φύσιν παριστάναι.

[20] *CE* II 354 (GNO I 329,20–22). Gregory's distinction between ἐκ φύσεως and ἐπινοητικῶς is met in Origen's *Selecta in Genesim* (PG 12, 100: φυσικῶς . . ., καὶ οὐκ ἐπινοητικῶς).

[21] Eunomius, *Apologia* 18 (Vaggione 54–56; SC 305, 266–268).

[22] *CE* II 246–292 (GNO I 298,17–312,25).

[23] A brief note on J. Daniélou's well-known and much-worn article on the alleged affinity of Eunomius' linguistic doctrine with that of Jamblichus' *De mysteriis Aegyptiorum* ("Eunome l'Arien et l'exégèse néo-platonicienne du *Cratyle*", *REG* 69, 1956, 412–432). Daniélou's argumentation for this affinity rests on two rotten premisses. Firstly, it takes for Eunomius' view whatever Gregory of Nyssa reports from his study of the lost Ὑπὲρ τῆς Ἀπολογίας ἀπολογία. Secondly, it mistakes Jamblichus' doctrine of the magical power of the sound of the traditional 'divine names' used in the pagan rituals for a doctrine of how humans acquire some knowledge of God, whereas, according to Jamblichus, the 'divine names' are effective in terms of their 'signifiant', even if their content is *not* understood by the auditors of the ritual.

APPENDIX

Ἐπίνοια in Basil of Caesarea's *Adversus Eunominum* I 6–7 and *intentio* in the *Paraphrasis Themistiana* (pseudo-Augustine's *Categoriae decem*), 27–29.[24]

Basil of Caesarea

Ὑπόλοιπον δ' ἂν εἴη [1] *δεικνύναι* {2}, *πῶς* [3] μὲν *ἡ συνήθεια* {4} καὶ ἐπὶ ποίων *πραγμάτων* {5} *τῇ ἐπινοίᾳ* [6] *χρῆται* [7], πῶς δὲ τὰ θεῖα λόγια *τὴν χρῆσιν* [7] αὐτῆς παρεδέξατο.

[1st definition of ἐπίνοια] Ὁρῶμεν *τοίνυν* [8] ὅτι ἐν *μὲν* [9a] *τῇ* κοινῇ *χρήσει* [7] τὰ ταῖς ἀθρόαις ἐπιβολαῖς *τοῦ νοῦ* [10] ἁπλᾶ *δοκοῦντα* [11] *εἶναι* [12a] καὶ *μοναχά* [12b], ταῖς *δὲ* [9b] κατὰ λεπτὸν ἐξετάσεσι ποικίλα φαινόμενα καὶ *πολλά* [13], ταῦτα *τῷ νῷ* [10] *διαιρούμενα* {14} *ἐπινοίᾳ* [6] μόνῃ *διαιρετὰ* [14a/b] λέγεται. Οἷον, *τὸ σῶμα* [15] ἁπλοῦν *μὲν* [9a] εἶναί *φησιν* {16a} ἡ πρώτη *ἔντευξις* {16b}, ποικίλον *δὲ* [9a] ὁ λόγος ἐπιὼν δείκνυσι, *τῇ ἐπινοίᾳ* [6] αὐτὸ εἰς τὰ ἐξ ὧν *σύγκειται* [17] *διαλύων* {14}, *χρῶμα* [18] *καὶ* σχῆμα *καὶ* ἀντιτυπίαν *καὶ* μέγεθος *καὶ τὰ λοιπά* {19} . . .

[2nd definition] . . . ὥστε μετὰ τὸ πρῶτον ἡμῖν ἀπὸ *τῆς αἰσθήσεως* [20]

Paraphrasis Themistiana

Restat [1] ut †*eorum quae sunt* {5} *quo pacto* [3] *Aristoteles* {4} *tractaverit* [7] *enarremus* {2}.

Sunt *igitur* [8] illa quae aut percipimus *sensibus* [20] aut *mente et cogitatione* [10] colligimus: *sensibus* [20] tenemus quae aut videndo aut contrectando aut audiendo aut gustando aut odorando *cognoscimus* [22]; *mente* [10] ut, cum quis equum aut hominem vel quodlibet animal *viderit* [11], quamquam *unum* [12b] *corpus* [15] *esse* [12a] *respondeat* {16a/b}, intelligit *tamen* [9a/b] *multis* [13] partibus *esse concretum* [17 *e contrario*] (siquidem alia sit pars capitis, alia pedum caeterorumque membrorum, in ipso capite partes suas aures habeant, habeat propriam lingua, ipsae quoque partes singulae *multa* [13] in se habeant quae *dividi et separari* [14a] *possunt* [14b], ut caro sit aliud, aliud corium, aliud venae, aliud nervi, capilli aliud; ergo haec *mente vel intellectu* [10] colligimus,

[24] Basil of Caesarea, *Adversus Eunomium* I 6,19–29; 41–51; 54–57; I 7,1–29 (SC 299, 184–190); *Pseudo-Augustini paraphrasis Themistiana* 27–29 (Minio-Paluello 139,9–140,6 [= PL 32, 1423]). The self-same parallels are marked with numbers in square brackets [1, 2, 3 . . .], whereas the synonym or inferred parallels (e.g., 4) are marked with numbers in hook brackets {1, 2, 3 . . .}.

ἐγγινόμενον *νόημα* [21] τὴν λεπτοτέραν καὶ ἀκριβεστέραν *τοῦ νοηθέντος* [21] ἐπενθύμησιν *"ἐπίνοιαν"* [6] ὀνομάζεσθαι· ὅθεν *ἡ συνήθεια* {4} καλεῖ "ἐπιλογισμόν", εἰ καὶ μὴ οἰκείως.[25] Οἷον τοῦ σίτου *νόημα* [21] *μὲν* [9a] ἁπλοῦν ἐνυπάρχει πᾶσι, καθὸ *φανέντα* {11} *γνωρίζομεν* [22]· ἐν *δὲ* [9b] τῇ ἀκριβεῖ περὶ αὐτοῦ ἐξετάσει *θεωρία* [23] τε *πλειόνων* [13] προσέρχεται καὶ προσηγορίαι διάφοροι *τῶν νοηθέντων* [21] σημαντικαί. Τὸν γὰρ αὐτὸν σῖτον *νῦν μὲν* [24a] "καρπὸν" λέγομεν, *νῦν δὲ* [24b] "σπέρμα", καὶ πάλιν "τροφήν"· "καρπὸν" μὲν ὡς τέλος τῆς παρελθούσης γεωργίας, "σπέρμα" δὲ ὡς ἀρχὴν τῆς μελλούσης, "τροφὴν" δὲ ὡς κατάλληλον εἰς προσθήκην τῷ τοῦ προσφερομένου σώματι. Τούτων δὲ ἕκαστον τῶν λεγομένων ... *κατ' ἐπίνοιαν* [6] *θεωρεῖται* [23].

[3rd definition] Καὶ ἁπαξαπλῶς πάντα τὰ *τῇ αἰσθήσει* [20] *γνώριμα* [22] καὶ ἁπλᾶ μὲν εἶναι *τῷ ὑποκειμένῳ* [25] *δοκοῦντα* [11], ποικίλον δὲ λόγον κατὰ *τὴν θεωρίαν* [23] ἐπιδεχόμενα, *ἐπινοίᾳ* [6] *θεωρητὰ* [23] λέγεται ...

Ἐγγὺς δὴ τοῦ τοιούτου *τρόπου* [3] *τῆς ἐπινοίας* [6] *τὴν χρῆσιν* [7] καὶ παρὰ τοῦ θείου δεδιδάγμεθα

ad quae nostri *sensus* [20] penetrare non possunt).

Consideramus [23] *et illa* [19], et *animi* [10] *intentione* [6] *cognoscimus* [22], vel hominem vel aliud animal crescere, senescere, *nunc* [24a] stare *nunc* [24b] movere gressum, *modo* [24a] angi curis *modo* [24b] securo pectore conquiescere, sanitate *alias* [26a] frui *alias* [26b] dolorem perpeti, ex nigro album, nigrum ex albo *colorem* [18] mutari, peritum ex imperito, ex indocto doctum, ex mansueto ferum, ex feroci mansuetum.

Cum igitur, *in iis quae sunt* {5}, alia *sensibus* [20], alia *mentibus* [21] colligantur, separari haec propriis nominibus homines eruditi maluerunt, et id quod *dinoscitur* [22] *sensibus* [20] *"usian"* [26b] dici, illud autem quod *animi* [10] *tractatu* [7] colligitur ac saepe mutatur 'συμβεβηκός' (id est "accidens") nominari voluerunt. Et quoniam in permanente *usia* [25b] ea quae accidunt inesse noscuntur, ipsam *usian* [25b] ὑποκείμενον' [25a] (id est "subjacens") et "non in subjecto" appellari voluerunt, illa vero quae accidunt, "ἐν ὑποκειμένῳ" (id est "in subjacenti") dixerunt.[26]

[25] For the genuineness of this semicolon on ἐπιλογισμός see my "The Sources of Content", 17–18.

[26] For a full analysis of the parallels (especially the *ad sensum* ones) see my "Stoic Epistemology".

λόγου . . . Ὁ Κύριος ἡμῶν Ἰησοῦς Χριστὸς . . . , *ἓν* [12b] *ὢν* [12a] κατὰ *τὸ ὑποκείμενον* [25a] καὶ *μία* [12b] *οὐσία* [25b] καὶ ἁπλῆ καὶ *ἀσύνθετος* {17 *e contrario*}, *ἄλλοτε* [26a/b] ἄλλως ἑαυτὸν ὀνομάζει *ταῖς ἐπινοίαις* [6] διαφερούσας ἀλλήλων τὰς προσηγορίας μεθαρμοζόμενος . . . Καὶ οὕτως ἄν τις τῶν ὀνομάτων ἕκαστον ἐφοδεύων ποικίλας εὕροι *τὰς ἐπινοίας* [6] *ἑνὸς* [12b] ἑκάστου τοῦ κατὰ *τὴν οὐσίαν* [25b] τοῖς πᾶσιν *ὑποκειμένου* [25a].

"HE BRANDISHES OVER US THIS ARISTOTELIAN WEAPON" (*CE* II 620). AN EXAMPLE OF (MIS)USE OF ARISTOTLE'S NAME IN THE CONTROVERSY OVER UNBEGOTTENNESS*

Ladislav Chvátal

> Ἢ τῶν Ἀριστοτέλους ὄντως ἡμῖν καὶ Χρυσίππου συλλογισμῶν ἔδει πρὸς τὸ μαθεῖν, ὅτι ὁ ἀγέννητος οὐ γεγέννηται;
>
> (Basil of Caesarea, *C. Eun.* I,5,43)
>
> ἁλιευτικῶς, ἀλλ' οὐκ Ἀριστοτελικῶς
>
> (Gregory of Nazianzus, *Or.* 23,12,12)

As the main topic of my paper, I have chosen an example of the use or misuse of Aristotle's name and his heritage in Gregory of Nyssa's *Contra Eunomium* II. This article could be regarded as a contribution both (I) to the debate about the reception of Aristotle and his philosophy by the Greek Fathers, and (II) to the discussion about the concept of 'unbegottenness' (ἀγεννησία) between the Cappadocians and the Eunomians.

Introduction

By attaching an appendix on "Aristotle in the Church Fathers" to his *L'idéal religieux des Grecs et l'Évangile* (1932), a text on both the philosophical and religious aspects of Greek culture,[1] A. J. Festugière stirred up discussion concerning the attitude of Greek patristics to

* I am greatly indebted to P. Dvořák and S. Douglass for their valuable comments and remarks about this essay.

[1] Cf. A. J. Festugière, *L'idéal religieux des Grecs et l'Évangile*, Paris ²1981, 221–263 (Excursus C. Aristotle dans la littérature grecque chrétienne jusqu'à Théodoret). This appendix is actually a question: how it could have happened that the Fathers so decisively rejected the philosophy which later was to form the foundation of the most successful and influential Christian philosophy ever devised? Cf. D. T. Runia, "Festugière Revisited: Aristotle in the Greek Patres", *VigChr* 43 (1989) 2.

Aristotelian philosophy.[2] David Runia has enlarged and elaborated on Festugière's conclusions.[3] The nucleus of Runia's paper is an extended list of all references to Aristotle and his school in the Greek Fathers.[4] According to this revised list of occurrences, the name of Aristotle (or Aristotelian or Peripatetic) is found eight times in Gregory of Nyssa and twice in the second book of the *Contra Eunomium*.[5]

In a section discussing the origin of words (*CE* II 403–442), Gregory mentions Aristotle as Eunomius' "champion and ally in doctrine".[6] This is because Eunomius argues for the divine origin of naming and words using a doctrine ascribed to Aristotle in the doxographic tradition which excludes divine providence from the sublunar world.[7] In this essay, I restrict myself to the second occurrence relating to an "Aristotelian weapon" (*CE* II 620). The first part deals with the formal structure of the "Aristotelian" argument, the second with its content and contextual aspects.

I. *Formal analysis: "Aristotelian weapon" in the* CE *II*

According to the division of Pottier, the tail end of *CE* II concerns "quelques thèses mineures d'Eunome" (*CE* II 561–627), amongst which he ranks a passage devoted to "Eunomius' dishonesty" (*CE* II 611–627).[8] This passage deals with the question of whether God

---

[2] Besides Festugière's and Ruina's essays mentioned above and below let us quote other influential studies: e.g. G. Lazzati, *L'Aristotele perduto e gli scrittori cristiani*, Milano 1937; H. A. Wolfson, *The Philosophy of the Church Fathers*, Cambridge (MA) 1956; J. Daniélou, *Message évangélique et culture hellénistique*, Tournai 1961; J. C. van Winden, *An Early Christian Philosopher*, Leiden 1971; L. J. Elders, "The Greek Christian Authors and Aristotle", *Doctor Communis* 43 (1990) 26–57.

[3] Cf. D. T. Runia, "Festugière Revisited", 1–34.

[4] Cf. D. T. Runia, "Festugière Revisited", 5–12.

[5] *CE* I 46; 55 (GNO I 37,20; 41,4); *CE* II 411; 620 (GNO I 346,5; 407,25); *CE* III/V 6 (GNO II 162,11); *CE* III/VII 15 (GNO II 220,4); *CE* III/X 50 (GNO II 309,9); *De an. et res.* (PG 46, 52b3–c1). However, the writings of Gregory show numerous reminiscences of Aristotle without naming him. E.g. only in the work *In Canticum canticorum* there are in Langerbeck's opinion about 40 places where the terms may have been taken over from Aristotle; cf. *In Canticum canticorum* (GNO VI 483–484).

[6] *CE* II 411 (GNO I 346,4–5): ὁ προστάτης αὐτοῦ καὶ σύμμαχος τῶν δογμάτων.

[7] *CE* II 411 (GNO I 346,4–15).

[8] B. Pottier, *Dieu et le Christ selon Grégoire de Nysse*, Namur 1994, 430. On the other divisions of *CE* II according S. Hall and L. Karfíková, see the results of this discussion above, p. 55–57; cf. A. Schindler, *Die Begründung der Trinitätslehre in der eunomianischen Kontroverse*, unpublished disertation thesis, Zürich 1964, 190.

comes from non-being. Eunomius had accused Basil of this assertion. After presenting his opponent's argument word-for-word, Gregory's immediate reaction to Eunomius' accusation is to exclaim: "He brandishes over us this Aristotelian weapon!", or in the translation of Stuart G. Hall: "Who agreed with the one threatening us with the Aristotelian spear?"[9] To answer the question what Gregory means by this "Aristotelian weapon/Aristotelian spear" (Ἀριστοτελικὴ αἰχμή), let us inquire into the statement of Eunomius.

> Ἵνα γάρ, φησί, μὴ κωλυθῇ τὸν υἱὸν ἐκ μετουσίας εἰπεῖν τοῦ ὄντος, λέληθεν ἑαυτὸν τὸν ἐπὶ πάντων θεὸν ἐκ τοῦ πάντη μὴ ὄντος εἰπών.
> εἰ γὰρ τὸ μηδὲν τῷ πάντη μὴ ὄντι ταὐτὸν κατὰ τὴν ἔννοιαν,
> τῶν δὲ ἰσοδυναμούντων ἀκώλυτος ἡ μετάληψις,
> ὁ λέγων ἐξ οὐδενὸς εἶναι τὸν θεὸν ἐκ τοῦ πάντη μὴ ὄντος εἶναι λέγει τὸν θεόν.[10]

In the translation of Stuart G. Hall:

> So that he may not be prevented, he says, from saying that the Son derives from participation in him who is, he [i.e. Basil] has inadvertently said that the God over all is from total non-being.
>
> For if A. 'nothing' is the same in meaning as 'total non-being',
> and B. the substitution of synonyms is unavoidable,
> C. one who says that God is from no one is saying that God is from total non-being.[11]

At first sight this assertion seems to be a syllogism, but it is not in the proper sense of the word. Proposition A affirms the identity (ταὐτόν [ἐστιν]) between the meanings of two predicates: 'nothing' (τὸ μηδέν) and 'total non-being' (τὸ πάντη μὴ ὄν).

---

[9] *CE* II 620 (GNO I 407,25–28): τίς ἔδωκε τῷ τὴν Ἀριστοτελικὴν ἡμῖν αἰχμὴν ἐπισείοντι, ὅτι τὸ λέγειν τινὰ πατέρα μὴ ἔχειν ταὐτόν ἐστι τῷ ἐκ τοῦ πάντη μὴ ὄντος αὐτὸν γεγενῆσθαι λέγειν.

[10] *CE* II 618 (GNO I 406,28–407,4).

[11] The other translation by A. Roberts – I. Donaldson, "Gregory of Nyssa, Answer to Eunomius' second book", in: *Nicene and Post-Nicene Fathers, Second Series: Volume V*, Oak Harbor (WA) 1997:

> We will allow him to say that the Son exists by participation in the self-existent; but (instead of this), he has unconsciously affirmed that the God over all comes from absolute nonentity.
>
> If A. the idea of the absence of everything amounts to that of absolute nonentity,
> and B. the transposition of equivalents is perfectly legitimate,
> then C. the man who says that God comes from nothing, says that He comes from nonentity.

Proposition B expresses the substitution rule which does not have to be stated explicitly[12] as long as the speaker does not put special stress on it as Eunomius does in our case.[13]

Prima facie, proposition C seems to be a compound statement. Nevertheless, whichever role the components of our statement play in Eunomius' argument, proposition C contains both the first premise ([ὁ λέγων] ἐξ οὐδενὸς εἶναι τὸν θεόν) and the conclusion ([λέγει] ἐκ τοῦ πάντη μὴ ὄντος εἶναι τὸν θεόν).

For a correct formalization, it is necessary to rearrange the individual components of the argument string as follows:

C1. God is from no one,
and A. 'nothing' is the same in meaning as 'total non-being'
[+ B. the substitution rule]
C2. God is from total non-being

Thus,[14]

O*ga* O . . . x is from y; *g* . . . God; *a* . . . nothing; *b* . . . total non-being;
a = *b* [+ B. the substitution rule]
O*gb*

It has also been said that this is not a classical Aristotelian syllogism, even if Gregory calls the above mentioned Eunomius' argument "the syllogism".[15]

---

[12] The substitution rule does not have to be expressed, because it falls along with the separation rule into the implicitly supposed rules.

[13] On the reason why Eunomius emphasizes the substitution rule, see below, p. 409.

[14] In this instance a problem has arisen with the predicates *a* and *b*, because they are not constants in the proper sense of the word: they do not denote individuals. In our formalization it could appear as if we describe 'nothing' as 'something' which is inadmissible. Since the modern predicate logic is not capable of writing down formally the term 'nothing' or 'total non-being' otherwise than by the statement

$$(x)(F)(\sim Fx) \text{ in contradiction to } \exists x\ \exists F\ (Fx)$$

("nothing has any property"; because of using the extensional interpretation, this statement means "nothing comes under any set"),
we fall back on the formalization 'nothing' and 'total non-being' as *a* a *b*, in the interest of clarity, being aware of that this is not substitution in a proper sense.

[15] Cf. for example *CE* II 617 (GNO I 406,24–25): "this vehement and irresistible web of syllogism" (τὴν σφοδρὰν ἐκείνην καὶ ἄμαχον τοῦ συλλογισμοῦ πλοκήν); *CE*

In Aristotle's work we can find two concepts of syllogism. In the *Prior Analytics*, Aristotle defines a syllogism as a discourse in which from certain propositions that are laid down something other than what is stated follows of necessity.[16] This describes syllogism in the broad sense of the word because this formula embraces almost any argument in which a conclusion is inferred from two *or more* premises.[17] But discussing syllogism in detail, Aristotle considers almost exclusively arguments in which there are two premises (αἱ προτάσεις) and, in his sense, a simple and general conclusion (τὸ συμπέρασμα). Speaking more precisely, every syllogistic conclusion follows from two premises which relate the terms of the conclusion to a third term called the middle.[18] The premises and the conclusion are simple statements because they affirm a predicate of the subject. Their internal structure corresponds to the manner of connection among individual terms. The number of statements (for Aristotle only 3) amounts to the number of terms (ὅροι). The same is also the number of symbols which Aristotle's syllogism uses to represent the terms.[19]

It follows that according to Aristotle's narrower usage of syllogism we may not apply the name 'syllogism' to any argument with a compound statement as a premise.[20] However, we have seen that Eunomius' argument does not contain a compound statement, even if it seemingly does.[21] The main reason why Eunomius' argument cannot be called an Aristotelian syllogism is that the word *is* in propositions C1 and C2 does not have the meaning of the Aristotelian copula, that of affirming a predicate of the subject. Instead, Eunomius uses *is* to convey the idea of origin, "comes from". It is not, therefore,

---

II 619 (GNO I 407,18–19): "that irresistible syllogism" (τὸν ἄμαχον ἐκεῖνον συλλογισμόν); *CE* II 623 (GNO I 408,19–20): "that invalid syllogism" (τὸν λελυμένον ἐκεῖνον συλλογισμόν); *CE* II 618 (GNO I 407,7): "the feeble illusion of his sophistic syllogism" (τὴν ψυχρὰν καὶ ὀνειρώδη τοῦ σοφίσματος συνθήκην); *CE* II 621 (GNO I 408,7–8): "the grip of your syllogism" (τὴν τοῦ σοφίσματός σου λαβήν); *CE* II 622 (GNO I 408,12–13): "that soggy web of your syllogism" (ἡ μαλθακὴ τοῦ σοφίσματος αὕτη διαπλοκή).

[16] Aristotle, *An. Pr.* I 1, 24b18–20: συλλογισμὸς δέ ἐστι λόγος ἐν ὧ τεθέντων τινῶν ἕτερόν τι τῶν κειμένων ἐξ ἀνάγκης συμβαίνει τῷ ταῦτα εἶναι.

[17] Syllogism in this inclusive sense had already been used in the *Topics*. Aristotle, *Top.* I 1, 100a25.

[18] Cf. Aristotle, *An. Pr.* I 25, 41b36–42a5.

[19] It is universally accepted that Aristotle's categorical syllogistic anticipates the modern predicate logic.

[20] Cf. W. Kneale – M. Kneale, *The Development of Logic*, Oxford 1984, 67.

[21] See above, p. 402.

a case of Aristotle's categorical subject-predicate statement but a relational one: the terms 'God', 'nothing', resp. 'total non-being' are members of a relation expressed by the predicate "is from/comes from". The Aristotelian logical apparatus was not able to cope with this kind of statement.[22]

If we work only with the English translation, it could be legitimately objected that both Eunomius' argument and our formalization make no sense. Proposition C runs in the translation of S. G. Hall: "one who says that God is from *no one* is saying that God is from *total non-being*", but proposition A asserts the identity of meaning of the terms *nothing* and *total non-being*. The translation, which is rather an explication here, is markedly limited by English language within its scope of expressing the relevant Greek terms. The masculine genitive of the negative indefinite pronoun οὐδείς ('no one, nobody') has the same form as that of οὐδέν ('nothing'): ἐξ οὐδενός.[23] Hence the expression ἐξ οὐδενός could be understood and translated

---

[22] Eunomius' relational argument is resolvable neither by Aristotelian logic nor by the apparatus of Megarian-Stoic logic. This logic school differs from the Paripatetic particularly in the fact that the propositions of a syllogism can be coumpounded with other propositions. The construction component of a syllogism is not a term as in Aristotle, but a statement. The form of syllogism rests only on the way of connection of propositions by propositional conjunction (*if, then, but* and *therefore*). The way the statements are connected with the help of conjunctions influences the rightness of the syllogism. However the basis of preposition remains still the (Aristotelian) scheme "S *is* P". On the Megarian and Stoic logic cf. W. Kneale – M. Kneale, *The Development of Logic*, 113–176.

Although the theory of relations and the solution of relational syllogisms is commonly (cf. for example W. Kneale – M. Kneale, *The Development of Logic*, 427) connected with Augustus de Morgan and his paper written in 1859 ("On the Syllogism IV and on the Logic of Relations", *Cambridge Philosophical Transactions* 10, 1864, 331–358), there is found in the history of philosophy in addition to minor attempts at a solution (for example Joachim Jungius [Junge] and his *Logica Hamburgensis* published in 1638) chiefly the book *Logica obliqua* written by Juan Caramuel of Lobkowicz (on the presentation of Juan Caramuel and his logic as the forerunner of de Morgan see P. Dvořák, *Jan Caramuel z Lobkovic*, Praha 2006; P. Dvořák, "Relational Logic of Juan Caramuel", in: D. M. Gabbay – J. Woods, eds., *The Handbook of the History of Logic*, II, Amsterdam, forthcoming).

[23] Being perfectly precise by formalization of Eunomius' argument, we should append another step which asserts the identity of the terms οὐδέν and μηδέν 'nothing', so that the record can be complete. The full version would look as follows:

C1. God is from 'οὐδενός',
[+ A1 [unexpressed]. 'τὸ οὐδέν/nothing' is the same in meaning as 'τὸ μηδέν/nothing']
and A2. 'τὸ μηδέν/nothing' is the same in meaning as 'τὸ πάντη μὴ ὄν/total non-being'
[+ B. the substitution rule]
C2. God is from 'τοῦ πάντη μὴ ὄντος/total non-being'.

both 'from no one', as Hall has done, and 'from nothing', as Roberts-Donaldson.[24] These two possibilities of understanding and translation are the root of the trouble: Did Eunomius understand the expression ἐξ οὐδενός as referring to οὐδέν 'nothing' or did he take advantage of the agreement of the genitive forms to twist the meaning of Basil's argument and to accuse him of asserting the scandalous opinion that God comes from nothing? Gregory positively tends towards the second alternative and aims to present the original meaning of Basil's words.

II. *Content analysis: Gregory's and Basil's explanations of unbegottenness*

Basil of Caesarea endeavours in a section of the first book of *Adversus Eunomium* to prove that the term 'unbegottenness' cannot express the divine essence as the Eunomians maintain.[25] He points to a biblical genealogy (*Lk* 3,23–27).[26] The origin of every human being is derived from his parents: Joseph was the son of Eli, Eli of Mattath, Mattath of Levi and so on, up to the first man Adam who is said to be from God (*Lk* 3,38). And there we have to stop going backwards. This is a clear sign for Basil, and should be to "the understanding of all" that "God is from no one (ἐξ οὐδενός)".[27] He is the beginning of all, there is nothing whatever preceding him.[28] To be from no one (τὸ ἐξ οὐδενός) is the same in meaning as to be unbegun (τὸ ἄναρχον), and to be unbegun amounts to being unbegotten (τὸ ἀγέννητον).[29]

---

[24] See above, n. 11.

[25] As regards the attitudes of Eunomius we have to rely particularly on Basil's and Gregory's reports in their works. Eunomius' well-preserved writings are gathered in R. P. Vaggione (ed.), *Eunomius. The Extant Works, Text and Translation*, Oxford 1987. On doubts if Gregory reproduces Eunomius' doctrine correctly cf. K.-H. Uthemann, "Die Sprache der Theologie nach Eunomius von Cyzikus", *ZKG* 104 (1993) 143–175.

[26] Basil of Caesarea, *Adv. Eun.* I 15,12–37(SC 299, 224–226); Gregory of Nyssa, *CE* II 614–615 (GNO I 405,21–406,5).

[27] *CE* II 614–615 (GNO I 405,21–406,1): ἐρωτήσωμεν ὁ δὲ θεὸς ἐκ τίνος; ἆρ' οὐχὶ πρόχειρόν ἐστι τῇ ἑκάστου διανοίᾳ ὅτι ἐξ οὐδενός.

[28] Cf. *CE* II 613 (GNO I 405,13–17): ἐπειδὰν γὰρ πάντα διεξελθόντες τὸν θεὸν μετὰ πάντα τῷ νῷ λάβωμεν, τὴν πάντων ἀρχὴν ἐνοήσαμεν. ἀρχὴ δὲ πᾶσα εἴπερ ἑτέρου τινὸς ἐξημμένη τύχοι, ἀρχὴ οὐκ ἔστιν. οὐκοῦν εἰ ἀρχὴ τοῦ παντὸς ὁ θεός, οὐδ' ὁτιοῦν ἔσται τῆς τῶν πάντων ἀρχῆς ὑπερκείμενον.

[29] Cf. Basil of Caesarea, *Adv. Eun.* I 15,25–26 (SC 299, 226): τὸ δὲ ἐξ οὐδενὸς τὸ ἄναρχόν ἐστι δηλονότι, τὸ δὲ ἄναρχον τὸ ἀγέννητον.

But Basil's explication of the connotation of 'unbegotten'[30] does not stop here. As in the case of humans, an expression of origin (τὸ ἔκ τινος) (e.g. to be from Peter and Mary) is not an expression of essence (οὐσία); the phrase "of unbegottenness" when it means "to be from no one" (τὸ ἐξ οὐδενός) cannot characterize the Divine essence.[31]

Basil and Gregory try to explain to Eunomius that the terms ἀγεννησία/ἀγέννητος do not have an exclusive status among the other predicates of God, as the Eunomians assert, but that it is possible to substitute synonyms for 'unbegottenness' such as 'to be from no one' (τὸ ἐξ οὐδενός) or 'to be unbegun' (τὸ ἄναρχον) without any change in meaning. 'Unbegottenness' is not the only proper name of the Divine essence or nature.[32] Against the singleness of Eunomian unbegottenness, Basil and Gregory put together a series of positive and negative terms by which they aim to describe what could not be grasped conceptually.[33] It is crucial for them that (1.) there are many predicates and (2.) there are both negative and positive expressions.

---

[30] Cf. *CE* II 613 (GNO I 405,17–18): αὕτη τοῦ διδασκάλου περὶ τῆς τοῦ ἀγεννήτου σημασίας ἡ ἔκθεσις.

[31] *CE* II 615 (GNO I 406,2–5): ὡς οὖν ἐπὶ τῶν ἀνθρώπων οὐκ ἦν οὐσία τὸ ἔκ τινος, οὕτως οὐδὲ ἐπὶ τοῦ θεοῦ τῶν ὅλων οὐσίαν ἔστιν εἰπεῖν τὸ ἀγέννητον.

[32] Cf. e.g. *CE* II 62 (GNO I 244,1–2): λέγουσι μηδὲν ἕτερον εἶναι τὴν θείαν φύσιν πλὴν τὴν ἀγεννησίαν αὐτήν, *CE* II 21 (GNO I 232,29–30): οὐσίαν τὴν ἀγεννησίαν ὁρίζονται, in a similar way Eunomius, *Apol.* 8 (Vaggione 42,17–18); *CE* II 23 (GNO I 233,15–17): τῆς φύσεως ὄνομα τὸ ἀγέννητον, καὶ ἔστιν οὐδὲν ἕτερον ἢ ἀγεννησία ἡ φύσις. The fact that only one appropriate expression about God can exist is derived by Eunomius from the divine origin of words (things are named by God and their names contain the substance of things in utterance – there is no comparison between the names given by God and those created by human reason, which cannot reflect reality; on the different Eunomian and Cappadocian semiotic models cf. T. Dolidze, "The Logic of Language in Gregory of Nyssa's Treatise 'Against Eunomius' ", *Phasis* (Tbilisi) 4, 2001, 15–25, see 16–19; L. Karfíková, "Die Rede von Gott nach Gregor von Nyssa: Warum ist Pluralität der theologischen Diskurse notwendig", *Graecolatina Pragensia* 18, 2000, 53–61, see 54–56) and from God's simplicity. God is simple and uncompound; that is why only one term can fully expresses him; cf. *CE* II 23 (GNO I 233,11–17); Eunomius, *Apol.* 19 (Vaggione 58,16ff). On the subject of connection of unbegottenness, simplicity and being cf. *CE* II 22–41 (GNO I 233,8–238,8).

[33] Cf. e.g. Basil of Caesarea, *Adv. Eun.* I 10,1–48; 14,1–2 (SC 299, 204–206; 220). But in the opinions of the Cappadocians not only the essence of God is unknowable, but the essence of all creatures as well; cf. e.g. *CE* II 71–78 (GNO I 236,14–239,1). This is a clear result of Gregory's conception of the cognitive status of language along with the ontological structure "infinite God—finite creatures" as T. Dolidze points out; cf. T. Dolidze, "The Logic of Language", 18; L. Karfíková, "Die Rede von Gott", 58.

1. According to Gregory, it is imperative that we name God by a great number of various predicates.[34] As there is not only one name describing the Divine essence, we must have recourse to a plurality of terms. Each of them expresses only a part of the Divine reality.[35] We are related to the inexpressible Divine essence by many thoughts and from many points of view.[36] Only the multiplicity and variety of individual terms could mediate to us at least a partial knowledge of God,[37] without knowing "the definition of his essence" (ὁ τῆς οὐσίας λόγος).[38] Individual names of God only refer our mind to God, nothing else.[39]

2. Gregory places alongside the expression unbegottenness a series of positive (ἡ πάντων ἀρχή, ἡ τοῦ παντὸς αἰτία) and negative (τὸ ἄναρχον, τὸ ἐξ οὐδενός) terms. The positive terms express what pertains to the Godhead,[40] the negative to what does not belong to it.[41] According to Gregory, the same idea can be expressed by both negation[42] and affirmation. The synonyms of 'unbegottenness' are mutually equivalent[43] and their meaning remains 'one and the same'.[44]

---

[34] On the necessary plurality of theological utterances in Gregory of Nyssa cf. L. Karfíková, "Die Rede von Gott", particularly 58–61.

[35] Cf. *CE* II 145 (GNO I 267,21–26): ἐπειδὴ γὰρ ἓν οὐδὲν ὄνομα περιληπτικὸν τῆς θείας ἐξεύρηται φύσεως κατ' αὐτοῦ τοῦ ὑποκειμένου προσφυῶς τεταγμένον, διὰ τοῦτο πολλοῖς ὀνόμασι, ἑκάστου κατὰ διαφόρους ἐπιβολὰς ἰδιάζουσάν τινα περὶ αὐτοῦ τὴν ἔννοιαν ποιουμένου, τὸ θεῖον προσαγορεύομεν. According to Gregory the God is ἀκατονόμαστος – unnameable; cf. *CE* III/V 59 (GNO II 182,2); *Ref.* 14–15 (GNO II 318,3–25).

[36] Cf. *CE* II 475 (GNO I 365,4–8): διὰ τὸ μὴ δύνασθαι τηλαυγῶς κατιδεῖν τὸ ζητούμενον πολλαῖς ἐννοίαις τῆς ἀφράστου φύσεως πολυτρόπως καὶ πολυμερῶς ἐπορέγεται, οὐ κατὰ μίαν τινὰ διάνοιαν τὸ κεκρυμμένον θηρεύουσα.

[37] Cf. *CE* II 145 (GNO I 267,26–28): ἐκ τῆς πολυειδοῦς καὶ ποικίλης κατ' αὐτοῦ σημασίας ἐναύσματά τινα πρὸς τὴν κατανόησιν τοῦ ζητουμένου θηρεύοντες.

[38] *CE* II 71 (GNO I 248,2).

[39] Cf. e.g. *CE* II 89 (GNO I 253,5–12). Cf. M. Canévet, *Grégoire de Nysse et l'herméneutique biblique*, Paris 1983, 54–59; B. Pottier, *Dieu et le Christ*, 180–181; L. Karfíková, Řehoř z Nyssy, Praha 1999, 182–187.

[40] *CE* II 131 (GNO I 263,27–28): τὰ μὲν [ὀνόματα] τῶν προσόντων τῷ θεῷ.

[41] *CE* II 131 (GNO I 263,28–29): τὰ δὲ τῶν ἀποπεφυκότων ἔχει τὴν ἔμφασιν.

[42] *CE* II 135 (GNO I 264,23): τὸ μὲν θέσιν τὸ δὲ ἀναίρεσίν τινος ἔχειν.

[43] *CE* II 137 (GNO I 265,16–21): εἴτε γὰρ ἀρχὴν αὐτὸν καὶ αἴτιον τοῦ παντὸς εἶναι λέγοις εἴτε ἄναρχον αὐτὸν ὀνομάζοις εἴτε ἀγεννήτως εἶναι εἴτε ἐξ ἀϊδίου ὑφεστάναι εἴτε τοῦ παντὸς αἴτιον εἴτε ἐξ οὐδενὸς αἰτίου μόνον, πάντα τὰ τοιαῦτα ἰσοστάσιά πως ἀλλήλοις ἐστὶ κατὰ τὴν δύναμιν τῶν σημαινομένων καὶ ὁμοτίμως ἔχει τὰ ῥήματα.

[44] *CE* II 136 (GNO I 265,6): τὸν δὲ νοῦν τοῖς λεγομένοις ἕνα καὶ τὸν αὐτὸν διαμένειν.

Gregory and Basil dilute the exclusivity of the term unbegottenness not only by connecting to it a plurality of positive and negative terms which express the same meaning, but also by attaching to 'unbegottenness' 'indestructibility' (ἀφθαρσία/ἄφθαρτος) as the polar term (which already does not have the same meaning!).[45] We predicate unbegottenness of God, if we approach God from the point of view of beginning; indestructibility, if we come up to Him from the point of view of end.[46] 'Unbegottenness', from being an absolute proper term which reveals the Divine essence itself, becomes one of the predicates expressing 'a peripheral property of the essence'.[47]

Conclusion

I have asked what 'the Aristotelian weapon' in *CE* II 620 means. Eunomius accused Basil of maintaining that God is from total nonbeing.[48] The detailed analysis of Eunomius' argument has shown that this is not an Aristotelian (subject-predicate) syllogism, even if Gregory calls it a syllogism in several passages[49] but a relational statement which the Aristotelian logical apparatus was not able to cope with. This 'Aristotelian weapon' is not the use of Aristotelian syllogistic or/and logic, but a 'syllogism' in the broad, general and rather inaccurate sense of the word: an elementary inferential rule of discur-

[45] Cf. *CE* II 366–386, 445–560 (GNO I 333,11–339,7; 356,17–390,16).

[46] To this subjectivizing step in Basil cf. Basil of Caesarea, *Adv. Eun.* I 7,35–44 (SC 299, 192); B. Pottier, *Dieu et le Christ*, 162–163.

[47] Cf. Basil of Caesarea, *Adv. Eun.* I 7,12–17.27–29 (SC 299, 188–190); B. Pottier, *Dieu et le Christ*, 166: "une qualité périphérique de la substance"; on the influence of Greek philosophical schools on Basil's theory of language and on the whole controversy cf. e.g. Th. Dams, *La controverse eunoméenne*, Paris 1951, 174; J. Daniélou, "Eunome l'Arien et l'exégèse néoplatonicienne du Cratyle", *REG* 69 (1956) 412–432; E. Cavalcanti, *Studi eunomiani*, Roma 1976, 34–46; J. M. Rist, "Basil's 'Neoplatonism': its background and Nature", in: P. J. Fedwick, (ed.), *Basil of Caesarea: Christian, Humanist, Ascetic*, I, Toronto 1981, 137–220; Th. Kobusch, "Name und Sein. Zu den sprachphilosophischen Grundlagen in der Schrift Contra Eunomium des Gregor von Nyssa", in: L. F. Mateo-Seco – J. L. Bastero (eds.), *El "Contra Eunomium I" en la Produccion Literaria De Gregorio De Nisa. VI. Coloquio Internacional sobre Gregorio de Nisa*, Pamplona 1988, 247–268; G. C. Stead, *Logic and the Application of Names to God*, in: L. F. Mateo-Seco – J. L. Bastero (eds.), *El "Contra Eunomium I"*, 303–320; L. Karfíková, "Die Rede von Gott", 53–56.

[48] *CE* II 611; 618 (GNO I 404,23–24; 406,28–407,4).

[49] Cf. above, n. 15.

sive thought. Aristotle's name is used less as a reference to his philosophy and intellectual heritage than as a contemptuous invective which the participants of dogmatic controversies in the 4th century C.E. often used as a curse.[50] Gregory's "insult" and its specific occasion are only a tiny fraction of the huge problem of argumentation in the debates between Eunomius and the Cappadocians.[51] To elaborate on this issue was not within the compass of this essay.

The fact that Eunomius' argument comes to the conclusion that God comes from non-being is a response to Basil's attempt to explain the term 'unbegottenness' as 'to be from no one' (τὸ ἐξ οὐδενός). We have to agree with Gregory that Eunomius took Basil's words out of context[52] because it must have been evident to Eunomius that τὸ ἐξ οὐδενός refers to οὐδείς 'no one, nobody' and not to οὐδέν 'nothing'. By the sequence ἐξ οὐδενός – τὸ οὐδέν/τὸ μηδέν – τὸ πάντῃ μὴ ὄν and the substitutability of these terms, Eunomius aims at the Cappadocian method of explaining the name unbegottenness[53] and turns it against Basil. On the basis of a list of synonymous names which are "the same in meaning" (ταὐτὸν κατὰ τὴν ἔννοιαν), Basil and Gregory aim to prove that 'unbegottenness' is not the only, exclusive term which reveals the Divine essence. It is only one of *several* names, either positive or negative, which are equivalent and through which we come to God from *our* point of view. He still remains unnameable and by our mind incomprehensible, not subject to being comprehended, grasped and expressed in His essence.

[50] On the association of Aristotelian dialectic with the origin and practice of heresy cf. D. T. Runia, "Festugière Revisited", 23–26; L. J. Elders, "The Greek Christian Authors and Aristotle", 47; J. Mansfeld, *Heresiography in Context*, Leiden 1992, passim.

[51] Cf. e.g. E. Vandenbussche, "La part de la dialectique dans la théologie d'Eunomius 'le Technologue' ", *RHE* 40 (1944–45) 47–72; R. J. De Simone, "The Dialectical Development of Trinitarian Theology: Augustine versus Eunomius' 'Technological' Theology", *Angelicum* 64 (1987) 453–475.

[52] Cf. *CE* II 611 (GNO I 404,24–27). This is one of the repeated objections to Eunomius; cf. e.g. Basil of Caesarea, *Adv. Eun.* I 5,69–78 (SC 299, 174–176). On the interrelationship of a signicative word and context cf. T. Dolidze, "The Logic of Language", 23.

[53] Cf. above p. 405.

GREGOR VON NYSSA UND PLOTIN ZUM PROBLEM DER GOTTESPRÄDIKATIONEN – EIN VERGLEICH

Theodoros Alexopoulos

1

Die Transzendenzbehauptung, Gott sei nicht nur dem Begreifen von Menschen, sondern auch dem von Engeln, ja, jedem überweltlichen Begreifen überlegen, er sei unaussprechlich, unsagbar, zu erhaben, als dass er sich durch Worte bezeichnen ließe,[1] siedelt das Göttliche jenseits jeden Bereichs des Denkens an.

Gregor fasst seinen Apophatismus mit folgenden Worten zusammen: "Zuerst lernen wir, was von Gott zu erkennen nötig ist: dieses Erkennen besteht darin, auf ihn nichts anzuwenden, was mit menschlicher Auffassungskraft erkannt wird."[2] Wenn aber Gott wesentlich unsagbar und unaussprechlich ist, fragt man sich billigerweise, ob das θεολογεῖν, die Rede von Gott, wirklich einen Sinn hat, und nicht bloß eine überflüssige, nutzlose Beschäftigung ist. Nach Gregor gibt es fünf wichtige Gründe, die den Prozess der Namensgebung legitimieren, und ihr einen besonderen Stellenwert verleihen:

1) Der erste Grund hängt eng mit der Perspektive der menschlichen Existenz zusammen. Diese Perspektive besteht vor allem in der Erkenntnis und der Betrachtung der Seienden.[3]

2) Von großer Bedeutung ist auch die Konzeption des Göttlichen als des Allerersehntesten (ποθεινότατον) und Reizvollsten (ἐρασμιώτατον)[4] (bzw. Anziehendsten).[5] Nach Gregor kann Gott nur das Ziel allen

---

[1] *CE* I 683 (GNO I 222,18–25).

[2] *VM* II (GNO VII/1 88,8–10).

[3] *CE* II 572 (GNO I 393,15–17): "Jede Tätigkeit und Bewegung des gesunden Denkens zielt nach Möglichkeit auf die Erkenntnis und die Betrachtung der Seienden ab."

[4] Vgl. *Cant.* I (GNO VI 31,5–6). S.u. Anm. 7. Dazu A. Meredith, "The Good and the Beautiful in Gregory of Nyssa", in: H. Eisenberger (ed.), ΕΡΜΗΝΕΥΜΑΤΑ. *FS H. Hörner*, Heidelberg 1990, 133–145. Vgl. auch Plotin, *Enn.* VI 7 [38] 32,25–26. Dazu G. Siegmann, *Plotins Philosophie des Guten. Eine Interpretation von Enneade VI 7*, Würzburg 1990, 101–108; 153–157.

[5] *An et res.* 54 (PG 46, 89b). Vgl. auch Plotin, *Enn.* VI 7 [38] 23,3.

Strebens sein (μόνον ὀρεκτόν),[6] was ein unendliches Fortschreiten zu Ihm verursacht.[7] Das absolut Gute ist dasjenige, das durch seine Anziehungskraft die Liebe der Seele weckt und nährt und sie als Quelle jeder Gutheit zu seiner Teilhabe ruft.[8]

3) Darüber hinaus ist man in der Lage über Gott zu sprechen wegen der ursprünglichen Verwandtschaft (συγγένεια)[9] zwischen der menschlichen Seele und Gott. Diese Verwandtschaft wird durch die εἰκών zum Ausdruck gebracht. Die εἰκών zeigt die von Gott gesetzte ursprüngliche Bestimmung des Menschen und sie ist die Voraussetzung für die Metousia.[10] Die Gottebenbildlichkeit des Menschen erklärt die innere Dynamik und den unaufhörlichen Drang der Seele nach Gott, der das endgültige Ziel aller Wünsche und Gedanken des Menschen ist. Wegen ihrer εἰκών-Haftigkeit ist die Natur des Menschen potentiell unendlich.

4) Gott verleiht uns Zeichen (ἴχνη) und (zündende) Funken (ἐναύσματα) durch seine Wirkungen, so dass wir das Unfassbare auf dem Wege der Analogie zu dem, was wir in der Wirklichkeit wahrnehmen, betrachten können.[11] Der Mensch erfährt die göttliche Energeia, die zu uns herunterkommt und die zur Grenze unseres Verständnisses von Gott wird.[12]

5) Die wichtigste Voraussetzung für die Gottesprädikation bezieht sich auf das außerordentliche und übernatürliche Ereignis der Menschenwerdung des Logos. Die Herablassung des Unveränderlichen ins Veränderliche hat Gott 'denen hienieden' (τοῖς κάτω)[13] zugänglicher gemacht. Die Seele verfügt jetzt über einen Wegweiser, einen Leiter, der sie nach oben emporführen kann.

---

[6] Vgl. *VM* II (GNO VII/1 40,24).

[7] Vgl. *Cant.* I (GNO VI 31,5–7).

[8] Vgl. *Cant.* V (GNO VI 158,12–14). Vgl. *Cant.* I (GNO VI 16,13).

[9] Vgl. *An et res.* (PG 46, 97b).

[10] *Infant.* (GNO III/2 79,14–16.21–22).

[11] Vgl. *Cant.* I (GNO VI 37,1). Um seinen Gedanke zu veranschaulichen, verwendet Gregor zur Auslegung der Stelle *Cant.* 1,3 (μύρον ἐκκενωθὲν ὄνομά σου) das Bild eines entleerten Salbölgefäßes, das aufgrung des Dampf-Rückstandes im Gefäß eine Vermutung über das ausgeleerte Salböl zuläßt. Mit allen theologischen Begriffen bezeichnen wir nicht das 'Salböl' der Gottheit selbst, sondern zeigen wir nur einen kleinen Rest vom 'Dampf' des göttlichen Wohlgeruchs (βραχύ τι λείψανον ἀτμοῦ τῆς θείας εὐωδίας) auf. Dazu F. Dünzl, *Braut und Bräutigam, Die Auslegung des Canticum durch Gregor von Nyssa*, Tübingen 1993, 64–65.

[12] Vgl. *Cant.* XI (GNO VI 334,5–9). Vgl. *Abl.* (GNO III/1 44,7–9).

[13] Vgl. *Cant.* X (GNO VI 304,17–305,2).

Die Zuschreibung verschiedener Prädikationen beeinträchtigt nach Gregor die göttliche Einfachheit nicht, und zwar aus folgenden Gründen:

1) Οὐ γὰρ ἐκ τοῦ καλεῖσθαί τι τὸ εἶναι γίνεται, ἀλλ᾽ ἡ ὑποκειμένη φύσις, οἵα δι᾽ ἂν οὖσα τύχῃ, διὰ τῆς προσφυοῦς τοῦ ὀνόματος σημασίας γνωρίζεται.[14] Der Name betrifft alles, was um das Seiende herum betrachtet wird.[15] Er umschreibt und umfasst das Ding ohne[16] sein Wesen zu bezeichnen. Er weist auf die jeweilige Eigenschaft (τὸ προσόν) des Dings hin, und erläutert das 'wie sein' (πῶς εἶναι) des Seienden.[17] Würden die vielen Namen, die wir, gestützt auf die Schrift, dem Göttlichen geben, sein Wesen bezeichnen, wäre die göttliche Natur 'vielartig' und zusammengesetzt.[18]

2) Darüber hinaus bleibt die Einfachheit der göttlichen Natur deshalb unaffiziert, weil jeder Name eine besondere Bedeutung hat, die nicht in Widerspruch zu einer anderen Bestimmung steht. Die vielen Benennungen verursachen nicht die Zerspaltung des Subjekts, weil sie nicht sein Wesen, sondern seine Eigenschaften auslegen.[19] Alle Namen sind einander gleichgewichtig und gleichwertig (ἰσοστάσια – ἰσότιμα).[20]

3) Es gibt eine Identität von Prädikationen, die sowohl dem Menschen als auch Gott zuzuweisen sind. Diese Art von Aussagen geschieht vom Sein her und entspricht der Tendenz, Bestimmungen des Niedrigeren auf das Höhere zu übertragen. Es besteht jedoch nur eine oberflächliche Ähnlichkeit, da die Bezeichneten so weit voneinander entfernt sind. In dem Maße, wie beide Naturen, die menschliche und die göttliche, voneinander entfernt sind, unterscheiden sich

---

[14] *Perf.* (GNO VIII/1 177,14–16): "Nicht dadurch, dass etwas benannt wird, kommt Sein zustande, sondern die zugrunde liegende Natur wird in ihrer jeweiligen Beschaffenheit durch die Bedeutung des von Natur aus zukommenden Namens erkannt."

[15] Vgl. *CE* III/V 56 (GNO II 180,23–24): ἄλλο μέν τι περὶ τοῦ ὄντος νοεῖν, ἄλλο δέ τι περὶ τοῦ ἐπιθεωρουμένου τῷ ὄντι (Es ist ein Unterschied zwischen dem Nachdenken über das Seiende und dem (Nachdenken) über das, was an dem Seienden zu beobachten ist). Vgl. ebd. *CE* III/V 60 (GNO II 182,9–13); vgl. *Abl.* (GNO III/1 42,21–43,2).

[16] *CE* III/V 55 (GNO II 180,7–10): "Jedes Wort, dass durch namentliche Bezeichnung die unbegrenzte Natur zu umfassen und auszulegen verspricht, gleicht einem, der sich einbildet, in seiner flachen Hand das ganze Meer einzuschließen."

[17] *CE* III/V 60 (GNO II 182,12–13).

[18] Vgl. *CE* II 302 (GNO I 315,11–13).

[19] *CE* II 477 (GNO I 365,19–22).

[20] *CE* II 137 (GNO I 265,19–21); vgl *CE* II 478 (GNO I 365,22–30).

auch die Eigenschaften der göttlichen Natur von den an uns feststellbaren und haben sich zum Erhabeneren und zum Gottangemesseneren gewandelt.[21] In dieser Hinsicht messen wir, wenn wir den Herrn 'Macht', 'Leben', 'Licht', 'Wort' nennen, diesen Bestimmungen eine gotteswürdige (θεοπρεπής)[22] Bedeutung bei und sind uns bewusst, dass die uns zugeschriebene Prädikation im Vergleich zu der, die dem Herrn zuzuschreiben ist, von niedrigerer Wertigkeit ist.

4) Gregor kennt zwei Weisen, von Gott zu reden: die positive und die negative. Sie sind durch eine Beziehung gegenseitiger Ergänzung gekennzeichnet. Die beiden sprachlichen Formen wechseln einander unablässig ab. Beide Formen bilden eine zusammenhängende, einheitliche[23] Redeweise, die zum besseren Verständnis des Göttlichen führt. Die positiven Bestimmungen haben die Bezüglichkeit Gottes durch seine Wirkungen auf die Seienden im Blick, eine positive Erfahrung der Wahrheit. Sie sind relationale Bestimmungen und Erklärungen und gehören zu den so genannten πρός τι λεγόμενα.[24] Diese Art von Prädikationen aber leidet an einer Schwäche. Sie trennt[25] nicht Schöpfer und Geschöpf. Diese Rolle spielen die verneinenden Bestimmungen. Sie haben eine 'abwendende' Wirkung, mahnen uns fernzuhalten, was Gott in seinsmäßig-naturhafte Beziehung zur Schöpfung bringen könnte. Sie sagen aus, was Gott nicht ist. Die negativen Namen bedeuten einen Verzicht auf alle Seinsbestimmungen und betonen genau die Stellung des Absoluten jenseits alles Seienden.

Positive und negative, kataphatische und apophatische Theologie sind gleichwertig.[26] Keine von beiden stellt die Teilhabe mit Gott sicher und keine beschreibt das Wesen Gottes als solches. Beide sind bestenfalls Annäherungen mit begrenzter Gültigkeit. In diesem Punkt

---

[21] *CE* II 235 (GNO I 294,21–24).

[22] *CE* III/I 135 (GNO II 49,7–12); vgl. *CE* III/I 129 (GNO II 47,4–9).

[23] *CE* I 588 (GNO I 196,4–10): "Jede Gottesprädikation und jeder erhabene Gedanke, jede Aussage und jede Annahme, sofern sie den Ideen von Gott gemäß ist, ist mit der anderen zusammengefügt und geeint; und sämtliche Annahmen bezüglich Gottes begreift man als fortwährend geeint und miteinander zusammengeschmiedet: Vaterschaft, Ungezeutsein . . ." Dazu Ch. Boukis, Ἡ γλῶσσα τοῦ Γρηγορίου Νύσσης ὑπὸ τὸ φῶς τῆς φιλοσοφικῆς ἀναλύσεως, θεολογικά δοκίμια 2, Θεσσαλονίκη 1970, 92–96.

[24] *CE* I 569 (GNO I 190,21).

[25] Vgl. *CE* II 579 (GNO I 395,16–17).

[26] *CE* II 137 (GNO I 265,19–21).

unterscheidet sich Gregor von dem Verfasser des *Corpus Areopagiticum*, der der Apophasis gegenüber der Kataphasis einen deutlichen Vorrang zuerkennt.[27]

2

Sehen wir uns jetzt die Lehre Plotins näher an. Das "Jenseits des Seins" hebt das Absolute Eine über das Sein hinaus und damit über alle überhaupt möglichen und denkbaren Bestimmungen. Plotin expliziert die absolute Transzendenz des Einen durch eine Reihe von negativen Prädikationen. In diesen Prädikationen werden dem Einen alle Bestimmungen des Intelligiblen wie des Sinnenfälligen abgesprochen. Die Negation versucht das Absolute nicht zu definieren und dadurch zu begrenzen, sondern durch Aphairesis aus dem Bereich der Seienden abzutrennen, auszugrenzen. Sie erweist sich dementsprechend als die Aussage, welche die Transzendenz des Absoluten zum Ausdruck bringt, und die seine vollkommene Unbezüglichkeit auf die Seinsordnung verdeutlicht. Die negative Methode aber sagt, was das Eine nicht ist, und nicht was Es ist. Das Eine wird an sich auch in der Negation nicht getroffen.[28] Die Negation aber hat den Vorrang vor der Position. Während die positive Aussage es unter einer Seinsbestimmung andeutet, macht die negative seine Seinstranszendenz sichtbar.

Die Negationen beziehen sich zwar auf das Absolute, vermögen es aber nur von außen zu umkreisen, ohne Es selbst zu erreichen.[29] Sogar der Name 'Eines', der schlechthin die Einfachheit anzeigt, und der, soweit möglich, treffend in Vergleich zu anderen Bestimmungen gesetzt ist, erweist sich als unangemessen,[30] um Es (Das Eine) an sich

---

[27] Vgl. *Div. Nom.* XIII 3 (PG 3, 981b = Suchla 230,1–2).

[28] Darum bleibt auch die Negation dem Absoluten unangemessen, "denn sie bezeichnet das Absolute wesentlich als das, was nicht das Sein ist, durch eine Relation also, in der das Absolute wesentlich doch nicht steht. Die Unwahrheit der negativen Transzendenzbehauptung ist ihre Unwesentlichkeit für das Absolute. Allein, über solche Unwesentlichkeit kommt keine Aussage hinaus." G. Huber, *Das Sein und das Absolute. Studien zur Geschichte der ontologischen Problematik in der spätantiken Philosophie*, Basel 1955, 82.

[29] *Enn.* VI 9 [9] 3,52–53: ἡμᾶς οἷον ἔξωθεν περιθέοντας. Vgl. *Enn.* VI 9 [9] 8,43–45.

[30] Vgl. *Enn.* V 5 [32] 6,31–34: . . . ἵνα ὁ ζητήσας ἀρξάμενος ἀπ᾽ αὐτοῦ, ὃ πάντως ἁπλότητός ἐστι σημαντικόν, ἀποφήσῃ τελευτῶν καὶ τοῦτο, ὡς τεθὲν μὲν ὅσον οἷόν

kund zu tun. Plotin gelingt es sogar zu sagen, die Bezeichnung Eines sei lügnerisch.[31] Im eigentlichen Sinne kommt dem Absoluten überhaupt kein Name zu, weil es in seiner absoluten Transzendenz über alle Namen erhaben ist. Wenn es keinen der Erhabenheit des Absoluten würdigen Namen gibt, dann muss man auf jeden Versuch Es zu benennen, verzichten. Plotin fordert uns immer wieder 'alles wegzunehmen' (ἄφελε πάντα),[32] um so zu einem einigeren Leben oder einem Leben auf Einheit hin zu gelangen:[33] Im Wegnehmen von allem wird die absolute Einfachheit des Einen bewahrt. Die Unaussagbarkeit des Einen ist nach Plotin in seiner Einfachheit begründet.

1) Das primäre Eine bestehe "ohne die Beifügung eines anderen" (ᾧ μηδὲν ἄλλο πρόσεστι) und sei infolgedessen von nichts aussagbar (οὐδενὸς ἂν κατηγοροῖτο τοῦτο).[34] Jede Ergänzung eines Prädikats würde eine Hinzufügung und daher eine Zerstörung der Einheit bedeuten.

2) Würde man versuchen, von dem Einen etwas zu prädizieren, dann würde es bedeuten, ihm ein Akzidens (συμβεβηκός) zuzuschreiben.[35] Das Eine weist nicht die für alles Sensible charakteristische Spaltung in οὐσία und συμβεβηκός auf; denn Es besitzt (im Unterschied zu diesem) seine Einheit nicht als einen Zusatz: οὔχ ὡς ἄλλο, εἶτα ἕν (nicht als sei es sonst etwas und dann erst Eines).[36]

τε καλῶς τῷ θεμένῳ οὐκ ἄξιον μὴν οὐδὲ τοῦτο εἰς δήλωσιν τῆς φύσεως ἐκείνης... K. H. Volkmann-Schluck (*Plotin als Interpret der Ontologie Platos*, Frankfurt 1966, 85) kommentieret die Stelle: "Das pythagorische Symbol A-pollon als der Un-viele trifft es ebenso wie die Bezeichnung 'Eines', wenn sie nicht mehr zu sein beanspruchen als Aufhebung der Vielheit und Bestimmtheit. Aber noch die angemessenste Bezeichnung führt zur Einsicht in die Unangemessenheit von Bezeichnung schlechthin."

[31] *Enn.* V 4 [7] 1,9.

[32] *Enn.* V 3 [49] 17,38. Vgl. auch V 5 [32] 13,11; V 5 [32] 6,20; VI 7 [38] 35,7; VI 8 [39] 21,26–28; VI 8 [39] 15,22–23; III 8 [30] 10,31.

[33] Die Gelassenheit ist somit die Bedingung der Möglichkeit der Einung. Die Abstraktionsbewegung (ἀφαίρεσις) darf nicht nur als logischer Prozess, sondern muss geradezu als ethischer Imperativ, als Lebensprogramm eines bewußten Lebens verstanden werden; dazu vgl. W. Beierwaltes, *Selbsterkenntnis und Erfahrung der Einheit. Plotins Enneade V 3* (Text, Übersetzung, Interpretation, Erläuterungen), Frankfurt 1991, 250–253; ders., *s. v.* "Erleuchtung", in: J. Ritter (Hrsg.), *Historisches Wörterbuch der Philosophie*, Bd. 2, Basel – Stuttgart 1972, 714.

[34] *Enn.* VI 2 [43] 9,6–7.

[35] Vgl. *Enn.* VI 9 [9] 3,49–51.

[36] *Enn.* VI 9 [9] 5,32–33. Dazu Chr. Horn, *Plotin über Sein, Zahl und Einheit. Eine Studie zu den systematischen Grundlagen der Enneaden*, Stuttgart – Leipzig 1995, 297, 325–326.

3) Das absolute Eine ist von nichts aussagbar auch deshalb, weil es durch seine strenge Einheit ein Unendliches ist, da es zu seinem Inhalt keine Grenze gibt. Denn eine externe wie eine interne Begrenzung, mithin eine Unterscheidung, wäre nur durch eine vorhergehende 'messende' Größe möglich, die von Plotin ausgeschlossen wird: das Eine ist weder gegen ein anderes, noch gegen sich selber begrenzt; denn dann wäre es schon Zweiheit.

Trotz der Grundhaltung, das Eine durch Negationen vom Seienden abzuheben, ist es unvermeidlich, dass vom Absoluten auch in positiven Aussagen die Rede ist. Wir nennen es so (z.B. ἀγαθόν), nicht weil ihm dies angemessen wäre, sondern weil wir nichts Besseres haben. Alle positiven Bestimmungen haben nur uneigentlichen und metaphorischen Charakter, sie haben einen rein didaktischen Sinn[37] und sind Hinweise auf das Unnennbare, die nur um unsertwillen nötig sind.[38] Sie sagen das Eine nicht aus, sondern sie weisen auf Es hin, denn die Sageweise der Aussage ist aufgrund ihrer zwiefältigen Struktur (etwas über etwas) dem absolut Einfachen unangemessen. Unter dem Vorbehalt der Uneigentlichkeit der Namen müssen wir in jeder Prädikation auch ein 'gleichsam' (οἷον) hinzufügen.[39] Alle Rede über das Eine, sowohl die bejahende als auch die verneinende, bringt nicht Es selbst zur Sprache, denn Es selbst ist absolut unsagbar: "Wir sprechen zwar über Es aber wir bringen nicht Es selbst zur Sprache. Denn wir sagen nur, was Es nicht ist, was Es aber ist, sagen wir nicht."[40]

3

Unser Vergleich zwischen den Konzeptionen beider Denker hat folgende Ergebnisse erbracht:

[37] Vgl. *Enn.* VI 8 [39] 13,4: τῆς πειθοῦς χάριν; VI 8 [39] 13,48: ἐξ ἀνάγκης ἐνδείξεως ἕνεκα.

[38] Vgl. *Enn.* VI 2 [43] 17,2–5: τὸ μὲν ἀγαθόν, εἰ τὸ πρῶτον, ἣν λέγομεν τὴν τοῦ ἀγαθοῦ φύσιν, καθ' ἧς οὐδὲν κατηγορεῖται, ἀλλ' ἡμεῖς μὴ ἔχοντες ἄλλως σημῆναι οὕτω λέγομεν. Vgl. auch *Enn.* VI 9 [9] 5,31–32; V 5 [32] 6,25–28; II 9 [33] 1,5–8; VI 7 [38] 38,4–6; V 3 [49] 13,5–6. Der Versuch, das Absolute affirmativ zu bestimmen, wäre, so Plotin, eine verwegene Rede (τολμηρὸς λόγος) und mit der absoluten Transzendenz nicht zu kombinieren. Vgl. *Enn.* VI 8 [39] 7,11.

[39] *Enn.* VI 8 [39] 13,50.

[40] *Enn.* V 3 [49] 14,5–8.

1) Für beide hat die Sprache einen relativen Charakter und basiert auf einer Vereinbarung. Sie ist nicht in der Lage, das absolut Unendliche in den engen Grenzen eines Wortes einzusperren. Die Wahrheit kann nicht in geschlossenen Begriffsbestimmungen, weder in positiven noch in negativen, bestimmt werden.[41]

2) Die Sprache hat primär eine semantisch-hinweisende Wirkung. Alle Prädikationen vermögen das Absolute nur von außen zu umkreisen,[42] darum beziehen sie sich zwar auf Es, aber ohne Es zu erreichen.

3) Alle Begriffe über Gott sind Anleihen aus dem Bereich des Seins. Diesen Begriffen verleihen wir einen Gottes Erhabenheit geziemenden Sinn.[43] Alles, was wir über Gott reden, reden wir daher uneigentlich (ἐκ καταχρήσεως),[44] gerade weil wir Ihn nicht anders bezeichnen können.[45]

4) Die Henologie Plotins ist nach Form und Gestalt wesentlich negativ. Plotin verwendet mit Vorsicht positive Prädikationen. Er legt keinen großen Wert auf die Kataphasis, und darin unterscheidet er sich stark von Gregor, der den Ausgleich zwischen den beiden Methoden festhält. Nach Plotin wäre jede positive Prädikation eine Hinzufügung und würde daher zur Zerstörung der Einfachheit führen. Dem Einen kommt aufgrund seiner Transzendenz das ἔστιν oder ὅ ἐστιν nicht zu.[46] Dagegen wird Gott von Gregor in der Auslegung von *Ex* 3,14 als das wahrhafte Seiende (ὄντως ὄν) bezeichnet.[47] Durch diese Bezeichnung kommt Gregors Gott auch der plotinischen zweiten Hypostase nahe[48] und unterscheidet sich von dem des Dionysius Areopagita, der eine stärkere Terminologie zur Betonung der Gottestranszendez verwendet.[49] Dazu kann man auch bemerken, dass bei Gregor der platonische Ausdrück 'jenseits des Seins' nicht zu finden

---

[41] Vgl. Plotin *Enn.* V 5 [32] 6,14–15. Vgl. *CE* III/I 103 (GNO II 38,19–21).

[42] Vgl. Plotin *Enn.* VI 8 [39] 8,6–7: περὶ αὐτοῦ. Vgl. Gr. Nyss., *Abl.* (GNO III/1 43,14–16).

[43] Vgl. *CE* III/I 128 (GNO II 47,4–5).

[44] Vgl. *CE* II 459 (GNO I 360,24).

[45] Vgl. Plotin *Enn.* VI 2 [43] 17,3–5.

[46] Vgl. Plotin *Enn.* VI 7 [38] 38,1–2.11; VI 8 [39] 8,14.20.

[47] Vgl. *VM* II (GNO VII/1 40,8). Dazu Th. Böhm, *Theoria – Unendlichkeit – Aufstieg. Philosophische Implikationen zu de Vita Moysis von Gregor von Nyssa.* Leiden – New York – Köln 1996, 94

[48] Vgl. S. R. C. Lilla, *Neuplatonisches Gedankengut in den Homilien über die Seligpreisungen Gregors von Nyssa*, Leiden – Boston 2004, 60, Anm. 216.

[49] Dionysius Areopagita bezeichnet Gott als μὴ ὄν. Vgl. *Div. Nom.* I 1 (PG 3, 588b = Suchla 109,16).

ist.[50] Trotz dieses wesentlichen Unterschieds, was die Terminologie angeht, stimmen Gregor und Plotin in der Behauptung überein, dass Gott jeden Bereich des Geistes transzendiert.[51]

5) Betreffs des Prozesses der Namensgebung (Gottesprädikation) setzt Gregor die göttliche Energeia voraus. Die Kataphasis hat auch für Gregor eine besondere Bedeutung, weil sie die Erfahrung der Wahrheit beschreibt. Sie beruht auf der göttlichen Wirkung, die der Mensch in seinem Aufstieg zu Gott erfährt und die er positiv zum Ausdruck bringt.[52] Auf die Würde der Kataphasis weist auch Gregor von Nazianz besonders hin, indem er sagt: "Es ist viel einfacher und kürzer zu zeigen, was etwas nicht ist, indem du sagst, was es ist, statt alles zu widerlegen was es nicht ist, um zu zeigen was es ist.[53] Derjenige, der sagt, was etwas nicht ist, und verschweigt, was es ist, verhält sich ähnlich jemandem, der, wenn er gefragt wird, wie viel zwei mal fünf macht, antwortet: es macht weder drei, noch vier, noch fünf usw." Plotin dagegen setzt kein göttliches Heilshandeln an der Welt und besonders für den Menschen voraus. Daher kann er sich nicht für eine Theologie einsetzen, die auf der Beschreibung der erfahrenen Wirkung beruht. In Plotins Betrachtung des Seienden auf seinen Einheitscharakter hin erkennt man Spuren[54] des Einen. Alles, was ist, ist dadurch, dass es am Einen teilhat.[55]

6) Für beide Autoren hat die Apophasis keinen privativen Sinn. Das Fehlen (στέρησις) ist das Ausbleiben dessen, was einem Wesen an sich zukäme; da Gott aber absolut einfach ist, kommt ihm an sich selbst überhaupt nichts zu. Gott ist völlig unbedürftig. Er bedarf nicht darüber hinaus noch der Benennung.

7) Als nächster, und zwar sehr wichtiger Punkt, in dem sich Gregor mit dem Gedanken Plotins berührt, ist die 'Unendlichkeit'[56] und

---

[50] *Lexicon Gregorianum* III 369–370, *s.v.* ἐπέκεινα.

[51] Vgl. *CE* III/VIII 2 (GNO II 238,18); *CE* III/I 105 (GNO II 39,5–6); *VM* II (GNO VII/1 87,16–17). Vgl. *Enn.* VI 7 [38] 41,32–38; III 9 [13] 9,10–12.

[52] Vgl. S. Papadopoulos, ΘΕΟΛΟΓΙΑ καὶ ΓΛΩΣΣΑ. Ἐμπειρικὴ θεολογία – Συμβατικὴ γλῶσσα, Athen 2002, 145.

[53] Vgl. *Or.* XXVIII 9 (PG 36, 37ab = SC 250, 118–120).

[54] Vgl. Plotin *Enn.* V 5 [32] 5,13–14: ὥστ' εἶναι τὸ εἶναι ἴχνος τοῦ ἑνός. Vgl. III 8 [30] 11,19–23; V 5 [32] 10,1–2; V 5 [32] 6,17. Vgl. Gr. Nyss., *Cant.* I (GNO VI 37,1).

[55] Vgl. *Enn.* III 8 [30] 9,23–24; V 5 [32] 10,3–4; VI 8 [39] 21,20–22.

[56] Über den Begriff der Unendlichkeit bei Gregor von Nyssa im Vergleich zu Plotin, siehe die eingehende Studie von Th. Böhm, *Theoria*, 108–149, 164–170, 195–198.

Unbegrenztheit Gottes – des Einen. Gregor von Nyssa geht davon aus, dass jedes Seiende vor allem dadurch gekennzeichnet ist, dass es durch gewisse Grenzen festgelegt wird (πέρασί τισιν ὡρισμένοις).[57] Diese Grenzen sind der Anfang und das Ende. Umschrieben von einer Arche und einem Telos ist jedes Seiende 'überschaubar' (ἐποπτεύσιμον).[58] Die Grenze ist die grundlegende Eigentlichkeit jedes Seienden. Sie bestimmt jedes Seiende zu einem umgrenzten Etwas, so dass dieses mit sich selbst identisch und von allem anderen unterschieden ist. Durch die Grenze wird jedes Seiende bestimmbar, definierbar und denkbar. Da der Mensch etwas nur als bestimmt bezeichnet erfassen kann und da Gott jede Seinsbestimmung wie Gestalt, Form, Größe, Qualität abgesprochen wird,[59] ergibt sich daraus, dass Er unfassbar und daher undefinierbar ist. Bei ihm erkennt man kein Maß. Im eigentlichen Sinn ist sein Maß die Unendlichkeit, d.h. die Fähigkeit, sich in jede Richtung auszudehnen und durch keine Grenzen beschränkt zu werden.[60] Wenn aber der Name eine Art von Umschreibung,[61] d.h. eine Art von Begrenzung ist, ist es selbstverständlich, dass sich Gott jeder Beschränkung durch die Worte entzieht.[62] Die oben erwähnte Vorstellung des 'Begrenzten' als grundlegende Eigenschaft des Seienden ist ein sehr wichtiger Anknüpfungspunkt zwischen Gregor von Nyssa und Plotin. Auch bei Plotin hat das Seiende einen bestimmten ontischen Inhalt, die Form (τὸ εἶδος). Alles was gestaltlos ist, ist keine Existenz, keine οὐσία. Und das ist so, weil die οὐσία ein 'etwas' (τι) sein muss und daher etwas Bestimmtes, Begrenztes. Ἀνείδεον ὂν οὐκ οὐσία· τόδε γάρ τι δεῖ τὴν οὐσίαν εἶναι· τοῦτο δὲ ὡρισμένον. (Ist das Eine gestaltlos, so ist es kein Sein; denn das Sein muss ein Dieses sein, und das heißt, ein Begrenztes.)[63] Die eidetische Bestimmtheit ist also der Grundzug des Seins und macht seine Erkennbarkeit für das Denken aus. Als absolut Einfaches kann

---

[57] Vgl. *VM* I (GNO VII/1 3,6–8). Gregor nennt als Beispiele im Bereich des Quantitativen die Elle oder die Zahl 'zehn', die jeweils an einem Punkt beginnen und an einem Punkt enden.

[58] Vgl. *CE* II 578 (GNO I 395,3–11).

[59] Vgl. *Beat.* III (GNO VII/2 104,15–19); vgl. auch *Virg.* X (GNO VIII/1 290,23–291,4); *Cant.* V; XII (GNO VI 157,14–21; 357,10–20).

[60] Vgl. *CE* I 345–346 (GNO I 129,11–13).

[61] Vgl. *Cant.* V (GNO VI 157,19). Vgl. auch Gr. Naz., *Or.* XVIII 10 (PG 36, 37d = SC 250, 120).

[62] Vgl. *CE* III/I 103 (GNO II 38,19–21); vgl. auch *CE* II 587 (GNO I 397, 29–30); *Abl.* (GNO III/1 52,15–53,3).

[63] *Enn.* V 5 [32] 6,5–6.

das Eine nicht eidetisch bestimmt sein; Das absolut einfache Eine liegt über jede Bestimmtheit hinaus und damit auch über das Sein, weil Sein wesentlich Bestimmtheit bedeutet. "Indem das Absolute das εἶδος transzendiert, transzendiert es *eo ipso* auch das Sein."[64] Indem das Eine nicht in bestimmten Grenzen eingeschränkt sein kann, kann es auch kein Gegenstand des Erkennens sein. Das Erkennen selber hat den Charakter der Einheit, aber den der bestimmten und relationalen Einheit (ἕν τι), nicht der absoluten und reinen. Denn Erkennen ist wesentlich intentional, es ist immer auf ein Bestimmtes (τί) gerichtet,[65] das als Bestimmtes auch erkennbar ist. Das absolute Eine als reine Einheit ist nicht Etwas – Eines, sondern vor dem Etwas (πρὸ τοῦ τί),[66] über jedes Was hinaus.

8) Abschließend: Einer der wichtigsten Punkte, in dem sich Gregor in Übereinstimmung mit Plotin befindet, besteht in der Überzeugung, dass Gott der direkten Erkenntnis für das ihm Nachgeordnete wesenhaft entzogen ist. In der Wirklichkeit kann dem Absoluten überhaupt kein Name zukommen. Die angemessene Weise der Gottesprädikation ist nicht die *theologia negativa*, sondern die *theologia superlativa* (übersteigende Theologie). Proklos und der Verfasser des *Corpus Areopagiticum* haben auf diese dritte Art der Theologie klar hingewiesen.[67] Spuren dieser Theologie, die zur Aufhebung jeder Erkenntnis führen, welche durch Kataphasis und Apophasis erreicht wird, sind sowohl bei Plotin[68] als auch bei Gregor zu finden. In unserem Fall, d.h. im zweiten Buch von *Contra Eunomium*, gibt es eine entscheidende Stelle,[69] an der diese Idee der Annäherung an Gott durch die Selbstüberschreitung des Denkens deutlich wird.

> Das menschliche Denken, indem es forschend und vielgeschäftig ist, begehrt und berührt, soweit möglich, durch Überlegungen die unüberschreitbare und erhabene Natur. Weder besitzt es eine Scharfsichtigkeit, um klar das Unsichtbare zu sehen, noch ist es völlig von

---

[64] G. Huber, *Das Sein und das Absolute*, 55.

[65] Vgl. *Enn.* VI 7 [38] 40,6: νόησις πᾶσα ἐκ τινός ἐστι καὶ τινός.

[66] *Enn.* V 3 [49] 12,52; dazu P. Crome, *Symbol und Unzulänglichkeit der Sprache. Iamblichos, Plotin, Porphyrios, Proklos.* München 1970, 87; J. Halfwassen, *Der Aufstieg zum Einen. Untersuchungen zu Platon und Plotin*, Stuttgart 1991, 165.

[67] Vgl. Proklos, *In Parm.* VII 7,9–10 (Cousin 1159f); dazu J. Halfwassen, *Der Aufstieg*, 181; W. Beierwaltes, *Proklos. Grundzüge seiner Metaphysik*, Frankfurt 1965, 361–366. Vgl. auch Ps. Dion. Areop., *MTh.* V (PG 3, 1048b = Ritter 150,7–9).

[68] Vgl. Plotin *Enn.* V 3 [49] 14,1–3.6–7.17–18; *Enn.* V 5 [32] 6,31–33; *Enn.* VI 8 [39] 8,6–8; dazu J. Halfwassen, *Der Aufstieg*, 181.

[69] *CE* II 138–139 (GNO I 265,28–266,3).

> der Annäherung ausgeschlossen, so dass es nicht in der Lage wäre, in sich ein Bild des Gesuchten zu formen. Ein Teil des Gesuchten hat es mit Hilfe der Vernunft aufgefasst, das andere aber hat es gewissermaßen durch die Schwäche, es deutlich zu erkennen, begriffen, indem es die Tatsache für eine Art des klaren Wissens hielt, dass das Gesuchte jede Erkenntnis übersteigt.

Das über das Sein Hinausgehende ist weder durch Worte auszudrücken noch der Vernunft zugänglich.[70] Gott kann weder durch die Kataphasis noch durch die Apophasis, d.h. nicht durch die Zugriffe der methodisch vorgehenden, alles erfassenden theoretischen Vernunft, erreicht werden. Gott wird in dem wissenden Nichtwissen[71] erreicht, d.h. im Verzicht und in der Ablösung von allem Denkbaren und Sinnlichen.[72] Im ekstatischen Nichtwissen wird der Geist selbst überschritten: hinausgehoben über sich selbst, wird er in der Erleuchtung durch das überhelle Licht mit Gott vereinigt.[73] Das Heraustreten des Geistes aus sich selbst, die Ekstasis, weist darauf hin, die höchste Erfüllung des Erkennens, die zugleich dessen Aufhebung ist.[74] Es handelt sich um eine lobenswerte ἀγνωσία, denn sie wird sich dessen bewusst, dass ihr alles Unbegreifliche über Gott unbekannt ist.[75]

[70] *CE* II 39–140 (GNO I 265,28–266,3).

[71] *VM* II (GNO VII/1 87,7). Vgl. Plotin, *Enn.* V 5 [32] 7,32: μηδὲν ὁρῶν θεάσεται.

[72] *VM* II (GNO VII/1 88,8–10).

[73] Vgl. *Beat* I (GNO VII/2 77,9–10); *Virg.* V (GNO VIII/1 277,11–12); *Ps.* I 7 (GNO V 44,2–4). Vgl. Ps. Dion. Areop., *Div. Nom.* I 1 (PG 3, 588a = Suchla 108,3–5), Vgl. Plotin. *Enn.* V 5 [32] 7,16–22; V 3 [49] 17,28–37.

[74] G. Huber, *Das Sein und das Absolute*, 88.

[75] Vgl. Maximus, *Schol. in Div. Nom.* IV 2 (PG 4,264a); Vgl. auch II 4 (PG 4, 216d–217a): εἶδος γὰρ καὶ αὐτὸ γνωριστικόν.

SIMPLICITÉ ET CARACTÈRE INENGENDRÉ DE DIEU SELON PLOTIN, EUNOME ET GRÉGOIRE DE NYSSE

Georgios Lekkas

Parmi les caractéristiques particulières de l'Un plotinien, celles qui dominent sont sa simplicité[1] et son caractère inengendré.[2] Tant la simplicité que le statut d'inengendré de l'Un plotinien s'expliquent par la place qu'Il occupe en tant que 'cause première' au sein du système plotinien. L'Un est inengendré parce que, du fait qu'Il est premier, il n'y a rien avant lui qui pourrait l'engendrer.[3] De même l'Un est ce qu'il y a de plus simple (ἁπλούστατον) puisqu'Il ne serait pas le premier s'Il était constitué de multiples.[4]

L'Un simple et inengendré est donc premier pour Plotin, tandis que le second rang revient à ce qu'Il engendre et qui est l'un-multiples, c'est-à-dire le *Noûs*,[5] ce dernier étant, en sa qualité de produit de l'acte de génération de l'Un, nécessairement[6] moins simple que son géniteur.[7] Le principe qui veut que l'engendré soit nécessairement inférieur à son géniteur constitue une constante de la métaphysique plotinienne[8] et n'est pas sans conséquences tragiques pour l'engendré dans la mesure où dès sa naissance celui-ci porte sur lui la marque de son incapacité à s'égaliser à son père,[9] de sorte que, comme l'observe pertinemment Jean Trouillard, le 'retour' de l'engendré est impuissant à le dédouaner pleinement de sa sortie hors de son géniteur.[10]

---

[1] Cf. *Enn.* V 2 [11] 1,3–4. *Ibid.* V 4 [7] 1,5. *Ibid.* V 5 [32] 6,30–33.

[2] *Enn.* VI 8 [39] 7,35–36. *Ibid.* V 4 [7] 1,18–19.

[3] *Enn.* VI 8 [39] 10,16–21.

[4] *Ibid.* II 9 [33] 1,8–9.

[5] *Enn.* V 4 [7] 1,20–21. *Ibid.* V 6 [24] 3,2–4.21–25.

[6] *Enn.* III 8 [30] 9,42–43. Cf. G. Lekkas, "Le concept positif de la nécessité et la production des êtres chez Plotin", *Les études philosophiques* 71,4 (2004) 554–557.

[7] *Enn.* VI 7 [38] 13,1–3.

[8] *Enn.* V 4 [7] 1,39–41. Cf. *ibid.* VI 9 [9] 2,29–32. *Ibid.* V 5 [32] 13,37–38. *Ibid.* VI 7 [38] 17,3–6. *Ibid.* V 3 [49] 15,3–11.

[9] "*L'unité cherche à compenser son inadéquation par la rigueur des relations idéales.*" J. Trouillard, *La purification plotinienne*, Paris 1955, 107 (les italiques sont de l'auteur).

[10] "Le processus de diversification est imparfaitement compensé par la démarche d'assimilation." J. Trouillard, *La purification plotinienne*, 108.

Néanmoins, nonobstant l'infériorité ontologique du *Noûs* engendré par rapport à l'Un qui lui donne naissance, les éléments qui, à notre sens,[11] prédominent dans toutes les métaphores utilisées par le philosophe alexandrin pour décrire la relation entre l'Un et le *Noûs* sont ceux-là même qui, dans son esprit, garantissent continuum et homologie entre le géniteur et les produits de sa procréation, c'est-à-dire entre l'Un et le *Noûs*.[12] On comprend ainsi pourquoi la différence entre l'Un et le *Noûs*, en d'autres termes la différence du père[13] d'avec les produits de sa génération qui lui sont inférieurs, est entre autres décrite par Plotin en termes de différence séparant tout et parties, tout qui n'est pas constitué de parties, à savoir l'Un et parties qui constituent un tout, à savoir le *Noûs*.[14]

Sur l'échelle plotinienne des êtres, les différents degrés ontologiques (*Noûs*, Âme, réalités sensibles) ne résultent pas simplement les uns des autres, mais constituent dans leur totalité l'œuvre d'une puissance autoproductrice et se déployant elle-même, puissance qui n'est autre que l'Un plotinien[15] dont le caractère transcendant est en propre celui du géniteur qui, tout en engendrant, demeure inentamé 'sur lui-même' (ἐφ' ἑαυτοῦ).[16] Plotin considère la relation de l'Un avec les produits inférieurs à lui de son acte de procréation sur base des présupposés de la doctrine platonicienne traditionnelle relative à la participation et à la séparation.[17] Par conséquent, les différents degrés ontologiques s'inscrivent, à son sens, dans la ligne des degrés différents auxquels les produits de l'acte de génération de l'Un participent de celui en qui tous trouvent leur origine.[18] L'Un plotinien ne constitue pas seulement l'origine de la sortie ouvrant par intellection à la multiplicité (νοερὰ διέξοδος),[19] mais également le point de rétrogression de toutes les réalités qui participent de lui.[20] À l'instar

[11] G. Lekkas, "Plotinus. Towards an ontology of likeness", *International Journal of Philosophical Studies* (Dublin), 13 (2005) 53–68.

[12] *Enn.* VI 8 [39] 18,36. Cf. *ibid.* 15–30. *Ibid.* VI 7 [38] 17,13–14. *Ibid.* V 9 [5] 2,26–27.

[13] *Enn.* VI 8 [39] 14,37–38. Cf. *ibid.* 9,29.

[14] *Enn.* VI 7 [38] 12,23–30.

[15] *Enn.* IV 8 [6] 6,11–16. Cf. *ibid.* 25–26.

[16] *Enn.* V 6 [24] 3,6–11. Cf. *ibid.* III 3 [48] 7,8–11.

[17] D. Koutras, *La notion de lumière dans l'esthétique de Plotin*, Athènes 1968, 24 et 26–27 (en grec).

[18] *Enn.* V 3 [49] 15,15–18. *Ibid.* VI 9 [9] 2,22–24. *Ibid.* VI 5 [23] 4,19–20.

[19] *Enn.* IV 8 [6] 7,17–23.

[20] *Enn.* VI 8 [39] 21,20–22. Cf. *ibid.* V 5 [32] 4,1–6.

du Bien dans la *République* de Platon,[21] l'Un plotinien n'est pas un principe agissant *du dehors* par rapport aux produits de sa procréation,[22] mais constitue au contraire pour eux une référence ontologique constante qui, par sa médiation (son effusion de lumière)[23] les pose ontologiquement et leur garantit la faculté de se connaître soi-même.

L'utilisation par Plotin de la participation platonicienne pour rendre compte en termes philosophiques du fait que tous les autres êtres proviennent de l'Un explique, à notre sens, que l'approche cataphatique (positive) de l'Un prenne décidément le pas dans l'œuvre plotinienne sur son approche apophatique.[24] L'Un se connaît lui-même,[25] mais non pas de la même manière que le *Noûs*.[26] L'Un n'est pas 'insensible' (ἀναίσθητον),[27] mais vivant.[28] L'Un ne pense pas mais est la pensée même.[29] Dès lors, nous sommes en droit de douter que, comme le soutient Georges Leroux, l'Un plotinien ne puisse recevoir de prédicats qui soient de l'ordre de l'intellection pure ("noétiques" écrit l'auteur),[30] mais, en tout état de cause, nous ne pouvons qu'être d'accord avec lui pour dire que Plotin recourt aux diverses acceptions positives du Bien platonicien pour démontrer qu'il est possible d'accéder positivement au principe premier (l'Un) au travers d'attributs relatifs à l'action ("éthiques") tels que la volonté et la liberté.[31] Il reste toutefois à faire clairement apparaître que loin de constituer simplement l'une des nombreuses possibilités particulières d'accès au premier principe plotinien, cet accès positif au dit principe est tout d'abord celui qui en fin de compte l'emporte dans l'œuvre plotinienne étant donné que le recours à la participation platonicienne pour les besoins de la cosmologie plotinienne fait du

---

[21] Platon, *République* 508a5–6, 508a11–12, 508b9–10, 508e1–3, 509b6–9 et 540a8.
[22] *Enn.* VI 7 [38] 16,33–35.
[23] *Ibid.* 21–24 et 27–31.
[24] G. Lekkas, "Plotinus", 58–59.
[25] *Enn.* V 4 [7] 2,15–16.
[26] *Enn.* V 3 [49] 15,27–31.
[27] *Enn.* V 4 [7] 2,15.
[28] *Ibid.* 16–17.
[29] *Enn.* VI 9 [9] 6,52–53.
[30] "Si on doit chercher une opposition à l'intérieur des prédicats de l'Un, on la trouvera principalement dans la polarité des prédicats noétiques, constamment niés et des prédicats éthiques que Plotin, avec force, leur substitue.". G. Leroux, *Plotin. Traité sur la liberté et la volonté de l'Un. Ennéade VI, 8 (39)*, Paris 1990, 38. Cf. *ibidem*, p. 37.
[31] G. Leroux, *Plotin*, 38–39.

rapport entre procréateur et procréé tel que le perçoit le philosophe alexandrin davantage un rapport de similarité ontologique que de différence radicale.[32]

Le point commun que l'ontologie plotinienne présente avec celle d'Eunome porte sur la détermination du 'quoi' (de l'essence) au départ du 'comment' (de la question du principe). Selon Eunome,[33] le Père inengendré représente une essence supérieure au Fils étant donné que c'est le Père qui engendre le Fils, de la même manière que l'Un plotinien est ontologiquement supérieur à ce qu'Il engendre, c'est-à-dire au *Noûs*. Toutefois, il y a lieu d'insister ici sur l'étroite filiation intellectuelle qui lie Eunome à Plotin : en effet, ce à quoi l'Un plotinien est ontologiquement supérieur, c'est le *monde intelligible* (le *Noûs*) dont lui-même est le créateur, tout comme Eunome, en faisant du Père le 'créateur' de son Fils, rejette le Fils du côté de la création (κτιστόν).[34] Suivant Grégoire de Nysse,[35] l'aberration où aboutit Eunome prend sa source dans l'identification des notions de 'père' et de 'créateur' et dans l'application du schéma de relation de cause à effet (le principe et ce qui en découle) au sein de la Trinité, et ce, en lui conférant le même contenu sémantique que celui que ce schéma a hérité de son application sur le plan cosmologique du Dieu créateur et du monde créé.

En appliquant à la Trinité le schéma philosophique bipolaire de la cause et de l'effet avec la portée sémantique que ce schéma tirait de son application dans les cosmologies d'inspiration platonicienne, Eunome ne pouvait parvenir à plus, en ce qui concerne le Fils, qu'a voir en lui un degré intermédiaire entre le Père et le monde, c'est-à-dire le degré ontologique d'un Dieu qui, n'étant Dieu qu'en tant que participant (ἐκ μετουσίας)[36] du Père, est nécessairement inférieur à lui.[37]

La question à laquelle il importe de répondre est de savoir quel est l'enjeu de l'application du schéma philosophique de la cause et de l'effet auquel Eunome procède sans distinguer le plan de la théo-

---

[32] G. Lekkas, "Plotinus", 53–57.

[33] *CE* II 52 (GNO I 241,7–9). Cf. *CE* II 65 ; 60 et 21 (GNO I 245,4f ; 243,18–20 et 232,29–233,1).

[34] *CE* II 15 (GNO I 231,11–14). Cf. B. Pottier, *Dieu et le Christ selon Grégoire de Nysse*, Namur 1994, 190.

[35] *CE* II 497–498 (GNO I 371,16–28).

[36] *CE* II 618 (GNO I 407,4–5). Cf. *CE* II 619 (GNO I 407,14–15).

[37] *CE* II 54–55 (GNO I 241,19–24).

logie trinitaire du plan cosmologique. Cet enjeu est purement et simplement l'égalité de rang divin du Père et du Fils. Grégoire de Nysse estime qu'Eunome a recours à l'argument du "caractère inengendré" du Père pour faire tort au Fils ;[38] aussi s'assigne-t-il pour principal objectif, dans la réfutation qu'il lui réserve, du moins dans le *CE* II, de démontrer l'égalité en dignité du Père et du Fils.[39]

Comme avant lui l'avait déjà fait Basile de Césarée,[40] le moyen qu'utilise Grégoire de Nysse pour atteindre son objectif est de dégager la question de l'essence de celle du principe[41] et de démarquer corollairement les noms qui se réfèrent à l'essence (telle la simplicité) de ceux qui désignent une relation ou une absence de relation avec un principe "suréminent" (ὑπερκειμένη) (tel le statut d'inengendré).[42]

Plus spécifiquement, pour Grégoire de Nysse, les termes d'engendré et d'inengendré désignent exclusivement une relation d'origine et non une essence.[43] Le Père est inengendré, mais ce statut qui est le sien n'est en rien constitutif de son essence.[44] Ainsi, ce qui se trouve exprimé par la distinction du Père inengendré et du Fils engendré, c'est une différence d'*hypostases*, celle du Père qui engendre le Fils et celle du Fils engendré par le Père, et non une différence d'essence.[45] La thèse soutenue par Grégoire de Nysse,[46] en accord avec Basile de Césarée,[47] c'est que ce que nous dit le qualificatif inengendré à propos du Père, ce n'est rien d'autre que l'absence de toute dépendance du Père à l'égard d'un principe qui lui serait "suréminent", mais sans rien nous apprendre sur son essence.

Ayant ainsi scindé la détermination, commune à Plotin et à Eunome, de l'essence au départ de la modalité marquant son origine (c'est-à-dire au départ de la question du principe), Grégoire de Nysse n'a désormais nulle peine à soutenir que, bien qu'engendré, le Fils est quant à son essence aussi simple que le Père inengendré.[48] Plus spécifiquement, le Père inengendré diffère de son Fils engendré quant

[38] *CE* II 15–16 et 58 (GNO I 231,19–21 et 242,26f).
[39] *CE* II 51 (GNO I 240,25–26).
[40] *CE* II 615 (GNO I 406,1–5).
[41] *CE* II 386 et 177 (GNO I 339,3–7 et 276,7–11).
[42] *CE* II 24–25 et 28–29 (GNO I 233,22–29 et 234,19–23).
[43] *CE* II 41 (GNO I 238,3–8).
[44] *CE* II 379–380 (GNO I 337).
[45] *CE* II 38–39 et 36 (GNO I 237,19–24 et 236,25–28).
[46] *CE* II 34 ; 18 et 192 (GNO I 236,17–20 ; 232,1f et 280,24–29).
[47] *CE* II 613 (GNO I 405,14–18).
[48] *CE* II 29 ; 42 et 30 (GNO I 234,23–24.26–29 ; 238,12–15 et 235,16f).

au 'comment' de son origine et non quant à sa simplicité.[49] De la sorte, alors que l'ontologie plotino-eunomienne excipait de la différence entre le Père et le Fils au niveau de la modalité propre à leur origine l'existence d'une différence subséquente au niveau de leur essence, Grégoire de Nysse conclut, quant à lui, à l'égalité d'essence du Père et du Fils à partir de la simplicité ontologique qui leur est commune.[50]

Il est intéressant d'observer combien différente est la façon dont les ontologies plotino-eunomienne et grégorienne tirent parti du schéma participatif platonicien relatif à la production du semblable à partir du semblable. En clair, dans le fait que le Fils doive son origine au Père Eunome voit une infériorité ontologique du Fils par rapport au Père attendu que, selon lui,[51] le Fils constitue l'effet d'un acte du Père qui, lui, "n'est pas le produit d'un acte" (μὴ ἐξ ἐνεργείας). En revanche, pour Grégoire de Nysse, d'avoir son origine dans le Père garantit au Fils le statut de "vrai Dieu né du vrai Dieu" avec une pleine égalité de dignité du Père et du Fils.[52] Ayant la "cause" de son origine dans le Père, le Fils se trouve avec lui dans un rapport d'"image" "vis-à-vis de l'original", ce rapport n'étant pas celui d'un inférieur à ce qui lui serait ontologiquement supérieur, comme le postulait la métaphysique plotino-eunomienne, mais bien un rapport d'égalité de rang ontologique entre le Père et le Fils[53] et, qui plus est, de plein et entier englobement réciproque sans aucune confusion de l'un avec l'autre.[54] Vrai Dieu, le Dieu-Logos[55] est, selon Grégoire de Nysse, tout aussi éternel[56] et incorruptible[57] que l'est le Principe de son origine.

Il apparaît donc clairement que par la scission qu'il opère au sein de l'identité plotino-eunomienne du principe et de l'essence, Grégoire de Nysse est parvenu à démontrer que, bien que simple (quant à

[49] *CE* II 29 (GNO I 234,30–235,3).
[50] *CE* II 489–490 (GNO I 369,5–15).
[51] *CE* II 376 (GNO I 336,11–15).
[52] *CE* II 377 (GNO I 337,18–22).
[53] *CE* II 215 (GNO I 288,4–6).
[54] *CE* II 215–216 (GNO I 288), (v. particulièrement : ἔχει ἐν ἑαυτῷ τὰ πατρῷα, μᾶλλον δὲ καὶ αὐτὸν τὸν πατέρα). Cf. *CE* II 214 (GNO I 288,1–3).
[55] *CE* II 236–237 (GNO I 295,7–13).
[56] *CE* II 610 (GNO I 404,16–20).
[57] *CE* II 369 (GNO I 334,7–8).

son essence) et sans principe qui le précède (quant à son origine), ce n'est pas parce qu'Il n'est subordonné à aucun principe que le Père est simple, comme le soutenait la métaphysique commune à Plotin et à Eunome. L'identification par Eunome de l'essence et du caractère inengendré du Père, affirme Grégoire de Nysse, fait de sa dialectique un pur nihilisme : en effet, en ce qui concerne le Père, cette dialectique prive le Père d'essence en identifiant ce qu'Il est à ce qu'Il n'a pas, c'est-à-dire un principe auquel Il serait ontologiquement subordonné, de même que, en ce qui concerne le Fils (ainsi que la création), elle le prive d'essence (tout autant que la création), dès lors que ne peut être essence, comme semble le soutenir Eunome selon Grégoire de Nysse, que le seul caractère inengendré du Père.[58]

Le problème philosophique central qu'examine le *CE* dans son ensemble est de savoir comment il y aura lieu de tirer parti du schéma ontologique traditionnel de la cause et de l'effet dans le cadre nouveau de la philosophie chrétienne. Eunome fait usage du schéma bipolaire grec traditionnel de la relation de cause à effet en le considérant sous l'angle de la métaphysique plotinienne et, plus spécifiquement, (a) de la subordination de la question de l'*essence* à celle du *principe* et (b) du continuum ontologique (du haut vers le bas) entre Dieu et le monde. Cependant, l'application du schéma ontogénétique plotinien de la cause engendrant et du produit engendré dans le cadre de la Trinité chrétienne aboutissait à des relations d'inégalité de rang ontologique entre les trois Hypostases, et ce, du fait que le schéma susmentionné n'était pas seulement un schéma théologique, mais également cosmologique destiné à permettre de rendre compte en termes philosophiques de l'origine du monde de la multiplicité au départ d'un principe premier un (et non pas trinitaire). La réfutation d'Eunome par Grégoire de Nysse se développe sur base d'une double stratégie et se trouve modalisée par un recours différent au schéma philosophique grec traditionnel de la cause et de l'effet suivant son domaine d'application, à savoir tantôt celui de la théologie trinitaire et tantôt celui de la cosmologie : il s'agit en clair (a) de récuser en faux la subordination de l'*essence* à la question du *principe* tout en rétablissant corollairement le primat de l'*essence* vis-à-vis du *principe* et (b) de rompre le continuum entre Dieu

[58] *CE* II 484–485 et 63 (GNO I 367,14–24 et 244,13–15).

et le monde en proclamant la différence ontologique radicale séparant le créé de l'increé.

(a) En ce qui concerne la réfutation de la subordination de l'*essence* au *principe*

Dans sa manière d'aborder la théologie trinitaire chrétienne sur la base des présupposés onto-cosmologiques plotiniens, Eunome conclut à un continuum à sens unique du type de la relation de cause à effet, continuum qui va du Père au Fils et selon lequel, au niveau ontologique, le Fils est nécessairement inférieur (ὑποβεβηκότα) au Père dans la mesure où ce dernier constitue sa cause, raison pour laquelle, d'après Eunome, il n'est pas possible d'attribuer au Fils par raison discursive (κατ' ἐπίνοιαν) l'égalité divine avec le Père.[59] Cependant, en dégageant le thème de l'essence divine de ses liens avec la question de la cause, ce que Grégoire récuse en faux, c'est en définitive la nécessité qui, pour Plotin et dans sa suite Eunome, régit l'essence quant à sa dépendance originaire à l'égard d'une cause supérieure à elle.[60] La relation de cause génitrice à produit engendré ne constitue pas nécessairement, aux yeux de Grégoire de Nysse, une relation de géniteur ontologiquement supérieur à produit ontologiquement inférieur de son acte de génération. D'après le penseur chrétien, du moins sur le terrain de la théologie trinitaire, la relation de cause génitrice à produit engendré ne prédétermine pas négativement le status ontologique de l'acte de procréation. Par conséquent, contrairement à ce qui prévaut de droit dans le cas de la philosophie plotinienne, la relation de cause engendrant à produit engendré ne présuppose pas qu'il existe entre l'une et l'autre une nécessaire différence dans l'ordre de l'essence. Loin d'aboutir à la différence ontologique séparant le procréé et son procréateur, comme c'est le cas pour l'ontologie adoptée par Plotin et Eunome, l'application par Grégoire de Nysse, dans le cadre de la Trinité, du schéma ontogénétique d'une relation de cause à effet lui permet, bien au contraire, de garantir l'identité essentielle de la cause et de l'effet, en l'occurrence celle du Père et du Fils. Cette identité, peut-être Grégoire de Nysse l'admettait-il comme naturelle à l'échelle du surnaturel,

[59] *CE* II 331–332 (GNO I 323,2–15).
[60] G. Lekkas, "Le concept positif de la nécessité", 556.

mais en aucun cas il ne l'eût volontiers acceptée en tant que pareillement nécessaire. Si nous devinons bien ce qui fait la teneur de sa pensée la plus intime, qu'il nous soit permis de supposer qu'il jugeait naturel que Dieu engendre Dieu (que le Père engendre le Fils) tout en faisant de lui son égal, sans cependant estimer que cela dût être semblablement nécessaire. Il est au contraire naturel mais également nécessaire pour Plotin que ce qui est divin par excellence (l'Un) engendre du divin (le *Noûs*) et, qui plus est, qu'il l'engendre en tant qu'inférieur à lui. Ce qui s'oppose ici, c'est, d'une part, une ontologie chrétienne de la liberté inspirée par les recherches d'Origène[61] et d'autre part, l'ontologie plotinienne de la nécessité.

(b) En ce qui concerne la rupture introduite dans le continuum ontologique unissant Dieu et le monde

Les réponses données après Platon par la philosophie grecque antique à la question de la création et de la conservation du monde créé ont été, d'une époque à l'autre et sous une forme plus ou moins modifiée, très souvent entérinées comme présupposée la doctrine platonicienne de la participation. Dans le contexte plus spécifique de la cosmologie plotinienne, le monde fait partie intégrante de la vie de Dieu[62] étant donné que Dieu est lui-même en puissance tout ce qu'Il crée. Pareille conception avait pour conséquence de rendre impossible la définition de limites strictes entre Dieu et le monde qu'Il crée. Au contraire, la réponse que la réflexion chrétienne de Grégoire de Nysse s'est efforcée de fournir à ce problème présupposait que Dieu et le monde fussent rigoureusement distingués sur le plan ontologique et qu'une solution de continuité s'inscrivît entre Dieu incréé et le monde créé.[63] De la sorte, Grégoire de Nysse est

[61] J. Gaïth, *La conception de la liberté chez Grégoire de Nysse*, Paris, 1953, 17–39 (particulièrement 31–32). Cf. B. Pottier, *Dieu et le Christ*, 204–205, et G. Lekkas, *Liberté et progrès chez Origène*, Turnhout 2001, 35–37 et 144–176.

[62] J. Rist, "Plotinus and Christian philosophy", in : L. P. Gerson (éd.), *The Cambridge Companion to Plotinus*, Cambridge 1996, 390–391.

[63] *CE* I 270–316 (GNO I 105–121). Cf. C. B. Skoutéris, "La distinction et l'union du créé et de l'incréé comme point central de la doctrine de saint Grégoire de Nysse", in : *Les Actes de la Rencontre organisée sur le thème "Saint Grégoire évêque de Nysse – Son œuvre pédagogique, anthropologique et théologique", Vouliagméni, 11/1/2003*, Athènes 2003, 17–23 (en grec). Cf. B. Pottier, *Dieu et le Christ*, 119–123, 149 et 180. Voir également M. Canévet, *Grégoire de Nysse et l'herméneutique biblique. Étude des rapports entre le langage et la connaissance de Dieu*, Paris 1983, 249–253.

parvenu non seulement à établir une distinction nette entre nature incréée et natures créées (et, partant, entre théologie et cosmologie, ce qui était inconcevable, par exemple, dans le cadre de la philosophie plotinienne), mais également à sauvegarder une nature commune de Dieu Trinitaire incréé en vue de satisfaire au postulat chrétien d'une égalité de rang ontologique des trois Hypostases divines.

ESSENCE AND ACTIVITY (ENERGEIA) IN EUNOMIUS AND ST. GREGORY OF NYSSA

Torstein Theodor Tollefsen

The terms οὐσία and ἐνέργεια play a lot of different roles in ancient philosophy as well as in the Christian theology of Late Antiquity. The terms are important, for instance, in the controversy over Neo-Arianism because they are central to Eunomius' theology as well as to the Cappadocian polemics against the position of Eunomius. They are also important because they even have a further history in Eastern Christianity, from the Cappadocians to St Gregory Palamas, and from him to modern Orthodox theology. The present paper is devoted to the Eunomian controversy. My intention is to discuss how the *concepts* of *ousia* and *energeia* function within Eunomius' theory of causation and how St Gregory of Nyssa responds to Eunomius' reasoning. I will end the paper, however, with some considerations about possible links between Gregory of Nyssa and the Palamite doctrine of uncreated energies.

In modern literature on 'Palamism', the word *energeia* is often translated as *energy*. I do not want to avoid this translation as a general rule, but I think it might be misleading in some instances. I prefer the more neutral and, perhaps, the philosophically more suitable term *activity*. The Eunomian doctrine of activity is a doctrine of causation, i.e. of divine causation. According to Eunomian theology, 'divine causation' means a doctrine of how God acts as the cause of created otherness. In the case of the Cappadocians, it refers to God as the cause of the uncreated divine hypostases of the Son and the Spirit as well.

In Eunomian theology, there is a hierarchy of three essences or primary beings.[1] The unbegotten God is the first, the only one that is God in the proper sense. The second is caused by the first, and the third is brought to being by the second. To make things quite clear, according to Eunomius, the second being, the Son of God, is

---

[1] Eunomius, *Apologia apologiae*, cf. *CE* I 151–153 (GNO I 71–72).

a *creature* (ποίημα).[2] The unbegotten God is his *cause*. The Son is, of course, not just any creature. He is created before all things as the Only-begotten God. He is, consequently, the most perfect creature that the primary, unbegotten God has ever made. The question is how God works as the cause of the Son.

It is in this connection we must analyze Eunomius' concept of divine activity.[3] How does the Son result from such activity? Eunomius denies that this activity is some kind of division or movement of the essence (μερισμὸν ἢ κίνησίν τινα τῆς οὐσίας τὴν ἐνέργειαν) of God.[4] This, for a start, is obviously a denial of central Nicene ideas in Cappadocian thought, i.e. the *homoousion* and divine generation. According to Eunomius, the divine essence cannot enter the causal relation in such a way that could divide itself and be portioned out like some kind of spiritual stuff. Nor can the activity be a movement of essence, because if essence is eternal, the activity would have to be eternal as well, and therefore the effect would be eternal. This corollary is clearly seen by Eunomius and, as a consequence, he denies its presupposition.[5]

Now, what is the exact relationship between the divine essence and the divine activity in the Eunomian theory of causation? In his *Apologia apologiae* Eunomius speaks of the activities that follow the essences (τῶν ταῖς οὐσίαις παρεπομένων ἐνεργειῶν and τῶν οὐσιῶν ἑπομένας ἐνεργείας).[6] The key terms are the verbs παρέπομαι (follows along side) and ἕπομαι (comes after, follows). If the activity is not an essential movement, one alternative strategy could be to emphasize the distinction between essence and activity in the way done here. The activity is not eternally stemming from the being of God, rather it has a loose connection with His essence as such. One could even speak of activities in the plural, and that they differ proportionately to the kind of work that is executed.[7] Higher products result from

[2] Eunomius, *Apologia* 20,17; 26,1–12 (Vaggione 60; 68–70).

[3] There is some material on the history of the causal sequence of *ousia-dynamis-energeia-ergon* in M. R. Barnes' paper "The background and Use of Eunomius' Causal Language", in: M. R. Barnes – D. H. Williams, *Arianism after Arius*, Edinburgh 1993. The paper lacks, however, comments on Neo-Platonist theories of causation.

[4] Eunomius, *Apologia* 22,9 (Vaggione 62).

[5] Eunomius, *Apologia* 22 (Vaggione 62).

[6] Cf. *CE* I 151–152 (GNO I 72,8–9.16). English translation by A. Roberts – I. Donaldson in: *Nicene and Post-Nicene Fathers, Second Series: Volume V*, Oak Harbor (WA) 1997, 50.

[7] *CE* I 152–153 (GNO I 72) (A. Roberts – I. Donaldson, 50). Cf. Eunomius, *Apologia* 23 (Vaggione 62–64).

more exalted activities, lower ones from more inferior activities. Whenever some thing has a *beginning* of being, this is a sure sign that the activity begins as well. Does this mean that activities have a temporal character?

Kopecek says the Neo-Arian Trinity consisted in discretely independent essences that have arranged themselves in a hierarchy of both *time* and *space*.[8] He qualifies this to mean 'pre-temporal time', a term that unfortunately is not explained. However, there are problems with this interpretation. According to Eunomius' *Expositio fidei* the Son is created and has a beginning, but even so he is "genuinely 'begotten' before the ages" (ἀληθῶς γεννηθέντα πρὸ αἰώνων).[9] For this reason I am sure that Eunomius would not have admitted 'time' (i.e. 'ages') into the spiritual realm. When it comes to space, Kopecek seems just to have taken an objection from Gregory at face value. Gregory points out the spatial indications in Eunomius' description of the hierarchy.[10] I think Eunomius could easily have defended himself against these charges. It is well known that temporal and spatial *metaphors* are frequent within Neo-Platonic as well as in Christian systems of theology. Such metaphors are unavoidable when speaking of intelligible being. When the productive activity takes place beyond the material world, any speaking of beginning and end or any thinking of entities existing discretely must be recognized as speaking and thinking metaphorically of something belonging to a realm that does not answer to our ordinary categories. This, of course, makes it more difficult to understand what it means that the Son is a *creature* in the realm transcending material creation. The Cappadocians fully accept that the Son is begotten, but not that he is οὐκ ἄκτιστον.[11] On the one hand, this makes it urgent to reflect on what is meant by beginning (ἀρχή): does it mean temporal beginning, source of movement (ἀρχὴ τῆς κινήσεως), source of being, that from which something originates? What is clear, though, is that, for Eunomius, the spiritual essences are separated to such a degree that only the first one is God in the proper sense. There must be an ontological gap, then, between God and the Son. This διάστημα is

---

[8] Th. A. Kopecek, *A History of Neo-Arianism*, Cambridge (Mass.) 1979, vol. 2, 453. This is repeated by M. R. Barnes, "The background", 221, cf. note 3.

[9] Eunomius, *Expositio fidei* 3,2–3 (Vaggione 152).

[10] *CE* I 166 (GNO I 76).

[11] Eunomius, *Expositio fidei* 3,4 (Vaggione 152).

one of the things that makes the Eunomian position heretical to the Cappadocians.

The Eunomian system requires a dimension of extended succession 'between' God's eternity and the temporality of material beings to make room for the Son and the Spirit.[12] The interesting thing is that God's activities themselves are 'located' to such a dimension. One might feel tempted to ask with St Gregory, 'how and whence did they arise' (πῶς ἢ παρὰ τίνος γενόμεναι)?[13] It strikes me as difficult to explain. On the other hand, a similar problem becomes acute for Gregory, himself, when he comes to the doctrine of creation: could we explain how the eternal divine activity becomes causative of temporal being? He is obviously aware of the difficulty, and simply drops a philosophical explanation of it.[14]

The activity that according to the Eunomian system results in the being of the Son has a loose connection with God's essence and has an ἀρχή. However, even if there should be good reasons for the distinction between divine essence and divine activity, in a doctrine of causation one would desire to know something more of the character of the cause as such. One would like to know what it is capable of and how it works. If the cause is a rational agent or artisan, one should like to know if the effect was intended by the cause or not, i.e. if it was *willed* by it. According to Eunomius, the divine activity is eternal in one special sense, i.e. as foreknown by God 'before' (a temporal metaphor, of course) the creation of 'the firstborn'.[15] God, in His foreknowledge, knew 'unbegottenly' what He was going to do, and 'when' He did it, the activity was executed as God's *will* (βούλησις) to do it.[16] In short, the cause, as a rational maker, was both capable of, knew and willed the work. At this point one might wish Eunomius to be confronted with the challenge to define more closely how he would avoid the *impression* that a kind of 'temporality' intrudes into the being of the first cause. There is an ἀρχή of

---

[12] I cannot develop the history of such a concept within the limits of this paper, but we are led back to the history of 'time'-concepts from Parmenides, through Plato (*Parmenides* and *Timaeus*) to Plotinus (*Ennead* III 7 [45]) and the requirements of a Christian doctrine of angelic being. Aquinas speaks of the *aevum*, cf. *Summa Theologiae* I 10,5 and I 63,6.

[13] *CE* I 207 (GNO I 87).

[14] Cf. *De anima et resurrectione* (PG 46, 121aff).

[15] Eunomius, *Apologia* 24,6–13 (Vaggione 64).

[16] Eunomius, *Apologia* 24,1–2 (Vaggione 64).

the activity and an ἀρχή of the Son. The divine will effects the creation of the Son: "... at the same moment he intends it (ἅμα τε βούλεται), whatever he willed comes to be".[17] There is simultaneity between the exercise of will and the existence of the work. Maybe we just have to say that God knew eternally that He would execute His external activity in such a way that the being of the Son emerged from non-being in ontological dependence on this act of will as his ἀρχή. There must be, then, a relation between God's foreknowledge and the activity of will.

It strikes me as rather odd to separate the being of God from the divine activity if the effect is willed by the causal agent. Of course, there is one doctrine of causality that to some degree could fit Eunomius' concerns, but eventually it would work very badly within a theology considered to be Christian. What I have in mind is the Plotinian doctrine of double activity.[18] According to this doctrine, the internal activity of a hypostasis (its activity of essence) is accompanied by an external activity (its activity out of the essence), like fire that generates heat. The external activity is both necessitated and accidental.[19] This paradoxical statement is, in fact, not very difficult to understand. The point is that the internal activity is executed for its own sake and is in this regard intransitive. If I go for a walk, the going for a walk could be my only objective. In connection with my preoccupation, external results are incidental. I do not, for example, intend to make footprints in the snow. On the other hand, whenever internal activity occurs, it necessarily leaves an external (transitive) result. Footprint-making is a necessary result of my walking in the snow.

God, according to such a theory, could be preoccupied eternally with His own internal contemplation and remain in His own intransient being. As a result of this, there occurs the external activity of making the Son, necessarily and incidentally. However, this doctrine of causality fits very badly with the image of God in the Scriptures, and as a scriptural theologian Eunomius could never have used it. God is obviously good and loving, and wills the economy of the

[17] Eunomius, *Apologia* 23,20 (Vaggione 64).

[18] Cf. *Ennead* V 4 [7] 2 and V 1 [10] 6. On double activity, cf. E. K. Emilsson, "Remarks on the Relation between the One and Intellect in Plotinus", in J. Cleary (ed.), *Traditions of Platonism*, Dortrecht 1999.

[19] Cf. *Ennead* V 4 [7] 2 and VI 1 [42] 22.

Son. There seems to be no reason for saying that Eunomius was 'influenced' by Neo-Platonism at all, even if this is what some patristic scholars suggested earlier.[20]

Terms like 'Father' and 'Son' lay claim to a definite relationship between two entities, so that we could imagine a kind of essential communication of being from the one to the other. As we have seen, however, this is explicitly denied by Eunomius.[21] Actually, Father is not a designation of the essence of God at all. It is the name of the divine activity. Son, on the other hand, reveals the essence of Christ.[22] One might be a bit surprised at the disproportion in the use of this Father-Son metaphor, but, of course, in accordance with the nature of the case (it is a 'mystery', I suppose), it would not be inadmissible in principle to use metaphorical language that shows limitations. The term 'Father' is sanctioned by Scripture and, I think, Eunomius uses it in the sense of 'generative activity'. In fact, for him, this would have the same sense as creative activity.

It is quite unsatisfactory to conceive of the activity of God as distinct from His essence the way Eunomius does. Further, it is difficult to understand how he will avoid God's essential involvement with the making of the Son. If God wills the creation of the Son, this must, even on Eunomian principles, be an essential act; if not, God's being cannot have the simplicity Eunomius thinks it has: the will would have to be some additional element in the being of God, and this would make Him into a composite.

The last point is, in fact, made by Gregory against Eunomius.[23] By 'activities', he says, Eunomius understands the powers (δυνάμεις) by which the Son and the Holy Spirit are produced. Are the activities something other, apart from the essences which they follow, or are they a part of these essences, belonging to their nature (ἄλλο τι παρὰ τὰς οὐσίας αἷς παρέπονται ἢ μέρος ἐκείνων καὶ τῆς αὐτῆς φύσεως)? If they are other than the nature, how and whence did they come into being? If they are the same, how were they separated from these essences, and how did they come to 'follow' them as something external (ἔξωθεν), instead of coexist with them? Gregory

[20] J. N. D. Kelly, *Early Christian Doctrines*, London 1977, 249; D. L. Balás, ΜΕΤΟΥΣΙΑ ΘΕΟΥ, Rome 1966, 25.

[21] Eunomius, *Apologia* 16 (Vaggione 52).

[22] Eunomius, *Apologia* 24,18–22 (Vaggione 66).

[23] *CE* I 205–209 (GNO I 86–88).

charges Eunomius with the view that the activity is expressed by a necessity of nature and that it occurs spontaneously, i.e. without God being engaged in the result. This, somehow, makes God into a composite being, i.e. an essence combined with an externally added activity. On Gregory's view, Eunomius should have to argue that the activity is not an accident contained in a subject (ὥς τι συμβεβηκὸς ἐν ὑποκειμένῳ). On the whole it is inadmissible to speak of the activity as an accident 'following' the essence – in this connection I think Gregory is correct. This is indeed a weak point in Eunomius' doctrine. It is more reasonable, from a philosophical point of view, to hold that an activity is what is expressed by a causal agent engaged in some work, than not to be able to state the relationship between cause and effect with any precision at all. According to Gregory, essences, deliberate and self-determined in their movement, produce by themselves the expected result (τὸ δοκοῦν). These free activities of forethought are not some kind of external results. We cannot separate the activity of a worker from the worker himself. When we conceive an idea of activity, Gregory holds that we comprehend simultaneously the one who is moved with the activity. And when we think of an agent, we include the idea of activity not explicitly put forward. This principle is sound, for instance if we conceive the idea of running or house-building, we would quite naturally include the idea of a runner or a carpenter.

Gregory, himself, tries to make his point clearer by an example. If we consider someone who works in metal, two aspects are comprehended, viz. the work done (activity) and the artificer. If we remove the one, the other has no existence either. An activity, it seems, is the self-expression of a cause. On this view, the activity must be essential and natural, in the sense that it is an actualization of potencies innate to the cause.

This ontological immediacy between cause and activity precludes any talk of activities 'going between' (μεσιτεύουσα) the first being (the cause) and the second (the effect). According to Gregory, on the other hand, the Eunomian scheme implies that the activity neither coincides with (συμβαίνουσα) the first nature, nor combines with (συναπτομένη) the second.[24] As we have seen, Gregory denies the first of these ideas. Whether the second point is made by Eunomius

[24] *CE* I 211 (GNO I 88).

or not, Gregory denies it as well, and on the whole it makes his theory of creative activity into an interesting philosophical doctrine. As a matter of fact, he comes close to Aristotelian doctrine. According to Aristotle, where the result of an activity is something existing apart for the exercise of an art, the *energeia* is in the thing made.[25] The artist or artisan has left the imprint of his art as a design or a form in the material.[26] In the 6th oration of *De beatitudinibus* there is a passage in which St Gregory shows how he reasons in this regard.[27] When we look at a work of art, we become aware of the artistic skill that the artist has left as an imprint of his art. This once more stresses the importance of identifying the cause of the activity as one who possesses potentialities in form of a power to act, an art or certain skills. Such *potentialities* would belong to the essence of something and carry the marks of essential being. The skills would not in the case of created being be included in the definition of the essence, but they would be properties in the sense that they are the kind of skills this kind of being is naturally apt to achieve. Further, a rational being, considered as one that possesses an art, would act from a plan (or a form in his mind), and by the work of his hands form a suitable material into a design of which one could say it carries the imprint of his art. It seems reasonable to say, on the basis of his writings, that Eunomius leaves much to be desired.

As far as I can see, this indicates that Gregory's concept of divine activity may be characterized as follows: (1) the activity is closely united with the entity that executes it. It springs from an inherent power of its being. (2) The activity is not some separate reality occurring 'between' the cause and the effect. (3) The activity does not terminate at the moment an external result is accomplished, but resides in the result as the imprint of the art of the maker.

One might wonder in what way this Gregorian concept of activity serves his own theological concerns. When Gregory in accordance with the Nicene faith speaks of the generation of the Son, this is viewed by him as a different kind of process than the creation of the Son spoken of by Eunomius. There is no 'sempiternal' beginning of the Son's being – if I may be allowed to speak of the dimen-

---

[25] Aristotle, *Metaphysics* IX 8, 1050a30.

[26] Cf. Aristotle, *Metaphysics* VII 7, 1032a32.

[27] *De beatitudinibus* VI (GNO VII/2 141).

sion 'between' eternity and time in this way. The Son is eternal and belongs to the sphere of the uncreated. Gregory admits, though, that the Son originates from divine will, this will, however, is not a separate activity called 'Father', but the activity of the hypostasis of the Father.[28] It is not admissible to conceive of this will as an extension (διάστημα) between the hypostases of the Godhead. According to Gregory, there is an immediate togetherness or union (ἄμεσος [. . .] συνάφεια) between Father and Son in the Godhead.

These consequences should not surprise one. If there is an eternal spiritual being that is the cause of two more eternal, spiritual beings – the one generated from it, the other proceeding from it – the intimate togetherness of the three is obvious. How could they be separated? There is no sempiternity, no time, no space, nor any other category of created otherness to separate such beings. This concept of Godhead differs heavily from the Eunomian one. According to Gregory's concept of divine activity, the movement of the essence or nature has no end at which it just stops, but resides in the product. If the being of God is thought to be simple, and if one argues for the establishment of a triune God, there would be no obstacle in principle to imagine the possibility that divine activity *ad intra* could culminate in a triad of hypostases.

I suppose one could challenge Gregory to explain why the divine activity results in a triad of hypostases on the same ontological level and not in a hierarchy of subordinated beings. According to the Plotinian scheme of causality, the doctrine of double activity is designed to explain a hierarchy of subordinated hypostases. Even if Eunomius' causal doctrine differs from that of Plotinus, I think it would be in Eunomius' interest to know Gregory's arguments. However, I cannot see there are any arguments. Gregory, I suppose, would just keep to an assertion that this is indeed a reasonable theory of causation, and why not? I think his doctrine is within the range of possible theories.

St Gregory's doctrine of divine activity has two aspects, the *ad intra* and the *ad extra*. *Ad extra*, God creates the world, works in relation to His own human nature in the Incarnation and is active in the human person on its way to salvation.[29] The richness of his

---

[28] *CE* III/VI 15–22 (GNO II 191–194).

[29] Cf. *In hexaemeron* (PG 44, 68dff); *De anima et resurrectione* (PG 46, 28a); *CE* III/III 51.64 (GNO II 126,6–9; 130,23ff); *De professione christiana* (GNO VIII/1 138);

doctrine makes it impossible to develop any of the aspects further within the limits of the present paper. Barnes, in a note in a paper on Eunomius' terminology of causation, quotes Lionel Wickham:[30] "As Dr. H. Chadwick once remarked to me, how bizarre it is that all this intense discussion about the divine energies should trace its source to Eunomius and Arius." The remark, of course, concerns the modern interpretation and discussion of St Gregory Palamas' doctrine of divine energies. Firstly, I think it could be fairly said that Gregory of Nyssa's doctrine of *energeia* is well integrated within his Christian system and owes nothing to a Eunomian concept. Secondly, the Palamitic concept of *energeia* is as dynamic as the one we find in the writings of Gregory of Nyssa. Finally, when Palamas appeals to the tradition for his concept of *energeia*, it strikes me that he does not have to distort the thought of Gregory in order to make the idea of *energeia* useful for his own purposes.[31] There is, I think, a positive link between the two Gregories, and what is bizarre is that some modern scholars have missed the real import of Palamas' theology.

De beatitudinibus VII (GNO VII/2 159f); *De oratione Dominica* (GNO VII/2 37 and 40f); *De instituto christiano* (GNO VIII/1 44 and 85).

[30] Cf. note 3 above.

[31] Cf. Gregory Palamas, *Capita CL*, 112 (Sinkewicz 210–212). This text depends in part on Gregory of Nyssa's *Ad Ablabium* (GNO III/1 47–48).

PART IV

SUPPORTING STUDIES

IV.2. THEOLOGICAL MOTIVES

THE COGNITIVE FUNCTION OF EPINOIA IN CE II AND ITS MEANING FOR GREGORY OF NYSSA'S THEORY OF THEOLOGICAL LANGUAGE

Tina Dolidze

In the background of the sharp controversy *contra Eunomium*, one can discern the outline of the cohesive epistemological doctrine of St. Gregory. It broadly considers the subject of the ability of human thought and language, and the mutual relation between them. The central epistemological term for St. Gregory, as well as for his brother, in their dogmatic polemics with Eunomius is ἐπίνοια in its various meanings and modifications. The different interpretations of this common term of philosophy of Late Antiquity correspond to two different epistemological models in the Cappadocian and Neo-Arian thought. Following classical semiotics, mainly Plato, Aristotle and the Stoics, the Cappadocian theologians developed a tripartite semiotic theory, that (1) distinguishes thing, human intelligence and linguistic annunciation as three components of reality and (2) simultaneously stresses the complex character of mental and linguistic entities in their dialectical ambivalence. *CE* II provides a theoretical frame for discussing these traditional philosophical issues in respect to Christian theology. In order to focus on positive issues of Nyssa's teaching, this survey presents the theoretical content of the interrelated topics of the *CE* II in a systematic exposition, excluding the discussion *in extenso* of the polemic context which provoked its development.

I. *Epinoia as conceptual thinking*

In the books of both Cappadocian brothers against Eunomius ἐπίνοια occurs in two main senses: it denotes a result of thinking, i.e. a conception, according to the patristic basis found largely in Origen's ἐπίνοια theory; and along with this, in St. Gregory and St. Basil, it concerns a faculty and a process of reasoning.[1] This latter sense,

[1] Cf. V. H. Drecoll, ἐπίνοια, *Lexicon Gregorianum* III, App. II, 793–799, esp. ἐπίνοια II and III.

although already implied in Origen's theory, was evidently coined in the polemic against the heterodoxy of Neo-Arians. Quite in accord with Origen's understanding of the term, Basil and with him both Gregories attach to it the faculty to analyze its object in mental categories through abstraction from sensible reality. In its particular theological usage, it means for the Cappadocians – as well as for their Alexandrian authority – that it is possible through rational reasoning to reach a valid idea of God and confess him in a manner that corresponds to His being. Gregory's own definition of ἐπίνοια is very important, inasmuch as it represents the semantic range of the term in a comprehensive form (both static and dynamic) and specifies its relevance in theological abstraction.[2] As significant as it is to the ability to conceive the world, man or God,[3] the role of rational conception is to both Cappadocians severely limited. The rhetorical cascade of questions is a common place in the attempt to persuade a reader that no scientific judgement can find either an answer to questions regarding the essence or the mode of existence of the supreme Being or define the essence, cause and mode of existence of various creatures. Another rhetorical technique, the ἀνακόλουθον, is used to convey the same epistemological reality, drawing the readers' attention to the greatness of God's creation and allowing them to experience its wonder only to bring them to the conclusion that scientific investigation and the logical designation of God's wisdom are pursuits doomed to failure.[4] The Cappadocian

[2] *CE* II 182 (GNO I 277,20–26): ἔστι γὰρ κατά γε τὸν ἐμὸν λόγον ἡ ἐπίνοια ἔφοδος εὑρετικὴ τῶν ἀγνοουμένων, διὰ τῶν προσεχῶν τε καὶ ἀκολούθων τῇ πρώτῃ περὶ τὸ σπουδαζόμενον νοήσει τὸ ἐφεξῆς ἐξευρίσκουσα. νοήσαντες γάρ τι περὶ τοῦ ζητουμένου τῇ ἀρχῇ τοῦ ληφθέντος διὰ τῶν ἐφευρισκομένων νοημάτων συναρμόζοντες τὸ ἀκόλουθον εἰς τὸ πέρας τῶν σπουδαζομένων τὴν ἐγχείρησιν ἄγομεν. Cf. the definition of demonstrative knowledge in Arist. *Anal. post.* 71b20. Basil's definition reflects a common philosophical account about noetic comprehension through the perception of sensible things: ὥστε μετὰ τὸ πρῶτον ἡμῖν ἀπὸ τῆς αἰσθήσεως ἐγγινόμενον νόημα τὴν λεπτοτέραν καὶ ἀκριβεστέραν τοῦ νοηθέντος ἐπενθύμησιν ἐπίνοιαν ὀνομάζεσθαι· ὅθεν ἡ συνήθεια καλεῖ ἐπιλογισμὸν, εἰ καὶ μὴ οἰκείως (*Adversus Eunomium* I 6, PG 29, 524b).

[3] *CE* II 181–195 (GNO I 277,7–21).

[4] *CE* II 71–81 (GNO I 247,4–250,28); 103 (GNO I 256,25). Basil, *Hex.* (PG 29, 28ab); Gr. Naz. *Or.* 20,11 (PG 35, 1077c–1080a); Gr. Naz. *Or.* 28,22–26; 28,28–31 (Mason 54,8–63,8; 64,15–72,2). The *figura sententia* of the classical rhetoric *interrogatio* (*subiection*) (cf. e.g. Quintil., *Inst. orat.* IX 2,6–14, Radermacher-Buchheit I 144,25–147,2) is used in the Cappadocian fathers as a topic when discussing the problem of the impossibility of knowledge of the essence of things. I express my gratitude to the late Prof. Andreas Spira for advice on this rhetorical figure. For

scepticism towards scientific knowledge is intensified in Gregory through his development of the primary ontological opposition between the infinite/adiastemic (God) and the finite/diastemic (man as creature), an opposition that characterizes the contradictory parts of being specifically in conjunction with the theoretical aspect of knowing.[5]

When Nyssa in *CE* II points to the great cognitive barrier between the subject and object of comprehension within the sensible universe while at the same time developing the idea that ἐπίνοια in the Divine realm can claim only to be a correct surmise, he actually prepares his reader for the suggestion of an alternative approach to the Transcendent. In addition, therefore, to their doctrinal disagreement, the Cappadocians understand Eunomius' error to be that he pretends to have knowledge where human reason can produce only hypothetical conclusions. Such a question concerns not only Eunomius' conclusions but his method of thinking. Eunomius, as the Cappadocians argue, proceeds from the false rationalistic premise that he can grasp in a concrete linguistic sign the divine being, and in order to rectify this rationalistic thesis turns to boundless logical artifices. When it concerns the realm of absolute transcendent nature, St. Gregory recommends as an alternative method to this kind of reasoning a simple deposit of faith (ἡ ἁπλῆ τῆς πίστεως παρακαταθήκη).[6] This has for him a unique capacity to neutralize in some degree the unbridgeable cognitive gap faced by dimensional human reasoning. The descriptive definition of faith in *CE* II presents it as a special spiritual power which mediates between subject and object of enquiry and, of itself, allows the inquiring mind to approach the incomprehensible nature.[7] There are peculiarities, opposite to those of bare rational reasoning, that Nyssa denotes in regard to the law of faith:

ἀνακόλουθον in Gregory see Ch. Klock, *Untersuchungen zu Stil und Rhythmus bei Gregor von Nyssa*, Frankfurt a.M. 1987, 211–214; H. M. Meissner, *Rhetorik und Theologie*, Frankfurt a.M. 1991, 207–210.

[5] *Locus classicus* *CE* II 67–70 (GNO I 245,18–247,4).

[6] E.g. *CE* II 91 (GNO I 253,23); *CE* II 93 (GNO I 254,5–10); *CE* II 100 (GNO I 255,24–25); *CE* II 13 (GNO I 230,26); *CE* II 78 (GNO I 250,1); *CE* I 371 (GNO I 136,14–17).

[7] *CE* II 91 (GNO I 253,25–28): . . . πίστεως μεσιτευούσης καὶ συναπτούσης δι' ἑαυτῆς τὸν ἐπιζητοῦντα νοῦν πρὸς τὴν ἀκατάληπτον φύσιν. This phrase in some way alludes to and neutralizes *CE* II 69 (GNO I 246,14) where Gregory speaks about the impenetrable ontological gap between uncreated nature and created being: πολὺ γὰρ τὸ μέσον καὶ ἀδιεξίτητον, ᾧ πρὸς τὴν κτιστὴν οὐσίαν ἡ ἄκτιστος φύσις διατετείχισται.

although by its inner intention it remains reverently at a distance from the object of affection, it operates in certainty and achieves what eludes the human understanding. Knowledge and faith accordingly have different premises: the first has an empirical approach based on that which is known (τὰ γινωσκόμενα), whereas Christian faith concerns things that are hoped for (τὰ ἐλπιζόμενα). St. Gregory sees the blasphemy of Eunomius in the fact that his opponent's model of thinking denies hope as the essence of Christian faith while determining the present existential status of man as already having reached salvation.[8] Nyssen explains the advantage of πίστις over γνῶσις through the goal of human life, which is ethical, not intellectual.

The allegorical interpretation of Abraham's migration as an ecstasy – one of the standard descriptions of mystical ascent to the divine beauty in St. Gregory – illustrates what he means by reasoning in faith.[9] In regard to the point of indicating a correct method of thinking, the passage is focused on structural elements of contemplation.

The way to God begins from following God's call in love and ignorance. That means Abraham begins via a detachment of mind from physical phenomena, as Basil had postulated in his definition of ἐπίνοια.[10] The further description of self-transcendence resembles the hierarchy of divine cognition in Platonic theology and the function of dialectic in it. From concentrating his mind on the beauty observed in sensible things, Abraham passes to the original model of beauty in God and, beholding only this idea, he grasps in abstract conception various features of the Godhead as human reasoning advances and uses all these as the foundation (ὑπόβαθρα) for his further apprehension of God.[11] He transcends all that his own intellect could grasp, surpasses every verbal description of God and resorts

[8] *CE* II 82 (GNO I 250,28); *CE* II 84 (GNO I 251,19); *CE* II 93–99 (GNO I 254,3–30).

[9] *CE* II 85–92 (GNO I 251,22–254,3).

[10] See above note 2.

[11] The description up to this point has a strong affinity with *Enn.* VI 7 [38] 36,1–27 even though Plotinus names in much more detail the stages of union with God (that is, through analogy, abstraction, knowledge of God in his acts, arts of ascent (ἀναβασμοί) – purgation, progress in virtue, entrance (ἐπιβάσεις), establishing (ἱδρύσεις) and banquet (ἑστιάσεις). Coming near to the Good the soul leaves behind all science, which brought it there, and concentrates itself only on the supreme beauty, thinking about nothing but beauty. The ascent in Plotinus ends as in Plato with supreme intuition, but not in terms of faith and not in the way of *sobria ebrietas* as Gregory understands it: on the highest stage of union with God

solely to faith, pure and unadulterated by any notion (ἔννοια). At the end of ecstasy, as Gregory says, Abraham reaches the supreme knowledge: he takes as an indicator of the knowledge of God that he believes him to be greater and higher than any cognitive indicator (γνωριστικὸν σημεῖον).

J. Daniélou sees in this passage a combination of two philosophical view points on beauty: a Stoic contemplation of divine beauty in the universe and the Platonic contemplation of intelligible beauty, as it is presented in the dialectic of Eros in the *Symposium*. Although he remarks that the movement of Gregory's thought is Platonic, he estimates Gregory's thought to be original.[12] The novelty consists in a new horizon of striving from Divine light to Divine darkness, as well as in a new mode of attitude to the object of contemplation. If the idea of Divine Being is absolutely transcendant to human intellectual grasp, dialectic is no longer the most relevant method for that 'upward journey'.[13] In accordance with the soul's movement in faith, Abraham's ecstasy is conducted, as Gregory stresses, to a great extent by the heart, rather than by the mind, as the center of pious intuition and the principle organ within which the irrational striving in love toward the absolutely unknowable can be accomplished.

If we, in addition, concentrate on the formal aspect of the ecstasy, precisely on Gregory's antithetical way of expression, it will be evident that here the ἀφαίρεσις of the Platonic tradition is framed and hence modified by the new context of a paradoxical Christian mentality.[14] This paradox is actually what Gregory lays out as the

---

soul in its introverted position becomes at the same time subject and object of its contemplation. See also *Enn.* VI 7 [38] 35,1–45; I 6 [1] 9,1–43 and the whole treatise III 8 [30]. Alcinoos (*Didasc.* X, (Whittaker H164,31–166,2) mentions abstraction (through synthesis and analysis), analogy and dialectical ascent which begins with contemplation of the Good in sensibles things, in its social aspects, in intelligible objects, up to contemplating the supreme Good by itself. The model goes back truly to Plato (cf. *Symp.* 210e, 212a; *Rep.* VI, 510b–511d).

[12] "Il va plus loin que Platon, qui identifie Dieu avec la sphère des intelligibles. Mais de même qu'il passait des φαινόμενα aux νοητά par la nuit des sens, il passe maintenant des νοητά à l'οὐσία par la nuit de l'esprit . . . La nuit de l'esprit . . . consiste à dépasser les attributs divins, à purifier l'esprit de tout concept, à s'enfoncer dans la ténèbre." J. Daniélou, *Platonisme et théologie mystique. Doctrine spirituelle de saint Grégoire de Nysse*, Paris 1944, 140–142.

[13] The priority of dialectic in Plato's view is that it operates in the intelligible world by making suppositions in due course reaching the ἀνυπόθετον (Cf. *Rep.* VI, 511b–d).

[14] A. Spira invites a vivid illustration in Gregory of Nazianzen, how upon the

structure of his ascensional hermeneutics, in the structure of his theology in general, and its specific role in his theory of theological language. From the many passages in St. Gregory of Nyssa's work that describe knowledge in faith, I refer to *CE* II 138–141.[15] It outlines the main attributes of the theological manner of reasoning and allows us to look at its criteria. Nyssa again discusses here the comprehension of the incomprehensible: although the religious mind knows God as "intangible, inconceivable, and beyond all rational comprehension", it investigates and searches

> by such reasoning as it is possible, reaches out (ἐπορέγεται) and touches (θιγγάνει τῆς ἀπροσπελάστου καὶ ὑψηλῆς φύσεως) the unapproachable and sublime Nature, neither seeing so clearly as distinctly to catch sight of the Invisible (ἰδεῖν τὸ ἀόρατον), nor so totally debarred from approaching (ἀπεσχοινισμένη τῆς προσεγγίσεως) as to be unable to form any impression (εἰκασία) of what it seeks.[16]

Knowledge achieved by the intention of the religious mind ends as in the allegorical interpretation of Abraham's ecstasy with cognitive paradox:

> By the reach of reason its goal is to discover what that is which it seeks, and in a sense understands that by the very fact that it cannot perceive it, inasmach as it acquires clear knowledge that what it seeks is beyond all knowledge.[17]

This way of thinking, which starts from the premise that God is beyond all knowledge and results in the same idea after all its efforts, has a cognitive value. The cognitive paradox elaborates the first criterion of true reasoning: comprehension of the incomprehensible is not knowledge. Being convinced of this epistemological reality, human reason passes on to the next criterion of true reasoning: the concrete positive action of mind in producing befitting conceptions of

---

impact of the paradoxical mystery of Incarnation the classical antithesis figure is transformed in holy Christian antitheta; see A. Spira, "The Impact of Christianity on Ancient Rhetoric. The Decay of Eloquence", *StPatr* 18/2 (1989) 137–153, esp. 147–149.

[15] GNO I 265,26–266,26. For further passages on Nyssa's pious *docta ignorantia* stressing the cognitive function of mystical paradox, see H. U. von Balthasar, *Presence and Thought. An Essay on the Religious Philosophy of Gregory of Nyssa*, San Francisco 1995, 97–108.

[16] *CE* II 138 (GNO I 265,29–266,3; tr. Hall 89).

[17] *CE* II 139 (GNO I 266,3–6; tr. Hall 89).

God by the Platonic synthesis, analysis and analogy.[18] That is, not being fixed on these concrete rational data of its own work, the mind employs them as a springboard for self-transcendence, where it can behold itself in pious distance from every designation of God. In this way the mind now comes through spiritual experience to its initial theoretical knowledge that God exists (ὅτι ἔστι καταλαμβάνεται). The very purpose of theology, St. Gregory sees, is exactly to reach a reverent conception of God by which it would be kept intact, what befits the conjecture of Him.[19]

II. *Epinoia as conceptual word (ὁ κατ' ἐπίνοιαν λόγος)*

If one turns now to Gregory's approach to the conceptual word, he can discover that conceptual thought and word are actually identified in Gregory, and hence own the same peculiarities. The most significant common feature of reason and language issues from their diastemic nature; both of them divide and classify their object and reflect it in multiplicity. Already Origen in his biblical hermeneutics took notice of that semiotic fact and drew from it a most productive idea of religious ἐπίνοιαι – respective thoughts and expressions reflecting through multiple indicators the fullness and perfection of God's simple being.[20] One of the principal components of Origen's hermeneutical doctrine finds a strong echo in the upholding of the cognitive power of ἐπίνοια as human thought and linguistic expression in the treatises of the Cappadocians against their great adversary. The multiplied representation of an integral object – explain St. Basil and his brother after Origen – is the specificity of the human mind. It

[18] Celsus maintains these three methods to be an achievement of philosophy. Cf. Orig., *C. Cels.* VII 42 (GCS 3, 192,22–193,22).

[19] *CE* II 136 (GNO I 265,7–10): ἐν τοῖς περὶ θεοῦ λόγοις ἐστὶν . . . εὐσεβῆ διάνοιαν ἐξευρεῖν δι' ἧς τὸ πρέπον τῇ ὑπολήψει τῇ περὶ θεοῦ φυλαχθήσεται. Cf. above the definition of ἐπίνοια by Nyssa.

[20] Orig., *Comm. in Ioh.* I 9–10 (GCS 10, 14,12–16,20); *De princ.* IV 4,1 (Görgemanns – Karpp 350,12). Vgl. *Comm. in Jer.* VIII 2 (GCS 6, 57,5–9). Cf. M. Harl, *Origène et la fonction révélatrice du verbe incarné*, Paris 1958, 121–123. The way for the Christian application of the idea was evidently prepared by Philo; cf. G. C. Stead, "Logic and the application of names to God", in: F. Mateo-Seco – J. L. Bastero (eds.), *El 'Contra Eunomium I' en la producción literaria de Gregorio de Nisa. VI. Coloquio Internacional sobre Gregorio de Nisa*, Pamplona 1988, 309–311.

is not misleading, however, but, when mentally and linguistically properly classified, can bring to knowledge the underlying object or can even supply a correct surmise on the Divine realm.[21]

Moreover, it was the paradoxical mode of narration in so much of Holy Scripture that first motivated the speculative mind of the Alexandrian master to produce its scientific interpretation and to explain the variety of obscure passages as indications on God's mystery. The sacred paradox, the essence of Origen's allegorical interpretation as it is, agitated, on the one hand, human reason to find integral sense in historical events that seemed literally independent or contrary, and to harmonize, on the other hand, the discrepancy between the sensible content of the biblical language and its spiritual dimension.[22] St. Gregory shared Origen's pathos for allegorical interpretation, and, therefore, the idea of sacred paradox is fundamental to Christian language and a Christian mentality. As in Gregory of Nyssa so in Origen intelligence and language are, nonetheless, things of different order. The Bishop of Nyssa had, in particular, to highlight it in his dogmatic controversy.

It was Origen who at first had to defend in his biblical hermeneutics the simple language of the Bible against Greek intellectuals and who insisted on the hidden spiritual 'treasures' in 'earthern vessels' of common language.[23] In contention with the Neo-Arian stance that naming God can express his divine essence, the Cappadocians had to move further in the direction of a sceptical approach to linguistic utterance. Ἐπίνοιαι ἀνθρωπίνων λογισμῶν, tells Gregory, are different in all men, but they assume even more diverse shapes in linguistic utterance. The process of dimensional multiplying of the object goes further in linguistic designations, as far as concluding that a number of signifiers can correspond to one signified. This is a strong argument for St. Gregory to uphold the conventional character of human language. The process goes actually into *reductio ad*

[21] *CE* II 271–276; 300; 475; 501–503 (GNO I 305,27–307,21; 314,22; 364,32; 372,16–373,8); Basil, *Adv. Eun.* I 6; I 7 (PG 29, 524b; 524d–525b).

[22] In more detail on the horizontal and vertical paradox in Origen's hermeneutic: T. Dolidze, "Der Glaube als Erkenntnis bei Origenes" in: W. Geerlings – C. Schulze (eds.), *Der Kommentar in Antike und Mittelalter. Neue Beiträge zu seiner Erforschung*, Leiden 2004, 185–211.

[23] Orig., *De prin.* IV 1,7; IV 3,14 (Görgemanns – Karpp 303,14–304,1; 345,5–347,4). Cf. *2 Cor* 4,7.

infinitum, if one takes into account that conceptual thought has even more diverse phonetic shapes in different languages.[24] Reminiscent of Basil's words, and in accord with Origen, Nyssa writes: "we have a faint and slight apprehension of the divine Nature through reasoning, but we still gather knowledge enough for our slight capacity through the words which are reverently used of it".[25]

This approximate knowledge issues from the main peculiarity of religious articulation: its equivocality. This equivocality is, in fact, a Christian religious paradox on the linguistic level and, as such, aims to mediate the contraries. In *De anima et resurrectione*, Nyssa introduces the anthropological background of equivocality. Man by his own choice abandoned his original uniform life (μονοειδὴς ζωή) in good and voluntarily became a nature compounded from opposites (σύμμικτος ἐκ τῶν ἐναντίων φύσις), that is of good and evil. This new existential status divides the whole human life into these two opposite poles and locates him permanently between opposite choices. After becoming twofold in nature, man becomes ambiguous having a homonymical understanding of good and evil in respect to his reason and senses.[26] Thus Gregory draws primarily on the traditional interpretation of equivocality as a principle of differentiation.[27] But this is only one aspect of the term, which was evidently used in contemporary school tradition, and along with this it pointed out the possibility of a correlation of two different things.[28] Already in Alcinoos equivocality is considered to be a logical analogy between a transcendent idea and its correlate in the world of phenomena.[29] Origen

---

[24] *CE* II 283–284; 406–410; 546 (GNO I 309,23–310,11; 344,25–346,4; 385,28); *CE* III/V 50–52 (GNO II 178,13–179,15). Nyssa's concept of the ambivalence and relativity of human epinoetic thought and language is a part of his profoundly dialectical theology.

[25] *CE* II 130 (GNO I 263,21–26; tr. Hall 87); cf. Basil, *Adv. Eun.* I 10 (PG 29, 533c); Gr. Naz., *Or.* 28,4 (Mason 26,12). In *C. Cels.* VII 42 (GCS 3, 192,22–193,22) Origen opposes his Christian position concerning the limited epistemological capacity of both reason and language to that of Plato; in *Timaios* 28c Plato maintains that it is impossible to express the metaphysical reality with human language, but ascribes the possibility of its comprehension to human reasoning.

[26] *De an. et res.* (PG 46, 81bc).

[27] Cf. Arist., *Cat.* 1a1; Arist., *Polit.* I 1,11, 1253a21.

[28] Clem. Alex., *Strom.* VIII 8,24,8 (GCS 17, 95). See M. Harl, "Origène et la sémantique du langage biblique", in: M. Harl, *Le Déchiffrement du Sens. Études sur l'herméneutique chrétienne d'Origène à Grégoire de Nysse*, Paris 1993, 61–87, esp. 65, note 13–14.

[29] Alcinoos, *Didasc.* XXX (Whittaker H183,17).

and the Cappadocians followed this model, but transposed and modified it according to their actual task. In Origen's biblical hermeneutics and Gregory's systematic reflection on religious language, the 'vertical' interpretation of the term 'homonyma' resulted in an ingenious solution to the problem: religious expressions combine in equivocality the common human vocabulary with the inspired sense, which transcends its literal meaning.[30]

According to Gregory of Nyssa, everything that is linguistically expressed of God is expressed equivocally of him, be it an affirmative or negative term. The first designates it in an equivocal analogy with human attributes or sensible things. It means that God communicates mysteries of divine truth in human terms so as to give instructions to mankind in accordance with the level of human capacity.[31] So are to be explained, in retrospective view to Origen and Judaic Hellenistic exegesis, all anthropomorphisms of God in the Bible.[32] Gregory repeats Origen's hermeneutical request to think about God in a manner that is worthy of God. The task of allegorical interpretation is, namely, to penetrate the sensible, verbal veil of Holy Scripture and to speak in a spiritual way spiritual matters concealed by it. Negative epithets belong to another type of linguistic multiplying of the transcendent Divine image. Nyssen, in a manner different to the negative theology of Platonism, gives no advantage to this kind of divine nomination; he finds it to be a conceptual expression of a special grammatical order that, through the prefix of privation, expresses God's divergence from the creature.[33] In theological language, both positive and negative articulations lead to the trans-

[30] Orig., *Comm. in Cant.* prol. (GCS 33, 64,16–20): "*Ostendere enim ex his volumus quod scripturis divinis per homonymas, id est per similes appellationes, immo per eadem vocabula et exterioris hominis membra ei illius interioris partes affectusque nominantur eaque non solum vocabulis, sed et rebus ipsis invicem comparantur.*" Cf. *CE* II 300f (GNO I 314,22–315,5). On equivocality in Origen, cf. R. Roukema, *The Diversity of Laws in Origen's Commentary on Romans*, Amsterdam 1988; M. Harl "Origène et la sémantique", 62–65; R. Gögler, *Zur Theologie des biblischen Wortes bei Origenes*, Düsseldorf 1963, 326–331; T. Dolidze, "Der Glaube als Erkenntnis", 204–210.

[31] *CE* II 130–147; 578–580; 104–105 (GNO I 263,21–268,18; 395,3–29; 257,2–21). The idea can be traced back to Philo; see J. M. Soskice, "Philo and Negative Theology", in: M. M. Olivetti (ed.), *Théologie négative*, Milan 2002, 491–504, esp. 500–503.

[32] Aristobulos was the first to originate the point; cf. R. Gögler, *Zur Theologie des biblischen Wortes*, 93–94.

[33] *CE* II 192–194 (GNO I 280,22–281,21).

gression of a multiplicity of designators in order to produce a comprehensive spiritual content under the condition that every designation is defined semantically through conceptual thought and properly applied to God. Correlated with each other, these terms imitate the integrity of our conception regarding God's life and then, through the intuition of reason, approximate the reality that surpasses the human intelligence. The correlating principle is valid also in biblical hermeneutics, as a part of theological language, but is shaped there in its specific way. There an interpreter and the common reader, led by him, primarily differentiate the biblical text into basic semantic parts (Gregory unlike Origen knows only of a twofold interpretation of text, spiritual and corporeal) with the aim to show a participation of a concrete historical event in the whole of God's economy. The same principle of mental and linguistic imitation of eternal reality is subjected to the manifold interpretation of biblical personages in typological and allegorical manner. In this sense, the hermeneutic interpretation of Solomon's *Canticum canticorum* – this *epoptic* of Christian theology – is most impressive. Likeness with the plenitude of God's mystery is achieved in commentaries of Nyssa and Origen through the complex meaning of figures and images, the accumulation of these meanings and the transposition from one to another in order to reveal their reciprocity.[34] The allegorical exegesis is thus an exercise of conceptual reasoning, which aims to overcome focusing on the variability of conceptual articulation and to reach methodically the understanding of the entire text as sacred metaphor.

This metaphysical perspective in St. Gregory's theory of language is supported by the biblical argument that, even if naming things is the invention of Adam,[35] the very faculty of expressing thoughts, as well as of reasoning, belongs to the work of God. It involves along with this an important ontological argument: that divine essence and its action are inseparable. As Gregory asserts, the created world is not a result of God's energy as something that is beyond his existence, but it is inherent to God and at the same time immanent to

[34] T. Dolidze, "Einige Aspekte der allegorischen Sprache in den Auslegungen von Origenes und Gregor von Nyssa zum *Hohenlied*", in: L. Perrone (ed.), *Origeniana Octava*, Leuven 2003, 1061–1070.

[35] *CE* II 402 (GNO I 343,25).

creation. Uncreated as it is, the divine energy is to be considered as a permanent spreading out of God's grace on creation. In the theory of theological language, this ontological doctrine is expressed in an identity of inspired word and divine energy and participation of human intelligence in this energetic union ideally.[36] This discrepancy was crucial to the Neo-Arian. Eunomius, entirely conditioned by Platonic tradition, divided divine energy from divine essence with the aim of legitimating the difference of Trinitarian persons in essence and dignity.[37] Presumably, his immediate source for doing this was Plotinus, who distinguished two kinds of energy in the intelligible world: essential, which coincides with the active being of divine hypostasis, and ἐνέργειαι, that issue from it's essence and are something external to it.[38] The dogmatic dispute had an intimate connection with the problem of Divine nomenclature. The ambiguity of the term ἡ ἐξ ἀναλογίας ὁμωνυμία ("homonymy based on analogy"), specifically, the question of its genuine meaning, played a key role, as each side attempted to control its essential theological meaning.

Eunomius, as we can judge from his *Apologia*, discerns two methods of approach to the Divine persons: (1) through the Platonic abstraction, oriented on examination and designation of their divine essence, and (2) through equivocal analogy, which depict them according to their activity. The first method, although it fails to provide a cataphatic definition of the first person of the Trinity because of the absolute transcendence of his essence and energy, comprehends Him in an apophatic designation. The inductive method of equivocal analogy enables the positivistic comprehension of the second and third

---

[36] Cf. *CE* II 298–299; 148–158; 581–587 (GNO I 314,8–20; 268,18–271,10; 395,30–397,31); *Beat.* VI (GNO VII/2 141,25ff); *De an. et res.* (PG 46, 124b). See Вл. Лосский, "Очерк Мистического Богословия Восточной Церкви" (пер. с франц.), in: *Мистическое Богословие*, Киев 1991, 142–143; H. U. von Balthasar, *Presence and Thought*, 84–85.

[37] Eun., *Apol.* 20,1–22; 25,1–26 (Vaggione 58–60; 66–68); Basil, *Adv. Eun.* I 5; I 6; I 24; II 32 (PG 29, 520c-521a; 521c–524a; 565a; 648b).

[38] Eun., *Apol.* 22,5–16; 24,1 (Vaggione 62; 64); cf. esp. *CE* I 205–211; 246–249 (GNO I 86,17–88,17; 98,27–99,24) with *Enn.* V 4 [7] 2,19–37 and V 3 [49] 12,1–52. Eunomius' phrase *CE* I 205 (GNO I 86,17) τῶν ταῖς οὐσίαις ἑπομένων ἐνεργειῶν καὶ τῶν ταύταις προσφυῶν ὀνομάτων resembles *Enn.* V 4 [7] 2,29: ἡ δὲ ἀπ' ἐκείνης (scil. τῆς οὐσίας T.D.), ἣν δεῖ παντὶ ἕπεσθαι ἐξ ἀνάγκης ἑτέραν οὖσαν αὐτοῦ. On metaphysical energy see also Porph. (?), *Comm. in Plat. Parm.* XIV 21 (Hadot 90); Porph., *Sent.* 43 (Lamberz 54,7–56,15); 44 (Lamberz 57,1; 58,4; 58,18; 59,1).

persons of the Trinity. The Son, the first and only result of God's energy, can be grasped through the extension of his creative energy in the universe.[39] The inspired language of the Scripture in Eunomius' eyes is based completely on equivocal analogy, but this linguistic phenomenon, itself, in his particuliar insistence, does not belong to human epinoetic language.[40]

The point argued by Gregory of Nyssa lies at the opposite pole to this thesis of the Neo-Arian. With the doctrine of the union of Divine essence and energy, and of common manifestation of energy in the Holy Trinity, Gregory of Nyssa gives another ontological reading to the notion of equivocal analogy.[41] He, like Basil, transposes the accent from the analogy between the created universe and the Son to the idea that the Triune God is not only transcendent, but also immanent to the world in its creative action. The equivocality of theological language in this context matches a flexible cognitive method; it can move in an act of energetic naming from divergence with the Divine to congruence with it.[42]

[39] Eun., *Apol.* 20,22; cf. 26,4; 28,1–26 (Vaggione 60; 68; 74). Further on the levels of Being and energeia in Eunomius' linguistic theory see: Th. Böhm, *Theoria. Unendlichkeit. Aufstieg. Philosophische Implikationen zu De Vita Moysis von Gregor von Nyssa*, Leiden 1996, 171ff; K.-H. Uthemann, "Die Sprache der Theologie nach Eunomius von Cyzicus", *ZKG* 104 (1993) 143–175; also his "Die Sprachtheorie des Eunomios von Kyzikos und Severianos von Gabala, Theologie im Reflex kirchlicher Predigt", *StPatr* 24 (1993) 336–344, esp. 339. In his method of thinking Eunomius tends actually to nominalism, inasmuch as his conclusions stem from the formal contradiction of 'generated/ungenerated', the most important opposition of his philosophy of language (Eun., *Apol.* 18,13–16.19; 19,12, Vaggione 56; 58). Cf. with the view of Cratylus, who asserted: "whoever knows the names knows the things" (Plat., *Crat.* 435d).

[40] Cf. Eun., *Apol.* 16,1–17,17; 18,6 (Vaggione 52–54; 54); *CE* II 306–312; 141 (GNO I 316,6–317,24; 266,25). In the extant fragments that came down to us, we can identify four categories of theological naming in Eunomius: (1) the naming of divine essence, which is an unequivocal designation ('Unbegotten', 'Being'), (2) the sacred language of the Bible, (3) theological language, based on the correct interpretation of the scripture and (4) false theological expressions, that are the product of human ἐπίνοια.

[41] *CE* II 238–240; 460 (GNO I 295,27–296,24; 361,10–12); *Ad Eustath.* (GNO III/1 11,3; 13,21–15,3); *Ad Ablab.* (GNO III/1 48,20–49,7); vgl. *CE* III/VII 9–14 (GNO II 206,28–208,21); *De an et res.* (PG 46, 124b). As E. Mühlenberg estimates, the idea that theological nomination does not denote essence, but denotes energies of God in the form of attributes, issues from Origen; E. Mühlenberg, "Die philosophische Bildung Gregors von Nyssa in den Büchern Contra Eunomium", in: M. Harl (ed.), *Écriture et culture philosophique dans la pensée de Grégoire de Nysse. Actes du colloque de Chevetogne (22–26 Septembre 1969)*, Leiden 1971, 230–244, esp. 241.

[42] Cf. e.g. Basil, *Adv. Eun.* I 16–22; II 10 (PG 29, 548c–561b; 589c); *CE* II 577 (GNO I 394,27); *CE* III/V 43–45 (GNO II 175,23–177,4); *CE* III/II 9–10 (GNO II 55,3–19).

It was Nyssen, while defending Basil's view of ἐπίνοια, who introduced for the first time the theory of theological language into patristic theology. He actually extended Origen's great hermeneutic construction on the whole linguistic corpus of reflexive theology. As significant as it is, the novelty consists not only in this. There also occurs in Gregory of Nyssa's theology of language a concept of silence, which brings a new element to the spiritual inheritance. The idea of silent adoration is evidently derived from the Bible, especially from Paul's and John's revelations, but, perhaps, supplemented by Plotinus' mysticism.[43] One can argue, that 'silence' has an essential weight in St. Gregory's theory of theological language. In *CE* II he says: the divine decree not to reveal his Being even in Sacred Scripture, is caused by his will to be honoured in silence, and hence to prohibit human enquiry into the deepest things.[44] Thus at its height faith's comprehension comes to actualization precisely in a verbal hiatus. In the context of Nyssen's intertextuality[45] this type of informative silence occurs not only in God's realm, or in the written Word in the Bible, but also in the whole universe created by the Word. Again in *CE* II, as well as in other treatises, this 'close at hand' silence is signified to have a higher degree of reality than the most reverent utterance about God.[46]

It has already been indicated in research into Gregory of Nyssa that the methodic conceptual reasoning in Nyssen ends in mystical silence.[47] Thus the theory of St. Gregory's theological language in its zenith comes to its negation. The doctrinal paradox is, however,

---

[43] Cf. *CE* II 268 (GNO I 304,25); *Enn.* III 8 [30] 4,1; III 8 [30] 6,10; VI 8 [39] 11,1.

[44] *CE* II 97–101; 105 (GNO I 255,1–256,15; 257,21).

[45] A. A. Mosshammer, "Disclosing but not Disclosed, Gregory of Nyssa as Deconstructionist", in: H. R. Drobner – C. Klock (eds.), *Studien zu Gregor von Nyssa und der Christlichen Spätantike*, Leiden 1990, 99–123, esp. 120–122.

[46] *CE* II 224–225 (GNO I 290,25–291,23); cf. *In Cant.* XV (GNO VI 455,10–456,15).

[47] Th. Kobusch, "Name und Sein. Zu den sprachphilosophischen Grundlagen in der Schrift Contra Eunomium des Gregor von Nyssa", in: F. Mateo-Seco – J. L. Bastero (eds.), *El 'Contra Eunomium I' en la producción literaria de Gregorio de Nisa*, 247–268, esp. 261. S. Douglass provides the conception of a sacred silence within the poles of paradoxical Christian metaphors in Nyssa; see S. Douglass "A Critical Analysis of Gregory's Philosophy of Language: The Linguistic Reconstitution of Metadiastemic Intrusions", in: H. R. Drobner – A. Viciano (eds.), *Homilies on the Beatitudes. Proceedings of the Eighth International Colloquium on Gregory of Nyssa (Paderborn, 14–18 September 1998)*, Leiden 1999, 447–465, esp. 454ff.

visible for it stays in full agreement with its ontological correlate – the divine infinity. This mutual contact, as Gregory attests, 'takes place' on the borders of extensive and inextensive existence, in the ἄδυτον, where man with his infinite desire of 'vision' of the Beloved, comes into participation with His infinity. As for the Christian theologian, the realm of sacred silence is for St. Gregory a realm of Unspoken Words.[48] There the human soul no longer needs the rules of logical discursive ἐπίνοια, while in sharp antithesis to them it begins to see the voice and move in stand.[49]

St. Gregory of Nyssa's idea of charismatic silence in theological language proved to be fertile: it can be traced through the thinking of Gregory Palamas, who laid silence as the ground of his mystical theory of the unspoken word as an area of God's uncreated energy.

[48] *CE* III/I 16 (GNO II 9,13); *CE* I 308–316 (GNO I 118,19–121,3).
[49] *De an. et res.* (PG 46, 25a; cf. *Apoc* 1,12; 10,4); *Vita Moysis* (GNO VII/1 118,1–24).

GREGORY OF NYSSA AND THEOLOGICAL IMAGINATION

Scot Douglass

Imagination is not entirely evil, it is evil and good, for in the midst of it man can master the vortex of possibilities and realize the human figure proposed in creation, as he could not do prior to the knowledge of good and evil... Greatest danger and greatest opportunity at once... To unite the two urges of the imagination implies to equip the absolute potency of passion with the one direction that renders it capable of great love and great service. Thus and not otherwise can man become whole.

Martin Buber, *Good and Evil*

I. *Situating ἐπίνοια in the gap*

Martin Buber's twentieth-century thoughts on the *dynamis* of imagination reflect a number of historical perspectives that are relevant to my reading of Gregory of Nyssa. At its very core, imagination has always been implicated in the notion of time, in the created order of existence. That is, it functions in the 'vortex of possibilities', in the flux of becoming, in the capacity to envision, evaluate and choose. As the substrate for the possibility of intentional change, it simultaneously looks back, summoning the never was, and looks forward, calling forth the yet to be and the never to be. By imposing a type of sovereignty over an infinite projection of potential futures and non-existent pasts, it is the servant of the present decision, the servant of yet another moment of becoming. Such service, as Buber notes, is deeply ambiguous. It is good and evil.

In addition to this ethical register of reading imagination, there has always been an epistemological interrogation of the role of imagination. Plato, for example, famously concluded that the creative offspring of imagination were "the poor children of poor parents". In the 'dividing line' between knowledge (ἐπιστήμη) and opinion (δόξα) in Book VI of the *Republic*, whereas reason (νοῦς) can contemplate truth, imagination serves the most inferior form of human opinion:

'illusion' (εἰκασία). Plato goes on to say: "Opinion is concerned with becoming and the exercise of reason with being . . . and what being is to becoming, the exercise of reason is to opinion."[1] Imagination for Plato is always implicated in becoming, and is, therefore, always inferior.

With the 1781 first edition of his *Critique of Pure Reason*, Platonic epistemology gets turned somewhat on its head as Kant claims that imagination precedes both rational thought and sensible intuition – imagination is the originating and productive root of both stems of knowledge: intuition and understanding. This re-orientation of the valuation of the role of imagination is reflected in the canonical metaphors used to describe them. Platonic imagination as mirror, the distorted and deformed reflection of reality, gives way to Modern imagination as lamp, the generation and creation of light. Heidegger comments on this first edition of Kant's *Critique of Pure Reason*:

> As a faculty of intuition, imagination is formative in the sense that it produces an image. As a faculty not dependent on objects of intuition, it produces, i.e. forms and provides, images. This 'formative power' is at one and the same time receptive and productive (spontaneous). In this 'at one and the same time' is to be found the true essence of the structure of the imagination. However, if receptivity is identified with sensibility, and spontaneity with understanding, then imagination falls in a peculiar way between the two.[2]

There are two notions here in Heidegger's reading of Kant relevant to reading Gregory's understanding of *epinoetic* invention: that imagination is "at one and at the same time receptive and productive" and that imagination "falls in a peculiar way between the two". In the lexicon of Gregory, ἐπίνοια, on an epistemological level, exists ("in a peculiar way") in the διάστημα between the reception of God's revelation and the production of theological discourse. That is, since created beings are limited to receiving revelation that is *diastemically* mediated, any theological discourse about the *adiastemic* God that attempts to speak beyond His activities must always be an *epinoetic* construction that consciously detours away from the goal of *mimesis*.[3]

---

[1] Plato, *Republic* 534a.

[2] M. Heidegger, *Kant and the Problem of Metaphysics*, tr. J. Churchill, Bloomington (IN) 1962, 135.

[3] For an extended examination of this type of *epinoetic* construction, see the chapter "The *Metadiastemic* Intrusion" in my *Theology of the Gap. Cappadocian Language Theory*

On an ethical level, ἐπίνοια functions in the διάστημα between the lives of ancient saints and the life-choices of contemporary believers. Richard Kearney summarizes the "three decisive claims" regarding the *dynamis* of imagination made within the phenomenological trajectory (i.e. Husserl, Heidegger, and their diverse heirs):

> (1) imagining is a productive act of consciousness, not a mental reproduction in the mind; (2) imagining does not involve a courier service between body and mind but an original synthesis which precedes the age-old opposition between the sensible and the intelligible; and (3) imagining is not a luxury of idle fancy but an instrument of semantic innovation.[4]

Gregory's valorization of ἐπίνοια in Book II of the *Contra Eunomium*[5] is rooted in the incredible scope of its productive capacity. Similar to the stolen fire of Prometheus, the source according to Aeschylus of "every art possessed by man", Gregory regards it as the most precious of all providential provisions and the source of every useful thought, skill and discipline of inquiry. It is the faculty that produces language and the capacity to discover, invent and construct. 'Επίνοια is even the source of "the very philosophy of being itself and metaphysical speculation" (αὐτὴ δὲ ἡ περὶ τοῦ ὄντος φιλοσοφία καὶ ἡ τῶν νοητῶν θεωρία). Very telling in his long list of the achievements of ἐπίνοια are the references to navigation. In a created order dominated by dimensionality (διάστημα) and motion (κίνησις), the *epinoetic* capacity enables created beings to move within the distanciated flux in a meaningful manner. In the explicitly theological thinking of Gregory, ἐπίνοια is the source of the greatest orthodoxies and the greatest heresies. As laid out in his sermons on *Ecclesiastes*, it is the ethical possibility of constitutionally *kinetic* beings exercising either good κίνησις and thus participating in the "Holy of Holies" or of exercising bad κίνησις and thus participating in the "Vanity of Vanities". As exemplified in his θεωρία of the life of Moses, it is the hermeneutical possibility of bringing together the life of an ancient saint with the radically different life of a fourth-century believer.[6]

---

and the Trinitarian Controversy, New York – Bern – Berlin – Bruxelles – Frankfurt am Main – Oxford – Wien 2005.

[4] R. Kearney, *Poetics of Imagining. Modern to Post-modern*, New York 1998, 6.

[5] See *CE* II 182–183 (GNO I 277,16–278,4).

[6] Gregory acknowledged a number of distanciations between his reader and Moses: cultural, historical and circumstantial. Since the *Textwelt* was 'other' to the

That is, *epinoetic* theologizing for Gregory was as equally concerned with the *noetic* as it was the *metanoetic*, with the knowledge of God as it was with the intentional transformation of a believer into the image of God.

II. *Epinoetic ambiguity in Gregory*

What Adam within the Hebrew tradition had to sin to get and Prometheus had to steal, God, according to Gregory, freely gave to humanity. This gift, like the gift of the Hebrew יצר, could be used for good or evil, but it was not implicated in the fall of humanity nor the creation of history in the same manner. To Gregory, *diastemic* and *kinetic* humanity were historical beings by nature, created as a function of alteration, always embedded in the process of becoming. In Gregory shorthand, "*Diastema* is nothing other than creation" (τὸ δὲ διάστημα οὐδὲν ἄλλο ἢ κτίσις ἐστίν)[7] and "to stop moving would mean to cease to exist altogether" (Εἰ δέ ποτε κινούμενον παύσοιτο, καὶ τοῦ εἶναι πάντως τὴν παῦλαν ἕξει).[8] The great gift of the δύναμις of ἐπίνοια – "the most precious of all gifts given to humanity"[9] – was necessary for there to be any possibility of connection, relationship and the avoidance of the empty abyss of absolute isolation. It is the divine gift that resists the total chaos and entropic dissemination of a universe constitutionally dominated by the chronotopic realities of διάστημα and κίνησις. As a *diastemic* gift given by God to help humanity overcome *diastemic* limitations, it shares in the very limitations it is meant to overcome. Gregory, therefore, shares the Platonic concern for the epistemological dangers of imagination, questioning whether it would not just be safer to reject it as a legitimate tool of theologizing.

worlds of Gregory and his readers, each of these distances constituted a *diastemic* barrier to the *metanoetic* project of imitating the life of a Jewish saint, of "placing [oneself] (ἐμαυτὸν καταστήσω) in their ranks" (*De vita Moysis*, GNO VII/1 6,5–14).

[7] *In eccl.* (GNO V 412,14).

[8] *De hominus opificio* (PG 44, 165a–b).

[9] καί μοι δοκεῖ πάντων τῶν κατὰ τὴν ζωὴν ταύτην ἐνεργουμένων ἐν ἡμῖν ἀγαθῶν τῶν ταῖς ψυχαῖς ἡμῶν παρὰ τῆς θείας προμηθείας ἐνυπαρχόντων τὴν ἐπίνοιάν τις προτιμοτέραν κρίνων μὴ ἂν τῆς πρεπούσης κρίσεως διαψευσθῆναι (*CE* II 183, GNO I 277,32–278,4).

> In another way, one might argue that safety lies in leaving the divine nature unexplored, as being inexpressible and beyond the reach of human reasoning. Speculating about the obscure and using the *epinoia* of human reason to search for some kind of knowledge of things hidden, allows admission and currency to false ideas, since speculation about the unknown understands not only what is true to be true, but often also what is false.[10]

Gregory's embracing of the ambiguous potential of ἐπίνοια meant that the act of addressing God was fraught with risk[11] and guaranteed to end in a certain type of failure. Gregory reads David's comment in *Psalm* 115,2: πᾶς ἄνθρωπος ψεύστης (all men are liars), not as a text about depravity (as does Paul in *Romans*), but rather as one about the constitutional limitations of dimensional being. All men lie οὐχὶ τῷ μίσει τῆς ἀληθείας, ἀλλὰ τῇ ἀσθενείᾳ τῆς διηγήσεως (not in any hatred of the truth, but in the feebleness of being able to set out a description).[12] Gregory of Nazianzus, in discussing the cost to Christ of His *kenosis*, tropes this same idea in a much more violent image. While proclaiming, Λόγος ἀκούεις, καὶ ὑπὲρ λόγον εἶ (You are called *Logos*, and You are beyond *Logos*),[13] the Theologian laments that, unavoidably and against his will, even his own reverent *logos* participated with those whom he regarded as heretics in casting stones at his Savior:

> And even now He bears being stoned, not only by those who are intentionally abusive, but also by we ourselves who seem to reverence Him. For to use corporeal names when discoursing of the incorporeal is perhaps to partake with those who intentionally abuse and stone Him; but be lenient, I say again, in respect to our weakness, for I do not willingly stone Him; but having no other words to us, we use what we have. You are called *Logos*, and You are above *logos*.[14]

---

[10] Καὶ ἄλλως δ' ἄν τις ἀσφαλὲς εἶναι φήσειεν ἀπολυπραγμόνητον ἐὰν τὴν θείαν οὐσίαν ὡς ἀπόρρητον καὶ ἀνέπεφον λογισμοῖς ἀνθρωπίνοις. τὸ μὲν γὰρ τῶν ἀδήλων καταστοχάζεσθαι καί τινα τῶν ἀποκρύφων γνῶσιν ἐξ ἐπινοίας ἀνθρωπίνων λογισμῶν ἐρευνᾶσθαι πάροδον καὶ ἀκολουθίαν καὶ ταῖς διεψευσμέναις τῶν ὑπολήψεων δίδωσιν, διότι τῶν ἀγνοουμένων ὁ στοχασμὸς οὐ μόνον τὸ ἀληθὲς, ἀλλὰ καὶ αὐτὸ πολλάκις τὸ ψεῦδος ὡς ἀληθὲς ὑπολήψεται (*CE* II 97, GNO I 255,1–8).

[11] Gregory's first 19 usages of ἐπίνοια and its cognates in *CE* I are uniformly negative, referring to Aetius' "scheming" to get money and Eunomius' "fictitious" heresies.

[12] Gregory of Nyssa, *De virginitate* (GNO VIII/1 290,13–14).

[13] Gregory of Nazianzus, *Oratio* 37,4 (PG 36, 285d).

[14] Φέρει καὶ νῦν λιθαζόμενος, οὐ μόνον ὑπὸ τῶν ἐπηρεαζόντων, ἀλλὰ καὶ ὑφ' ὑμῶν αὐτῶν τῶν εὐσεβεῖν δοκούντων. Τὸ γὰρ περὶ ἀσωμάτου διαλεγόμενον, σωματικοῖς

The status of *epinoetic* theological discourse (the only theological discourse Gregory thought possible within the *diasteme*) is that every truth about God is also a lie about God and that every theological utterance aimed at accurately 'hitting' the truth of God unavoidably also contains fragments of the very same stones hurled at God by the heretics.

Although Gregory shares with Plato the notion of an absolute realm of Being, there remains in Gregory a decisive διάστημα between humanity and God that can never be bridged. All we can ever see is the διάστημα in something.[15] As a result, all truth is mediated via the constitutional realities of creation. Truth "from above" always appears, as it were, "from below". That is, *epinoetic* theology is always, in Derridean terms, from the χώρα. As such, truth takes a detour, a detour always marked by a type of *kenosis* that denies itself a complete noetic return to its absolute source. Imagination, therefore, cannot be delimited (as with Socrates) as being a helpful ladder to be discarded once it has been climbed, leaving the seeker in a realm where pure reason can contemplate essence. To be sure, Gregory defends the use of analogy at times in these very terms, but this must always be situated within the larger structure of his construction of a *diastemic* episteme in which any noetic access to essence is structurally denied.[16] As a result, there is no choice but to utilize ἐπίνοια, despite its risks, limitations and its being always implicated in becoming. The cost of this choice is a recalibration of the possibility of theological discourse and a subsequent increased investment in the impact of theology. Such an investment, the move away from a Eunomian valorization of what Heidegger would later call *die Wahrheit als Richtigkeit*, created more space for the operation of theological imagination.

κεχρῆσθαι ὀνόμασι, τυχὸν ἐπηρεαζόντων ἐστὶ καὶ λιθαζόντων· ἀλλὰ συγγνώμη, πάλιν λέγω, τῇ ἀσθενείᾳ. Λιθάζομεν γὰρ οὐχ ἑκόντες, ἀλλὰ τὸ φθέγγεσθαι ἄλλως οὐκ ἔχοντες, ᾧ δὲ ἔχομεν χρώμενοι. Λόγος ἀκούεις, καὶ ὑπὲρ λόγον εἶ (Gregory of Nazianzus, *Oratio* 37,4, PG 36, 285cd).

[15] οὕτω καὶ πᾶσα ἡ κτίσις ἔξω ἑαυτῆς γενέσθαι διὰ τῆς καταληπτικῆς θεωρίας οὐ δύναται, ἀλλ' ἐν ἑαυτῇ μένει ἀεὶ καὶ ὅπερ ἂν ἴδῃ, ἑαυτὴν βλέπει· κἂν οἰηθῇ τι ὑπὲρ ἑαυτὴν βλέπειν, τὸ ἐκτὸς ἑαυτῆς ἰδεῖν φύσιν οὐκ ἔχει. οἷον τὴν διαστηματικὴν ἔννοιαν ἐν τῇ τῶν ὄντων θεωρίᾳ παρελθεῖν βιάζεται, ἀλλ' οὐ παρέρχεται. παντὶ γὰρ τῷ εὑρισκομένῳ νοήματι συνθεωρεῖ πάντως τὸ συγκαταλαμβανόμενον τῇ ὑποστάσει τοῦ νοουμένου διάστημα· τὸ δὲ διάστημα οὐδὲν ἄλλο ἢ κτίσις ἐστίν (*In eccl.*, GNO V 412,6–14).

[16] See my *Theology of the Gap* for a development of what I am calling a "*diastemic* episteme".

> The purpose of theology is not to think (ἐπινοῆσαι) up resounding and harmonious verbal beauty, but to identify a reverent notion by which what befits the thought of God may be kept intact.[17]

The *epinoetic* faculty cannot construct a harmonious whole whose *diastemic* fractures and *kinetic* disseminations are sutured and overcome.[18] To the contrary (as will be seen in the next section), governed by a greater concern for reverence than correctness, *epinoetic* theology must use *epinoetic* thinking to guard against (φυλαχθήσεται) the inherent risks of thinking *epinoetically*. Such a stance has earned him the reputation amongst many scholars of simply being a bad philosopher. This paper is a brief consideration of the possibility that this is, at least at times and in part, more a function of his acknowledged reliance upon a certain type of theological imagination than it is upon poor thinking.

III. *Silence, presence and the productive theological imagination*

The question of imagination and its utility in the production of theology is closely related to two problems with which Gregory wrestles: the problem of silence and the problem of presence. Language first emerges in order to negotiate the constitutional distanciation of the created order.[19] It is an *epinoetic* maneuver to confront the

[17] τὸ γὰρ σπουδαζόμενον ἐν τοῖς περὶ θεοῦ λόγοις ἐστὶν οὐχὶ ῥημάτων εὐφωνίαν εὔκροτόν τε καὶ ἐναρμόνιον ἐπινοῆσαι, ἀλλ' εὐσεβῆ διάνοιαν ἐξευρεῖν δι' ἧς τὸ πρέπον τῇ ὑπολήψει τῇ περὶ θεοῦ φυλαχθήσεται (*CE* II 136, GNO I 265,7–10).

[18] Gregory of Nazianzus invoked the same type of *epinoetic* sensibility in his judgment of what constituted the "best theologian": καὶ οὗτος ἄριστος ἡμῖν θεολόγος, οὐχ ὃς εὗρε τὸ πᾶν, οὐδὲ γὰρ δέχεται τὸ πᾶν ὁ δεσμός, ἀλλ' ὃς ἂν ἄλλου φαντασθῇ πλέον, καὶ πλεῖον ἐν ἑαυτῷ συναγάγῃ τὸ τῆς ἀληθείας ἴνδαλμα, ἢ ἀποσκίασμα, ἢ ὅ τι καὶ ὀνομάσομεν (*Oratio* 30,17, PG 36, 125c). Gregory of Nazianzus recognized the *diastemic* bondage that made an analytical approach to truth impossible. It was beyond his capacity to construct a totalizing discourse (τὸ πᾶν) because it was beyond his ability to discover or receive τὸ πᾶν.

[19] This hope is central to Basil's high regard for the capacity of language. Τοῦ λόγου τὴν χρῆσιν δέδωκεν ἡμῖν ὁ κτίσας ἡμᾶς θεὸς, ἵνα τὰς βουλὰς τῶν καρδιῶν ἀλλήλοις ἀποκαλύπτωμεν . . . τῶν τῆς καρδίας κρυπτῶν προφέροντες τὰ βουλεύματα. Εἰ μὲν γὰρ γυμνῇ τῇ ψυχῇ δειζῶμεν, εὐθὺς ἂν ἀπὸ τῶν νοημάτων ἀλλήλοις συνεγινόμεθα· ἐπειδὴ δὲ ὑπὸ παραπετάσματι τῇ σαρκὶ καλυπτομένη ἡμῶν ἡ ψυχὴ τὰς ἐννοίας ἐργάζεται, ῥημάτων δεῖται καὶ ὀνομάτων πρὸς τὸ δημοσιεύειν τὸ ἐν τῷ βάθει κείμενα (*Hom. in illud, Attende tibi ipsi* 1, PG 31, 197c–d). Nouns and verbs bear the desire to overcome secrets, the yearning to transcend the alienation of distanciation – the longing to know and be known.

problem of the ever-present διάστημα that makes the experience of presence impossible.

> For things have their names, not for His sake but for ours. For as we cannot always have all things before our eyes, we take knowledge of some of the things that are present with us from time to time, and others we register in our memories. But it would be impossible to keep memory unconfused unless we had the notation of words to distinguish the things that are stored up in our minds from one another. But to God all things are present, nor does He need memory, all things being within the range of His penetrating vision. What need, then, in His case, for parts of speech, when His own wisdom and power embrace and hold the nature of things distinct and unconfused? Whereas all things that exist substantially are from God, all things that exist are provided with names to indicate them for our guidance. And if any one says that such names were imposed by the arbitrary usage of mankind, he will be guilty of no offense against the scheme of Divine providence.[20]

God's access to presence, indeed that all things are always present to Him, eliminates His need for memory and language. For humanity, on the other hand, language is the very condition for the possibility of memory.[21] The *kinetic* aspects of dimensional thinking must be stabilized by the arbitrary assignment of words, ἄλλως δὲ οὐκ ἔστιν ἀσύγχυτον φυλαχθῆναι ἡμῖν τὴν μνήμην ("otherwise there would not be the guarding of our memory as unconfused"). There is a certain *kinetic* entropic force at play in human thinking that must be arrested, even momentarily, to guard against (φυλαχθῆναι) complete disseminated confusion. In the mind of God, though, there is no

[20] οὐδὲ γὰρ ἐκείνου χάριν, ἀλλ' ἡμῶν ἕνεκεν ἐπίκειται τοῖς πράγμασι τὰ ὀνόματα. διὰ γὰρ τὸ μὴ πάντοτε δυνατὸν ἡμῖν εἶναι πάντα ἐν ὀφθαλμοῖς ἔχειν τὰ ὄντα τὸ μέν τι τῶν ἀεὶ παρόντων γινώσκομεν, τὸ δὲ τῇ μνήμῃ ἐναπογράφομεν. ἄλλως δὲ οὐκ ἔστιν ἀσύγχυτον φυλαχθῆναι ἡμῖν τὴν μνήμην, μὴ τῆς τῶν ὀνομάτων σημασίας διαστελλούσης ἀπ' ἀλλήλων τὰ ἐναποκείμενα τῇ διανοίᾳ πράγματα. θεῷ δὲ πάντα πάρεστι καὶ οὐδὲν δεῖ μνήμης αὐτῷ, πάντων τῇ διορατικῇ δυνάμει περικρατουμένων τε καὶ θεωρουμένων. τίς οὖν ἐπ' αὐτοῦ χρεία ῥήματος ἢ ὀνόματος, αὐτῆς τῆς ἐν αὐτῷ σοφίας τε καὶ δυνάμεως ἀσύγχτόν τε καὶ διακεκριμένην τὴν τῶν ὄντων φύσιν περιεχούσης; οὐκοῦν παρὰ θεοῦ μὲν τὰ ὄντα καὶ ὑφεστῶτα πάντα, τῆς δὲ ἡμετέρας ἕνεκεν ὁδηγίας ἔπεστι τοῖς οὖσι τὲ σημειωτικὰ τῶν πραγμάτων ὀνόματα. ταῦτα δὲ κατὰ τὸ ἀρέσκον ταῖς τῶν ἀνθρώπων συνηθείαις γίνεσθαί τις εἰπὼν οὐδὲν εἰς τὸν τῆς προνοίας πλημμελήσει λόγον (*CE* II 281–283, GNO I 309,14–310,1).

[21] Although the Cappadocians make distinctions between thinking and speaking, passages like this seem to implicate an inextricable relationship between thought and language – both being rooted in ἐπίνοια.

potential for confusion, no possibility of kinetic slippage between one concept and another, because all things and their natures are always present to Him. As a result, there is no need of the guardian service of language. God, therefore, does not speak, save in His relationship with *diastemic* beings.

In defending the dynamic unity of the Trinity, Gregory developed the following ratios: *diastema* – language; no *diastema* – no language.

> But where no separation is conceived, close conjunction is surely acknowledged; and what is totally conjoined is not mediated by voice and speech. By 'conjoined' I mean that which is totally inseparable; for the word 'conjunction' does not imply a kind of bodily affinity in what is essentially intelligent, but the union of wills between one intelligent being and another.[22]

Where there is a full 'conjoining' between two beings (that is, no διάστημα, total and complete presence), the mediating function of language is not needed (φωνῇ καὶ λόγῳ οὐ μεσιτεύεται). As constitutionally *diastemic* and *kinetic* beings, as beings who can never experience being "fully conjoined" (συνημμένον) with anything, humanity can neither comprehend nor experience *adiastemic* and *akinetic* being nor function within the *diasteme* without *diastemic* and *kinetic* language – nor, as a result, can they ever experience the οὐσία of other *diastemic* beings.[23] Widening the scope of Plato's concern in the *Phaedrus* for the ambiguous, *pharmakological* role of writing in preserving orphaned speech, Gregory presented language as the vehicle of not being orphaned from oneself and, more importantly, not being orphaned from God.

Much of what Gregory says about ἐπίνοια and theological language, especially in Book II of the *Contra Eunomium*, is rightly circumscribed within the realm of similitude, within the context of working with analogies, of what he refers to above as 'affinities'. He

---

[22] ὅπου δὲ διάστασις οὐκ ἐπινοεῖται, τὸ συνημμένον πάντως ὁμολογεῖται, τὸ δὲ διὰ πάντων συνημμένον φωνῇ καὶ λόγῳ οὐ μεσιτεύεται. συνημμένον δὲ λέγω τὸ ἐν πᾶσιν ἀχώριστον. οὐ γὰρ σωματικήν τινα συμφυΐαν ἐπὶ τῆς νοερᾶς φύσεως τὸ ὄνομα τῆς συναφείας ἐνδείκνυται, ἀλλὰ τὴν τοῦ νοητοῦ πρὸς τὸ νοητὸν διὰ τῆς ταὐτότητος τῶν θελημάτων ἕνωσίν τε καὶ ἀνάκρασιν (*CE* II 214, GNO I 287,26–288,3).

[23] Διὰ τοῦτο πᾶσάν τις θεόπνευστον φωνὴν ἐρευνώμενος οὐκ ἂν εὕροι τῆς θείας φύσεως τὴν διδασκαλίαν οὐδὲ μὴν ἄλλου τινὸς τῶν κατ' οὐσίαν ὑπεστηκότων· ὅθεν ἐν ἀγνοίᾳ πάντων διάγομεν πρῶτον ἑαυτοὺς ἀγνοοῦντες οἱ ἄνθρωποι, ἔπειτα δὲ καὶ τὰ ἄλλα πάντα (*CE* II 106, GNO I 257,26–258,1).

advocates a type of 'non-total' conjoining, similar to the use of analogy by Socrates, that seeks helpful illustrations of truth.[24] Most of this has to do with finding *diastemic* analogs to God's *diastemically* mediated ἐνέργειαι. In addition to this, though, there is also the attempt to conjoin that which resists conjoining, a bringing together of the dissimilar. Christ is ὁμοούσιος with the Father. Christ is fully human and fully divine. Mary is a virgin and the mother of God, etc. This type of theologizing finds great expression in the theological poetry of Gregory of Nazianzus, as well as in the liturgy of Basil. In such a maneuver, there is always the creation of space, a moment of reflection upon the incommensurable. There is no language in this space, only silence. There is no accessible presence, only the desire for presence and the positing of a presence that remains out of reach. But this silence is not merely a moment of defeat. It is a carefully crafted silence that bears the status of somehow being an orthodox silence. That is, it is a silence that has a value. When Gregory states that "we have learned to honor with silence what transcends speech and thought" (σιωπῇ τιμᾶν τὰ ὑπὲρ λόγον τε καὶ διάνοιαν μεμαθήκαμεν),[25] there is something more than a complete agnosticism and something far less than a totalizing noeticism. There is, in this moment of worship, both an imaginative creation and entrance into this space – an entrance barred to reason and language, but one that retains for the worshipper some sense of worshipping someone. In the language of mathematics, worship is always a vector and never merely a scalar (i.e. it has direction as well as magnitude). This space, though, is decisively not *mimetic*; the space does not aspire to be a copy. The silence of the space has already acknowledged its inability to be a replica. It is the result of a productive moment of imagination and the believer's experience of it is a function of a type of pious imagination.

The creative *epinoetic* drive for Gregory is not a Platonic remembrance of pre-embodied access to truth; it is a productive activity that brings together what can be known within the *diasteme* in a manner that produces new knowledge.[26] In this manner, ἐπίνοια func-

---

[24] *CE* I 213; 622 (GNO I 88,23–28; 205,19–25).

[25] *CE* III/I 105 (GNO II 39,5–6).

[26] ἔστι γὰρ κατά γε τὸν ἐμὸν λόγον ἡ ἐπίνοια ἔφοδος εὑρετικὴ τῶν ἀγνοουμένων, διὰ τῶν προσεχῶν τε καὶ ἀκολούθων τῇ πρώτῃ περὶ τὸ σπουδαζόμενον νοήσει τὸ ἐφεξῆς ἐξευρίσκουσα (*CE* II 182–183, GNO I 277,16–278,4 for the full context of this comment).

tions in an originary manner that is similar to that ascribed to imagination by Kant in the 1781 first edition of the *Critique of Pure Reason*, but it is put by Gregory into the service of worship, obedience and the production of theological reflection. As opposed to discovering the true knowledge of God's being, ἐπίνοια creates what Wittgenstein might have called an "*epinoetic* style".

SERVICE OR MASTERY? 'THEOLOGY' IN GREGORY OF NYSSA'S *CONTRA EUNOMIUM* II

Ari Ojell

I. *Introduction*

In this presentation, I discuss the concept of θεολογία in Gregory of Nyssa in light of his use of the title θεολόγος in his *Contra Eunomium* II and in relation to some of his other works, especially *CE* III and *De vita Moysis*. As a concept, *theologia* is most often read and understood in Gregory as synonymous and interchangeable with the concept of *divine knowledge*, θεογνωσία.[1] As an activity, it is most commonly regarded as a human approach to God, as contemplation, θεωρία, or, to use the words of Werner Jaeger,[2] as something that "Hellenic striving for a philosophic understanding of what we believe" has "called into being". That one finds much philosophic striving in Gregory – whether 'Hellenic' or more universally human – is nothing less than sure. It seems, however, that it is not the *human* striving and speculative approach to God what can properly be called 'theology' according to Gregory. Consistent with this understanding, Gregory does not use the word θεολογία in *CE* II, but instead, he speaks of a "word coming down"[3] in the words of the saints of the Holy Scripture. Gregory's idea is that in the human words of the Scripture, the divine Word comes down for the benefit of the hearers, that they may know God's will and God according to His will. This, if anything, is 'theology' according to Gregory.

In the second book of *Contra Eunomium*, Gregory also explains how language, according to his view, is based on two things: on the divine gift of abstract conception (ἐπίνοια), and on human conventions concerning how to use the words we people are able to produce in

[1] See J. Daniélou, *Platonisme et théologie mystique*, Paris 1944, 200–201, 159 translating both θεολογία and θεογνοωσία as '*la connaissance de Dieu*.'

[2] W. Jaeger, *Two Rediscovered Works of Ancient Christian Literature: Gregory of Nyssa and Macarius*, Leiden 1965, 73.

[3] *CE* II 431 (GNO I 352).

expressing the thoughts we are able to think.[4] Our prevailing scholarly custom invites us to speak of the 'theology of Gregory of Nyssa' with no second thoughts. As a result, it is quite natural for us, according to our modern conventions of language, to compare 'Gregory's theology' to the theologies of Basil, Origen, Augustine, Eunomius, Plato, etc. In doing so, we make it appear as if there really were some speculative construction, a train of thought or 'inventive approach'[5] that Gregory *himself* might have called 'my theology' in contrast to 'other theologies' of the 'other theologians', whether Christian or pagan.[6]

However, for Gregory, himself, it seems there can be but *one* theology, common for us all, expressed in the "divine words (or statements: θεολογίαι) of the Holy Scripture, set out for us by the persons inspired by the Holy Spirit". Gregory uses this expression in his *Homilies on the Beatitudes*,[7] and it is this idea that his conception of theology is built on: many words but only one 'speaking body' of several members. One seeks in vain from Gregory any positive concept of an individual 'theology of Basil', 'my theology' or 'the natural theology of Plato'. In *CE* II, Gregory consistently indicates that according to his conception of theology – which implicitly was his suggestion for a 'convention' how to use the concept[8] – any identification of himself as a theologian, any claim 'according to my theology' with a reference to his personal speculations concerning God, would be the same as admitting that he is a heretic having his own private God, an idol that he has made up of his own theory.

[4] *CE* II 183–186; 395–402 (GNO I 277f; 341–344).

[5] H. U. von Balthasar, *Presence and Thought. An Essay on the Religious Philosophy of Gregory of Nyssa*, San Francisco 1995, 172f. Von Balthasar importantly pays attention to the significance of the "strict and definitive correlation between the *word* of God and what the creature *hears*" as well as the idea of "the God who speaks" (Θεὸς λέγων) in Gregory. He nevertheless goes on talking about the "theology of Gregory of Nyssa" as (human) "inventive approach" having its object in what God wants us to hear.

[6] See H. Drobner, *Gregory of Nyssa as Philosopher*, Halifax 2000, 67–101. Drobner correctly points out that the modern separation of theology and philosophy does not apply in ancient authors. However, I do not think Drobner is right when he indicates that Gregory regarded Plato as a theologian.

[7] *De beat.* 7 (GNO VII/2 150).

[8] Θεολογία is not a biblical term. Clement and Origen were the first Christian authors to use it extensively. W. Jaeger, *Two Rediscovered Works*, 72–73, n. 3.

II. *Gregory's heroes: Gregory the Wonderworker and Basil*

Unlike Gregory of Nazianzus, Gregory of Nyssa nowhere in his writings calls himself a theologian or indicates in any way that he is one – despite his elaborate discussions of theological issues.[9] He is not just being humble. Instead, he is deliberately making a point: he never uses the designation 'theologian' for any of the Fathers of the Church he greatly respected – those *we* are accustomed to call theologians. Gregory does not attach the title of *theologos* even to those whom he calls 'great' (μέγας), respects as 'teachers' (διδάσκαλος) and regards as saints (ἅγιος) after the type (τύπος) of Moses: the 'second Moses' Gregory the Wonderworker[10] and Gregory's brother Basil whom he introduces as a contemporary Moses.[11] Instead, as mighty imitators of Moses, the perfect 'servant of God' (οἰκέτης θεοῦ) serving in the ministry of God (οἰκονομία τοῦ θεοῦ),[12] their greatness lies in that they may be regarded – like Moses – as God's servants.[13] Paul, as Gregory well knew, also identified himself as a servant, διάκονος κατὰ τὴν οἰκονομίαν τοῦ θεοῦ announcing the λόγος τοῦ θεοῦ – the mystery (τὸ μυστήριον) revealed to his saints for the benefit of Christ's Body: Christ in us (*Col* 1,24–29). Accordingly, Gregory identifies Basil as a *diakonos* of the mysteries of Christ whose tongue was taught by God.[14] Furthermore, the utmost Christian perfection, according to Gregory, is not to be called *theologos* but a servant (οἰκέτης) of God whom the Lord himself calls his friend (φίλον).[15]

[9] The namesakes agreed that speculation in theological issues is not for everyone. There is, however, a difference in how they use the terms θεολογία and θεολόγος. That Nazianzen had no problem in calling 'theologians' those found qualified for theological reflection, becomes clear in his Theological Orations.

[10] *Thaum.* 25 (GNO X/1 14).

[11] Also in the opening of *CE* II there is an implicit equalisation of Moses and Basil leading "Lord's army in the battle", *CE* II 10 (GNO I 229). Defending God's people against idolatry was an important virtue of Moses. See also *Hex.* (PG 44, 61f) and *Bas.* (GNO X/1 109–134).

[12] *VM* II 317; 279 (SC 1bis, 133; 120).

[13] For Gregory as a servant, see *Thaum.* 41 (GNO X/1 23–24).

[14] Basil as διάκονος μυστερίων Χριστοῦ setting forth divine mystery διὰ τῆς θεοπαιδεύτου γλώττης, see *CE* III/VI 57 (GNO II 206). In this definition, Gregory combines the elements of Paul's formulations in *Col* 1,25 and *1 Cor* 4,1. Basil belongs to Paul's 'order' (τάξις) as his successor with the same eminence as Sylvanus and Timothy. *Bas.* (GNO X/1 110–111).

[15] *VM* II 305–321 (SC 1bis, 129–135). The title θεολόγος preaches by its absence in this Gregory's mature work.

These are the things that one can become by imitating and following the saints – not by aspiring to be a 'theologian'. Since the era of the biblical saints – 'the architects of faith' (ἀρχιτέκτονες τῆς πίστεως) who laid the foundation of the faith in Christ[16] – no *individual thinker* can authoritatively 'contribute' to theology; only the *apostolic Church* as one terrestrial Body of Christ having Christ himself as its head, can do this. It always maintains its centre in Christ and through this centre ecclesiastically culminates in the confession, ὁμολογία, of the faith in the Triune God.

III. *Eunomius as a 'new theologian'*

Gregory makes one, very revealing exception to his rule. Indeed, there is one among his contemporaries whom he calls a theologian: *his adversary Eunomius* – and it is no compliment. It is a serious accusation and mockery. When Gregory calls Eunomius a theologian,[17] always with epithets like new (καινός), wise (σοφός) and corporeal (ὁ σωματικὸς θεολόγος),[18] his point is not simply that Eunomius is a lousy theologian or unorthodox theologian. The point is that Eunomius is not and simply *cannot* be a theologian at all. He is not one of the saints of the Bible above whom he is elevating himself[19] by *replacing* the 'God-fitting' names given by them with his new ones. Everyone still has a right to express some reverent notion concerning God – according to the actions he performs for our lives – with whatever words and names, new or old, one finds to suit the reverent purpose best,[20] but Eunomius greatly exceeds in his desire to contribute to theology as though he were a theologian, even over and against the authority of the Word of truth itself.[21] He is naming the Father anew, κατὰ φύσιν, as ἀγέννητος, 'Unbegotten', whose being is ἀγεννησία,

[16] *CE* III/I 55 (GNO II 23). The apostles enjoyed an order (τάξις) which formed prophets, shepherds and teachers: the Only-begotten Son's theophany through his birth from a virgin. *Bas.* (GNO X/1 109).

[17] Altogether sixteen times in *CE* I–III and *Ref. Eun.* Five times in *CE* II: 42, 326, 365, 389, 409 (GNO I 238; 321; 333; 339; 345).

[18] *CE* III/VI 43 (GNO II 201).

[19] *CE* II 82; 97–105 (GNO I 250f; 255ff).

[20] *CE* II 130–136; 148–150 (GNO I 263ff; 268f).

[21] *CE* II 50–66 (GNO I 240–245). Eunomius' actual aim, according to Gregory, is to degrade Christ.

'unbegottenness', in order to establish a difference of nature between the Father as ἀγέννητος and the Only-begotten Son as γεννητός, 'begotten'.[22] He is revealing them as 'the God' and 'created God' and is thus openly inviting people to worship creation. In proclaiming the divine nature, Eunomius claims for himself a supreme knowledge far more 'excellent' than the knowledge of the saints – the saints never claimed to know God's unnameable essence. Obviously, according to Gregory, he is in the business of making a new revelation, not proclaiming or interpreting the old. This can be nothing but a revelation of his private God, a new and strange God[23] – an idol that he has made up of his own theory.[24]

Gregory, therefore, does have a concept of 'my theology' but he relates it negatively to the endeavours of Eunomius. 'His theology' is actually *only* a human theory, a result of his own philosophic striving, a harmonious construction of words leading up to 'God' as the result of human reasoning. But Gregory demands that it must be acknowledged 'what our word is compared with the Word that truly Is' – nothing.[25] Eunomius is mistaken in how he thinks vanishing human words serve the subsisting Word of God. The purpose of περὶ θεοῦ λόγοι is not to 'think up' God but to 'bring down' a reverent notion befitting the thought of God (περὶ θεοῦ).[26] Philosophic speculation is not a bad thing as long as it does not, instead of following it in order to serve it, become an attempt to master the divine Word. Eunomius' theory by which he worships and services human *logos* instead of the Divine is an open violation against the 'theology of John'.

IV. *Theology of St. John*

Following the custom that had become traditional by his time, Gregory allows St. John the title ὁ θεολόγος.[27] As such, he is the 'voice of

[22] *CE* II 21 (GNO I 232).
[23] *CE* II 204–205 (GNO I 284f). Gregory regards Eunomius attempt to capture the essence God in one human word as θεοποιΐα.
[24] *CE* II 100 (GNO I 255f).
[25] *CE* II 235–237 (GNO I 294f).
[26] *CE* II 136, 154–158 (GNO I 265; 270f).
[27] *Theod.* (GNO X/1 71).

thunder' who 'shouts out', 'proclaims' and 'celebrates' the 'mystery of theology' in the most open manner. He proclaims Christ, the Only-begotten Son, as the λόγος τοῦ θεοῦ who in the beginning was *in* God, *with* God and *was* God, the Logos through whom everything is created, the Logos who is Life and Light and who became flesh. The whole Gospel according to John is written from the perspective of Christ's divinity. For Gregory, St. John – the beloved disciple who rested on Christ's chest, hearing secrets – is the embodiment of his idea that there is one divine origin behind all *theologiai* of the Holy Scripture. John is the leader of the choir of the saints *in* theology:[28] to him it was given to scale the summit of τὸ περὶ τῆς θείας φύσεως κήρυγμα[29] as handed down in the Scripture by making the pre-existence and the divinity of the Incarnated One open and manifest. But *all* the saints of the Bible – in their several God-fitting statements constituting the one Body of the Holy Scripture – actually share and proclaim the one and same theology which is identical with the 'theology of John'. They all reveal the one and same God in Christ. They all proclaim the one and the same Word of God in their own due part, as much was given to each of them to reveal according to the instruction of the Spirit. One summit of *theologia* and one human *theologos* – according to his God-given mission so entitled[30] – points beyond itself to the *one and single source* of all *theologia*: to God who speaks his own Word of truth about himself in the Spirit, making himself known to men according to his will.

V. *The choir of the saints*

It is quite certain that Gregory did not regard himself as a theologian according to his own understanding of how to use the term. Technically, he wanted to preserve this particular title, *if* and when applied to some collective of human agents, for those whom he calls in his *De vita Moysis* the 'trumpets'[31] of divine mysteries, those who

---

[28] *CE* III/I 11–14 (GNO II 7f). *Cant.* (GNO VI 39–42).

[29] *VM* II 158 (SC 1bis, 79).

[30] John does have a 'type' in the Old Testament – Isaiah. Neither of them is superior to Paul, but not even Isaiah or Paul are actually entitled *theologos* by Gregory. However, they both, like John, *proclaim* theology laying down the law of *worship*. *CE* III/III 8–11 (GNO II 109ff); *CE* III/II 40–41 (GNO II 65).

[31] *VM* II 159–161 (SC 1bis, 79–80).

proclaim the divine nature as pure-sounding instruments of God's will – the saints of the Bible. In *CE* II, when accusing Eunomius of idolising his own mental processes, Gregory introduces against him the saints as 'one choir' by using biblical verses: "The prophets and patriarchs in whose time the *Word of truth* spoke in diverse parts and manners (*Heb* 1,1), and thereafter those [apostles] who became the *eyewitnesses and servants of the Word* (*Lk* 1,2)." It is safest, Gregory appeals, and also necessary to "respect the reliability of those attested by the Spirit himself" and "stay within the limits of their learning and knowledge".[32] Their authority rests in the Word of truth.

VI. *Divine speaking: Holy Scripture as the loving* oikonomia *of the Spirit*

Gregory's point is that we may still hear the Word of truth himself, speaking in the words of his prophets and apostles in the God-inspired Scripture. We are not expecting additions from some new 'revealers of God' to what has been revealed in Christ, what the Spirit reveals of God through him. In *CE* II Gregory says that the reason why God converses with his servants is his love of man, φιλανθρωπία. God himself has no need of words. But like a compassionate mother joins in the baby-talk of her babies, the divine philanthropic Power passes on to the human race that which we are capable of receiving.[33] These are the human words of the inspired saints. The saints were silently instructed by the Spirit in *what* to express: for them it was left to decide which ordinary human words to use to match the divine purpose. They became pure instruments of God's will – not like marionettes but as his faithful and morally responsible servants and co-workers – in dispensing the divine will for the benefit of all men, by applying words to the wordless speaking of God through his own Word in his Spirit. While God himself does not use words, he nevertheless authorises all things said about him in the Scripture.

In *CE* III, Gregory is very clear on this issue. In Christ, "the God who was in the beginning" descended out of his love of man – in the οἰκονομία of φιλανθρωπία – to commune with our lowliness and

[32] *CE* II 101 (GNO I 256).
[33] *CE* II 417–420 (GNO I 348f).

weakness; [he] *was seen upon earth and conversed with men* (*Bar* 3,38). In the Holy Scriptures, the eye-witnesses and servants of the Word deliver to us what they saw and heard.[34] Scripture is the "philanthropic οἰκονομία of the Spirit" through which theology reaches our hearing and understanding. The divine dispensation of the Spirit "delivers to us the divine mysteries and conveys its instruction on those matters which transcend language, by means of what is within our capacity". "Divine intention lies hidden under the body of the Scripture" where "all things said are utterances of the Holy Spirit"; it is the "teaching of divine afflatus", given to benefit men. "If the bodily veil of the words were removed, that which remains is Lord and life and Spirit."[35]

VII. *Gregory – an imitator of the servants of the Word*

Gregory's idea in *CE* II is that those who proclaim the Word of truth in the Bible – inspired and instructed by the Spirit – can be regarded as theologians in relation to *us*: it is their learning and knowledge expressed in their *theologiai* or *peri theou logoi* we must trust when hoping to share with them in the knowledge of God (*theognosia*). For us, the God-inspired Holy Scripture with its saints proclaiming Christ represents what the Holy Mountain of the divine trumpets was for Moses. But in relation to the Word of truth – i.e. Christ himself who is the Fathers' Word, Will and Wisdom that the Spirit communicates, and who himself speaks in the Body of the Scripture – no man can ever be identified as a theologian. If and when we follow and imitate the saints, as much as we grant them authority in theology in relation to us, we must not identify ourselves as 'theologians', authoritative God-speakers, but *notice how the saints identified themselves in relation to the Word.* Gregory hears and follows the instruction of St. Paul, the imitator of Christ in whom Christ spoke, and who himself is to be imitated:[36] "People should

[34] *CE* III/III 33–40 (GNO II 119f). Importantly, 'conversation' is discussed in relation to '*oikonomia* of *philanthropia*' and '*oikonomia* of the Cross'. In *Trid. Spat.* (GNO IX 299–303) Gregory introduces the Cross as a theologian.

[35] *CE* III/V 7–16 (GNO II 162–166); *CE* III/VI 32–41 (GNO II 197–200).

[36] *1 Cor* 11,1; *2 Cor* 13,3. For Paul as an imitator of Christ, see *CE* I 546 (GNO I 184); *CE* II 259 (GNO I 302); *Perf.* (GNO VIII/1 174–175); *Inst.* (GNO VIII/1 50); *Cant.* (GNO VI 46; 212); *Tunc et ipse* (GNO III/2 3; 15; 23).

consider us as servants of Christ and stewards of God's mysteries" (*1 Cor* 4,1).[37] It is this advice through which Gregory identifies his own teachers, his brother Basil (as well as his sister Macrina), Gregory the Wonderworker and all the rest who faithfully teach, proclaim and serve the Word in the apostolic tradition of the Church. This is also how Gregory wished himself to be identified: as a servant of Christ and steward of God's mysteries, an imitator of those who heard the Word of truth speaking and who became eyewitnesses and servants of the Word.

VIII. *Looking, hearing and seeing the Word:* θεωρία – θεολογία – θεογνωσία

As an imitator of the "servants and *eyewitnesses of the Word*", Gregory desired to share their vision of God: to share in their "knowledge and learning" in order to be a servant of Christ in their order and sequence (τάξις καὶ ἀκολουθία) according to God's will (θέλημα). The biblical coupling of Word and vision – of listening and looking, hearing and seeing, the functioning of ears and eyes – in receiving knowledge of God in faith[38] is what constitutes Gregory's idea of Christian contemplation (θεωρία) as a following (ἀκολουθία)[39] of the divine Word in a continuous dialectic of hearing and seeing the essentially spiritual divine Word.

The *akolouthia* of the contemplation of the divine nature begins by *looking* at the *oikonomia* of incarnation[40] as it is presented in the *oikonomia* of the Spirit, the God-inspired Scripture. One then distinguishes between conceptions (ὑπολήψεις) concerning the divinity (περὶ τὸ θεῖον) and the humanity (περὶ τὸ ἀνθρώπινον) of Christ Jesus,[41] in order to

---

[37] Ὑπηρέτης for 'servant' and οἰκονόμος for 'steward'.

[38] Through and through, Gregory writes, the Divinity is sight and hearing and knowledge. So it is with the divine Word – but not so with human receiver of the Word. *CE* II 211–212 (GNO I 286f).

[39] For *akolouthia* as *Leitmotiv* of Gregory's thought, see J. Daniélou, *L'être et le temps chez Grégoire de Nysse*, Leiden 1970, 18–50.

[40] Cf. *VM* I 20–21 (SC 1bis, 9–10); *VM* II 19–26 (SC 1bis, 37–39).

[41] *CE* III/I 54 (GNO II 22f). By this method Gregory improves Basil's technical *theologia-oikonomia*-distinction. While defending it for its intention, he actually uses another technical distinction, ἄκτιστον – κτιστόν for discussing the *two natures of the one person* Christ Jesus.

hear "the *preaching* (κήρυγμα) concerning the divine nature".[42] This is *theologia* which becomes perfectly heard according to its spiritual meaning and divine intention when the bodily veil of human words that surround the Word becomes completely removed. In this process,[43] the Word enters the heart of a believer through the *spiritual* sense of *hearing*.[44] The receiving of the Word makes the soul open up for the divine Light and become perceptive of God. The Word becomes an object of spiritual and intellectual visions as it indwells the heart. Spiritual *seeing* and vision – knowledge partly communicable to the intellect – is *theognosia*. Every vision becomes a new 'look' towards the Word that one still hears calling and willing: ἀκολούθει μοι![45]

In the divine contemplation, the soul always follows behind the 'divine voice' (θεοῦ φωνή) – and the soul's happiness consists of seeing God. In the final state of beatitude, both seeing and hearing of the Word become purely spiritual and immediate. One has then fully received the divine Spirit and entered, by faith, through intellectual not-seeing and not-knowing, the "inner sanctuary of *theognosia*" – Christ himself – beyond the 'sound of the trumpets', *beyond theologia*.[46] *In Christ* the hearing of the Word is no longer mediated by human words. Instead, as the soul is now in Christ and Christ dwells in the soul, 'hearing' is a result of becoming perfectly *one in will* with Christ – just as between the Father and the Son (and the Spirit) there is a *perfect union and commingling* (ἕνωσις καὶ ἀνάκρασις) *between two* (three) *individual intelligent existents* (τοῦ νοητοῦ πρὸς τὸ νοητόν) *through the identity of their wills* (διὰ τῆς ταὐτότητος τῶν θελημάτων) in their action.[47] This is how the human soul eventually learns to know and see God, and, accordingly, speak about him: not according to his infinite essence but according to his will. The Father's will is his Son – loving and sharing of his Goodness in and through his Son, our Lord Christ, the Wisdom and Power of God.

---

[42] *VM* II 158 (SC 1bis, 79). 'Climbing' importantly relates to θεολογία, but theology *itself* is the 'trumpet blast' to be more and more clearly *heard*.

[43] See *CE* III/II 16–25 (GNO II 57–60).

[44] Even the 'natural theology' of divine Power proclaimed silently by 'the heavens' is to be *heard*. *CE* II 219–225 (GNO I 289ff).

[45] *VM* II 250–255 (SC 1bis, 112–114). *Theognosia* in *CE* II 232; 259–261 (GNO I 293; 302).

[46] *VM* II 152–175 (SC 1bis, 77–86).

[47] *CE* II 214–218 (GNO I 287ff). Cf. *Abl.* (GNO III/1 48–49); *Tunc et ipse* (GNO III/2 22–23).

IX. *Theology as divine philosophy and the Mother-tongue of worship*

As a Christian, Gregory knew that true Wisdom has an identity and knew how to identify her – or him – as Christ.[48] As φιλόσοφος, Gregory was φιλόχριστος, a lover of Christ.[49] In Christ, a Christian wisdom-lover loves the same Wisdom that the Father has always loved when loving his own Son. As a result, the human Christ-loving movement of the intellect, desiring to *ascend* to divine Wisdom and God's man-loving movement, *descending* to share his own Wisdom, meet in Christ. The essentially divine, descending 'philosophic' movement of God's Word may be called 'divine philosophy' and 'theology' alike, but the essentially human, ascending philosophic movement can only adequately be called philosophy. When the Christian philosopher receives the down-coming Word and gives it a body in human words, this participation is most adequately to be called 'serving the Word' according to God's will: it is διακονία in the οἰκονομία τοῦ θεοῦ.

When theology becomes natural human expression and spiritual movement 'up' in the conversation between man and God, it is not human speculation but already a *response of worship and praise* to the initial address of God. In its natural state, all creation is an expression of God's will, manifesting and proclaiming God's glory, wisdom and power. As God's work, the whole *oikonomia* is a 'saying of God' named by men.[50] Humankind in its natural state as God's image and likeness is a manifestation of God's Wisdom and Power as Love – of God himself as loving nature. As much as it has now received the divine Word in the Spirit, it proclaims Christ Jesus as the Lord and glorifies God in the Church's 'Mother-tongue' of worship: in the name of the Father, the Son and the Holy Spirit. The Church[51] already participates in 'divine philosophy' where Christ loves the

[48] For identification, see Gregory's first work *De virg.* 20 (GNO VIII/1 328).

[49] *VM* II 31; 176 (SC 1bis, 40; 86).

[50] *CE* II 219–225; 265–267 (GNO I 289ff; 303f); *VM* II 168–169 (SC 1bis, 83–84).

[51] Gregory discusses the ecclesiological and eschatological dimensions of human perfection in *Tunc et ipse* (GNO III/2 3–28) and *Cant.* (GNO VI). For further discussion of the eschatological dimensions in *Tunc et ipse*, see A. Ojell, "El *telos* escatológico de la vida cristiana. La vida en Christo según San Gregorio de Nisa", in: C. Izquiero – J. Burggraf – J. L. Gutiérrez – E. Flandes (eds.), *Escatología y Vida Cristiana*, Pamplona 2002, 353–373.

Church (and each faithful soul) as his Bride and she loves him as her Bridegroom – and the Father loves man in his Son as he loves his natural Son. In the eschatological consummation, the whole πλήρωμα of ἄνθρωπος – as μονάς then called ἐκκλησία – becomes subjected, through the Son, to the loving will of the Father, and 'Man' as one Body of Christ is exalted to the subsisting reality of Divine Philosophy – the Father loving his Son. Then *Sophia* calls *Ecclesia* her friend whom she knows in the same manner as if she was looking at her own image in the mirror. Man then finally leads the chorus of all creation celebrating God – and in one voice joins the Angels[52] in *the singing of God's glory*: θεολογία.

[52] *In diem lum.* (GNO IX 241). 'Angels singing' is the 'natural theology' of the created intelligible order.

EUNOMIUS' *APOLOGIA* AND BASIL OF CAESAREA'S *ADVERSUS EUNOMIUM*

Anne Gordon Keidel

The theological challenges of the fourth century provided the exercize ground which allowed orthodox theologians to work out clear statements of orthodox Christian faith. This process began with Arius and the Arian movement, which resulted in preliminary statements of faith at Nicaea in 325 A.D. But it was with the second generation Arians and their best spokesman, Eunomius, that major issues were argued and faith statements were more clearly defined. The efforts of Basil and his brother Gregory culminated in the Constantinople/Nicaean Creed at the Council of Constantinople in 381. This achievement brought an end to the Arian challenge and represented the triumph of orthodoxy.

Eunomius and Basil shared a lot in common. They were both born in Cappadocia around the same time, and both were intelligent, articulate and well-educated. Where Basil and Eunomius differ in their background, is in the social standing in which they were born. Basil's family was part of the landed aristocracy, the elite of Cappadocian society. Eunomius was born in northwest Cappadocia into a family of peasants and craftsmen.[1] While we have not specific information concerning Eunomius' education, we can deduce from the writings of his accusers that he moved through the Greek educational system to its highest level, from grammar school through the study of Greek philosophy. Basil accuses him of basing his ideas on Aristotle and Chrysippus, and Gregory of Nyssa, in challenging his second *Apologia*, accuses him of Neo-Platonism. It is interesting to note that his experience provides evidence of the possibility at that time for those born into the poorest class of society to achieve upward mobility and influence within that society.

Eunomius was a disciple of Aetius, the leader of the second generation Arians called Anomoeans, who held an extremist position

[1] W. V. Harris, *Ancient Literacy*, Cambridge (Mass.) – London 1989, 284, 288.

concerning Father and Son. Eunomius followed Aetius from Antioch to Alexandria studying philosophy and dialectics under him during the years 356–358. Intellectually he outshone his master. In 358, the two of them together with the Arian Eudoxius participated in the Arian council held in Antioch. Here, they alarmed the more moderate Arians such as Basil of Ancyre, who was able to get them exiled to Phrygia. Two years later the tables turned, Eudoxius was made bishop of Constantinople, and the emperor called a synod in 360 in that city to solidify the Arian position. Eunomius came as a deacon, having been ordained by Eudoxius at the Council of Antioch in 358,[2] and Basil came accompanying Dianius, who ordained him reader on their return to Caesarea. It was at this synod that Eunomius delivered his *Apologia* and stirred up a lot of commotion, challenging and stimulating the Cappadocian Fathers to produce some of their most important works.

I. *Eunomius'* Apologia

Eunomius' *Apologia* begins with a rhetorical and methodological preamble and a preliminary confession of faith. The principal body of the work sets out to explain the tenets of this confession of faith and leads to a more developed confession of faith at the end. The three principal sections address 1) God as unique and ungenerated, 2) the Son as product and creature of the Father, and 3) the Spirit as creature of the Son, Paraclete and third in order of nature. We will briefly consider the main points.

God as unique and ungenerated: The central point of Eunomius' thesis is that ungenerated denotes the substance of God. He claimed that God himself and the nature of being ungenerated were correlative. From this he deduces that because God is ungenerated he cannot generate. Eunomius responds to objections by saying that neither time, century, nor order is able to differentiate the essence of God, thus proving God's simplicity of essence (οὐσία).[3]

---

[2] B. Sesboüé, Introduction to Basil's *Adverus Eunomium*, SC 299, 19.

[3] Eunomius, *Apol.* 7 (SC 305, 244–246). (For Eunomius' *Apologia*, the edition used was SC 305, with Introduction, French translation and notes by Bernard Sesboüé and Georges-Matthieu de Durand. It will be abbreviated *Apol.*, followed by the section(s) numbers.)

The Son, product and creature of the Father: According to Eunomius, the Son was not generated within the divine nature, but was produced, made, created by the Father. This enabled him to have creative power and only in this way to resemble the Father. Concerning the generation or non-generation of the Son, Eunomius first makes the point that the opinion in opposition to his own implies that the Son must have been generated while he was already existing. But this does not make sense Eunomius says, because whoever is existing does not need generating. He believes that God's essence does not allow for generation, since God himself is not generated, and as he is incorruptible, his essence can neither be separated nor split. This would eliminate the only essence that could serve as a substratum for generation of the Son. Concurrently, those who would teach the generation of the Son would be saying that the Son has been generated when he was not yet in existence. This is the reasoning which leads Eunomius to say that the Son, being product and creature of the Father, is excluded from being of similar essence as the Father.[4]

Two ways of knowing: Next, Eunomius describes two ways of knowing. First, he says, we examine the essences (substances) themselves, and judge each one by means of pure reason. The second way is knowing by examining the activities and judging them from their created works and the effects of these works. From this he concludes that neither of these ways show evidence of similarity in essence.[5] To demonstrate his position Eunomius cites Scripture, where he says that the Law and the Prophets announce One God. He specifically cites the place where the Savior and Only-begotten himself confesses that he is going to his God and to our God (*Jn* 20,17).[6]

Eunomius does say however that the Son is in the image of the Father by reason of the similarity of activity. But, he hastens to add that the activity of the ungenerated is not the same thing as the substance of the ungenerated. The statement that the Son is in the image of the Father, is explained by the identity of the Son's will and activity, with the activity being separate to his essence. As the Monogenes is under the will of the Father, so his activity is the same as the Father's, while their two essences remain different.[7]

---

[4] Eunomius, *Apol.* 18 (SC 305, 268–270).
[5] Eunomius, *Apol.* 20 (SC 305, 274–276).
[6] Eunomius, *Apol.* 21 (SC 305, 276–278).
[7] Eunomius, *Apol.* 22–24 (SC 305, 278–284).

The Spirit: Paraclete, third in order of nature: According to Eunomius, the Spirit is the first creature of the Son, different in nature from the Son, and has no creative power. However, the Son has given the Spirit the power to sanctify and to teach. Thus, the hierarchy is represented by the Son being the creature of the Father, and the Spirit being the creature of the Son. And, just as the Son's nature is different from the Father's, so the Spirit's nature is different from the Son's. Here, Eunomius replaces the word 'essence' with the word 'nature' (φύσις).[8]

Confession of Faith developed: With this confession of faith Eunomius summarizes and concludes the thesis he has just presented, with the principal points being as follows: God of the universe is unique and alone true God. God is ungenerated, without principle, incomparable, superior to all cause and the cause of the existence of all beings. God did not constitute the created world from a community, together with others. And before everything else, he created the Son.[9]

According to this statement of faith, the Son, the Monogenes, Our Lord Jesus Christ, by whom everything is made, is in the image of the Father by reason of power and activity, but not by substance. The Son is without end, and so without error. As product of the Father, the Son is obedient, a very perfect minister, who served in order to accomplish all of the Father's work and decisions. The Son does this for the 'Economy', to realize God's plan of salvation. He was engendered by the holy virgin, and lived under human laws. The Spirit is the first work of the Son, a product by order of the Father, but product by the activity of the Son. The Spirit is the servant of the Son for the sanctifying and teaching and confirming of believers.[10]

II. *Basil's Adversus Eunomium*

Basil, along with many other orthodox participants at the Synod of Constantinople, was profoundly disturbed by the challenge of the Anomoeans, represented in particular by Aetius and Eunomius' pre-

---

[8] Eunomius, *Apol.* 25 (SC 305, 284–286).
[9] Eunomius, *Apol.* 26 (SC 305, 288–290).
[10] Eunomius, *Apol.* 27 (SC 305, 290–294).

sentation at the Synod. He most likely is referring to this experience, when he writes in one of his earliest works, the *De judicio Dei*:

> "In the Church of God alone, I saw a great and exceeding discord . . . I saw its very leaders differing so much from one another in sentiment and opinion, and so hostile to the commandments of our Lord Jesus Christ, and so mercilessly rending the Church of God, and unsparingly agitating his flock, that now, if ever, when the Anomoeans had sprung up, was fulfilled the saying: 'From among your own selves shall men arise, speaking perverse things, to draw away the disciples after them' (*Acts* 20,30)."[11]

Basil was persuaded by other concerned Christians to write, in time for the Council of Lampsacus in 364 a rebuttal to Eunomius' *Apologia*. He undertakes the task, while saying that he is "of words absolutely unpracticed in such kinds of things".[12] Basil's response to Eunomius is divided into three parts, addressing Eunomius' three main sections, on Father, Son, and Holy Spirit.[13]

Book One. Basil begins by characterizing Eunomius as a liar and his *Apologia* as a fiction. Eunomius is called vain for presenting himself as a model of courage, and an opponent of the [Christian] tradition for correcting the confession of faith. Basil accuses Eunomius of contradicting himself, when he states that the two terms, 'ungenerated' and 'essence' are mutually related.[14] For them to be related they must be two separate things, with 'ungenerate' existing outside the essence. Basil says that which is exterior to God cannot be God's substance.[15]

Eunomius says that because ungenerate is not a concept but rather the substance of God, saying that the Son was generated precludes

[11] Basil, *De judicio Dei* 1 (PG 31, 653ab).

[12] Basil, *Adv. Eun.* I 1 (SC 299, 140–146).

[13] W. K. L. Clarke, *St. Basil the Great*, Cambridge 1913, 92, n. 2; Jean Gribomont dates *Adversus Eunomium* about 370, just before he became a bishop, believing that Basil would have had to have had more experience in dealing concretely with the problems in the Church before writing such a dogmatic work. See J. Gribomont, "Notes biographiques sur s. Basile le Grand", in: P. J. Fedwick (ed.), *Basil of Caesarea. Christian, Humanist, Acsetic*, I, Toronto 1981, 38. However, most scholars date this work (Books 1–3) to immediately before the Synod of Lampsacus (364), citing the clear evidence of the Council that Basil had brought the writings with him when he came. See P. J. Fedwick, "A Chronology of the Life and Works of Basil of Caesarea", in: P. J. Fedwick (ed.), *Basil of Caesarea*, I, 10, and M. V. Anastos in his article in the same volume, "Basil's Κατὰ Εὐνομίου", 70, n. 8.

[14] Eunomius, *Apol.* 7,11–14 (SC 305, 246).

[15] Basil, *Adv. Eun.* I 5 (SC 299, 168–182).

the Son from being of the same substance as God. The word 'concept' is convenient for Eunomius, Basil says, because it signifies nothing more than the act of enumeration. Basil illustrates the nature and usage of this concept by citing Scripture, where the Lord gives himself certain names, such as 'door', 'way', 'bread', 'vine', 'shepherd', and 'light'. The Lord is one essence (μία οὐσία) and the names indicate, not essence but properties.[16] Basil says that Eunomius' use of language causes confusion, and cites his statement that the body is simple, when reason tells us that it is complex.[17]

Eumomius uses the term, στέρησις, privation, negation, in reference to God, saying that the word refers to privation of natural attributes. Basil replies that 'ungenerate' designates an absence in God, that there does not exist a unique name which suffices to embrace the complete nature of God, and explain it in a satisfactory manner. But we do speak of God in negative terms, 'invisible', 'incorruptible', 'immortal'. Basil shows by this the limitations, not of God, but of our language and comprehension when considering God's essence. This essence is known only by the Son and the Spirit, but is beyond human comprehension. Likewise, the essence of earth is not revealed in Scriptures. Because of this we say that God is incomprehensible, totally inexpressible, and that we are thus faced with the inaccessibility of God. What is revealed in Scripture is God's goodness and wisdom. This means that we can know the properties of God, but are unable to know God's essence. Ungenerate indicates the 'how' of God but not God's essence.[18]

In response to Eunomius' claim that ideas of order, time and century can exist in the substance of God, Basil says that consubstantiality is eternal in the order of the persons in God, because there can be no Father without the Son.[19] Eunomius' premise that the divine simplicity suggests the inequality of Father and Son, Basil says that, on the contrary, this shows the sameness of Father and Son. Eunomius refers to the words, "the Father is greater than I," to substantiate his claim that the Father is first in the hierarchy, and greater in power than the Son. Basil says that 'greater' refers to cause and

[16] Basil, *Adv. Eun.* I 7 (SC 299, 188–192).
[17] Basil, *Adv. Eun.* I 8 (SC 299, 192–198).
[18] Basil, *Adv. Eun.* I 9–12 (SC 299, 198–216).
[19] Basil, *Adv. Eun.* I 19 (SC 299, 238–242).

principle, meaning the term 'Father' as cause and principle of the term 'Son' is said to be greater. However, Basil totally rejects the assumption that greater refers to power, that Christ can be said to have less power than God, and cites the passages where Christ states, "The Father and I are one", saying that this refers to the equality and identity of Father and Son according to power.[20] At the same time, Basil says that it is a contradiction to say that God is greater and incomparable,[21] and at one point states:

> I am not able to believe that even in full delirium you would ever affirm that the Son is other than incorporal, without form, without figure and all that you would say of the Father.[22]

Book Two: the Son. Against the thesis that the Son is product (γέννημα) and creature (ποίημα) of the Father, Basil says that Eunomius misuses Scripture by trying to use the passage, "God made this Jesus Lord and Christ" (*Acts* 2,36) to prove his point. This passage rather envisages a moment in the Economy of God (God's work of salvation).[23] Basil asks where Eunomius got such an idea of the Son being a product and creature of the Father, saying that it is something extraneous to Scripture. The fruits of the earth are products, Basil says, but a child is not a product.[24]

Against the thesis that the Son was generated, when he was not, meaning that if the Son was generated, then there was a time when the Son was not. Basil answers this by saying that that which is good is always present in God, that God the Father always possessed the Son by reason of his always willing that which is good. The Father is Father from all eternity. The Father is not Father without the Son. Thus, the Son is co-eternal with the Father and never had a beginning.[25]

Against the thesis that the Son is a creature of the Father, and the Spirit is a creature of the Son. Basil responds by saying that if the Son knows the essence of the Father then it is impossible for him to have been created. One is able to ascertain God's power by knowing his works, but one cannot understand that which is his

---

[20] Basil, *Adv. Eun.* I 25 (SC 299, 260–262).
[21] Basil, *Adv. Eun.* I 26 (SC 299, 264–266).
[22] Basil, *Adv. Eun.* I 23 (SC 299, 252–256).
[23] Basil, *Adv. Eun.* II 3 (SC 305, 16–18).
[24] Basil, *Adv. Eun.* II 8 (SC 305, 30–34).
[25] Basil, *Adv. Eun.* II 12 (SC 305, 44–46).

essence. God's power (δύναμις) is the same as his essence.[26] We know God through his works, but not through his essence.[27] The Spirit is at the same time Spirit of God and Spirit of Christ. He calls the Spirit, the Spirit of Truth, because he himself is Truth.[28]

Book Three: the Spirit. Basil counters Eunomius on the Spirit by saying that the difference in order and dignity doesn't suggest a difference in nature. The names, 'Holy' and 'Paraclete' prove that the Spirit is divine. The Holy Spirit not only shares the designation 'holy' with God, but also the designation 'Spirit': "God is Spirit, and those who worship him must worship him in spirit and in truth" (*Jn* 4,24).[29] The activities are on the same level as the activities of the Father and the Son. The divine character of the Spirit is shown in the words: "All these are activated by one and the same Spirit, who alots to each one individually just as the Spirit chooses" (*1 Cor* 12,11).[30]

The indwelling of the Spirit, Basil says, is a divine indwelling, citing: "Go baptise in the name of the Father, the Son, and the Holy Spirit" (*Mt* 28,19). Baptism is the seal of faith and faith is an assent to the divinity. Basil rejects Eunomius' claim that the Spirit is something made, a creature created by the Son,[31] and says that although not generated, the Spirit belongs to the Trinity.[32]

In conclusion we can say that Basil's response to Eunomius resulted in the following statements of orthodox faith: We cannot know the essence of God, and so we speak of the unknowability of God, the inaccessibility of God to the human mind. This theological statement, along with Gregory of Nyssa's theology on the same subject was to underpin Christian apophatic spirituality. However, we can know God through his works, we can know God's properties. Basil also articulated the eternal generation of the Son, and that the Son is co-eternal with the Father, and states that the divine character of the Spirit is shown in the Scriptures, citing *1 Cor* 12,11. While this early response to Eunomius did not silence the challenge, it did help

[26] Basil, *Adv. Eun.* II 32 (SC 305, 132–136).
[27] Basil, *Adv. Eun.* II 32,18–27 (SC 305, 134).
[28] Basil, *Adv. Eun.* II 34 (SC 305, 140–142).
[29] Basil, *Adv. Eun.* III 2–3 (SC 305, 150–153).
[30] Basil, *Adv. Eun.* III 4 (SC 305, 156–162).
[31] Eunomius, *Apol.* 26,24–26 (SC 305, 290).
[32] Basil, *Adv. Eun.* III 5 (SC 305, 162–164).

provide a framework of basic principles, which Gregory of Nyssa would later develop, when, after Basil's death, he continued the work of providing what would become the orthodox response to the Arian challenge.

DIE ALLEGORESE IN DER SCHRIFT *LEBEN DES MOSE* GREGORS VON NYSSA IM KONTEXT SEINER EPINOIA-THEORIE

Tamara Aptsiauri

Der Begriff ἐπίνοια hat sich in der Lehre der kappadozischen Kirchenväter während der Debatten gegen Eunomius formiert. Die Kappadozier unterscheiden in epistemologischer Hinsicht zwischen einer positiven und einer negativen Bedeutung. 'Epinoia' bezeichnet einerseits eine phantastische Erfindung,[1] andererseits ein Konzept, Sinn, eine Vorstellung, wenn es sich mit dem Denkvermögen verbindet, womit Gott die intelligible menschliche Natur ausgezeichnet hat.[2] Nach Gregor von Nyssa ist gerade ἐπίνοια, der bekannte Terminus der antiken Erkenntnistheorie, allgemein die Grundlage der Wissenschaft und so auch des spekulativen theologischen Wissens.[3] Das Denksystem des kappadozischen Kirchenvaters stellt eine eng miteinander verbundene Ideenkette dar: Zwischen Gregors Idee der Unendlichkeit Gottes, der epinoetischen Beziehung des Menschen zum göttlichen Wesen und der allegorischen Auslegung der Heiligen Schrift soll ein sachlicher Zusammenhang gesehen werden.

Obwohl der Terminus ἐπίνοια im *Leben des Mose* nicht im Besonderen erläutert wird, bietet diese Schrift, eines der wichtigsten allegorisch-mystischen Werke Gregors von Nyssa, eine Möglichkeit zu betrachten, wie im allgemeinen Kontext der Epinoia-Theorie die grundlegenden Fragen der Hermeneutik von Gregor beantwortet werden: Die Notwendigkeit des tiefen Durchdenkens der Heiligen Schrift, die Eigenart und die Aufgabe der allegorischen Sprache.

---

[1] *CE* II 187 (GNO I 278): τὸ δὲ λέγεσθαι παρὰ τῶν ὑπεναντίων τὰ μυθώδη πλάσματα καὶ τὰ ψευδῆ τερατεύματα παρὰ τῆς ἐπινοίας λογοποιεῖσθαι καὶ πλάσσεσθαι, οὐδὲ αὐτὸς ἀντιλέγω.

[2] *CE* II 186 (GNO I 278): νοῦς δὲ ἔργον θεοῦ. οὐκοῦν ἐκ θεοῦ πάντα ὅσα διὰ τοῦ νοῦ ἡμῖν πεπόρισται. *CE* II 189 (GNO I 279): οὕτως φαμὲν καὶ τῆς ἐπινοίας τὴν δύναμιν ἐπ᾽ ἀγαθῷ μὲν ἐντεθεῖσθαι παρὰ τοῦ θεοῦ τῇ ἀνθρωπίνῃ φύσει.

[3] *CE* II 181–182 (GNO I 277).

I. *Die Notwendigkeit der allegorischen Auslegung der Heiligen Schrift*

Das Hauptthema der Auseinandersetzung der Kappadozier mit dem Neoarianer Eunomius ist bekanntlich dessen Lehre, dass die einzig wahre Definition des göttlichen Wesens das selbst von Gott offenbarte Prädikat 'ungezeugt' (ἀγέννητος) sei. Die Idee der Unendlichkeit Gottes, seiner Transzendenz und Unerreichbarkeit ist das wichtigste Konzept, mittels dessen sich Gregor von Nyssa mit dieser Theorie des Eunomius auseinandergesetzt hat.

Für Gregor von Nyssas Schema ist es spezifisch, dass er scharf zwischen der geschaffenen und ungeschaffenen Natur unterscheidet. Um den zwischen der geschaffenen vernünftigen und der ungeschaffenen Natur existierenden Erkenntnis- und ontologischen Abgrund zu bezeichnen, führt Gregor den Begriff διάστημα ein. Gott, als die adiastematische Natur, ist unerreichbar und unbegreiflich für die geschaffene Natur, die diastematisch ist; nicht nur für die körperliche Schöpfung – für den Menschen –, sondern auch für die unkörperlichen Wesen.[4] Das Erkennen des Wahrhaftseienden bedeutet gerade die Anerkennung seiner Unerkennbarkeit, Unerreichbarkeit und Unendlichkeit; und auch der mystische Aufstieg zu ihm ist ein unendlicher Prozess, wie es dem Mose während der zweiten und dritten Theophanien geoffenbart wurde.[5] Durch dieses ontologische Schema wird das unmittelbare Begreifen Gottes, wie Gott von Natur ist (denken wir an Moses Wunsch, Gott von Angesicht zu Angesicht zu sehen),[6] von selbst ausgeschlossen. Der einzige Weg zur Betrachtung des Schöpfers ist für den sich in der zeitlichen und räumlichen Dimension befindenden Menschen das geschaffene Universum, das als Offenbarung der göttlichen Energie selbst vom Schöpfer zeugt.

Der Teilung der Welt in diese zwei ontologischen Pole (geschaffen/ungeschaffen) entspricht Gregor von Nyssas Konzept von Erkenntnis und von der diskursiven und bedingten Natur der Sprache. Die menschliche Vernunft und die Fähigkeit der Benennung sind Teil der geschaffenen Natur und begrenzt als eine diastematische Schöpfung. Die Sprache, so Gregor, ist eine menschliche Schöpfung[7] und hat

---

[4] *CE* II 67 (GNO I 245). Auch *De vita Moysis* II (GNO VII/1 87,10–13): θεὸν οὐδεὶς ἑώρακε πώποτε, οὐ μόνον τοῖς ἀνθρώποις ἀλλὰ καὶ πάσῃ τῇ νοητῇ φύσει τῆς θείας οὐσίας τὴν γνῶσιν ἀνέφικτον εἶναι τῇ ἀποφάσει ταύτῃ διοριζόμενος.

[5] *VM* II (GNO VII/1 66,20–67,8).

[6] *VM* II (GNO VII/1 110,6–15).

[7] *CE* II 392.395–402 (GNO I 340–344).

einen diastematischen Charakter. Deshalb vermag die Sprache nicht jedes Phänomen des intellektuellen Bereichs wiederzugeben, umso weniger das ewige und unendliche Wesen zu bezeichnen. Unter den Bedingungen von Gregor von Nyssas Teilung der Welt in einen sinnlichen und einen vernünftigen Bereich gibt es folgende Alternative der Erkenntnis der Dinge. Einerseits, wenn es um den sinnlichen Bereich geht, gibt die sinnliche Wahrnehmung der Dinge die Möglichkeit, über sie ein wahrhaftes Wissen zu erhalten.[8] Andererseits, wenn das zu untersuchende Objekt zum intelligiblen Teil der Welt gehört, spielt im Prozess seiner Erkenntnis und Benennung διάνοια die entscheidende Rolle, die in diesem Fall eine intellektuelle Vorstellungsfähigkeit des Menschen, eine konzeptionelle Vermutung über das Objekt darstellt.[9] Die dem transzendenten höchsten Wesen entsprechende menschliche Vorstellung und die wörtliche Bezeichnung dieser Vorstellung kann nur bedingt und teilweise zutreffend sein. So hat Mose auf dem Berg Sinai die göttliche Anordnung erhalten, dass es vor allem auf der Tugend geziemende Vorstellungen (τὰς πρεπούσας ὑπολήψεις) von der Natur Gottes ankommt, da diese jenseits alles erkennenden Verstehens und jenseits aller Beispiele liegt (ὑπέρκειται παντὸς γνωριστικοῦ νοήματός τε καὶ ὑποδείγματος), und mit nichts zu vergleichen ist, was erkannt wird (οὐδενὶ τῶν γινωσκομένων ὁμοιουμένη).[10] Die Betrachtung Gottes bedenkt, dass sein Wesen mit nichts gleichzusetzen ist, was durch die menschliche Erkenntnis erlangt wird.[11] Unsere Erkenntnis und Vorstellung des göttlichen Wesens erzeugt nichts anderes als ein εἴδωλον θεοῦ[12] keine Bezeichnung des Wesens Gottes. Wenn jemand meint, es sei möglich, die göttliche Natur zu begreifen, sinkt er schon von dem wirklich Seienden zu dem, das durch die erfassende Vorstellung verstanden wird.[13] Da die differenzierte Sprache unfähig ist, direkt auf das

[8] *CE* II 572–573 (GNO I 393).

[9] *CE* II 574–576 (GNO I 393f).

[10] *VM* II (GNO VII/1 22,14–18).

[11] *VM* II (GNO VII/1 88,7–10): μαθὼν ἐν πρώτοις ἃ χρὴ περὶ τοῦ θεοῦ γινώσκειν· τὸ δὲ γινώσκειν, τὸ μηδὲν περὶ αὐτοῦ τῶν ἐξ ἀνθρωπίνης καταλήψεως γινωσκομένων εἰδέναι.

[12] *VM* II (GNO VII/1 88,2–5): παντὸς νοήματος τοῦ κατά τινα περιληπτικὴν φαντασίαν ἐν περινοίᾳ τινὶ καὶ στοχασμῷ τῆς θείας φύσεως γινομένου εἴδωλον θεοῦ πλάσσοντος καὶ οὐ θεὸν καταγγέλλοντος.

[13] *VM* II (GNO VII/1 115,6–8): ὁ τοίνυν τῶν γινωσκομένων τι τὸν θεὸν εἶναι οἰόμενος, ὡς παρατραπεὶς ἀπὸ τοῦ ὄντως ὄντος πρὸς τὸ τῇ καταληπτικῇ φαντασίᾳ νομισθὲν εἶναι, ζωὴν οὐκ ἔχει.

einfache göttliche Wesen hinzuweisen, wird von einem jeglichen zu Gott gerichteten apophatischen oder kataphatischen Terminus unsere Epinoia über die göttliche Natur bezeichnet.[14] Ausgehend von dieser Überlegung, ist für Gregor der von Eunomius eingeführte Terminus 'ungezeugt' völlig annehmbar als eines der Prädikate des göttlichen Wesens, obwohl er kategorisch verneint, dass die 'Ungezeugtheit' als der bezeichnende Begriff selbst das göttliche Wesen sei.[15] Wenn der Verfasser das Symbol des ungeschaffenen Zeltes auslegt, weist er auf das relative Prinzip der Namensgebung der göttlichen Natur hin, dass durch jeden für Gott gebrauchten Namen nur die Wirkung (Energie) Gottes bezeichnet wird: "Wie alle anderen Namen im religiösen Sinn zur Bezeichnung der Macht Gottes gebraucht werden, wie z.B. Arzt, Hirte, Schützer . . . und was sonst noch von Ihm gesagt wird, so wird Er auch mit einem Namen, der der göttlichen Natur angemessen ist (κατά τινα θεοπρεπῆ σημασίαν), 'Zelt' genannt."[16] Nimmt man auf diese Idee Rücksicht, wird deutlich, dass, obwohl die Heilige Schrift inspiriert worden ist, sie trotzdem durch die menschliche Sprache spricht und so imstande ist, Wahrheit durch eine rätselhafte Aussage (δι' αἰνίγματος) wiederzugeben.[17] Die Teilung der inspirierten Heiligen Schrift in historische und theoretische Teile übernimmt Gregor von Origenes als etwas völlig Selbstverständliches.[18] Gregors Hermeneutik der biblischen Bücher geht von der Koexistenz von Historie und Theorie aus. Der Mensch erhebt sich durch eine Interpretation der Geschichte zur Betrachtung des Höchsten Wesens. Durch die Suche nach dem hinter dem einfachen Wort und der Erzählweise der Heiligen Schrift versteckten tieferen Sinn führt die biblische Geschichte zur mystischen Betrachtung,[19] was wiederum den Menschen auf den unendlichen Weg der geistigen Vervoll-

---

[14] *CE* II 130–136.446–449 (GNO I 263–265.356f).

[15] *CE* II 177 (GNO I 276): ἀγέννητόν φασι τὸν θεὸν εἶναι· τούτῳ καὶ ἡμεῖς συντιθέμεθα. ἀλλὰ καὶ τὴν ἀγεννησίαν οὐσίαν εἶναι· πρὸς τοῦτο παρ' ἡμῶν ἀντίρρησις. ὄνομα γὰρ τοῦτό φαμεν ἐνδεικτικὸν εἶναι τοῦ ἀγεννήτως τὸν θεὸν ὑφεστάναι, οὐ τὴν ἀγεννησίαν εἶναι θεόν.

[16] *VM* II (GNO VII/1 92,8–18).

[17] *VM* II (GNO VII/1 62,10; 65,10; 72,8).

[18] S. T. Dolidze, "Einige Aspekte der allegorischen Sprache in der Auslegung von Origenes und Gregor von Nyssa zum Hohenlied", in: L. Perrone (Hrsg.), *Origeniana Octava*, vol. II, Leuven 2003, 1061–1070.

[19] Dazu s. Th. Böhm, *Theoria Unendlichkeit Aufstieg. Philosophische Implikationen zu De Vita Moysis von Gregor von Nyssa*, Leiden – New York – Köln 1996, 212–227.

kommnung und zur Erkenntnis der göttlichen Schönheit führt. Ein deutliches Beispiel dafür bietet Gregors spirituelles Nachdenken über jedes Detail des Lebens des Mose.

Damit ist aber die Allegorie auch ein Mittel zum Aufstieg vom Sinnlichen zum Sittlich-Geistigen. Für Gregor von Nyssa ist die allegorische Betrachtung der biblischen Bücher untrennbar von der Gewinnung der Tugend d.h. vom sittlichen Leben.[20] Wenn beim buchstäblichen Verstehen der Heiligen Schrift die biblische Geschichte in eine Art Widerspruch mit der göttlichen Gerechtigkeit gerät, wird es notwendig, diese Geschichte sittlich-allegorisch zu reflektieren. Dieser Gedanke Gregors von der scheinbaren Unangemessenheit der Schrift stammt aus der Hermeneutik des Origenes. Im *Leben des Mose* weist Gregor oft auf die Unangemessenheiten hin, die entstehen würden, wenn der Exeget nicht von einer konkreten Geschichte abstrahiert und dem Leser so beim Begreifen des tieferen Sinnes des inspirierten Textes hilft.[21] Indem er die Tötung der ägyptischen Erstgeborenen, die Aneignung des Schmucks der Ägypter, den Hinweis auf den Aufenthaltsort Gottes während der dritten Theophanie und mehrere anderen Passage auslegt, macht der kappadozische Kirchenvater durch eine Verbindung der überzeugenden Logik und der rhetorischen Verfahren deutlich, dass die Allegorie der einzige richtige Weg für die Auslegung der biblischen Bücher sei.[22]

II. *Die Eigenart der allegorischen Sprache*

Mit Blick auf die Lehre Gregors von Nyssa von der Sprache und insbesondere von deren Differenziertheit und Konventionalität entsteht die Frage: Welche Gemeinsamkeiten und welche Unterschiede bestehen zwischen der theologischen Sprache und der Sprache schlechthin?

---

[20] Th. Kobusch, "Metaphysik als Lebensform bei Gregor von Nyssa", in: H. R. Drobner – A. Viciano (Hrsg.), *Gregory of Nyssa: Homilies on the Beatitudes. An English Version with Commentary and Supporting Studies, Proceedings of the Eighth International Colloquium on Gregory of Nyssa (Paderborn, 14–18 September 1998)*, Leiden – Boston – Köln 2000, 467–485. Auch T. Dolidze, "Einige Aspekte", 1063.

[21] Allegorese als Abstand von dem Sinnlich-Konkreten, s. T. Dolidze, "Einige Aspekte", 1065–1066.

[22] Vgl. *VM* II (GNO VII/1 110,24–111,17; 60; 68).

Weil für Gott in seiner transzendenten Natur Sprache – dieses für den diastematischen Bereich bestimmte Phänomen – etwas völlig Fremdes ist, spricht der Herr mit uns in unserer Sprache durch die Heilige Schrift. Die Propheten und Apostel sind Instrumente des Heiligen Geistes.[23] Einer davon ist Mose durch sein ganzes Wirken und dadurch, dass er Mittler zwischen Gott und den Menschen wird, wenn er vom Berg Sinai Gottes Gebote für sie mitbringt. Die Propheten und Apostel geben nicht ein konkretes Konzept von der göttlichen Natur, sondern eine Vielfalt an Namen und Analogien, damit der Mensch die für ihn entsprechenden Vorstellungen (ἡ θεοπρεπὴς ἔννοια) über Gott zu schaffen vermag.[24]

Durch die Unendlichkeit und Transzendenz des göttlichen Wesens einerseits, andererseits aber durch die gegliederte Struktur der menschlichen Sprache und ihre Bedingtheit wird die Vielfältigkeit der durch die epinoetische Fähigkeit des Menschen gewonnenen Analogien und göttlichen Namen bedingt. Die göttliche Natur offenbart sich dem Menschen nicht nach ihrem wahren und absoluten Wesen, sondern nach dem Vermögen des Empfängers (οὕτως ἐμφαινομένη καθὼς ἂν χωρῇ τὸ δεχόμενον).[25] Dementsprechend ist für die Sprache der inspirierten Schrift Mehrdeutigkeit und Mannigfaltigkeit charakteristisch.

Gregor von Nyssa gebraucht im *Leben des Mose* den Begriff 'Homonymie' in Bezug auf die Allegorie. Dieser Begriff erscheint in einigen anderen seiner Werke bei der Auslegung der hermeneutischen Fragen. Mit diesem Terminus ist eine Reihe von Fragen verbunden, die noch nicht erforscht sind, wie es in der wissenschaftlichen Spezialliteratur der letzten Jahre bemerkt wurde.[26] Wegen der Kompliziertheit der Frage wollen wir sie diesmal nicht genauer erforschen, ich möchte nur bemerken, in welchem Kontext hier der Terminus 'Homonymie' erwähnt wird. Ausgehend von der bedingten und veränderlichen Natur der Sprache, hält Gregor die Ambivalenz von Worten für möglich in dem Sinn, dass eine lexikalische Einheit in verschiedenen Kontexten eine gegensätzliche Bedeutung haben

---

[23] *CE* II 393–394 (GNO I 341).

[24] *VM* II (GNO VII/1 22,14–16); *CE* II 168 (GNO I 273f).

[25] *VM* II (GNO VII/1 70,8–11).

[26] M. Harl, "Origène et la sémantique du langage biblique", in: *Le déchiffrement du sens*, Paris 1993, 65. T. Dolidze, "Der Glaube als Erkenntnis bei Origenes", in: W. Geerlings – C. Schulze (Hrsg.), *Kommentar in Antike und Mittelalter. Neue Beiträge zu seiner Erforschung*, Leiden 2003, 205.

kann. So spricht er im *Leben des Mose* über Aaron: Das Wort 'Bruder' wird vom Autor in einem Fall als eine Metapher für den Herrenengel erläutert, in einem anderen aber als Anführer des Götzendienstes und als Allegorem des bösen Trachtens. Gregor betont: τῆς οὖν ἀντιθέσεως οὔσης . . . κἀκεῖ μετρίως παρεδήλου τὴν τῆς ἀδελφότητος ὁμωνυμίαν ὁ λόγος, ὡς οὐχὶ πάντοτε τοῦ αὐτοῦ σημαινομένου ἀπὸ τῆς αὐτῆς φωνῆς ὅταν ἐπὶ τῶν ἐναντίων νοημάτον τὸ αὐτὸ λαμβάνηται ὄνομα.[27]

Das *Leben des Mose* belegt, genauso wie der Kommentar Gregors von Nyssa über das *Hohelied*, die komplexe Natur der allegorischen Sprache des kappadozischen Kirchenvaters. Die Polysemantik ist eine wichtige Eigenschaft der theologischen Sprache, die nicht nur auf der Ebene der Metapher erforscht werden soll.[28] Die Vielfältigkeit der allegorischen Sprache wird bei der mehrdeutigen Auslegung von mehreren sprachlichen Bildern deutlich. Die Heilige Schrift bietet (in Analogie zum unendlichen göttlichen Wesen) die Möglichkeit unendlicher Hermeneutik. In dieser Hinsicht ist es für Gregor völlig annehmbar, dass von verschiedenen Auslegern eine und dieselbe biblische Passage individuell und unterschiedlich erläutert wird. Bei der Interpretation der hyazinthblauen Kleidung zum Beispiel bemerkt er: Manche, die diese Stelle vor uns betrachtet haben, sagen, dass mit dieser Farbe die Luft gemeint sei. Ich für meine Person vermag nicht genau zu entscheiden, ob die Farbe dieser Blume etwas mit der Farbe der Luft gemein hat. Jedoch weise ich diese Auslegung nicht zurück.[29]

Die Mehrdeutigkeit der Konzepte ist nicht nur bei der Erläuterung des Unterschieds zwischen verschiedenen Interpreten zulässig, sie tritt auch bei einem einzelnen Exegeten auf. Aufgrund der Vielfältigkeit der Erscheinungen des göttlichen Wesens ist Gregor bei der allegorischen Auslegung der Schrift nicht kategorisch. Dies wird deutlich zum Ausdruck gebracht durch die Metapher vom himmlischen Manna. Dies symbolisiert für Gregor das Wort Gottes, das seine Kraft mannigfach verändert, entsprechend dem Verlangen derjenigen, die

---

[27] *VM* II (GNO VII/1 106,11–16).

[28] Die Frage der Polysemantik in der Allegorese von Origenes und Gregor von Nyssa wird bei T. Dolidze besonders beachtet, s. T. Dolidze, "Einige Aspekte", 1061–1070.

[29] *VM* II (GNO VII/1 98,15–19).

es zu sich nehmen.[30] Das *Leben des Mose* ist voll von Metaphern komplexen Charakters, bei denen verschiedene allegorische Bedeutungen mit erstaunlicher Meisterschaft innerhalb eines Symbols wechseln. So ist Mose einerseits für die auf dem Weg der Tugend wandelnden Menschen das Vorbild, das gleich bei der geistigen Geburt nach seinem freien Willen die Tugend wählt, andererseits ist er als Führer der Hebräer ein Typus des wahren Erlösers und Gesetzgebers – Jesu Christi.

Wie Gregor von Nyssa im *Leben des Mose* bemerkt, ist die Vertiefung in das inspirierte Wort und danach die Betrachtung des göttlichen Wesens ein unendlicher Prozess, so wie für den Suchenden der geistigen Vervollkommnung, der sich auf Jakobs Leiter stellt, auf der jede Stufe eine andere folgt, bis ins Unendliche.[31] Die Komplexität der allegorischen Sprache und die endlose Möglichkeit der Auslegung der Bilder dienen der anagogischen Funktion der Heiligen Schrift.[32] Bei Gregor von Nyssa bekommt die Möglichkeit der vielfältigen und unbegrenzten Hermeneutik der biblischen Geschichte, genauso wie die Idee der Unendlichkeit und der Transzendenz des göttlichen Wesens, eine positive Bedeutung. Jeder auf dem Weg der Vervollkommnung gemachte Schritt ist die Grundlage eines nächsten, jede beliebige Interpretation ist der Anfang einer neuen Interpretation, obwohl der Abstand bis zum höchsten Wesen unveränderlich bleibt. Und "wieder führt die Schrift unseren Geist aufsteigend zu höheren Stufen der Tugend".[33] Am Beispiel des Vorausgehenden soll der Wahrheitssuchende seine eigene spekulative Erfahrung gewinnen, so wie Mose zum Wegweiser und Führer für die in der Tugend Wandelnden wurde. Nach der Hermeneutik Gregors im *Leben des Mose* ist jedes sprachliche Bild von anagogischem Charakter und wird im Allgemeinen protreptischen Kontext gelesen.

Zusammenfassend lässt sich sagen: Wie in anderen Werken von Gregor von Nyssa wird auch im *Leben des Mose* die Notwendigkeit der allegorischen Interpretation der biblischen Bücher und ihr komplexer Charakter zusammen mit Gregors Idee der Unendlichkeit des göttlichen Wesens auch durch die Diastemie des Denkens und der

[30] *VM* II (GNO VII/1 78,1–3; vgl. 51,24; 17,10–20).
[31] *VM* II (GNO VII/1 113,3–6).
[32] *VM* II (GNO VII/1 76,12–14; 82,17–18).
[33] *VM* II (GNO VII/1 82,4–5).

Sprache bedingt. Das geistliche Nachdenken über die Heilige Schrift als das einzige richtige Verfahren der Erkenntnis und Hermeneutik des inspirierten Wortes dient zur Verwirklichung der soteriologischen Mission des Erlösers, und die Allegorese soll im Werk Gregors von Nyssa als die logische Folge seiner Epinoia-Theorie verstanden werden.

DIE BEDEUTUNG DER EPINOIAI IN DEN PREDIGTEN GREGORS VON NYSSA

Jochen Rexer

Die Predigten des 4. Jh. sind eine wichtige Quelle, um Informationen über das Verständnis reichskirchlicher Theologie zu erhalten. Dabei muss grundsätzlich unterschieden werden zwischen den vielen gehaltenen Predigten in den verschiedenen Gemeinden jener Zeit und den dann auch publizierten sowie uns heute noch zugänglichen, d.h.: zwischen der verbreiteten Predigtpraxis und der eingeschränkten Predigtpublikation, die dann auch noch tradiert werden musste. Es ist also immer zu berücksichtigen, dass in dieser Zeit einmal nur die Predigten der bekanntesten *Prediger* – meist waren es die Bischöfe in den größeren christlichen Zentren[1] – niedergeschrieben wurden, dass dabei wiederum allein ihre herausragendsten *Predigten* weitertradiert wurden, und dass schließlich auch bei den *Hörern* von einem überdurchschnittlich gebildeten und interessierten Publikum ausgegangen werden muss.[2] Deshalb sind die heute noch zugänglichen Predigten immer als Musterreden anzusehen, die zu besonderen Anlässen und mit einer bestimmten Absicht vorgetragen, aufgeschrieben und weitertradiert wurden. Auf diesem Hintergrund gelten die Predigten, die bis heute gesichert dem Bischof Gregor von Nyssa zugeschrieben werden, als ein repräsentatives Beispiel und Muster der Predigtpraxis seiner Zeit. Die reichskirchlichen Predigten und im Besonderen die

[1] Predigtrecht und -pflicht hatte zunächst allein der Bischof, der für die Verkündigung und den Glaubenshalt seiner Gemeinde verantwortlich war. In der östlichen Kirche wurde es – sicher bezeugt ab dem 4. Jh. – üblich, auch Presbyter und Diakone zu beauftragen, den Bischof im Predigtdienst zu vertreten (z.B. Johannes Chrysostomus). Im Westen setzt diese Entwicklung erst mit Augustinus ein; vgl. E. Dassmann, *Kirchengeschichte* II/2. *Theologie und innerkirchliches Leben bis zum Ausgang der Spätantike*, Stuttgart 1999, 129.

[2] Zur Überlieferung der christlichen Predigt vgl. B. Studer, *Schola christiana. Die Theologie zwischen Nizäa (325) und Chalzedon (451)*, Paderborn 1998, 114f; zum liturgischen Ort und dem Verhältnis Predigt – Prediger – Hörer vgl. H. G. Thümmel, "Materialien zum liturgischen Ort der Predigt in der Alten Kirche", in: E. Mühlenberg – J. van Oort (Hrsg.), *Predigt in der Alten Kirche*, Kampen 1994, 115–122; L. Brottier, *Predigt* V. *Alte Kirche*: TRE 27 (1997) 244–248.

Festtagspredigten sind bedeutsam sowohl für die Predigt –, als auch für die Liturgiegeschichte. Darüber hinaus spiegeln sie aber immer auch die theologische Diskussion ihrer Zeit wider.

Daher wird zuerst die Rolle der Festtagspredigten Gregors im Allgemeinen behandelt, um zweitens die ἐπίνοιαι in seinen Predigten darzustellen und drittens den erkenntnistheoretischen Hintergrund aufzuzeigen.

I. *Die Festtagspredigten Gregors von Nyssa*

Gregor von Nyssa bezeugt als der erste bis heute bekannte Prediger mit seinem umfangreichen *Corpus* an tradierten Festtagspredigten einen abgeschlossenen Oster- und Weihnachtsfestkreis.[3] Daneben hat er zahlreiche Märtyrerpredigten sowie Lob- und Trostreden hinterlassen.[4] Die Predigten sind in seiner produktivsten Zeit zwischen 379 und 386 entstanden. Gregor von Nyssa entwickelte zwar keine explizite Theorie des Festes, gibt aber in seinen Festtagsreden deutliche Hinweise auf eine angemessene Theologie des Festes. Er reflektiert selbständig die Festpraxis seiner Zeit, nimmt dabei seine theologische Tradition kritisch auf und rezipiert ganz selbstverständlich allgemein anerkannte Festelemente seines soziokulturellen Umfelds.[5]

[3] Sieben Predigten zu den christlichen Herrenfesten werden Gregor von Nyssa sicher zugeschrieben: die Osterpredigten *Sanct. Pasch.* (GNO IX 245–270) und *Trid. spat.* (GNO IX 273–306) mit dem Epilog *Salut. Pasch.* (GNO IX 315–319); die Himmelfahrtspredigt *Ascens.* (GNO IX 323–327); die Pfingstpredigt *Pent.* (GNO X/2 287–292); die Weihnachtspredigt *In diem nat.* (GNO X/2 235–296), sowie die Epiphaniepredigten *In diem lum.* (GNO IX 221–242) und *Bapt.* (GNO X/2 357–370). Vgl. dazu den tabellarischen Überblick bei J. Rexer, *Die Festtheologie Gregors von Nyssa. Ein Beispiel reichskirchlicher Heortologie*, Frankfurt 2002, 6.

[4] *Bas.* (GNO X/1 109–134); *Flacill.* (GNO IX 475–490); *Mart.* Ia (GNO X/1 137–142); *Mart.* Ib (GNO X/1 145–156); *Mart.* II (GNO X/1 159–169); *Melet.* (GNO IX 441–457); *Pulcher.* (GNO IX 461–472); *Steph.* I (GNO X/1 75–94); *Steph.* II (GNO X/1 97–105); *Thaum.* (GNO X/1 3–57); *Theod.* (GNO X/1 61–71). Zu den Märtyrer- und Heiligenreden Gregors von Nyssa vgl. die Beiträge des Sammelbandes: A. Spira (Hrsg.), *The Biographical Works of Gregory of Nyssa. Proceedings of the Fifth International Colloquium on Gregory of Nyssa, Mainz 6–10 September 1982*, Cambridge (Mass.) 1984.

[5] In welcher Art und Weise die Kirche über ihre Festpraxis reflektierte, d.h.: Welche Überzeugungen, Bedürfnisse und Vorstellungen hinter der sich entwickelnden kirchlichen Festpraxis stehen, führt in den Themenbereich der *Heortologie*, der Rede über das Fest, genauer in den Themenbereich der Theologie des Festes, der Rede von Gott am Fest. Zur Praxis und Theorie des christlichen Festes vgl. Rexer, *Festtheologie*.

Die Festtagspredigten bezeugen einmal, wie über das Mittel des sich entwickelnden liturgischen Jahres der Kirche das Christusgeschehen in die Zeitstrecke des Jahres vermittelt werden sollte, d.h.: Die Predigten sind *erstens* ein Ausdruck der damaligen spirituellen bzw. geistlichen Reflexion. Zum anderen sind sie aber immer auch eine Reflexion der damaligen theologischen Auseinandersetzungen und spiegeln *zweitens* die theologische Diskussion ihrer Zeit wider. In den Festtagspredigten Gregors von Nyssa finden sich deutliche Spuren der dogmatischen, speziell trinitarischen und christologischen Kontroversen des 4. Jh.: Arianismus und Apollinarismus.

So behandelt etwa die Osterpredigt *De tridui spatio* (nicht vor 386) im ersten Hauptteil vier Fragen,[6] deren Art der Darstellung wie der Lösung nach Hubertus R. Drobner "nur aus Gregors großen polemischen Traktaten *Contra Eunomium* und *Adversus Apolinarium* zu erklären sind".[7] Die Pfingstpredigt *In sanctam Pentecosten* (388) richtet sich im Rahmen der zeitgenössischen Diskussion explizit gegen die Pneumatomachen, welche die Göttlichkeit des Heiligen Geistes leugnen. Ebenso setzt sich Gregor in seiner ersten Lobrede auf den Protomärtyrer Stephanus *In sanctum Stephanum I* (386) mit den Pneumatomachen über die Göttlichkeit des Heiligen Geistes und dem damit verbundenen richtigen Schriftverständnis auseinander.[8] In diesem Zusammenhang wendet sich Gregor dann auch gegen die Neuarianer, die er parallel zu den Pneumatomachen Christomachen nennt, weil sie den Sohn dem Vater unterordnen.[9] Die christologische Diskussion scheint in Gregors Weihnachtspredigt *In diem natalem Salvatoris* (386) durch, wenn er gegen eine doketische Position unterstreicht, dass Christus wahrer Gott und wahrer Mensch ist und Christus wirklich die menschliche Natur annahm.[10] Schließlich wendet sich Gregor in seiner

---

[6] Erstens die Frage *Was* während der drei Tage geschah: der Descensus Christi als Sieg über Tod und Teufel (*Trid. spat.*, GNO IX 280,14–283,9); zweitens die Frage nach dem *Warum* der drei Tage (*Trid. spat.*, GNO IX 283,10–286,12); drittens die Frage *Wie* die prophetischen drei Tage und Nächte zu berechnen sind (*Trid. spat.*, GNO IX 286,16–290,17) und viertens die Frage des *Wie* sich Christus an diesen Tagen gleichzeitig Dreien geben konnte (*Trid. spat.*, GNO IX 290,18–294,13).

[7] H.R. Drobner, *Die drei Tage zwischen Tod und Auferstehung unseres Herrn Jesus Christus*. Eingel., übers. u. kommentiert, Leiden 1982, 172.

[8] Vgl. *Steph.* I (GNO X/1 88,23–94,7).

[9] Vgl. *Steph.* I (GNO X/1 91,10–94,7).

[10] Vgl. *In diem nat.* (GNO X/2 266,14–269,7).

Epiphaniepredigt *In diem luminum* (383) zugleich gegen Pneumatomachen, Eunomius und Neuarianer, wenn er sagt, dass kein Unterschied in der Heiligung durch drei Hypostasen bestehe, weil alle drei gleich göttlich seien. Die drei Hypostasen seien nicht drei Götter, die einander unähnlich (ἀνομοίους; 229,17) sind. Deshalb dürften die drei Hypostasen nicht in verschiedene Naturen zerstückelt werden, da ein und dieselbe Gnade von allen drei ausgehe.[11]

Zweifellos entwickelt und vertieft Gregor von Nyssa sein Festverständnis im Rahmen seines trinitarischen und christologischen Denkens. Deshalb verwundert es nicht, dass sich in seinen Festtagspredigten ἐπίνοιαι finden.

II. *Der Begriff der ἐπίνοιαι in den Festtagspredigten Gregors von Nyssa*

Aufgrund der Vielfalt der biblischen Begriffe für Jesus Christus entfaltet Origenes seine Lehre von den ἐπίνοιαι, die Gregor von Nyssa und die anderen Kappadokier übernehmen. Nach Origenes vermittelt Christus zwischen der Einheit Gottes und der Vielfältigkeit der geschaffenen Welt. Er erweist sich als Mittler, der zugleich an der Einheit Gottes in der Vielfalt der Geschöpfe teilnimmt. Christus als die Weisheit Gottes und als Wort für die Menschen in der Welt zeigt sich nach Origenes in verschiedenen Aspekten der Bibel, die er als ἐπίνοιαι bezeichnet: z.B. als Arzt, Hirte, König oder Licht, Weg und Wahrheit, aber auch als Sohn, Erlöser und Auferstehung.[12] Hermann Josef Sieben wies nach, dass Origenes im engsten Zusammenhang mit seiner Epinoiailehre die Auffassung vertritt, Christus

---

[11] Vgl. *In diem lum.* (GNO IX 228,26–229,18).

[12] Vgl. zur ἐπίνοια-Lehre bei Origenes und ihrer Rezeption durch die Kappadokier ausführlich H. J. Sieben, "Vom Heil in den vielen 'Namen Christi' zur 'Nachahmung' derselben. Zur Rezeption der Epinoiai-Lehre des Origenes durch die Kappadokischen Väter", *ThPh* 73 (1998) 1–28, der 2–11 die Epinoiailehre des Origenes referiert und Literaturangaben zum Status quaestionis gibt. Origenes unterscheidet im einzelnen folgende ἐπίνοιαι: 1. Bezeichnungen, die Christus sich selber gibt, die er dann noch weiter differenziert in solche, die in den Evangelien festgehalten sind (Licht, Auferstehung, Weg, Wahrheit, etc.), solche, die die geheime Offenbarung bezeugt (Erster, Letzter, Lebender, Alpha und Omega), sowie solche, die sich bei den Propheten befinden (Pfeil, Gottesknecht, Licht der Völker, Lamm); 2. Bezeichnungen, die Christus von Autoren des Neuen Testaments zugeschrieben werden; 3. solche, die ihm schon die Propheten gegeben haben; 4. die ihm von Johannes gegebene Bezeichnung 'Logos' (vgl. ebd., 4, mit ausführlichen Stellenangaben).

offenbare sich den Menschen je nach ihrer Erkenntnismöglichkeit oder ihrem Tugendgrad in verschiedener Gestalt. Die Polymorphie Christi sei eine Variante der Epinoiailehre. Folglich hänge unsere menschliche Erkenntnis Christi davon ab, wie nahe wir ihm kommen, diese Nähe wiederum vom Grad unserer Tugend.[13]

Hinter Gregors Festtheologie steht die von Origenes rezipierte ἐπίνοιαι-Lehre, wenn er in seiner Weihnachtspredigt *In diem natalem Salvatoris* die Lehre der Heilsordnung (τὸν λόγον τῆς οἰκονομίας, 267,14) erläutert und sagt, die Gottheit besitze alle Dinge, die zum Aspekt, Begriff, Konzept oder Gedanken (κατ' ἐπίνοιαν, 267,17) 'gut' gehören, d.h.: Macht, Gerechtigkeit, Güte und Weisheit seien alles Begriffe, die Gott würdig bezeichneten.[14] Die ἐπίνοια 'gut', fährt Gregor fort, sei den Menschen in Christus während seiner irdischen Wirksamkeit offenbart worden, der in seiner Güte (ἀγαθότης, ἀγαθός, 268,4f) die Abgefallenen liebte und in seiner Weisheit (σοφία, σοφός, 268,4f) den Gedanken (ἐπίνοιαν, 268,6) fasste, die Geknechteten zu befreien. In seiner Gerechtigkeit (δικαιοσύνη, δίκαιος, 268,4.7) hätte er sich daher als Lösegeld (ἀντάλλαγμα, 268,9) für die menschliche Schuld hingegeben, um schließlich in seiner Macht (δύναμις, δυνατός, 268,4.11) den Tod zu überwinden, indem er leiblich auferstand.[15] Gregor gebraucht den Terminus ἐπίνοια im Zusammenhang der Festrede also nicht wie Origenes für die biblischen Aspekte Christi, sondern im erkenntnistheoretischen Sinne. Macht, Gerechtigkeit, Güte und Weisheit sind 'Gedanken' oder 'Begriffe', ἐπίνοιαι, die Gregor aus der Schöpfung ableitet und nicht mehr nur aus der Bibel wie Origenes. Für Gregor vermitteln die ἐπίνοιαι den Menschen die Möglichkeit, das Heilswirken Gottes in Christus zu erkennen. Ebenso bezeichnet Gregor in anderen Festreden mit ἐπίνοια allgemein den Gedanken oder Einfall.[16]

In seiner am frühest bezeugten Osterpredigt *In sanctum Pascha* (382) hebt Gregor im Hinblick auf die menschliche Erkenntnis Gottes aber zugleich hervor: Es sei nicht möglich, allein durch menschliches

---

[13] Vgl. Sieben, "Zur Rezeption der Epinoiai-Lehre", 8–11.

[14] Vgl. *In diem nat.* (GNO X/2 267,14–268,2).

[15] Vgl. *In diem nat.* (GNO X/2 268,2–14).

[16] Z.B. Gregors erste Lobrede auf die 40 Märtyrer *Mart.* II (GNO X/1 163,23) von 379; seine Lobrede zum zweiten Todestag seines Bruders *Bas.* (GNO X/1 133,4.5) von 381; die Festrede auf Gregor den Wundertäter *Thaum.* (GNO X/1 10,19; 15,13; 27,3; 29,3), die nicht genau zu datieren ist; etc.

Nachdenken (ἐπινοίαις ἀνθρωπικαῖς, 255,24) die Wirksamkeit Gottes (θεοῦ ἐνεργείας, 255,25) zu erforschen. Der Mensch könne zwar einzelne Wirkungen Gottes, die *Oikonomia*, wahrnehmen und auf Gottes Allmacht schließen, aber die Heilsursache, Gott selbst, müsse er glaubend anerkennen.[17] Gregor wahrt damit wie bereits Origenes die transzendenten Eigenschaften in Gott Vater, der absoluten Einfachheit, in der strenggenommen keine Mehrzahl von Namen zu finden ist. Hingegen lässt Christus in origenischer Sicht "als *multiplex in constitutione*, also wegen seiner Zusammensetzung, Platz für eine Vielzahl solcher Benennungen",[18] wie Alois Grillmeier feststellt. Daraus lässt sich schließen: Christus vermittelt den Menschen die eine Wirklichkeit Gottes in vielen Einzelheiten, in ἐπίνοιαι.

Die durch Christus offenbarten ἐπίνοιαι als Weg des Menschen zu Gott sind offensichtlich der Hintergrund für das allgemeine Verständnis der Theologie des Festes bei Gregor. Denn zu Beginn seiner zweiten Osterpredigt *De tridui spatio* spricht Gregor von den Strahlen der alttestamentlichen Verheißungen, die sich mit den Fackeln der gegenwärtigen Festfeier zu einem großen Gnadenlicht Gottes verbinden, d.h.: Wie Gott seine Gnade uns Menschen in Christus offenbarte, so bereits in den Verheißungen des Alten Testaments und so auch gegenwärtig am Fest. Damit ist das Fest wie das Zeugnis der Schrift als geschichtliche Offenbarung Gottes Teil der *Oikonomia*, der Dinge also, die Gott zum Heil der Menschen unternimmt.[19]

Schließlich zeigt sich in Gregors Predigten sogar die Verbindung der ἐπίνοιαι-Lehre mit der Nachahmung Christi, die er in einer eigenen, systematisch aufgebauten Schrift mit dem Titel *De perfectione* entfaltet.[20] Formal gesehen ist *De perfectione* ein Kommentar, der sechsundzwanzig aus den Paulusbriefen und vier aus weiteren biblischen Schriften entnommenen ἐπίνοιαι Christi behandelt.[21] Inhaltlich interpretiert Gregor die Epinoiailehre des Origenes dort aber entscheidend neu, wenn er aufgrund der ἐπίνοιαι Christi zur Nachahmung (ἡ μίμησις) auffordert.[22] Der Weg zur christlichen Vollkommenheit, so

[17] Vgl. *Sanct. Pasch.* (GNO IX 255,24–256,7).

[18] A. Grillmeier, *Jesus der Christus im Glauben der Kirche* I. *Von der Apostolischen Zeit bis zum Konzil von Chalcedon (451)*, Freiburg im Breisgau [3]1990, 270.

[19] Vgl. *Trid. spat.* (GNO IX 273,5–274,2).

[20] Vgl. H. J. Sieben, "Zur Rezeption der Epinoiai-Lehre", 18–28.

[21] Vgl. ebd., 22.

[22] Vgl. *Perf.* 4 (GNO VIII/1 178,11): "Merkmale eines wahren Christseins sind

Gregor, bestehe in der 'Nachahmung' der ἐπίνοιαι Christi, der Aspekte unseres Erlösers.[23]

So nennt Gregor in seiner Osterpredigt *In sanctum Pascha* das gegenwärtige Fest das wahrhafte Abbild oder die wirklichkeitsgetreue Nachahmung (ἡ μίμησις) des zukünftigen Tages der eschatologischen Vollendung.[24] Das gegenwärtige Fest sei die richtige, angemessene und passende (καλῶς) Form, um die geistige Wirklichkeit sinnlich wahrnehmbar zu machen. Explizit geht Gregor auf die Nachahmung der ἐπίνοιαι Christi in der Lobrede auf seinen Bruder *In Basilium fratrem* (381) ein, wenn er von dem Gedanken (ἡ ἐπίνοια, 133,5) spricht, der Wort und Tat verbindet:[25] Das Wort als solches, sagt er, das von der Tat getrennt ist, sei nichtig (μάταιος, 133,6) und ohne sichere Grundlage (ἀνυπόστατος, 133,7), also irreal. Hingegen zeige die Natur der Werke in Verwirklichung und Wahrheit (ἐν ὑποστάσει καὶ ἀληθείᾳ, 133,7)[26] sinnlich wahrnehmbar das geistliche und gedankliche Konzept, das hinter dem gesprochenen Wort stehe, d.h.: Die Werke offenbarten ὑπόστασις und ἀλήθεια (Verwirklichung und Wahrheit) der ἐπίνοιαι. Deshalb sei Basilius als Vorbild in der Nachfolge Christi höher geehrt durch Werke als durch die Lobrede. Die Nachahmung seines Lebens sei wertvoller als dessen Erinnerung in Worten.

aber alle die, die wir an Christus erkannt haben. Davon ahmen wir nach (μιμέομαι), was uns möglich ist, was unsere Natur davon nicht nachahmen kann, das verehren wir. Alle Namen also, die die Bezeichnung 'Christus' näher ausdeuten, müssen im Leben eines Christen aufleuchten, entweder durch Nachahmung oder durch Verehrung". Dazu meint Sieben, "Zur Rezeption der Epinoiai-Lehre", 24: "Es handelt sich um eine Neuinterpretation, insofern als die ἐπίνοιαι nicht mehr einfach als im Glauben geschenktes Heil, als Heilsgüter in Christus konzipiert sind, wie das bei Origenes der Fall war, sondern als durch Bemühung, durch willentliche, aszetische Bemühung anzueignende Tugenden und Haltungen."

[23] Daher stellt Sieben, "Zur Rezeption der Epinoiai-Lehre", 28, als Ergebnis fest: "Der Traktat *De perfectione* stellt ein wichtiges Zeugnis für die Rezeption der origenischen Epinoiailehre dar, er dokumentiert sowohl die Kontinuität mit dem genialen Alexandriner als auch die neuen Akzente, die die Kappadokischen Väter in diese Lehre eintrugen. Sah Origenes das Heil noch in eben diesen vielen Namen Christi geschenkt, so sind sie für Gregor von Nyssa nicht nur Heilsgabe, sondern auch ein aszetisches Programm, eben Tugenden, die nachzuahmen sind."

[24] Vgl. *Sanct. Pasch.* (GNO IX 250,2–14).

[25] Vgl. *Bas.* (GNO X/1 133,5–18).

[26] Zur Bedeutung von ὑπόστασις bei Gregor vgl. R. J. Kees, *Die Lehre von der Oikonomia Gottes in der Oratio catechetica Gregors von Nyssa*, Leiden 1995, 93ff, bes. 94 Anm. 10.

III. *Der erkenntnistheoretische Hintergrund der Festtheologie Gregors von Nyssa*

In seinen Festtagsreden nimmt Gregor von Nyssa das allgemeine erkenntnistheoretische Problem der Erkennbarkeit Gottes durch den Menschen auf, wenn er in seiner Osterpredigt *In sanctum Pascha* sagt:[27] Gott ist allmächtig (παντοδύναμος, 256,26), seine Schöpfung das Bild seiner unaussprechlichen Wirksamkeit, die bereits das menschliche Denkvermögen zur Verzweiflung bringt und somit zeigt, dass sich der Mensch das Wesen Gottes nicht vorstellen kann. Der Mensch könne zwar einzelne Wirkungen Gottes wahrnehmen, niemals aber Gottes Wesen erfassen, er müsse an Gottes Allmacht glauben. Damit kann der Mensch nach Gregor von der Wirkung Gottes zwar auf seine Allmacht schließen, nicht aber sein Wesen erkennen. Nach Gregor ist die Offenbarung Gottes in der Welt und die Erkennbarkeit Gottes durch den Menschen immer eine Bewegung, die von Gott aus zu den Menschen geht. Als Beweise der Allmacht Gottes, die dann auch die zukünftige leibliche Auferstehung bewirken kann, nennt Gregor neben der Schöpfung bereits geschehene Totenauferweckungen, wie die des Lazarus und vieler anderer.[28] Schließlich habe Gott sogar den Aposteln die Kraft verliehen, Tote aufzuerwecken.[29] Daher werde der Vernünftige nachvollziehen können, dass der Mensch, wie er durch Teile der Schöpfung auf den allmächtigen Schöpfer schließen könne, so auch aufgrund der geschehenen Auferweckung des einzelnen, wie des Lazarus, an die zukünftige Auferstehung vieler glauben dürfe.[30]

---

[27] Vgl. *Sanct. Pasch.* (GNO IX 256,23–26).

[28] Vgl. *Sanct. Pasch.* (GNO IX 257,7–13); Joh 11,44.

[29] Vgl. *Sanct. Pasch.* (GNO IX 257,14–16).

[30] Vgl. *Sanct. Pasch.* (GNO IX 258,2–15); zu Glaube und Gotteserkenntnis bei Gregor von Nyssa vgl. I. Escribano-Alberca, *Glaube und Gotteserkenntnis in der Schrift und Patristik*, Freiburg 1974, 91–105 u. 111–115, der 103 zum Paradox in Gregors θεωρία sagt: "Jedes Schauen des Göttlichen, sei es noch so erhaben und einem eminent fortgeschrittenen Entwicklungsstadium angemessen, gipfelt in der Einsicht, dass die eigentliche Schau eine erst zu gewährende Gnade ist, deren Zustandekommen sowohl die menschliche Begrenztheit als auch die göttliche Andersartigkeit hindernd im Wege stehen. Zur Darstellung dieses nicht leicht erfaßbaren Sachverhaltes ist Gregor als Stilmittel die Paradoxie – mit ihren verneinend-bejahenden Imponderabilien – ein willkommener Ausdruck: Einsicht in das Wesen Gottes ist Einsicht in die Unerfaßbarkeit Gottes durch θεωρία; die eigentliche Erkenntnis steht in der Einsicht, dass man von Gott keine Einsicht haben kann – ἰδεῖν ἐν τῷ μὴ ἰδεῖν."

In seiner ersten Lobrede auf den Protomärtyrer Stephanus *In sanctum Stephanum I* beweist Gregor dann auf seiner erkenntnistheoretischen Grundlage den Wahrheitsgehalt der Trinitätslehre mit dem Bild der platonischen Ideenlehre:[31] Die Sinneinheit des Bildes (ὁ τῆς εἰκόνος λόγος, 93,16), sagt er, bleibe erhalten, wenn geglaubt wird, dass dieselben Dinge, die im Bild vorgestellt und angeschaut werden, auch im Urbild (ἐν τῷ ἀρχετύπῳ, 94,1) vorhanden sind. Denn wie im Guten das Gute und im Licht das Licht sinnlich wahrgenommen wird, so werde in allen Dingen die ursprüngliche Schönheit (τὸ πρωτότυπον κάλλος, 94,2) durch das ihr Eigentümliche im Bilde (ἐν τῇ εἰκόνι, 94,2) ausgeprägt. Im Bild drücke sich das Urbild sinnlich wahrnehmbar aus. Dieses philosophische Konzept überträgt Gregor auf die Trinitätslehre und erklärt:[32] Damit die Sinneinheit des Bildes (τῆς εἰκόνος ὁ λόγος, 94,5f) nicht auseinanderfällt, dürften die Eigentümlichkeiten des Bildes gegenüber dem Urbild (ἐν τῇ ἀπαλλάξει τῶν ἰδιωμάτων τοῦ ἀρχετύπου, 94,6) nicht verändert und entfremdet werden. Deshalb werde im Sitzen des Sohnes – welche Vorstellung auch immer dieser Begriff (τὸ ὄνομα, 94,4) hervorrufe – auch das Sitzen des Vaters mit einbegriffen, und im Stehen das Stehen. Gregor spricht also von einem Aussagentausch der Eigentümlichkeiten zwischen Vater und Sohn, weil der Sohn dasselbe Urbild oder Wesen (οὐσία) habe wie der Vater. Die Eigentümlichkeit, die entweder nur vom Vater oder nur vom Sohn ausgesagt wird, ist für Gregor als *tertium comparationis* immer von beiden anzunehmen. Folglich symbolisiere das Stehen oder Sitzen des Vaters und des Sohnes immer dieselbe göttliche Herrlichkeit,[33] d.h.: Die Dinge oder Vorstellungen (ἐπίνοιαι), die über den Sohn ausgesagt werden, können nach Gregor auch über den Vater ausgesagt werden und umgekehrt.

---

[31] Vgl. *Steph.* I (GNO X/1 93,16–94,7).

[32] Zur Bildtheologie im allgemeineren bei Gregor vgl. I. Escribano-Alberca, *Glaube und Gotteserkenntnis*, 111–115, der 111f zur erkenntnistheoretischen Bedeutung der Bild-Theologie, dass Gott im Bild wirklich erkennbar ist, sagt: "Als Verständigungsmittel mit der Philosophie ist Gregor der εἰκών-Begriff willkommen. An einer beachtenswerten Stelle heißt es, alle Philosophie komme überein in der Anerkennung, dass alles eine Ursache und ein Prinzip hat. Das, fügt Gregor hinzu, kommt dem gleich, was die Schrift behauptet (*Gen* 1,26): Der Mensch wurde geschaffen nach dem Bilde Gottes."

[33] Vgl. *Steph.* I (GNO X/1 92,10–94,6).

IV. *Schluss*

Die Untersuchung der ἐπίνοιαι in den Predigten Gregors von Nyssa zeigt, dass die Rezeption der Epinoiailehre des Origenes hinter seiner Festtheologie steht.

Gregor gebraucht den Begriff der ἐπίνοιαι in seinen Festpredigten jedoch anders als Origenes: nicht nur für die biblischen Aspekte Christi, sondern in einem umfassenderen erkenntnistheoretischen Sinn für den 'Gedanken' oder 'Einfall'. Die ἐπίνοιαι sind Begriffe, die Gregor allgemein aus der Schöpfung ableiten kann. Die ἐπίνοιαι als Weg des Menschen zu Gott bleiben aber auch für Gregor geschichtliche Offenbarungsweisen Christi, d.h.: Christus vermittelt den Menschen in vielen Einzelheiten die eine Wirklichkeit Gottes, die teilweise erkannt, aber letztlich geglaubt werden muss. Diesen geschichtlich offenbarten ἐπίνοιαι Christi soll der Mensch nachfolgen und sie in seinem Leben nachahmen, um Christus nahe zu sein.

Damit nimmt Gregor in seinen Festtagsreden das allgemeine erkenntnistheoretische Problem der Erkennbarkeit Gottes durch den Menschen auf. Im Anschluss an seinen Bruder und damit gegen Eunomius betont er, dass die ἐπίνοιαι immer nur die Wirkungen einer Sache, aber niemals ihr Wesen benennen können. Die ἐπίνοιαι sind Aspekte, die letztlich auf einen menschlichen Denkakt zurückgehen, um einzelne geschichtliche Wirkungen Gottes in Jesus Christus zu benennen. Über die ἐπίνοιαι Christi kann der Mensch zwar auf Gott-Vater schließen, aber niemals sein Wesen erkennen.

Trinitarisch gesprochen geben die ἐπίνοιαι ein Bild davon, *wie* der Vater und der Sohn sind, aber niemals *was* sie sind. Über den Sohn bekommt der Mensch zwar ein Bild vom Vater. Der Sohn ist aber zugleich auch mehr als dieses Bild, weil er vom Vater kommt und dasselbe Wesen hat wie er, d.h.: Die Dinge oder Vorstellungen (ἐπίνοιαι), die über den Sohn ausgesagt werden, können nach Gregor auch über den Vater ausgesagt werden und umgekehrt.

Die Festtagspredigten Gregors von Nyssa spiegeln die theologische Diskussion seiner Zeit wider. Diesen Schluss legt bereits die gemeinsame Entstehungszeit der drei Bücher *Contra Eunomium* (380–383) und der Festtagspredigten (379–386) nahe. Von daher ergänzen Gregors Aussagen über die ἐπίνοιαι im Rahmen seiner Festtheologie das grundlegende Verständnis der ἐπίνοιαι im Hinblick auf die Kontroverse um Eunomius.

ABBREVIATIONS

A. *Periodicals and series*

BGL	Bibliothek der griechischen Literatur, Stuttgart
CAG	Commentaria in Aristotelem Graeca, Berlin
CCL	Corpus Christianorum. Series Latina, Turnhout
CPG	Clavis Patrum Graecorum, Turnhout
FC	Fontes Christiani, Freiburg i.Br.
GCS	Die griechischen christlichen Schriftsteller der ersten drei Jahrhunderte, Berlin
GNO	Gregorii Nysseni Opera, Leiden
JThS	*Journal of Theological Studies*, Oxford
PG	Patrologiae cursus completus. Accurante Jacques-Paul Migne. Series Graeca, Paris
PGL	G. W. H. Lampe, *A Patristic Greek Lexicon*, Oxford 1961
PL	Patrologiae cursus completus. Accurante Jacques-Paul Migne. Series Latina, Paris
RAC	*Reallexikon für Antike und Christentum*, Stuttgart
REG	*Revue des études grecques*, Paris
RHE	*Revue d'histoire ecclésiastique*, Louvain
SC	Sources chrétiennes, Paris
StPatr	*Studia patristica*, Berlin u.a.
SVF	Stoicorum Veterum Fragmenta, Stuttgart
ThPh	*Theologie und Philosophie*, Freiburg i.Br.
ThQ	*Theologische Quartalschrift*, Tübingen
TRE	*Theologische Realenzyklopädie*, Berlin
TU	Texte und Untersuchungen zur Geschichte der altchristlichen Literatur, Berlin
VigChr	*Vigiliae Christianae*, Amsterdam
ZKG	*Zeitschrift für Kirchengeschichte*, Stuttgart

B. *Others*

ad loc.	*ad locum*
Anm.	Anmerkung

Bd.	Band
bes.	besonders
bzw.	beziehungsweise
cf.	confer
ders.	derselbe
d.h.	das heißt
Diss.	Dissertation
e.a.	*et alii*
e.g.	*exempli gratia*, for instance
ebd.	ebenda
ed.	editor
éd.	éditeur
eds.	editors
éds.	éditeurs
esp.	especially
ET	English translation
f, ff	folgender, folgende, following
Fr.	Fragment
FS	Festschrift
Hrsg.	Herausgeber
ibid.	*ibidem*
Lit.	Literatur
LXX	Septuaginta
MS	Manuscript
MSS	Manuscripts
p.	page
par	parallel
s.	siehe
s.v.	*sub voce*
tr.	translated by
u.a.	und andere, unter anderem
usw.	und so weiter
vgl.	vergleiche
z.B.	zum Beispiel

INDICES
(Ladislav Chvátal)

I. INDEX LOCORUM

I.1. BIBLIA

I.1.A. VETUS TESTAMENTUM

I.1.B. NOVUM TESTAMENTUM

I.2. AUCTORES ANTIQUI ET MEDII AEVI

II. INDEX NOMINUM

III. INDEX VERBORUM

III.1. VERBA GRAECA

III.2. VERBA LATINA

SUPPLEMENTS TO VIGILIAE CHRISTIANAE

67. Carriker, A. *The Library of Eusebius of Caesarea*. 2003. ISBN 90 04 13132 9
68. Lilla, S.R.C., herausgegeben von H.R. Drobner. *Neuplatonisches Gedankengut in den 'Homilien über die Seligpreisungen' Gregors von Nyssa*. 2004. ISBN 90 04 13684 3
69. Mullen, R.L. *The Expansion of Christianity*. A Gazetteer of its First Three Centuries. 2004. ISBN 90 04 13135 3
70. Hilhorst, A. (ed.). *The Apostolic Age in Patristic Thought*. 2004. ISBN 90 04 12611 2
71. Kotzé, A. *Augustine's* Confessions: *Communicative Purpose and Audience*. 2004. ISBN 90 04 13926 5
72. Drijvers, J.W. *Cyril of Jerusalem: Bishop and City*. 2004. ISBN 90 04 13986 9
73. Duval, Y.-M. *La décrétale* Ad Gallos Episcopos*: son texte et son auteur*. Texte critique, traduction Française et commentaire. 2005. ISBN 90 04 14170 7
74. Mueller-Jourdan, P. *Typologie spatio-temporelle de l'*Ecclesia *byzantine*. La Mystagogie de Maxime le Confesseur dans la culture philosophique de l'Antiquité. 2005. ISBN 90 04 14230 4
75. Ferguson, T.J. *The Past is Prologue*. The Revolution of Nicene Historiography. 2005. ISBN 90 04 14457 9
76. Marjanen, A. & Luomanen, P. *A Companion to Second-Century Christian "Heretics"*. 2005. ISBN 90 04 14464 1
77. Tzamalikos, P. *Origen – Cosmology and Ontology of Time*. 2006. ISBN 90 04 14728 4
78. Bitton-Ashkelony, B. & Kofsky, A. *The Monastic School of Gaza*. 2006. ISBN-13: 978 90 04 14737 9, ISBN-10: 90 04 14737 3
79. Portbarré-Viard, de la G.H. *Descriptions monumentales et discours sur l'édification chez Paulin de Nole*. Le regard et la lumière (*epist.* 32 et *carm.* 27 et 28). 2006. ISBN 90 04 15105 2
80. Ziadé, R. *Les martyrs Maccabées: de l'histoire juive au culte chrétien*. Les homélies de Grégoire de Nazianze et de Jean Chrysostome. 2007. ISBN-13: 978 90 04 15384 4, ISBN-10: 90 04 15384 5
81. Volp, U. *Die Würde des Menschen*. Ein Beitrag zur Anthropologie in der Alten Kirche. 2006. ISBN-13: 978 90 04 15448 3, ISBN-10: 90 04 15448 5
82. Karfíková, L., S. Douglass and J. Zachhuber (eds.). *Gregory of Nyssa: Contra Eunomium II*. An English Version with Supporting Studies Proceedings of the 10th International Colloquium on Gregory of Nyssa (Olomouc, September 15-18, 2004). 2007. ISBN-13: 978 90 04 15518 3, ISBN-10: 90 04 15518 X
83. Silvas, A.M. *Gregory of Nyssa : The Letters*. Introduction, Translation and Commentary. 2007. ISBN-13: 978 90 04 15290 8, ISBN-10: 90 04 15290 3
84. Tabbernee , W. *Fake Prophecy and Polluted Sacraments*. Ecclesiastical and Imperial Reactions to Montanism. 2007. ISBN-13: 978 90 04 15819 1, ISBN-10: 90 04 15819 7
85. Tzamalikos, P. *Origen: Philosophy of History & Eschatology*. 2007. ISBN-13: 978 90 04 15648 7, ISBN-10: 90 04 15648 8